Darbyshire on the English Legal System

Darbyshire on the English Legal System

Penny Darbyshire PhD, MA, FRSA

Professor, Kingston Law School, Kingston University

SWEET & MAXWELL

THOMSON REUTERS

First Edition	1971
Second Edition	1977
Third Edition	1982
Fourth Edition	1987
Reprinted	1990
Fifth Edition	1992
Sixth Edition	1996
Seventh Edition	2001
Reprinted	2003
Eighth Edition	2005
Ninth Edition	2008
Tenth Edition	2011
Eleventh Edition	2014
Twelfth Edition	2017

Published in 2017 by Thomson Reuters trading as Sweet & Maxwell. Registered in England & Wales, Company No.1679046.
Registered Office and address for service: 5 Canada Square, Canary Wharf, London, E14 5AQ.

For further information on our products and services, visit *www.sweetandmaxwell.co.uk*

Typeset by Letterpart Limited, Caterham on the Hill, Surrey, CR3 5XL.

Printed and bound by CPI Group (UK) Ltd, Croydon, CR0 4YY.

No natural forests were destroyed to make this product; only farmed timber was used and re-planted.

A CIP catalogue record of this book is available for the British Library.

ISBN: 978-0-414-05785-2

Thomson Reuters and the Thomson Reuters logo are trademarks of Thomson Reuters.

Sweet & Maxwell ® is a registered trademark of Thomson Reuters.

Crown copyright material is reproduced with the permission of the Controller of HMSO and the Queen's Printer for Scotland.

Preface

My aim is to explain the legal system of England and Wales to the reader who knows nothing about it. There is a lot more about the law and the legal system to learn and I hope you will enjoy your voyage of discovery as much as I still do.

Studying law requires an enormous amount of reading. Remember, however, that law exists in the real world, not just in books. Read about the courts here, then take yourself off to watch them. They are a free source of entertainment, Monday to Friday. You will learn a lot, especially if you visit a variety. While you are there, speak to a lawyer or a magistrate or a judge but read the relevant chapters of this book first so that your conversation is better informed. You can also watch tribunal proceedings, or ask to work-shadow a lawyer, or para-legal, or judge, or magistrate for a day or more.

Learning about the English common law and the legal system is exciting, because its long history and worldwide importance are awesome. It has been developing since before the Norman invasion of 1066. It changes continually so remember to keep up to date with the news. By the time you read this book, it will be out of date, like every law book.

Have fun!

Penny Darbyshire

Kingston, July 2017

Online Updates

A free online updating service is available in conjunction with this text. It can be accessed by going to the Sweet & Maxwell academic website at *http://uklawstudent.thomsonreuters.com*. This service will provide periodic updates from 2018.

Acknowledgments

Grateful acknowledgment is made to the following authors and publishers for permission to quote from their works:
Cambridge University Press

* H. Genn, *Judging Civil Justice* (Cambridge: 2010)
* R.M. Jackson, *The Machinery of Justice in England* (Cambridge: 1940)

The Incorporated Council of Law Reporting for England and Wales

* *Arab Monetary Fund v Hashim (No.7)* [1993] 1 W.L.R. 1014
* *Inland Revenue Commissioners v McGuckian* [1997] 1 W.L.R. 991
* *Pepper (Inspector of Taxes) v Hart* [1993] A.C. 593
* *R. v Chief Constable of the RUC Ex p. Begley* [1997] 1 W.L.R. 1475
* *R. v Horsman* [1998] Q.B. 531
* *R. v International Stock Exchange Ex p. Else* [1993] Q.B. 534
* *R. v Preddy* [1996] A.C. 815
* *R. Sheffield Crown Court Ex p. Brownlow* [1980] Q.B. 530
* *Stock v Frank Jones (Tipton) Ltd* [1978] 1 W.L.R. 231

The following have been reproduced by permission of Reed Elsevier (UK) Limited, trading as LexisNexis:

* All England Law Reports
  — *R. v McIlkenny* [1992] 2 All E.R. 417
  — The Practice Statement [1966] 3 All E.R. 77
* New Law Journal
  — G. Bindman, "Spead the Wealth" (2014) 164 N.L.J. 22
  — Lightman J, "The case for judicial intervention" (1999) 149 N.L.J. 1819
  — K.M. Qureshi, "International Law and the English Courts" (2001) 151 N.L.J. 787

Wiley

* L. Barnes and K. Malleson, "The Legal Profession as Gatekeeper to the Judiciary: Design Faults in Measures to Enhance Diversity" (2011) 74(2) M.L.R. 245

ACKNOWLEDGMENTS

- J. Donoghue, "Reforrming the Role of Magistrates: Implications for Summary Justice in England and Wales" (2014) 77(6) M.L.R. 928

While every care has been taken to establish and acknowledge copyright, and contact the copyright owners, the publishers tend their apologies for any accidental infringement. They would be pleased to come to a suitable arrangement with the rightful owners in each case.

TABLE OF CONTENTS

CONTENTS

CONTENTS

CONTENTS

CONTENTS

TABLE OF CASES

TABLE OF CASES

TABLE OF CASES

TABLE OF CASES

TABLE OF CASES

TABLE OF CASES

TABLE OF CASES

TABLE OF CASES

TABLE OF CASES

TABLE OF CASES

TABLE OF CASES

TABLE OF CASES

TABLE OF CASES

TABLE OF STATUTES

TABLE OF STATUTES

TABLE OF STATUTORY INSTRUMENTS

TABLE OF INTERNATIONAL AND EUROPEAN
CONVENTIONS AND LEGISLATION

Regulations

Directives

The importance of English law and UK legal services and the legal consequences of Brexit

In this little note, I explain importance of UK legal services. I describe the three jurisdictions in the UK state and the historic and modern worldwide importance of English law and the English legal system. I examine the legal ramifications of Brexit. This requires leaving aside, for a moment, the rage and depression prompted by the word "Brexit". As my American students have reminded me, "Trump is for four years but Brexit is forever".

This note was prompted by a query in an email from Alan, a student of the University of Notre Dame, Indiana, sent to the ND London Law Centre (where I teach visiting American law students), on the morning of 23 June 2016, as the Brexit referendum result was emerging. I replied. Here, I reproduce our exchange and I expand on my reply, because I have no doubt that other law students and would-be students from all over the world are asking Alan's question.

The email exchange

"Dear Professor...
Brexit is upon us, good or bad. I was up all night watching the referendum. Startling outcome! But I had a gut feeling that Leave would win. Just to follow up, I am currently enrolled in the class entitled "English Legal System". Although obviously an important class, if English laws are in limbo due to Brexit, is there any way one more class can be added to the course listing to replace English Legal System...?
Best regards,
Alan Grigorian"

"Dear Alan,
I'm delighted to hear that you are coming to ND London and that you are thinking of studying ELS. Your email has been copied to me, as I am the ELS Professor. Your concern about Brexit is understandable. I am writing to explain the position and importance of the ELS. It is the mother of the world's biggest family of legal systems, including the whole of North America, Australia, New Zealand, India, the rest of the Commonwealth, all the former British Empire and indeed the whole English speaking world. English common law has been under construction since well before 900 and forms the basic law in all of those countries. The UK Parliament passed the European Communities Act in 1972. This has added to the sources of English law but has not affected the ELS in any other respect. I attach a flyer for my textbook, which is used for the class. Of its 17 chapters, only two will

need tiny modifications in the next edition. The UK will not be exiting the EU until at least 2018, if ever. UK lawyers are the most mobile in Europe and all UK businesses and law firms will still need a profound understanding of EU law because the EU will remain a primary trading partner of the UK.

Good luck!

Professor Penny Darbyshire FRSA"

Alan took the ELS class. He was a joy to teach, as were all my class of 2016. Alan came top of the class and we all had lots of fun together in the pubs of London.

The UK's global importance in legal services

The best source is the City UK's *Legal Services Report 2016*, which I paraphrase:

- The UK accounts for 10% of the global market for legal services, second only to the USA.
- The UK is the world's most international market for legal services because of the almost unrestricted access to foreign lawyers in establishing practices in the UK.
- There are 200 foreign law firms from 40 jurisdictions, including, of course, all major US law firms.
- The UK is the main base for 2 of the 4 biggest international law firms, based on a head-count.
- The UK is the leading international centre for dispute resolution.

Expanding on this last point, they mean court disputes, arbitration and alternative dispute resolution. London's Commercial Court was established in 1895 and has been instrumental in developing international law in trade, insurance, banking, shipping and aviation, insurance and so on. Over 80 per cent of its cases involve one foreign party or foreign sovereign state. In 50 per cent of its cases, both parties are foreign. Arbitration grew alongside the industrial revolution, which started in the UK.

The international pre-eminence of the UK in the law and legal services rests on not just the importance of English common law but the UK's history as a maritime and trading hub. London was a Roman port but the land mass called The British Isles was a trading hub in pre-Roman times: Orkney was a Viking trading hub.

In a July 2017 speech, Lord Neuberger said:

"The common law ... will remain as attuned to the demands of international business as it ever was ... Brexit does not alter the fact that lawyers and judges in the UK are as internationally minded and expert as they ever have been. Indeed, like any significant change, Brexit is operating as a spur to encourage all involved in the provision of legal services in London to strive to ensure that those services are even better than they already are."

The Legal Consequences of Brexit

The Constitution

The UK is one of three countries in the developed world without a written constitution.

The UK is the nation state. It contains three domestic legal systems, those of England and Wales, Scotland, a hybrid common law and civil law jurisdiction, and Northern Ireland. The UK Parliament is its legislature. While Wales and Northern Ireland have assemblies and Scotland has a parliament, *all* of the law that they make is delegated legislation, acting under powers devolved by the UK. Very few UK citizens understand this point. The Acts of the devolved legislatures are all judicially reviewable and can be struck down by the UK Supreme Court, unlike Acts of the UK Parliament, which are not reviewable because of the doctrine of parliamentary supremacy, parliamentary sovereignty, which is the fundamental principle of the unwritten constitution. Scotland, Northern Ireland and Wales cannot choose to act independently. The UK is the member state of the EU. Nevertheless, in the event that a future Scottish referendum results in a vote to leave the UK, the UK Parliament would be highly likely to pass an Act conferring independence on Scotland. Scotland would then have to apply to join the EU and would be obliged to join the Eurozone.

Legislation

The UK has passed 50,000 laws since joining the EU. The European Union [Withdrawal] Bill 2017 will, if enacted, keep all "EU-derived domestic legislation" as part of domestic law, then decide which to keep, repeal or amend. This applies to all EU Regulations and decisions in effect immediately before "Exit Day" which is proposed in 2019. Obviously, lawyers and legislative bodies will focus a sharp eye on the development of EU law in the future because if we wish to sell our goods and services to Europe, we will have to comply with their regulations as we do with exports elsewhere.

Most UK law is unaffected by EU law. The main areas of EU activity are social and market regulation, free movement of workers, competition and single market, the environment, VAT, data protection, and extradition.

The UK Parliament has a number of committees contemplating the implications of Brexit, such as foreign affairs, the economy, students, women and equalities, tourism, the digital single market and the Ireland/Northern Ireland border but the ones that concern lawyers, whose investigations and reports we need to monitor are: The Joint Committee on Human Rights and the House of Lords EU subcommittee on EU-UK security and police co-operation. Once the European Union [Withdrawal] Bill is enacted Parliament and government ministers will need to enact considerably more legislation in order to fully implement Brexit.

Precedent and case law—the common law

The common law as we now know it emerged in the twelfth century (Baker). The stability of the common law is one of the reasons why people all over the world choose to use or resolve their disputes by it. As Lord Chief Justice Thomas was at pains to explain in 2017:

> "In some quarters it has even been suggested that Brexit makes the law of the UK uncertain. This is all quite wrong. Brexit will have no effect on London's key strengths. Let me take English contract law as an example. Brexit has no effect, unsurprisingly, both because the common law is used by nearly 30% of the world's legal jurisdictions and because English contract law has at its centrepiece respect for parties' intentions, as has the Commercial Court in London. That English contract law is well-established, well-understood and freely circulates contributes to its being a law of choice; and in terms of arbitration, the law of choice for 40% of all global corporate arbitrations. English contract and commercial law remains as the UK's 'national treasure'... London's Commercial Court is and will remain the ideal commercial court for litigation. It is both 'international in outlook' and 'commercial in skill'. London remains and will remain to the fore as a centre of international dispute resolution."

In October 2016, Lord Neuberger, The President of the UK Supreme Court, told me and my ND students that he has a working party on how to cope with Brexit. In future, the UKSC will be free to depart from precedents that it set down whilst the UK was bound by EU law. After Brexit, UK judges, who are overtly pro-EU are, I suggest, highly likely to keep as part of judge-made law those concepts that they adopted from Europe, such as proportionality, which is not a common law concept. Over its nine centuries, the common law has behaved like a "discriminating magpie", as Lord Neuberger put it in 2016, collecting glittery pieces of law and procedure from other legal systems, such as Roman law, equity, discovery, mercantile and admiralty law. EU law concepts were just more silver trinkets to bedeck the common law nest. After "Exit Day" UK courts will not be bound by future principles laid down by the Court of Justice of the EU.

Human Rights

Our membership of the Council of Europe is unaffected by Brexit. Many UK citizens, including journalists and politicians, do not understand that the European Convention on Human Rights 1950 is not a treaty of the EU. There are 47 contracting states. This treaty was passed before the common market was formed by the Treaty of Rome 1957. The Convention was drafted by UK lawyers, from an idea by Winston Churchill after WWII. The UK was the first signatory and the first to ratify the Convention. The Convention was naturally partly modelled on the common law, for example, art.6 was based on the rules of natural justice; art.5 was based on the old English writ of habeas corpus. After the Brexit vote, the Conservative government dropped their discussions about human rights. They have always been split on human rights but it is highly unlikely, in my opinion, that Parliament would repeal the Human Rights Act 1998 that made the Convention enforceable in the English Courts.

The UKSC's judgments have influenced the Strasbourg court, which has regularly adopted its reasoning or conceded that UK judges had interpreted the Convention correctly, when interpretation has conflicted. This dialogue with the Strasbourg court will doubtless continue. As Lord Neuberger pointed out, European human rights law has been much more influential over English common law than EU law, injecting concepts such as privacy and freedom of expression.

Pan-European Criminal Procedure and Cooperation

The most useful analysis is Spencer's article, published before the Brexit referendum. The punchline is that the future of the UK's relationship with the EU in this respect is uncertain, of course, as it is in all spheres of EU activity. Nevertheless, given that crime is international, it seems obvious to me that it is in our interests to keep cross-border police co-operation, putting us in the same position as other countries now outside the EU who have agreements with the EU but of course without the power to shape EU procedure.

He lists the five elements of criminal justice:

1. Agencies: OLAF on fraud, Europol (representative of Member States' police forces) and Eurojust, a collegiate body of national prosecutors aiming at cross-border co-ordination.
2. Legal instruments to improve cooperation, such as databases.
3. Legal instruments requiring mutual recognition, such as enforcement of judgments and sentences, and the European Arrest Warrant.
4. Twenty instruments aimed at harmonising criminal law, such as on terrorism and people trafficking.
5. Instruments aimed at harmonising procedure, such as minimum rights of suspects and victims.

The UK's attitude to these has been contrary and contradictory. David Cameron's Coalition opted out of some criminal justice measures, to pander to Brexiteers, only to opt back in again immediately, under pressure from the UK police, who make extensive use of the European Arrest Warrant.

Implications for lawyers, judges and law students

The City UK has reported that UK legal services saw a drop in revenue recently because of uncertainty caused by Brexit. While law firms, like financial services and other UK based global enterprises, will establish strategic satellite offices in other EU countries, I suggest that it is highly unlikely that there will be a mass exodus from the City of London. Most of the legal services and other services that they provide do not involve EU law.

Lawyers and judges will need an acute knowledge of EU law way beyond my lifetime. For example, take a hypothetical 20 year old, employed by a UK or EU firm, in 2017. Her pension rights are regulated by EU law. In 50 years' time, in the event of a dispute about her pension coming before the courts, the lawyers and judges involved will need to understand EU law as it was in 2017.

As I said, UK lawyers are the most mobile in Europe, the most likely to take advantage of the EU Directives that allow lawyers to establish practices in other EU states. UK judges were at the heart of Europe, developing pan-European judicial dialogue, conferences and exchanges and they will continue to spearhead human rights in this way, even though they now find themselves jettisoned from the EU.

How is Brexit being started?

In July 2017 the government published the European Union [Withdrawal] Bill. If enacted, it will repeal the European Communities Act 1972, and take the UK out of the EU on "Exit Day" in 2019. All future EU Law will not be binding on the UK. The opposition parties and Scottish and Welsh politicians have, however, threatened to decimate the Bill so Brexit may take longer than planned.

The online updates of this book will give further detail and track progress.

Bibliography and further reading

Department for Exiting the EU, *The Repeal Bill Factsheets*, especially 1, 2 and 3, online from *http://www.gov.uk* "publications", accessible, along with further information, via links on the departmental press release, 13 July 2017.
J.H. Baker, *An Introduction to English Legal History*, 4th edn (Oxford: Oxford University Press, 2002).
"Brexit" [2017] P.L. 124.
Lord Neuberger, President of the UK Supreme Court, "Has the identity of the English Common Law been eroded by EU Laws and the European Convention on Human Rights?" speech, Singapore, 16 August 2016, UKSC website; "Welcome address to Australian Bar Association Biennial Conference", July 3, 2017, UKSC website.
J.C. Spencer, "What would Brexit mean for British criminal justice?" [2016] 5 *Archbold Review* 6.
Parliament website.
Thomas LCJ, "Commercial Dispute Resolution: Courts and Arbitration", speech, Beijing, 6 April 2017.

PART 1

SOURCES

CHAPTER 1

Understanding the English Legal System

"Some 27% of the world's 320 legal jurisdictions use English common law...in part driven by the UK's reputation as the leading centre for international dispute resolution – whether through litigation, arbitration or mediation...

The largest international law firms in London have between 45% and 65% of their lawyers based outside the UK...Nearly 7,000 solicitors from England and Wales are located abroad;

...London's reputation as a leading global centre for international dispute resolution through the courts is underlined by the fact that in 2015, nearly 1,100 claims were issued in the Commercial Court, of which more than two-thirds involved at least one party whose address is outside of England and Wales. Furthermore, London is viewed as the leading preferred centre for arbitration. The number of commercial and civil disputes resolved through arbitration, mediation and adjudication in the UK totalled over 22,000 in 2015." (From The City UK, UK Legal Services Report 2016).

The English legal system is the mother of all common law legal systems, worldwide, the globe's biggest family of legal systems. They all apply English common law alongside their own laws. UK judges are highly outward looking and proactive in understanding and absorbing foreign legal concepts and in developing the common law, international law and European human rights law. They are very influential. It is no accident, then, that London is one of the world's pre-eminent centres of international law and of legal services and dispute resolution, as can be seen from the quotation above and the Brexit note above. This makes the study of the English legal system and the law of England and Wales very exciting. Before we examine the importance of English law in its international context, below, we need to understand what law is because, for many readers, this will be the first law book they touch.

1-001

1. WHAT IS LAW? THE RULE OF LAW

Societies and their subcultures govern themselves by countless sets of rules, written or unwritten. These include our own internalised moral code, rules of etiquette and expectations of civilised behaviour.

1-002

We may adhere to the tenets of a religion and a particular church. We may belong to a private organisation, such as a political party or a sports club with its own constitution and membership rules but none of these codes, however complex, carries the force of law. The constitution of the California Parent Teachers' Association is lengthier and much more complex than the Savings

(Government Contributions) Act 2017 but it is not law. It cannot be interpreted or enforced by a court unless there is a contractual relationship between the parties. Courts refuse to enforce non-legal rules. For example, in *R. (on the application of Proud) v Buckingham Pubwatch Scheme* (2008), it was held that a public house is a private place so, under the Licensing Act 2003, licensees were entitled to make decisions as to whom to admit. The applicant had been banned by pubs in the Buckingham Pubwatch area. He was refused judicial review. The ban unarguably fell into an area of life with which the courts do not interfere.

What, then, is special about legal rules? A rudimentary definition of law is a rule that is backed by a sanction for its breach, ultimately enforceable by a court, a tribunal or other public body with enforcement powers. There is considerable overlap between non-legal rules and the law. For instance, the basic rules of most major religions are astonishingly similar. They condemn murder, as do all legal systems, although what constitutes murder and how it is punished differs from one legal system to another. In another overlap, dropping litter in the street would be condemned by most people as inconsiderate behaviour but it is also illegal and subject to a fine enforceable in a criminal court. Nevertheless, many forms of bad manners, such as spitting in a crowded street, might offend people as a breach of the rules of civilised behaviour but are not illegal. We must also distinguish between the immoral and the illegal. Adultery used to be illegal but morals changed and Parliament decided it should no longer be an offence. It is, however, a breach of many people's religions or moral codes. Sanctions for breach of the law take many forms, apart from the obvious example of sentences passed for breaches of the criminal law. When part of the Merchant Shipping Act 1988 was found by the European Court of Justice, in the *Factortame* cases, to be in breach of the Treaty of Rome, the operation of the offending sections of the Act had to be suspended. The UK government had to compensate Spanish fishermen who had been prevented from plying their trade in UK coastal waters. The UK was in breach of public international law, notably EU law. This story is told in Ch.3. If I breach my contract with you, you can ask a civil court to compensate you by awarding damages against me, or to enforce my obligations under the contract. If a government minister makes a new set of regulations, they can be quashed by the High Court if she failed to follow procedure prescribed in the enabling Act of Parliament which gave her the power to make the regulations, such as consulting affected parties.

Modern democracies claim to adhere to "the rule of law" and in Spring 2017, a number of judges in the USA produced judgments which effectively tried to explain this to Donald Trump. This concept was emphasised by the illustrious constitutional lawyer, Dicey, in 1885 but he did not invent it. It can be traced back to Aristotle. The best modern definition and analysis is provided by Lord Tom Bingham, senior law lord 2000–2008, one of the greatest ever British judges. His book, *The Rule of Law*, was his parting gift to us just before his death in 2010. Every law student should read it and certainly every politician. What follows is a summary of Lord Bingham's thesis. Dicey's first meaning is very well known: no-one can be punished or made to suffer "in body or goods", except for a distinct breach of the law, established in a legal manner, before the ordinary courts. The roots of this are the famous cl.39 of Magna Carta 1215:

"No free man shall be seized or imprisoned, or stripped of his rights or possessions, or outlawed or exiled, or deprived of his standing in any other way, nor will we proceed with force against him, or send others to do so, except by the lawful judgment of his equals or by the law of the land."

Magna Carta was declared void by the Pope within 10 weeks but it was reissued in 1216, 1217 and 1225. In any event, these principles were not a novelty. The writ of habeas corpus was available before Magna Carta and used from the fifteenth century to challenge unlawful detention. Dicey's second meaning is also universally accepted in democracies: everyone, of whatever rank, is subject to the ordinary law of the land; no-one is above the law. As Dr Thomas Fuller said, in 1733, "Be you never so high, the law is above you". As Lord Bingham pointed out, after the English Bill of Rights 1689, "(n)o monarch could rely on divine authority to override the law" (p.24). He modified and expanded Dicey's definition, as follows:

1-003

1. "The law must be accessible and so far as possible intelligible, clear and predictable" (Bingham, Ch.3). The common law assumes that everyone knows the law. Ignorance of the law is no defence. This rule is a requirement of fairness.
2. "Questions of legal right and liability should ordinarily be resolved by application of the law and not the exercise of discretion" (Bingham, Ch.4), meaning that legal rights should be based on stated criteria and amenable to legal challenge.
3. "The laws of the land should apply equally to all, save to the extent that objective differences justify differentiation" (Bingham, Ch.5). While modern democracies have generally grasped and applied some definition of equality, in terms of gender, ethnicity and sometimes age and sexuality and disability, the UK and the USA and others seem reluctant to apply equal rights to non-citizens.
4. "Ministers and public officers at all levels must exercise the powers conferred on them in good faith, fairly, for the purpose for which the powers were conferred, without exceeding the limits of such powers and not unreasonably" (Bingham, Ch.6). There is an irrebuttable presumption that decisions will be made in accordance with the law. The High Court applies this requirement when reviewing the legality of administrative action. The rules of natural justice (fair trial), originally applied in testing the legality of proceedings in the lower courts, have been extended to government action. Decision-making must be unbiased. Everyone liable to have an adverse decision made against them has a right to be heard.
5. "The law must afford adequate protection of fundamental human rights" (Bingham, Ch.7). This is a twentieth century addition which Dicey would not have recognised. We examine the European Convention on Human Rights in Ch.4.
6. "Means must be provided for resolving, without prohibitive cost or inordinate delay, bona fide civil disputes which the parties themselves are unable to resolve" (Bingham, Ch.8). This encompasses what has fashionably become known as "access to justice". There is no point in having a civil right if you cannot enforce it through the courts. Chapter 10

of this book has much to say about this. Chapter 6 discusses the controversy between judges and government about the cost of civil court fees. The phrase has also been used to denote access to legal advice and legal services, discussed in Ch.17. I have argued for many years in previous editions of this book that these services must, logically, be provided by the State as a requirement of the rule of law.

7.   "Adjudicative procedures provided by the state should be fair" (Bingham, Ch.9). Some requirements go beyond the rules of natural justice. For instance, the European Court of Human Rights requires "equality of arms". Bingham says "in retrospect most legal systems operating today will be judged to be defective in respects not yet recognised". There is no universal interpretation of fair trial. For instance, while judges in England and Wales have been careful to distance themselves from party politics from about the mid-twentieth century, the American judicial system is shot through with party politics. Judicial independence has become a multi-faceted concept and is examined in Ch.14 of this book but its modern root is the Act of Settlement 1701.

8.   "The rule of law requires compliance by the state with its obligations in international law as in national law" (Bingham, Ch.10). International law is examined, briefly, in Ch.2.

The United Nations puts the rule of law at the heart of its mission. The World Bank deploys some staff exclusively on promoting the rule of law, including judicial independence. They try to persuade borrowing countries of the need to respect the rule of law. The UN Declaration of Human Rights 1948 and the European Convention on Human Rights 1950, discussed in Ch.4, refer to the rule of law.

2.   DISTINGUISHING BETWEEN DIFFERENT TYPES OF LAW

Substantive and procedural

1–004   Substantive law prescribes, proscribes and regulates areas of human activity. Procedural rules prescribe how substantive law can be enforced. The Theft Acts and many leading cases define what conduct and mental elements constitute the offence of theft but the procedures for arresting the suspect, questioning, charging and trying him are contained in several, quite different, Acts of Parliament, cases and procedural rules, plus codes which are not law, but the breach of which may be taken account of by a court.

Private and public

1–005   The former governs relations between private citizens or bodies. The latter applies to public bodies which are publicly regulated and normally created by an Act of Parliament, including the departments of local and central government, and public services, such as the Highways Agency. The twentieth century, especially since 1981, saw the massive growth in public law in the form of administrative law, the body of law regulating the conduct of public bodies. The grounds of challenge have been expanded by the Human Rights Act 1998, as described in Ch.4.

Domestic and international

Our domestic law is applicable in and enforceable by the courts of England and Wales and, sometimes, throughout the UK. International law, also described in Ch.2, is contained in conventions and treaties devised, signed and *ratified* by countries concerned to regulate activities in which they have a common interest or which take place across national boundaries, covering everything from air traffic to drug trafficking. Its interpretation and enforcement may be the task of an international court, recognised in or established by such a treaty. Frequently, detailed laws giving practical effect to treaty requirements are enacted into domestic law. The Misuse of Drugs Act 1971 constitutes domestic UK law in accordance with the requirements of the international conventions on narcotics. It is very important to understand that EU law and the law of the European Convention on Human Rights are *not* foreign law, as I write in 2017. They are types of international law that have been incorporated into UK law, but in different ways, as explained in Chs 3 and 4.

1–006

Civil and criminal

Private civil law regulates relations between private persons or bodies, normally invoked only by those parties seeking to protect their private rights or interests. For instance, if I commit a tort against you by, say, negligently backing my muck spreader over your gatepost, the State, as such, has no interest in taking me to court to sue for damages on your behalf but you may sue me in a civil court, for a fee. The State simply provides the courts to enable you to enforce your private rights, as required by Magna Carta. It is not going to step in if you do not act. Having said that, elements of the State, such as government agencies, have a vast range of statutory and common law powers to invoke the civil law against private individuals and, of course, a private party may take a civil court action against an element of the State, such as suing the police over a death in custody, but all of these activities between citizen and State are subject to the rules of public law as well.

1–007

By contrast, a criminal offence is a wrong against the State and punishable as such, in the criminal courts. Criminal law is a type of public law. The State has no interest in pursuing your civil claim for damages but if you are a victim of a crime, such as theft, the State may prosecute the offender, regardless of your views. The aim of taking a criminal case to court is to punish the wrongdoer, rather than to compensate, although judges and magistrates may attach a compensation order to any sentence they pass. In English law, victims of crime retain the right of private prosecution and so may prosecute the offender in the criminal courts, if the State chooses not to prosecute.

All of this is very confusing but the new law student will soon be able to recognise the difference. Suffice it to say that virtually all the foundation subjects studied in a law degree, such as tort, contract, land law, equity, most of public law and most EU law are elements of civil law. Most of criminal law is taught under the heading of "criminal law". A true story may help the reader to distinguish between the two. When I was a law student, I was cycling to college to sit the last of my finals when the driver of a car knocked me off my bike. The police arrived on the scene and took details of the accident and interviewed her and the witnesses. She was prosecuted in *criminal* proceedings in Kingston Magistrates' Court, pleaded guilty to the criminal offence of careless driving, and was fined. My solicitor, acting on my behalf, threatened to sue her in *civil* proceedings in Kingston County Court for damages for the losses I had suffered, as a result of her negligent driving, a tort. I needed the cost of a new bike, and damages for the pain and shock of my injuries. Luckily, the driver's motor insurance company, acting on her behalf, agreed to settle out of court for the sum we sought. This was typical. As we shall see in Ch.10, the vast majority of civil disputes are settled out of court, following negotiations between the parties or their representatives. What is also typical was my solicitor's tactic of waiting for the outcome of the criminal case before threatening a civil action against her. A civil case is much easier to prove than a criminal one. The civil quantum, standard, of proof is lower, so my solicitor knew that the driver's criminal conviction would make the civil case easy to prove. A crime must be proven beyond reasonable doubt, whereas civil liability need only be established on the balance of probabilities.

Civil and criminal cases: getting the language right

1–008   Here is a list of the correct terminology used in most civil and criminal cases. Try to get it right.

CIVIL	CRIMINAL
The claimant sues the defendant in the County Court or High Court.	The prosecutor prosecutes the defendant in the magistrates' court or Crown Court.
Most cases are settled without a trial, as no defence is entered.	Most cases are heard without a trial, as the defendant pleads guilty. Many crimes are not taken to court. An offender may be offered an official caution.
If a defence is entered, the case goes to trial and it is heard by a district judge who determines fact and law. In exceptional cases, a jury decides.	If the defendant pleads not guilty the case goes to trial and is heard before a professional magistrate called a district judge, or lay magistrates, who determine facts and law. In the Crown Court, the jury determines issues of fact (the verdict) and the judge rules on points of law.
If the judge finds the case proven, she enters judgment for the claimant.	If the magistrates or jury find the case proven, they bring in a verdict of guilty and convict the defendant.
She may make an order, such as an award of damages, against the defendant.	The magistrates or judge may pass sentence on the defendant, e.g. a fine.

CIVIL	CRIMINAL
If the judge does not find the case proven, she enters judgment for the defendant.	If the magistrates or jury find the case is not proven, they acquit the defendant.

In either case, if the losing party appeals, she becomes "the appellant" and the other side "the respondent". If she seeks judicial review of the legality of proceedings, she becomes "the applicant".

Common law and equity

These two used to be separate systems of law and legal remedies until the common law absorbed equity in 1873–1875. Modern lawyers need to understand this simple point: if a claimant proves her case at common law, she has a *right* to a remedy but if seeking an equitable remedy, such as an injunction to stop a threatened breach of the law, she has no right to it. The judge has a *discretion* and will examine the claimant's *behaviour*. An example from a case where a plaintiff (claimant) sought specific performance of a contract is *Milward v Earl Thanet* (1801), where Lord Alvanley MR said "A party cannot call upon a Court of Equity for specific performance, unless he has shewn himself ready, desirous, prompt, and eager". Chapter 8 gives a full explanation and see Neuberger.   1–009

3.   WHAT IS THE ENGLISH LEGAL SYSTEM?

The study of the English legal system applies to the powers, procedures and activities of the group of courts and statutory tribunals in England and Wales and the people who work in them and/or whose job it is to resolve legal problems. The State is the UK, comprising Great Britain (England, Wales and Scotland), plus Northern Ireland. The legal systems of Scotland and Northern Ireland are separate. They have distinct court structures, different procedures and sometimes apply different rules of substantive law. The Isle of Man and the Channel Islands are not part of the UK. They are self-governing Crown Dependencies, part of the group of islands known, geographically, as The British Isles.   1–010

We speak of the English legal system as if it were a coherent structure with the constituent parts working in a smooth, interrelated fashion but it is very important to bear in mind that no-one has custom-designed it. Think of it as a heap of Lego bricks, some of which are joined together, rather than a sophisticated construction of Lego Technic. It has been given to us in little boxes, over the last 11 centuries or more. Parts have been deconstructed and reconstructed from time to time. We fiddle with it. For instance, in the 1990s, Lord Woolf was asked to consider how to enhance access to justice by reforming civil procedure and in 1999–2001, Lord Justice Auld was asked to consider reforms to the practices, procedures and rules of evidence applied by the criminal courts, but no-one ever examines the workings of the whole English court structure. We take it for granted that we need two levels of first instance court (trial court). We take it for granted that we need both a Court of Appeal and a Supreme Court because it has been that way beyond living memory. The general issues paper of the *Civil Justice Review*, 1986, raised the radical question of whether we really need both the county courts and the High Court dealing with civil cases and the Master of the Rolls asked this again, in 2005. It is true to say, however, that, considering nothing much had happened in the English legal system since the 1870s, we have scrutinised and reconfigured an enormous number of bricks in our Lego pile since 1985, largely thanks to the radical Conservative Lord Chancellor, Lord Mackay, and his Labour successors, Lord Irvine and Lord Falconer. Since then, Coalition and Conservative Lord Chancellors busied themselves from 2010 in deconstructing much of the legal aid structure put in place from the mid-twentieth century.

Hallmarks of the English legal system

The common law

1–011   The English legal system is a "common law" system. This means that many of our primary legal principles have been made and developed by judges from case to case in what is called a system of precedent, where the lower courts are bound to follow principles established by the higher courts in previous cases. The term "common law" historically distinguished the law made by judges in the royal courts in Westminster and commonly applicable throughout the kingdom, from canon law (ecclesiastical law) and the local systems of customary law which predominated until 1066 and survived beyond. This is examined in Ch.8.

Judge-made law is at least as important to us as statute law made by Parliament. For instance, there is no statute telling us that murder is a crime and defining it for us. It is a common law crime. The required guilty act, of causing death, and the necessary degree of guilt, malice aforethought, have been prescribed and defined, over the centuries, by judges, on a case-by-case basis. Similarly, the civil law of negligence was the invention of a judge who wanted to find a remedy for a woman who had suffered gastro-enteritis when she drank from an opaque bottle of ginger beer, wherein lurked the decomposing remains of a stray snail. She was given the ginger beer and thus had no contract with the retailer or manufacturer. The judge, Lord Atkin, decided that, as a matter of principle, she should have a right to damages against the manufacturer, as they owed her a "duty of care". Thus, he invented what became the law of negligence.

Adversarial procedure

1–012   Another characteristic of the English legal system and all common law systems is that basic trial procedure is essentially adversarial. This means that the two parties to the case are left to their own devices to prepare and present their cases unaided by the court. Crass comparisons are made between this typical common law procedure and the type of "inquisitorial" procedure, with officials of the court involved in the fact finding process, which is said to be a hallmark of continental European legal systems. As we shall see, however, our trial system has not always been adversarial, and inquisitorial elements are appearing at many points in the system. Also, it is wrong to label European procedural systems as "inquisitorial". See Ch.9.

Jury trial and orality

Historically, and certainly since 1215, jury trial was central to the English legal system in both criminal and civil cases, although its use in civil cases is now rare and it is confined to a small percentage of cases, including all serious cases, in the criminal courts. The need to argue cases before a jury has shaped our rules of evidence, procedure and substantive law and has meant, historically, that most arguments were presented to the court orally, by the parties, through examination and cross-examination of witnesses. Again, the emphasis on orality is rapidly disappearing, with the admission of more and more written statements and documentary evidence in hard copy and electronically retrievable form. Since 1995, in civil cases, lawyers now have to present the court with a skeleton argument so the advocate's art of oral storytelling has been replaced by a scene in a typical civil court room where all heads are face-down in "the bundle" of documents and the "skeleton" (argument), flicking through hard copy or more usually an electronic tablet, to make cross references, incomprehensible to the casual observer. It has taken some fun out of court watching, because it is difficult to follow the story.

1–013

Lay magistrates

The bulk of criminal cases are heard in magistrates' courts, mostly by lay justices. There are almost 18,000 of them. No other legal system makes such heavy use of laypeople as decision-makers. In exporting the common law, we exported the concept of magistrates but they tended to be professionals. When you add to lay justices (magistrates) the thousands of lay arbitrators, tribunal panel members and jurors, you start to realise how many important decisions are taken by laypersons in the English legal system.

1–014

4. THE MOTHER OF ALL COMMON LAW SYSTEMS

Just as England has been called "the mother of parliaments", because so many others have been modelled on the UK Parliament, I have called the English legal system the mother of all common law legal systems, worldwide. English common law is the most widespread legal system in the world, governing 30 per cent of the world's population. Twenty seven per cent of the world's 320 legal jurisdictions use common law, according to research by Wood (2009). We exported the common law and our legal system, along with the English language, into our old colonies and the Commonwealth. The common law daughters of the English legal system include the USA, Canada, Australia, New Zealand and most of India and Pakistan but we maintain our direct link with the living common law of many Commonwealth countries, through the Judicial Committee of the Privy Council. This court sits in London and is the highest court of appeal for those

1–015

jurisdictions. Since it is mainly composed of UK Supreme Court Justices, this provides for harmonious development of principle throughout all of these common law jurisdictions. Decisions of the Judicial Committee (JCPC) are persuasive and not binding precedents on the English courts but they are very heavily influential, since everyone realises that when those senior judges metamorphose back into UKSC Justices, they are not likely to contradict legal principles which they carefully established when doing their job as privy councillors.

This common law cross-fertilisation is by no means confined to Commonwealth countries, however: see Cooke (1997). Certain areas of the common law, such as tort and criminal law, have developed globally, with judges in the courts of one country sometimes persuaded by the reasoning of their brethren in another jurisdiction. You only have to flick through the pages of an English text on criminal law to see how other countries tackle some of the interpretive problems facing our criminal courts. Where no precedent exists, English judges may be persuaded by a precedent from America, Australia or Canada, and so on, such as the trial judge in a manslaughter judgment: *R. v Pagett* (1983). In this case, P used his pregnant girlfriend as a shield in a police shoot-out and she was shot dead. There was no precedent as to whether he could be found guilty of her murder so the courts were persuaded by a New York precedent that he could.

Of course, enabled by the European Convention on Human Rights, obliged by membership of the EU and facilitated by the internet, UK judges have also enthusiastically adopted attractive reasoning and principles from jurisdictions outside the common law world into English common law. As Lord Dyson MR explained in a fabulously interesting 2015 speech, "The Globalisation of Law":

> "An interesting and difficult question is: by what criteria does a national court decide whether to adopt the views of academic writers or the decisions of other national courts? In our courts at least, a passage from a textbook or a judgment in a foreign case is often cited to reinforce a conclusion that has already been reached by independent detailed reasoning. Sometimes, however, the passage sets out reasoning which the judge considers to be so compelling that he or she simply adopts it. The willingness of judges to borrow from each other is now an accepted and, in my view, welcome fact of judicial life. There is much that we can learn from each other, and not merely in relation to the interpretation of international treaties. In recent years, the development of the common law of England has benefited hugely from decisions of courts of other common law jurisdictions."

The whole speech, on the judiciary website, is well worth reading, on how UK courts crafted a definition of "refugee", by borrowing. He also mentioned that England copied a new way of handling expert witnesses from Australia and New Zealand. In turn, we exported to them the concept of proportionality in civil litigation, and judicial case management to Norway. There is now a global traffic in legal ideas, as judges read one another's judgments and meet at international conferences. At the same time, though, I found from teaching in California and buying property in Colorado that much of old English common law is still alive throughout her common law daughters, including the USA, even in forms which have been replaced in England. For instance, the actions constituting an attempted crime in California are determined by old English case law, replaced in England by the Criminal Attempts Act 1981. US property law uses concepts straight out of medieval English property law, abolished by the English in the Law of Property Act 1925. If you buy property or sign a contract in the USA, you may be astonished by ancient English terminology.

To mark the transformation of the UK's top court from "law lords" into the Supreme Court, in 2009, the Canadian Chief Justice, Beverley McLachlin and South African Justice Kate O'Regan wrote an article, "Views from Canada and South Africa: We owe a great debt to the work of the judges", acknowledging the contribution of the law lords to the worldwide spread of common law. The law lords and now the UKSC play a prominent role in the development of international common law and human rights, evidenced by dozens of sources, not least in some of the 51 essays in *Tom Bingham and the Transformation of the Law*. For instance, Michael Kirby, former Justice of the Australian High Court said "Decisions have no binding force whatsoever ... the greatest tribute to the House of Lords can be found in the fact that ... they continue to be cited in so many fields." Similarly, Andenas and Fairgrieve, referring to his judgments on liberty and anti-terror, said "Lord Bingham persuades through his reasoning ... his judgments are comparative law sources, as persuasive authority, all over the world". Zeno-Zencovich, in the same book, detailed the court's internationalism. Of 475 decisions in 2000–2007, 250 centred on interpretation of or made use of transnational or international law, including 100 human rights and 50 EU law cases, plus a number citing American, Canadian and Commonwealth authorities. He said, "A comparativist finds in the House of Lords reports a bonanza for his classes and case-books". Andenas and Fairgrieve claimed Bingham to have been a pioneer in developing comparative law in modern court practice. They pointed to his willingness to use European human rights law to develop the common law.

The globalisation of law, especially English law, is not a new thing and judges with an interest in history remind us that the ancient English common law was an avid borrower. As Lord Neuberger said in 2015:

> "We have to preserve and to defend our common law systems and traditions, of which we have every right to be proud and whose value is plain from the volume of international contracts which are expressed to be subject to English law and pursuant to which disputes end up in English courts or arbitrations. However, the common law has survived and has led by learning partly by lifting good ideas from Europe – examples include the jury in the 11th century, the writ in the 12th century, disclosure in the 13th century and the *lex mercatoria* in the 18th century."

Sir Edward Coke was highly instrumentally in this borrowing, as Attorney General and then a judge and Chief Justice, in his arguments, judgments and writing. He thought nothing of adopting Roman law principles as if they were long-established common law principles and no-one challenged him because he was so well-read and prolific. For example, we all think of the phrase "an Englishman's home is his castle" as quintessentially English. Dyson pointed out that it originated in England from Coke's argument in *Semayne's case* in 1604 but it came from Roman law.

As the mother of all common law systems, with a stable system of law and courts over 940 years old and a generally incorruptible judiciary, English law and

1–016

English courts are heavily influential worldwide, and London is an international litigation and arbitration centre, as can be seen from the quotation at the top of this chapter.

5. THE COMPARISON WITH OTHER EUROPEAN SYSTEMS

1–017 Since, in our popular rhetoric and our legal analysis, we are always comparing ourselves with continental legal systems, notably the French, and since we, along with all other EU Member States, now and for the time being have to absorb EU law into our domestic legal systems, we students of the English legal system need to understand something more about the world's second most extensive "family" of laws, the "Romano-Germanic" family, as David and Brierley describe it, in *Major Legal Systems in the World Today*. Apart from Ireland, a common law country, the legal systems of all of our EU partners are, historically, members of that other major family. Thanks to the globalisation of law and legal ideas, highlighted in recent judicial speeches, the differences in substantive law and procedure are shrinking, as can be seen in the tiny Ch.9 of this book.

Different roots …

1–018 Law applied in the Romano-Germanic family was developed by scholars in the European universities from the Renaissance of the twelfth and thirteenth centuries. There was a need for an autonomous law, independent of canon (Church) law, to replace inadequate and bitty customary law. This is called civil law, as distinct from canon law but here the phrase "civil law" has this different meaning from the phrase "civil law", meaning non-criminal law, described above. Renaissance scholars latched onto Roman law as a neat, pre-existing body of rules and set about refining it. Law was seen as a fairly abstract body of principles of justice, and its teaching was linked to the teaching of philosophy, theology and religion. It emerged from France and Italy but was taught in this way in Spain, Portugal, Scandinavia and even Oxford and Cambridge. The teaching of national law was not taken up until the seventeenth and eighteenth centuries. The flexibility and abstract nature of this civil law, refined and taught in Europe, can be contrasted with the rigidity of the common law rules developing in the Westminster courts in London. Eventually, Roman law was translated into the basis of national laws for practical application. This could not be done in England because the rules of common law were already too entrenched. From the thirteenth to the sixteenth centuries, the law as taught in European universities had considerable influence. Jurists, not governments, developed the law, so the countries of the Romano-Germanic family had jurists and legal practitioners who derived their concept of law, approach and reasoning from Roman law.

The study and refinement of Roman law naturally progressed to its codification. Codes were developed independently but the most influential of these was the Napoleonic Code of 1804. The French code was received in Belgium, the Netherlands, the Rhenish provinces, Luxembourg, Poland and Italy.

Thanks to colonisation by the Spanish, Portuguese, French and Dutch, elements of Romano-Germanic civil law spread throughout South America, parts of North America (Louisiana and Quebec) and Africa. The French influence extends to Turkey, Egypt, Iran, Syria, Iraq, Japan, Taiwan, Vietnam and Cambodia. Certain countries have a mixture of common law and civil law. Examples are Scotland, Israel, South Africa, Zimbabwe and Botswana. Because the French Napoleonic Code was absorbed into so many legal systems, this made France another mother of a family of legal systems. Notice that Germany did not adopt the French code but devised one of its own, so some comparativists talk of a French family and a German family.

... and different branches

The same divisions of law can be found throughout the Romano-Germanic legal systems and some of them, such as "the law of obligations", are alien to the common lawyer.

1–019

Written constitutions

The UK is one of only three countries in the developed world without a written constitution. Consequently, there is almost no awareness amongst the public at large of what the UK constitution amounts to. There is no talk of fundamental constitutional rights, as is drummed into every small child's memory in the USA, because we do not think we have any. We have only spoken in terms of human rights since the Human Rights Act 1998 came into force, in October 2000, making our *existing* rights under the European Convention on Human Rights enforceable in the UK courts. In most other jurisdictions, the legality of the law of the land can be tested against a written constitution in the courts and struck down if it offends against some constitutional requirement. In the UK, we are used to the idea that the law of our land is untouchable. Parliament is supreme, sovereign, and, prior to 1973, only Parliament could undo what a previous parliament had done. It is this inability to conceptualise any law superior to that made by Parliament which partly explains why we reacted so badly to the effrontery of the rulings of the European Court of Justice (ECJ) in the *Factortame* cases, which resulted in the suspension of part of an Act of the UK Parliament (see Ch.3). Similarly, the Blair government protested loudly in December 2004, when the law lords condemned the Anti-Terrorism, Crime and Security Act 2001 as contravening the European Convention on Human Rights (see Ch.4).

1–020

Public law and private law in Europe

Romano-Germanic legal systems all recognise the distinction between public and private law which, historically, English common law did not acknowledge. The French, for instance, have a separate set of courts, headed by the Conseil d'État, administering a separate body of public law developed by those courts to a sophisticated level by the first half of the twentieth century. French law has, in this respect, been highly influential over Belgian and Dutch law. Those countries also have courts which are modelled on the Conseil d'État. In the English legal

1–021

system, however, the development of public law was stifled, until the enactment of the Crown Proceedings Act 1947, by the rule that the Crown could not be sued, and until 1981 by the procedural difficulties in applying for judicial review. It is only since the 1960s that we have acknowledged the separate existence of a body of public law, worthy of being taught as an independent subject. We still do not have a separate set of public law courts, along French lines, but at least we now list most applications for judicial review to be heard in the Administrative Court (and now the Upper Tribunal), with a simplified procedure, which has allowed the rapid development of a coherent body of public administrative law.

The concept of law

1–022   The very way in which law is conceived of in the legal systems of the Romano-Germanic family is radically different from the way we approach it and it has developed in the common law countries, and this goes a very long way towards explaining why EU law and the judgments of the European Court of Justice were, in the early days, so much easier for our European partners to assimilate than for us. This is how David and Brierley, in their classic analysis, explain *la différence*:

> "In countries of the Romano-Germanic family, the legal rule is formulated, characterised and analysed in the same way. In this family, in which doctrinal writing is held in high esteem, the legal rule is not considered as merely a rule appropriate to the solution of a concrete case. It is fashionable to view with a certain disdain, and as casuistic, the opposite view which places the rule of law at the level of concrete cases only. Digests of decided cases, form books and legal dictionaries are certainly useful working instruments for practitioners, and they provide much of the raw material for jurists in their work. But these compilations do not enjoy the high prestige associated with legal scholarship. The function of the jurist is to draw from this disorganised mass first the rules and then the principles which will clarify and purge the subject of impure elements, and thus provide both the practice and the courts with a guide for the solution of particular cases in the future." (p.94)

In common law countries, just about the opposite is going on. The initial approach is one of pragmatism in individual cases, rather than abstract principle. The common law is developed, whether the judges are dealing with a judge-made law or interpreting a statute, on a case-by-case basis. The concern of the judge is to find the solution to the instant case. When a sufficient body of case law has developed, through the application and extension of judicial reasoning in the system of precedent, then it may be possible to elevate these judicial rulings to the level of principle. In other words, judicial reasoning in a common law country is said to work from "bottom up" and in a civil law country it is from "top down".

Because judicial reasoning is such an important source of law, common lawyers throughout the world are heavily dependent on law reports. Academics certainly comment on judicial reasoning but scholars cannot be said, for the most part, to be the source of legal doctrine themselves. Indeed, there was a convention that judges did not cite living authors. The exception is that, where there is no precedent, the courts would resort to examining what are known as "books of authority"—early writings in the common law. It is now quite common for judges to refer to modern textbooks or articles.

Sources of law and the judicial approach

The primary source of law in the Romano-Germanic legal systems is codified   1–023
law, the drafting and interpretation of which is influenced by, or is the task of,
academic jurists. In common law countries, we depend on a mixture of
judge-made law (common law) and statute, as interpreted by judges, whose
reasoned opinions we must read in the law reports. If we take the French legal
system as a contrasting example, we can see that the judge is not considered to be
a source of law. Indeed, following the revolution, judges' powers were curtailed
and they were prohibited from creating binding rules of precedent. Of course, this
is constitutional theory but in reality, French judges have had to make law, to a
certain extent, and some critics say that the notion that they do not make law is an
academic myth. While even the judgments of the Cour de cassation are not meant
to form binding precedents, they are followed by the lower courts in most cases.
Certainly French public law is almost entirely judge-made since it was developed
after the Napoleonic era of codification. The French ambivalence is illustrated by
the way law is taught. Textbooks emphasise codified law (legislation), with cases
relegated to footnote illustrations, yet tutorials concentrate on case commentaries.

The nature of a French judgment is very different. Whereas some of our
leading UKSC decisions contain the reasoned opinions of five to nine Justices,
distinguishing and applying a long list of precedents and stretching through over
100 pages in the law reports, French judgments, even emanating from the Cour
de cassation, are very short. They are in the form of a syllogism: they set out the
facts, the legal issue in context and the conclusion, usually without citing any
previous case authority. Because judgments are so short, they are normally
published accompanied by academic commentary.

Procedural differences

We most commonly see the English legal system contrasted with European   1–024
systems in terms of procedure, notably criminal procedure. Broadly speaking,
European systems were characterised by common lawyers as "inquisitorial", with
the examining magistrate, then the court, taking a significant part in fact-finding
and examining witnesses. This caricature was contrasted with the adversarial or
accusatorial system, which the common law population likes to insist is so much
fairer, with the judge acting as an unbiased umpire, permitting both sides to
prepare and present their cases and examine witnesses, independent of court
interference. Both the English and continental legal systems have recently
departed from the purity of their respective models, however, especially with the
procedural changes of the 1980s and 1990s. The Italian criminal process has
recently become much more adversarial and in 2009, French President Sarkozy
announced the abolition of investigating magistrates.

Bad Europeans

I have endeavoured to explain at some length the contrast between the English   1–025
legal system and the Romano-Germanic systems of our EU partners for two
reasons. First, we need to see where the English legal system sits, in worldwide

terms, and secondly, we need to understand why EU law seems a bit more difficult for us to get used to than for our European counterparts. EU procedural law and its concept of law are derived directly from the French legal system.

The French influence can be seen in the procedure of the Court of Justice of the European Union. French was the original working language of the court. Lawyers' oral submissions are strictly limited to 30 minutes' argument. Common lawyers, trained in the tradition of oral advocacy, had to be helped by the court's staff to reduce their arguments into writing, in the early days. The roles of the advocate-general and judge-rapporteur are modelled on the French. They have no common law equivalent. The system of references for preliminary rulings bears a direct similarity to references of questions of law from the French inferior courts to the Cour de cassation. Again, there is no common law equivalent. The early judgments of the European Court of Justice (ECJ) looked just like French judgments, with very little reasoning and no precedents cited. This was one of the most difficult aspects of EU law for the common lawyer to comprehend but the Court of Justice has now changed. For the sake of consistency, it takes serious account of its own precedents and cites them in its judgments, and reported decisions contain much more reasoning than they formerly did, thus looking much more like common law judgments. The court certainly accepts and applies broad principle in the same way that a court in a Romano-Germanic legal system would.

6. WHO RUNS THE ENGLISH LEGAL SYSTEM?

1–026 The Lord Chancellor (Secretary of State for Justice) is the cabinet minister in charge of the Ministry of Justice. It is the successor of the Department for Constitutional Affairs, formerly the Lord Chancellor's Department. On its surprise creation in 2007, it also took many functions from the Home Office. It is responsible for corrections (prisons and so on), criminal justice, HM Courts and Tribunals Service, tribunals, judicial diversity, family justice, coroners' courts and legal aid. The Home Office is responsible for immigration and passports, the police, drugs policy, crime and counter-terrorism. HM Courts and Tribunals Service is an independent agency, formed in 2011, running the courts and tribunals. The minister in charge of prosecutions is the Attorney General. Prosecutors are described in Ch.12. The judiciary is independently run by the Lord Chief Justice, under the Constitutional Reform Act 2005, as described in Ch.14. Lawyers are regulated by a variety of bodies, overseen by the Legal Services Board, described in Ch.13.

7. KEEPING UP-TO-DATE WITH THE ENGLISH LEGAL SYSTEM

1–027 Most of the law changes frequently and this subject changes most often. Like all law books, this one, finished in Spring 2017, and proofread in July 2017, will be out of date by the time you read it. Here are some tactics for keeping up-to-date:

- Never read out-of-date law books. They are as dangerous as last week's cream cakes.

- Show tutors/examiners that you have kept up to date by scan-reading a quality newspaper, such as *The Times*, *The Financial Times*, *The Guardian* or *The Independent* (or at least the Reuters or BBC news websites, as these do not make fake news). *The Times* has the most legal content. It also contains brief law reports of recent cases, which are super-useful and can be accessed via the CASES on *Lexis*. *The Guardian* contains useful analysis of social issues in the legal system, as does *The Independent*. You can also search all newspapers in various subscriber databases, which most libraries have, or abstracted on *LexisNexis* or *Westlaw*. By keeping abreast of the news, you can make the law more interesting for yourself by understanding how law is about real people, in the real world. Law is not just in books.

- Take yourself to court. The courts are a free source of daily entertainment, Mondays to Fridays. Justice in England and Wales is meant to be open to the public. Courts and tribunals are everywhere. Go and see how law operates in practice, in solving people's disputes and responding to their offences. In this way, you will learn a lot about procedure, the court structure, lawyers, magistrates and judges.

- Regularly browse the legal news journals, such as *The New Law Journal*, *Legal Action*, the Law Society's *Gazette* or *The Lawyer*.

- Listen to *Law in Action* on BBC Radio 4. Old programmes are on iPlayer Radio and you can download the BBC iPlayer Radio App.

- Visit relevant websites and check on "What's New?" and the press releases. You can sign up to email alerts from Westlaw, Lexis, the Ministry of Justice and so on.

ELS Websites (checked in July 2017)

Association of Women Barristers *http://www.womenbarristers.com*　　　1–028
Association of Women Solicitors London *http://www.awslondon.co.uk/*
Attorney　　General　　*https://www.gov.uk/government/organisations/attorney-generals-office*
Bar Council *http://www.barcouncil.org.uk/*
British and Irish Legal Information Institute *http://www.bailii.org/*
Centre for Effective Dispute Resolution (ADR) *http://www.cedr.com*
Citizens Advice Bureau *http://www.citizensadvice.org.uk/*
Civil Justice Council: see judiciary website
City UK: *https://www.thecityuk.com/*
Criminal Cases Review Commission *http://www.ccrc.gov.uk/*
Criminal Courts Review (archived) *http://webarchive.nationalarchives.gov.uk/+/ http://www.criminal-courts-review.org.uk/*
Crown Prosecution Service *http://www.cps.gov.uk/*
Department for Constitutional Affairs (archived), the predecessor of the MoJ, very informative *http://webarchive.nationalarchives.gov.uk/20100512160448/ http://www.dca.gov.uk/index.htm*
European Court of Human Rights *http://www.echr.coe.int/Pages/home.aspx?p= home*

European Union institutions and documents, including European Commission and Court of Justice of the EU *http://europa.eu/*

European Commission Representation in the UK, for EU news, publications and information *http://ec.europa.eu/unitedkingdom/*

Gov.UK Government Information *https://www.gov.uk/*

Her Majesty's Courts and Tribunals Service *http://www.justice.gov.uk/about/hmcts/*

Home Office https:*//www.gov.uk/government/organisations/home-office*

International Courts of Justice are best accessed via the United Nations website *http://www.un.org/*

Judicial Appointments Commission *http://jac.judiciary.gov.uk/*

Judicial Committee of the Privy Council *http://www.jcpc.uk/*

Judiciary *http://www.judiciary.gov.uk/*

JUSTICE (lawyers advocating law reform and human rights) *http://www.justice.org.uk/*

Law Commission *http://lawcommission.justice.gov.uk/*

Lawlinks, links to legal internet resources *http://www.kent.ac.uk/library/subjects/lawlinks/*

Law Society, including the Gazette *http://www.lawsociety.org.uk/*

Legal Abbreviations *http://www.legalabbrevs.cardiff.ac.uk/*

Legal Action Group, including items from Legal Action *http://www.lag.org.uk/*

Legislation *http://www.legislation.gov.uk/*

Liberty *http://www.liberty-human-rights.org.uk/*

National Assembly for Wales http*://www.assemblywales.org/*

UK National Statistics *http://www.statistics.gov.uk/*

UK Parliament *http://www.parliament.uk/*

UK Supreme Court *https://www.supremecourt.uk/*

US Supreme Court *https://www.supremecourt.gov/*

Welsh Government *gov.wales*

Bibliography, further reading and sources for updating this chapter

1–029   Free updates of this book are available on the Sweet & Maxwell website: *http://uklawstudent.thomsonreuters.com*.

Summary and revision: P. Darbyshire, *Nutshells English Legal System*, 10th edn (London: Sweet & Maxwell, 2016).

M. Andenas, and D. Fairgrieve (eds), *Tom Bingham and the Transformation of the Law* (Oxford: Oxford University Press, 2009).

T. Bingham, *The Rule of Law* (London: Penguin, 2011).

The Right Hon The Lord Cooke of Thorndon KBE, Hamlyn Lectures: *Turning Points of the Common Law* (London: Sweet & Maxwell, 1997).

R. David, and J. Brierley, *Major Legal Systems in the World Today*, 3rd revised edn (Steven & Sons Ltd, 1985).

Department of Constitutional Affairs, *A Guide to Government Business involving the Channel Islands and the Isle of Man*, (2002).

Lord Dyson M.R., "The Globalisation of Law", 6 November 2015.

P. Glenn, *Legal Traditions of the World*, 5th edn (Oxford: Oxford University Press, 2014).

T. Honoré, *About Law: An Introduction*, 1st edn (New York: Oxford University Press, 1995).
Chief Justice B. McLachlin and Justice K. O'Regan, *Timesonline*, 1 October 2009.
Lord Neuberger, "Developing equity—a view from the Court of Appeal", speech, January 20, 2012; "Some thoughts on the post-LASPO civil judge's role before and during trial", Manchester, 22 January 2015.
Professor Philip Wood's research for Allen and Overy, reported at (2009) 159 N.L.J. 245.

It is not used here but a really entertaining and wide ranging book, giving a brilliant introduction to English law in general, is G. Rivlin, *Understanding the Law*, 7th edn (Oxford: Oxford University Press, 2015).

CHAPTER 2

Sources of English and Welsh Law

"The inevitable duty of the Courts is to make law and that is what all of us do every day." (Lord Cooke of Thorndon, cited by Lord Bingham (2000), p.34).

"We're a common law court. Of course we 'make' law as we go along." (US Supreme Court Justice Sandra Day O'Connor, quoted by Toobin (2007), p.97).

"The days are long gone when anyone could expect to find the text of the law set out clearly in an Act of Parliament." (D.A. Thomas 2012).

The sources of Welsh and English law are statute law (Acts of the UK   2–001
Parliament and statutory instruments), other delegated legislation including
Welsh Acts, common law (mainly in case law made by judges), EU law (until
Brexit happens in *law*), the European Convention on Human Rights 1950, other
international law, royal prerogative (including orders in council), books of
authority and custom. Law making and law reform are discussed in Ch.5. Very
importantly, note that EU law and The European Convention on Human Rights
are *such* important sources of law that they are not examined in this chapter but
each has their own chapter: Ch.3 and Ch.4 respectively.

1. LEGISLATION

Acts of the UK Parliament (Primary Legislation)

The most obvious source of codified law is an Act of the UK Parliament, the   2–002
legislature. In the unwritten UK constitution, "parliamentary sovereignty" is
fundamental. It recognises that supreme power is vested in Parliament and that
there is no limit to its law-making capacity. This is currently tempered by
membership of the Common Market since 1973 (now EU) and the further effect
given to the European Convention on Human Rights by the Human Rights Act
1998, from 2000. Nevertheless, for the time being, unless it conflicts with EU
law, the courts will always apply an Act of Parliament. Where statute law
provides a remedy, the citizen is expected to use that, not a common law remedy:
Marcic v Thames Water Utilities Ltd (2003). A person whose property was
flooded by overflowing sewers had an adequate statutory complaints procedure,
without resorting to the tort of nuisance. The same applies to criminal law. In *R. v
Goldstein, R. v Rimmington* (2005), the law lords held that good practice and
respect for primacy of statute over the common law required that people should

23

be prosecuted for a statutory offence where possible. Therefore, prosecutions for common law offences such as public nuisance should be rare.

The courts' acceptance of parliamentary supremacy is derived from the seventeenth century conflict between the Stuart kings and Parliament. In that conflict, the courts took the side of Parliament and have since acknowledged Parliamentary sovereignty, whilst Parliament has, in turn, readily allowed the independence of the judiciary. This was established in the Act of Settlement 1701 and is discussed in Ch.14. The contrast with countries with a written constitution (most countries) is, however, very marked. Their Supreme Courts have the power to overrule legislation as being "unconstitutional". No such power exists in the UK. The only role of the courts is to "interpret" statutory provisions to the circumstances of any given case. They must, where possible, interpret Acts so as to give effect to the European Convention on Human Rights and they are currently obliged to recognise EU law as supreme, if it conflicts with UK law. The courts can judicially review and quash delegated legislation but not primary legislation.

In *British Railways Board v Pickin* (1974), an unsuccessful attempt was made to persuade the top court, the House of Lords appellate committee, to intervene, on the grounds that the Board had obtained powers in a private Act of Parliament by misleading Parliament. Another unsuccessful attempt was made in *R. (on the application of Jackson) v Attorney General* (2005). In this case, pro-hunt supporters challenged the validity of the Hunting Act 2004, arguing that it was invalid because it was passed under the procedure laid down by the Parliament Act 1949 which they argued was also invalid. The 2004 Act, banning fox hunting, was hotly controversial. The Government had used their powers under the 1949 Act to pass the Bill through the House of Commons only, without the consent of the House of Lords, who had rejected a previous version. The 1949 Act had amended the Parliament Act 1911, which permitted a Bill to be passed by the House of Commons alone, in certain circumstances, provided a two-year period had elapsed. The 1949 Act reduced that period to one year. Lord Woolf CJ in the Court of Appeal (CA) remarked that it was very rare for the courts to entertain a challenge to an Act but the challenge *was* permissible because the 1911 Act was very unusual. The House of Lords, House of Commons and the King had used the machinery of legislation to make a fundamental change to the constitution. The law lords agreed with the CA: while *Pickin* sought to investigate the internal workings of Parliament, this case questioned whether the Parliament Acts were correctly enacted law. Importantly, the CA held that the UK's unwritten constitution *could* be amended by the legislature and it was clear that such an amendment was intended by the 1911 and 1949 Acts. The decision was upheld on appeal to the law lords.

The Queen in Parliament

2–003   The UK Parliament is made up of three constituent elements: the monarch, the House of Lords and the House of Commons. An Act normally has approval of all three elements. Under certain conditions, it can be passed without the approval of the Lords, using the Parliament Acts 1911 and 1949. This has only been done a few times and occurred in 2004 with the Hunting Act. The monarch's place in

Parliament is a formality. She attends the opening of each new Parliamentary session and after each General Election when a new government is elected. She reads the "Queen's speech" from the throne, which is the Government's statement of its legislative proposals for the coming Parliamentary session. It is written by the Prime Minister and does not reflect her views. All legislation must receive Royal Assent before it becomes law. Royal Assent has not been refused since the reign of Queen Anne in 1707, because of the constitutional convention (custom) that the monarchy does not interfere in politics.

Procedure

An Act starts off as a Bill. Most are Public Government Bills. Their clauses will have been agreed by the "sponsoring" government department, usually after considering responses to consultation papers placed on the departmental website. Consultation papers were called "green papers", as they were green, in the days when they were only published in hard copy. The Bill will have been drafted by parliamentary counsel and often a "white paper" is published alongside it, explaining the government policy reflected in the Act. For example, from 2010, the Justice Minister consulted on proposed changes to legal aid and civil justice, most of which were incorporated into the Legal Aid, Sentencing and Punishment of Offenders Act 2012, which he had introduced into Parliament as a Bill.

2–004

Before a Bill becomes an Act, and the clauses become sections, it must undergo five stages in each House. It may start off in the Commons or Lords. Once the Bill with any amendments has been approved both by the Commons and, normally, the Lords, it needs only the Royal Assent to become an Act. It comes into immediate effect unless it contains its own commencement date, or it has a provision which allows different parts to be brought into force at different times, by statutory instrument. For instance, parts of the Criminal Justice Act 2003 were still being brought into force in 2005 and some have not been brought into force by 2017. Some sections will probably never be implemented. Some have been repealed without having been brought into force. The Human Rights Act 1998 did not come into force until 2000, to give the courts, public bodies and the public time to prepare. For a comprehensive explanation of Parliamentary procedure, Bills and Acts, in plain English, visit the UK Parliament website, especially "Making Laws", under "How Parliament Works". Even better, go and watch proceedings yourself. Alternatively, you can watch a choice of live proceedings or archived debates via the website. There is an explanation of Welsh law on the National Assembly for Wales website.

The form of an Act of Parliament

Statutory language must be precise. Every Act must relate to existing legislation on the subject. Therefore, sections or schedules often amend old Acts or cross-refer to others. For example, the Tribunals, Courts and Enforcement Act 2007 Pt 2, changing the eligibility conditions for judicial appointments, alters the wording of dozens of statutory provisions, to which it cross-refers. This makes it difficult to read and understand. Further, although the modern aim is to draft the law in plain English, the endeavour to close loopholes also makes Acts complex.

2–005

The reader can browse Acts on the Legislation website for evidence of this. In 1995, I watched an argument between a parliamentary draftsman and a tax lawyer, at a conference on legislation. The tax lawyer accused the draftsman of making the annual Finance Acts too complicated for ordinary people to understand. The draftsman retorted that if clients stopped paying tax lawyers large amounts of money to find loopholes, he could draft them in simpler language. Controversial or big Bills suffer many amendments, especially by the Government who introduced them. They respond to criticisms made in Parliament by making hundreds of amendments. These factors combine to make statutes complicated and notoriously difficult for the lay person to understand. Although the earliest statutes had long titles and preambles, since the Short Titles Act 1896, Acts of Parliament have been given a short title and a long title. To try and make Acts more comprehensible, governments since 1998 publish explanatory notes alongside many new Acts. The Coroner Reform Bill 2006 contained a plain English translation alongside each clause. It spelled out in full the relevant sections of previous legislation, instead of just making a reference and forcing the reader to look up the old statute. In the autumn of 2006, it was reviewed by a panel of 15 members of the public who had had recent experience of using the court. The Plain English Campaign called it a "great step forward". Luckily, on the legislation website, we can now read the amended versions of *some* Acts. Readers with access to *Westlaw* or *Lexis*, via university or law firms' libraries, can read statutes in an extremely useful updated and annotated form and that is by far the best approach.

Citation and publication

2–006   From 1963, every Act is given a sequential chapter number for the year in which it receives the Royal Assent. It is possible to identify a statute simply by year and chapter number. They are now referred to by their short title and chapter number: for example, The Children and Families Act 2014 (c.6). Acts are published by The National Archives. They make new legislation available for sale as soon as it has been given Royal Assent. It is available free online, including all public Acts from 1988 and some from 1801–1987.

Public Bills and Private Bills

2–007   A Public Bill affects the public at large, and generally applies throughout England and Wales. Most Bills are Public and sponsored by the Government. A Private Bill affects a limited section of the population, either by reference to locality or by reference to a particular family or group of individuals. These are known respectively as Local and Personal Bills. A Private Member's Bill is a Public Bill introduced by a back-bench Member of Parliament, who has been successful in the ballot. A Hybrid Bill may cover work of national importance but in a local area. Examples are the Channel Tunnel Bills of the 1970s and 1980s and the High Speed Rail (Preparation) Act 2013 enabling the proposed HS2 railway.

Consolidation, codification and statute law revision

Consolidation is the process by which provisions in a number of Acts are brought together and re-enacted in one Act. It is not a method for changing the law but it does make the law easier to find. In order to ease the passage of such measures, they go through Parliament in a special procedure. For example, legislation concerning sentencing was consolidated in the Powers of the Criminal Courts (Sentencing) Act 2000. The Government's Discrimination Law Review published a consultation paper in June 2007 which identified nine pieces of discrimination legislation and concluded that we needed a single Equality Act. This was enacted in 2010.

2–008

Codification means using an Act to bring together all the existing legislation and case law to form a complete restatement of the law. It can involve changes in the law and is thus one method of law reform. The Law Commission, which was set up under the Law Commissions Act 1965, has the responsibility to keep under review all the law with a view to its systematic development and reform, including codification. The Commission also has overall responsibility for advising the repeal of obsolete and unnecessary enactments. Since 1993–1994, a "fast-track" procedure has been used for legislation proposed by the Commission and other non-contentious Bills. We return to all of this in Ch.5 on law reform.

Pre-legislative scrutiny

Pre-legislative scrutiny has been favoured since Tony Blair PM came to power in 1997. Gordon Brown PM took this further by announcing the contents of the next autumn's Queen's speech in July 2007, in a Green Paper. This followed his undertaking to "modernize and open up the legislative process". Some departments published draft bills for consultation. Later governments have continued this practice so you can now see draft Bills and Bills on the UK Parliament website.

2 009

Post-legislative scrutiny

In 2006 the Law Commission supported extending and formalising post-legislative scrutiny. The aim is to "improve the accountability of governments for the legislation they pass and ultimately lead to better and more effective law". Consequently, Parliamentary Select Committees do this all the time now. They are composed of all-party backbenchers, who are watchdogs over government action. They conduct post-legislative assessment on recent Acts, exploring how the Act has been used, whether it achieved its objectives and what impact it has had on public authorities. For example, as will be seen in Ch.17, in 2013–2014, the Justice Committee conducted such an assessment of the heavily criticised changes made to the legal aid scheme in a 2012 Act.

2–010

Delegated (secondary, subordinate) legislation

2–011 This is the name given to law made in documentary form by subordinate authorities acting under powers delegated by Parliament. Parliament does not have time or expertise to fill in the details or technicalities of the law so most big Bills are mere frameworks. The big difference between Acts of the UK Parliament (primary legislation) and subordinate or delegated legislation is that the courts can quash the latter if it is outside the remit of the power delegated by the enabling Act (substantively ultra vires) or if it has not been made procedurally correctly (procedurally ultra vires). Such legislation can take the following forms.

Statutory instruments

2–012 The most common form of delegated legislation is a statutory instrument (SI), made under power given to a minister to make law for a specified purpose. As each SI is published, it is given a number for the year, for example, the Greenhouse Gas Emissions Trading Scheme (Amendment) Regulations (SI 2004/3390). Much more of our law is contained in SIs than Acts. Almost all EU law has come into English law via SIs, like the one just mentioned.

Byelaws

2–013 Parliament, via its Acts, delegates to local authorities and other public bodies the power to make local laws or laws limited to their particular functions. Therefore, local authorities can make byelaws for their areas. For instance, there are often rules governing behaviour in parks or leisure centres. The authority has to obtain confirmation from the named central government minister before the byelaws take effect. The power to make byelaws is also conferred on public bodies such as the Civil Aviation Authority. Like statutory instruments, byelaws can be quashed on judicial review by the High Court if they are ultra vires. Their illegality can also be used as a defence where someone is prosecuted for infringing them. This happened to Lindis Percy, a protester against US defence forces in the UK. She appealed to the Crown Court against her conviction for breach of byelaws by repeatedly entering a secure defence installation. The Crown Court upheld her appeal, holding the byelaws to be ultra vires the Military Lands Act 1892, the enabling Act: *Secretary of State for Defence v Percy* (1999).

Welsh law

2–014 Wales gained considerable autonomy in making delegated legislation, from 1999. Under the Government of Wales Act 1998 and subsequent legislation, this includes areas of government such as agriculture, planning and the environment, health and social services, education and industry, housing and local government, sport and leisure, and the Welsh language. In turn, the Assembly has delegated many of its powers to its First Minister, who leads the Welsh Assembly Government. Under the Government of Wales Act 2006, the Welsh Assembly was given enhanced legislative power from 2011. The need to refer back to the UK Parliament was dispensed with. The Wales Act 2017 amends the 2006 Act. It provides that the UK Parliament will not normally legislate on devolved matters without the Assembly's consent. Also, the Act devolves far more power to Wales as it will confer *general* legislative power on the Assembly, with certain exceptions, instead of just power over the current limited list of topics. (Welsh law now has its own user-friendly, explanatory website). It should be remembered, however, that Welsh Acts, like Acts of the Scottish Parliament, are delegated legislation. They are thus reviewable by the UK Supreme Court. The validity of Scots law was tested for the first time in this way in *Martin (Sean) v HM Advocate* (2010) and I give a 2016 example in Ch.4 on human rights.

Comment on delegated legislation

Since the early twentieth century, there has been increasing concern that Parliament, the *legislature*, has been delegating too much law-making power to the *executive* government. This is perceived as undesirable because it breaches the separation of powers of the three organs of government (legislature, executive and judiciary) and separation is considered essential for democracy and the rule of law. Lord Chief Justice Hewart complained of this creeping growth of executive power in *The New Despotism* in 1929. Acts are often mere frameworks, giving substantial powers to Ministers to fill in the details through delegated powers. For instance, the Energy Act 2010 provides for carbon capture and storage and places duties on the relevant minister (Secretary of State) in relation to gas and electricity markets, empowering him to licence producers of electricity and provide a scheme of financial assistance, but it leaves it up to him to devise the schemes and the regulations.

2–015

Hewart was also concerned about the use of "Henry VIII" clauses in Acts which permit a single minister to amend an Act through a statutory instrument. For instance, the Legislative and Regulatory Reform Act 2006 permitted any minister to amend *any* legislation to get rid of red tape (see Burns (2006)). In 2010, Lord Chief Justice Judge repeated his predecessor's concern, castigating the Government for introducing a new Bill with sweeping Henry VIII clauses. The Government backed down. Bodies like the Law Commission were listed in Sch.7 of the Public Bodies Bill, a Henry VIII clause that would have allowed them to be merged or abolished by secondary legislation. (There were *seven* Henry VIII clauses in the Bill.) All of this has serious implications for independence in the distribution of resources and for scrutiny of the government, which is what these public bodies were created to do. In his Mansion House speech, in 2010, Lord Chief Justice Judge told the Lord Chancellor that Henry VIII clauses should be "confined to the dustbin of history", reminding us that in 1539 Henry persuaded Parliament to pass the Statute of Proclamations, giving his proclamations the same force as acts of the legislature. It was repealed on Henry's death. Lord Chief Justice Judge had tried to find out how many there were: 120 had been passed in the last session of Parliament alone. In December 2010, he then warned the Constitution Committee in the House of Lords that schedules of the Bill could potentially be used to abolish such important bodies as the Judicial Appointments Commission, Criminal Cases Review Commission and so on, bodies whose independence from government was vital. The Government backed down, announcing that it would not abolish public bodies using a Henry VIII clause, after all. Lord Chief Justice Judge, now retired from the judiciary, is a member of the House of Lords Select Committee on the Constitution which repeated these concerns in its ninth report for the 2015–2016 session and added that governments were using delegated legislation inappropriately:

> "This Committee and others have noted a trend whereby delegated legislation has increasingly been used to address issues of policy and principle, rather than to manage administrative and technical changes."(Summary).

The courts also criticise some delegated legislation. For example, the UK Supreme Court was "troubled" by incomprehensible immigration rules that the Home Secretary herself could not interpret consistently, (*R. (on the application of Iqbal) v Secretary of State for the Home Department* (2016)). In 2017, lawyers and politicians expressed outrage about the number of Henry VIII clauses in the European Union [Withdrawal] Bill.

2. STATUTORY INTERPRETATION

"Rules" for statutory interpretation

2–016   Disputes arise as to the meaning or application of primary or delegated legislation and the judges' task is to interpret it but do not neglect the obvious—the rest of us need to interpret statute law too: law lecturers and students; lawyers advising their clients; judges of the lower courts, for their own judgment-formation and sometimes for juries, and magistrates' clerks (legal advisers) need to advise their bench. Civil servants and local government officers need to know how to apply the law to us. Most importantly, as ordinary citizens, all of us are presumed to know the law. Therefore, we need to understand the way our business and social lives are regulated and what are our rights (for instance, as employees) and duties (for instance, to pay tax). Ignorance of the law is no defence so if Supreme Court Justices, with reputedly some of the world's most astute legal minds, struggle to interpret delegated legislation, then I suggest that affected individuals suffer from a serious shortfall in access to justice and this surely has implications for the rule of law, discussed in Ch.1.

Before considering the "rules" for interpretation, we should note that two experts on statutory interpretation, Cross and Bennion, insisted that there were no such "rules". In Bennion's first edition of *Statutory Interpretation* (1984) he said "Instead there are a thousand and one interpretive criteria". Nevertheless, judges have developed a set of common law *principles* to help them interpret statutes that are sometimes known as the rules of statutory interpretation. Judges do not describe themselves as applying these "rules" but they do tend to apply them sequentially.

The first tactic judges use is to look for definitions of contentious words. The Interpretation Act 1978 is used. One of its better-known sections provides that "unless the contrary intention appears (a) words importing the masculine gender include the feminine (and vice versa) (b) words in the singular include the plural, and words in the plural include the singular". Most statutes contain definitions of the words they use, especially if they are novel, so the Guardianship (Missing

Persons) Act 2017 s.24 defines "the missing person". Sometimes words are left undefined, though, and it is for the courts to determine their application. The Protection from Harassment Act 1997 did not define harassment but the High Court decided it did not include the activities of Microsoft, intimidating a software counterfeiter by provoking police raids, conducting oppressive litigation and telephoning the claimants at night: *Tuppen v Microsoft Corp Ltd* (2000).

The first principle (*the literal rule*) of interpretation is that the judge should apply the words according to their "ordinary, plain and natural meaning". In *Clarke v Kato* (1998) the law lords held that as a matter of ordinary language, a car park did not qualify as a road for the purposes of the Road Traffic Act 1988 so as to be an area in respect of which a motor insurance policy had to provide cover. In *Welsh v Stokes* (2007) the CA gave the word "normal" its "core" meaning of "conforming to type". The appellants lost their appeal against liability under the Animals Act 1971 s.2(2)(b), making the keeper of an animal liable for damage unless due to characteristics not normally found in animals of the same species. It was *normal* for a horse to bolt in certain circumstances and in this case a safe horse had thrown its rider who had suffered a serious head injury. In *Boss Holdings v Grosvenor West End Properties* (2008), the House of Lords applied a literal interpretation to the definition of a "house". It was originally "designed or adapted for living in" in the 1730s and so satisfied this definition in the Leasehold Reform Act 1967, even though it had become dilapidated. In *Day v Hosebay Ltd* (2012), the UK Supreme Court held that a building used entirely for non-residential purposes could not be a "house".

2–017

The Law Lords applied a common sense and literal interpretation in *R (on the application of National Grid Gas Plc (formerly Transco Plc) v Environment Agency* (2007). The case concerned liability for the cost of removing harmful coal tar residues found beneath the gardens of 11 homes, deposited by private gas companies before gas was nationalised in 1948. The phrase "person ... who has caused or knowingly permitted" pollution, in the Environmental Protection Act 1990 s.78F was not to be construed as including every person who became a successor in title to the polluters.

> "This is, in my opinion, a quite impossible construction to place on the uncomplicated and easily understandable statutory language. The emphasis in section 78F ... is on the actual polluter, the person who '... caused or knowingly permitted ...'." (per Lord Scott at [20]).

The courts will always construe penal legislation restrictively, applying limited meaning to statutory language, as can be seen from *R. v Johnson, R. v Hind* (2005), cited in Ch.12.

Unfortunately, the courts sometimes find themselves bound by the literal words of an Act into an interpretation which they consider leads to a daft result. In *R. v Horsman* (1998) Waller LJ said

> "however anomalous, if the words of the section are clear, there is no room for construing them in any other way ... the question whether there should not be some amendment [by Parliament] should be looked at with some haste".

R. v Smith (Wallace Duncan) (No.3) (2002) was another case where the CA reluctantly felt itself bound by a literal interpretation of statute. Section 14(5) of the Criminal Appeal Act 1995 seemed to say that once the Criminal Cases Review Commission (CCRC), on whatever grounds, had made a reference to the court, the appellant might add any further grounds, including those expressly rejected by the CCRC. Their Lordships were "very surprised indeed" at this and respectfully suggested that Parliament should make an amendment.

2–018 Sometimes judges are frustrated that a legislative oversight can produce a harsh result in unforeseen circumstances. A poignant example was *R. v Human Fertilisation and Embryology Authority Ex p. Blood* (1996). Diane Blood and her husband had decided to have a baby. Before she got a chance to conceive, her husband died of meningitis. While he was still in a coma, a sample of sperm was removed and frozen. His widow wanted to use it to conceive. The Human Fertilisation and Embryology Act required a man's written consent for the storage or use of his sperm in the UK. Much as the judge and the public had "universal sympathy" (Stephen Brown J) for the weeping Mrs Blood's "double bereavement", he could not surmount the clear requirement of the Act. Baroness Warnock, whose committee's finding led to the Act, blamed herself for not foreseeing such a case. Lord Winston, the famous fertility specialist, called the result "cruel and unnatural". The Court of Appeal also felt that "all the courts . . . can do is give effect to the clear language of the Act" (per Woolf MR). Happily, they allowed her appeal on a separate argument, a point of EU law. They ruled that she had the right to take the sperm for insemination elsewhere in the EU: (1997). She conceived in 1998 and had a second child in 2002.

Judges are more liberal in giving broad interpretations to words now than they used to be, if they feel they can produce a just result. The CA held that a generous interpretation should be put on "building", under the Cremation Act 1902, to permit Hindu open air funeral pyres. There was no reason not to give the word its natural and *relatively wide* meaning. They thought it should be possible to make a building in a private location with substantial openings: *R. (on the application of Ghai) v Newcastle City Council* (2010). The outcome here was surely fairer than the outcome of the very narrow interpretation in *Hobbs v Robertson (CG)* (1970), below.

Sometimes a case can be spared a bad outcome which would result from a literal interpretation, because a second principle, which became known as *the golden rule*, is that the literal application need not be applied, if to do so would lead to absurdity or to inconsistency within the statute itself. An outstanding example of the golden rule occurred in *Re Sigsworth* (1935), where a man was found to have murdered his mother. In the statute dealing with the distribution of the mother's estate it was laid down that the estate was to be distributed amongst "the issue" (children). The son was her only child. The judge held that the common law rule that a murderer cannot take any benefit from the estate of a person he had murdered prevailed over the apparently clear words of the statute.

A third principle is that if the so-called literal or golden rules fail to assist, the judge is entitled to consider *the mischief rule*. This rule, which was first settled in *Heydon's Case* (1584), allows the judge to consider: (1) what was the common law; (2) what was the defect or mischief in the common law; and (3) what remedy Parliament has provided in the legislation under scrutiny. Here, a judge is entitled to examine existing legislation and case law before coming to a decision, with the intention that the ruling will "suppress the mischief and advance the remedy." In *R. v Bournewood Community and Mental Health NHS Trust Ex p. L* (1999), the House of Lords held that the statutory predecessor to s.131(1) of the Mental Health Act 1983 was designed to cure the mischief caused by the assumption that compulsory powers had to be used unless the patient could express a positive desire for treatment.

The court is not easily persuaded to reject the plain words of the statute, **2–019** though. Lord Scarman in *Stock v Frank Jones (Tipton) Ltd* (1978) explained that

> "if the words used by Parliament are plain there is no room for the anomalies test, unless the consequences are so absurd that without going outside the statute, one can see that Parliament must have made a drafting mistake ... but mere manifest absurdity is not enough; it must be an error (of commission or omission) which in its context defeats the intention of the Act".

An example was *Inco Europe Ltd v First Choice Distribution* (2000). The House of Lords said the courts must be able to correct obvious drafting errors. In suitable cases, the court can add, omit or substitute words. Before doing so, they must be abundantly sure of three matters: the statute's intended purpose; that the draftsmen and Parliament had inadvertently failed to give effect to that purpose; and the substance of the provision that Parliament would have made, had the error been noticed.

Drafting errors and omissions may occur because of the number of amendments made as a big Bill passes through Parliament. A famous example of this is s.16 of the Theft Act 1968, which became known as "a judicial nightmare" and remained uncorrected until the Theft Act 1978. Lord Goff closely examined *Hansard* and recounted its messy legislative history in *R. v Preddy* (1996) and commented

> "hurried amendments to carefully structured comprehensive Bills are an accident-prone form of proceeding; and the new s.16 ... proved to be so incomprehensible as to be unworkable in practice".

Lord Denning used to say "we fill in the gaps" (in legislation). Sometimes the courts have to rewrite statute law in order to make sense of it. In *R. v Zafar* (2008), the Lord Chief Justice redrafted s.57 of the Terrorism Act 2000 to require an *intention* to use an article for a terrorist purpose.

Other "rules" (aids to interpretation)

It is accepted practice that "(t)he policy and objects of the Act must be **2–020** determined by construing the Act as a whole": *Padfield v Minister of Agriculture, Fisheries and Food* (1968). It follows that a judge must relate a word or phrase in a statute to its place in the context of the whole measure. Where specific words are followed by general words, the general words must be given effect in the light of the foregoing specific words. This is called the *ejusdem generis rule*. An example is *Hobbs v CG Robertson Ltd* (1970) where the Court of Appeal had to construe the following phrase concerning the provision of goggles in the

Construction (General Provisions) Regulations 1961 "breaking, cutting, dressing or carving of stone, concrete, slag or similar materials", in circumstances where a workman injured an eye, through the splintering of brickwork from a chimney breast which he was required to remove. The court applied the ejusdem generis rule in holding that brick was not "a similar material" to stone, concrete or slag; the provision of goggles was, therefore, not compulsory and the workman's claim failed. This narrow interpretation, producing such a harsh result, would not be the likely approach of modern judges.

A connected rule is that where, in a statute, there is a list of specified matters, which is not followed by general words, then only the matters actually mentioned are caught by this provision of the Act. The Latin phrase for this is *expressio unius est exclusio alterius*. In *R. v The Inhabitants of Sedgley* (1831), a statutory provision for rating occupiers of "lands, houses, tithes and coal mines" was held not to apply to any other kind of mine and in *B v DPP* (1999), the CA applied the rule (without saying they were doing so) in interpreting the Sexual Offences Act 1956. The inclusion of a specific statutory defence in two sections demonstrated conclusively that Parliament did not intend that the defence should be available for other offences where a defence was not mentioned. The rule *noscitur a sociis* means that where two or more words follow each other in a statute, they must be taken as related, for the purpose of interpretation. For example, in *Inland Revenue Commissioners v Frere* (1965) the House of Lords held that in the phrase, "interest, annuities or other annual payments" the word "interest" meant annual interest.

Presumptions

2–021 Judges apply well-known presumptions in interpreting legislation, unless rebutted by clear words.

(1) There is no change in the existing law beyond that expressly stated in the legislation.
(2) The Crown is not bound unless the Act specifically makes it so. The Windsors can only be prosecuted for speeding because the Road Traffic Acts spell out that they bind the Crown.
(3) Legislation is not intended to apply retrospectively, unless expressly stated. This is rare. An example was the War Crimes Act 1991, designed to target Nazi war criminals.
(4) Any change in the law affecting the liberties of the subject must be expressly and specifically stated.
(5) Any liability for a criminal offence must be on the basis of fault, unless the words of the statute clearly intend otherwise.
(6) The legislation applies throughout the UK unless an exemption for Scotland, Northern Ireland or Wales is stated. Because Scotland, in particular, has its own legal system, it is common for Parliament to legislate for Scotland separately and now much of this legislative power has been passed to the Scottish Parliament. As explained above, Welsh legislative power was enhanced from 2011, then 2017.

(7) If the provisions of two Acts appear to be in conflict, the court will
     endeavour to reconcile them, since there is no presumption of implied
     repeal. If reconciliation is not possible, logic demands that the later
     provision be given effect. For instance, in *Padmore v Inland Revenue
     Commissioners (No.2)* (2001), the court had to resolve a conflict between
     two inconsistent tax provisions. The Chancery Division held that where the
     Act being construed is a consolidating Act, it is only permissible to take
     into account the earlier legislation if the later language is ambiguous,
     obscure or would lead to an absurdity. Where there is a conflict between
     two sections in the same statute, the court must do its best to reconcile them
     and may read words into the statute, to give effect to plain legislative intent.
(8) Legislation must be construed so as not to conflict with EU law (for the
     time being).
(9) Legislation must be construed so as to give effect to the European
     Convention on Human Rights *where possible*. (If not possible, then a senior
     court may make a declaration of incompatibility.)
(10) Parliament intends to give effect to international treaties to which the UK is
     a contracting party.

Intrinsic (internal) aids

The judge may be assisted by components of the statute. These include the long
title, marginal notes, headings, which may be prefixed to a part of the Act, and
schedules, which are part of the Act, although they do not affect words used in the
body of the Act unless these are ambiguous. Punctuation is referred to in
interpreting the meaning of a sentence in the same way as we use it as an
essential guide to the sense of normal everyday English. In *R. v Montila* (2004),
the House of Lords ruled that headings and side notes could be used in
interpretation but less weight should be attached to them than to parts of the Act
that are open to debate in Parliament. Preambles may be used. EU legislation
makes regular use of preambles. The famous "Eurobananas" Regulation of 1994,
regulating standards of bananas, contains a preamble longer than the text. The
Court of Justice of the EU examines preambles as a matter of course, in
interpreting EU legislation.

2–022

Extrinsic (external) aids

Judges refer to other statutes on the same subject and to general knowledge. They
decided that, as a general rule, they would refrain from consulting *Hansard,* the
report of debates on a Bill through Parliament, and would only permit reference
to preparatory documents to interpret the Act they sought to remedy. They set out
guidelines in *Black-Clawson International Ltd v Papierwerke Waldhof-
Aschaffenburg AG* (1975). The reason for this rule is that people should be
entitled to know the law by taking an Act at face value. Furthermore, the
intentions of, say, the Lord Chancellor, in introducing the Legal Services Bill
differed significantly from the "intention of Parliament", in passing the 2007 Act,
after it had been hotly debated and repeatedly amended for months. Because of
this rule, judges were unable, theoretically, to make use of Parliamentary debates,

2–023

reports of committees or commissions, or what the government ministers involved had said about the measure, as evidence of Parliamentary intent. This rule, that no extrinsic aids would be used, ensured that Parliament had a complete obligation to express itself precisely when making new law.

Serious inroads into this rule, altering the judicial role in statutory interpretation, were made by the law lords in *Pepper (Inspector of Taxes) v Hart* (1993). In this case, the question arose whether, under the Finance Act 1976, Parliament had intended school teachers at private schools to be taxed on the full value of the "benefit in kind" of the private education offered to their own children. The House of Lords ruled, erroneously, that this had been Parliament's intention. Their Lordships' attention was later drawn to the statement of the minister who sponsored the Bill through Parliament. From this, it became clear that the true intention was that the teachers should only be taxed on the cost to their employers, which was minimal, so an Appellate Committee of seven law lords was reconvened and the case reargued, with reference to *Hansard*. Their Lordships held that Parliamentary materials should only be referred to where:

"(a)   legislation is ambiguous or obscure or leads to an absurdity;
(b)   the material relied on consists of one or more statements by a minister or other promoter of the Bill together if necessary with such other Parliamentary material as is necessary to understand such statements and their effect;
(c)   the statements relied on are clear" (per Lord Browne-Wilkinson)."

Despite their Lordships' warnings that this new activity was to be the exception, judges and counsel have made frequent use of the *Pepper v Hart* principle, even where there is little ambiguity in a statute, and case law has extended the rule to allow reference to preparatory material, such as green papers and white papers, and reports of the Law Commission and Royal Commissions. Even back in the 1970s, the Master of the Rolls, Lord Denning, and the Lord Chancellor, Lord Hailsham, said they always consulted *Hansard*. Drawing attention to the dangers of all this, the editors of *Cross on Statutory Interpretation* (1995) said it created more work for lawyers, in advising clients and preparing litigation. Resorting to all these extrinsic aids was no substitute for the clearest possible drafting of the text of the statute. Dame Mary Arden, when chairman of the Law Commission, warned of the dangers of *Pepper v Hart*. In *R. v Secretary of State for the Environment, Transport and the Regions Ex p. Spath Holme Ltd* (2001), the law lords tried to put a stop to this. They deprecated the frequent citation of *Hansard* and said that the conditions laid down in *Pepper v Hart* should be strictly insisted upon. They were concerned with the cost of fruitless *Hansard* searches.

2–024   An example of the application of *Pepper v Hart* appears in *R. v Mullen (No.2)* (2000), where Auld LJ resorted to parliamentary debates to interpret the Criminal Appeal Act 1995. The case appears in Ch.12 on criminal procedure. Looking at *Hansard*, he decided that the meaning of "unsafe" conviction in the amended form of the Criminal Appeal Act 1968 was meant to be the same as before the 1995 amendment. A very important example of the CA and the House of Lords referring to *Hansard* to help them in statutory interpretation was the case challenging the validity of the Hunting Act, *Jackson*, referred to above. Lord Woolf CJ, in the CA, said the 1911 Parliament Act, which allowed legislation to be passed through the House of Commons only, in certain circumstances, was passed to resolve a constitutional crisis. An examination of *Hansard* disclosed beyond doubt that both the Commons and the Lords fully appreciated the extent of the constitutional change to which they were agreeing.

In *Westminster City Council v National Asylum Support Service* (2002), the law lords held that explanatory notes accompanying an Act could be used in interpretation, even if there were no ambiguity. They are more useful than other materials because they are updated as a Bill passes through Parliament and changes its wording and meaning. Judges seem to be much more ready, nowadays, to use other preparatory material, such as reports of reform bodies, to help them interpret the law. In both *Jackson* and *R. v G. & R.*, on recklessness, below, the law lords referred to a variety of background material. Different considerations apply in the case of a statute which incorporates an international convention. Here, exceptionally, the court *must* have regard to the full background so reference may be made to relevant material. For a discussion of the approach of the English courts in interpreting international law, including the *Pinochet* cases, see Qureshi (2001).

The move towards a broader, contextual, "purposive" approach

From about the 1960s or 1970s, Cross and other commentators argued that judges took a "contextual approach". (See *Cross on Statutory Interpretation* (1995)) In doing this, judges claim to be searching for "the will of Parliament" and sometimes they articulate this. For instance, in *R v Chief Constable of the Royal Ulster Constabulary Ex p. Begley* (1997), Lord Browne-Wilkinson explained this limit on the law lords' role in developing the common law, as he saw it: 2–025

> "It is true that the House has power to develop the law. But it is a limited power. And it can be exercised only in the gaps left by Parliament. It is impermissible for the House to develop the law in a direction which is contrary to the expressed will of Parliament."

Nevertheless, a legislature of over a thousand people cannot be said to have a single intention. Judges have to look for the true meaning of what Parliament said, not what it meant: Lord Reid in *Black-Clawson* (1975), as cited by Bell and Engle (1995), p.17. If the words of a statute fail to deal with a particular situation, there is no power in a court to fill the gap, despite Lord Denning's claim. Only Parliament may do so, with a new Act. Some judges get frustrated, though, because Parliament is too busy to amend faulty legislation. Eventually, the law lords became more bold, giving a purposive construction to legislation. In *Fothergill v Monarch Airlines Ltd* (1981) Lord Diplock was explicitly critical of previous judges' "narrowly semantic approach to statutory construction, until the last decade or so". Judging from the wide application given to *Pepper v Hart*, many modern judges agree with this criticism. Taking a broad, purposive approach, they apparently relish the opportunity to consult extrinsic aids. On the other hand, they may decline to do so in the face of clear language. An example is the *Kato* case above. Here Lord Clyde rejected an invitation to include car parks in the definition of "road" to give a purposive construction, because it would strain the word "road" beyond what it meant in ordinary usage. Some commentators have made sweeping statements that judges now favour a broad purposive approach but this is not really true in many instances, as the above cases demonstrate and as can be seen from any trawl through recent law reports. The simple reason is that judges cannot use the purposive approach to avoid clear words. Lord Steyn said in *Inland Revenue Commissioners v McGuckian* (1997):

> "During the last 30 years there has been a shift away from the literalist approach to purposive methods of construction. When there is no obvious meaning of a statutory provision the modern emphasis is on a contextual approach designed to identify the purpose of a statute and to give effect to it."

He applied a purposive approach in *R. v A* (2001) which I analyse in depth in Ch.4 on human rights. But Dame Mary Arden, quoting him, added that the courts could only apply a purposive approach where the purpose is sufficiently clear. One can identify some cases where judges clearly articulate that they are taking a purposive approach and they explain why. In one such case, judges were anxious to enforce safety on the railways and rejected the literal interpretation sought by Railtrack to excuse itself: *Railtrack Plc v Smallwood* (2001). The *Jackson* fox hunting case, above, provides another example of a broad, purposive approach, with the courts fully examining the political background and history of the Parliament Acts. Also, taking a practical view, Lord Woolf pointed out that a number of Acts had been passed according to the procedure the Parliament Acts had established. Unravelling all of them would not be easy.

Both the European Court of Human Rights and the Court of Justice of the EU take a broad purposive approach to interpretation, described as "teleological". English and Welsh judges are well aware of this and use it themselves in relevant cases. A purposive approach can lead to a different interpretation of words from a literal construction. In *Laroche v Spirit of Adventure (UK) Ltd* (2009), the CA held that a hot air balloon was an "aircraft" according to the Pocket Oxford Dictionary but the plain, ordinary meaning was not necessarily determinative. On a purposive construction of the Carriage by Air Acts (Application of Provisions) Order 1967, it was reasonable to suppose that Parliament intended such balloons to be included, as they were capable of being used for international transport.

The topics of interpreting EU law and the UK's obligations under the European Convention on Human Rights are dealt with in the next two chapters.

3. CRITIQUE OF LEGISLATION

2–026   The attempt to make legislation more comprehensible has a long and somewhat fruitless history. The Statute Law Society was formed in 1968. Its main object was to procure technical improvements in the form and manner in which legislation is expressed and published so as to make it more intelligible. Its first report, in 1970, said procedures must be governed by the needs of the user. This was approved in 1975 by the Renton Committee. The Rippon Commission followed almost 20 years later and listed the following principles:

- Laws are made for the benefit of citizens.

- All citizens should be involved as fully and openly as possible in the way statute law is prepared.
- Statute law should be as certain and intelligible as possible.
- Statute law should be rooted in the authority of Parliament and thoroughly exposed to democratic scrutiny.
- Ignorance of the law being no excuse, statute law had to be as accessible as possible.
- Although governments need to be able to secure the passage of their legislation, to get the law right and intelligible is as important as getting it passed quickly.

In a 1992 critique, *Making The Law*, the Hansard Commission recommended that Bills should be published with explanatory notes, updated when the Bill became an Act, and this was done from 1998. In the meantime, tax lawyers, among others, were still frustrated by the complexity of Finance Acts. In 1996, the Inland Revenue admitted that tax law could be simplified and a rewrite project was launched. The Capital Allowances Bill 2001 was subjected to a four-stage consultative process involving users of tax legislation. Also in 2001, the Lords and Commons set up a Joint Committee on Tax Simplification Bills. Tax lawyers and taxpayers are not the only people who get frustrated by confusing legislation. The group which undoubtedly has the biggest struggle and suffers from the greatest volume of legislation—as well as some of the most ill-drafted, complex and often unworkable legislation—is magistrates' clerks (legal advisers).

Sometimes legislation proves to be completely unworkable and this has repeatedly occurred in the area of criminal procedure and sentencing, which has been the subject of far too much legislation, as discussed below. For instance, the Criminal Justice and Public Order Act 1994 purported to do away with committals from magistrates' courts to the Crown Court and to replace them with transfer proceedings. When Epsom Magistrates' Court tried to use the new transfer scheme in September 1995, the bench and clerk found it did not work. Eventually, the section was abandoned and a new scheme created in 1998. Academics and the Law Commission get very frustrated when they have warned that there are gaps in a Bill, or defects, and ministers just ignore or even ridicule them. This frustration is expressed by Ashworth (1996). In *R. v Chambers* (2008), the CA realised that for seven years no-one had noticed that the law on confiscating smuggled tobacco had changed, so over 1,000 confiscation orders were flawed. The CA said this was symptomatic of a wider problem—that the law was inaccessible to everyone today, because most of it was secondary legislation and the volume of legislation had increased. 2–027

This brings us back to Lord Bingham's first meaning of "the rule of law", that the law must be accessible, discussed in Ch.1 of this book. In his third chapter, he examined what this required. He cited Sir Menzies Campbell, who, as leader of the Liberal Democrats in 2007, pointed out that there had been 382 Acts in the previous 10 years, including 29 Criminal Justice Acts, and more than 3,000 new criminal offences had been created. He cited the well-known description of the Criminal Justice Act 2003 and other legislation on criminal procedure as "labyrinthine", which refers to two problems. There is layer upon layer of criminal justice legislation, often produced for the sake of a news sound bite, depicting the minister as "tough on crime", with new Acts being passed before the previous one has been fully implemented. Secondly, the law's obscurity is exacerbated by parliamentary drafting where new Acts cross-refer to old Acts and statutory instruments, so that we cannot make sense of an Act by reading it alone.

4. CASE LAW

2–028   Remembering that the English legal system is a common law system, indeed the mother of all common law systems, the significance of judge-made case law, i.e. common law, in creating and refining our laws cannot be underestimated. The law produced by the courts, laying down principles to be followed in later cases can be just as important as that produced by Parliament. The common law has been under development since about the ninth century and many books and modern judges' speeches remind us that English common law has borrowed so many concepts from Roman and ecclesiastical law, equity and other sources. (See Hale, Neuberger (cited in the previous chapter) and Dyson). The common law is constantly developing to meet new circumstances and social and moral expectations. For instance, in 1991, in *R. v R.*, the law lords abolished the rule protecting a husband from criminal responsibility for raping his wife.

In 2016, Sir Henry Brook, retired appeal judge, quoted Lord Reid, the intellectual giant among twentieth century law lords:

> "Lord Reid, who played such a key role between 1949 and 1975 in rescuing the judiciary from decades of torpor: 'The Common Law has not been built by Judges making general pronouncements: it has been built by the rational expansion of what already exists in order to do justice in particular cases.' Thus landmark decisions like Donoghue v Stevenson [creation of the tort of negligence] or Hedley Byrne v Heller [establishing liability in tort from pure economic lass caused by negligent misstatement] did not emerge out of thin air: they emerged from the application of principle to the case with which the court was currently concerned."

Describing the method of reasoning of common law judges, Lord Goff said:

> "We tend to avoid large, abstract, generalisations, preferring limited, temporary, formulations, the principles gradually emerging from concrete cases as they are decided. In other words, we tend to reason upwards from the facts of the cases before us, whereas our continental colleagues tend to reason downwards from abstract principles embodied in a code."

I referred to this contrast in Ch.1. Common law judges reason from the bottom up. Judges in civil law countries, notably European jurisdictions, reason from the top (principles) down.

The meaning of precedent

2–029   The doctrine of judicial precedent is known as stare decisis (to stand by decisions). In a system of *binding* precedent, when a judge comes to try a case, she *must* always look back to see how previous judges in the senior courts have dealt with cases (precedents) involving similar facts in that branch of the law. She expects to discover relevant legal principles. She tries to apply those principles to reach a decision consistent with the precedents and if the facts of her case are slightly different, she may need to develop the principle a little further. The advantages and disadvantages of precedent are straightforward and set out in the law lords' 1966 practice statement, cited below.

The doctrine of precedent in operation

The system operates as a hierarchy.   2–030

The Court of Justice of the EU and the European Court of Human Rights

Decisions of the former are currently binding on all English and Welsh courts,   2–031
until Brexit. Decisions of the latter will be unaffected by Brexit and must be "taken account of", following the Human Rights Act 1998 but the UK Supreme Court has now determined that they are *not* binding. Indeed, in some cases, a dialogue has arisen between the ECtHR in Strasbourg and the UK's top court. In *R. v Horncastle* (2009), the UKSC Justices declined to follow the ECtHR on art.6 (fair trial), in a case on hearsay evidence, yet previously, their predecessors, the law lords, had said the UK *was* bound, in a case on control orders, *Home Secretary v AF* (2009). There is a useful commentary by Craven and Pennington-Benton. In the *AF* case, Lord Hoffmann felt that the Strasbourg court's decision was wrong but that the UKHL had to submit, or be in breach of our Convention obligation. In the later case, however, the seven-panel UKSC expressed concern as to whether the Strasbourg court fully understood the domestic (English) procedure or took account of common law safeguards against an unfair trial. It recognised the possibility of a "dialogue" between the two courts and, in turn, the ECtHR adjourned its final decision pending the UKSC decision. The authors point out that judicial dialogue between the two courts has occurred before, on art.8 and housing possession proceedings, notably in *Manchester CC v Pinnock* (2010). In *Doherty v Birmingham City Council* (2008), the law lords declined to follow the ECtHR in *McCann v UK* (2008), Lord Hope commenting that the Strasbourg decision was "almost useless". In 2011, in *Al-Khawaja v UK*, the ECtHR agreed with the UKSC that their interpretation was correct. The ECtHR President, Sir Nicolas Bratza, "said the decision was a 'good example of the judicial dialogue between national courts and the European court' that Lord Phillips, president of the UK Supreme Court, had called for two years ago" (Rozenberg 2011) and see Ashworth's comment in 2012. In the past, the ECtHR has overturned its own previous decision, following "clarifications" of domestic law by the law lords: *Osman v UK* (2000), which is a testament to the powerful international influence of the UK's top court, discussed in Ch.1. The latest statement reflecting and refining the approach of the UKSC came in *R. (on the application of Chester) v Secretary of State for Justice* (2013). The website's press summary says:

"Under the HRA, the Supreme Court is required to 'take into account' decisions of the ECtHR, not necessarily to follow them. This enables the national courts to engage in a constructive dialogue with the ECtHR. However, the prohibition on prisoner voting in the UK has now been considered by the Grand Chamber of the ECtHR twice and, on each occasion, found to be incompatible with A3P1. In these circumstances, it would have to involve some truly fundamental principle of law or the most egregious oversight or misunderstanding before it could be appropriate for the Supreme Court to refuse to follow Grand Chamber decisions of the ECtHR. The ban on prisoner voting is not a fundamental principle of law in the UK, and the circumstances do not justify a departure from the ECtHR's caselaw [25–35]."

In a 2014 speech quoted in Ch.4, Lord Neuberger said the UK courts should be more ready not to follow Strasbourg decisions because:

"It is a civilian court under enormous pressure, which sits in chambers far more often than in banc, and whose judgments are often initially prepared by staffers, and who have produced a number of inconsistent decisions over the years."

The House of Lords Appellate Committee/UK Supreme Court

2–032 Decisions of the House of Lords (law lords), and now the UK Supreme Court that replaced it in 2009, are binding on all the courts lower in the hierarchy. Until 1966, the law lords considered themselves bound by their own precedents but, by a formal Practice Statement, they announced that in future they would not regard themselves as necessarily bound by their own previous decisions. The Practice Statement (1996) is worth quoting at length, as it gives us a neat summary of the arguments for and against a rigid system of binding precedent.

"Their Lordships regard the use of precedent as an indispensable foundation upon which to decide what is the law and its application to individual cases. It provides at least some degree of certainty upon which individuals can rely in the conduct of their affairs, as well as a basis for orderly development of legal rules. Their Lordships nevertheless recognise that too rigid adherence to precedent may lead to injustice in a particular case and also unduly restrict the proper development of the law. They propose, therefore, to modify their present practice and, while treating former decisions of this House as normally binding, to depart from a previous decision when it appears right to do so. In this connection they will bear in mind the danger of disturbing retrospectively the basis on which contracts, settlements of property and fiscal arrangements have been entered into and also the especial need for certainty as to the criminal law. This announcement is not intended to affect the use of precedent elsewhere than in this House."

There have not been many instances of the top court departing from a previous decision. In *Herrington v British Railways Board* (1972) the House revised a long-standing legal principle concerned with the duty of care owed to a child trespasser. Under the old law, child trespassers were unprotected and by 1972, the law lords considered this rule far too harsh. In *R. v Shivpuri* (1987) the House departed from a decision given only one year earlier when reconsidering the law relating to criminal attempts. A very significant instance was *R. v G & R* (2003) which reversed the effect of *R. v Caldwell* (1982), which had redefined and broadened the meaning of "recklessness" in the Criminal Damage Act 1971 (and consequently criminal law in general) to include offenders who had not foreseen a risk. The House noted that *Caldwell* had been subject to forceful academic, judicial and practitioner criticism, as producing unfair results. They examined the Law Commission's Draft Criminal Code Bill and its working paper prior to the 1971 Act and decided Parliament had never intended to broaden the ambit of the criminal law in this way. In this case, the House clearly saw themselves as morally justified in departing from precedent in correcting its unfair effects. In *A. v Hoare* (2008), on the urging of the CA, the law lords overruled *Stubbings v Webb* (1993), to avoid the harshness of the limitation period and thus allow victims to sue in historic abuse and rape claims—another decision driven by morality. See, similarly *Horton v Sadler* (2006). By way of contrast, in *Jindal Iron & Steel Co Ltd v Islamic Solidarity Shipping Co Jordan Inc* (2004), the House declined to overturn a 1957 precedent, because it had stood for 50 years, had worked satisfactorily, had not produced unfair results and an enormous number of transactions had taken place assuming that it was the law. In the final case heard by the law lords, in July 2009, before transforming into the UKSC, *R. (on the application of Purdy) v DPP*, they ruled that art.8(1) of the European Convention on Human Rights *was* engaged, when a terminally ill person sought assisted suicide, departing from their previous decision in *R. (on the application of Pretty) v DPP* (2001) and instead following the ECtHR in *Pretty v UK* (2002). These cases are discussed in Ch.4 on human rights.

The UKSC has followed the practice of the law lords, in departing from its previous decisions where it sees fit, and confirmed this general intention in *Austin v Mayor and Burgesses of the London Borough of Southwark* (2010). In *Manchester CC v Pinnock* (2010), the court considered a number of ECtHR cases expressing the principle that in housing possession cases, the proportionality principle must apply, and they departed from previous HL judgments. In *Spiller v Joseph* (2010), they renamed the defence of "fair comment" in defamation actions to "honest comment" because it was too narrow and "society and its concerns" had changed because "millions now talk and thousands now comment in electronically transmitted words, about recent events . . ." (per Lord Walker). Another example is the decision that the armed forces *can* rely on their rights under the European Convention on Human Rights, when they are outside UK territory: *Smith (FC) v The Ministry of Defence* (2013), departing from *R. (on the application of Smith) v Oxfordshire Assistant Deputy Coroner* (2010). In *R. v Jogee and Ruddock* (2016), the UKSC made a highly significant change to the mental element required to convict someone as an accomplice to an offence, reversing 32 years of law.

The Court of Appeal

Unless they conflict with the Human Rights Act 1998, House of Lords and UKSC decisions are binding on the CA, even if the court is very unhappy with an unjust result, as in *A v Hoare* (2006), referred to above, but below, I describe a 2006 case where the CA decided to follow the *persuasive* precedent of the Judicial Committee of the Privy Council (JCPC), rather than the *binding* precedent of the HL, because it knew the JCPC decision represented the views of contemporary law lords, sitting as the JCPC.

2–033

The Civil Division of the CA binds all courts except the UKSC. The CA binds itself for the future, according to the decision in *Young v Bristol Aeroplane Co* (1944), although it may escape if: (i) a later decision of the House of Lords (or UKSC) applies; (ii) there are previous conflicting decisions of the CA; or (iii) the previous decision was made *per incuriam*, i.e. in error, because some relevant precedent or statutory provision was not considered by the court. An example of such a decision, which the Divisional Court of the Queen's Bench Division considered was decided *per incuriam*, was *Thai Trading Co v Taylor* (1998), on the legality of a contingency fee agreement entered into by a solicitor. The House of Lords authority of *Swain v Law Society* (1983) had not been cited. It was obviously binding on the CA and they decided wrongly, in ignorance of it, so *Thai Trading* is a *per incuriam* decision and not binding on any court. Note that the respondents in the case were unrepresented and, without a lawyer to do the legal research, the binding precedent had been overlooked. With an increasing number of litigants in person, this problem is bound to occur, which is why judicial assistants were invented, in the 1990s, to do background research for judges in cases like this. Litigants in person (LIPs) are examined in Ch.10 on civil procedure. Later case law added another exception: (iv) the CA is not bound by an interlocutory decision of two CA judges. There appear to be more exceptions: (v) where a CA decision conflicts with an earlier HL or UKSC decision; (vi) where a previous CA decision conflicts with international law; and (vii) where the CA is the court of last resort, with no appeal available to the UKSC. Furthermore, (viii) the CA will not follow its previous decision which conflicts with the Human Rights Act 1998.

The Criminal Division of the CA does not consider itself always bound by its own decisions. Where the liberty of the subject is concerned, the court feels itself free to overrule a previous decision if it appears that the law was misunderstood or misapplied "and if a departure from authority is necessary in the interests of justice to an appellant": *R. v Spencer* (1985). An example occurred in *R. v Shoult* (1996). The court declined to follow *R. v Cook* (1996), in considering an appeal against a prison sentence for a drink-driving conviction. This flexible approach has especially applied since October 2000, where the court has chosen to modify the law in accordance with the European Convention on Human Rights and can clearly be seen in the case law on the Criminal Appeal Acts 1968 and 1995 discussed in Ch.12 on criminal procedure. A court of five may overrule a bench of three.

The High Court

2–034   Decisions of a single judge in the HC are binding on the lower courts but not on other HC judges. They are only persuasive. This can cause conflicting decisions. On the same day in 2013, two courts produced conflicting judgments about the freezing of company assets. Decisions by a Divisional Court of the HC are binding on judges of the same Division sitting alone but not necessarily on future Divisional Courts: *R. v Greater Manchester Coroner Ex p. Tal* (1985). The Upper Tribunal and Administrative Court should follow one another's decisions, because of judicial comity (reciprocity) and the common law method, despite the fact that HC judges do not normally bind one another: *R. (on the application of B) v Islington LBC* (2010).

The County Court, the Crown Court and magistrates' courts

The decisions of these courts are seldom reported and not binding.   2–035

Binding and persuasive

Depending on the status of the court, a precedent may be binding or persuasive. 2–036 Precedents which come from the JCPC or other common law jurisdictions are persuasive, and the adoption of concepts developed in other common law courts has influenced English common law, as described in Ch.1. Sometimes, the top court considers developments in other common law jurisdictions but decides not to adopt them into English law. This occurred in *Transco Plc v Stockport MBC* (2003). The House restated the rule in *Rylands v Fletcher* (1868), rejecting a submission that this tort had been absorbed into the law of negligence, as held in the Australian High Court.

In a unique decision, *R. v James, R. v Karimi* (2006), the Court of Appeal decided to follow a JCPC decision instead of an earlier HL decision. The JCPC had decided in *R. v Holley* (2005), an appeal from Jersey, that the House of Lords precedent on provocation in murder, *R. v Smith (Morgan James)* (2000) had been wrongly decided. The board of the JCPC consisted of 9 of the 12 Lords of Appeal in Ordinary (law lords), the UK's top court, and this fact and their lordships' comments indicated to the CA that they had decided to use the case as a vehicle to review *Morgan Smith* as it applied in *English* law, not just in the law of Jersey. The Lord Chief Justice said that if they followed *Morgan Smith*, the law lords would be sure to overrule them and the law would be reduced to a game of ping-pong. In *Willers v Joyce* (2016), the UKSC said that, even though not bound to do so, a court in England and Wales should *normally* follow a Privy Council ruling unless there was a decision to the contrary effect by a superior court. The 2016 *Jogee* case in the UKSC, just mentioned, was joined to a Privy Council case, *Ruddock*, with the UKSC Justices sitting in both their capacities as top UK judges and Privy Council judges, and they changed the law on criminal accessories in the UK and Jamaica simultaneously.

Terminology

Where a judge finds that a precedent to which she is referred is not strictly 2–037 relevant to the facts of the case before her, she is said to "distinguish" that case. As such, the case is not binding upon her. If, on the other hand, she holds that a precedent is relevant, and applies it, she is said to "follow" the reasoning of the judge in the earlier case. When an appeal court is considering a precedent, it may "approve" or "disapprove" of the principle of law it established. It can "overrule" the principle if the case was decided by a court junior in status. A decision is said to be "reversed" when a higher court, on appeal, comes to the opposite conclusion to the court whose order is the subject of the appeal.

Ratio decidendi and obiter dicta

2–038 The most important and binding element of a judgment is the legal principle which is the reason for the decision, the ratio decidendi. The remainder of the judgment, such as explanatory statements and other legal principles argued before the court, are called obiter dicta or things said "by the way". The whole of a dissenting (disagreeing minority) judgment is obiter. It is the ratio of a decision which constitutes the binding precedent, or "rationes" if there is more than one reason. When a court is referred to a precedent, the first task is to decide what was the ratio of that case, and to what extent it is relevant to the principle to be applied in the present case. Whilst an obiter dictum is not binding, it can, if it comes from a highly respected judge, be very helpful in establishing the legal principles in a later case. Of course, most cases are decided in the lower courts, according to their facts. The judge assesses the strength of the evidence and makes findings of fact. These do not form part of the ratio.

Trying to extrapolate the ratio from multiple judgments with differing sets of reasoning is a miserable task, as the CA complained in *Doherty v Birmingham City Council* (2006), when they had to make sense of six law lords' judgments. They referred to the rule of law: the law should be accessible and intelligible. Since *Doherty*, there have been many judicial speeches and articles on this subject. Carnwath LJ, Arden LJ and Neuberger MR were critical of multiple judgments and urged the UKSC to give single judgments. Most UKSC Justices are sympathetic with this. They claim they try to give simple judgments more often but cannot always achieve it. At the UKSC's first anniversary seminar, in September 2010, Baroness Hale was campaigning for single judgments. She presented a paper, "Judgment Writing in the Supreme Court" (UKSC website). She said the Judicial Assistants had rated the *Jewish Schools* case as the lowest point in the first year, because of its nine judgments. She said that when they had been law lords, the judges rarely tried to devise jointly authored or "plurality" opinions, though *R. (on the application of Aweys) v Birmingham City Council* (2009) was a joint effort between her and Lord Neuberger. In the UKSC, they could deliver judgments in whatever order they chose. A judicial assistant had examined the first 57 decided cases.

> "He found that in 20, there was a 'judgment of the court'; and in a further 11, there was either a single judgment (with which all the other Justices agreed), or a single majority judgment (with which all the Justices in the majority agreed), or an 'effectively' single or single majority judgment (because separate judgments were simply footnotes or observations). So 31, or more than half, came out as plurality or effectively plurality judgments."

2–039 Baroness Hale examined the well-known arguments for and against multiple judgments. For instance, Lord Reid felt that single judgments were undesirable because they were treated as if they were words in an Act of Parliament. He and Lord Bingham had criticised single JCPC judgments as inferior in quality for developing the law. Nevertheless, said Baroness Hale:

> "I suggest that we should have a flexible approach in which each Justice is free to write but a climate of collegiality and co-operation in plurality judgments is

encouraged. At the very least, however many judgments there are, there should never be any doubt about what has been decided and why."

She said that if you had plurality judgments, you could still have certain sorts of concurring judgment. This approach to judgment-writing is common elsewhere in the world: the USA, Canada and the ECtHR. This is not the same as prohibiting dissent, as in the US Supreme Court and the Court of Justice of the EU. Baroness Hale said it promotes "much more collegiality". Lord Neuberger, in the annual 2012 Bailii lecture, said judgments should be shorter and clearer to enable "reasonably intelligent non-lawyers" to understand the case and in the 2012 Chancery Bar Association conference, he said "Greater brevity, and with it clarity, could be obtained through adopting the single majority judgment approach, with a reasoned dissent and short, reasoned concurring judgments." Lord Neuberger is now the President of the UKSC and Lord Carnwath is a UKSC Justice. Students can see for themselves from the UKSC website whether Neuberger, Carnwath and Hale have succeeded in generating more combined judgments. In 2013, the trend towards single judgments continued, at 57 per cent (Dickson (2014)) but went down to 44 per cent in 2015 (Dickson (2016)).

Law reports

A system of binding precedent is dependent on the publication of reported cases dating back to the thirteenth century. The earliest case summaries were collected in manuscript form in the *Year Books*. These were prepared by students or practitioners and circulated among the judges and leading barristers. The use of printing, from the sixteenth century, made law reporting common and more reliable. These are published under the reporters' names and have been republished in a series called *The English Reports*, covering 1220–1865.

In 1870, the Incorporated Council of Law Reporting was established. It publishes the Official Law Reports. They are published some time after the judgment has been given, but are regarded as authentic because the judges have corrected them. Approved judgments handed down in the HC or CA can be copied immediately. Unapproved judgments are only given to the parties involved. HC and CA decisions are available online, via HM Courts & Tribunals Service website, and UKSC decisions are available on the UKSC website. The *Weekly Law Reports* and *All England Law Reports* are published commercially by firms of law publishers. They are in hard copy and online on subscriber databases. All decisions of the Crown Court, HC and above, whether or not reported elsewhere, are stored on *Westlaw* and *Lexis*. The best free source of full law reports is the British and Irish Legal Information Institute website. As well as these full reports, a number of law magazines carry summaries of recent case decisions, and the short law reports in *The Times* are outstandingly useful, and available on *Lexis*. From 2001, all judgments of the senior courts (High Court, Court of Appeal and UKSC) are numbered and have numbered paragraphs. This "neutral citation of judgments" caters for those cited from electronic sources.

2–040

Citation of judgments

2–041 To try to control the multiple citation of precedents of different value in reports of varying accuracy, the Lord Chief Justice has issued a number of Practice Directions. No more than 10 authorities should be included in the bundle. Unreported cases may not be cited without permission. Advocates are now required to state, in their skeleton argument, the proposition of law demonstrated by each authority they wish to cite and they must justify citation of more than one authority for each proposition. If advocates wish to cite foreign authorities they must justify doing so and certify that there was no English authority on the point. The CA is constantly reminding careless advocates of these requirements: *TW v A City Council* (2011). In *R. v Erskine; R. v Williams* (2009), the CA reminded the advocates who swamped the court with authorities of a great aphorism from Viscount Falkland in 1641: "if it was not necessary to refer to a previous decision of the court, it was necessary not to refer to it". Doubtless this attempt by the judges to limit citations stems from the uncontrolled growth in the number of precedents lawyers will incorporate in their arguments, as demonstrated by a small piece of statistical research by Zander. Advocates have a common law duty to the court to achieve and maintain appropriate levels of competence and care: *Harley v McDonald* (2001). They still have a duty to draw to the attention of the court authorities which support their *opponent's* case.

5. PREROGATIVE POWER

2–042 As the monarch no longer has any power under our unwritten constitution, her residual power is exercised by the Prime Minister and other ministers. The prerogative includes the power to conduct foreign relations, enter treaties, declare war and peace, confer honours, issue pardons, secretly vet jurors and a list of more uncertain activities. Where a statute deals with an activity previously exercised by way of prerogative power, the courts will presume that the statute has eclipsed and replaced it. In 2004, Professor Jeffrey Jowell suggested that they should be codified. In 2006, The House of Lords Constitutional Affairs Committee examined the Government's use of prerogative power to declare war, prompted by the UK's involvement in Iraq. The Committee called for evidence on whether a statutory framework should be introduced and whether the Prime Minister should be required to explain the legal justification for war. In 2009, the Ministry of Justice published a *Review of the Executive Royal Prerogative Powers*, now in the National Archives. Useful information is summarised in a House of Commons Library Note.

Orders in Council are laws made by the Prime Minister, using prerogative powers, within the Privy Council. In *R. (on the application of Bancoult) v Secretary of State for Foreign and Commonwealth Affairs (No.2)* (2008), the law lords held that an Order in Council was *primary* legislation, like an Act of Parliament, but did not share the characteristics of an Act of Parliament. Sovereignty of Parliament was founded on the unique authority of Parliament which derived from its representative character. An OC was an act of the executive and was thus reviewable by the courts, unlike an Act. Smith (2009) pointed out some concerns about OCs. They bypass Parliamentary debate and thus the procedure for certification of compliance with the Human Rights Act (and see JUSTICE 2009). Orders in Council are often used in controversial circumstances. Margaret Thatcher used one to ban union membership at the Government Communication Headquarters. An OC was also used to frustrate a court ruling and prevent the Chagos islanders returning home, which was unsuccessfully challenged in the *Bancoult* case, above.

6. CUSTOM

English "common" law was derived from the different customary laws of the existing Anglo-Saxon tribal groups, and was developed into a common, nationally applicable law, after England became one nation, with one king and one government, hence the phrase "common law". Custom then continued to play a part over the medieval period. Customs were absorbed into the legal system, sometimes in the form of legislation and sometimes, particularly in the earliest period, by the judges giving decisions which were based on custom. The gradual result was that custom virtually disappeared as a creative source of law. Nowadays, exceptionally, custom may be recognised by a court if it can be convinced that a particular local custom applies. Custom may be pleaded as a defence. The rules for its acceptance are strict. Recognised custom does, however, play a very important part in the interpretation of international law, below.

2–043

7. BOOKS OF AUTHORITY

Certain books of antiquity can be regarded as a source of law, though they are seldom relied on nowadays. The following, mostly written by judges, are accepted as books of authority.

2–044

Blackstone, *Commentaries on the Laws of England* (1765): a survey of the principles of English law in the mid-eighteenth century, intended for students. It was meant as a commentary but was taken as a statement of the law by early American lawyers.

Bracton, *De Legibus et Consuetudinibus Angliae* (c.1250): mainly commentaries on the forms of action with case illustrations; a major study of the common law.

Coke, *Institutes of the Laws of England* (1628): an attempted exposition of the whole of English law.

Fitzherbert, *Nature Brevium* (c.1534): a commentary on the register of writs.

Foster, *Crown Cases* (1762): criminal law.

Glanvill, *De Legibus et Consuetudinibus Angliae* (c.1189): authoritative on the land law and the criminal law of the twelfth century.

Hale, *History of the Pleas of the Crown* (1736) (60 years after Hale's death): the first history of the criminal law.

Hawkins, *Pleas of the Crown* (1716): a survey of the criminal law and criminal procedure.

Littleton, *Of Tenures* (c.1480): a comprehensive study of land law.

Modern textbooks are not treated as works of authority although they are frequently referred to in court. Advocates are permitted to adopt a textbook writer's view as part of their argument. Judges will often quote from a textbook in the course of giving judgment. In *R. v Shivpuri* (1987) the law lords paid tribute to an article in the *Cambridge Law Journal* by Professor Glanville Williams which persuaded them to reverse their previous ruling on criminal attempts. The reason why no textbooks since Blackstone's *Commentaries on the Laws of England* have been accepted as works of authority seems to be that: (i) case reports have become fuller and much more easily accessible; and (ii) by that time the original principles of the common law were fully established.

8. INTERNATIONAL LAW AS A SOURCE OF ENGLISH LAW

2–045   There are two types of international law: private and public. The former deals with such things as family law—what happens when there is a divorce between nationals of two different jurisdictions, who has care and control of the children and what happens if one kidnaps the children and takes them abroad. It also determines, for instance, what law should govern a dispute arising out of a car accident between nationals of two different states which takes place in a third state. Private disputes between individuals or commercial organisations, such as those arbitrated in London, discussed in Ch.11, may also be governed by elements of international law. Public international law (PIL) governs relations between states and the entities of states and creations of states, such as the United Nations and the World Bank. In the twentieth century and even before, we have created a number of fora to resolve international disputes. The War Crimes Tribunal for the former Yugoslavia, in the Hague, tried the former President Milosovic in 2005 and in 2014, tried Radovan Karadzic for war crimes in the 1990s Bosnia war. Public international law regulates such matters as the carriage of goods by air and sea, use of illegal drugs, and war crimes. As individuals become more mobile in their domestic, social and working lives and with globalisation of the market place, so UK governments sign up to more and more treaties obliging us to enact domestic legislation giving effect to them and so we see more international litigation in the English courts. In Ch.1, we saw that Lord Bingham regarded the rule of law as requiring compliance by states with their obligations under international law and Ch.10 of his book, *The Rule of Law*, is an informative plain-English analysis of the position of international law. Qureshi's very useful articles examine the attitude of the English courts to PIL issues. One fascinating aspect of PIL explained in these articles is the recognition of custom. We bind ourselves to the explicit obligations of treaties but are also bound by the tacit rules of custom. Customary international law (CIL) is law which is a product of consensus amongst the community of nations. States regard it as binding in their dealing with other states. English courts have regarded CIL as part of the common law since *Triquet v Bath* (1764). Qureshi quoted Lord Lloyd in the first *Pinochet* case (2000) on the effect of CIL in English law:

"The application of international law as part of the law of the land means that, subject to the overriding effect of statute law, rights and duties flowing from the rules of [customary international law] will be recognised and given effect by the English courts without the need for any specific act adopting those rules into English law."

In applying and interpreting international conventions, the courts will apply a purposive construction, as the House of Lords did in *Sidhu v British Airways Plc* (1997). This case also determined that domestic common law cannot override a convention to which the UK is a contracting party. In this case, the parties sought to sue for damages at common law but the Lords held that their remedies were limited to those available for international carriage by air according to the Warsaw Convention. It provided a comprehensive code with a uniform international interpretation which could be applied in the courts of contracting parties, exclusive of any reference to domestic law. Remember this case the next time your luggage goes missing or gets damaged when you fly.

9. THE EUROPEAN CONVENTION ON HUMAN RIGHTS AND EU LAW

Reminder: these are such important elements of international law in the UK that they merit their own chapters of this book (so read on ...).   2–046

Bibliography

Dame Mary Arden, "Modernising Legislation" [1998] P.L. 65.   2–047
A. Ashworth, editorial of the March 1996 *Criminal Law Review* and comment on *Al-Khawaja v UK* [2012] Crim. L.R. 375.
J. Bell and G. Engle, *Cross on Statutory Interpretation*, 3rd edn (London: LexisNexis, 1995).
T. Bingham, *The Business of Judging: Selected Essays and Speeches* (Oxford: Oxford University Press, 2000).
Sir Henry Brooke, "Human Rights and English Common Law" [2016] EHRLR 329.
S. Burns, "Tipping the Balance" (2006) 156 N.L.J. 787.
E. Craven and R. Pennington-Benton, "When Strasbourg speaks" 160 (2010) N.L.J. 377.
B. Dickson, "A Supreme education" (2014) N.L.J. February, p.17, "Reigning Supreme", (2016) 166 N.L.J. 19.
Lord Dyson MR, "The Globalisation of Law", lecture, 6 November 2015.
Editorial on post-legislative scrutiny, *Statute Law Review*, April 2008, p.1.
Lord Goff, "The Future of the Common Law" (1997) 46 I.C.L.Q. 745 at 753, as cited by Bell, above (2008), at p.13.
Baroness Hale, "Magna Carta: did she die in vain?" speech, 19 October 2015.
House of Commons Library Note "The Royal Prerogative" SNPC 03861, by L. Maer and O. Gay.
House of Lords Select Committee on the Constitution, *9th Report of Session 2015–16 Delegated Legislation and Parliament: A response to the Strathclyde Review* (2016).

Professor Jowell was appearing on BBC Radio 4 in the *Unreliable Evidence* series.

Lord Judge CJ, speech at the Mansion House dinner for HM judges, on the tyranny of Henry VIII clauses, 13 July 2010.

JUSTICE, *The Constitutional Role of the Privy Council and the Prerogative* (2009).

K.M. Qureshi, "International Law and the English Courts" (2001) 151 N.L.J. 787; "A global view" (2012) 162 N.L.J. 351.

J. Rozenberg, "Bin Henry VIII clauses Ken Clarke told", *Guardian*, 15 July 2010; comment on *Al-Khawaja*, *Guardian*, 15 December 2011.

R. Smith, "Beyond satirical debate?" (2009) 159 N.L.J. 212.

The Governance of Britain—*The Government's Draft Legislative Programme* (2007, CM 7175).

D. Thomas, editorial, [2012] Crim. L.R 405.

J. Toobin, *The Nine: Inside the Secret World of the Supreme Court* (New York: Doubleday, 2007).

M. Zander, "What precedents and other source materials do the courts use?" (2000) 150 N.L.J. 1790.

Sources for updating this chapter

2–048   Free updates of this book are available on the Sweet & Maxwell website: *http://uklawstudent.thomsonreuters.com*.

Summary and revision, P. Darbyshire, *Nutshells English Legal System*, 10th edn (London: Sweet & Maxwell, 2016).

British and Irish Legal Information Institute

Parliament

Scottish Parliament

Welsh Law *http://law.gov.wales*

Welsh Assembly Government

CHAPTER 3

EU Law

"DETERMINED to lay the foundations of an ever closer union among the peoples of Europe." (The first aim of the preamble of the Treaty of Rome 1957)

"The Treaty is like an incoming tide. It flows into the estuaries and up the rivers. It cannot be held back." (Lord Denning MR in *HP Bulmer Ltd v J Bollinger SA (No.2)* (1974))

"The rise of the City firms of solicitors (and parallel firms in other cities) has made Britain the legal capital of Europe." (Stevens (1994))

1. EU LAW IS PART OF UK LAW, FOR THE TIME BEING

Until the UK formally leaves the EU and the European Communities Act is repealed, it is still part of UK law. As explained in the Brexit note opening this book, in future, and indeed beyond my lifetime, UK lawyers and law students will still need to acquire a deep understanding of EU law, for the following reasons. The EU remains our biggest trading partner so people selling goods and services will need to comply with EU law and those buying goods will need to know how their rights are affected by EU law; UK lawyers are the most mobile in Europe and the most likely to practice and set up business elsewhere in the EU; there are millions of EU citizens still living, studying and working in the UK, and vice versa (UK citizens living and working in the EU), all affected by the law; many UK workers are employed by EU companies; EU law will still have to be applied by lawyers and the courts to future cases coming before them for advice or litigation, which relate to contracts, problems or events that arose during the period when the UK was part of the EU. For example, for many decades to come, workers will need to know what their current and future pension rights are and how they were regulated during the time that the UK was in the EU and how this affects the pension that they will receive. London has been one of the major world trading and maritime hubs for centuries, and an international capital of banking and insurance. Multinational law firms have established themselves there as a consequence and although they will move some of their employees and operations, they are not about to depart entirely.

Membership of the European Union, formerly the Common Market, has curtailed the sovereignty of Parliament, in those areas of EU activity, until the UK formally leaves the EU. Apart from the Treaties and Regulations, which are directly applicable in all Member States without further ado (and made binding in UK law by the European Communities Act 1972 s.2), most EU law came into the

3–001

UK "by the back door", through UK delegated legislation, but it was scrutinised in Parliament by committees in both Houses. See UK Parliament website.

The interpretive and other judgments of the Court of Justice of the European Union (CJEU) are also a source of EU law and they and the EU Treaties and secondary legislation have to be interpreted by the English and Welsh courts. All magistrates and judges must currently treat questions as to the meaning or effect of the Treaties and EU instruments as questions of law to be determined in accordance with principles laid down by the Court of Justice. On any such question, they must take judicial notice of the Treaties, the *Official Journal* and decisions or opinions of the Court of Justice or General Court. This is laid down in the European Communities Act 1972 s.3, as amended. This means that all CJEU rulings are binding precedents to be applied in the English and Welsh courts, until Brexit occurs in law. Here, I provide a simple and very basic guide to the institutions of the EU and the sources of EU law. Until 2009, EU law was officially known as "Community law". In this chapter, the term Community law is used in case law and instruments created before then.

2.   THE TREATIES

3–002   The Common Market was created by the signing of the Treaty of Rome in 1957. The primary aims of its first six members were economic but as the Treaty states, its signatories were "determined to lay the foundations of an ever closer union among the peoples of Europe … by … pooling their resources to preserve and strengthen peace and liberty". The Treaty of Rome, EC Treaty, now consolidated with the amending Reform Treaty (Treaty of Lisbon 2007) became known as the Treaty on the Functioning of the EU (TFEU), in 2009. The TFEU remains an essential source of EU law, as well as the EU's constitution. Incorporation of the Treaty of Rome and the other EU Treaties into UK law was brought about by the European Communities Act 1972 so that Act must be repealed to take the UK out of the EU. This will be done by the European Union [Withdrawal] Bill, if enacted. The other major EU Treaties are the Single European Act of 1986, which created the single European market, effective from 1992; the Treaty on EU (TEU, Maastricht Treaty), ratified in 1993, which extended the scope of EU competence and provided for economic and monetary union and Union citizenship; the Treaty of Amsterdam 1997, in force from 1999 and the Treaty of Nice, in force from 2003, which expanded the Union from 15 Member States to 25. The EU used to consist of three pillars: the European Community, the central law making and law enforcing unit, and the two outside pillars, Justice and Home Affairs and Foreign and Social Policy. This structure went, thanks to the Lisbon Treaty. The Nice Treaty 2000 provided for enlargement, and for alterations to the Council and Commission, and increasing the Parliament.

In 1991, the European Economic Area was created, including States subjected to EU law on the internal market and competition, but not represented in the institutions. Ten of them joined the Union after the Treaty of Nice. Bulgaria and Romania joined in 2007. After a failed attempt to introduce an EU constitution, The Treaty of Lisbon 2007 came into force in 2009. The detail is on the Europa website. Its headlines are:

"*A more democratic and transparent Europe*, with a strengthened role for the European Parliament and national parliaments, more opportunities for citizens to have their voices heard and a clearer sense of who does what at European and national level ...

A more efficient Europe, with simplified working methods and voting rules, streamlined and modern institutions...

A Europe of rights and values, freedom, solidarity and security, promoting the Union's values, introducing the Charter of Fundamental Rights into European primary law...ensuring better protection of European citizens ...

Europe as an actor on the global stage... The Treaty of Lisbon gives Europe a clear voice in relations with its partners worldwide. It harnesses Europe's economic, humanitarian, political and diplomatic strengths to promote European interests and values worldwide, while respecting the particular interests of the Member States in Foreign Affairs." (From "The Treaty at a Glance".)

There are 28 Member States, until the UK leaves. The six Common Market founders were France, Germany, Italy, Belgium, Luxembourg and The Netherlands, in 1957. The UK joined in 1973. By 2002, the Union consisted of 15 states, after the accession of Denmark, Greece, Spain, Ireland, Austria, Portugal, Finland and Sweden. In 2004, 10 more joined: Estonia, Lithuania, Latvia, Poland, Hungary, the Czech Republic, Slovakia, Slovenia, Malta and Cyprus. Romania and Bulgaria joined in 2007 and Croatia in 2013.

---

3. INSTITUTIONS

There are seven basic EU institutions. We are concerned with the Parliament, the Council, the European Council, the Commission and the Court of Justice. Details of the Court of Auditors and European Central Bank are on the Europa website.　　　3–003

The European Parliament (arts 223–234 TFEU)

The 751 MEPs are directly elected by their Member States. They are not delegates but representatives. Unlike conventional Parliaments on the Westminster model, this is *not* the legislature of the EU, although its powers were enhanced by the Single European Act 1986, the Treaty on the European Union 1992 and the Treaty of Lisbon 2007. This has gone some way to remedy the institutional imbalance and the "democratic deficit" complained of by critics: the fact that the unelected Council is the primary legislature. Parliament now has a legislative role on several levels, advisory and consultative, a right to participate in conciliation and co-operation procedures and a right of co-decision in over 40 fields, so co-decision, between the Parliament and Council, has become the normal method of law-making. The Parliament has a supervisory role over the Commission, which must report to it, submit proposals when requested, and answer questions. Acting with the Council, it fixes the Union's annual budget. It may set up a committee of inquiry to investigate maladministration or breaches of EU law.　　　3–004

The Council (the Council of the European Union) (arts 237–243 TFEU)

3–005   This is really the legislature of the European Union, though Parliament has gained much more legislative power since 2009. It is composed of one minister from each Member State. These *delegates* change according to the nature of the subject under discussion. On agricultural policy, states will send their agriculture ministers. On economic issues, finance ministers will attend. There are indeed 10 configurations of the Council. These are chaired by a President on a six-month rota. The exception is the Foreign Affairs Council, which, since 2009, is chaired by a High Representative of the Union for Foreign Affairs and Security Policy. The Council's job is to ensure the Treaty objectives are attained. The website summarises its role as follows:

> "•   *Negotiates and adopts EU laws*, together with the European Parliament based on proposals from the European Commission
> •   *Coordinates* EU countries' policies
> •   Develops the EU's *foreign & security policy*, based on European Council guidelines
> •   Concludes *agreements* between the EU and other countries or international organisations
> •   Adopts the annual EU budget – jointly with the European Parliament."

It has the final say on most EU secondary legislation but, in most cases, can only act on a proposal from the Commission. Since the Lisbon Treaty, it can act on a proposal signed by a million citizens. Voting strength is specified by the Treaties in accordance with the population size of each Member State. The UK *was* one of the four most powerful states. Not only is the Council criticised for being unelected (the democratic deficit) but it used to lack transparency. This was the only legislature outside North Korea and Cuba to sit in secret. At long last, thanks to years of British political pressure, from 2009 the Council sits in public when voting on legislative proposals or conducting a general debate and this is broadcast live on the internet. Discussions on foreign affairs are not public. Since it is not a permanent body, much of its day-to-day work, initially sifting and scrutinising Commission proposals, is delegated to COREPER, the committee of permanent representatives of the Member States (civil service). It delegates its workload to working groups. Again, COREPER lacks accountability and transparency.

The European Council (arts 235–236 TFEU)

3–006   When the Council is composed of heads of state or government it is known, confusingly, as the European Council. It became an EU institution under the Lisbon Treaty from 2009. It has a President and meets at least twice a year, with the Commission President. It can invite the President of the Parliament to speak. The High Representative takes part in its work. It does not legislate. It develops Union policy and priorities, in effect setting the EU agenda.

The Commission (arts 244–250 TFEU)

This is the EU executive and employs a large civil service. There is no separation   3–007
of powers in the EU and it also has legislative power delegated to it by the
Council. There is one Commissioner from each of the Member States but each
must act independently of state control. They are appointed for five years,
renewable. Each has a portfolio for a particular Union activity and heads a
Directorate General. The Commission's functions are as follows:

The motor

It takes the initiative on proposing new law and policy. The Council may request   3–008
the Commission to undertake studies and submit proposals. This power of
initiative makes it very influential in setting the agenda of the Council and
Parliament. It consults widely. It draws up the budget for approval by the
Parliament and Council and supervises how money is spent.

The watchdog

The Commission enforces the Member States' Treaty obligations and may take an   3–009
errant Member State to the Court of Justice, under art.258 TFEU, should
persuasion fail. An example is the Court's decision against Italy in 2002 that it
was in breach of the Treaty and Directive 89/48 in failing to provide foreign
lawyers with the infrastructure and freedom to provide their services in Italy:
Commission v Italy (2002). Another example was the 2003 Court of Justice ruling
that Italy was in breach of its treaty obligations in insisting that British chocolate
should be called "chocolate substitute" because it contained vegetable fat other
than cocoa butter: *Commission v Italy* (2003). The Commission can impose big
fines and penalties on those in breach of EU competition law, or those who ignore
decisions taken against them. Accordingly, it has extensive investigatory powers.
For instance, because Germany failed to comply with rulings on water purity and
protection of birds, it imposed a daily fine of £350,000 while the infringement
continued.

The executive

Policies formed by the Council need detailed implementation by the Commis-   3–010
sion. Much of this is done by legislation, which requires a final decision by the
Council. The Commission has its own decision-making powers and enforces
competition policy.

Negotiator and representative

In relation to the EU's external policies, the Commission acts as a negotiator,   3–011
leaving agreements to be concluded by the Council, after consulting the
Parliament, where this is required by the Treaty. It represents the EU
internationally, especially in relation to trade policy and humanitarian aid.

What does the EU do? It makes law and policy on: trade and enterprise, customs, consumer affairs, economic and monetary union, agriculture, fisheries, competition, freedom of movement of workers, freedom to establish business, education and training, energy, the environment, climate change, food safety, employment and social affairs, sex equality, public health, regional policy, transport and tax. It also makes policy and encourages co-operation on justice and home affairs, including human rights, foreign policy and security, external trade and humanitarian aid. See the Europa website for the full list.

The Court of Justice of the European Union (arts 251–281 TFEU)

3–012   Along with the General Court (formerly Court of First Instance) the Court of Justice is now part of the Court of Justice of the European Union. From 2016, the Civil Service Tribunal was integrated into The General Court.

Do not confuse the Court of Justice with the European Court of Human Rights (ECtHR), described in Ch.4. The Court of Justice sits in Luxembourg and interprets EU law for the Member States. The ECtHR is *not* an institution of the EU. It interprets and enforces the European Convention on Human Rights 1950 for the 47 contracting states that have ratified the Convention. It sits in Strasbourg.

Composition

3–013   The main court, the Court of Justice, consists of one judge for each Member State, one of whom is elected President for six years. They are assisted by 11 advocates general (AGs). It is an AG's task to assist the court by making a detailed analysis of all the relevant issues of fact and law in a case listed before the court and submitting a report of this, together with recommendations, to the court. Thus, they can express their personal opinions, which the judges cannot, and they can examine any related question not brought forward by the parties. Article 253 TFEU stipulates that both judges and AGs "shall be chosen from persons whose independence is beyond doubt and who possess the qualifications required for appointment to the highest judicial offices in their respective countries or who are jurisconsults of recognised competence" (such as academic lawyers). Each judge and advocate general is appointed for a renewable term of six years.

Procedure (reformed)

3–014   The court's workload has increased since 1970 when 79 cases were lodged, to 1,711 lodged (in the three courts) in 2015 (including the very important 436 references for preliminary rulings) and it completed 1,755. This is very good news, as it means the court is at last matching its workload and clearing its backlog, despite receiving its biggest ever case load. The President said in his annual report that this was the most productive year ever. The Court of Justice completed 616 cases in 2015 and the General Court completed 987, which, happily, was more than it received (831). The General Court was created to help with the increasing workload but, still, it proved necessary to devise another coping mechanism. In the past, the UK has been a constant critic of the court's slowness and a 2011 committee of the House of Lords (in the UK Parliament) reported that the court was in "crisis" and urgently needed to appoint more advocates general. At last, there are now 11, since 2015, and the court implemented further reforms from 2011. They now hear cases before a chamber of three or five judges, reserving the Grand Chamber of 13 judges for the more important cases (8 per cent in 2015). It is currently taking an average of 15.6 months to deal with a case, which is a few weeks faster than three years earlier. Case throughput has accelerated thanks to the adoption of an expedited procedure for urgent preliminary references (which now take 1.9 months, on average) and a simplified procedure, without a hearing, and giving some judgments without an AG's opinion (43 per cent in 2015). The case for each party is submitted in written pleadings. The President allocates one of the judges to act as a juge-rapporteur in each case. She prepares a public report after the written procedure, ready for the short oral hearing. It contains a summary of the facts and legal argument. She prepares a private report to the judges, containing her view of whether the case should be assigned to a chamber.

Meanwhile, an advocate general may also have been assigned to the case. This is now only done in about half of all cases. They are not assigned to cases brought by or against their native Member State. The AG prepares an opinion which is delivered orally, at the end of the oral hearing. It contains a full analysis of relevant EU law, which may give a more complete and accurate account than that produced in argument by the parties, since the lawyers appearing in the case may appear before the Court of Justice only once in their legal careers. The AG also gives his opinion as to how the court should decide the case. The court does follow this opinion in most cases and it provides an essential explanation of the reasoning behind the court's decision but this *opinion* should never be referred to as a "ruling". After this, the AG drops out of the picture and the judges deliberate in secret, without interpreters, in a common language (traditionally, French). After deliberations, the assigned juge-rapporteur will draft and refine the decision. There is no charge to use either court. Legal aid is available to persons of "insufficient means", under their national rules.

Function

The court is the supreme authority on all matters of EU law. Its practices and procedure draw on continental models, notably French procedure, but in substantive law, it borrows principles from all Member States. The TFEU is a framework, generally speaking, with few of its provisions spelled out in detail. This gives the court latitude as a court of interpretation, in effect creating EU law and jurisprudence. Its boldness used to be a matter of controversy in the early days but since we were watching the emergence of a whole new legal system and body of law, it is hardly surprising that decisions contained sweeping statements of principle, especially given that the Treaty of Rome was silent even on such fundamentals as the relationship between EU law and national law (see, for instance *Costa v ENEL* (1964)).

3–015

When developing new principles, the court's reference points are the objectives of the EU and the articles of the TFEU. Over time, it has built up a body of reported decisions. Like the UK Supreme Court and many other top courts, it is not bound by its own previous decisions but usually follows them. The judgment is a single one but without much indication of the reasoning behind it (especially in the older cases). This is where the submission of the AG comes in useful, as an explanation.

Jurisdiction

3–016   The Court of Justice's work consists mainly, but not exclusively, of the following:

1.   References for preliminary rulings on the interpretation of EU law from Member States' courts (art.267 TFEU).
2.   Actions brought by the Commission or a Member State against Member States for failure to fulfil obligations under EU law (art.258 TFEU).
3.   Judicial review actions for annulment of legislative or other acts of the Council, Commission or Bank, other than recommendations or opinions (art.263 TFEU). The Lisbon Treaty widened the scope for judicial review. For instance, the Committee of the Regions may challenge measures on the basis that they violate the subsidiarity principle. This principle means that, where possible, the EU should leave the member states to make their own laws.
4.   Actions for failure to act, in infringement of the Treaties, against the Council, European Council, Commission or Parliament (art.265 TFEU).
5.   Disputes between Member States under the Treaties (art.273 TFEU).
6.   Determining the procedural legality of acts of the European Council (art.269 TFEU).
7.   Appeals on points of law from The General Court (art.256 TFEU).
8.   Actions for damages (art.268 TFEU).

The Court of Justice of the EU does not have jurisdiction over common foreign and security policy (art.275 TFEU), or police and law enforcement operations within Member States, or their internal security (art.267 TFEU). Point 1 above is very important, as this is the mechanism through which EU law is developed and *interpreted* in its domestic context, throughout the EU. Any case may be referred to the Court of Justice from any court or tribunal, under art.267 TFEU (formerly art.234 EC), where there is an item of EU law to be interpreted. The Court of Justice gives its interpretation and then remits the case to the domestic court, leaving them to apply that interpretation and then decide the case accordingly. UK courts made 16 applications in 2015 and have made 589 since 1974. Germany has made 2,216 since 1965.

General Court (art.225)

3–017   The Single European Act (1986) provided for the establishment of a Court of First Instance, now called the General Court, and it began its work in 1989. Its 47 judges usually hear cases in chambers of three or five, any of whom, apart from the President, may be called upon (unusually) to act as advocate general. Its jurisdiction was quite limited. In 1992, however, the TEU provided that the

Council could transfer any area of the top court's jurisdiction down to the CFI, except for preliminary rulings. A lot of work was transferred in 1993, to relieve pressure on the European Court of Justice, as the upper court was then called. By 1996, the CFI was hearing as many cases as the top court. The General Court's current jurisdiction is listed on the Europa website and detailed in its annual report.

Article 267 TFEU Preliminary Rulings (Formerly art.234 EC)

"The Court of Justice of the European Union has jurisdiction to give preliminary   3–018
rulings on the interpretation of European Union law and on the validity of acts of the institutions, bodies, offices or agencies of the Union." (Information note 2009/C 297/01). Any court or tribunal of any Member State may make a reference. The court's ruling on the point is then sent back to the national court to be applied in the pending case, which will have been suspended in the meantime. All national courts have a duty to apply and enforce EU law but this ability to refer when they are uncertain is designed to prevent divergent interpretation throughout the EU. These references are a significant volume of the court's workload, as can be seen from the statistics above, and they have proven to be the essential vehicle for the court to develop its principles and precedent. The wording of art.267 TFEU is very important:

> "The Court of Justice of the European Union shall have jurisdiction to give preliminary rulings concerning:
> (a) the interpretation of this Treaty;
> (b) the validity and interpretation of acts of the institutions, bodies, offices or agencies of the Union;
> Where such a question is raised before any court or tribunal of a Member State, that court or tribunal *may*, if it considers that a decision on the question is *necessary* to enable it to give judgment, request the Court to give a ruling thereon.
> Where any such question is raised in a case pending before a court or tribunal of a Member State against whose decisions there is no judicial remedy under national law, that court or tribunal *shall* bring the matter before the Court.
> If such a question is raised in a case pending before a court or tribunal of a Member State with regard to a person in custody, the Court of Justice of the European Union shall act with the minimum of delay." (My emphasis.)

Paragraph (b) includes all art.288 TFEU legislative acts, and also includes most non-binding recommendations and opinions. The court cannot rule on facts or questions of national law so cannot rule that a national provision is incompatible with EU law but has said it will provide the national court with all necessary criteria to enable it to answer such a question. It will not rule on how law is to be applied by the domestic court but will offer guidance. It has interpreted international treaties entered into by the EU but cannot rule on the validity of the EU Treaties.

National courts or tribunals that may refer

Where the law (as opposed to a private contract) imposes an arbitrator to resolve   3–019
disputes, then a question can be referred. It does not matter if the court is at the

lowest level. In *McCall v Poulton and Motor Insurers Bureau* (2008), the English Court of Appeal upheld a county court decision to refer a question on the obligations of the Bureau to compensate victims of uninsured drivers. Even a body exercising functions preliminary to its judicial function may refer. In *Pretore di Salo v Persons Unknown* (1987), an Italian public prosecutor, who would later act as examining magistrate, was allowed to refer. In *El-Yassini v Secretary of State for the Home Department* (1999), the court permitted a reference from an Immigration Adjudicator, because he was determining disputes according to statutory powers. In *Dorsch Consult* (1997) the court held:

> "The Court takes into account a number of factors, such as whether the body is established by law, whether it is permanent, whether its jurisdiction is compulsory, whether its procedure is inter partes, whether it applies rules of law and whether it is independent."

The discretion to refer

3–020   It is essential for the national court to explain why it considers a ruling to be *necessary* and define the factual and legislative context of the question. The timing of a reference is left to the national court, though the Court of Justice has issued guidance. A national court or tribunal cannot be prevented from making a reference by a national law that it is bound to follow the decision of a higher court on the same question of EU law. In other words, the Court of Appeal (CA) of England and Wales could still make a reference, if they considered it *necessary*, despite the existence of a House of Lords or UKSC precedent on the same question of EU law. The court emphasised in the *Rheinmuhlen-Dusseldorf* case (1974) that, as the object of art.267 is to ensure that the law is the same in all Member States, domestic law cannot limit the lower court's power to make a reference if it considers the superior court's ruling could lead it to give judgment contrary to EU law.

"Necessary in EU Law"

3–021   Before exercising its discretion to refer, the national court must consider a reference *necessary*. The court defined this in *CILFIT Srl v Italian Ministry of Health* (1982). There is no need to refer if:

1.   the question of EU law is irrelevant; or
2.   the provision has already been interpreted by the court, even though the questions at issue are not strictly identical; or
3.   the correct application is so obvious as to leave no scope for reasonable doubt.

This matter must be assessed in the light of the specific characteristics of EU law, the particular difficulties to which its interpretation gives rise and the risk of divergences of judicial decisions within the Community.

"Necessary" in English Law

In *HP Bulmer Ltd v J Bollinger SA (No.2)* (1974) Lord Denning MR set out   **3–022**
guidelines for English courts, for deciding when it was necessary to make a
reference. They did not meet with uncritical approval. Bingham J warned that the
Court of Justice was in a better position to determine questions of EU law
because, for instance, of their expertise, their unique grasp of all the authentic
language texts of that law and their familiarity with a purposive construction of
EU law. Once he became Master of the Rolls, he set out this important dictum in
*R. v International Stock Exchange of the United Kingdom and the Republic of
Ireland Ex p. Else (1982) Ltd* (1993).

> "if the facts have been found and the Community law issue is critical to the court's
> final decision, the appropriate course is ordinarily to refer the issue to the Court of
> Justice unless the national court can with complete confidence resolve the issue
> itself. In considering whether it can with complete confidence resolve the issue
> itself the national court must be fully mindful of the differences between national
> and Community legislation, of the pitfalls which face a national court venturing into
> what may be an unfamiliar field, of the need for uniform interpretation throughout
> the Community and of the great advantages enjoyed by the Court of Justice in
> construing Community instruments. If the national court has any real doubt, it
> should ordinarily refer."

Commenting on this case, Weatherill and Beaumont, in *EU Law*, praised Lord
Bingham for doing a great service in creating a presumption that national courts
and tribunals should make a reference if they are not completely confident as to
how the issues can be resolved.

> "This is a communautaire approach consistent with the spirit of judicial co-operation
> that is needed if the Article 234 system is to do its job of ensuring uniform
> interpretation of EU law throughout the Community" (3rd edn, 1999).

It is, nevertheless, a rebuttable presumption, so the English law reports have
many examples of the courts declining to refer. An example is *R. v Ministry of
Agriculture, Fisheries and Food Ex p. Portman Agrochemicals Ltd* (1994).
Brooke J, in declining to refer, took account of the guidelines in previous case
law but was influenced by the fact that neither of the parties wished for the case
to be referred and that, given the usual 18-month delay to be expected in
receiving the court's interpretation, the answer would be redundant by the time
they would receive it. Some judges have warned that English courts should
exercise great caution in relying on the doctrine of "acte clair" in declining to
make a reference. The court accepts that national courts will apply this doctrine,
borrowed from French law, when the interpretation of a provision is clear and
free from doubt. It is possible, in the English legal system, for an appeal to be
made against a lower court's decision to refer. Such an appeal was successfully
made in *Ex p. Else* (above), the CA holding that it was not necessary to refer.

The obligation to refer

3–023   Two questions arise here. Firstly, when is a court "a court or tribunal of a Member State against whose decisions there is no judicial remedy under national law"? There are two theories, abstract and concrete. Under the former, only the UK Supreme Court would be obliged to refer. Under the more practical concrete theory, any court from whom there is no appeal or from which appeal has been refused should be obliged to refer. The rulings of the Court of Justice seem to support the latter: *Costa v ENEL* (1964) (obiter). This seems to be fairer to the parties, especially where they have been refused permission to appeal and it seems more likely to achieve the harmonisation of law that art.267 is aiming at. The matter has been resolved by the court itself in *Lyckeskog* (2003). It held that courts which could be challenged did not fall into the category of court under an obligation to refer. Some critics were disturbed by this result in terms of access to justice because it presupposes the parties have the time and money to litigate right through to the last possible court before being able to obtain a reference.

The second question relates to the circumstances in which the obligation to refer arises. Although the wording of this paragraph looks mandatory, as top courts *must* refer every point of EU law to the court, it has ruled, in the *Costa v ENEL* case (see below) that this is not necessary where the question raised is materially identical to a question which has already been the subject of a preliminary ruling in an earlier case. In *CILFIT* (above) the court said that courts of last resort have the same discretion as others, to decide whether a reference is necessary, and that there is no obligation to refer if the criteria laid down are satisfied.

Satisfying the conditions for the application of the third *CILFIT* criterion (the law's interpretation is obvious) will not, however, be easy, as the court laid down the condition that the national court must be convinced that the matter is equally obvious to the courts of the other Member States and to the Court of Justice and they reminded courts that, in satisfying themselves of this criterion, they should bear in mind the plurilingual nature of that law and the court's use of purposive and contextual construction. While many domestic judges would not shy away from a purposive and contextual approach (especially the UKSC) I am at a loss to see how any domestic top court has the facilities to delve into the domestic law reports of the other Member States to see how a point has been variously interpreted by other national courts, in their many national languages.

There are examples of the UK law lords refusing to refer a case to the court, mainly relying on the first *CILFIT* exception, that the EU law point was irrelevant, including a case in which they refused to follow the *Von Colson* principle: *Finnegan v Clowney Youth Training Programme Ltd* (1990). In the very important case of *Three Rivers DC v Bank of England (No.3)* (2003), the law lords declined to refer. Another example occurred in *Abbey National Plc v OFT* (2009). Of course the danger of not referring lies in the risk that different Member States will resolve the same issue in different ways. The "Recommendations" information note on the website (2012/C 338/01), tells us when it is appropriate to make a reference but it really states the existing principles, as set out by case law. It is (for the time being) cross-referred to in the civil, criminal and specialist practice directions applicable in English and Welsh courts and tribunals (HMCTS website). UK courts have always been very confident to interpret EU law themselves and do so frequently. For example, in *Mirga v Secretary of State for Work and Pensions; Samin v Westminster City Council* (2016), the Supreme Court ruled that an EU citizen who moved to the UK but was not a worker, jobseeker, student, self-employed or self-sufficient could validly be denied a right of residence in the UK and could therefore be excluded from a right to income support or to housing assistance as a homeless person.

4. SOURCES OF EU LAW

The sources of EU law are as follows: 3–024

1.   The Treaties.
2.   EU secondary legislation (regulations, directives and decisions).
3.   International agreements entered into by EU institutions on its behalf, using their powers under the Treaty.
4.   Decisions of the Court of Justice and General Court, including general principles, developed over the years.

Article 10(5) of the EC Treaty obliged all Member States to "take all appropriate measures, whether general or particular, to ensure fulfilment" of all these obligations. This obligation, reworded, is now in art.4(3) of the Treaty on European Union.

Secondary Legislation (Legislative Acts) art.288 TFEU

The law-making powers of the EU institutions are laid down in art.288 TFEU: 3–025

> "To exercise the Union's competences, the institutions shall adopt regulations, directives, decisions, recommendations and opinions.
>   A *regulation* shall have general application. It shall be binding in its entirety and directly applicable in all Member States.
>   A *directive* shall be binding, as to the result to be achieved, upon each Member State to which it is addressed, but shall leave to the national authorities the choice of form and methods.
>   A *decision* shall be binding in its entirety. A decision which specifies those to whom it is addressed shall be binding only on them.
>   *Recommendations and opinions* shall have no binding force."

These are all called "acts". Distinguish between binding and non-binding acts. Only the first three are binding.

Regulations are generally applicable and designed to apply to all situations in the abstract. Since they are binding in their entirety and directly applicable in all Member States, they may give rise to rights and obligations for states and individuals without further enactment.

Directives are binding as to the result to be achieved, upon each Member State to which they are addressed. The State thus fills in the details, by enacting domestic law in accordance with the principles it is directed to put into law.

Decisions are individual acts, addressed to a specified person or persons or States. They have the force of law and, therefore, have effect without further expansion.

Acts which do not conform with procedural safeguards may be annulled.

5. DIRECT APPLICABILITY AND DIRECT EFFECT

3–026   To understand the application of EU law, it is necessary to have a basic grasp of the distinction between the principles of direct applicability and direct effect. It is also necessary to understand the distinction between horizontal and vertical direct effect, that is, between provisions directly effective between individuals, giving rise to rights or obligations enforceable between individuals, and provisions giving rise to rights of individuals against the Member States. When the European Communities Act 1972 took the UK into the EU, or Common Market, as it then was, EU law became directly applicable, in international law terms, as if it were domestic law. The terminology becomes confusing, however, because provisions of international law which are found to be capable of application by national courts at the suit of individuals are also termed directly applicable. To spare confusion, therefore, all UK writers on EU law have adopted the term "directly effective" to express this second meaning, that is, to denote provisions of EU law which give rise to rights or obligations which individuals may enforce before the national courts.

Whether a particular provision of EU law gives rise to directly effective, individually enforceable rights or obligations is a matter of construction, depending on its language and purpose. Since principles of construction vary from State to State, the same provision may not be construed as directly effective everywhere. For lawyers in the English legal system, until Brexit, whether a provision is directly effective is crucially important because, thanks to the concept of primacy of EU law, a directly effective provision must be given priority over any conflicting principle of domestic law. The Treaty specifies, in art.288 TFEU, that regulations are directly applicable, but it has been left to the Court of Justice to set out, in a group of leading cases, which and when other EU provisions can have direct effect.

Treaty Articles

3–027   The issues of whether and when a Treaty Article could have direct effect were first considered in *Van Gend en Loos* (1963). The question arose as to whether former art.12 EC, which prohibited States introducing new import duties, could confer enforceable rights on nationals of Member States. The court held that it could do because the text of the article set out a clear and unconditional duty not to act. The prohibition was, thus, perfectly suited by its nature to produce direct effects in the legal relations between Member States and their citizens. The court clearly thought it desirable that individuals should be allowed to protect their rights in this way, without having to rely on the European Commission or another Member State to take action against an offending Member State.

This case involved a flouted *prohibition* but Court of Justice case law soon extended direct effect to *positive* Treaty obligations, holding that an article imposing upon a Member State a duty to act would become directly effective once a time-limit for compliance had expired. The Court of Justice has found a large number of Treaty provisions to be directly effective, in relation to free movement of goods and persons, competition law and discrimination on the grounds of gender or nationality. The court applies the following criteria to test whether a provision is amenable to direct effect. It must:

- be clear and precise, especially with regard to scope and application;
- be unconditional; and
- leave no room for the exercise of implementation by Member States or EU institutions.

The court has, however, applied these conditions fairly liberally, with results as generous as possible to the individual seeking to rely on the article. Although the *Van Gend* case involved vertical direct effect, that is, a citizen enforcing rights against a State, later case law, notably *Defrenne v SABENA* (1981), demonstrated that Treaty Articles could also have horizontal direct effect, that is, could be relied on between individuals, such as private employer and employee. A good example of the invocation of vertically directly effective Treaty Articles is the *Factortame* case, discussed below.

Regulations

Regulations are, as stated above, designed to be directly applicable and, thus, directly effective. This means both vertically and horizontally.   3–028

Directives

Directives are instructions to Member States to enact laws to achieve a certain   3–029
end result, so it was originally assumed they could not be directly effective. Nevertheless, in *Grad v Finanzamt Traunstein* (1970) the court held that no such limitation applied. Here, a German haulier was allowed to rely on a directive and decision on VAT which the German government had ignored. The direct effect of directives was confirmed in *Van Duyn v Home Office* (1975). The court held that Mrs Van Duyn, a Scientologist, was allowed to rely on a directive to challenge the UK's refusal to allow her to enter the UK. The conditions for effectiveness are the same as those applied to test Treaty provisions: clarity, precision, being unconditional and leaving no room for discretion in implementation. Once a time-limit for implementation has expired, the obligation to implement it becomes absolute but a directive cannot be directly effective before that time-limit has expired: *Pubblico Ministero v Ratti* (1979). Directives have to be interpreted and applied by domestic courts and tribunals in the same way as domestic statutes do. Unlike UK statutes, however, we are given lengthy preambles to help us interpret them. Directives provide effective rights, in practice. In 2007, The Royal Cornwall Hospital Trust tried sacking 36 people of over 65 on the day before the UK age discrimination regulations came into force

and had to reinstate them when the Trust learned it was bound by the directive on age discrimination, even before it became part of national UK law.

Horizontal or vertical direct effect?

3–030   One of the most difficult issues before the court has been the issue of whether directives can be declared effective *horizontally*, that is, to enforce rights and obligations between private parties. All the case law above relates to the enforcement of private rights against a State, giving *vertical* direct effect. This is unproblematic, since the court is merely enforcing rights and obligations against a State which it has failed to implement in its domestic law. The court is not so keen to hold private parties bound by a directive which a State has neglected to implement, when the default is clearly the State's.

The leading case is *Marshall v Southampton and South West Hampshire AHA* (1986) but, as we shall see, subsequent case law, in particular the *Marleasing* case and *Foster v British Gas*, left the law in a position which is far from clear. The decision in the *Marshall* case is clear enough. Mrs Marshall was an employee of the Area Health Authority and she challenged their compulsory retirement age of 65 for men and 60 for women as discriminatory and in breach of the EC Equal Treatment Directive 76/207. Different retirement ages were permissible in domestic English law, under the Sex Discrimination Act 1975. On a reference from the Court of Appeal, the court held that the different retirement ages did indeed breach the directive and that Mrs Marshall could rely on the directive against the State (the Area Health Authority) regardless of whether they were acting in their capacity as a public authority or her employer. The issue of horizontal and vertical effect of directives had been fully argued before the court and they determined that "a directive may not of itself impose obligations on an individual and that a provision of a directive may not be relied upon as such against such an individual". This looks like a very straightforward refusal to permit directives to have horizontal direct effect but problems remain.

- Here, Mrs Marshall could rely on the directive against her employers because they were a part of the State so how is "State" to be defined?
- Was the time now ripe for directives to be given horizontal direct effect?
- Has the Court of Justice permitted individuals to avoid the harshness of this ruling against horizontal effect by requiring domestic courts to apply directives indirectly, as a matter of interpretation (the *Von Colson* principle)?

What is the State?

3–031   In *Marshall* then, a Health Authority was regarded as an arm of the State, as was the Royal Ulster Constabulary in *Johnston v RUC* (1987), but what of other publicly funded organisations such as universities or publicly run corporations? The House of Lords sought a preliminary ruling from the court on the status of the British Gas Corporation and in their response, in *Foster v British Gas Plc* (1991), the court took the opportunity to provide a definition, although it is not definitive. The court ruled that a directive may be relied on as having direct effect against "a body, whatever its legal form, which has been made responsible, pursuant to a measure adopted by the State, for providing a public service under the control of the State and has for that purpose special powers beyond those which result from the normal rules applicable in relation between individuals."

The court ruled that:

1. It was up to them, the Court of Justice, to rule which categories of body might be held bound by a directly effective directive.
2. It was up to the domestic court to decide whether a particular body fell within that category.

On the second point, the refinement of the concept of State is laid open to differences of interpretation by Member States' domestic courts. The UK's definition of a state body was addressed in *Doughty v Rolls Royce Plc* (1992). Here, the CA ruled that Rolls Royce did not qualify as part of the State, within the *Foster* definition, because they did not provide a public service, nor possess any special powers, despite being wholly owned by the State. The issue as to what is an emanation of the State was addressed again by the ECJ in *Kampelmann v Landschaftsverband Westfalen-Lippe* (1997) and seems to have been expanded. The court defined it by repeating the exact words they had used in *Marshall* but then added "or other bodies which irrespective of their legal form, have been given responsibility, by the public authorities and under their supervision, for providing a public service". See Tayleur. This was confirmed in *Rieser* (2004). A private company undertaking a public duty fell within *Marshall*.

Should horizontal direct effect be extended to directives?

In three cases in 1993 and 1994, advocates general separately argued that the court should reverse its decision in *Marshall* and give horizontal direct effect to directives. In *Faccini Dori v Recreb Srl* (1994), an Italian student sought to rely on a 1985 directive, unimplemented by Italy, to cancel a contract she had entered into with a private company and now regretted. A number of reasons had been put forward by the AGs in these cases and by academic commentators for an extension of the concept. For instance, first, the court is prepared to give horizontal direct effect to Treaty Articles, despite the fact that, like directives, they are addressed to Member States. Secondly, the emergence of the single market in 1993 necessitated enforcing equality of the conditions of competition and the prohibition on discrimination. Thirdly, the TEU had amended the EC Treaty to require publication of directives in the *Official Journal* (so private persons had less excuse not to know their responsibilities under a directive). A full court of 13 judges nevertheless declined to adopt this reasoning and extend the concept of horizontal direct effect. They reiterated that the distinguishing basis of vertical direct effect was that the State should be barred from taking advantage of its own failure to comply with EU law, confirmed in *Pfeiffer* (2004).

3–032

Decisions

3–033   The *Grad* case, discussed above, confirmed that decisions could be directly effective, provided they met all the required criteria. This does not pose any of the moral problems of horizontal direct effect of directives, since decisions are, in any event, only binding on the addressee. Where the addressees of a decision are Member States, an individual cannot rely on it in legal proceedings in contract, against another individual: *Carp* (2007).

International Agreements

3–034   As to whether international agreements to which the EU or a Member State is party can be given direct effect, the case law is inconsistent.

6.   THE *VON COLSON* PRINCIPLE AND *MARLEASING*: INDIRECT EFFECT

3–035   Where individuals seeking to rely on a directive cannot show that their opponent is a branch of the State, all may not be lost, because of a principle developed in *Von Colson and Kamann* (1984). Miss Von Colson was claiming that the German prison service had rejected her job application in breach of the Equal Treatment Directive 76/207 and German law provided inadequate compensation. At the same time, another claimant, Miss Hartz, was making the same claim against a private company. Thus, the issue of horizontal/vertical direct effect and the public/private distinction was openly raised. The court avoided opening up these distinctions by ingenious reliance on art.5 EC. Article 5 required States to "take all appropriate measures" to ensure fulfilment of their EU obligations. This obligation fell on all parts of a State, said the court, including its courts. Thus, the *courts* in a Member State must interpret national law in a manner which achieves the results referred to in art.189 EC (now art.288 TFEU), that is, the objectives of a directive. The German courts were thus obliged to interpret German law in such a way as to enforce the Equal Treatment Directive. The court added an important qualification to this obligation: "it is for the national court to interpret and apply the legislation adopted for the implementation of the directive in conformity with the requirements of EU law, in so far as it is given discretion to do so under national law". These qualifying words were moderated in *Marleasing* (below) to "as far as possible". The significance of this case is that it provides horizontal effect in an indirect way. Even though EU law is not applied directly, it may still be applied indirectly through the medium of the court's domestic interpretation.

The principle was extended in a significant way by the case of *Marleasing SA v La Comercial Internacional de Alimentacion SA* (1990). The court held that a national court was required to interpret its domestic legislation, whether it was legislation adopted prior to or subsequent to the directive, as far as possible within the light of the wording and purpose of a directive, in order to achieve the result envisaged by it. Some argue this case is a large step towards accepting the horizontal direct effect of directives. The end result of such interpretation certainly appears to be the same, as far as the individual litigants are concerned.

This principle has been applied many times over. One example was *Oceano Grupo Editorial SA v Quintero* (2000). Oceano sought to rely on Spanish law to bring an action in a Barcelona court. Part of the Unfair Contract Terms Directive, which only became enforceable in Spanish law after their claim arose, would have deprived the Barcelona court of jurisdiction. The court reaffirmed that a national court is obliged, when it applies national law provisions, predating or postdating a directive, to interpret those provisions, so far as possible, in the light of the wording of the directive, even if this meant ruling that it did not have jurisdiction to entertain the claim.

The court has qualified the principle. It declined to apply the principle to extend criminal liability: *Pretore di Salo v Persons Unknown* (1987). It is unclear to what extent national courts are required to depart from national law in order to achieve the result sought by a directive. To achieve such a result may involve the national court departing significantly from the wording of national law. For instance, in the *Von Colson* case, the national law clearly limited the compensation payable to the two women to a nominal amount, whereas the court held that the directive required the amount to be effective. It does seem, however, that the national court is not required to override the clear wording and intent of national law in order to make it comply with a directive which cannot be construed as directly effective.

7. DAMAGES FROM A TARDY STATE: THE *FRANCOVICH* PRINCIPLE

Another remedy is available for a citizen who has suffered as a result of the non-implementation of a directive but where the conditions for direct effect are not satisfied. In another case giving a bold interpretation to former art.5, the court held that, in certain conditions, the aggrieved citizen may have a remedy against the State in damages. In *Francovich v Italy* (1991), the applicants were employees of businesses which became insolvent, leaving substantial arrears of unpaid salary. They brought proceedings in the Italian courts against Italy, for the recovery of compensation provided by Directive 80/987, which Italy had not implemented. The directive should have guaranteed payment of unpaid remuneration in the case of insolvency by the employer. The applicants could not rely on the concept of direct effect, because the directive's terms were insufficiently precise. Happily for the applicants, the court held that they were entitled to compensation from the State. Inherent in the Treaty, they said, was the principle that a Member State should be liable for damage to individuals caused by infringements of EU law for which it was responsible. Their interpretation rested, in particular, on art.5, which placed a duty on Member States to take all appropriate measures to ensure the fulfilment of Treaty obligations. The court argued that to disallow damages against the State in these circumstances would weaken the protection of individual rights. The court laid down three conditions for an individual claiming damages against a Member State for failing to implement or incorrectly implementing a directive:

3–036

1. The result laid down by the directive involves the attribution of rights attached to individuals.
2. The content of those rights must be capable of being identified from the provisions of the directive.
3. There must be a causal link between the failure by the Member State to fulfil its obligations and the damage suffered by the individuals.

The court has left it up to each Member State to determine the competent courts and procedures for actions for damages against the State. The procedures must be not less favourable than those relating to similar claims under domestic law and must not make it difficult or practically impossible to obtain damages from the State. In *Becker v Finanzamt Munster-Innenstadt* (1982), the court held that provisions of directives could be invoked insofar as they define rights which individuals are able to assert against the State. Only a person with a direct interest could invoke a directive but this might include a third party: in *Verholen* (1991), a husband could bring a claim where his wife was discriminated against in a social security benefit, as it disadvantaged him.

Damages from a state whose legislature flouts EU law

3–037   In *Factortame (No.4)*, properly known as the joined cases *Brasserie du Pecheur SA v Federal Republic of Germany and R. v Secretary of State for Transport Ex p. Factortame Ltd (No.4)* (1996), the Court extended the *Francovich* principle to permit a claim of damages against a State whose national *legislature* had passed a law which was in serious breach of EU law. In the first case, French beer manufacturers were claiming damages against Germany for passing beer purity laws that effectively excluded the import of their beer. In the second case, the UK Parliament had passed the Merchant Shipping Act 1988, promoted as a Bill by Margaret Thatcher's government, which effectively excluded foreign fishing vessels, notably Spanish, from their right to fish in UK coastal waters, by laying down registration conditions of residence, nationality and domicile of vessel owners. Spanish fishermen complained that the Act offended against art.52 EC (now art.49 TFEU), which guaranteed freedom of establishment (freedom to establish a business). In prior cases, the court had already ruled the domestic legislation to be in breach of EU law. What was now at issue was whether the aggrieved parties could claim *damages* against the respective states in the national courts. The *Factortame* case had been referred by the Queen's Bench Divisional Court for a preliminary ruling. The Court of Justice decided the following, (paraphrased).

1. The *Francovich* principle applied to all state authorities, including the legislature.
2. The conditions of a damages claim were:
    a. that the rule breached was intended to confer rights on the individuals who had suffered loss or injury;
    b. that the breach was sufficiently serious;
    c. that there was a causal link between the breach and the damage sustained by the individuals.

3.   The State must make reparation, in accordance with its national law on liability but the conditions laid down must not be less favourable than for a domestic claim and must not make it excessively difficult to make a claim. (In the context of English law, it was virtually impossible for the Spanish fishing vessel owners to claim damages in the English courts, because we had no substantive or procedural law enabling a claim for damages against Parliament.)

4.   Such a claim could not be made conditional on establishing a degree of fault going beyond that of a sufficiently serious breach of EU law.

5.   Reparation must be commensurate with the damage sustained and this might include exemplary damages. It was left to the domestic legal system to set the criteria.

6.   Damages could not be limited to those sustained after a judgment finding such an infringement of EU law.

The upshot of these cases was that the onus was on the UK to create some procedure, in the English courts, for making a claim against the State for a breach of EU law by Parliament. The UK was obliged to devise some substantive cause of action in damages. In 1997, the Spanish brought their claim through the Queen's Bench Divisional Court and were awarded damages. This was upheld by the CA then the law lords so the Secretary of State for Transport lost in all three courts. The law lords found that the Thatcher Government, in introducing this legislation, had deliberately discriminated on grounds of nationality in the face of a clear and fundamental provision of the EC Treaty art.7 (now art.18 TFEU). This was done in good faith and to protect UK fishing communities rather than to harm the Spanish but inevitably it took away or seriously affected their rights to fish. There was a fundamental breach of Treaty obligations. It was a sufficiently serious breach to entitle Factortame and 96 others to compensation in damages: *R. v Secretary of State for Transport Ex p. Factortame Ltd (No.5)* (2000).

3–038

Factortame (No.4) was swiftly followed by a case which clarified how bad the breach of EU law had to be before damages could be claimed. In *R. v HM Treasury Ex p. British Telecommunications Plc* (1996), the Court of Justice repeated the rule that damages could be claimed by individuals who had suffered loss as a consequence of a State's enacting a directive incorrectly (this much was not new) but here the breach of EU law was not sufficiently serious to merit damages. The UK had acted in good faith and simply made a mistake in its enactment into UK law of the relevant directive. The wording of the directive was ambiguous and several other Member States had also misinterpreted it so there was no manifest and grave breach of EU law, as required by *Factortame (No.4)*. In 2003, the same cause of action was extended to a supreme court, in *Köbler v Republik Osterreich* and to courts and tribunals in *Ferreira da Silva e Brito v Portugal* (2015). Here, the State was being sued for damages caused by a court or tribunal against whose decisions there was no domestic remedy. The domestic law requiring that court's judgment to be set aside when it was impossible to achieve this should be ignored. This is the principle of effectiveness. *Factortame (No.4)* was applied and damages were awarded in the UK courts in *Byrne v Motor Insurers Bureau* (2008), in relation to restrictions on claiming compensation of victims of untraced drivers, and *Thin Cap* (2009), about faulty tax rules.

8.   DIRECT EFFECT OF EU LAW IN THE UK

3–039   The European Communities Act 1972 gave legal effect to EU law in the UK and it will be repealed when Brexit occurs. Pay close attention to the wording of s.2(1):

> "All such rights, powers, liabilities, obligations and restrictions from time to time created or arising by or under the Treaties, and all such remedies and procedures from time to time provided for by or under the Treaties, as in accordance with the Treaties are without further enactment to be given legal effect or used in the United Kingdom shall be recognised and available in law, and be enforced, allowed and followed accordingly; and the expression 'enforceable Community right' and similar expressions shall be read as referring to one to which this subsection applies."

In *Factortame (No.1)* (1990), the House of Lords interpreted "enforceable Community right" to mean directly effective legal right. This section gives effect to all directly effective EU law, whether made prior to or after the passing of the Act.

Section 3 binds all our courts, for the time being, to interpret matters of EU law in accordance with the rulings of the court and requires our courts to take judicial notice of EU legislation and the opinions of the Court of Justice. Our courts have had no problem in applying directly effective provisions. They seem to have been reluctant in some cases, however, to apply the *Von Colson* principle. In *Duke v GEC Reliance Ltd* (1988), Duke complained that she had been forced to retire at 60, despite the fact that her male colleagues were permitted to work until 65. Equal Treatment Directive 76/207 was not enacted into domestic law until the Sex Discrimination Act 1986. Duke could not rely on the directive as being directly effective because her employer was a private company. She argued that the English courts should construe the unamended Sex Discrimination Act 1975 in a manner consistent with the Equal Treatment Directive, treating her enforced retirement as unlawful dismissal. The House of Lords considered the case of *Von Colson* but opined that it did not provide a power to interfere with the method or result of the interpretation of national legislation by national courts. They noted that the Equal Treatment Directive post-dated the Sex Discrimination Act 1975 and thought it would be unfair on Reliance to "distort" the construction of the Act to accommodate it. Nevertheless, the House was prepared to make a distinction when construing national legislation that has been passed *in order to implement a directive*. In *Pickstone v Freemans Plc* (1989) the House adopted a purposive construction in interpreting an amendment to the Equal Pay Act 1970, in order to make it consistent with the UK's obligations under the Equal Pay Directive. The same purposive approach was taken in *Litster v Forth Dry Dock & Engineering Co Ltd* (1990). In this case, Lord Templeman said he thought the *Von Colson* principle imposed a duty on the UK courts to give a purposive construction to UK legislation which had been passed to give effect to directives. In *Webb v EMO Air Cargo (UK) Ltd* (1993), Lord Keith said it was the duty of the UK court to construe domestic legislation in accordance with the Court of Justice's interpretation of a relevant EU directive "if that can be done without distorting the meaning of the domestic legislation". He noted that, according to the European Court of Justice, this obligation on the domestic courts only arose where domestic law was open to an interpretation consistent with a directive. The House ruled that the applicant had not suffered discrimination under English law. They nevertheless asked the Court of Justice to construe the relevant directive and the application of the principle of equal treatment to the circumstances of the case. The Court of Justice sent back its interpretation, flatly disagreeing with the House and ruling that the case disclosed discrimination. The House applied the court's ruling in 1995. The report provides an interesting example of how the House had to construe an English statute in accordance with EU law in a way which seemed to run contrary to the instincts of domestic courts at all levels, at that time. (The Employment Appeal Tribunal and CA had reached the same conclusion.)

9.   SUPREMACY OF EU LAW

Curiously, the founding Treaty of the Common Market (European Community, EU), the Treaty of Rome 1957, did not prescribe the supremacy of EU law over national law. It was left to the embryonic European Court of Justice in developing its limbs, to describe the conception of its supremacy in *Costa v ENEL* (1964). This principle is as oft-cited and as jurisprudentially significant as Lord Atkin's famous neighbour principle, which developed the English law of negligence. In addition, the words below are so constitutionally significant, they should be learned and absorbed by every EU citizen.

3–040

> "By creating a Community of unlimited duration, having its own institutions, its own personality, its own legal capacity and capacity of representation on the international plane and, more particularly, real powers stemming from a limitation of sovereignty or a transfer of powers from the States to the Community, the Member States have limited their sovereignty rights, albeit within limited fields, and have thus created a body of law which binds both their nationals and themselves.
>
> The integration into the laws of each Member State of provisions which derive from the Community, and more generally the terms and the spirit of the Treaty, make it impossible for the States, as a corollary, to accord precedence to a unilateral and subsequent measure over a legal system accepted by them on a basis of reciprocity."

By 1970, the court had asserted the supremacy of EU law, even over Member States' constitutions (the *Internationale Handelsgesellschaft* case). By 1976, in *Simmenthal*, the court had explained that this meant that every domestic court, however lowly, was under a duty to disapply national law in favour of EU law, where there was a clear conflict. Furthermore, in the *Brasserie du Pecheur/ Factortame (No.4)* case, the court added that national courts must be capable of protecting claimed EU law rights in the face of clear contrary provisions in national law, pending the Court of Justice's final ruling on the precise nature of those rights.

The effects of EU sovereignty within the UK

3–041   In the European Communities Act 1972, the UK Parliament effectively gave away its legislative sovereignty in matters within the EU's sphere of activity, recognising the principle of supremacy of directly effective Community (EU) law. The crucial words of s.2(4) are both retrospective and prospective: ". . . any enactment passed or to be passed . . . shall be construed and have effect subject to the foregoing provisions of this section". This means that, where domestic law conflicts with directly effective EU law, the latter must be applied and the only way of altering this position is to repeal this subsection. The House of Lords, in *Factortame (No.1)* recognised that this was the effect of this subsection, when they disapplied part of the Merchant Shipping Act 1988, the clear words of which flew in the face of established EU law rights, including freedom of establishment and non-discrimination.

In this case, as explained above, Spanish owners of fishing vessels sought to register as British so that they would have access to the UK fishing quota under the common fisheries policy. The 1988 Act attempted to limit registration to British managed vessels. *Factortame* and others sought a judicial review in the High Court of the legality of the Act. The HC referred the question of Community (EU) law to the Court of Justice but, meanwhile, the procedural question of how to grant interim relief found its way up to the House of Lords (law lords). They declined to grant an interim injunction against the Crown, as an injunction could not, in English law, bind the Crown. Furthermore, the applicants' EU law rights were "necessarily uncertain" until determined by the court of Justice and appeared to run directly contrary to Parliament's sovereign will. They sought a preliminary ruling from the Court of Justice. The court answered by saying that where the sole obstacle preventing a national court from granting interim relief based on EU law is a rule of national law, that rule must be set aside. Not surprisingly, when the court ruled on the substantive question, they upheld Factortame's complaint that part of the Merchant Shipping Act ran contrary to Community (EU) law.

A comment on *Factortame (No.4)*

3–042   The UK media reacted especially badly to the *Factorame (No.4)* ruling, affronted at the thought of having to pay damages to the Spanish for stopping them coming and raiding "our" fish stocks. What is so ridiculous is that the UK politicians and journalists reacted as if the ruling were a surprise. When the UK Parliament passed this piece of protectionist legislation in 1988, the Thatcher government was warned formally by the Commission, in 1989, acting under their former art.169 powers (now art.258 TFEU), that the UK was in breach of the EC Treaty so it should have been obvious that the ultimate punch line would be that the UK would have to pay damages to the Spanish. The UK reacted with the same indignant horror to *Factortame (No.1)*, in 1990, which effectively ruled that a part of the Merchant Shipping Act would have to be suspended, as if we were shocked at this assault on the legislative sovereignty of Parliament. Apparently, many UK citizens, especially some politicians and journalists, had not noticed, or worked out, that we had given part of this away, on joining the common market, as it then was, in January 1973. As if to rub salt into the wound made by *Factortame (No.4)*, in March 1996, the BSE beef crisis broke out within days of the judgment. We reached the hypocritical position of arguing that the court's powers should be curbed, by the 1996 Intergovernmental Conference (the renegotiation of Maastricht); yet at the same time lodging a claim before the court against the Commission for losses caused by the export ban on British beef.

10. GENERAL PRINCIPLES OF LAW

The Court of Justice has built up and interpreted a body of general principles. **3–043** They must be applied in interpreting EU law, including elements of domestic law. These principles, developed by the court just as the English courts have developed the common law, should be distinguished from the fundamental principles of the Treaty (e.g. free movement of goods and persons; non-discrimination). In part, the general principles are derived from fundamental rights in individual Member States. The court looks for principles common to Member States' constitutions and is guided by international treaties to which Member States are signatories, the most obvious and important being the European Convention on Human Rights. The Luxembourg and Strasbourg courts look to one another's judgments and usually but not always harmonise the interpretation of rights. The EU rights include, for example:

- proportionality: administrative authorities must not use means more than appropriate and necessary to achieve their ends;
- legal certainty: includes the principle of legitimate expectation (same as English law) and the principle of non-retroactivity;
- natural justice: the right to a fair hearing (same as English law), the duty to give reasons, due process;
- the right to protection against self-incrimination (same as English law);
- equality;
- subsidiarity: the EU can only act if its objectives cannot be achieved by the Member States.

11. THE EU AND THE EUROPEAN CONVENTION ON HUMAN RIGHTS AND THE CHARTER OF FUNDAMENTAL RIGHTS OF THE EUROPEAN UNION (2010/C 83/02)

All the Member States are signatories of the Convention so one would think the **3–044** obvious way for the court to guarantee rights would be for the EU to be a signatory of the Convention. An early attempt to do this was initially declared invalid by the court. The 1996 Intergovernmental Conference failed to have accession incorporated into the Treaty of Amsterdam. The Court of Justice nevertheless continues to apply the Convention rights within its jurisdiction, as part of its general principles. In the meantime, the Lisbon Treaty provided for the EU to accede to the Convention. In 2013, the Member States agreed a draft agreement on acceding to the Convention but, on a reference from the Commission, in 2014 the Court of Justice published an opinion that the draft agreement was incompatible with the treaties. Yet again, then, the EU has failed to become a signatory to the Convention, though it has been trying to get this procedure right for decades.

Also, the EU Charter was signed at the end of 2000. It was declaratory. It was given binding legal effect, on a level with the Treaties, by the Treaty of Lisbon, in 2009. It puts social and economic rights on the same footing as civil and political rights. Examples of the rights are listed below.

1. Dignity (e.g. right to life, prohibition on torture).
2. Freedoms (e.g. liberty and security, respect for private and family life, right to marry, freedom of thought, religion, expression; right to education).
3. Equality (e.g. non-discrimination, cultural, linguistic and religious diversity; rights for children, the disabled and the elderly).
4. Solidarity (e.g. workers' rights to information and consultation; social security, health care, environmental and consumer protection).
5. Citizenship rights (e.g. voting, good administration, access to documents, the Parliament and the Ombudsman and diplomatic and consular protection).
6. Justice (e.g. effective remedy, presumption of innocence and fair trial).

The full text can be seen on the Eur-Lex section of the Europa website. As can be seen, there is an overlap with the European Convention on Human Rights, described in the next chapter, which is *not* a treaty of the EU. The Charter preamble explains that it includes the Convention rights, subject to the principle of subsidiarity. The UK and Poland think they secured a sort of opt-out, in Protocol 30 to the Treaties, restricting the interpretation of the Charter by the Court of Justice and national courts, in those two countries.

12. HARMONISATION OF LAWS: THE CORPUS JURIS PROJECT AND THE CREATION OF A EUROPEAN AREA OF JUSTICE

3–045

In 2005, Europol, the EU police coordinating agency, claimed there were 4,000 criminal gangs operating in Europe. According to the International Monetary Fund, the profits of organised crime account for 2.5 per cent of the world's gross domestic product.

Corpus juris would be a common law of Europe in certain fields if it were ever achieved, but it would take decades to achieve and would be technically and politically extremely difficult. The phrase seems to be little used in the EU nowadays, probably because it is so provocative. Two examples are contract law and the small claims procedure. A new cross-border procedure for claims under 2,000 Euros was agreed by justice ministers in 2006. This was increased to 5,000 Euros in 2017.

Most importantly, the Commission has always pressed for a greater measure of control over criminal investigation and prosecution within Member States, to combat organised crime. The aim is to protect the financial interest of the EU (protecting the budget; tax evasion). It is directed at crimes such as fraud, market rigging, abuse of office, misappropriation of funds, disclosure of secrets derived from office-holding, money laundering and receiving and conspiracy. This is now extended to protect citizens and so includes such matters as child pornography and terrorism. The Europa website explains all the Commission bodies and other agencies responsible for justice in the EU, under the heading of "justice and fundamental rights", on the Commission's web-pages. They are outlined perfectly in Spencer's 2016 article, cited in the Brexit note at the opening of this book.

As an example of EU activity in this field, in May 2011, Justice Commissioner Viviane Reding proposed a directive on minimum standards for victims in the EU. In 2002, the Council established Eurojust, to enhance the development of Europe-wide co-operation in criminal justice cases. A European arrest warrant came into effect, as a result of a decision in 2002. It replaced extradition proceedings between Member States with a system of surrender between judicial authorities. In 2004, the Commission adopted a proposal for a Council framework decision on certain procedural rights in criminal proceedings throughout the EU. There are directives providing a right to interpretation and translation and access to information in criminal proceedings. A 2016 directive aims to strengthen the presumption of innocence and the right to be present at one's trial. From 2014, a new directive facilitated judicial authorities in requesting investigations to gain evidence from another member state. Another directive, when implemented, will make it easier to trace, freeze and confiscate criminal assets across borders. All of these developments rest on the principle of mutual recognition where criminal justice systems operate differently, as they all do because, in practice, the interpretation of what constitutes a fair trial differs fairly radically throughout Europe. There have been examples of English courts refusing extradition to France, on the ground that the suspect would not get a fair trial, and a similar refusal by a French court to extradite to Spain, on the ground that the suspect might be tortured. The problem with some of these proposed new rights, as Alegre points out, is their vagueness, so a right to legal advice does not even extend to a right to have a lawyer present during questioning. For further discussion see Alegre and for detail, see the Commission website.

Stephen Jakobi, who for many years ran Fair Trials Abroad, a group of lawyers who endeavour to help those detained and tried abroad, was all too familiar with the shortcomings of other legal systems. He warned, in 2002, that efficiently administered justice systems would be forced to recognise decisions made by under-funded and ill-managed courts. JUSTICE wanted the UK Government to take a lead on harmonisation. The then Director, Roger Smith, said the UK "has a generally creditable record in the defence of suspects and defendants. Our citizens have much to gain from all countries in the EU attaining the same standards." In December 2013, however, the UK Government decided that the proposal to establish a European Public Prosecutor's Office was a step too far. In the Lisbon Treaty, the UK secured an opt-out of 133 police and criminal justice measures. At the time of writing, 2017, no-one yet knows the effects Brexit will have on mutual co-operation in criminal justice between the UK and the EU.

Obviously, instruments like the European Arrest Warrant will be invalid in the UK but the UK will, in my opinion, become a "partner" of Eurojust, not least because the UK police services will insist on it, as explained in the Brexit note at the opening of this book. As I write, in July 2017, almost every aspect of the potential impact of Brexit is uncertain but I have endeavoured to explain there some of the inevitable legal consequences.

Bibliography

3–046   S. Alegre, "EU fair trial rights—added value or no value?" (2004) 154 N.L.J. 758.

S. Jakobi, "Tattered Justice", *Counsel*, April 2002, p.18.

D. Ormerod, "Editorial—EU Criminal Justice" [2012] Crim. L.R. 907.

N. Padfield, "The Spread of EU Criminal Law", *Archbold News*, August 2006.

R. Smith, "Fundamentally right" (on the EUCFR) (2005) 155 N.L.J. 229 and (2006) 156 N.L.J. 206.

R. Stevens, "On being nicer to James and the children" (1994) 144 N.L.J. 1620.

T. Tayleur, "Emanations of the State" (2000) 150 N.L.J. 1292.

Further reading and sources for updating this chapter

3–047   Free updates of this book are available on the Sweet & Maxwell website: *http://uklawstudent.thomsonreuters.com*.

Summary and revision: P. Darbyshire, *Nutshells English Legal System*, 10th edn (London: Sweet & Maxwell, 2016).

Europa, EU website and portal: *http://europa.eu*. Start here because it has links to all other web-pages and sites.

European Charter of Fundamental Rights.

European Commission: *https://ec.europa.eu/commission*.

European Commission in the UK: *http://ec.europa.eu/unitedkingdom/*.

Court of Justice of the EU: *http://curia.europa.eu/jcms*. See annual reports and press releases.

Eurojust: *http://www.eurojust.europa.eu/*.

Portal to European Union Law, Eur-Lex: *http://eur-lex.europa.eu/*.

The UK Parliament: http://*http://www.parliament.uk*.

Refer to the latest editions of the following*

3–048   *Cambridge Yearbook of European Legal Studies*.

P. Craig and G. De Burca, *EU Law*.

N. Foster, *Blackstone's EU Treaties and Legislation 2016–2017*.

S. Weatherill, *Cases and Materials on EU Law*.

*Note: please refer to the Publisher's website for the latest editions.

CHAPTER 4

The European Convention on Human Rights

"He regarded the European Convention as 'a gift from victory' in the Second World War, a product of victory over the principles and governance of wicked men, led by Adolf Hitler" (Attorney General Lord Goldsmith QC, obituary for Lord Scarman, law lord 1977–1986, *Counsel*, February 2005).

In Ch.1 we saw that Lord Bingham considered the rule of law as requiring adequate protection of fundamental human rights.   4–001

1. INCORPORATION INTO UK LAW

The European Convention on Human Rights 1950 (the Convention) was drafted   4–002 by British lawyers, notably Sir David Maxwell-Fyfe, who had been a prosecutor at the Nuremburg trials of World War II Nazi war criminals. It followed the Universal Declaration of Human Rights by two years and grew out of disgust with fascism and an anxiety to protect basic freedoms. It is a Treaty of the Council of Europe, which was formed in London in 1949 from a 1946 idea of Winston Churchill that we needed a "United States of Europe" to make all of Europe "free and happy" and peaceful. (See Council of Europe website.) The UK was the first state to ratify. Many Convention rights reflect the common law and the 1689 English Bill of Rights. I emphasise these points so that the reader understands that the Convention rights are not foreign ideas inflicted on the British by "Europe", the impression now given by some politicians and elements of the UK media. The Human Rights Act 1998 and the Convention are often criticised in the UK and there is confusion over the ambit of the Convention and EU law. In 2007, Frances Lawrence, widow of a murdered head teacher, expressed concern that his murderer would not be deported at the end of his sentence because of the Human Rights Act but the decision was based on EU law, not the HRA. As it happens, the EU has adopted the Convention rights as part of its general principles of law but it must be understood that the Convention is *not* an EU treaty. It was created independently, years before the Common Market (now EU) was formed in 1957.

From 1966, individuals were permitted to bring claims to the European Court of Human Rights (ECtHR) against the UK. By 1998, 99 cases had been taken to Strasbourg, more than any country except Italy, and the UK had been found to be in violation of the Convention 52 times. It was a frequent defendant before the court, partly because the UK lacks a written constitution or modern Bill of Rights. Prior to 2000, however, the individual could not assert their Convention rights through the domestic (UK) courts. Judges of the UK were powerless to apply it. The courts, in any event, took a fairly conservative approach. Modern judges, from 1990, grew more outspoken in their concerns about human rights. Lord Chief Justice Bingham urged incorporation of the Convention into UK law and in the Court of Appeal (CA) he and his fellow judges expressed dissatisfaction with their powerlessness to allow appeals in a case which raised Convention issues: *R. v Morrisey* (1977). In the meantime though, the Conservative governments of the early 1990s had set their face against incorporation. They had grown hostile to the Strasbourg court, especially because of decisions such as the damages award against the UK in favour of the families of IRA members assassinated by the UK Government, in Gibraltar, in the Death on the Rock case. Minister Michael Heseltine called this decision "ludicrous" and called for an alteration to the powers of the ECtHR. The Government were dilatory in enforcing the judgments of the court that they did not like, as Bindman explained.

4–003   In 1996, the Labour opposition published their plans to allow the domestic courts to enforce Convention rights. The Conservatives argued that UK citizens were adequately protected by the common law. Enacting a Bill of Rights would give the courts wide discretion over matters which were properly the preserve of Parliament. The generalised wording of the Convention would leave too much scope for judicial interpretation and litigation. (As we shall see in this chapter, the same point has been revived in arguments about the Human Rights Act, from 2009.) Lord Irvine, Shadow Lord Chancellor, pointed out that the UK was virtually alone amongst the major nations of Western Europe in failing to give its citizens the means to assert Convention rights in their courts (see Hudson). Once in Government, in 1997, New Labour swiftly published a White Paper, *Rights Brought Home*. The newly appointed Lord Chancellor Irvine said:

> "The Human Rights Bill … will be a constitutional change of major significance, protecting the individual citizen against erosion of liberties … It will promote a culture where positive rights and liberties become the focus and concern of legislators, administrators and judges alike". (The Tom Sargeant Memorial Lecture).

The Bill would, he said, require judges to produce a decision on the morality of conduct, not simply its compliance with the bare letter of the law. He thought the traditional common law approach to the protection of liberties, described as a negative right (the right to do anything not prohibited by law), offered little protection against creeping erosion of individual liberties by a legislature.

The Human Rights Act 1998

4–004   The Human Rights Act 1998 (HRA 1998) gave *further effect* to the Convention rights in UK and thus English law from 2000 and made them enforceable in UK courts and tribunals. Section 1 and Sch.1 of the HRA 1998 did *not* incorporate the Convention rights but restated the Conventions and Protocols as part of UK law with the exception of art.13. Article 13 would have given a remedy for violation in any court or tribunal. The Government did not want to give them sweeping, new, inappropriate powers. People have to seek monetary remedies in the *senior* courts or UKSC, on appeal or in judicial review proceedings. The relationship between the Convention and the HRA 1998 is explored in *Al-Skeini v UK* (2007). The objective of the Act was to create rights that are co-extensive with Convention rights, except where expressly excluded by the Act. The Convention could apply to state acts in an area outside its jurisdiction, over which it exercised "effective control". The geographical extent of the HRA 1998 is co-extensive with the Convention.

> *Very importantly*, s.2 of the HRA 1998 provides that when a court or tribunal is determining a question in connection with a Convention right it "must take into account" judgments, decisions or declarations of the ECtHR, and opinions or decisions of the Commission or the Committee of Ministers. This does *not* mean that the court's decisions are binding, as explained in Ch.2 and emphasised by the UKSC in *R. v Horncastle* (2009). This is in distinct contrast with the binding decisions of the Court of Justice of the EU, as provided by the European Communities Act 1972, until repealed. Furthermore, s.3 of the HRA 1998 says *"(s)o far as possible*, primary legislation and subordinate legislation must be read and given effect in a way which is compatible with the Convention rights".

Notice that this applies to all of us in interpreting legislation, not just the courts, but the obligation is qualified. Section 6 makes it unlawful for any public authority, including any court or tribunal, to act in a way incompatible with a Convention right. The lack of clarity in the meaning of "public authority" has been criticised. Any party to any legal proceedings can rely on a Convention right. This means, for example, that it can be used to apply for a stay (stop) of proceedings, or as a defence, or a ground of appeal, or to found an application for judicial review. If a court or tribunal is satisfied of a violation, they may award anything appropriate within their jurisdiction. Damages or compensation may only be awarded by those courts or tribunals empowered to do so (s.8).

Where courts cannot interpret a piece of legislation as compatible, then some **4-005** higher courts may make a *declaration of incompatibility*, under s.4(2), meaning the High Court, Court of Appeal, UKSC, Judicial Committee of the Privy Council and the Courts Martial Appeal Court. A lesser court or tribunal must apply the incompatible law and the case will have to be taken on appeal until one of these courts is reached. This may take two levels of appeal. For instance, the Employment Appeal Tribunal does not have this power. The declaration of incompatibility does not affect validity of the law and is not binding on the parties (s.4). In any case where a court is considering making a declaration of incompatibility, the Crown (meaning the Government) is entitled to notice and to be joined as a party to the proceedings (s.5). Section 11 provides for a fast-track legislative procedure designed to remove the incompatibility, so a minister can use a statutory instrument to amend offending primary legislation and, as I explained in Ch.2, these "Henry VIII" sections of Acts are controversial. Declarations of incompatibility are discussed below. Most defects in UK law have been remedied by legislation or policy changes, as will be seen in the last section of this chapter. This, and the UK's compliance record and government and political attitudes towards the Convention are discussed below. People can still apply to the ECtHR in Strasbourg but they have to show that they have exhausted all domestic remedies.

When any new Bill is published, s.19 obliges the sponsoring minister to make a written statement that it is compatible with the Convention, or decline to make a statement but indicate that the Government wishes to proceed. A Joint Parliamentary Committee on Human Rights scrutinises Government Bills for their human rights implications and compatibility. (Parliament website.)

Like the Court of Justice of the EU, the Strasbourg court takes a highly purposive approach to legislative interpretation. Examining relevant case authorities since the Act came into force in 2000, we can see that UK judges have, to an extent, taken this approach themselves. It was obvious in 1998 that there would be an impact on precedent and judicial interpretation of statute and this has proven to be the case. In order to enforce a Convention right, the Court of Appeal may consider itself not to be bound by previous binding precedents which are incompatible with Convention rights. This was explained in the 1997 White Paper. Examples appear in Ch.12 on criminal procedure. A number of extra judges were created to deal with what the Government predicted would be a heavy workload generated by the HRA 1998 but this did not occur. Many far-fetched claims fail. We can find some amusement in these, like the hilarious claim mentioned in Ch.1 that a pub ban constituted a breach of human rights.

2.   THE CONVENTION RIGHTS

4–006   These are appended to the HRA 1998 as Sch.1, where they are spelled out in full. Briefly, they are, by article:

2.   Right to life.
3.   Prohibition of torture.
4.   Prohibition of slavery and forced labour.
5.   Right to liberty and security.
6.   Right to a fair trial.
7.   No punishment without law.
8.   Right to respect for private and family life.
9.   Freedom of thought, conscience and religion.
10. Freedom of expression.
11. Freedom of assembly and association.
12. Right to marry.
13. Right to an effective remedy—not incorporated into English law (see above).
14. Prohibition of discrimination.
16. Restrictions on political activity of aliens.
17. Prohibition of abuse of rights.
18. Limitation on use of restrictions on rights.

Some rights are absolute, such as 3. Some admit exceptions, such as 2, and most are subject to restrictions to ensure respect for other rights and freedoms.

Subsequent protocols added protection of property, rights to education, free elections, freedom of movement within a state, prohibitions on imprisonment for debt, the expulsion of nationals, the collective expulsion of aliens, abolition of the death penalty, a right of appeal in criminal cases and compensation for wrongful conviction, the right not to be punished twice, equality between spouses, and a general prohibition on discrimination.

3. THE EUROPEAN COURT OF HUMAN RIGHTS

Do not confuse the ECtHR with the Court of Justice of the EU, described in Ch.3. The latter sits in Luxembourg and interprets EU law for the Member States of the EU. The ECtHR is *not* an institution of the EU. It interprets and enforces the Convention for the 47 contracting states that have ratified it. It sits in Strasbourg.

4–007

The court first sat in 1959 and the fulltime Strasbourg court, designed by London architect Sir Richard Rogers, was opened in 1998. Its composition is described in Ch.6 on civil courts. Procedure is described on its website. Each application is assigned to a section and a rapporteur. Three judges filter applications, with most decision-making done on the papers. Admissible cases go to panels of seven judges. Initially, or at any time in proceedings, a case may be referred to a Grand Chamber of 17 judges "where a case raises a serious question of interpretation of the Convention or where there is a risk of departing from existing case-law". Any judge in the panel is entitled to append to the judgment a separate opinion, concurring or dissenting. Within three months of the judgment, any party may request that the case be referred to the Grand Chamber if it raises a serious question of interpretation or application, or a serious issue of general importance. Following a finding of a breach of the Convention, the State is legally obliged to make reparation.

One practical drawback is the court's backlog. The Interlaken Conference on Reform of the European Court of Human Rights 2010 devised an action plan. Since 2010, the ECtHR can strike out cases where the applicant has not suffered a "significant disadvantage". Judges are now elected for nine years maximum and may not seek re-election. After further conferences and more reforms, the court's 2016 annual report said that the backlog had been reduced to 80,000, from 160,000 in 2011. At last, by June 2017, the backlog was cleared. Rejected applicants get a reasoned decision by a single judge. From 2014, all incomplete applications are rejected and the time limit has been reduced. The states agreed to strengthen domestic remedies, to resolve the problem of massive batches of cases on a single issue bulking up the backlog. By 2013, Turkey and others had already implemented this plan. The 2016 Annual Report details some remarkable reforms in the court's functioning and communications, which will hopefully satisfy critics such as the UK and others. In 2015 they formed the Superior Courts Network of top courts in 17 contracting states (hopefully 30 by 2017). Dialogue with these top state judges now allows the Strasbourg court to get information on comparative domestic laws, which helps them interpret the Convention. In turn, the states' top courts can get information and commentary on ECtHR case law and they can submit questions. This is a forerunner to formal cooperation which will occur once new Protocol 16 is implemented. This will permit a preliminary reference procedure for advice, copying the similar reference procedure in EU cases. This was another reform prompted by the Brighton Declaration 2012, on further reform. Multilateral dialogue was extended to different forms too. The Strasbourg judges also had their first meeting with the Network of the Presidents of the Supreme Courts of the EU. The UK is part of this but (tragically in my opinion) will cease to be so on Brexit. The court is also trying to improve its communications by issuing factsheets on its case law, rapidly providing an overview on specific topics. They have imported a new principle of consultation into the court's procedural rules, again responding to calls for reform. We return to the issue of the court's role and functioning, below, in the last section.

The Committee of Ministers is the decision-making organ of the Council of Europe and is composed of the foreign Ministers of the contracting States. (*Remember, these are not EU institutions.*) It supervises the execution of the court's judgments and can check that a State has taken steps to amend offending legislation. The court may, at the request of the Committee of Ministers, give advisory opinions on legal questions concerning the interpretation of the Convention and Protocols. A.T.H. Smith explained the principles upon which the ECtHR has acted.

1.   A generous approach is taken when determining what comes within the scope of the rights.
2.   There are four requirements before conditions can be imposed on a right:
      ● interference must be lawful;
      ● it must serve a legitimate purpose;
      ● it must be necessary in a democratic society;
      ● it must not be discriminatory.
3.   The Convention is a "living instrument", so the court may depart from its previous decisions, to suit changing circumstances.

The court has held that the Convention, not the domestic court, determines whether proceedings are civil or criminal.

4.   EXAMPLES OF THE CONVENTION'S APPLICATION IN THE UK

4–008   It should be understood that cases against any State before the ECtHR are of equal value to the English and Welsh courts in assisting them to apply the Convention. Below, I list just a few cases, most of which involved the UK as a respondent, as well as some in domestic courts. This is only a sample, so the reader can start to understand the impact of Convention law on the law of the three UK domestic jurisdictions. As can be seen in the last section of this chapter, by 2016, the UK has a very good record of compliance with human rights judgments. The 2016 Report of the Ministry of Justice that I summarise there provides detailed examples of how UK law and policy have been changed to respond to judgments in 2014–2016.

Article 2 Right to Life

As Lord Bingham pointed out, in his book *The Rule of Law*, while English law   4–009
has long outlawed murder, manslaughter, infanticide and so on, the ECtHR has
gone further and interpreted art.2 as imposing on states a positive obligation to
establish legal frameworks to protect life.

Coroners' juries and inquests into deaths in custody

In *R. (on the application of Middleton) v HM Coroner for West Somerset* (2004),   4–010
the House of Lords held that the State's procedural obligation to investigate a
death which might have violated the right to life because it was a death in custody
(in a state-run institution) required an inquest jury to draw conclusions on the
central factual issues of the case. The word "how" in the Coroners Act 1988 and
the Coroners' Rules should be interpreted as meaning not simply "by what
means" but also "in what circumstances" the person died. The State has a duty to
ensure a reasonably prompt, effective investigation before an independent body
with an opportunity for the relatives of the deceased to participate: *R. v Secretary
of State for the Home Department Ex p. Amin* (2003). In this case, where the
victim had been killed by his cellmate in Feltham Young Offenders Institution,
there had been an investigation into the death by the Prison Service, the police
and the Commission for Racial Equality but the Minister had refused the family's
request for an independent public inquiry. It was held that the Minister had not
met minimum standards set down by the ECtHR in other cases involving deaths
in custody in the UK. One of these was *Edwards v UK* (39647/98) (2005), in
which the ECtHR held that the authorities had failed to protect the life of the
applicants' son who was stamped on and kicked to death whilst sharing a cell at
Colchester police station. These decisions have caused changes in detention
practices and in the conduct of inquiries and inquests, following deaths in public
institutions. The coronial system has been restructured, as explained in Ch.6.
These cases also engage art.8, by requiring that the family be involved and
informed.

Armed forces

The HRA 1998 *does* apply to armed forces on foreign soil: *Smith (FC) v The*   4–011
Ministry of Defence (2013). The UKSC departed from their previous decision in
R. (on the application of Smith) v Oxfordshire Assistant Deputy Coroner (2010).
Parents of dead soldiers have also been given remedies under art.2 in relation to
gunshot deaths of young recruits at Deepcut Barracks. Article 2 also offered a
remedy to parents of recruits who died of heat exhaustion on Brecon Beacons in
2015.

Witnesses

Articles 2 and 8 were breached where the police failed to protect a prosecution   4–012
witness, who was shot dead days before he was due to give evidence: *Van Colle v
Chief Constable of Hertfordshire* (2007).

The right to die

4–013   In *Pretty v UK* (2002), the dying Diane Pretty took her case to the ECtHR in Strasbourg, after the law lords refused to rule that the Director of Public Prosecutions (DPP) should be told by the courts to grant her husband immunity from prosecution in assisting her planned suicide. Her application was unanimously declared inadmissible. Article 2, right to life, did not extend to a right to die. Article 8 (private and family life) *was* engaged because under it, notions of the quality of life took on significance but there was no violation, because, in regulating behaviour for the protection of public morals, the state's "margin of appreciation" was important (in other words, the state had a lot of discretion) so the Suicide Act 1961, criminalising assisting a suicide, did not amount to a disproportionate interference with the applicant's right. Mrs Pretty died a few days later. In *R. (on the application of Purdy) v DPP* (2009), the circumstances were almost identical. Mrs Purdy wanted clear guidelines as to whether her husband would be likely to be prosecuted if he assisted her suicide. The law lords accepted the ECtHR ruling in *Pretty*, on art.8, and ruled that the DPP *was* obliged to publish his policy identifying the facts and circumstances he would take into account in deciding whether to prosecute someone for assisting the suicide of a terminally ill person. (See this now on the Crown Prosecution Service website).

Death penalty

4–014   In *Al-Saadoon and Mufdhi v UK* (2009), the applicants were transferred to Iraqi courts, regardless of the ECtHR and the fact that they risked the death penalty, which breached art.2, and they made no attempt to negotiate this with the Iraqi courts.

Article 3 Prohibition of torture and inhuman or degrading treatment or punishment

4–015   As described below, the English have long outlawed judicial torture. Indeed, they have been boasting since the fifteenth century that this is one of the many aspects of their criminal procedure that makes them superior to continental jurisdictions, notably the French.

Prohibition of reliance on evidence derived from torture

4–016   In *A v Secretary of State for the Home Department* (2005) the law lords ruled that evidence obtained by torture was inadmissible. Although their Lordships relied on art.3 of the Convention, their primary authorities were the common law and international law. (Torture was prohibited by statute in England in 1640. The Bill of Rights 1689 prohibited cruel and unusual punishments.) Examining the ancient sources of common law on repugnance to torture, Lord Bingham concluded that it was a constitutional principle, not just a rule of evidence. Lord Bingham's judgment is a great education on ancient common law sources, modern relevant precedents and international law on the point.

The State's duty to protect people

The UK failed to protect children against serious long-term neglect and abuse: *Z*   **4–017**
v UK (2001). The Court of Appeal held that police failure to investigate a serial
rapist, "the Black Cab Rapist" was a breach: *D v Commissioner of Police of the
Metropolis* (2014).

Minimum standards of treatment in custody

Breaches of art.3 were found in detaining a disabled prisoner in cells without   **4–018**
suitable facilities, in *Price v UK* (2002), and failing to monitor the condition of an
asthmatic heroin addict who died in prison, in *McGlinchey v UK* (2003). In the
2017 case of *Hutchinson v UK (No 2)*, the Grand Chamber of the Strasbourg
court ruled that a whole-life tariff imposed on a prisoner could be regarded as
compatible with art.3, as there was a prospect of review and release.

Article 4 Prohibition of slavery and forced labour

English law already prohibited these. There are exceptions, such as compulsory   **4–019**
military service, in other contracting states, and forced work in prisons.

Article 5 Liberty and Security

The text is set out in the criminal procedure chapter. It is clearly modelled on the   **4–020**
English writ of habeas corpus.

Parole procedure, immigration detention, terror suspects and "kettling" demonstrators

See also Ch.12 on criminal procedure. In *The Rule of Law*, Lord Bingham   **4–021**
acknowledged that the article had enabled the courts to go further in protecting
liberty than the common law, Magna Carta, habeas corpus and other English
remedies. Strasbourg court rulings below have forced the UK to reorganise its
parole procedure.

In *Hussain v UK, Singh v UK* (1996), breaches were found when juveniles
were sentenced indeterminately "at Her Majesty's pleasure". They were unable to
have the lawfulness of their continued detention reviewed by a court. The lack of
adversarial proceedings before the Parole Board prevented it from being a court
or court-like body.

In *Stafford v UK* (2002) the Home Secretary decided to keep S in prison longer
than recommended by the Parole Board. The fact that this decision was taken by
a politician rather than a judge went against the "spirit of the Convention" as too
arbitrary. This was one of a series of cases diminishing the power of the Home
Secretary over sentencing. Home Secretary David Blunkett expressed disappointment but no other country in the Council of Europe allowed a Government
minister to determine sentence length for individuals. See also many other
decisions condemning proceedings before the Parole Board, such as *Waite v UK*
(2003) and the House of Lords in *R. v Parole Board Ex p. West* (2005). In *Reid v*

UK (2003), breaches of art.5(4) were found in placing the burden of proof on R to establish that his continued detention in a mental hospital did not satisfy conditions of lawfulness and in the four-year-long delay in determining his appeal.

In *Austin v UK* (2012) the Strasbourg court found no violation where demonstrators and innocent passers-by were "kettled" (contained in a confined space) to prevent a demonstration getting out of control.

In 2016, The ECtHR ruled that the UK's system of immigration detention did not violate art.5 but delay in deporting a detainee did: *JN v UK*. It also ruled that there was no breach in using closed court hearings where terror suspects challenged the lawfulness of their detention: *Sher v UK*. The UK Supreme Court ruled there was no breach of arts 5, 6 and 8 by the Terrorism Act 2000, which permits detention of people at borders for questioning, without suspicion, for nine hours: *Beghal v DPP* (2015).

Indefinite internment—The Belmarsh Case

4–022   2004 saw nine law lords taking a radical decision on a very controversial piece of legislation: *A (FC) v Secretary of State for the Home Department*. The appellants challenged the lawfulness of their indefinite detention under the Anti-Terrorism, Crime and Security Act 2001, which enabled the internment without trial of foreign nationals who the Home Secretary suspected were terrorists. This Act was passed swiftly after the terrorist destruction of the New York World Trade Centre on 11 September 2001. There were no similar powers over UK citizens. The Government had derogated from (opted out of) its obligations under art.5, as provided for by the Convention where there is "a public emergency threatening the life of the nation". No other European country had done this in the wake of "9/11". Seven law lords ruled that indefinite detention without trial was unlawful because it was a disproportionate interference with liberty (art.5) and equality (art.14). Lord Hoffmann went further, claiming the nation was not under threat, as required for derogation. Like his fellows, he saw the Act as offensive to fundamental constitutional principles:

> "The real threat to the life of the nation, in the sense of a people living in accordance with its traditional laws and political values, comes not from terrorism but from laws such as these. That is the true measure of what terrorism may achieve. It is for Parliament to decide whether to give the terrorists such a victory."

Baroness Hale said "We have always taken it for granted that we cannot be locked up in this country without trial or explanation". Lord Hope said it was impossible to overstate the importance of liberty in a democracy. Lord Scott said "Indefinite imprisonment, on grounds not disclosed, is the stuff of nightmares, associated with … Soviet Russia in the Stalinist era." They were not persuaded by the Government's argument that the Act did not offend against art.5 because it allowed for review by the Special Immigration Appeals Commission, which could hear the evidence against the accused (too sensitive to be admitted in a court) and overrule the Home Secretary. Nor, unsurprisingly, were they at all impressed by the Attorney's argument that they, the judges, were an unelected and undemocratic body who should not second guess ministers.

The Government then faced what much of the media portrayed as a constitutional crisis. Backbenchers threatened trouble. Some of the special government-appointed advocates for the detainees said they would resign. In 2005, Parliament passed the Prevention of Terrorism Act to replace the offending 2001 Act but it was ferociously debated. Opponents, including civil liberties groups, did not cite the Convention so much as ancient liberties fundamental to the UK constitution, such as habeas corpus, which they claimed was laid down in Magna Carta. (Historians know that this is erroneous but writs with the same effect can be traced back to the twelfth century). The Prevention of Terrorism Act 2005 again derogated from the requirements of the Convention. It allowed British and foreign terrorist suspects to be placed under a control order (meaning house arrest), by the Home Secretary. Although this was reviewed by a judge, it did not satisfy critics who said it amounted to detention without trial. They asked why we were the only country in Europe which considered it necessary to do this. Other countries' laws permitted the admission of evidence obtained by surveillance, such as telephone tapping, so such suspects could be tried for say, incitement or conspiracy to commit terrorist offences. The conditions of detention under a control order were much more draconian than those of house arrest under the old apartheid regime in South Africa. Control orders provoked more challenges in the courts. See, for example, under art.6, below. The 2005 Act was repealed by the Terrorism Prevention and Investigation Measures Act 2011.

Article 6 Fair Trial

Lord Steyn said in *R. v DPP Ex p. Kebilene* (2000) "when article 6 of the Convention becomes part of our law, it will be the prism through which other aspects of our criminal law may have to be re-examined". The biggest cluster of cases and legislative changes generated by the HRA 1998 have been those on criminal procedure, mostly art.6. Some are dealt with here and the rest in Ch.10 on criminal procedure, where the text of art.6 is set out. See further Ashworth (2014). Nevertheless, the most dramatic impact of art.6 was that it necessitated wholesale constitutional reform to the office of Lord Chancellor and the replacement of the law lords by a new UK Supreme Court, explained in Ch.14. 4 023

Courts martial—appearance of bias

The ECtHR repeatedly found against the UK in relation to courts martial proceedings. Systems of military adjudication which had been in place for over 600 years had to be altered. Since a defendant's commanding officer and other officers participated in proceedings, they were considered insufficiently independent. In response to *Findlay v UK* (1997), the Armed Forces Act 1996 was passed but it was inadequate to remedy the defect. The Armed Forces Discipline Act 2000 was an attempt to make the system compliant with the Convention but in 2002 it had to be suspended and investigated further. 4–024

Delay

4-025   The ECtHR has frequently found a breach of art.6 in cases where it takes a long time to bring proceedings to a conclusion. The art.6 requirement that justice be reasonably swift applies to civil as well as criminal proceedings. A 2016 example is *O'Neill and Lauchlan v UK*, where criminal proceedings took nine years.

Legal aid—equality of arms

4-026   In *McVicar v UK* (2002), Linford Christie sued the applicant journalist for defamation in alleging that he used performance-enhancing drugs. The ECtHR held that the unavailability of legal aid did not violate arts 6 or 10, as a well-educated journalist was capable of forming a cogent argument. Defamation law was not so complex as to require representation. The same issue arose in an application made by the two defendants in the famous "McLibel case", the longest trial in English legal history, lasting 313 days in 1994–1996. The saga was finally resolved in *Steel and Morris v UK* (2005). The ECtHR held that there had been a breach of art.6 here, because the applicants (members of London Greenpeace) were denied legal aid, in defending themselves against a defamation action by McDonalds, after distributing leaflets attacking them. The court said it was central to the concept of a fair trial that a litigant was not denied the opportunity to present his or her case effectively before the court and that he or she was able to enjoy *equality of arms* with the opposing side. The question whether legal aid was necessary was to be determined on the facts. It depended on what was at stake for the applicant, the complexity of law and procedure and the capacity of the applicants to represent themselves. The applicants argued they were severely hampered by lack of resources (note-taking and photocopying) not just legal advice. The facts were complex, involving 40,000 pages of documentary evidence, as was the law. Extensive legal and procedural issues had to be resolved even before the trial started. Although the applicants were articulate and they had some help from pro bono (free) lawyers, they mainly acted alone. The trial length was a testament to their lack of skill and experience. They had been deprived of the opportunity to present their case effectively. See also art.10. In *Ezeh and Connors v UK* (2002), the ECtHR found a breach of art.6(3) where prisoners were denied legal aid or advice before a disciplinary hearing which could have resulted in detention for an extra 42 days.

Separation of powers and judicial independence

4-027   In *R. (on the application of Anderson) v Secretary of State for the Home Department* (2002), the law lords held that the Home Secretary's power to determine the length of a life sentence was incompatible with art.6. He was not independent of the executive. Complete functional separation of the judiciary from the executive government was "fundamental", since the rule of law depended on it. Home Secretary David Blunkett promised that the Government would establish a clear set of principles to fix minimum tariffs and a new judicial authority would consider tariffs for current lifers. Similarly, see *Easterbrook v UK* (2003). In *Whitfield v UK* (2005), the applicant complained of unfairness in prison disciplinary proceedings. The applicants were denied legal aid and the opportunity to consult a lawyer and there was a lack of judicial independence. The Prison Governor, answerable to the Home Office, had drafted the charges, investigated, prosecuted and tried the case, determining the applicants' guilt and innocence, and sentences.

Terror suspects

In *Secretary of State for the Home Department v AF* (2009), the law lords ruled that the appellant's rights had been violated, as he had been the subject of a control order (house arrest plus), as a terror suspect, pursuant to the notorious Prevention of Terrorism Act 2005 s.2, for three years, and his detention had been based on "general assertions". Trial procedure could never be considered fair if a party was kept in ignorance of the case against him, applying *A v UK* (2009). Where the interests of national security were concerned, in combating terrorism, it might be acceptable not to disclose the source of the evidence. The law lords had already ruled that the 18-hour curfew in control orders breached the Convention. These cases received intense publicity. There were repeated calls for control orders to be banned, and they were, as described above.

4–028

In a 2016 case before the ECtHR, the "7/7" (2005) London suicide bombers challenged the lawfulness of their questioning. The court ruled that denying them access to a lawyer under police questioning, using terrorist legislation, had been a justified interference with the right to legal assistance. Admitting their statements in evidence had not prejudiced their right to a fair trial as guaranteed by art.6(1). Nevertheless, taking self-incriminating statements from a suspected accomplice without legal advice or cautioning him as to his rights, contrary to UK law, and allowing the statements to be admitted at trial, was a breach of his art.6 rights: *Ibrahim and Others v UK*. In 2015, on a challenge from a terrorist convicted of conspiracy to murder by taking explosive liquids onto an aircraft, the court held that adverse pre-trial publicity did not violate art.6 as there was a time lapse between media coverage and the trial, and the judge gave adequate guidance to the jury: *Abdulla Ali v UK*.

Teachers

R. (on the application of G) v X School Governors (2010): professionals who faced disciplinary proceedings should have a right to legal representation. Here a school applied for a teacher to be subjected to a lifetime ban on working with children.

4–029

Article 7 No punishment without law

In *The Rule of Law*, Lord Bingham remarked that this was a simple rule which a child could understand and it had featured in most legal systems since Roman times. As explained in Ch.2 of this book, in English law, it is a presumption of statutory interpretation.

4–030

Article 8 Right to respect for private and family life

4–031   This is qualified, like arts 9, 10 and 11, by a community exception. Rights can be restricted in the interests of the community at large. In his book, Lord Bingham explained that the protections afforded by English common law have been patchy. Although Coke famously said in his *Institutes*, 1628, one of the ancient common law books of authority, listed in Ch.2, that "a man's house is his castle", a 2007 pamphlet by the Centre for Policy Studies found 266 ways that the State was empowered to enter one's home. Lord Bingham added that this was a considerable understatement. One very important omission in the common law is that it has never protected privacy. For instance, there is no tort of invasion of privacy and there is no freestanding right of privacy. In *Douglas v Hello!* (2005), below, the CA tagged it onto the tort of breach of confidence. Mr Justice Rabinder Singh examined proportionality in a 2016 lecture. He explained that the courts must deal with issues under art.8 in a structured way, asking: 1. Has there been an interference with the right? 2. Authorised by law? 3. And is it proportionate? Proportionality was established by the Strasbourg court from the 1970s, emphasising the word "necessary" but since 2000 the concept has become highly developed. The courts have settled on a series of questions, adopted from Canada, South Africa, Zimbabwe and elsewhere. In *Huang v Secretary of State for the Home Department* (2007), the law lords clarified the four-part test. You can read these criteria and his extensive discussion of later case law on proportionality in his speech.

Gay People in the Armed Forces

4–032   Military investigations into the sexuality of gay members of the armed forces and their subsequent dismissal were grave breaches: *Lustig-Prean and Becket v UK (No.1)* (2000).

Transsexuals' rights

4–033   In gender reassignment cases, where applicants born as males sought to be re-registered as females, the ECtHR held that the Government was under no positive duty to amend its system of birth registration: *Sheffield and Horsham v UK* (1998) but in *Goodwin v UK* (2002), a Grand Chamber of the Court took a different approach. Where G had undergone gender re-assignment surgery, it was a breach of art.8 for the State not to recognise a change of legal gender. Since the surgery was provided by the State, this was illogical. The very essence of the Convention was respect for human dignity and freedom. It was unsatisfactory for post-operative transsexuals to live in an intermediate zone. Since 1986, the court had emphasised the importance of keeping the need for appropriate legal measures under review, having regard to scientific and societal developments. There had also been a breach of arts 8 and 12, in denying the applicants a right to marry someone the opposite of their new sex. The State could not bar a right to marry. See also art.12, below.

Gross indecency in private

A conviction for gross indecency, when it took place in private, constituted an unnecessary interference with the right to respect for private life. Following a search of his premises, police had seized photos and videos of the applicant and other consenting men engaging in oral sex and mutual masturbation. The acts took place in the applicant's home and did not involve physical harm: *ADT v UK* (2000). **4-034**

Prisoners' Rights and Deaths in Custody

A policy that prisoners must be absent when privileged legal correspondence held in their cells was examined by prison officers was unlawful. The House of Lords reached this conclusion by applying the common law but it was supported by the art.8(1) right to respect for correspondence: *R. v Secretary of State for the Home Department Ex p. Daly* (2001). This case is very important as the House ruled that the courts must apply a proportionality test in judicial review cases, including Human Rights cases, as *proportionality* is now a principle of English law. **4-035**

In *Dickson v UK* (2006), the UK policy of requiring exceptional circumstances to be demonstrated before a life prisoner could have access to artificial insemination was a violation.

The law lords, in *Wainwright v Home Office* (2003) took a restrictive approach to the issue of privacy rights. Prison visitors had been strip searched in 1997 because the authorities suspected that their relative, the prisoner, had been dealing in drugs in prison. This was a very important case, as the House held that there was no general tort of invasion of privacy at common law and art.8 did not guarantee a right to privacy, as such. Lord Hoffmann said there was nothing in the jurisprudence of the ECtHR which suggested the adoption of some high-level right of privacy.

The series of cases involving deaths in custody, described above, showed that art.8 was engaged, requiring families to be fully informed and involved, in any inquest or inquiry. Coronial procedure has now been significantly reformed, in the Coroners and Justice Act 2009.

Supermodel in rehab

The House did not depart from this principle in *Campbell v Mirror Group Newspapers Ltd* (2004). This case arose from the *Daily Mirror*'s disclosure that supermodel Naomi Campbell was secretly attending meetings of Narcotics Anonymous. "Put crudely," said Baroness Hale, "it is a prima donna celebrity against a celebrity-exploiting tabloid newspaper". Where art.8 was engaged, the court had to carry out a carefully focused and penetrating balancing exercise to reconcile the restrictions that the art.8 and art.10 rights imposed on one another, applying the principle of proportionality. In media cases where both articles were engaged, it was necessary to conduct a parallel analysis, looking at the comparative importance of the rights being claimed in the individual case and at the justifications for interfering with or restricting each right, and applying the **4-036** proportionality test to each. The majority held that, on the facts, the *Mirror* had gone too far in the details they had published.

Celebs again

4–037   In the long running saga of litigation arising out of *Hello!* magazine's use of surreptitious photos of the wedding of Michael Douglas and Catherine Zeta-Jones, in *Douglas v Hello!* (2005), the Court of Appeal accepted that art.8 privacy rights had to be enforced via "the cause of action formerly described as breach of confidence". It was no longer necessary for the information to have been imparted in circumstances "importing a duty of confidence". See also *Murray v Express Newspapers Plc* (2008): J.K. Rowling's son's privacy was breached. A child had a reasonable expectation that he would not be targeted in order to obtain photographs.

Embryos

4–038   *Evans v UK* (2007) went to the Grand Chamber of the ECtHR. Miss Evans lost her sad fight to preserve embryos belonging to her and her ex-boyfriend. The court held that in such sensitive moral and ethical issues, the state had a wide margin of appreciation. Evans had known as a matter of law that her boyfriend could withdraw consent to the use of the embryos. Also, embryos did not have an independent right to life under art.2.

Fingerprints

4–039   Storing suspects' DNA samples and fingerprints, when they have not been convicted, was disproportionate interference with art.8 rights: *S and Marper v UK* (2009). This case provoked a political controversy.

Stop and search

4–040   *Gillan and Quinton v UK* (2010): police stop and search powers under the Terrorism Act 2000 violated art.8. The interference with the right of respect to private life was different from an airport search, as anyone could be stopped, any time. There was no requirement that the stop and search be necessary, only "expedient". The officer's decision to stop was based on hunch or intuition. This was remedied by a remedial order on 17 March 2011. "Police will only be able to stop and search people without reasonable suspicion where it's considered necessary to prevent terrorism." (Home Office press release.) Additionally, the UK Supreme Court ruled that suspicionless searches were compatible with art.8, where officers were looking for offensive weapons. There was a risk that young black and minority groups would be targeted but it was mostly young, black lives who would be saved if there were less gang violence in London and other cities: *R. (on the application of Roberts) v Commissioner of Police for the Metropolis* (2015).

Housing possession

Hounslow LBC v Powell (2011) confirmed that in housing repossession cases, an independent tribunal must consider *proportionality* before evicting. See also *Manchester City Council v Pinnock* (2010). The UKSC considered a number of ECtHR cases expressing the above principle and departed from previous HL judgments. This case was mentioned in Ch.2, in the section on precedent.

4-041

Sex offenders

In *R. (on the application of F) v Secretary of State for the Home Department* (2010), the Supreme Court held that sex offenders had a right to some form of review of the requirement to be on the register. Placing them on a register for life, with duties of notification, was a disproportionate invasion of privacy. Provisions to review exist in other jurisdictions. Some politicians and news media reacted as if "review" meant "release". This is silly. Dangerous mass-murderers such as the Yorkshire Ripper and Rosemary West have a right to have their prison sentences reviewed but that does not mean that they are about to be released.

4-042

Article 9 Freedom of thought, conscience and religion

Lord Bingham summarised the Convention's position as

> "you may believe what you like provided you keep your beliefs to yourself or share them with like-minded people, but when you put your beliefs into practice in a way that impinges on others, limits may be imposed, if prescribed by law, necessary in a democratic society and directed to one of the specified purposes." (*The Rule of Law*, pp.76–77.)

4-043

Islamic dress

The ECtHR held there to be no breach of art.9 in a ban placed on Islamic headscarves by the University of Istanbul. Turkey's Constitutional Court guaranteed democratic values, including the freedom of religion but restrictions could be placed on this freedom if necessary, to defend other values and principles, including secularism and equality: *Sahin v Turkey* (2004). In 2014, the ECtHR ruled that the French ban on the full-face veil was lawful. In *R. (on the application of Begum) v Denbigh High School Governors* (2006), a girl insisted on attending school wearing a jilbab. The law lords dismissed her appeal. There was evidence that her family had chosen a school outside their catchment area. There was no evidence of any real difficulty in her attending one of the three schools in her catchment area that permitted the wearing of the jilbab. The shalwar kameeze was worn by B for her first two years, without objection. On the facts, there was no interference with B's right to manifest her belief in practice or observance.

4-044

Corporal punishment

4-045   Although the statutory ban on corporal punishment in UK schools was capable of interfering with art.9 rights, Parliament was entitled to take the view that the ban was necessary in a democratic society to protect children: *R. (on the application of Williamson) v Secretary of State for Education and Employment* (2005).

Articles 10 Freedom of expression and 11 Freedom of assembly and association

4-046   At common law, people could say or write what they liked, unless it breached a law, for instance in constituting the torts of libel or slander. Journalists have always felt that the law of defamation, enforced by these torts, unduly hampered their free speech. Lord Bingham said art.11 went far beyond the common law, which provided no positive right of assembly or association but relied on the absence of prohibitions.

The tension between freedom of expression and protection from defamation

4-047   In *Steel and Morris v UK*, the successful appeal by the McLibel two, discussed above, the ECtHR said the central issue on an art.10 application was whether the interference with freedom of speech was necessary in a democratic society. Even small and informal campaign groups, like London Greenpeace, to which the pair belonged, had to be able to carry on their activities effectively. The fact that the burden of proof was on them, the defendants, to prove the truth of their allegations was not incompatible with art.10, though.

Public demonstrations

4-048   In *R. (on the application of Laporte) v Chief Constable of Gloucestershire* (2006), Lord Bingham said that while arts 10 and 11 rights were not absolute, they were fundamental in a democratic society. Coaches full of demonstrators had been intercepted and turned away from Fairford RAF base, after having given the required notice of their plans.

Article 12 Right to marry

Transsexuals

4-049   In *Bellinger v Bellinger* (2003) the House of Lords ruled that a transsexual could not be legally recognised in her new gender so her marriage was void under the Matrimonial Causes Act 1973. The House was bound by this UK statute but it declared UK law to be incompatible with the Convention, arts 8 and 12. The Government promised a Bill to give transsexuals legal recognition. This was done via the Gender Recognition Act 2004.

Article 13 Effective remedy

In a number of the cases above, such as those arising out of deaths in custody, the ECtHR also held there was a breach of this article, because the inquests held were an ineffective remedy.

4–050

Article 14 Prohibition against discrimination in enjoying Convention rights

As can be seen, this is not a free-standing prohibition on discrimination. For a detailed example on homosexual rights, see *Ghaidan v Godin-Mendoza* (2001) and (2004), analysed below in Pt 6.

4–051

Widowers

Bereaved fathers were equally entitled to the "widowed mother's allowance", conceded the UK, in *Cornwell v UK* (2000). The Government dealt with this problem by introducing the Welfare Reform and Pensions Act 1999.

4–052

Bedroom Tax

The UK Supreme Court held that the rule reducing housing benefit where social tenants were deemed to have more bedrooms than necessary, was a breach of art.14, when taken in conjunction with art.8, right to private and family life, specifically in a case where it failed to take account of a disabled person's proven medical needs: *R. (on the application of Carmichael) v Secretary of State for Work and Pensions* (2016).

4–053

Protocol 1, article 3

Prisoners' Voting Rights

The blanket ban on prisoners' voting was a disproportionate interference in rights: *Hirst v UK (No.2)* (2006). The UK Labour government considered this decision repugnant and ignored it. In *Green v UK* (2010), and in 2016, in *Millbank and Others v UK*, the Strasbourg court reiterated that the UK must remove the ban. This issue is now proving extremely controversial and we will come back to this point, below, in the last section.

4–054

5. THE APPROACH OF ENGLISH COURTS TO CONVENTION RIGHTS AND INTERPRETATION OF DOMESTIC LAW

Does the Convention allow judges to make law?

4–055 Prior to the implementation of the HRA 1998 in October 2000, the Government sought to stop fears that the courts would be swamped with claims by pointing out that the Convention had been in force in Scotland since May 1999 and 98 per cent of challenges had failed. There was a great deal of speculation in the Parliamentary debates on the Bill and in law journals as to how the courts might or should approach the Convention. Emmerson is reported as predicting "a major shift of power from Parliament to judges. They will, in effect, be able to rewrite sections of Acts by reading into them words that are not there and by massaging away any potential conflicts with the Constitution." (1998). Nevertheless, in 1999, the law lords were swift to point out, in *Kebilene*, that the Convention gave way to Parliamentary sovereignty. In the words of Lord Steyn:

> "It is crystal clear that the carefully and subtly drafted Human Rights Act 1998 preserves the principle of Parliamentary sovereignty. In a case of incompatibility, which cannot be avoided by interpretation under section 3 (1), the courts may not disapply legislation. The court may merely issue a declaration of incompatibility which then gives rise to a power to take remedial action: see section 10."

As for common law remedies, Irvine LC said in Parliament:

> "In my view, the courts may not act as legislators and grant new remedies for infringement of Convention rights unless the common law itself enables them to develop new rights and remedies. I believe that the true view is that the courts will be able to develop the common law by relying on the existing domestic principles of trespass, nuisance, copyright, confidence and the like, to fashion a common law right to privacy."

A clear exposition of the approach of the courts in the years immediately following the importation of Convention rights in 2000 was set out by Kavanagh in 2004. She made the following observations, paraphrased:

1. Section 3 does not require any ambiguity before it comes into operation: *R. v Lambert* (2001).
2. It is only a rule of interpretation, not legislation, according to many judges.
3. Section 3 does require judicial law-making but it is much more limited in scope and effect than law-making by the legislature.
4. The way judges interpret s.3 and the word "possible" will affect their interpretive approach.
5. The interpretive issues posed by the Convention cannot be resolved linguistically. For instance, there is no point in using a dictionary to determine whether the right to life in art.2 includes a right to death.
6. If judges merely declared the law, all they could do in some cases was to say that the HRA is indeterminate on the matter.

7. Broad evaluative terms in the Convention necessitate the judges engaging in moral reasoning.
8. Interpretation combines applying and making the law.
9. Where there is no previous case law on the point, judges are required to make the law.
10. Judges are also under a duty to arrive at a just decision in the instant case.
11. HRA case law shows that even where judges are engaged in innovative decision-making, they are still concerned to preserve continuity, authority and stability to the greatest possible degree.
12. When judges make law under s.3, they do so by interpretive reasoning.
13. Legislators, on the other hand, are entitled to create new frameworks or radically alter existing ones.
14. Much judicial law-making is by way of filling in the gaps in legislation and they will read in words in order to make legislation Convention-compliant but they cannot rewrite a whole statute.
15. The fact that judicial law-making is incremental places limits on the ability or willingness of the judges to reform the law, as in *Bellinger v Bellinger*, above, where Lord Nicholls said the recognition of gender assignment for the purposes of marriage is part of a wider problem which should be considered as a whole so it was preferable to leave this to Parliament.
16. Judges are trained to resolve legal issues and are ill-equipped to make decisions about general policy.
17. A "possible" meaning of legislation is not necessarily its ordinary meaning, nor is it unlimited.
18. Where there is an outright contradiction between the words of a statute and Convention rights, then judges cannot "read or give effect" to those terms. Lord Steyn, in *R. v A* (2001), below, pointed out that Parliament rejected the New Zealand legislative model whereby judges find a "reasonable interpretation".

An Example from 2001

R. v A (2001) was a landmark precedent because it demonstrated how the law   **4–056**
lords were prepared to interpret and apply their own duty under s.3 of the HRA 1998. The House had to construe s.41 of the Youth Justice and Criminal Evidence Act 1999, restricting evidence and questioning about the victim's sexual history, and determine whether it conflicted with the Convention. A man accused of rape wanted to bring evidence of his previous sexual relationship with the complainant, to support his defence that she had consented. The trial judge had ruled this out because of the 1999 Act but considered that his ruling breached art.6 (fair trial). The law lords applied their interpretive duty under s.3 of the HRA 1998 and gave proper regard to the protection of the complainant but effectively "read into" the 1999 statute some protection for the accused under art.6. They told the trial judge he could proceed with the case in the light of their ruling—in other words, telling him to make a bold interpretation and allow this evidence in for the sake of protecting the accused under art.6. I will analyse Lord Steyn's interpretive methods sequentially, with my explanations italicised.

1. *He plunged straight into a purposive construction of the 1999 Act*: in the criminal courts, outmoded beliefs about women and sexual matters lingered on. *Referring to approaches in another common law country, in Canadian jurisprudence*: they had been referred to as discredited twin myths "that unchaste women were more likely to consent to intercourse and in any event, were less worthy of belief".

2. *Statement of moral principle*: "such generalised, stereotyped and unfounded prejudices ought to have no place in our legal system". It resulted in an absurdly low conviction rate in rape cases.

3. *Interpretation of purpose of the 1999 Act*: The Sexual Offences (Amendment) Act 1976 did not achieve its object so "(t)here was a serious mischief to be corrected".

4. *Statement of the problem before the House*: the blanket exclusion of prior sexual history between the complainant and the accused posed an acute problem of proportionality.

5. *Applying what he called "common sense"*: a prior relationship between accused and accuser might be relevant to the issue of consent in rape.

6. *His interpretation of the court's duty under the HRA 1998*: when a question arose as to whether, in a criminal statute, Parliament had adopted a legislative scheme which made an excessive inroad into the right to a fair trial, the court was qualified to make its own judgment and had to do so.

7. *Application of ECtHR jurisprudence*: it was well established that the guarantee of a fair trial under art.6 was absolute. A conviction obtained in breach could not stand. The only balancing permitted was in respect of what the concept of a fair trial entailed. Applying proportionality, in determining whether a limitation was arbitrary or excessive, a court should ask itself whether:
    a. the legislative objective was sufficiently important to justify limiting a fundamental right;
    b. the measures designed to meet that objective were rationally connected to it, and
    c. the means used to impair the right or freedom were no more than necessary to accomplish the objective.

8. Two processes of interpretation had to be distinguished. Ordinary (traditional, English) methods of purposive and contextual interpretation might yield ways of minimising the "exorbitant breadth" of the section, i.e. the blanket ban on questioning a woman about her sexual history. The second was the interpretative obligation of HRA 1998 s.3(1) (so far as possible, primary legislation had to be given effect in a way compatible with the Convention).

9. *He applied the first method, looked at the wording of the section and relevant domestic cases on evidence prior to the HRA 1998 and concluded this could not solve the problem.*

10. *Interpreting s.3 of the HRA 1998*: he cited *Kebilene*. The HRA 1998 s.3 obligation went far beyond the rule which enabled the courts to take the Convention into account in resolving any ambiguity in a legislative provision. Parliament specifically rejected the legislative model requiring a reasonable interpretation. It placed on a court a duty to strive to find a

possible interpretation compatible with Convention rights. It was much more radical than the ordinary method of interpretation which permitted a departure from language of an Act to avoid absurd consequences. In accordance with the will of Parliament when they enacted the HRA 1998, it would sometimes be necessary to adopt an interpretation which linguistically might appear strained. The techniques to be used would not only involve the reading down of express language in a statute but also the implication of provisions.

11. *Interpreting s.4 of the HRA 1998*: a declaration of incompatibility was a measure of last resort.

12. *Conclusion, inferring Parliamentary intent*: the legislature, if alerted to the problem, would not have wished to deny the accused the right to put forward a full defence by advancing probative material. It was possible to read into s.41 of the 1999 Act the implied provision that any evidence or questioning required to ensure a fair trial under art.6 should not be inadmissible.

13. *Implications for future trials*: sometimes logically relevant evidence of sexual experience might be admitted but where the line was to be drawn was up to the trial judge.

An example from 2004, reading words into a statute

The same bold approach, demonstrating that the courts are prepared to read words into a statute, effecting quite substantial rewriting, was adopted by the Court of Appeal and then the House of Lords in *Ghaidan v Godin-Mendoza* (2001; 2004). Here, M, the homosexual partner of the deceased tenant of a flat, appealed from a decision that he could not be awarded a statutory tenancy under the Rent Act 1977. He could not qualify as a "spouse" under the Act and thus did not enjoy the benefit granted to an unmarried heterosexual partner in the same position. The Court of Appeal held that, in cases involving art.14, four questions must be asked:

4–057

1. Do the facts fall within the ambit of one or more of the substantive rights under the Convention?

2. If so, was there different treatment as respects that right between a complainant and other persons put forward for comparison?

3. Were the chosen comparators in an analogous situation to the complainant's situation?

4. If so, did the difference have an objective and reasonable justification? Did it pursue a legitimate aim and bear a reasonable relationship of proportionality to the aim sought to be achieved?

Deference to Parliament has a minor role to play, said the Court of Appeal, where issues of constitutional importance, such as discrimination, arise. Discrimination on grounds of sexual orientation was now impermissible, on the same level as any others under art.14. Section 3 of the HRA 1998 required that words should be read into the Rent Act 1977. The words defining "spouse" as "his or her wife or husband" should be read to mean "as if they were his or her wife or husband". In the House of Lords, it was held that s.3, wide statutory interpretation, was the core remedy provided by the HRA 1998 and the s.4 declaration of incompatibility should only be a last resort. As long as it did not go against the grain of the legislative measure, there was *no limit to the words that could be read in or out of a legislative measure* (my emphasis).

Judicial Review and Proportionality

4–058   Above, we examined the importation of the concept of proportionality into English law. The High Court's traditional power to review the legality of executive action and decisions of the lower courts was developed and refined by the courts in the twentieth century. The courts had traditionally declined to examine the merits of a decision, provided it had been taken procedurally correctly and provided the decision-maker had taken account of all relevant factors and decided rationally. This was known as the *Wednesbury* test of irrationality or unreasonableness, based on the test laid down in *Associated Provincial Picture Houses v Wednesbury Corp* (1948). In *Kingsley v UK* (2002), the ECtHR held that this was inadequate. The nature of judicial review proceedings which restricted the court to examining the quality of the decision-making process rather than the merits of the decision meant that an applicant alleging bias had not had a fair hearing. Here, the CA had held that the Gaming Board of GB had taken a biased decision but had no power to remit the decision to the Board. The reviewing court should not confine itself to examining the quality of the decision-making process and not the merits. The reviewing court must ask itself whether:

1.   the objective is sufficiently important to justify limiting a fundamental right;
2.   the measures designed to meet the objective are rationally connected to it; and
3.   the means used are no more than necessary to accomplish the objective.

In *Kay v UK* (2011), the ECtHR welcomed the UKSC's statements in *Kay* and elsewhere that expanded conventional judicial review grounds beyond *Wednesbury* reasonableness to proportionality.

6.   WHO CAN BRING AN ACTION AND AGAINST WHOM CAN ACTIONS BE BROUGHT?

4–059   The person deprived of their right can bring an action, usually in the High Court, for judicial review, but other groups would like to join in on public interest test cases. The Civil Procedure Rules were amended to enable "any person" to apply to file evidence or make representations at the judicial review hearing. The UKSC welcomes multiple interveners regularly. There were five in the 2009 Jewish Schools case. It was accepted by the House of Lords in *R. (on the* *application of Rusbridger) v Attorney General* (2003) that the courts were prepared to grant a declaration, to clarify the law, where no wrong had been alleged.

As for the persons against whom an action can be taken, the HRA 1998 does not explain "public authorities" but it includes central and local government departments, non-departmental public bodies and the courts and tribunals. Section 6(3)(b) of the Act provides that it shall be unlawful for a private person exercising a public function to act in a way incompatible with a Convention right. There have been many academic articles on whether the Act provides rights against private bodies. This debate is fuelled by the ambiguous HRA 1998. On the one hand, s.3 requires primary and subordinate legislation to be read as far as possible in a way which is compatible with Convention rights but this instruction is not limited to public authorities or just the courts. Under s.2, courts and tribunals must take into account ECtHR jurisprudence. The Government could have specifically excluded private parties from the scope of the Act, as other jurisdictions have done, but did not. On the other hand, ss.6 and 7 only allow challenges to actions of public authorities, generally, with the exception of any person exercising "functions of a public nature". We are not helped by the statements made by the Lord Chancellor who sponsored the Bill through the House of Lords.

Dawn Oliver pointed out that, by 2004, the case law was very confusing. **4-060** "Public functions", mentioned in some cases did not equate to "functions of a public nature". It was unclear whether liability arose when a private contractor was working for a public authority, gardening or cleaning. These, she suggested, are "functions of a private nature". The contractors enjoy Convention rights which have to be balanced against the recipients' rights. Putting them under HRA duties might have negative implications for many charitable or not-for-profit organisations, providing services for the disabled, the elderly and the homeless. She was diametrically opposed to the suggestion in the seventh report of the Joint Parliamentary Committee on Human Rights (2003–2004) that a broader approach should be taken by the courts. Many academics have expressed opinions on the broader issue of whether Convention rights apply "horizontally" between private parties. These can be found in textbooks and articles on public law.

In *YL v Birmingham City Council* (2007), two of five law lords decided that a private care home was not conducting public functions for the purposes of the HRA 1998. See comment by Parkhill and Murray. They pointed to "a sharp difference of opinion" between the law lords. The jurisprudence of the ECtHR was referred to in interpreting s.6(3)(b). The section emphasises the function, not the body. The judges were agreed that whether there was a statutory basis for its operations or powers to support its operations was a relevant consideration. The issue of whether it applied to particular functions would have to be decided on a case-by-case basis. The writers were lawyers for Birmingham City Council and commented that this result left uncertainty and was unsatisfactory for the public sector. In *R. (on the application of Weaver) v London and Quadrant Housing Trust* (2009), the CA held that although the Trust was a private body, a number of its activities, taken together meant that it was carrying out public acts and had to comply with the HRA 1998, though they reiterated that liability had to be decided on a case-by-case basis.

7. EVALUATIONS OF THE HUMAN RIGHTS ACT AND THE UK'S RELATIONSHIP WITH THE EUROPEAN COURT OF HUMAN RIGHTS

Expanding Common Law Rights and Recognising New Ones: The Common Law and Convention Law

4–061   As I have demonstrated in this chapter, through examples, the Act has had an impact on a broad spectrum of English law, enhancing and extending rights for diverse groups from terror suspects to teachers. More examples can be seen in later chapters, such as 6, 10 and 14. Not only has statute law been amended and reinterpreted, as seen above, but also the common law has absorbed the concept of proportionality and the criteria for judicial review have had to expand. The HRA 1998 came into force in 2000. Lord Irvine LC, in a November 2002 speech, said the courts had not dissolved into chaos; there was not a politicised judiciary or the inauguration of the rule of lawyers. We had developed a domestic "margin of appreciation". The Convention had reinvigorated the common law and "legal reasoning applied here carries weight in Strasbourg—as we hoped it would when drafting the Bill".

Sir Henry Brooke, a retired appeal judge, listed the shortcomings of the common law:

> "I have even heard it suggested that if Parliament repealed the Human Rights Act without replacement, the English common law would…fill the gaps. I found that sentiment puzzling…There was no English common law right to privacy. There was no English common law right not to be exposed to a humiliating strip-search. There was no English common law right to be protected from telephone hacking. The state had no positive obligation to protect people's rights." (2016)

Writing in the same volume, Bowen, in an excellent and detailed article, agreed that the common law would not fill the gap, were the HRA 1998 to be repealed, because the Convention reached further than the common law; it protected more rights; the common law was unclear and it protected privileges, values and liberties rather than rights. Also, because of the unwritten constitution and Parliamentary sovereignty, common law rights enjoyed no special constitutional status and the courts lacked democratic legitimacy to expand them.

The civil liberties group, Liberty, welcomed decisions such as *A (FC) v Secretary of State for the Home Department* (2004), the *Belmarsh* case on terrorist suspects, above. Lord Woolf CJ, in a 2002 speech, said that if people rejected the 1998 Act's values, then they were rejecting the standards of Western society. Speaking at the Strasbourg court in 2003, he said the Convention had had a "remarkably smooth transition into English law". English lawyers and judges felt "instinctively at home with Strasbourg jurisprudence". Senior judge Sir John Laws said that the Convention embodied "values which no democratic politician could honestly contest". The Human Rights Lawyers Association, in a pamphlet celebrating 10 years of the 1998 Act, 2000–2010, said it had enabled the courts to balance the competing rights of different groups. People were spared the expense and delay of taking a case to the Strasbourg court. It had strengthened rights without weakening Parliament by allowing judges to read legislation compatibly with the HRA 1998. Decisions of the UK courts on human rights had been cited in Canada, India, New Zealand, South Africa and Australia. They gave further specific examples of groups who had benefited from the Act.

Lord Bingham, in his judgments as Senior Law Lord, and even before that in the Court of Appeal, dealt with human rights questions by applying a mixture of common law, Strasbourg jurisprudence and international law and this seems to have become the conventional approach nowadays. In his 2014 speech, Lord Neuberger said that recently, the judges had been trying to bring the common law back to centre stage, citing *Kennedy v Charity Commissioners* (2014), where the Justices sent the case back to the trial judge, remarking that there was a stronger case based on common law, than the Convention point that had been argued. In a 2016 lecture, Lord Neuberger said that the Human Rights Act had made some lawyers act as if they were playing with a novel new toy and had to be reminded that the common law could often be relied on. In 2012, Toulson LJ in the Court of Appeal decided a case on common law grounds where it had been argued purely on human rights points. Judges are divided as to whether the common law should be developed so as to incorporate Convention rights. If they are kept separate then there is a danger that the common law of rights will stop growing, as Friedman has argued.

The judicial role and the balance of power between them, the legislature and the government

Essential reading on this subject is a 2014 speech by Lord Neuberger. I quote him at length:

4-062

> "this new judicial power of quasi-interpretation [in the HRA s.3] can be said to involve a subtle but significant adjustment to the balance of power between the legislature and the judiciary of the UK...the UK approach can be seen as effectively conferring a law making function on the judiciary. The UK courts have developed new rules which control the way in which this power can be exercised. For instance, the section 3 power cannot be used in a way which would involve an apparently incompatible statutory provision having a meaning which was inconsistent with the scheme of the Statute concerned, or if it is not clear how an apparently incompatible statutory provision would have been rewritten.
>
> Even the power to make a declaration of incompatibility represents an important shift in the balance of power in a country whose institutions have such a deep respect for the rule of law such as the UK...a common law judge's power to make a declaration of incompatibility is revolutionary, as it does not affect the rights of the parties to the relevant case, and it is ultimately advisory...in that sense it can be said to represent a role for the judiciary which is subordinate to that of parliament...In more practical terms, however, the power now given to judges in the UK by section 4 of the HRA is demonstrated by the fact that, with one exception, Parliament has always acted on every such [declaration] and cured any incompatibility. The one exception is prisoners' right to vote..."

Despite accusations (by a few politicians) of power-seeking and behaving in a politically motivated manner, judges will decline to grant declarations of incompatibility when they think moral issues should be left to Parliament. A classic example is *Nicklinson v Ministry of Justice* (2014), on whether the blanket ban on assisting suicide breached art.8. While the Supreme Court held that the issue fell within the "margin of appreciation", in other words the local discretion of each contracting state, four Justices said that Parliament was much better qualified to deal with questions like this and three more declined to make a declaration of incompatibility.

Some politicians do not and did not share these positive views expressed by civil libertarians and judges. Parliamentary debates on such controversial areas as terrorism and asylum, during 2000–2003 demonstrated some hostility, even among Labour ranks. Home Secretary David Blunkett was especially hostile to the judicial interpretations of the Convention, especially when they limited his ministerial power. With the Conservatives in power, the HRA 1998 is under threat of repeal. Nevertheless, the parliamentary Joint Committee on Human Rights has been very proactive in drawing parliamentarians' attention to human rights issues. It decided to scrutinise all Bills.

In 2001, the UN Human Rights Committee called for the UK to establish a body to monitor human rights. The Equality and Human Rights Commission at last started work during a Labour administration, in 2008. It has a duty to promote and monitor human rights and enforce and promote equality.

4–063   In opposition, in 2007–2009, the Conservatives kept saying they would repeal the Human Rights Act and replace it with a Bill of Rights. Director of Public Prosecutions, Kier Starmer QC, an internationally renowned human rights expert (who is now a Labour MP and spokesperson for Brexit in 2017), heavily criticised those who attacked the HRA 1998 in the CPS Annual Lecture, 2009. He referred to

> "those who … propose to replace the Human Rights Act … with other human rights which they consider to be more appropriately geared to 'British' society … the United Kingdom played a major role in the design and drafting of the European Convention … The idea that these human rights should somehow stop in the English Channel is odd and, frankly, impossible to defend."

Immediately before the 2010 election, the Conservative plans on human rights were unclear. Their spokesperson said on Radio 4, "I don't know. I haven't drafted the Bill yet". Conservative lawyers had established a HR Commission in 2007 and it had been divided. Ken Clarke, a liberal Conservative, who became Minister of Justice in 2010, had said in 2006 that to replace the HRA 1998 with a HR Bill was "xenophobic and legal nonsense". In the meantime, Prime Minister Cameron wrongly said in 2010 that the HRA 1998 had enabled a prisoner to have hard core porn, and that the police were not allowed to put criminals' faces on wanted posters. He was corrected by the police in 2007, after making the same speech to the Police Federation but had apparently forgotten. See Smith. The Labour Ministry of Justice launched a Green Paper Bill of Rights in March 2009. It included rights such as health care and rights for crime victims. It listed citizens' responsibilities too. In 2009, retiring law lord, Lord Hoffmann, expressed strong views about the role of the ECtHR. He said the Strasbourg Court had been unable to resist the temptation to aggrandise its jurisdiction and impose uniform rules on member states. David Pannick QC said there were two answers to this. (1) The ECtHR took account of contracting states' margin of appreciation, and (2) The UK courts were not bound by ECtHR decisions. Under s.2 of the HRA 1998, courts only had to take into account its judgments. In 2010, the Conservative party formed a Coalition government with the Liberal Democrats who would never allow the HRA 1998 to be repealed, therefore the Conservative threat became academic; but Cooper and Warburton listed the reasons why the UK could not repeal the HRA 1998:

- It would not benefit anyone.
- Following the Lisbon Treaty, EU member states were obliged to comply with the EU Charter of Fundamental Rights, which built on the Convention.
- The common law had a long tradition of protecting basic rights. Human rights thinking was highly influential before the HRA 1998.

In March 2010, the UK Parliamentary Joint Committee on Human Rights published a report, *Enhancing Parliament's role in relation to human rights judgments*. They said the UK's compliance record was generally good but there were lengthy delays, up to five years, in implementation in some cases. The UK should be "leading by example". The Coalition Government responded in July 2010, in Cm.7892. They said:

> "The Government remains committed to the European Convention on Human Rights ... [but] ... wants to look afresh at how human rights are protected in the United Kingdom to see if things can be done better and in a way that properly reflects our traditions ... a Commission will be created to investigate the creation of a Bill of Rights that incorporates and builds on all our obligations ... ensures that these rights continue to be enshrined in British law, and protects and extends British liberties. The Government will also seek to promote a better understanding of the true scope of these obligations and liberties" (p.5).

In November 2010, a new row broke out. Prime Minister David Cameron said the ECtHR ruling in *Green*, above, that the UK was breaching the Convention by not giving prisoners voting rights, made him feel "physically ill". In February 2011, the Commons, in debate, rejected the *Green* ruling. Apparently, it is common in the other contracting states to find rulings of the ECtHR repugnant. Some MPs were also offended by the UKSC ruling that people should have the right to appeal for removal of their names from the Sex Offenders' Register. The then Home Secretary Theresa May said "It is time to assert that it is Parliament that makes our laws, not the courts, and that the rights of the public come before the rights of criminals and above all that we have a legal framework that brings sanity to cases such as these". The second Human Rights Commission, launched in 2011, disintegrated without agreement, like its predecessor.

4-064

In 2011, the Attorney General, Conservative Dominic Grieve, interviewed on Radio 4's *Law in Action*, said there was no chance that we would be departing from our commitment under the European Convention on Human Rights. He said there was concern about the ECtHR's case backlog. Some of the judges were "not very well focussed" on their work. "The court appears to be far too willing to try to micro-manage Convention rights in individual states." By 2014, criticism of the ECtHR had increased. Politicians continued to be affronted by its decisions on prisoners' voting rights and the rights of terrorists. In 2013, three top judges—Laws LJ, Lord Judge and Lord Sumption said the court had overstepped its powers. See Sumption's F.A. Mann lecture 2011. These judges and politicians argued that domestic legislatures of the contracting states should decide on matters such as votes for prisoners, without being dictated to by the ECtHR. The 46 other states appeared to share this view and the concern about the court's judges and working method, because in 2012, the contracting states agreed to The Brighton Declaration, reforming the court in five ways. These include amending the preamble to the Convention to refer to the principle of subsidiarity and the margin of appreciation, meaning maximising the legislative freedom of the contracting states, as well as reforming the court's procedures, as discussed above. In 2013, the contracting states agreed to a new procedure, permitting states to seek an advisory opinion from the ECtHR. Also resulting from the Brighton Declaration, the Council of Europe consulted, in 2013–2014, on the long-term future of the court. Some UK politicians continue to call for the UK to leave the Convention. This would be a "political disaster" said the court's President, Judge Dean Spielmann, speaking on *Law in Action* in 2013. It would ruin the UK's credibility when it comes to promoting human rights worldwide. At the time of writing, 2017, the Government has frozen its plans to repeal the Human Rights Act 1998 and enact a UK Bill of Rights as it is too preoccupied with Brexit. In 2017, the Parliamentary Joint Committee on Human Rights, which is an all-party group of backbenchers whose job is to be a watchdog over government policy, are conducting an inquiry into the Government's plans to derogate from the Convention.

4–065   Despite the current anti-Strasbourg rhetoric of certain Conservative MPs and news media, the UK has a very good compliance record, as demonstrated by a 2016 Ministry of Justice publication, *Responding to human rights judgments*, one of its regular reviews. This shows that:

- Applications against the UK peaked in 2010 and declined by 79 per cent by 2015. By 2016, only 0.4 per cent of pending applications (in Strasbourg) were being made against the UK.
- Since 2010, most applications have been declared inadmissible by the ECtHR.
- Judgments against the UK show a downward trend and reached an all-time low in 2015 of *four*.
- 2016 statistics showed that, of the 22 finalised declarations of incompatibility made by UK courts since 2000, 17 had been remedied by legislation; three had been remedied by a remedial order and one was about to be, and one was under consideration about how to remedy the incompatibility. This is the issue of prisoners' voting rights. The Ministry's 2016 report insisted that prisoner voting was a matter for Parliament. (The report gives useful details.)
- As for implementing the ECtHR's judgments, the report showed that by 2015, the UK had 19 outstanding judgments still under supervision of the Committee of Ministers, compared with 2,421 in Italy.

Pro human rights Conservatives, like the former Attorney General, Dominic Grieve (see his 2016 article) doubtless appreciate that the very idea of repealing the Human Rights Act and derogating from the Convention is repugnant to most

UK lawyers who understand the simple point that I made at the beginning of this chapter: the Convention was drafted by UK lawyers and much of it was modelled on the common law.

Bibliography

A. Ashworth, "A Decade of Human Rights in Criminal Justice" [2014] Crim. L.R. 325. **4–066**

G. Bindman, "Contempt of the European Court", *New Statesman*, November 15, 1996.

T. Bingham, *The Rule of Law* (London: Penguin, 2011).

P. Bowen, "Does the renaissance of common law rights mean that the Human Rights Act 1998 is now unnecessary" [2016] E.H.R.L.R. 361.

Sir Henry Brooke, "Human Rights and the English Common Law" [2016] E.H.R.L.R. 329.

J. Cooper and C. Warburton, "HRA 1998: irreversible?" (2010) 160 N.L.J. 1605.

Emmerson was reported in *The Times*, 26 November 1998.

D. Friedman, "A common law of human rights: history, humanity and dignity" [2016] E.H.R.L.R. 378.

D. Grieve QC MP, "Can a Bill of Rights Do Better than the Human Rights Act?" [2016] P.L. 223.

Lord Hoffmann, "The Universality of Human Rights", speech, 1 April 2009.

R. Hudson, (1996) 146 N.L.J. 1029.

Human Rights Lawyers Association, "*Ten Years of the Human Rights Act: Providing Protection, Participation and Accountability*", 2010.

Lord Irvine, "The Human Rights Act Two Years On: An Analysis", speech delivered on 1 November 2002, reproduced at [2003] P.L. 308.

The Joint Committee on Human Rights report and government responses are on the Parliament website.

A. Kavanagh, "The Elusive Divide between Interpretation and Legislation under the Human Rights Act 1998" (2004) 24 (2) *Oxford Journal of Legal Studies* 259.

Ministry of Justice, *Responding to Human Rights Judgments—Report to the Joint Committee on Human Rights on the Government's response to human rights judgments 2012–13* (Cm.8727); *Responding to Human Rights Judgments—Report to the Joint Committee on Human Rights on the Government's response to human rights judgments 2014–16* (Cm.9360).

Lord Neuberger, "Protecting human rights in an age of insecurity" (discussion of the judiciary's role), speech, 7 February 2011, judiciary website and "The role of judges in human rights jurisprudence: a comparison of the Australian and UK experience", speech in Melbourne, 8 August 2014; "The Role of the Supreme Court Seven Years On – Lessons Learnt", 21 November 2016; "Has the identity of the English Common Law been eroded by EU Laws and the European Convention on Human Rights?" speech, Singapore, 16 August, 2016, UKSC website.

D. Oliver, "Functions of a Public Nature under the Human Rights Act" [2004] P.L. 329.

D. Pannick, "The European rights court has its uses—to keep us on our toes", *The Times*, 7 May 2009.

L. Parkhill and C. Murray, "A difference of opinion", (2007) 157 N.L.J. 1378–1379.
Sir Rabinder Singh, "Making Judgments on Human Rights Issues", University of Nottingham 2016, Judiciary website.
A.T.H. Smith, "The Human Rights Act and the Criminal Lawyer: The Constitutional Context" [1999] Crim. L.R. 251 and see other articles in the same issue.
R. Smith, "Executive decision" (2010) 160 N.L.J. 296.
Lord Woolf, "Human Rights: Have the Public Benefited?" speech, 15 October 2002.
M. Zander, "Could do better" (2010) 160 N.L.J. 1249.

Further reading and sources for updating this chapter

4–067   Free updates of this book are available on the Sweet & Maxwell website: *http://www.uklawstudent.thomsonreuters.com*.
Summary and revision: P. Darbyshire, *Nutshells English Legal System*, 10th edn (London: Sweet & Maxwell, 2016).
Council of Europe: *http://hub.coe.int/*.
European Court of Human Rights: *http://www.echr.coe.int*. See Annual Reports, press releases and judgments.
European Human Rights Law Review (*Westlaw*).
Human Rights Lawyers Association: *http://www.hrla.org.uk/*.
Judges' speeches on the judiciary website and the UKSC website.
JUSTICE (pressure group): *http://www.justice.org.uk/*.
Regular updates in *Legal Action*.
Public Law, *Westlaw*.
Times Law Reports (on *Lexis* and in newspaper databases like UK Newsstand).
UK Parliament website, notably the reports of the Joint Committee on Human Rights.

CHAPTER 5

Law Reform and the Changing Legal System

"Everyone nowadays regards law reform as 'a good thing'. It was not always so. It was a proud boast of Lord Bathurst the 18th century Lord Chancellor that when he left office he had left English law exactly as he had found it." (Carnwath LJ, the then Chairman of the Law Commission, 2002.)

1. THE INEVITABILITY OF CHANGE

How much easier the lawyer's life must have been in the eighteenth century. All areas of law are characterised by change nowadays. New governments want to make their mark and with a powerful majority they will succeed in having most of the Bills implementing their policies passed into Acts by Parliament. Parliament is choking with the sheer volume of legislation it is expected to scrutinise. To the 15,000 annual pages of domestic legislation we can barely digest, we have to add 5,000 pages of EU regulations and directives, most of which are enacted through statutory instruments. This will continue until Brexit becomes law. Indeed, Brexit itself has massively added to the workload of Parliament and government departments as they need to decide what EU law to keep and what they wish to modify. The senior courts also develop and change the common law. There are more judges and more cases than ever before. The more complex the society, the more complex the law and the disputes that arise.

5–001

2. METHODS OF LAW REFORM

Parliament

Most Acts result from Government Bills, sponsored by the relevant chief Minister. Education legislation, for example, is drafted by that department then introduced by the Secretary of State for Education. Very few ordinary Members of Parliament succeed in getting a Public Act passed. Pressure groups and specialised interest groups lobby for changes in the law. Some, like the Confederation of British Industry, are very powerful organisations with wide national support but sometimes small pressure groups are successful. Bills may be introduced, or delegated legislation passed, following the report of a Royal Commission or advisory committee, or another ad hoc review body, as described

5–002

below. Parliament is so busy that it can take decades to close a legal loophole. The Domestic Violence, Crime and Victims Act 2004 s.5 closed the gap in the law of murder which allowed parents or carers to get away with murdering children and the vulnerable, where two or more carers both denied the offence and there were no witnesses to the harm. This problem was well known even before it was discussed by the Royal Commission on Criminal Justice Report 1993.

The judiciary

5–003   Judges can effect dramatic changes in the law through statutory interpretation and reinterpretation of the common law. In 1991, the law lords abolished the rule that a husband could not be guilty of raping his wife: *R. v R.* We saw in Ch.2 that the law lords, now UK Supreme Court (UKSC), will readily change the common law to keep up with social change, as they did in recognising pre-marital contracts. The higher courts have been forced to change their approach to statutory interpretation and become much more proactive, by the Human Rights Act 1998 and by our membership of the EU, as can be seen from the previous two chapters. As demonstrated in Ch.4, by reading words into statutes, the law lords and UKSC have extended people's Convention rights.

Judges sometimes draw attention to anomalies and call for change, as can be seen in Ch.2. An example occurred in *R. v Kai-Whitewind* (2005), where the Court of Appeal (CA) highlighted defects in the law on infanticide and complained that it was unsatisfactory and outdated. Also, senior judges make public speeches calling for law reform. They sometimes spoke in law reform debates in the House of Lords, before the Constitutional Reform Act 2005 removed them. Nowadays, retired judges are very active in the upper chamber and serving judges are frequently summoned to appear in front of Parliamentary select committees. As well as contributing to, or even provoking, the debates on constitutional reform, from 2003, senior judges turned out in force in the debate on the Human Rights Bill. All judges also have the Judges' Council as a vehicle for discussing and lobbying about proposed changes in law and policy. For example, in 2011, they condemned the Minister of Justice's plans to cut legal aid.

The Law Commission—a story of frustration and wasted taxpayers' money, but have things changed?

5–004   This is an independent body established by the Law Commissions Act 1965 with a duty under s.3(1)

> "to take and keep under review all the law with which they are … concerned with a view to its systematic development and reform, including in particular the codification of such law, the elimination of anomalies, the repeal of obsolete and unnecessary enactments, the reduction of the number of separate enactments and generally the simplification and modernisation of the law".

It does this through codification of the law, consolidation of statutes and statute law revision. The commissioners are five lawyers (practitioners and academics) seconded for a five-year period. The chairperson is always a High

Court or Court of Appeal judge. Following criticism, there are now two lay people, non-executive board members. They are supported by a Chief Executive, about 20 members of staff, including members of the Government Legal Service, two Parliamentary Counsel who draft Bills for them, an economist, as they have to produce impact assessments, and some research assistants.

They conduct many projects simultaneously and these are all on "lawyers' law", not emotive moral or social topics. They consult widely when establishing a new law reform programme. They research an area of law which has been criticised by judges, lawyers, government departments or the public, to identify defects, then publish proposals in a consultation paper. Once responses have been considered, they publish a report, usually with a draft Bill appended. Uncontentious law reform measures can be speeded through Parliament in the "Jellicoe" procedure, which allows the use of a Special Public Bill Committee, without using parliamentary time allocated to normal Bills. Since 2010, such bills start in the House of Lords. Their projects and reports are on their website.

They have repealed over 6,000 redundant Acts. For instance, in 2013 a Statute Law (Repeals) Act repealed 817 Acts, dating back to 1322. Codification is inevitably a long-term plan, since in each case the objective is a single self-contained code, which will be "the statement of all the relevant law in a logical and coherent form".

The annual report and now the Ministry of Justice's annual implementation reports show which of their recommendations have been made into law. Until the 1990s, the Commission was especially frustrated in their lack of progress in persuading governments to allocate parliamentary time to Bills designed to enact their Draft Criminal Code, which they published in 1989. In the 1990s, successive chairmen of the Commission complained bitterly at the backlog of their reports ignored by governments. The 1994 Annual Report complained that the work of the Commission was being neglected. The chairman, then Sir Henry Brooke, said there were 36 reports "stuck in the log-jam".

The Jellicoe procedure was introduced in 1994. Disappointingly, the next **5–005** chairman, Dame Mary Arden, commented in 1998 "the procedure has not worked quite as had been hoped as it makes very heavy demands on the time of members of the committee and of ministers and their officials". In the 1996 Annual Report, in an open letter to the Lord Chancellor, she accused the Government of wasting taxpayers' money by delaying implementation of law reforms. One of the reports ignored was on conspiracy to defraud, noting defects in the law. In *R. v Preddy* (1996), the House of Lords ruled that mortgage fraud was not covered by the law of theft. Eleven prosecutions had to be dropped and many others were not brought. At last, the Fraud Act 2006 placed most common law fraud and conspiracy to defraud on a statutory footing. Most of the Bill was drafted by the Law Commission to accompany its 2002 paper on fraud.

Another scandal relates to the state of "offences against the person", embodied in the decrepit, inappropriate, contradictory and archaically-worded Offences Against the Person Act 1861, upon which the Commission reported in 1993. Commissioner Stephen Silber QC complained of inaction in 1996. He illustrated it with the example of stalking. Had their proposals been implemented, there would have been none of the uncertainty that arose in the courts as to whether it was a criminal offence. In 2005, 80,000 cases per year were being prosecuted under this anachronistic Act. This issue is still trundling on. In 2015, the Commission produced yet another comprehensive report to Parliament, setting out the defects of these nineteenth century laws and the case for reform, and appending the 1998 draft bill, yet again.

In March 2003, the Department of Constitutional Affairs (DCA) published the *Quinquennial Review of the Law Commission*. John Halliday, its author, recommended strengthening its relationships with government. The aim should be to maximise public benefits derived from law reform. Performance would be at its best, he said, when:

- the projects selected were those most likely to result in law reform;
- government committed itself in advance to act on the outcomes;
- projects were managed to the highest standards, with regular reviews to ensure timelines;
- links between the Commission and its stakeholders (mainly Government departments) were strong;
- the Commission's internal systems and systems for managing the relationship with Government were strong; and
- the Commission and the DCA had the necessary vision, commitment, skills and resources.

5–006   He made a number of recommendations to improve the work and organisation of the Commission and its links with government and the public. Most had been implemented by 2005. In 2007, the Chairman reported improved publicity, "we are raising our profile in Westminster and Whitehall, and sending more clearly our message to those who need to hear it" but the second bullet point is a precondition for success and this has yet to be achieved. In 2008, the Minister of Justice made a welcome announcement. He expressed the Government's intention to put a stop to the Law Commission's perpetual frustration.

> "For 40 years the Law Commission has played a vital role … but I intend to strengthen its role by placing a statutory duty on the Lord Chancellor to report annually to Parliament on the government's intentions regarding outstanding Law Commission recommendations."

The chairman welcomed this as the most important structural change between the Commission, Parliament and the executive since 1965. This led to the Law Commission Act 2009 which now requires an annual report by the Ministry of Justice to be laid before Parliament on implementation of the Commission's proposals. Also, resulting from the 2009 Act, in 2010, a protocol was laid before Parliament on the relationship between the Commission and the Lord Chancellor (Minister of Justice). Government departments will undertake to take forward relevant law reform, keep the Commission up to date on policy developments that may impact on its proposals and provide an interim response within six months of Commission's proposals and a full response within a year. In its turn, the Commission will consult ministers about potential law reform projects in their fields, support all its final reports with an impact assessment and take full account of the minister's views in deciding whether and how to continue with a project, at agreed review points. Thus, by 2011, it looked as if the Government had at long last understood that it is a pointless waste of public money to establish a body of experts to painstakingly plan and consult on law reform and then just ignore it. By 2017, it looks from the annual reports as if the reforms are working, with Government departments engaging with its work. In his 50th anniversary lectures in 2015, the then Chairman, David Lloyd Jones LJ, listed it achievements. It had:

"●   ...published 202 law reform reports of which approximately 69% have been implemented in whole or in part.
●   ...been responsible for 222 consolidation Acts of Parliament.
●   ...[and] 19 Statute Law Repeal Acts which have repealed 3,117 statutes in their entirety and 3,982 in part because they are no longer of any practical utility."

See further his 2015 speeches, the annual reports and the rest of the website.

Advisory committees

Committees and "councils" of experts and interested parties are statutorily appointed to keep specific areas of law and policy under review and to provide information and recommendations. They range through such diverse topics as disabled persons, technology, nutrition, drugs, low pay, equality, social mobility, pesticides, nuclear safety, medicines, construction, advertising and industrial injuries. An example from this book is the Civil Justice Council.   5–007

Royal Commissions

These were appointed ad hoc, to conduct major reviews of the law or legal system. The recommendations of the Royal Commission on Criminal Procedure (1980) led to the passing of the Police and Criminal Evidence Act 1984 (PACE), protecting crime suspects. In 1991 the Royal Commission on Criminal Justice was established, at the height of public concern over famous miscarriages of justice. It reported in 1993 and some of its recommendations have been followed, such as those on appeals, in the Criminal Appeal Act 1995. Others have been ignored, such as those on the right to silence. Royal Commissions are very expensive and since the mid-1990s governments have preferred to appoint individuals to recommend legal system reform, as below.   5–008

Other bodies and individuals

On legal system reform, for example, the Lord Chancellor (Minister of Justice) is advised by several permanent and some ad hoc committees, such as the Youth Justice Board. Several of these non-departmental public bodies have been abolished under the Public Bodies Act 2011, known as "the bonfire of the quangos". They include the Administrative Justice and Tribunals Council. There are committees re-drafting and monitoring family, civil and criminal procedure rules. The Justice Minister also appoints non-statutory working parties. The Research Secretariat of the Ministry sets a research agenda, and funds projects often executed by academics. Since 1994, three judges and a retired judge were appointed to report on reforming the work and organisation of the civil courts   5–009

(Lord Woolf and Lord Justice Jackson), the criminal courts (Auld LJ) and tribunals (Sir Andrew Leggatt). This book contains countless examples of specially commissioned reports, such as the Leveson Review of criminal courts efficiency.

(Green) Consultation Papers and (White) Policy Papers

5–010   All government departments commonly publish Green Papers, now known as consultation papers, setting out their proposals for legislative change. Published online, these are invitations for comment by the interested public at large. Once gathered in, these responses help to modify final legislative proposals, which are set out in a White Paper.

Statute law revision

5–011   Dame Mary Arden, who chaired the Law Commission, provided an interesting account of this. The Renton Committee on the Preparation of Legislation 1995 made detailed recommendations on the drafting of statutes, parliamentary procedure and statutory interpretation. In 1992 the Hansard Commission reported on the legislative process. Dame Mary said badly drafted legislation encouraged litigation and was, therefore, expensive. Unclear legislation transferred the power to determine the law from an elected legislature to the courts and, furthermore, it was a fundamental civil liberty that people should be able to know and understand the laws that govern them. She told the story of the Tax Law Rewrite. In 1995, the Inland Revenue published two documents listing criticisms of the 6,000 pages of tax legislation, including:

- Complicated syntax, long sentences and archaic or ambiguous language.
- The principles underlying the rules were not apparent. This forced the courts to interpret strictly according to wording.
- Too much detail, covering every conceivable situation.
- Many sections could not be understood in isolation.
- Some rules were wide and, therefore, uncertain.
- It was difficult to find all the rules.
- Definitions were inconsistent and spread throughout different statutes.
- There was an imbalance between primary and secondary legislation.
- There was a lack of consultation and openness in drafting statutes.

The Inland Revenue decided to organise a project, a five-year, plain English rewrite, consulting representative bodies and taxpayers and employing 40 lawyers. A special joint committee of the Lords and Commons would scrutinise Bills.

Consolidation and codification

5–012   Consolidating statutes endeavour to simplify the law by replacing multiple statutes (Acts) with a single Act. Thus, for example, the whole of the legislation concerned with tribunals and inquiries was brought together and updated in the

Tribunals and Inquiries Act 1992. The consolidating procedure is not possible where the Bill involves changes of substance in the law, known as "codification". A codifying measure brings together the existing statute and case law, in an attempt to produce a full statement as it relates to that branch of law. The main examples of successful codification date from the end of the nineteenth century when the following four statutes were passed: the Bills of Exchange Act 1882, the Partnership Act 1890, the Sale of Goods Act 1893 and the Marine Insurance Act 1906. The Bills of Exchange Act 1882 involved the consideration of 17 statutes and 2,500 decided cases. These were compressed to make a statute 100 sections long. After these Acts were passed, there was no more codifying legislation until the Theft Act 1968.

The difference between consolidation and codification is classically illustrated by the example of the Powers of Criminal Courts (Sentencing) Act 2000, designed to pull together all the dozens of legislative strands of sentencing, which baffled judges, magistrates and their advisers. Annoyingly, this neat new fabric was already unravelling, thanks to a new statute in 2001, and has been further unwound annually, by later Acts. Governments can never resist the temptation to pick away at sentencing and criminal procedure, every year. What the Law Commission, Lord Chief Justices and academics are clamouring for is a proper criminal code, which would include all substantive criminal statute law, criminal procedure and sentencing, like the California Penal Code and that of every other US state. Then, anyone could buy or download the latest version every year and governments would have to weave their amendments into the existing cloth of such a code.

The Law Commission, frustrated at inaction on a criminal code, pointed out on its website in 2001 that we are almost the only country in the world without one. Lord Chief Justice Bingham told this pathetic history of English criminal law in exasperated tones, "The plea for such a code cannot, I fear, startle by its novelty":

- 1818, both houses petitioned the Prince Regent to establish a Law Commission to consolidate statute law.
- 1831, Commission established to inquire into codifying criminal law.
- 1835–1845, it produced eight reports, culminating in a Criminal Law Code Bill, ultimately dropped.
- 1879, Royal Commission recommended a code containing 550 clauses.
- 1844–1882, Lord Brougham and others made eight parliamentary attempts to enact a code.
- 1965, Law Commission established.
- Criminal Code Team established, including Professor Sir John Smith "the outstanding criminal lawyer of our time" (Bingham).
- Code published 1985, revised and expanded 1989.

He concluded   5–013

    "even the most breathless admirer of the common law must regard it as a reproach that after 700 years of judicial decision-making our highest tribunal should have been called upon time and again in recent years to consider the mental ingredients of murder, the oldest and most serious of crimes" (at p.695).

Spencer added a plea for a code of criminal procedure, because in this context English inaction looks even more inexcusable, in the face of a 1995 Scottish code

" ... the sources are at present in a shocking mess, as a result of which the law is not readily accessible to those who have reason to discover it ... dispersed among ... some 150 statutes ... even the modern ones are mainly messy and unsystematic and hard for the user to find his way around: a succession of Criminal Justice Acts, each a disparate jumble of new rules, or of new amendments to old ones" (at p.520).

Almost all the law of evidence was uncodified and our haphazard way of creating rules resulted in "all sorts of astonishing contradictions".

At last the government announced, in 2001–2002, that they intended to start work on a criminal code. Reacting quickly, the Law Commission started updating its 1989 Draft Criminal Code. In 2009, however, they abandoned the project because of "complexity of the common law, the increasing pace of legislation, layers of legislation on a topic being placed on another with bewildering speed and influence of European legislation": Ian Dennis, (2009). He also said piecemeal codification of the criminal law, such as the common law on self-defence was "a pointless exercise" (2008). Lawyers already know the law and it will not help non-lawyers to work out what they can reasonably do to fend off a burglar or assailant. The Commission still favours codification, as did the Lord Chief Justice Thomas, according to his 2016 speech at Her Majesty's Judges Mansion House Dinner.

There is reason for optimism. In 2005 the bold step was finally taken of reducing all the rules of criminal *procedure* to one set. They have now been set out in one place, on dedicated web-pages, but are still a bit of a mish-mash. They are re-issued regularly so the latest, at the time of writing, are the Criminal Procedure Rules 2015 but by now (July 2017), there are seven sets of amending rules. Disappointingly, however, the Government established a committee to work on the codification of *primary* legislation on criminal procedure but withdrew funding for the project, to Spencer's frustration (2007).

Bibliography, further reading and sources for updating this chapter

5–014   Free updates of this book are available on the Sweet & Maxwell website: *http://www.uklawstudent.thomsonreuters.com*.

Summary and revision: P. Darbyshire, *Nutshells English Legal System*, 10th edn (London: Sweet & Maxwell, 2016).

Dame Mary Arden, "Modernising Legislation" [1998] P.L. 65.

Rt Hon Lord Bingham of Cornhill CJ, "A Criminal Code: Must We Wait for Ever?" [1998] Crim. L.R. 694.

Interview with Sir Henry Brooke, *The Magistrate*, February 1994.

Carnwath LJ, "The art of the possible" *Counsel,* February 2002, p.20.

I. Dennis, editorial [2009] Crim. L.R. 1; [2008] Crim. L.R. 507.

M. Dyson, J. Lee and S. Wilson Stark, *Fifty Years of the Law Commissions*, Hart Oxford 2016.

Law Commission website, especially annual reports and speeches.

A.T.H. Smith, "Criminal Law and the Law Commission", [2016] Crim. L.R. 381.

J.R. Spencer, "The Case for a Code of Criminal Procedure" [2000] Crim. L.R. 519.

J.R. Spencer, editorial [2007] Crim. L.R. 331.
Sir Roger Toulson, "Law reform in the twenty-first century" (2006) 26 (3) *Legal Studies* 321–328.

PART 2

INSTITUTIONS

THE COURT STRUCTURE

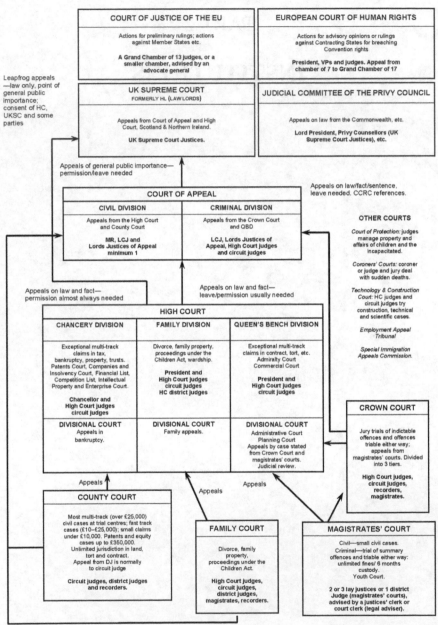

CHAPTER 6

Civil Courts

"I don't give a fuck whether we're peers or not" (Senior Law Lord, Lord Bingham, on being asked by Boris Johnson MP, a journalist, whether he would not miss being in "the best club in London" if the law lords moved out of Parliament and into a new Supreme Court, 2002).

"The Online Court project offers a radically new and different procedural and cultural approach to the resolution of civil disputes which, if successful, may pave the way for fundamental changes in the conduct of civil litigation over much wider ground than is currently contemplated by its first stage ambition, to resolve money claims up to £25,000 subject to substantial exclusions." (Lord Justice Briggs, 2016).

"Citizens, whether litigants or not, are not supplicants coming to the high hand of judgment. They are rights bearers...this is not about local buildings or the court and tribunal estate – that would be an entirely superficial and simplistic way of characterising access to justice. This is about recognising the way that we live in a digital society and responding accordingly. With modern methods, effective use of IT, we ought to be creating – recreating – local justice." (Sir Earnest Ryder, Senior President of Tribunals, 2016).

"Three months ago, we began the central part of what has been described as the most radical and ambitious programme of courts and tribunal reform anywhere in the world...but we must keep an eye on what is happening elsewhere in the world. Many states are now developing their own commercial courts." (Lord Chief Justice Thomas, 2016).

"[T]he reputation of the lawyers, judges and courts of the UK or England & Wales...remains high in the international commercial community. The unique selling points... of the English courts are the integrity of our judges: i.e. the complete absence of corruption, our compliance with the rule of law, the consistently high quality of judges, and the certainty and quality of English law. These USPs and high repute do not, however, mean the UK is immune to competition from other commercial court centres seeking to prise dispute resolution business away from the UK to other jurisdictions in Europe, the US and Asia. We should take this competition very seriously indeed." (Vos C, 2016).

"To no-one will we sell, to no-one deny or delay right or justice." (From Magna Carta 1215 cl.40.)

The work of the civil courts was reformed from 1990. Following the *Civil Justice Review* 1988, the Courts and Legal Services Act 1990 shifted most civil business down into the County Courts from 1992, as the High Court was clogged up with trivia. The Woolf Report 1996 recommended an overhaul of civil procedure, implemented by the Civil Procedure Rules (CPR) 1998. In 2009, a new UK Supreme Court was created. The Lord Chancellor (Secretary of State for Justice) and his department, the Ministry of Justice, created in 2007, run the

6–001

courts, court staff and buildings. Under the Courts Act 2003, he is under "a duty to ensure that there is an efficient and effective system to support" the running of the courts. A unified courts agency, Her Majesty's Courts and Tribunals Service, administers the day-to-day running of the courts. This replaces the Court Service and local committees of magistrates who were responsible for running their courts. The hot news in 2017 is Briggs LJ's *Civil Courts Structure Review* 2016, recommending an Online Court handling all money claims up to £25,000, and a 2016 "vision paper" authored by the Minister of Justice, Lord Chief Justice and President of Tribunals, *Transforming our Justice System*, which promises (or threatens) a massive shift out of court buildings and into a virtual world:

> "The revolution in technology will characterise tomorrow's justice system. We will provide online access by developing a single online system for starting and managing cases across the criminal, civil, family and tribunal jurisdictions."

Eighty six more local court buildings will be closed (civil, criminal and family). The Ministry says it will spend £970 million modernising courts and tribunals and enhancing technology. This is a transparent cost-cutting exercise, sold to us in an optimistic "vision" that we will be able to sue someone for up to £25,000, or be left to defend ourselves, using our iPad, without getting out of bed. The provisions for open, public justice in this plan are somewhat farcical, to say the least, and as Padfield remarked:

> "Extraordinarily, there appears to have been no thought given to the impact on justice of 'virtual courts', to the limitations of justice by video link, to the importance in terms of legitimacy of judges and offenders meeting in a public forum etc."

Obviously, after the closure of so many court buildings, the people who will find it most difficult to travel to distant courts will be the poor and the disadvantaged: the unemployed, those in poor mental or physical health, substance abusers, the homeless, asylum seekers and so on. As is starkly portrayed in the empirical research reported in my book, *Sitting in Judgment*, these are exactly the people who populate the criminal, civil and family courts—the dispossessed. Naturally, they will also struggle to do *anything* online.

The descriptive text in this chapter and the next one explains the court structure diagram opposite this page so you need to cross-refer to it. We will examine civil procedure in depth in Ch.10.

1. MAGISTRATES' COURTS

6–002   Trial courts, where cases start off, are called "courts of original jurisdiction" or "courts of first instance". There were over 400 magistrates' courts in England and Wales in the 1970s, reduced to 330 by 2011 but there has been an extensive court closure programme, leaving just 236 by 2017. Another 43 magistrates' courts are scheduled to close from 2017.

From around 1200, a number of knights were appointed in each county to keep the peace. By a series of statutes in 1327–1377, they became known as justices of the peace, the predecessors of modern JPs, also known as magistrates. Cases are heard by two or three lay magistrates or a professional district judge (magistrates' courts). Most cases are criminal. Their civil work includes enforcement of payments for income tax, council tax and national insurance. In 2015, there were almost 64,000 civil claims in magistrates' courts. In 2005, the magistrates lost their liquor licensing administrative work to local authorities. This was a logical change. Magistrates used to carry out all local government functions until the Local Government Act 1888 created most local councils. Licensing was a relic of this administrative work, inappropriate for a section of the judiciary. The family work shifted to the new unified family court in 2014 but the magistrates went with the work.

2. COUNTY COURTS

Since their establishment by the County Courts Act 1846, they have provided a local and relatively inexpensive alternative to the High Court for civil business only. They do not follow county boundaries. Their name is historical. The Crime and Courts Act 2013 created a single County Court, from 2014, which mirrors the single Crown Court. It sat at 216 locations in 2011 but by 2017, there are now only 172, with more closures planned. Circuit judges specialise in the more complex work. District judges are the powerhouse of the County Court. Their jurisdiction to assess damages is now unlimited, unless otherwise directed. They preside over the small claims court, where the limit is £10,000. They handle most pre-trial case management and hear 80 per cent of contested County Court trials. Circuit judges generally hear the more serious matters. Recorders are lawyers who sit part time, doing similar work. Deputy district judges are lawyers sitting part-time. All judges sit alone, although circuit judges and recorders may sit with a jury of eight, in categories of case described in the chapter on the jury. Specialist circuit judges are nominated to sit in the mercantile (meaning commercial), chancery, and technology and construction courts. Designated Civil Judges manage civil judges in their area.

    Under the Courts and Legal Services Act 1990 s.3, the County Court was given almost all the powers of the High Court, with some restrictions. They try the bulk of civil cases, such as tort, contract, property, insolvency and bankruptcy, with the High Court reserved for a few special cases. The civil justice statistics are woefully unhelpful so Briggs LJ commissioned special analysis which showed that in 2015/16, 1,521,624 claims were started (compared with 1,900,000 in 2000). Most of these were money claims, the others being social landlord repossessions, mortgage repossession claims, personal injury and insolvency petitions. Ninety per cent of cases are always undefended so only a tenth, 152,184 were defended and thus allocated to a trial track. Most cases do not get to trial because the parties settle, so only one in 30 of the claims issued went to trial: 50,638 (compared with 60,000 in 2009). Confusingly, these statistics include High Court cases heard in County Courts outside London. Some County Courts have the jurisdiction to hear "equity" cases, about trusts, and contested probate up to the value of £30,000. Under the Civil Procedure Rules 1998, cases are divided into small claims, fast track and multi-track and the County Courts hear all small claims, most fast track and most multi-track claims. The County Court includes

6–003

five specialist mercantile courts (the provincial equivalent of the Commercial Court) and a patents County Court, all of which have specialist circuit judges. Some big city County Court locations have been renamed Civil Justice Centres, as they offer ADR (alternative dispute resolution) as well as litigation facilities.

3. THE HIGH COURT OF JUSTICE

6–004   The High Court of Justice (HC) and the Court of Appeal (CA) were brought into being as the Supreme Court of Judicature under the Judicature Acts 1873–1875. At that time, the HC consisted of five Divisions representing the old separate courts it replaced, the Queen's Bench, Chancery, Probate, Divorce and Admiralty (PDA), Exchequer, and Common Pleas. The last two were merged in the Queen's Bench Division (QBD) in 1880 and the remaining three continued unaltered from then until the 1970 redistribution of the PDA functions created the Family Division. The Constitutional Reform Act 2005 renamed the HC and CA as the Senior Courts of England and Wales.

The HC sits at the Royal Courts of Justice in the Strand and elsewhere. Commercial, admiralty, chancery and technology and construction cases, as well as Financial List cases, Companies and Insolvency and Patents Court cases and cases from the Competition List, are now heard in the new Rolls Building in Fetter Lane, nearby. These are known as "The Business and Property Courts of England and Wales" from June 2017 and those courts will deploy judges flexibly, from the QBD and Chancery Divisions, for the first time. For the convenience of litigants, there are a number of High Court district registries at County Court trial centres in the larger cities in England and Wales. Therefore, for example, Business and Property Courts will also sit at Birmingham, Manchester, Leeds, Bristol and in Cardiff, with expansions to Newcastle and Liverpool in the future. High Court judges have been travelling on circuit since the twelfth century with the aim that the monarch's justice is administered evenly throughout the land. There are 100 High Court judges, 18 in Chancery, 18 in Family and 64 in the QBD. Trials may be conducted by deputy HC judges (lawyers sitting part-time) and circuit judges authorised ("ticketed") to hear HC cases. All HC judges generally sit alone, with the exception of certain judicial review cases and commercial arbitrations. Jury trial with 12 jurors is permitted in the QBD in five torts and at the discretion of the judge but is very rare in other cases. The most common and well-publicised jury trials are defamation actions and actions against the police.

The Queen's Bench Division

6–005   This, the great common law court, takes its name from the fact that the early royal judges sat on "the bench", "en banc", at Westminster. It absorbed the whole common law jurisdiction, when the High Court was reformed. The present jurisdiction of the Division is thus both civil and criminal, original and appellate and the QBD is much larger than the other two Divisions.

In its general civil jurisdiction, most cases are contract or tort. It is headed by a President. Cases are managed, pre-trial, by Masters of the HC in London (in a part of the Royal Courts of Justice called "the Bear Garden") and by County Court district judges outside London. The QBD contains the Commercial Court and the Admiralty Court and 13 QBD judges are nominated ("ticketed") to hear those cases, among others. The Admiralty Court hears cases relating to ships, such as collisions and damage to cargo. A "commercial list" was established in the High Court in 1895, now the Commercial Court. The cases normally involve over £1 million, on contracts relating to shipping, commerce, insurance, banking, international credit and questions arising from arbitrations. Commercial Court cases outside London are mainly heard by nominated circuit judges at nine Mercantile Courts outside London, and are now under the Business and Property Court umbrella.

As explained at the beginning of this book, to understand the international importance of the English legal system both right now and historically, one needs an appreciation of the Commercial Court, its popularity with litigants, its relationship with the world's other international commercial courts, and the importance of London in developing the common law and global commercial law. In 2016–2017, Thomas LCJ is trying to promote common international codes and procedures, and transnational commercial court hearings through video-link. As he said in Beijing in 2017, he is trying to get commercial courts and international arbitral centres to work together to develop this and persuaded foreign courts to join a Standing International Forum, with a first meeting in May 2017, in London. For a penetrating and highly informative consideration of London's Commercial Court and its relationship to foreign commercial courts and to arbitrators in London see Thomas LCJ's April 2017 Beijing speech and his 2016 speeches he cites therein, delivered in Dubai, Singapore and the Cayman Islands. On the globalisation of commercial law and commercial courts, see his February 2016 speech in Dubai.

A specialist (and extremely busy) Administrative Court was added to the QBD in 2000 and a Planning Court was added in 2014. The Administrative Court sits in five cities. From 2015, cases over £50 million requiring expertise in financial markets were allocated to a new Financial List. Most QBD judges spend half their time sitting on circuit hearing serious criminal Crown Court cases or civil cases outside London. The QBD administers the Technology and Construction Court (TCC) which hears such things as technical construction disputes, computer and sale of goods litigation, torts relating to the occupation of land and questions arising from arbitrations in building and engineering disputes. Some full-time TCC circuit judges sit in London, supervised by HC judges. Over 40 circuit judges and recorders are nominated, "ticketed" to hear TCC cases in 11 provincial centres. Specialist QBD judges also sit in the Employment Appeal Tribunal.

The Divisional Court of the Queen's Bench Division

In its appellate jurisdiction, the QBD, like the other two Divisions, has what is confusingly called a Divisional Court. This is mainly an appeal court. Its jurisdiction includes:

6–006

- appeals on a point of law by way of case stated from magistrates' courts and the Crown Court;
- judicial review—the supervisory jurisdiction of the HC over the lower courts and tribunals and, most importantly, over governmental and other public bodies. The Administrative Court hears applications, for instance, challenging the closure of a hospital, or a decision to evict gypsies from public land; and
- applications for habeas corpus (challenging the legality of detention).

Around half the QBD judges are nominated ("ticketed") to hear these cases, mainly in the Administrative Court. Some matters are determined by a single judge, such as applications for leave to apply for judicial review (on paper or in person) and others must be heard by at least two judges, usually a HC judge and a Lord Justice of Appeal. There was a 60 per cent increase in the caseload of the Administrative Court in 2004–2008, because of asylum and immigration claims, which formed two thirds of its workload. In 2007–2012, there was an 86 per cent increase in judicial review applications, again driven by immigration and asylum. Ninety per cent are found to have no merit in law. By contrast, only 13,000 proceedings started in the QBD general list in 2015 (resulting in 199 trials), compared with over 112,000 in 1996, because of the shift of work down to the County Court. Judicial review reconsideration applications were transferred to the new Upper Tribunal in 2010 and some immigration and asylum work was also eventually transferred there.

The Chancery Division

6–007   This is the direct descendant of the Lord Chancellor's equity jurisdiction, and the pre-1873 Court of Chancery. It also has statutory responsibility for such matters as the winding-up of companies and revenue cases. Its 18 specialist judges are headed by the Chancellor. Case management is done by HC Masters in London and district judges outside. Its jurisdiction is:

- disputed intellectual property, copyright or patents;
- the execution or declaration of trusts;
- the redemption and foreclosure of mortgages;
- conveyancing and land law matters;
- partnership actions and other business and industrial disputes;
- the administration of the estates of deceased persons (contested probate);
- revenue issues, i.e. taxation cases;
- insolvency;
- professional negligence claims against solicitors, accountants, surveyors and others.

It contains three specialist courts: the Patents Court and the Intellectual Property Enterprise Court, handling intellectual property disputes, and the Bankruptcy and Companies Court, handling company insolvency. It sits in the Rolls Building in the City of London and provincial HC centres. Most of the substantial work in the provinces is handled by circuit judges "ticketed" for HC

Chancery work. The Divisional Court of the Chancery Division heard tax appeals from the Commissioners of Taxes and from the County Courts in bankruptcy cases. Some of these have shifted into the Tax and Chancery Chamber of the Upper Tribunal. Because of its intellectual property and copyright jurisdiction, the litigants we are most likely to hear of in Chancery are involved in the music industry, such as the Spice Girls, Bruce Springsteen and the late George Michael. The development of the Rolls Building which contains all the specialist business courts of the Chancery Division and QBD, plus the launch of the Financial List and the radical modernisation programme currently underway are long overdue attempts to preserve the competitive edge of London as the forum of choice for international commercial litigation, as explained in many speeches in 2016 by the Lord Chief Justice and others. Sir Geoffrey Vos, Chancellor of the High Court, said this in the speech quoted at the opening of this chapter:

> "First, there was the introduction of the Financial List on 1st October 2015. This has, thus far, been a huge success. The List uses the most highly qualified judges from both the Chancery Division and the Commercial Court and offers the twin advantages of speed and efficiency. It has introduced a market test case procedure to resolve an uncertain point where resolution of the issue would benefit the financial markets...We intend to keep the procedures of the Financial List continuously under review so as to make sure that they meet the needs of the international commercial community whether based here or abroad. We will listen to what you have to say at our briefing events or through our Users Group, but also by making sure that the courts are accessible and responsive, and the IT that we are using works effectively for the users."

Senior judges' speeches show that they are always worried about losing international litigation and arbitration to other countries. For the best evidence-based analysis, see the 2016 speech by Blair J, head of the Commercial Court.

The Family Division

This Division shared family jurisdiction with the magistrates' court and the County Court, until most work shifted into the unified Family Court from 2014, leaving wardship and international cases. Its 18 High Court judges and 7 HC district judges are headed by a President. High Court judges sit in the Royal Courts of Justice and some hear cases while travelling on circuit. High Court district judges sit in the Central Family Court, in Holborn. Most cases outside London are heard by authorised ("ticketed") circuit judges. In the Family Court, the judges continue to sit in the same buildings as before. High Court judges' main work is:

6–008

- complex defended divorce cases;
- complex applications relating to children, under the Children Act, for instance applications for care orders, adoptions, and child arrangement orders, where the contest is acrimonious or complex or one or more parties lives abroad. Only this court may deal with wardship applications, in which the court orders a child to be made a ward of court and subject to its control; and

- the grant of probate or letters of administration to authorise the disposal of a deceased person's estate where the matter is uncontested.

The Family Court

6–009   A unified family court has been debated since the 1960s and was recommended by the Finer Committee in 1974, but proceedings remained divided between the three courts (HC, County Court and magistrates' courts), which causes immense confusion and stress to some parties and delay, inefficiency and consequent expense. Repeated claims by politicians and judges that we were on the verge of creating a family court were an exaggeration and lacked insight into this chaos. At long last a family court was created from April 2014, following the Family Justice Review 2011. It deals with all family cases and comprises the HC, circuit and County Court district judges and district judges of the High Court, recorders (part-timers) plus district judges (magistrates' courts) and magistrates and their legal advisers. Cases are still divided geographically and a designated family judge oversees judicial deployment in each locality. Hearings still take place in the existing magistrates' courts and the County Court so parties will still be as confused as they always were.

Under the Children Act 1989, magistrates' domestic courts were renamed "family proceedings courts" but these were replaced in 2014 with the single Family Court. Specially trained magistrates can make and enforce financial provisions following a family breakdown and can make orders protecting adults and children. They share children cases with High Court judges, County Court district judges and circuit judges but magistrates cannot grant divorces. A number of circuit and district judges are authorised, "ticketed" to sit in the Family Court. Family cases are allocated to different levels of judge according to complexity. Judges can make a range of orders relating to children, including care, supervision, adoption and child arrangements. From 2014, the single Family Court hears all family cases, except wardship and international cases, which will stay in the HC. Almost all divorces were granted by the County Court and in 2014, this work shifted to the Family Court.

4.   THE COURT OF APPEAL (CIVIL DIVISION)

6–010   The Court of Appeal (CA) was created by the Judicature Acts 1873–1875 and now forms part of the senior courts. It was intended that the CA should be the final appeal court, but a change of plan led to the Appellate Jurisdiction Act 1876, under which the House of Lords in its judicial capacity was retained as the highest appeal court (until 2009).

Thirty-nine Lords Justices and the five heads of division sit in the CA. The Master of the Rolls heads the Civil Division. It hears appeals on fact and law from the HC and the County Court. The CA (Civil Division) was composed of three Lords Justices but, since the Access to Justice Act 1999, the Court may be composed of one, two or three judges, depending on the importance and complexity of the case. In a case of great importance a "full court" of five judges is convened. It sits in the Royal Courts of Justice in the Strand and in Cardiff. The court disposed of 1,055 appeals in 2015 and there has been no significant increase since 2003 but there has been a 50 per cent increase in applications for permission to appeal in 2011–2016. The cases are taking more time, especially applications for permission to appeal in immigration and asylum cases, and much of the judges' time is spent on administration and management jobs so the court has accrued an increasing backlog, criticised by Lord Briggs in his 2016 report. Some reforms commenced in late 2016 and he recommended others.

5. THE HOUSE OF LORDS APPELLATE COMMITTEE TRANSFORMS INTO THE SUPREME COURT

From the Appellate Jurisdiction Act 1876 until July 2009, the Appellate Committee of the House of Lords was the final court of appeal in civil matters from all courts in the UK and in all criminal cases except those from Scotland. There were 12 Lords of Appeal in Ordinary, known colloquially as the "law lords". Other senior judges could sit with them. By constitutional convention, members of the House of Lords who were not judges did not take part. Normally, five judges heard an appeal. If a case was exceptionally important, seven or nine would sit. The court sat in two committee rooms in the Palace of Westminster. The appeals always raised a point of law of general public importance, the sole ground for obtaining leave. Because the court originated as, and was still technically, a committee of the House of Lords the judgments were called "opinions" and were delivered to the Lords, in the chamber.

6–011

The Constitutional Reform Act 2005 replaced the Appellate Committee with a UK Supreme Court from October 2009. The Act resulted from a Government announcement in 2003 that it was determined to reform the constitution, by abolishing the Lord Chancellor (they did not achieve this but reformed his role), reforming judicial appointments and transforming the law lords into a Supreme Court. The Act and these reforms were the most dramatic consequence of the Human Rights Act 1998 and the attention that this drew to the requirement for an independent judiciary, under art.6 of the European Convention on Human Rights.

The problem with the law lords, apart from their inclusion of the Lord Chancellor, a government minister, was their place in the legislature and consequent perceived danger that they could be involved in debates on Bills which they might later have to interpret and apply in court. Further, despite the constitutional convention that law lords should not take part in political debates in the House of Lords chamber, some law lords had done so, albeit very rarely. Both in reality and in appearances, the law lords breached the separation of judicial and legislative powers required by art.6. In 2003, the Government was persuaded by the reform campaigners, the radical and outspoken intellectuals, law lords Bingham and Steyn. Lord Steyn invoked the words of the famous constitutionalist Walter Bagehot, that the "the Supreme Court of the English people ... ought not to be hidden beneath the robes of a legislative assembly". He was alarmed at the confusion of functions in the eyes of the public and foreign observers, reminding us that when the law lords delivered their judgments in the first *Pinochet* case, in the Lords' chamber, foreign television viewers thought Lady Thatcher was a judge, part of the dissenting minority, opposing the extradition of General Pinochet in 1998. He reminded us of the requirements for judicial independence under art.6 of the Convention, as well as the UN, the Council of Europe's Charter of the Statute for Judges and the Universal Charter of the Judge.

Although it had been mooted many years earlier that the law lords should be abolished, leaving the CA as the final appellate body, that argument was rarely heard by 2000. Stevens pointed out, in various of his works, cited in Ch.14, that the 1873 Judicature Act abolished appeals to the House of Lords and set up "the Imperial Court of Appeals", sitting in the Strand. It was only a group of Tory mavericks that led the court back to the House of Lords, three years later, for the purpose of "dignity". In the comment examined below, Baroness Hale also examined the option of abolishing the top court.

6–012   The 2003 Government announcement that they intended to abolish the 1,400 year old office of Lord Chancellor, convert the law lords into a Supreme Court, reform the system of judicial appointments and consider abolishing Queen's Counsel was a surprise to almost everyone. These plans were presented as decisions, as a fait accompli, without consultation or forewarning.

For those of us who had watched politics very closely, however, the announcements were an acceptance of the inevitable. It had become apparent that the tripartite role of Lord Chancellor, holding significant power in all three organs of government, was untenable, under the Convention. A series of cases had made it clear that art.6 (fair trial) was breached if a member of the executive (government) sat as a judge and the Lord Chancellor was both head of the judiciary and an important Cabinet minister.

The reasons for questioning the future of the law lords were, said Lord Bingham in 2002, the recent reforms of the House of Lords as a parliamentary chamber, the Human Rights Act and the new role of the Privy Council in devolution issues, after the Devolution Acts of 1998. The last development raised the issue of whether the law lords and the Judicial Committee of the Privy Council (JCPC) should be merged. He examined the four different models for a Supreme Court, as he saw them:

1.   Amalgamating the law lords and JCPC as a UK Supreme Court.
2.   A new constitutional court, operating alongside courts in the three UK jurisdictions (Northern Ireland, Scotland and England and Wales).
3.   A court modelled on the European Court of Justice, giving authoritative rulings on points of law referred to it by other courts, as opposed to appeals.
4.   Simply severing the law lords from the legislature, re-housing and renaming them but with their powers unchanged and with the JCPC continuing alongside.

He preferred the fourth option.

Also speaking in 2002, Lord Steyn was much more strident. Most of his attack was directed at the Lord Chancellor's position, although his speech was entitled "The Case for a Supreme Court". Lord Steyn, a South African, took a comparative view, examining the lack of a functional separation of powers in the UK, compared with the rest of the democratic world "nowhere outside Britain, even in democracies with the weakest forms of separation of powers, is the independence of the judiciary potentially compromised in the eyes of citizens by relegating the status of the highest court to the position of a subordinate part of the legislature. And nowhere outside Britain is the independence of the judiciary potentially compromised in the eyes of citizens by permitting a serving politician to sit as a judge, let alone in the highest court which fulfils constitutional functions."

He dismissed British defences of the status quo. His brilliant exposition of the separation of powers is well worth reading.

"Justice Brandeis said that the separation of powers serves, not to promote efficiency but to prevent the exercise of arbitrary power ... For protection, citizens must look to the courts. Tensions between these ideals arise from time to time. The executive and the judiciary are not on the same side. The stability of democratic institutions ultimately depends on public confidence."

The last straw was an attack by the Parliamentary Assembly of the Council of Europe (the watchdog for the European Convention on Human Rights, *not* an EU institution). They published a report in April 2003: **6–013**

"Whilst the office of Lord Chancellor may be venerable and as yet remain unchallenged before the European Court of Human Rights, continuation of the current system creates real problems of lack of transparency and thus of lack of respect for the rule of law."

In the previous month, the author, Erik Jurgens, Rapporteur to the Council, had appeared before the newly formed House of Commons Committee on the Lord Chancellor's Department. He was polite enough not to use the word hypocrisy and recognised that the ancient British constitution was venerated, but his evidence shows exasperation:

"Every day in my Council of Europe work I am in confrontation with new democracies from central and Eastern Europe, who I tell they should not do certain things, and they say, 'What about the British? They have these appointed Members of Parliament in the upper House. They have a Lord Chancellor' ... If you say he is a link between the Cabinet and the judges I think you are saying something very dangerous ... I do not think judges should say anything to the Cabinet except in public and I do not think the Cabinet should say anything to the judges except in public because transparency is just about the most important point."

Countries who had been on the other side in World War II had made great efforts to develop new constitutions in compliance with the Convention. It was time to review the old, unchanged constitutions. Mr Jurgens' evidence was broadcast on the media. On hearing his words, I realised the Lord Chancellor's role would have to be dismantled. Only three years earlier, New Labour had "brought Convention rights home" in the Human Rights Act 1998. They could hardly be seen to be ignoring its very guardian, the Council of Europe.

Two months later, Tony Blair's government announced their intention to form a Supreme Court. In the consultation paper, *Constitutional Reform: a Supreme Court for the United Kingdom*, they relied heavily on Lord Bingham's ideas. Below, I paraphrase and summarise the main questions it raised and the responses. The Government did not ask *whether* there should be a Supreme Court. "The Government *will* legislate to abolish the jurisdiction of the House of Lords" (my emphasis) but they said they had no intention of creating a US style supreme court, with the power to strike down legislation:

> "Parliament is supreme in our constitution and must remain so. Nor, in the absence of a codified, clearly delineated body of constitutional law, do we see a role for a Constitutional Court" (Department of Constitutional Affairs Press Release 296/03).

The paper asked the following questions:

1. Should the UKSC's jurisdiction include the devolution cases dealt with by the JCPC? 86 per cent of respondents were in favour.
2. Do you agree that its members should remain at 12, with access to a supplementary panel? 74 per cent agreed.
3. Should retired Supreme Court members be appointed to the House of Lords (i.e. the upper House of Parliament)? 68 per cent agreed.
4. Should the court sit in panels, as the law lords did, or should every member sit on every case (as in the US Supreme Court)? 69 per cent thought the court should sit in panels. Several respondents cited Lord Bingham's concern that if all members of the court decided all cases, the appointing authority might try and influence decision-making when filling vacancies.
5. Should the court decide for itself which appeals it hears? 64 per cent said not.

6–014   Six law lords considered the proposals unnecessary and harmful. They believed the law lords' presence in Parliament to be mutually beneficial. The cost would outweigh any benefit. One of the new ones, in 2004, was Brenda Hale, for whom the planned UKSC was not radical enough (see below). By 2008, some law lords had retired and been replaced, so by then only two opposed a new court. All were agreed that a Supreme Court should enjoy an independent budget.

There were formidable critics. New Zealander, Lord Cooke, former Lord of Appeal, said law reform debates in the Parliamentary chamber had benefited from the contribution of serving and former law lords. Lord Bingham's own maiden speech, urging incorporation of the European Convention, cited in Ch.4 of this book, was a perfect model. The most outspoken critic was Lord Chief Justice Woolf. He delayed retirement to stay and "fight for the independence of the judiciary". In the 2004 Squire Centenary Lecture, he remarked that the proposed court would be a "poor relation" of the world's other supreme courts, because of its more limited role:

> "We will be exchanging a first class Final Court of Appeal for a second class Supreme Court . . . Separating the House of Lords in its legislative capacity from its activities as the Final Court of Appeal could act as a catalyst causing the new court to be more proactive than its predecessor. This could lead to tensions. Although the law lords involvement in the legislative chamber is limited, the very fact that they are members of the legislature does provide them with an insight and understanding of the workings of Parliament."

Lord Chancellor Falconer responded in the House of Lords, introducing the Constitutional Reform Bill for its second reading:

> "The Law Lords are appointed to the final Court of Appeal, not the legislature. They are judges. We ... believe in the supremacy of Parliament. Ultimately, laws must be made by Parliament. The judges ... must construe and interpret those laws. However, unlike systems such as that in the United States of America, we do not want policy issues such as capital punishment, abortion or racial discrimination to be decided by judges ... That most certainly does not make our system any worse or better than that in the United States of America; it is simply different ..." (*Hansard*, 7 March 2004).

The Bill was almost defeated but the Government rescued it by promising that it could be scrutinised by a Parliamentary select committee. It was delayed. The committee made 400 amendments. Lord Woolf, placated by the Government's promise of £45 million to fund the new building, decided to support the Bill. By Christmas 2004, it was clear there would be a separate supreme court and the only outstanding issue was to find a prestigious building.   **6–015**

Some academics and others had advocated a supreme court for years. To them, the reforms were too hasty and ill-thought-through. Their writings (the best collection being in a 2004 special edition of *Legal Studies*, as cited in the bibliography) show frustration that the proposals did not go far enough. They either wanted a US style constitutional court or they considered that the UKSC would be one in disguise. Robert Stevens (in that volume) was cynical, considering the Government's reasoning to be Alice in Wonderland "if we say often enough that our judges are apolitical they will be". The consultation paper emphasised the supremacy of Parliament, yet the reality was that the Human Rights Act and the European Communities Act had required the law lords to apply a fundamental law and act as a type of constitutional court.

Baroness Hale, former academic, the first ever female Lord of Appeal (law lord), carefully examined the ramifications of abolishing the top court altogether, an option ignored by most other commentators. The main argument for retaining the new court's jurisdiction over ordinary civil cases was uniformity of approach (in England and Wales, Scotland and Northern Ireland) but she was cynical. The opportunity for error-correction in such cases only arose rarely and randomly, dependent on whether one of the parties wanted to appeal. The argument for retaining a final appellate court rested on the deficiencies of the Court of Appeal, which worked under a great deal of pressure and was heavily dependent on the quality of the arguments prepared before it.

She asked, "If we are to have all the upheaval this will entail, is it not worth contemplating doing something a little more radical?" A supreme court was there to bridge the gap between law and society and to protect democracy. She argued that it could be confined to cases of constitutional importance, on human rights, devolution, Europe, international treaties and perhaps adding in those ordinary cases where a serious inconsistency had arisen between the UK's jurisdictions. Such a transformation would raise an argument for fundamental change in composition. It was commonplace for members of other supreme courts to come from much wider professional backgrounds than the law lords. As a consequence, the style of judgments might change and be more comprehensible.

Professor John Bell, writing in the same collection, complained that there had been no attempt at strategic thinking. "It is constitutional reform by way of incremental change." Considering continental supreme courts, he raised these questions (paraphrased):

1. Why have a single Supreme Court? European courts have specialist panels and some jurisdictions have separate courts to apply and interpret administrative law. Do we need a larger range of expertise? Is there a case for a specialist reporting judge?
2. How should it act as the authoritative interpreter of the law? The principal role of other supreme courts is to quash, rather than re-decide, wrongly decided cases. The suggestion of a referral for a preliminary ruling on a point of law (like the Court of Justice of the EU) was dismissed in the consultation paper without discussion but this might be a more efficient way of securing decisions on significant points of law. If the court was to be limited to difficult or important points of law, should these not be paid for by public funding?
3. Was it to be a constitutional court? Under the devolution legislation, abstract review of legislation is permitted. On the other hand, the European Convention is pervasive. It might be difficult to separate out constitutional cases.
4. Should it give advisory opinions? Some European supreme courts did. The concept was not alien to our courts, as they could give declaratory rulings.
5. How did it relate institutionally to law reform? The Swedish Supreme Court could make suggestions for law reform, technically scrutinise Bills and comment on proposed reforms. The annual reports of French supreme courts make suggestions for law reform.
6. What would be its place within the judiciary? European supreme courts used younger judges as judicial assistants, helping them to learn judicial technique.

6–016 Many more opinions were expressed on court composition and the selection of judges. We return to this in Ch.14. The Bill was passed as the Constitutional Reform Act 2005, after months of Parliamentary scrutiny, debate and amendment. Part 3 provided for a UK Supreme Court, and transferred to it the judicial functions of the Appellate Committee of the House of Lords and the devolution jurisdiction of the Judicial Committee of the Privy Council (JCPC). It opened in October 2009. It consists of 12 Justices appointed by her Majesty. It has a President and Deputy. The others are called Justices of the Supreme Court. They are not lords but given the courtesy title "Lord" or "Lady". The law lords were the first Justices. Selection and appointment is detailed in Pt 3 of the Act, and discussed in Ch.14. The bench should generally consist of an uneven number of judges and a minimum of three. Supplementary acting judges may be appointed, drawn from the CA or equivalent in Scotland and Northern Ireland and others. For instance, Lord Judge CJ and Lord Neuberger MR sat with them. The court may appoint and hear from a special adviser. The rules are made by the President, with a view to securing that the court is "accessible fair and efficient" and they must be "both simple and simply expressed". The Lord Chancellor appoints a

Chief Executive, in consultation with the President, and the President appoints other staff. The Lord Chancellor (Minister of Justice) is responsible for providing appropriate resources. The building is Middlesex Guildhall, across Parliament Square from the Palace of Westminster. It was very contentious, since the law lords wanted a dedicated new building, not a converted Crown Court. It annoyed building historians and conservationists, since they consider its interiors to have been one of the most important examples of gothic revivalist architecture (SAVE 2006).

The Act lays down the rules on precedent. An appeal from one jurisdiction in the UK is not binding on the courts of another UK jurisdiction so a Scottish appeal is not binding on England and Wales. In devolution proceedings, however, all cases are binding throughout the UK, except on the court itself. The statute is silent on the details of procedure and, indeed, on the court's power to select cases it wishes to hear, so the Justices are free to devise their own practice. The transformation into the UKSC made the law lords think about their procedures. For example, I have noted the following points, gleaned from my observations, discussions with UKSC Justices (casually and in the course of research), and the many articles listed in the bibliography below.

- They are now more inclined to sit as a panel of seven or nine, though this is the continuation of a law lords' trend. This can be seen from case reports on their website though the percentage of such cases declined again from 2013.
- They are endeavouring to give more unified judgments, though this does not always work. There was a debate raging about unified judgments. This was discussed in Ch.2.
- They are more ready to hear interveners, giving them each a maximum of 15 minutes' argument.
- One aim is that the UKSC should be much more accessible to the public and they are probably one of the most transparent and user-friendly courts in the world. They actively welcome visitors and have a really useful website, with details of upcoming cases and excellent press releases summarising their judgments. The court attracts many visitors and they are proud of their TripAdvisor rating. They have a dedicated YouTube channel, though there is astonishingly little media interest, given that they can make use of the continuous TV feed, for free.
- All Justices may now comment on applications for leave to appeal, though these are still determined in secret by three Justices, as they were in the law lords. Critics complain that there is still no public list of *reasoned* decisions on permission to appeal and parties' written submissions are not made public.
- Proper conference rooms now enable them to do a tiny bit of pre-deliberation before case hearings.
- A blog commentary has been established by lawyers.

There was a well-publicised clash of opinions in Autumn 2009 on the nature of the UKSC. Lord Neuberger MR said it might become a constitutional court, with power to overrule legislation. Lord Phillips, its first President, and Lord

6–017

Bingham, previous Senior Law Lord were adamant that it would not. The argument is summed up by Lord Neuberger MR in a 2009 speech.

"In the light of this climate, I have expressed the concern that one unintended consequence of the Supreme Court's creation might be the eventual emergence of a constitutional court; that it would in time consider that it had, like other Supreme Courts, had the power to review the legality of law, to declare Acts of Parliament unconstitutional. Might we see a UK Supreme Court at some time in the future have its own *Marbury v Madison* moment, with a future Supreme Court President declaring like US Chief Justice Marshall, that a particular law was 'repugnant to the constitution' and therefore no law at all. Let me be clear I am not saying that this will or that it should happen. I am saying it may happen. Many eminent people, Lord Phillips and Lord Bingham among them, say that it won't, and they may well be right … Section 40(5) of the Constitutional Reform Act 2005 could imply a power to review the constitutionality of statutes. It provides that the Supreme Court 'has power to determine any question necessary to be determined for the purposes of doing justice in an appeal to it under any enactment.' What if the question is whether an Act of Parliament is contrary to a fundamental right, a constitutional right? It might, I suppose, be argued that this provides more than the US Constitution does as a guide as to whether constitutional judicial review lies within the ambit of the Supreme Court" (paras 23–24).

The transformation of the law lords into a UKSC has provoked a large amount of academic commentary. For a synopsis of this material and empirical research on the way the top court works, including interviews with and observations of the Justices, see Ch.15 of Darbyshire, *Sitting in Judgment: The Working Lives of Judges* (2011). See also Darbyshire (2015).

6.   THE COURT OF JUSTICE OF THE EU

6–018   This is described in the chapter on EU law.

7.   THE EUROPEAN COURT OF HUMAN RIGHTS

6–019   This is described in Ch.4. Remember it is totally separate from the EU.

8.   THE JUDICIAL COMMITTEE OF THE PRIVY COUNCIL

6–020   The JCPC was established in 1833, by the Judicial Committee Act. It is composed of Privy Councillors who have held or now hold high judicial office, mostly the UKSC Justices. It sat in Downing Street but moved to the Supreme Court building in 2009. Its primary job is as the ultimate appeal court from some UK overseas territories (such as the Cayman Islands) and Crown dependencies (Jersey, Guernsey and the Isle of Man) and from some Commonwealth states. In 2003, New Zealand withdrew from the JCPC's jurisdiction and created its own supreme court, having debated it for 100 years. The Committee hears appeals from certain ecclesiastical and domestic courts and tribunals in England and Wales, such as the Disciplinary Committee of the Royal College of Veterinary

Surgeons. It acquired jurisdiction over devolution issues in 1998 but lost that to the UKSC in 2009. Each case must be heard by a "board" of three to five, although one group of exceptional cases in 2004, on the constitutionality of the Jamaican death penalty, was decided by a board of nine. It usually consists of five UKSC Justices. Its civil work is varied.

9.   OTHER CIVIL COURTS

Ecclesiastical courts

They exercise control over the Church of England clergy. In each diocese there is   6–021
a consistory court, or equivalent, the judge (Chancellor) of which is a barrister or
a judge appointed by the bishop. Appeal lies to the Arches Court of Canterbury or
the Chancery Court of York, and further appeal lies to the JCPC.

Court of Protection

Under the Mental Capacity Act 2005, the Court of Protection is a superior court   6–022
of record, with a President, VP and specialised circuit and district judges, sitting
in London and various provincial centres.

The Coroner's Court

The Coroner's Court is used to inquire (by an inquest) into unexplained deaths.   6–023
Its proceedings are inquisitorial, unlike those of a court. The coroner may, and
sometimes must, call a jury of seven to eleven, to return a verdict as to the cause
of death. The coroner must be legally or medically qualified. In 2003, the
Government published a fundamental review of the coronial system and in 2004
started a programme of reform, taking account of case law on coroners'
proceedings that had arisen under the Convention, described in Ch.4 on human
rights. The Review recommended:

- all coroners should be legally qualified;
- inquests should be held into deaths in custody, traumatic workplace deaths, public transport crashes and certain deaths of children;
- exceptionally complex or contentious inquests should be conducted by a circuit judge or High Court judge;
- the outcome should be a factual account of the cause and circumstances of death and an analysis of whether there were systemic failings;
- coroners should report findings swiftly to any relevant body;
- families should have a right to meet the investigator and be kept informed;
- juries should be used in most cases where art.2 of the Convention is engaged, such as deaths in custody.

By January 2005, the new system for these penetrating, inquiry-like inquests was in use. In 2007–2008 a high profile inquest into the deaths of Princess Diana and Dodi Al-Fayed was conducted by Scott Baker LJ and a jury and in 2010–2011, Hallett LJ presided over the "London 7/7 bombings" inquest.

The Employment Appeal Tribunal

6–024   This was established by the Employment Protection Act 1975 to hear appeals from decisions of Industrial Tribunals (now employment tribunals), in particular those relating to unfair dismissal, equal pay and redundancy. The composition of the court for a hearing is one High Court judge, or a "ticketed" circuit judge, sitting with two lay people who have specialised employment knowledge. It sits at the level of the High Court. This means its decisions are not subject to judicial review. Appeals on points of law go direct to the Court of Appeal.

10.   ARGUMENTS ABOUT COURT MANAGEMENT: JUDGES V GOVERNMENT

6–025   Note the quotation from Magna Carta that heads this chapter. Judges, the Civil Justice Council and lawyers are highly critical of successive governments' policy to make the civil courts self-funding. There are also pockets of severe problems about court facilities of all types, understaffing and poor IT, caused by radical cuts in funding. For a picture of the dismal state of the impoverished courts see empirical research reported in Ch.17 of Darbyshire (2011). There have been more severe cuts in funding since then.

   Since the 1990s, governments have thought that a good solution to lack of money is for court users to pay for the real cost of the courts. Judges, however, strongly feel that the courts should be run as a public service. In a 1997 speech, Sir Richard Scott, head of the Chancery Division, said the idea that the civil courts should be self-financing was "indefensible from a constitutional point of view". In 2002, Lord Woolf CJ accused the Government of "flawed thinking". No other country had such a policy. Its effects were "pernicious and dangerous". In 2003, Mance LJ said that civil justice would never pay for itself. In New Zealand and Australia, fee income paid for less than half the cost. High fees put people off bringing their cases to court and would mean that commercial cases would subsidise family cases. Nevertheless, MoJ research published in 2014 concluded that "participants bringing civil and family cases to court typically felt that court fees were affordable, and they would not have been deterred from starting court proceedings if court fees had been set at … higher levels". This is not borne out by statistics. Lord Briggs emphasised in his 2016 report that a recent increase in civil court fees for multitrack (complex) cases had caused a significant drop in claims. Fees continue to increase and critics continue to complain. In 2016, the Ministry of Justice went ahead with a 500 per cent increase in fees for immigration and asylum claims, despite criticism by the reforming judge Jackson LJ, in his 2016 book, *The Reform of Civil Litigation*. In his 2016 Annual Report, Thomas LCJ expressed concern that hikes in court fees would deny access to justice and put off international litigants bringing their commercial cases to London. In a 2015 speech, he had said that they imperilled the principle in Magna Carta, at the opening of this chapter. The Parliamentary select committee on

Justice published a report in 2016/17 on *Courts and Tribunals Fees* and the Ministry of Justice responded in November 2016.

At the same time, judges are frustrated at poor court facilities in every respect. Their IT provision still does not equate with that recommended by Lord Woolf in his 1996 review of civil procedure, *Access to Justice*. In a 2004 speech, Brooke LJ said he had spent 19 years promoting IT in the courts. In 2007, on the BBC news, Judge Paul Collins, of the Central London Civil Justice Centre said: "We are operating on the margins of effectiveness, and with further cuts looming we run the risk of bringing about a real collapse in the service." In a 2008 *Review of the Administration of the Courts*, the Lord Chief Justice complained that the courts suffered from a serious shortage of judges, a high turnover of under-paid staff, unreliable statistical information and continuing IT problems. Nevertheless, civil court fees were ramped up dramatically in 2008. The cost of taking child care proceedings rose from £150 to £5,225 so local authority applications to protect children at risk reduced by 25 per cent. By 2009, there was a £90 million shortfall in collection of fees. The maintenance backlog in courts amounted to £200 million. In 2014, in the *Chancery Modernisation Review*, Biggs LJ called for better IT. In his 2016 *Civil Courts Structure Review* he said there had been a serious under-investment in civil justice outside London. There was a lack of access to justice because of cost, a reliance on "the tyranny of paper" and obsolete and inadequate IT, and a shortage of judges. Gross LJ, the outgoing Senior Presiding Judge said in a September 2016 speech:

"In terms of funding for the courts, there has been a 25% cut between 2010 – 2015…636 buildings in 2011 have reduced to 471 by March 2015. Finally, HMCTS staff numbers have reduced from 22,000 in 2009/10 to 17,000 in 2014/15…there has been a painful loss of institutional knowledge flowing from the departure of some very experienced managers and the downgrading of some posts."

There have been decades of complaint that London's commercial courts had inadequate facilities and this risked losing international business litigation from London to foreign destinations. Until 2011, the Commercial Court sat in office blocks around the Royal Courts of Justice and in St. Dunstan's house, nearby, described by one judge as "a public disgrace", because of its cramped courtrooms and lack of waiting and consultation facilities. The London business community shared the judges' frustration. Judges' IT systems were extremely poor, compared with those of large London law firms. The court attracts foreigners in to use London's lawyers. In 2005, Lord Phillips MR, said that the number of trials had recently dropped by one third thanks to the availability of better facilities in Amsterdam, Dublin and elsewhere. At long last, the spangly new Rolls Building was opened in 2011. It houses the Business and Property Courts. It claims to be the world's biggest business court. In his 2012 report, Lord Chief Justice Judge said:

6–026

"Its presence underpins the City of London's position as the world's pre-eminent financial centre for both international and national dispute resolution and spearheads the contribution of some £25.6 billion to the gross national product made by the provision of legal activities."

But by 2014, the Minister of Justice was required to cut the Ministry's budget by a further £2.5 billion, having cut it by billions since 2010. He said the Government's policy on fees had been one of "full costs recovery" but that had not been working as intended so court fees would rise again. (There is, incidentally, a fee remission system for all courts. People with low incomes can get full or partial waivers of court fees.) Very importantly, at the same time, he announced a reform programme for IT, buildings and working practices, costing £75 million a year for five years from 2015, in order to save £100 million per year. Court users should, in future, only need to attend a court or tribunal where absolutely necessary. They will increase digital working and allow users to complete forms and make payments online. His remarks, in a letter to all judges and court staff *looked* as if he was responding to some of the judges' persistent criticisms.

> "*The rule of law and the economy*
> Citizens, businesses and other organisations and individuals within the UK rely on our justice system to uphold the rule of law, enforce their rights, provide timely access to justice and support and enable enterprise. Implementation of the Reform Programme will also help to maintain the UK's competitiveness internationally in providing legal services, supporting the already significant contribution that the legal sector makes to the country's economy."(28 March 2014.)

6–027   The reform programme is underway, as I write, in 2017. In the 2016 vision paper, *Transforming our Justice System*, the Ministry of Justice promised £970 million to modernise the courts and transfer all case management to an online system.

There is, however, another problem about access to justice, apart from high civil court fees and lack of facilities: the loss of localised justice. The current reform programme will make this worse. At the lower levels of the court structure, judges complain that court closures reduce public access to justice. The Ministry of Justice always portrays this as a benefit but by concentrating courts in a few larger centres, it is difficult and expensive for parties, witnesses, lawyers and other court users to get to the few remaining courts. In the 1970s, there were over 400 magistrates' courts. One of the vital advantages of lay justices used to be their familiarity with their locality, for instance, scenes of crime. In 2002, John Killah, writing in *The Times*, complained that 110 local courts had closed in the previous 10 years. It was already difficult enough to get witnesses to turn up to court, without making it worse. Kingston people petitioned the Queen and fended off plans to close their magistrates' court, which has sat in Kingston since 1230 but in 2011, the Minister of Justice closed it. Courts are sometimes replaced with modern combined court centres. This is because the old buildings lack adequate facilities, such as access for the disabled and consultation rooms. Sadly, some of the grand old courthouses are listed buildings, where even the interiors are listed and cannot be altered so some are left to rot. SAVE Britain's Heritage reported on the problem in 2004. Eight hundred courts had closed since 1945. Despite protests, the Lord Chancellor announced, in 2005, the closure of the historic and iconic Bow Street Magistrates' Court (1879) and its famous police station next door, home of the first police service, the Bow Street Runners. Oscar Wilde, Reggie Kray and Dr Crippen all appeared before the court.

In 2011, matters took a dramatic turn for the worse for those who emphasise the important of localised justice. Following consultation, the Ministry announced on 14 December 2010, the closure of 49 County Courts and 93 magistrates' courts. They claimed they would save £41 million and may make £38 million from the sale of assets. The Ministry said:

> "Her Majesty's Courts Service currently operates out of 530 courts, many of which do not meet the needs of modern communities. Their number and location does not reflect recent changes in population, workload or transport and communication links over the many years since they were originally opened ... Some courts lack appropriate facilities for victims and witnesses such as separate waiting areas, do not have secure facilities for prisoners, or are not accessible to disabled court users, limiting the type of case that can be heard."

The Ministry said that magistrates' courts sat for 64 per cent of their available time and County Courts sat on average for 130 days per year. Senior Presiding Judge, Goldring LJ, drew attention to a series of "significant errors" in the proposal. For instance, Abergavenny MC was listed for closure, because it was said not to have been used since 1999, yet it was refurbished and re-opened in 2010. He said that poor public transport meant many court users would not be able to get to court before 10.00 am. Highlighting the impact of closing 93 magistrates' courts, is the Magistrates' Association National Response to Consultation on Court Closures, 2010, and see news media from 2010. In response to a freedom of information request, the Law Society exposed the fact that £2.5 million per year was being spent on maintaining closed court buildings. John Fassenfelt, chairman of the Magistrates' Association, said that magistrates were having to travel long distances. Some magistrates had chosen to leave the Bench (Hyde 2012). On 11 February 2016, in a written statement to Parliament, the Ministry of Justice said 86 courts were being closed because 48 per cent of the 460 court buildings were only used for half their hearing time. In 2015, the Chief Executive of Her Majesty's Courts and Tribunal Service said the Service spent a third of its budget on buildings maintenance. The impact assessments of these closures say that people will be able to "appear" in court via video link so will not need to travel much. In 2016, the *Guardian* reported that a whistleblowing district judge was suing the Ministry of Justice for the harm she suffered as a consequence of court closures and increasing workload. The 2016 Justice Committee report on the role of magistrates, discussed in Ch.15, recommended that the government should ensure that 90 per cent of court users can reach the nearest court by public transport in an hour. A novel suggested solution to the loss of localism caused by court closures that has been repeatedly made in 2016–2017, including in Briggs LJ's Review, is the idea of pop-up courts. In a fascinating and unusual 2016 study of "Attitudes to Justice in a Rural Community", Newman reported that, of the 163 courts closed in 2010–2015, only 52 had been sold. The Law Society had rebutted the Ministry's argument that courts were accessible to most people within one hour's travel. IT systems were not in place to substitute virtual hearings. Given that most people never need to go to court, it is not surprising that many of his Welsh interviewees did not know where their local court was and were unaware of proposed court closures but, along with police station closures and so on, it was seen as the loss of another

6–028

piece of history and community. The loss of police presence caused much more concern. As magistrates, the Law Society and family lawyers repeatedly point out, the people who will find it most difficult to travel to court are those on low incomes and the vulnerable (Bowcott 2016), as I explained at the opening of this chapter.

6–029   As we will see in the next chapter, on criminal courts, and in Ch.12 on criminal procedure, the House of Commons Public Accounts Committee produced a forthright and alarming report on efficiency, in May 2016, including an attack on HM Courts and Tribunals Service for not having a credible plan for producing value for money from its estate.

There is yet another criticism of court administration. New courts vary in design and there have been ample examples of design defects which have delayed court openings or irritated judges, court users and court staff, such as in South Wales in 2004–2005. For instance, some courts have jury boxes facing public galleries. Bizarrely, the *Court Standards Design Guide* was only published as recently as 2004 and some courts opened from 2011 do not comply with it. The guide follows a key recommendation of the Auld Review 2001. All new Crown Courts, County Courts and magistrates' courts should now have a standard layout. The guide should ensure better access for all users, including the disabled and parents with young children. It recommends separate waiting areas for witnesses and defendants. Court designers and architects are expected to incorporate IT such as video links, video conferencing, email, in-court intranet and public display screens in their designs.

In a 2016 working party report, *What is a Court?* The pressure group JUSTICE made recommendations which seem to me to be the only logical conclusion following court closures and the promise of digital by default: flexible justice spaces for crime, family, civil and tribunal hearings, in "flagship", "local" and pop-up courts. Thus we return back the clock to when the quarter sessions and visiting assizes sat in the local Guildhall...

11.   OPEN JUSTICE?

6–030   At my time of writing, Summer 2017, one of the huge question marks over the current radical plans to transform civil, criminal and family proceedings into a virtual world, is how on earth justice is to be kept open to the public. At the same time, research in 2016 showed a 40 per cent drop in court reporting since 2012 (Robins).

As Lord Neuberger pointed out in a 2011 speech, the principle of openness is central to English justice and the concept of the rule of law and goes back to "time immemorial", i.e. before 6 July 1189. In a democracy, government, including the judiciary, derives its authority from the people. Members of the public should, therefore, have a right to attend court. After all, justice is administered on their behalf and paid for by the taxpayer. Public scrutiny is an incentive for judges and other court professionals to behave politely, fairly and competently. It should encourage consistency in the conduct of proceedings and in the decisions made, such as sentencing. Openness and approachability should encourage civil litigants to take their cases to court, thus enhancing access to justice. In criminal cases, if the apprehension, conviction and sentencing of offenders is to have any generally deterrent effect then they must be reported, locally and nationally.

Furthermore, most international judicial instruments emphasise the litigant's right to a public trial. Of course, a civil litigant may not want publicity, hence the popularity of arbitration and other forms of alternative dispute resolution, described in Ch.11. Nevertheless, art.6(1) of the European Convention on Human Rights (right to a fair trial) provides:

> "In the determination of his civil rights and obligations or of any criminal charge against him, everyone is entitled to a fair and public hearing within a reasonable time by an independent and impartial tribunal established by law. Judgment shall be pronounced publicly but the press and public may be excluded from all or part of the trial in the interests of morals, public order or national security in a democratic society, where the interests of juveniles or the protection of the private life of the parties so require, or to the extent strictly necessary in the opinion of the court in special circumstances where publicity would prejudice the interests of justice."

Some proceedings are closed to the public. Where a defendant is refused bail in a criminal case by magistrates and applies to the Crown Court, he appears before a judge in chambers, as he is technically innocent, pre-trial. Reporting restrictions are imposed, under the Contempt of Court Act 1981, in some other Crown Court proceedings. The youth court, in the magistrates' court, is closed to members of the public, to protect the young defendant (aged 10–17). Proceedings may be reported but the youngster and all child witnesses will not be named, unless the justices or district judge give exceptional permission.

Procedure in all civil courts is regulated by the Civil Procedure Rules 1998 **6–031** (CPR). Rule 39.2: states that "(1) The general rule is that a hearing is to be in public". Under (3), a hearing, or any part of it, may be in private if publicity would defeat its object, or it involves national security, or confidential information, or it is necessary to protect a patient or child, or for various other reasons, or where the court considers it necessary, "in the interests of justice". The Rules direct the judge to art.6 of the Convention. In *Al Rawi v Security Service* (2010), the CA held that was not open to a court to use a closed procedure to examine the defendant's evidence in the course of an ordinary civil trial. In this case, former Guantanamo Bay inmates, including Moazzam Begg and Binyam Mohamed were suing the UK Government in tort, claiming it had been complicit in their torture. Lord Neuberger MR relied on the common law, not art.6. It was a fair trial (natural justice) requirement for a party and their lawyer to see and hear all the evidence and argument in open court. In principle, a litigant should know the reasons why he has won or lost his case and this should enable the judiciary to provide sufficient reasons. Trials should be conducted and judgment delivered in public. A party was entitled to know the elements of his opponent's case in advance and of the documents in his control. These rules were so "embedded in the common law" that no judge should override them in an ordinary civil claim without parliamentary authority. Also, the CPR provided no authority for a closed material procedure and it was precluded by the overriding objective of the Rules. See further Gibb and Wellington. It was upheld by the Supreme Court: (2011). The Government hastily promoted The Justice and Security Bill (now Act) s.6

through Parliament to provide for closed material procedures in civil proceedings. In 2016, the ECtHR said that a terror suspect's art.5 rights Convention right were not infringed by closed proceedings, because of the threat of an imminent terrorist attack: *Sher v UK*.

Bearing in mind that small claims and most other proceedings are heard by district judges in the County Court, in the judge's own room ("chambers"), these all took place behind closed doors until 1999. They have now had to be opened up to the public, because this is required by art.6 and by the Civil Procedure Rules. I suggest that the present position is far from satisfactory, however. Many civil district judges have key coded security doors on their chambers so a member of the public is likely to be deterred from asking if they could watch proceedings, even if they were aware that they are open to the public.

6–032   One of the greatest anomalies was related to family proceedings, the closed nature of which became very contentious, since 2000. While these were open in the magistrates' court, identical cases in the County Court and High Court were closed to the public and unreported. This is a reversal of the position in the early twentieth century, when the newspapers would print salacious details exposed in divorce cases. Hewson explained that the judges of the time thought such cases ought to be open, as a matter of principle. In *McPherson v McPherson* (1936), the Privy Council said that a divorce pronounced in private was voidable, because the judge had denied the public their right to be present. Lord Blansbourgh said "publicity is the authentic hallmark of judicial, as distinct from administrative procedure". In *Ambard v Att Gen for Trinidad and Tobago* (1936), Lord Atkin remarked "Justice is not a cloistered virtue". The history of publicity in family cases and the inconsistent position in different courts was described in *Allan v Clibbery* (2002). The judges recognised in this and other cases that the courts have to effect a balancing exercise between the right to respect for family life and privacy in art.8 of the European Convention and the right to freedom of expression in art.10. They remarked that it is widely recognised in European jurisprudence that the balance in children cases is in favour of confidentiality, see *B v UK*, *P v UK* (2001). In *Allan v Clibbery*, Allan, described as a prominent businessman, lost his appeal against his former mistress being permitted to disclose to the *Daily Mail* and Hong Kong media the details of their private lives that came to light in the property dispute that arose after their relationship broke down. It had become apparent at the hearing that she was one of several mistresses and the appellant claimed to have paid her to be at his disposal, for sex. In *Blunkett v Quinn* (2004), Ryder J decided to deliver in open court his judgment in a case involving the then Home Secretary, David Blunkett and his ex-lover and her child. He said he did this in order to correct false information already in the public domain, in the publicity surrounding the case.

In 2004–2005, many fathers' groups, such as the aggressive Fathers 4 Justice, represented by Spiderman, Batman and other demonstrators, argued that more family proceedings should be open to the public. They were aggrieved at what they saw as the courts' failure to enforce contact orders allowing them to see their children where a mother disobeys court orders. They considered that publicity would expose the unreasonableness, as they saw it, of disobedient mothers and ineffectual judges. Some judges also argued for greater publicity, for different reasons. For example, Thorpe LJ, a passionate and devoted, pioneering family judge, was quoted by Gibb, in 2005, as considering that it would be "healthy" to remove privacy. Exposing the system to public scrutiny would reveal the family justice system to be in good condition. He reminded us that in Scotland, family proceedings have always been in public. "Campaigners say that the judges have a vested interest in maintaining privacy because it enables them to carry on making these 'wicked' decisions in private". In 2005, the House of Commons Constitutional Affairs Select Committee published a report, *Family Justice: the Operation of the Family Courts*. They concluded that a greater degree of transparency was required in family courts. They suggested the press and public should be allowed into the courts subject to the judge's discretion to exclude them.

In 2008, following consultation, the Minister of Justice announced that **6–033** accredited media would be able to visit all family courts, removing inconsistencies. The courts are able to restrict access, for the welfare of children or safety of parties. A pilot project was then started to

> "place anonymised judgments online, give parties involved a copy of the judgment and look at the practicalities of retaining judgments so that children involved in proceedings can access them when they are older".

A fresh consultation was launched in 2008, called *Family Justice in View*. It proposed to allow parties to disclose information about their case to advisors (including MPs) while a case was still in progress and to allow "more information to be made accessible to the public about the way the family courts work and how decisions are made" (MoJ website). In 2010 the Ministry of Justice announced that parts of the Children, Schools & Families Bill were aimed at encouraging media attendance at family courts. Research showed that rule changes in April 2009, permitting journalists to report anonymised proceedings had had some impact—25 per cent of court staff said journalists had attended at their court. The Bill would permit broader reporting of family proceedings but included an indefinite ban on identifying the parties. A pilot scheme operated at three courts, publishing the results of family cases on the internet. The Bill was enacted in 2010. In the meantime, there was an enormous amount of comment (see bibliography). In 2009, Geoffrey Robertson QC said that although the courts were opened to journalists from that April, no-one went into family courts because they "could not report anything" but it had encouraged people to settle their disputes because they did not want their affairs exposed to the public. James Munby LJ was always outspoken on family justice. Now that he is President of the Family Division he has issued draft guidance, in 2013, reversing the 2005 position. Judgments *should* be published unless there are compelling reasons not to. Judgments are now published on Bailii (British and Irish Legal Information Institute) but this is meaningless because the public are unaware of this website. The *Guardian* reported in December 2016 that Munby LJ would announce in Spring 2017 an experiment with public family hearings and releasing documents to the media. This provokes strong arguments. Some women's groups maintain that the secrecy of the family courts has allowed their abusing partners to carry on the abuse but most family lawyers argue that openness will be harmful to vulnerable people. The Court of Appeal has reiterated the principle that the default position in cases involving children is privacy, the reverse of the normal presumption of openness in court proceedings: *In Re W (Children) (Care Proceedings: Publicity)* (2016).

The courts are a source of free, public entertainment and education. Until the late twentieth century, public galleries were routinely populated by local onlookers. Now that TV and the internet are more fun, courts are rarely visited, with exceptions such as the great international tourist attraction, The Old Bailey, and certain cases in the Royal Courts of Justice. In the 1980s, the Bar Council campaigned to televise court proceedings. They gave up. In 1994, Bingham MR spoke in favour, while an experiment was being conducted in Scotland. In 2004, Falconer LC launched a consultation and at the same time, an experiment started in recording the proceedings of the CA (Civil Division). Footage was not broadcast but used for evaluation. With the exception of the UKSC, it has been illegal since 1925 to take photographs or record proceedings in court, or even to make drawings. Court artists, whose depictions appear in the news media, have to leave the courtroom and sketch from memory. Mohammed Zahir, who used his mobile phone to take pictures of defendants in the dock of Birmingham Crown Court, was jailed for nine months in 2004.

6–034 In the USA, all 50 states permit cameras in some courts and 39 allow them into trial courts. Court TV broadcasts high profile trials. Some are broadcast internationally, such as the Rodney King beatings trials and the OJ Simpson trial in the 1990s but Falconer LC remarked, in 2004, "We don't want our courts turning into US-style media circuses . . . Justice should be seen to be done but our priority must be that justice is done." Judge LJ (later LCJ), took part in a seminar debating broadcasting the courts in 2005. He said he was deeply committed to open justice but was worried that witnesses would be deterred and for that reason, he distinguished televising the courts from televising Parliament. Also in 2005, the Government announced the results of its consultation on broadcasting the courts. Opinion was divided but there was a very strong view that witnesses, victims and jurors should not be filmed. The second murder trial of Sion Jenkins at the Old Bailey in July 2005 saw a new form of instant court reporting. Sky News broadcast an almost instantaneous transcript of Rafferty J's summing up. Under a protocol agreed by the Lord Chancellor and broadcasters, the latter may, with the judge's permission, make news from the live feed from the court stenographer's transcript. Under a 2011 practice direction, people can, in certain circumstances, send live text, such as email and Twitter, from the courtroom. Interestingly, the Constitutional Reform Act 2005 exempts the UKSC from the ban on photography. They make available a free broadcast feed of all proceedings, for anyone who wants to make use of it and two TV documentaries on the UKSC were broadcast in 2011. By 2013 the lead Justice's five-minute summing up in each case is now on a dedicated YouTube channel.

In a 2011 lecture, Neuberger MR advocated televising civil hearings. From 2013, delegated legislation permits the broadcasting of Court of Appeal proceedings. Broadcasters have to cover the cost. Five CA courtrooms are wired. The media seldom use this facility. In 2016, filming of the judge's sentencing remarks was piloted in eight Crown Court venues, but not broadcast.

As proceedings are rapidly being digitised and conducted online, following the 2016 "vision paper", *Transforming our Justice System*, and the Briggs Review, this raised the problem of how to keep them open to the public and transparent. The response appears in the Ministry press release announcing the (now defunct) Prisons and Courts Bill 2017:

> "To ensure justice is also open and seen to be done, video booths will be installed in courts across England and Wales to allow members of the media and public to observe virtual hearings from court buildings anywhere in the country. Lists and results of cases that have taken place online, as well as those concluded in a physical courtroom, will also be available digitally."

This conjures a vision of the lone observer in a booth, a bit like a voyeur of a sheep-bestiality DVD in an Amsterdam shop. As almost no-one watches real courts nowadays, it is difficult to visualise anyone bothering to do this. Since the 1980s, courts have been holding open days to try and help the public to understand the courts. The initiative started in the magistrates' courts and has spread to the Crown Court and combined court centres. Visitors can explore the courtrooms and prison vans and participate in mock sentencing exercises. We should be strongly in favour of this and of televising the courts because research has shown that members of the public are shockingly ignorant of their justice system and this should be a cause of concern since their taxes pay for a system that purports to be administering justice on their behalf.

Chapter 10 continues the theme of civil justice.

Bibliography

The articles on the UKSC remain especially valuable. Those by Professor Robert   6–035
Stevens, Baroness Hale, Sir Thomas Legg and Professor John Bell all appear in a special issue of *Legal Studies*, on the proposed Supreme Court, Vol.24, March 2004.

J. Battle, "Filming courts: time to lift the ban" *The Times*, 3 October 2006.

Lord Bingham was being interviewed by Boris Johnson in *The Spectator*, May 2002.

Rt Hon. Lord Bingham of Cornhill CJ, "A New Supreme Court for the United Kingdom", 1 May 2002, The Constitution Unit, University College, London; *http://www.ucl.ac.uk/spp/publications/unit-publications/90.pdf*, and see his 2001 speech "The Evolving Constitution", Law Society, 4 October 2001.

Sir William Blair, "Contemporary Trends in the Resolution of International Commercial and Financial Disputes", speech, 2016.

Lord Justice Briggs, *Civil Courts Structure Review: Final Report* 2016. The opening quotation of this chapter is from p.115).

O. Bowcott, "Whistleblower judge: austerity politics have made courts dangerous" *The Guardian*, 23 January 2016; "Ministry of Justice to Close 86 Courts in England and Wales", *The Guardian*, 11 February 2016.

Council of Europe, *Office of the Lord Chancellor in the constitutional system of the United Kingdom* (2003, Doc. 9798).

P. Darbyshire, *Sitting in Judgment: The Working Lives of Judges* (Oxford: Hart Publishing Ltd, 2011); "The UK Supreme Court—is there anything left to think about?"; (2015) 21(1) *European Journal of Current Legal Issues*, free, online; a later version is in *The UK Supreme Court Yearbook Legal Year 2014–2015* (2015).

Department for Constitutional Affairs, *Constitutional Reform: a Supreme Court for the United Kingdom*, CP 11/03, July 2003 and responses, archived on the Department of Constitutional Affairs website, along with Lord Falconer's press release 296/03.

H. Genn, *The Hamlyn Lectures: Judging Civil Justice* (Cambridge: Cambridge University Press, 2010).

Sir P. Gross, "Providing Sufficient Resources for the Courts and Judiciary as a Fundamental Constitutional Obligation", speech, 19 September 2016.

F. Gibb and J. Killah, "Magistrates will be packaged off to vast justice factories in large urban centres", *The Times*, 2 July 2002.

J. Hyde, "News: millions spent on empty court buildings" (2012) L.S. Gaz, 23 February.

Lord Justice Jackson, *The Reform of Civil Litigation* (London: Sweet & Maxwell, 2016).

J. Jaconelli, *Open Justice: A critique of the Public Trial* (Oxford: Oxford University Press, 2002).

JUSTICE, "What is a Court? (2016).

A. Le Sueur, *Building the UK's New Supreme Court: National and Comparative Perspectives* (Oxford: Oxford University Press, 2004).

Lord Mance, "Constitutional Reforms, the Supreme Court and the Law Lords", (2006) 25 *Civil Justice Quarterly* 155–165.

R. Masterman, "A Supreme Court for the United Kingdom: two steps forward, but one step back for judicial independence" [2004] P.L. 48; *Democracy Through Law* (2004).

D. Newman, "Attitudes to Justice in a Rural Community" (2016) 36 LS 591.

N. Padfield, Editorial The Prisons and Courts Bill, [2017] Crim. L.R. 343.

I. Periera and others, *The role of court fees in affecting users' decisions to bring cases to the civil and family courts: a qualitative study of claimants and applicants*, Ministry of Justice, 2014.

Lord Neuberger MR, "Insolvency, internationalism and Supreme Court judgments", speech, November 11, 2009, from para.20; "Is the House of Lords losing part of itself?", speech, December 2009; "Open Justice Unbound?" JSB annual lecture 2011, 16 March 2011, Judiciary website.

G. Robertson was speaking on the Radio 4 *Today* programme, on 30 June 2009.

J. Robins, "The Demise of Court Reporting", (2016) 180 JPN 768 and *Proof*, December 2016, *http://www.thejusticegap.com*

J. Rozenberg, "Britain's new Supreme Court" *The Times Literary Supplement*, 2 September 2009.

Sir Earnest Ryder, Senior President of Tribunals, "The Modernisation of Access to Justice in Times of Austerity", speech, 3 March 2016.

Save Britain's Heritage, *Silence in Court, the future of the UK's historic law courts* (2004); *The Guildhall Testimonial* (2006).

H. Schleiff, "Cameras in courts" (2004) 154 N.L.J. 1745.

Sir Richard Scott's 1997 speech is quoted at (1997) 147 N.L.J. 750.

R. Stevens, *The Independence of the Judiciary* (Oxford: Oxford University Press, 1993); "On being nicer to James and the children" (on independence, countering attacks on Mackay LC) (1994) 144 N.L.J. 1620; "Reform in haste and repent at leisure: Iolanthe, the Lord High Executioner and Brave New World" (2004) 24 *Legal Studies* 1.

Lord Johan Steyn, "The Case for a Supreme Court" (2002) 118 L.Q.R. 392.

Thomas LCJ, "Commercial Justice in the Global Village: the Role of Commercial Courts", Dubai, speech, 1 February 2016; "Dinner for Her Majesty's Judges", speech, Mansion House, 6 July 2016; "Commercial dispute resolution: courts and arbitration", speech, 6 April 2017, and the speeches he cites therein. All are on the Judiciary website.

Transform Justice, *Managing Magistrates' Courts—has central control reduced local accountability?* (2013).

The Magistrate, for articles on magistrates' court closures (and the Magistrates' Association website).

Sir Geoffrey Vos, Chancellor of the High Court, "A Look at the Future for Insolvency and Business Litigation in London", speech, 9 November 2016.

Lord Windlesham, "The Constitutional Reform Act 2005: The Politics of Constitutional Reform Part 2" [2006] *Public Law* 35–57.

Lord Woolf CJ, Squire Centenary Lecture, March 4, 2004, Cambridge, "The Rule of Law and a Change in the Constitution", Judiciary website.

On open family courts: F. Gibb, "Fathers winning battle to have custody hearings in public." *The Times*, 10 January 2005; B. Hewson, "Why have secrecy in the family courts?" (2003) 153 N.L.J. 369; G. Morris, (2008) 158 N.L.J. 750; F. Gibb, *The Times*, 27 April 2009; *The Times* leading article, "In Open Court", April 27, 2009; E. Floyd, (2009) 159 N.L.J. 451; R. Newitt, (2009) 159 N.L.J. 843; T. Roberts and S. J. Boon, (2010) 160 N.L.J. 126; S. Palin, "The Slur of Secrecy" (2007) 157 N.L.J. 1224; E. Harris, (2007) 157 N.L.J. 1225; D. Pannick, "Family courts should be led out of the dark ages" *The Times*, 17 July 2007 and many other news and law journal articles.

Further reading and sources for updating this chapter

Free updates of this book are available on the Sweet & Maxwell website: *http://uklawstudent.thomsonreuters.com*.   **6–036**

Summary and revision: P. Darbyshire, *Nutshells English Legal System*, 10th edn (London: Sweet & Maxwell, 2016).

Architectural heritage, including campaigns against the destruction of old courts: *http://www.savebritainsheritage.org*.

Department of Constitutional Affairs website (the predecessor of the Ministry of Justice for documents to mid-2007), archived in the National Archives.

Her Majesty's Courts and Tribunals Service, especially annual reports of various courts.

Family Justice Council, Judiciary website.

Court of Justice of the EU.

European Court of Human Rights.

Judicial Committee of the Privy Council.

Judges' speeches and annual reports are on the Judiciary website.

Magistrates' Association.

Ministry of Justice website, including Court Statistics and HMCTS pages.

UKSC Blog *http://www.ukscblog.com*.

UKSC on YouTube *http://www.youtube.com/user/UKSupremeCourt*.
UKSC website.

CHAPTER 7

Criminal Courts

"The very idea of a Magistrates' Court is that it should administer summary justice locally." (Lord Judge CJ 2008)

"Here, the closure of Cardigan Magistrates' Court means that there is one court in the whole of Ceredigion, to cover potential users across a distance of 100 miles in each direction." (Newman 2016)

"The government is investing over £850 million to modernise and digitise the courts, and preserve the full majesty of the physical courtroom for cases that require it, in addition to around £250 million to deliver a fully connected criminal courtroom. This will result in savings of £252 million a year for the taxpayer". (Prisons and Courts Bill press release, Ministry of Justice, 20 March 2017. The Bill was dropped but the plan seems to be proceeding.)

The last chapter covered controversial and sweeping plans to digitise civil **7–001** family and criminal courts and the tribunals, following a massive court closure programme. In 2016, the House of Commons Justice Committee reported on the role of magistrates, as discussed in Ch.15 on magistrates. In evidence to them, various people and groups pointed out that many court users lead chaotic lives. One magistrate said that in her area, the level of deprivation was so high that 34 per cent of people did not have access to a car so it was not reassuring that the government claimed that after further closures 98 per cent of locals would be able to access a court within an hour's drive.

The previous chapter also discussed the perpetual argument between judges and government about whether courts should be provided as a public service or funded by court users. The chapter also covered the story of the creation of the UKSC and the issue of open justice. All of those topics are highly relevant to this chapter but not repeated here.

There are two criminal trial courts (courts of original jurisdiction, or "courts of first instance") in England and Wales, the magistrates' court and the Crown Court. Auld LJ, in his *Review of the Criminal Courts of England and Wales* recommended a unified criminal court divided into three tiers, or failing this, a unified courts administration. The first was rejected but this last recommendation was fulfilled there is now a unified HM Courts and Tribunals Service. Part 7 of the Courts Act 2003 defines criminal courts (s.68). The Act is one of the outcomes of the Auld Review. Criminal procedure is examined in Ch.12. In reading this chapter, the reader should cross-refer to the courts diagram, preceding Ch.6.

1. MAGISTRATES' COURTS

7–002   As explained in the previous chapter, in 2011, there were 330 magistrates' courts, although their numbers have diminished to 236 in 2017 because of court closures and bench amalgamations since the 1980s, and 43 more magistrates' courts are threatened with closure. Over 80 per cent of defendants to criminal charges are tried at the magistrates' courts (1.17 million in 2015–2016, according to the Criminal Justice Statistics). It should be obvious from this statistic that magistrates' courts do not deal with trivia, although many members of the public and even lawyers and judges underestimate their importance. Proceedings in the magistrates' court are known as summary proceedings. Trials are called summary trials. Most cases are heard by lay magistrates and the fact that they hear the bulk of criminal cases makes the English legal system unique in this respect, worldwide. Until 1949 these courts were known as police courts and many are or were situated close to police stations. This is unfortunate since it conveys the impression that the court sits at the convenience of the police to distribute punishment in accordance with police evidence. As the police inevitably figure prominently in the magistrates' court, it is not surprising that the public has tended to think of it as the police court (see Darbyshire, "Concern", 1997). Happily, there are not so many uniformed police officers in today's courts as there were prior to 1985. The Prosecution of Offences Act 1985 replaced police prosecutors with Crown Prosecutors and the 1990s saw private security officers replacing police court security officers. Nevertheless, from April 2014, video links were installed into all courtrooms to link them to the police stations so that defendants and police witnesses can "appear" in the courtroom without attending and in reality, as far as the defendant is concerned, the virtual court is now *inside* the police station.

For most people who appear in a criminal court, as a defendant, witness or victim, the court involved will be the magistrates' court. The least serious category of offence is the summary offence. Almost all summary offences must be heard in the magistrates' court. They are all statutorily defined. They include the vast bulk of traffic offences, the most trivial of which many people wrongly assume not to be normal criminal offences. We do not have a third species of law, "violations", as they do in the US. Common assault is a summary offence, as are many regulatory offences, prosecuted by government departments. The category of offences of medium seriousness is called "triable either way" and most of them are tried in the magistrates' court. Here, the defendant may elect trial in the magistrates' court or in the Crown Court, unless the magistrates insist on a Crown Court trial. Most defendants in the "either way" category opt for summary trial in the magistrates' court and one quarter were tried summarily in 2015–2016.

Magistrates' jurisdiction is statutory. They can send an offender to prison for up to six months, or a maximum of twelve months for more than one offence. This was fixed by the Powers of the Criminal Courts (Sentencing) Act 2000 but if the Criminal Justice Act 2003 s.154 ever comes into force, magistrates' sentencing powers will double to one year's imprisonment. At the time of writing, 2017, this seems unlikely. Until 2012, the maximum fine they could impose was £5,000 but this cap was removed by the Legal Aid, Sentencing and Punishment of Offenders Act 2012. The statutory maximum varies between offences. If, after conviction, the bench feels their powers of sentence are inadequate, they may send the offender to the Crown Court for sentencing. A district judge (magistrates' court), sitting alone, generally has the same powers as a bench of two or three lay justices. At the hearing of any case, the bench is assisted by the justices' clerk or, more usually, a court clerk (commonly called a legal adviser). The former and many of the latter are legally qualified. The magistrates' legal adviser may advise the magistrates on the law. Magistrates and their clerks are discussed in Ch.15.

Throughout the nineteenth and twentieth centuries, more and more work has been shifted down onto the shoulders of the magistrates, by reclassifying offences as summary only or by shifting them out of the indictable category into the "triable either way" category. It is a big mistake, therefore, to think of this court as dealing with trivia. Of course, if magistrates' sentencing powers are ever increased, under the 2003 Act, even more work will shift out of the Crown Court and into the magistrates' court. For discussion see Darbyshire "Neglect", 1997. In 2009, virtual courts were being piloted, and from 2012 flexible courts, including weekend courts were piloted, as discussed in Ch.12 on criminal procedure.

The community justice centre

In December 2004, a pilot project commenced, establishing a Community Justice Centre in North Liverpool. The aim in establishing it was to engage the local community in finding solutions to anti-social behaviour, social exclusion and crime. It was modelled on the Red Hook Project in New York. The court started with the jurisdiction of the magistrates' court. It was meant to act as an outreach centre for the local community, using the court building for community activities. It was accompanied by a programme of community consultation and engagement. One of its themes was restorative justice. The first judge was a local circuit judge who was formerly a district judge (magistrates' court). The judge monitored the progress of the sentences passed. For more details of the Red Hook project and other models, see Brimacombe. The Liverpool CJC closed in 2014, because of reduced workload. This idea was copied in 10 new centres, including London, Nottingham, Wales, Yorkshire and the South West. Local people help to select the judges.

7–003

Domestic violence courts

There were 140 but one sixth were closed since 2011.

7–004

"The specialist domestic violence court programme promotes a combined approach to tackling domestic violence by the police, the Crown Prosecution Service (CPS), magistrates, courts and probation together with specialist support services for victims." (MoJ, 19 March 2010.)

Mental health courts

7–005 They were piloted at two magistrates' courts in 2009, to identify defendants with mental health issues. The process evaluation was published in September 2010 and found the court "strengthened collaboration between health and criminal justice agencies enabling needs to be addressed at an early stage" (MoJ).

Drugs courts and family drug and alcohol courts

7–006 These commenced with two experimental courts and were expanded. Offenders convicted of low level crime can be sent there for sentencing. The sentencing judge reviews their progress every six weeks (they are drug tested twice weekly). They might get a hug and a bagel from the judge. See Tendler. The Dedicated Drug Courts Pilot Evaluation Process Study was published in 2011 (MoJ research 1/11). They found the courts were perceived as useful, in providing goals and enhancing offenders' self-esteem, making offenders accountable and facilitating agency partnerships. Continuity of the bench (magistrates or DJs) was a key element. Though the courts were helpful, staff and offenders thought courts' ability to reduce reoffending was limited. By 2014, their availability had declined due to court closures and centralisation. There are 13 Family Drug and Alcohol Courts within the Family Courts. The Parliamentary Justice Committee examined the benefits of them in 2016 and received considerable evidence in support of them.

Problem solving courts

7–007 In the 2016 joint vision statement *Transforming our Justice System*, referred to in the last chapter, the Lord Chancellor (Minister of Justice) and senior judges said they wanted to explore the use of problem-solving courts, which tackle the underlying causes of criminal behaviour, such as drug misuse and mental illness. It is a great pity, then, that availability of some of the courts listed above has been reduced. In response, the Centre for Justice Innovation, a charity and think-tank, published *Problem-solving courts: A delivery plan*, calling for the development of 10 criminal courts, from 2017. This was cited and problem-solving courts were strongly supported by the Parliamentary Justice Committee in its 2016 report.

2.   THE YOUTH COURT

7–008 In the UK, the age of criminal responsibility is ten. Ten to seventeen-year-olds are almost all tried in the Youth Court, which is a special court within the magistrates' court, although the majority of young offenders are diverted from the criminal process by the official cautioning scheme, first put on a statutory basis by the Crime and Disorder Act 1998. Notably, the number of young offenders processed through the criminal justice system has fallen dramatically since 2006, with first-time entrants declining by 83 per cent. 66 per cent of first-timers received a caution and were thus diverted from the youth court, in 2015. The bench comprises specially trained lay magistrates (lay justices), who usually sit in mixed gender threesomes, or a district judge (magistrates' court). The predecessor of the court, the juvenile court, was formed in 1908, by the Children Act. It was thought desirable to keep adult defendants separate from juveniles. Ideally, the Act's progenitors would have liked to have seen a separate system of courts for young offenders. Separate courts have never been developed, except in large cities like London, Nottingham, Birmingham and elsewhere, where the caseload warranted it. Instead, it became the habit at smaller courts to convene the juvenile court on a separate day from the adult court. Eventually, this was whittled down to an hour's gap between adult and juvenile courts but this was abandoned. This is a great pity. It seems to have been forgotten that the original aim was to protect children from contact with adult criminals. Recently, the Magistrates' Association expressed disquiet that juveniles were being put into the adult list. The 1908 courts originally dealt with the "deprived" as well as the "depraved". In other words, in addition to criminal cases, it heard civil applications by the local authority, to take the child into care for its own welfare. This civil work was given away to the family proceedings court (in the magistrates' court) when the youth court was created by the Children Act 1989 and it has now gone to the Family Court from 2014 so the youth court now has a purely criminal jurisdiction. Importantly, the public are excluded from the youth court and procedure is more informal than that of the adult court. The youth court has a variety of powers. For example, as well as fining the child and/or parent, it can impose a supervision order, which is like a probation order for children, or order detention and training for up to two years, so magistrates are more powerful in this court than in the adult court.

Only those youngsters who commit "grave crimes" or those tried with an adult may be sent up for trial in the Crown Court (explained in Ch.12). This means something like murder. Auld LJ recommended, in his *Review of the Criminal Courts* (2001), that serious crimes should be heard in a youth court composed of a judge and two youth panel magistrates. In the Courts Act 2003, all judges were given the jurisdiction to sit in the magistrates' court but there are no current plans to carry out Auld LJ's suggestion and remove children from the Crown Court altogether. The Youth Justice Board oversees the youth justice system in England and Wales, including the harvesting and publication of statistics.

3. THE CROWN COURT

The Courts Act 1971, which abolished assizes and quarter sessions, replaced them with one unified Crown Court. England and Wales are divided into six circuits, Midlands, Northern, North Eastern, South Eastern, Wales and Western. There are 76 main Crown Court Centres (plus 15 satellite centres) of three types. First tier centres are visited by High Court judges for serious Crown Court work and High Court civil business (though this is normally heard in County Court trial centres nowadays). Second tier centres are visited by HC judges for Crown Court criminal business only. Third tier centres are not normally visited by a High Court judge. Circuit judges and recorders (part-time judges) sit at all three. At least two presiding High Court judges are appointed to each circuit and they help to organise judicial deployment in the Crown Court. Indictable offences are

7–009

recognised at common law or by statute and are the most serious type of offence. "Triable either way" offences, of medium seriousness, can also be tried at the Crown Court. By Practice Direction, the Lord Chief Justice directs that Crown Court business should be classified into three.

Class 1: the most serious offences are generally tried by a HC judge, unless released by the presiding judge to an authorised ("ticketed") circuit judge. They include treason and murder.

Class 2: these are generally also tried by a HC judge and include manslaughter and rape.

Class 3: these include all other offences and are normally tried by a circuit judge or authorised recorder. They include kidnapping, burglary, grievous bodily harm and robbery.

The Crown Court also hears appeals against conviction and/or sentence from those convicted in the magistrates' court. Appeals are usually heard by a circuit judge and two magistrates. The Crown Court also sentences defendants who have been committed for sentencing by magistrates, after having been summarily convicted of an either-way offence. In 2015–2016, over 86,000 cases were disposed of by the Crown Court. The most famous Crown Court Centre is the Central Criminal Court, known as the "Old Bailey" in the City of London. It has a fascinating and gruesome history over several centuries and is a world famous tourist attraction. It deals with the most serious offences from London and the south of England. About 95 per cent of its workload is heard at other Crown Court Centres, such as Kingston, so it is left with only the most serious cases of murder, fraud, terrorism, rape and so on.

As part of a modernisation programme the Crown Court has been linked to prison service video conferencing facilities so that prisoners can "appear" from secure conditions in preliminary hearings without having to be transported to court. Prisoner transport is notoriously expensive and the cause of frustrating delays. The same technology allows vulnerable witnesses to give evidence from outside the courtroom. Another part of the programme was the installation of XHIBIT which allows all trial participants to track the progress of a case through modern technology, using the internet and sending texts to mobile phones. Witnesses and police officers do not need to wait around in court but can come when needed. During the 1990s the courts endeavoured to make themselves more user-friendly, to court users and visitors. Court buildings contain notices indicating the standards of service that can be expected and detailing related sources of help. Details of how courts have provided better facilities for users are listed in the press releases on the MoJ website. Examples include: training staff in sign language; sending staff into solicitors' offices to learn how the court could improve its service; providing consulting rooms and dedicated Witness Support suites with separate entrances. HMCTS Annual Report gives updates on the modernisation programme. Nevertheless, a 2016 House of Commons Public Accounts Committee report, *Efficiency in the Criminal Justice System*, disclosed a depressing statistical analysis, discussed in Ch.12 on criminal procedure.

4. THE DIVISIONAL COURT OF THE QUEEN'S BENCH DIVISION

This court hears prosecution and defence appeals "by way of case stated" on points of law from the magistrates' courts and the Crown Court, excluding appeals relating to trial on indictment, which go to the Court of Appeal. It conducts judicial reviews of the legality of proceedings in magistrates' courts In doing this it is exercising the High Court's prerogative power to review the legality of proceedings in the lower courts. These are discussed in Ch.6. **7–010**

5. THE COURT OF APPEAL (CRIMINAL DIVISION)

The CA (Criminal Division) (CACD) was established by the Criminal Appeal Act 1966 to replace the Court of Criminal Appeal. Its jurisdiction is contained in the Criminal Appeal Act 1968, as amended by the Criminal Appeal Act 1995 and the Criminal Justice Act 2003. Its work is described in Ch.12. It usually sits only in the Royal Courts of Justice in the Strand but in 1999, Lord Bingham CJ took it to sit in Liverpool and Bristol, and it sat at Snaresbrook in 2002. The court is made up of the Lord Chief Justice, the Vice-President of the Criminal Division, Lords Justices of Appeal, the judges of the Queen's Bench Division and a number of circuit judges specially nominated by the Lord Chief Justice. It normally sits as a bench of three: one Lord Justice of Appeal and two High Court judges, or one Lord Justice of Appeal, one High Court judge and a circuit judge. Sentencing appeals are heard by pairs of HC judges. The jurisdiction of the CACD is: **7–011**

1. to hear appeals against conviction on indictment with the leave of the CA or if the trial judge certifies that the case is fit for appeal (Criminal Appeal Act 1995 s.1);
2. to hear appeals against sentence pronounced by the Crown Court provided that the sentence is not one fixed by law and provided that the court grants leave. An application for leave may be determined by a single judge, but if leave is refused, the appellant can require a full court, i.e. two or more judges to determine the matter;
3. to hear appeals referred to it by the Criminal Cases Review Commission, under the Criminal Appeal Act 1995;
4. to hear appeals against a verdict of "not guilty by reason of insanity" or against findings of fitness and unfitness to plead;
5. to hear an appeal by the prosecution against an acquittal on a point of law at the trial in the Crown Court. This provision involves an application by the Attorney General for the opinion of the court on the point of law and is known as an "Attorney General's Reference". The result cannot affect the acquittal and the defendant is not named in the appeal;
6. to hear an appeal by the prosecutor, again as an "Attorney General's Reference" against a lenient sentence. In this case the court will set out sentencing guidelines for the future but may also increase the actual sentence imposed; and

7.   to hear prosecution appeals against judge's rulings, under the Criminal Justice Act 2003, as described in Ch.12.

The CACD publishes an annual review, providing statistical details of its caseload. It has a big case load and the judges who sit in it are under enormous pressure to deal with long lists of appeals very swiftly. According to the Royal Courts of Justice Statistics, in 2015, it heard 1675 full appeals against conviction (305) or sentence (1370), compared with a peak of 2906 in 2003. It is normal for a bench of three judges to deal with a mixed list of sentencing appeals and applications for leave to appeal all morning (eight cases or more) and a substantive appeal in the afternoon. High Court judges normally sit in the court for a maximum shift of three weeks at a time, as the pressure of work is so great, usually requiring the judges to work long hours into the night and at weekends, reading papers and writing judgements. Bear that in mind the next time you read the law report of a criminal appeal. Even though the workload has decreased, the Annual Report says that the increased number of unrepresented appellants has now had an impact on all aspects of the CACD's work. They aim to face this by giving appellants more guidance and applying stricter case management.

6.   THE UK SUPREME COURT AND THE JUDICIAL COMMITTEE OF THE PRIVY COUNCIL

7–012   The UKSC and its predecessor, the Appellate Committee of the House of Lords, are described in Ch.6. It hears appeals from the CACD and those that have leapfrogged from the High Court. Either prosecutor or defendant may appeal, provided the CA certifies that a point of law of general public importance is involved and that either court feels that the point should be considered by the UKSC and grants leave. The UKSC, in disposing of the appeal, may exercise any of the powers of the CA, or remit the case to it (Criminal Appeal Act 1968, as amended).

The JCPC is described in the previous chapter. Its criminal jurisdiction in death penalty appeals from the Caribbean is very important and controversial. Since the 1990s, its liberal-minded judges, hostile to the death penalty, have provoked the impatience of the governments of independent Caribbean countries who send appeals to it in death penalty cases. It frequently allows appeals against conviction (e.g. *Boodram v State of Trinidad and Tobago* (2001)), or against the imposition of the death penalty. In one decision, *Lewis* (2001), it ruled that hundreds of death row prisoners in the Caribbean should be given a stay of execution. Similarly, in *Reyes v The Queen* (2002) and two other murder appeals in 2002, the JCPC ruled that the imposition of the mandatory death penalty was unconstitutional in seven Caribbean countries. Its automatic imposition for some crimes was held by the JCPC to be inhuman or degrading treatment, offending against international standards of human rights. A similar decision was reached on the unconstitutionality of the death penalty of Jamaica, by a nine judge JCPC, in *Watson v The Queen* (2004). In two cases decided on the same day, however, their Lordships felt constrained by the wording of the constitutions of Barbados and Trinidad and Tobago. "The language and purpose of [the relevant constitutional provisions] are so clear that whatever may be their Lordships' views about the morality or efficacy of the death penalty, they are bound as a court of law to give effect to it", said Lord Hoffmann, in giving the majority judgment in *Boyce and Joseph v The Queen* (2004).

These death penalty cases were argued by the pro bono units of large London law firms and English human rights barristers. They had a very high success rate since the mid-1990s. Consequently, governments and some judges in Caribbean countries see the JCPC as a group of unduly liberal judges who undermine their efforts to tackle high murder and violence rates and drug trafficking on their islands. They have long debated whether to abolish the JCPC's jurisdiction and replace it with a regional court of appeal. In 1970, at the Sixth Heads of Government Conference in Jamaica, the home delegation proposed the establishment of a Caribbean Supreme Court. In 2001, an agreement was signed to establish it and a building was set aside in Trinidad. It was obvious that as a consequence of its formation, many people then waiting on death row would be executed. In a 2005 ruling of great constitutional significance, *Independent Jamaica Council for Human Rights v Marshall–Burnett* (2005), however, the JCPC ruled that three Acts of the Jamaican Parliament, designed to give effect to the agreement to establishment of the Caribbean Court of Justice were not enacted in accordance with the procedure laid down in Jamaica's constitution and were thus void. In *Bowe v The Queen* (2006), the court abolished the death penalty in the Bahamas. Keir Starmer, then a famous human rights QC, said this was the culmination of a 10-year litigation strategy to abolish the death penalty in the English-speaking Caribbean. In 2001, however, the Caribbean Court of Justice was established and took over appeals from some Caribbean countries. On *Miguel v Trinidad and Tobago* (2011), Jeremic concluded:

> "Miguel should mark the end of what has been a veritable saga [of] … acrimony between local courts and the Privy Council, but in the end resolved on orthodox principles of sound constitutional jurisprudence. It is elementary that laws enacted subject to a Constitution must conform with it or be struck down. Here for the time being at least should end the saga of the death penalty in Caribbean constitutional jurisprudence."

The decision in *Hunte v Trinidad and Tobago* (2015) might be interpreted as something of a reversal of the trend. The JCPC dismissed two death penalty appeals on the ground that it had no jurisdiction to commute a lawfully passed death sentence on the ground that it would be unconstitutional for the sentence to be carried out. The Privy Council's only power to commute a death sentence for such reason was on appeal from a constitutional motion.

7. THE COURT OF JUSTICE OF THE EU AND THE EUROPEAN COURT OF HUMAN RIGHTS

These are described in Chs 3 and 4.   7–013

8. COURTS MODERNISATION

7–014   Below, I quote at length from a 2015 speech of the Chief Executive of HM Courts & Tribunals Service, on what is promised in the criminal courts. As I mentioned in the last chapter, the "vision" of digital by default looks great on paper and logically obvious. But, as I learned as an undergraduate, whose hobby was court watching, there is a massive difference between law in books, or especially law in departmental aspirational form, and the operation of law in the real world. The speech below reminds me of Lord Woolf's 1996 vision of a digitised civil justice system but, conducting empirical research in civil courts a decade later, district judges showed me the frustrating uselessness of experimental digital case management software: see *Sitting in Judgment*. Observing youth courts in 2016, another decade later, I was reminded of what I had already seen all too often. The technology did not work. Police witnesses turned up late with a DVD of CCTV in a shoplifting case, only to discover that it would not play on the court's viewing screens. Everyone had to gather round the prosecutor's laptop... so everything planned below looks laudable but I will believe it when I see it.

> "We have court buildings across the country which are no longer fit for purpose...[with staff handling] ...mounds of paper . . .Police officers come to court to give 10 minutes of evidence in person, giving up half a day from the beat...we transport prisoners across the country, at huge cost, for a 5 minute bail hearing...
>
> ...In our criminal courts, witness, victims and defendants can wait years for a case to come to trial...Court and tribunal reform has been talked about for some years now. There has been work happening – including installing Wi-Fi and screens in our criminal courts, and the start of an ambitious IT programme to create a common case flow infrastructure to enable information to flow seamlessly from the police, to the CPS and then to the courts. But what we need to do is far more radical than adding a few new screens and digitalising today's processes. We need to fundamentally rethink our model for the 21st century.
>
> Today's court system has been built around a physical paradigm. We spend a third of the court and tribunal service budget on running and maintaining our buildings. And last year, over a third of courts sat for less than 50% of the time available to them. But for many of our services, that physical paradigm no longer feels like the right answer, not just because it's expensive, but because it is no longer the right answer for good justice. Britain has the highest rate of online service usage in the world...We need to enable a police officer give evidence by video, taking 10 mins of time...
>
> We clearly need the full majesty of our criminal courts for our most complex and our most horrific criminal trials. But...they feel disproportionate and unnecessary for traffic offences...we could deal with many cases...in a far more proportionate way – using modern technology to consider evidence, using hearings only where necessary...
>
> Over the past year we've installed Wi-Fi into court rooms...We're equipping magistrates' courts with the equipment they need to display digital material – videos, photos, maps, audio files, CCTV footage, emails. Presenters...can quickly link up their own devices to our system, and display material on a large wall-mounted screen...
>
> Over the last six months we've upgraded the video link between police sites, prisons and 64 of our most business-critical Crown and magistrates' courts. This is a cost-effective and safer alternative to the large-scale movement of people between

police stations, prisons and the courts. Significantly, we've already achieved a lot: 45% of all relevant hearings are already being managed in this way, a figure that has risen every month so far.

To reduce the amount of court time spent on low-level, uncontested offences, we've introduced an online service for people who want to plead guilty to a driving offence...

We're piloting extended sitting hours...We're introducing new facilities so victims of sexual crime can give evidence from somewhere they feel safe and comfortable...Magistrates will soon be able to book their hearings online...

This investment will primarily go into digital infrastructure...moving work from underutilised buildings into better nearby buildings which we believe will give a better service. This will free up buildings that we don't need, which we can sell. The proceeds of these sales will go straight into this reinvestment into our future IT infrastructure and modernisation programme."

Despite this upbeat vision, the House of Commons Public Accounts Committee published a blistering report in May 2016, concluding:

"HMCTS does not yet have a credible plan for securing value for money from its estate. HMCTS began consulting on a programme of court closures in July 2015, but told us it only started working on a long term asset management plan to prioritise investment in its estate in December 2015. We were surprised to hear that HMCTS has continued to spend limited resources on courts which are now being closed, for example £600,000 on Torquay Magistrates Court over the last six years...We agree that an estate comprising fewer, bigger courts has the potential to provide more flexibility in scheduling trials, but remain concerned that the impact on all court users has not been properly considered. It can be difficult, for example, for jurors to get to court due to lack of public transport or funds for a taxi."

Lawyers are highly critical of the plan for evening courts, to be piloted in six places in 2017. Solicitors say they will be working longer hours for the same pay. The Bar Standards Board says it is a bad idea and they will be monitoring the effects on diversity in the profession. Ministers and judges who have revived the idea seem ignorant of the fact that experimental evening courts were dropped in the 1970s because they inconvenienced all professional court users.

See further Padfield and the 2016 JUSTICE report she cites, *What is a Court*, recommending the reconceptualising of courts and tribunals as "justice spaces".

Bibliography

H. Brimacombe, "Bringing justice closer to the community", *Legal Action*, December 2004, p.10.   7–015
Centre for Justice Innovation *justiceinnovation.org*.
Natalie Ceeney, Chief Executive of HMCTS, "Modernising Courts and Tribunals", speech, 23 September 2015.
P. Darbyshire, "An Essay on the Importance and Neglect of the Magistracy" [1997] Crim. L.R. 627; "For the New Lord Chancellor—Some Causes of Concern About Magistrates" [1997] Crim. L.R. 861; *Sitting in Judgment: The Working Lives of Judges* (Oxford: Hart Publishing Ltd, 2011), Chs 8, 9, 14 and 17.

House of Commons Committee of Public Accounts, *Efficiency in the Criminal Justice System – First Report of Session 2016–2017*, May 2016, Parliament website.

Justice for All, White Paper, July 2002.

J.S. Jeremie, "The final act of the Caribbean death penalty saga?" (2012) 128 L.Q.R. 485.

D. Newman, "Attitudes to justice in a rural community" (2016) 36 L.S. 591.

Lord Judge CJ, "The Criminal Justice System in England and Wales—Time for Change?" speech, 5 November 2008.

N. Padfield, "Reforming the Courts", editorial [2016] Crim. L.R. 517.

S. Tendler, "Sentenced to a hug and a bagel", *The Times*, 15 March 2007.

Further reading and sources for updating this chapter

7–016   Free updates of this book are available on the Sweet & Maxwell website: *http://uklawstudent.thomsonreuters.com*.

Summary and revision: P. Darbyshire, *Nutshells English Legal System*, 10th edn (London: Sweet & Maxwell, 2016).

Auld LJ, *Review of the Criminal Courts of England and Wales* (2001).

Annual Reports of HMCTS and the annual review of the CACD on HMCTS website.

Ministry of Justice website, especially news releases, consultation papers, research and the Criminal Justice Statistics.

Sources as listed at the end of Ch.6.

CHAPTER 8

History

"However, the common law has survived and has led by learning partly by lifting good ideas from Europe – examples include the jury in the 11th century, the writ in the 12th century, disclosure in the 13th century and the lex mercatoria in the 18th century." (Lord Neuberger 2015)

1. CONTINUITY

The UK's system of government, and the legal institutions which form part of it, are only explicable in terms of their long history. Whereas most continental legal systems rely heavily on legal principles derived from Roman law, adopted during the Renaissance (see Ch.1), the English legal system has remained comparatively uninfluenced by this source. The reason for this is the unbroken historical development of the system in England, where at no time was it felt necessary to look outside the principles of common law or equity for assistance. Inevitably, through the ecclesiastical courts in particular, some Roman law influence can be traced but in general terms this is very limited. Indeed, the reason why England resisted the "invasion" of Roman law, was that a unified common law system was already growing in strength prior to the Norman Conquest.   8–001

2. EARLY HISTORY

Anglo-Saxon laws

The earliest English laws of which there is documentary evidence date from the Anglo-Saxon period. These are not strictly English laws; more accurately they relate to a particular tribal area such as Kent, Wessex or Mercia. They were based on the customs of the local settlers.   8–002

The Norman Conquest (1066)

The Anglo-Saxon divisions were just giving way to a national entity when the Norman invasion of England occurred. The result of the Battle of Hastings in 1066 led to William the Conqueror ascending the English throne, determined on a process of centralisation. William's tactics were to impose strong national government and this he did by causing his Norman followers to become the   8–003 major land-owners throughout the country. The system used was "subinfeudation" under which all land belonged to the monarch and was by him granted to his followers on certain conditions. In turn they could grant their land to their tenants. Subject to conditions, those tenants could make similar grants and so on, down the ladder. This method created the complete feudal system under which tenants owed duties to their lord, whilst he owed duties to his lord and so on up to the monarch, as the supreme point of the feudal pyramid. Nevertheless, the system never became as firmly entrenched in this country as it did, for instance, in France.

Feudal courts

8–004   A characteristic benefit to the feudal lord was the right to hold his own court. This provided financial benefits and effective power over the locality. So far as the ordinary individual was concerned this local manor court was the one which affected him most. Bearing in mind that the concept of central legal and governmental authority was still comparatively new, it took a long time before the royal courts were able to exercise control over these local courts. Although the passage of centuries saw the transfer of real power from local to national courts, these feudal courts remained in many instances until the property legislation of 1925. Until then, there was a feudal court relic, a tenure of property called "copyhold", which involved the registration of the transaction in the local court roll so that the person held the land by "copy" of the court roll.

Royal Courts

8–005   Following the Norman Conquest, monarchs soon realised that besides the need for strong national government there was also a need for a national law and order system. To this end the closest advisers of the monarch—the "*curia regis*", or "King's council"—encouraged the establishment of three separate royal courts which sat at Westminster. These were:

- the Court of Exchequer which was mainly concerned with cases affecting the royal revenue, but which also had a limited civil jurisdiction;
- the Court of King's Bench which, taking its name from the original concept of the monarch sitting with his judges "en banc"—on the bench—at Westminster, dealt with civil and criminal cases in which the King had an interest; and
- the Court of Common Pleas, which was established to hear civil cases brought by one individual against another.

In the Court of Exchequer sat judges called Barons, with a presiding judge known as the Chief Baron. This court appears to be the oldest, emerging in recognisable form in the early thirteenth century, having developed out of the financial organisation responsible for the royal revenues. The Court of King's Bench had its own Chief Justice and judges, and was closely linked with the monarch and the Great Council. This was due to the understanding that this court followed the King's person. The Court of Common Pleas had a Chief Justice and dedicated judges and left records from the early thirteenth century. All three courts were required by the monarch, said Stow in his survey of London in 1224, to make their base in Westminster Hall, and there arose continuing conflicts between them over jurisdiction. The importance of getting more and more work was largely brought about by the fact that the judges were paid out of the court fees. At any rate these three royal courts, later added to by the introduction of a Court of Chancery, survived five centuries before being reconstructed into the present High Court of Justice in the Judicature Acts 1873–1875. The ultimate merger of Exchequer and Common Pleas into the Queen's Bench Division came about in 1880.

3. THE COMMON LAW

Origin

As a centralised system of law and order developed, so customary laws gave way to national law, which became known as the common law. It was called "common" because it was common to the whole country, as opposed to the local customs. Since inevitably the different customs at times conflicted, the judges' decisions, absorbing certain customs and rejecting others, came to be of predominant importance. They were creating "the law of the realm". The common law was thus derived entirely from case law.

8–006

Development

The Norman Kings, in attempting to weld the country together, made use of royal commissioners to travel the country to deal with governmental matters. The production of the *Domesday Book*, in 1087, as a property and financial survey, is the best known example. The extension of these activities to the judicial field seems to have arisen not long after the Conquest. The king appointed judges as royal commissioners, charged with certain royal powers, to travel the country to deal with civil and criminal cases. This system of "itinerant justices in Eyre" dates from not long after the Conquest; but the assize system, as later developed, really dates from the reign of Henry II (1154–1189). It only ended with the Courts Act 1971 *but* High Court judges of all three HC divisions still travel the six circuits, endeavouring to demand high standards of the advocates who appear before them and ensuring that undesirable localised practices do not get established. It was an important part of the work of these judges to formulate the principles of the common law, by meeting together formally and informally to resolve problems which had arisen in the cases coming before them. As these judges were linked with the courts in Westminster Hall, this helped to develop national laws. Nevertheless, the common law never completely supplanted local custom. As we saw in Ch.2 on sources, custom remains a source of law today but it is most significant in the development of international law.

8–007

Forms of action and the meaning of common law

8–008   In addition to settling national legal principles, the courts began to establish formal procedural rules. Actions were commenced by the issue of a royal writ. The claim had to be set out in an accepted fashion. This was called a form of action. Eventually, the system became rigid. The judges ruled that unless a claimant could fit their claim into an appropriate "form of action" it was not one known to the law. The court officials responsible for issuing writs tried initially to satisfy the demands of claimants by drawing up new forms of action, but the judges frowned on this and the practice was stopped by the Provisions of Oxford 1258. So great was the resulting dissatisfaction that almost 30 years later, by the Statute of Westminster 1285, this strict approach was slightly relaxed, so that the officials could issue a new writ, where the new situation was closely related to that covered by an existing writ. These new writs became known as writs "*in consimili casu*". The effect which the writ system had on the development of the legal system is seen below in the section on equity. The common law is still being developed today, via the system of precedent, case law, as explained in Ch.2. Thanks to Parliamentary sovereignty, legislation supplements it, codifies it and replaces it. There are several different meanings attaching to the term.

- In the historical sense, explained above, common law refers to the national law, as opposed to local law or custom. It is the law "common" to England and Wales.
- The law made by the judges, in contrast to legislation.
- The law not historically derived from the courts of equity.
- A "common law country" or "common law jurisdiction" is one that originally applied English law.

4. EQUITY

Origin

8–009   The difficulty of bringing cases in the common law courts, thanks to the rigidity of the writ system, led to increasing dissatisfaction. Litigants petitioned the monarch. He handed these petitions on to the Lord Chancellor, who, as Keeper of the King's Conscience and an ecclesiastic, seemed to be a suitable person. He set up his own Court of Chancery where he, or his representative, would sit to determine these petitions. He would be guided by equity, or fairness. The legal principles which successive Lord Chancellors made came to be known collectively as equity. The system became well established in the fifteenth century. Because of the rapid increase in judicial work, it was soon found necessary to have a lawyer as Lord Chancellor. The discretion vested in early Lord Chancellors gradually gave way to a system of precedent, but it was a long time before the common law joke died, about equity being as long as the Chancellor's foot (meaning the outcome depended on the mood of the LC). Both common law and equity came to operate as parallel systems, with each set of courts regarding itself as bound by its own judicial precedents.

Development

Equity soon found itself establishing a jurisdiction over matters where the common law had failed, and continued to fail, to recognise legal rights and duties. Equity was always a "gloss" on the common law; it always presumed the existence of the common law and simply supplemented it where necessary.

8–010

New rights

The whole of the law of trusts owed its existence to the willingness of equity to recognise and enforce the obligation of a trustee to a beneficiary. Equity accepted the use of the mortgage as a method of borrowing money against the security of real property, when the common law took a literal view of the obligation undertaken by the borrower. It introduced the "equity of redemption" to enable a borrower to retain the property which was the security for the loan, even where there was default under the strict terms of the mortgage deed.

8–011

New remedies

At common law, the only remedy for breach of contract was damages, a money payment as compensation for the loss suffered. Equity realised that in some cases damages was not an adequate remedy, and therefore proceeded to introduce the equitable remedies of injunction and specific performance. An injunction is used to prevent a party from acting in breach of their legal obligations; a decree of specific performance is used to order a party to carry out their side of a contract. A party to a contract cannot just decide to break it and pay damages. Other equitable remedies are the declaratory order or judgment; the right to have a deed corrected by the process known as rectification and the right to rescind (withdraw from) a contract. The willingness of equity to intervene where fraud was proven and its preparedness to deal with detailed accounts in the law of trusts and the administration of estates, also gained it wide jurisdiction. The appointment of a receiver is an equitable solution to the problem of the management of certain financial matters.

8–012

New procedures

In contrast to the rigidity of common law remedies, equity favoured a flexibility of approach. Consequently it was prepared, by a "subpoena", to order witnesses to attend, to have them examined and cross-examined orally, to require relevant documents to be produced, known as discovery of documents, to insist on relevant questions being answered, by the use of interrogatories, and to have the case heard in English, where the common law for centuries used Latin. In the event of a failure to comply with an order, equity was prepared to impose immediate sanctions for this contempt of court.

A classification sometimes employed is to define the jurisdiction of equity as exclusive, concurrent and auxiliary. In the exclusive jurisdiction sense, equity recognised actions, as in trusts and mortgages, where the common law would provide no remedy; in the concurrent jurisdiction sense equity would add to the

8–013

remedies provided by the common law, as by the introduction of the injunction and the decree of specific performance; in the auxiliary jurisdiction sense equity employed a more flexible procedure than the common law.

Maxims

8–014   Among the most famous principles are:
He who comes to equity must come with clean hands;
Equity will not suffer a wrong to be without remedy;
Delay defeats equity; and
Equity looks to the intent rather than to the form.

The maxims emphasise that equity, based in fairness and natural justice, attempted to maintain this approach throughout its later history. Judges retained their personal discretion so that equitable remedies were not, and are not, obtainable as of right. It is very important to understand that, whereas the litigant has a right to a remedy, at common law, once she has proven her case, this is not so with equity. All equitable remedies are still discretionary.

Relationship between common law and equity

8–015   Early relations between the two systems were comparatively strained. The common lawyers regarded equity as an interloper, lacking the firmly-based principles with which they were familiar. They were unable to see that equity was invaluable in remedying deficiencies in the common law and in encouraging the latter to develop its substantive law and procedure. As the Court of Chancery built up its jurisdiction and the two systems could be seen to be operating on a parallel basis, the question arose as to what was to happen in the unusual instance when there was a conflict. This problem was solved by James I, in the *Earl of Oxford's* case (1615), by a ruling that where there was such a conflict, the rules of equity were to prevail. The later history of equity was dogged in the eighteenth and nineteenth centuries by the courts of Chancery becoming overburdened with work, with increasing reliance being placed on judicial precedent and consequent delays. Dickens' attack in his novel, *Bleak House*, on the delays and costs in the system, seems to have to been thoroughly justified, with some examples of cases awaiting judgment dragging on for scores of years until both parties were dead. In the 1850s, Parliament endeavoured to ease the position, by the Common Law Procedure Acts 1852–1854 and the Chancery (Amendment) Act 1858 but the dual systems continued, sometimes to the substantial detriment of litigants, until 1873–1875.

5. NINETEENTH-CENTURY DEVELOPMENTS

The Supreme Court of Judicature Acts 1873–1875

This legislation reorganised the existing court structures completely and formally   **8–016**
brought together the common law courts and the courts of Chancery. In the
Supreme Court of Judicature set up by the Acts, the three original royal courts
became three divisions of the new High Court of Justice. The Court of Chancery
which administered equity became the fourth division, i.e. the Chancery Division
of the High Court, and a fifth division, dealing with those matters not within
common law or equity, became the Probate, Divorce and Admiralty Division. By
Order in Council in 1880, the three royal courts were merged to form the Queen's
Bench Division, thus leaving the three Divisions of the High Court—Chancery,
Queen's Bench, and Probate, Divorce and Admiralty—which remained
unchanged for 90 years. The Acts placed on a statutory basis the old rule that
where common law and equity conflict, equity shall prevail. It gave power to all
the courts to administer the principles of common law and equity and to grant the
remedies of both, as circumstances in a case demanded. Consequently, the old
conflict no longer arises, although common law and equity principles still exist.

By bringing the two systems together administratively, and allowing the High
Court judge to exercise the principles, procedures and remedies of common law
and equity in a single case, it seemed that the two systems had merged. That this
was somewhat superficial is borne out by the exclusive jurisdictions left to the
Queen's Bench and Chancery Divisions. The work formerly done by the Court of
Chancery is exactly that dealt with in the Chancery Division. The whole of the
legislation has now been consolidated in the Supreme Court Act 1981, now
renamed Senior Courts Act.

Probate, Divorce and Admiralty jurisdiction

These three important legal topics fell neither within the common law nor equity   **8–017**
jurisdictions, since probate (which is concerned with wills) and divorce were, for
centuries, treated as ecclesiastical matters, and there was a separate Admiralty
Court inevitably influenced by international shipping practices. Probate and
divorce were transferred from the ecclesiastical courts to the ordinary civil courts
in 1857 by the setting up of a Court of Probate and a separate Divorce Court. The
ancient High Court of Admiralty gradually lost its widest jurisdiction to the
common law courts, but retained powers over collisions at sea, salvage and prize
cases. All other aspects of the law merchant, that is the law affecting traders had,
over the centuries, been transferred to the common law courts.

Appeal courts

As described in Ch.6, the Judicature Acts, in creating a Court of Appeal alongside   **8–018**
the new High Court of Justice, had intended that this court with its specially
designated Lords Justices of Appeal should be the final appellate court for civil
matters. Political considerations intervened, however, and the proposal to remove
judicial functions from the House of Lords was shelved. The Appellate

Jurisdiction Act 1876 provided for the retention of the House of Lords as the final appeal court in civil cases and for the creation of special judges, Lords of Appeal in Ordinary, as life peers to staff the court.

6.   TWENTIETH-CENTURY DEVELOPMENTS

Criminal courts

8–019   In 1907, the Criminal Appeal Act established the Court of Criminal Appeal to provide for the first time a general right of appeal for persons convicted and sentenced in indictable criminal cases. A further appeal in matters of general public importance lay to the House of Lords. The Court of Criminal Appeal became the Court of Appeal (Criminal Division) by the Criminal Appeal Act 1966. The role of the Queen's Bench Divisional Court in ruling on points of law arising by way of case stated in summary criminal cases was amended by the Administration of Justice Act 1960. This Act enabled an appeal in a case of general public importance to go to the House of Lords (now UKSC) if the Divisional Court granted a certificate and leave was obtained from the top court. The court structure for trying indictable criminal cases was substantially changed by the Courts Act 1971 which abolished the historically derived Court of Quarter Sessions and Assizes and replaced them with a single Crown Court.

Civil courts

8–020   The Administration of Justice Act 1970 created a Family Division of the High Court and amended the jurisdiction of the Queen's Bench and Chancery divisions, redistributing the functions of the former Probate Divorce and Admiralty Division. One novel change in appeal provisions was the introduction by the Administration of Justice Act 1969 of a possible "leapfrog" appeal from the High Court to the House of Lords (now UKSC), bypassing the Court of Appeal. The procedure was, however, made subject to stringent conditions which in practice limit its use. The Courts and Legal Services Act 1990 gave concurrent jurisdiction in civil matters to the High Court and the County Court, with the exception of judicial review, an exercise of prerogative power vested in the High Court. Twenty-first century developments are dealt with in the other chapters of this book.

Further reading and sources for updating this chapter

8–021   Free updates of this book are available on the Sweet & Maxwell website: *http://uklawstudent.thomsonreuters.com*.

Summary and revision: P. Darbyshire, *Nutshells English Legal System*, 10th edn (London: Sweet & Maxwell, 2016).

J.H. Baker, *An Introduction to English Legal History*, 4th edn (London: Butterworths, 2000).

Lord Neuberger, "Some thoughts on the post-LASPO civil judge's role before and during trial", speech, 22 January 2015.

PART 3

PROCEDURES

CHAPTER 9

The Adversarial Process

"Anglo-American culture has long been beset with a pervasive myth about the conduct of criminal justice in European States. Continental criminal procedure is thought to be unjust and oppressive. It is called "inquisitorial", a term that has lost its neutral meaning and is now largely an epithet harkening back to the witchcraft trials and heresy persecutions of distant centuries. Among English speaking peoples the belief is widespread (and quite mistaken) that in Continental procedure the accused is presumed guilty until he proves himself innocent." (Langbein, 1977)

A contrast used to be drawn between the English legal system as "adversarial" and continental European systems, mostly daughters of the French legal system as "inquisitorial", as is explained in Ch.1. That comparison is crude and somewhat inaccurate. Nevertheless, procedure under common law legal systems is accurately described as adversarial. Historians like Langbein attribute it to the rise of lawyers, in the eighteenth century.

9–001

1. ELEMENTS OF THE ADVERSARIAL (ACCUSATORIAL) SYSTEM

The judge as umpire

It has traditionally been said that the role of the English judge, or magistrate, is as an unbiased umpire whose job it is to listen to evidence presented by both sides, without interfering in the trial process. This was contrasted with the role of the juge d'instruction, the French first instance judge who performed an inquisitorial role in some criminal cases, directing investigations, cross-examining the defendant and compiling a dossier of evidence for the trial court. There is no comparable common law equivalent. Similarly, the role of the German judge is to take an active part in the assembling of evidence and the questioning of witnesses, before and at trial. Nevertheless, the European Convention on Human Rights, binding on continental systems and ours, provides that a fair civil or criminal trial, required by art.6, must be adversarial. The European Court of Human Rights has ruled that the "equality of arms" principle requires equal access to information (with strict exceptions), adequate notification of the case that the defendant has to answer, equal opportunities to present evidence and challenge other evidence, and free legal representation and interpretation where

9–002

necessary to achieve this. See, for instance, *Rowe and Davis v UK* (2000), a criminal case, and *McVicar v UK* (2002), a civil case described in Ch.4 on human rights.

It has been said that the English judge's traditional role, as a non-interfering umpire, is a reflection of the English sense of fair play: each side has an equal opportunity to win the litigation "game" (in civil cases) by convincing the judge of the merits of their argument, collecting supporting evidence and citing favourable case authorities. The judge does not interfere in the presentation of evidence by examining and cross-examining witnesses. This is left to the parties or their advocates. The role of the judge was set down clearly by Lord Denning MR in *Jones v National Coal Board* (1957) and can be summarised thus. The judge should:

1. listen to all the evidence, only interfering to clarify neglected or obscure points;
2. see that advocates behave and stick to the rules;
3. exclude irrelevancies and discourage repetition;
4. make sure he understands the advocates' points; and
5. at the end, make up his mind where the truth lies.

If the judge interferes unduly in the advocates' speeches or adduction of evidence, it may constitute a ground of appeal. As Jackson explained, his research, with Sean Doran, demonstrated that the presence of a jury encourages the judge to be especially passive. Very few civil trials are determined by a jury but juries determine the verdict in almost all Crown Court criminal trials. As we shall see, thanks to civil procedure reforms and the increase in unrepresented litigants, judges have had to become much more proactive in respect of managing the case and the trial and since 2005, the same expectation is now made of judges in criminal cases.

The parties control the evidence

9–003   Prior to the 1990s the parties generally brought whatever evidence they saw fit to prove their case. The court would seldom limit it. The parties would decide which and how many witnesses to call. The court has power to call witnesses but seldom does so. Parties were able to "keep their cards close to their chest" pre-trial, which was sometimes likened, mixing metaphors, to "trial by ambush". This, plus the complexity of English procedural rules, plus the rigid adduction of evidence by examination and cross-examination, meant that unrepresented parties were at a disadvantage and it was sometimes the case that the best lawyer or richest party won. All of this is explained in graphic detail by Lightman J, in the 2003 lecture cited in Ch.10 on civil procedure.

The stronger case wins

9–004   It is the court's job to determine the relative strength of the parties' cases, according to the law, on the evidence presented, not to determine where the truth lies. Having said that, the Court of Appeal has sometimes said in recent cases that its job is to do justice, as can be seen in Ch.12 on criminal procedure. It is up to the person bringing the case (claimant in a civil case, or prosecutor in a criminal case) to prove it (called the burden of proof), to the satisfaction of the court, according to the required standard or *quantum* of proof. In civil cases, the standard is proof "on the balance of probabilities", meaning the claimant must show his version of events is more likely than not to be correct. In criminal cases, there is a massive power imbalance between the prosecutor (the State, normally the Crown Prosecution Service) and the defendant. This is one reason why the standard is much higher. The prosecutor must satisfy the magistrates or jury of the accused's guilt "beyond reasonable doubt", giving the benefit of any doubt to the defendant. Historically, the burden of proof in the English adversarial system meant that the defendant was entitled to see the (civil) claimant's or (criminal) prosecutor's case in full before starting to defend himself.

The principle of orality

This is often seen as a relic of jury trial but was elevated to the level of principle. **9–005** Most cases were argued by word of mouth, from start to finish. Witnesses were (and in criminal cases most still are) publicly examined by their own side and cross-examined by the opposition. Evidence, such as exhibits and documentation, was, and is, brought out in open court and acknowledged orally. Reported speech, such as the transcription of a suspect's interrogation, is brought in evidence and often re-enacted in court before the jury. All of the evidence has to be summarised, acknowledged or adduced in open court and must be clearly audible. The oral trial proceedings are routinely tape-recorded in all courts, civil and criminal, except the magistrates' court, which is not a "court of record". Rock argued that the principle of orality did not apply in magistrates' courts.

2. CRITICISM OF THE ADVERSARIAL SYSTEM

Lightman J's 2003 criticisms of the adversarial nature of English civil procedure **9–006** are typical.

1. Success turns very much on the performance on the day. If a party or witness underperforms or counsel lets him down, there is no chance of a replay.
2. Performance at trial turns on investment in the litigation "money talks loud and clear". Cases are won or lost by the quality of representation.
3. The limitation on the role of the judge means his search for truth is confined to the evidence placed before him by the parties.
4. The adversarial system is expensive and time-consuming. He attacked the silk system—the high fees paid to QCs, as can be seen from the quotations in Ch.13 on lawyers.
5. The deficiencies of the adversary system are aggravated by the case law system: "judges are increasingly ... bombarded ... with torrents of authorities. The judges make too little efforts to keep their judgments as brief as the reasoning requires."

Added to this is the problem that it is left to the parties to select witnesses. This means that there may be a witness who could give damming evidence against both sides, so the court does not get to know of their existence, or testimony, or a crucial witness is not called because of a lack of defence resources in a criminal case, resulting in a wrongful conviction, as can be seen in the chapter on criminal procedure.

The plight of the unrepresented in criminal cases has been well documented in socio-legal research (Dell (1971); Carlen (1976); Darbyshire (1984)). Lay people find it very difficult to present their "story" to the court by means of examining witnesses. To add to this problem, they are often very nervous and in unfamiliar surroundings. Where a defendant is unrepresented, mostly in the magistrates' court, he is wholly dependent on the goodwill and expertise of the bench or, more realistically, the clerk (legal adviser), to help him put his case and examine witnesses and explain what is being asked of him, for example, choice of venue in a triable-either-way offence. Some clerks are much more prepared and skilled to help than others. The same problem occurs in a civil case where one or both sides is a litigant in person. The increasing numbers of litigants in person have created difficulties for judges, in our adversarial process, as explained in Ch.10 on civil procedure.

The Royal Commission on Criminal Justice 1991–1993 (RCCJ), was concerned that the English criminal trial, allowing the accused to keep his defence secret until having seen the whole of the prosecution case, permitted him to "ambush" the prosecution with an unpredictable defence. As Jackson explains, the English adversarial criminal trial has concentrated on the opposing interests of prosecution and defence, with victims and witnesses given too little independent protection. (See Rock's research and other research to which he refers.) From the 1990s, victims' involvement in the criminal process has been enhanced, as explained in Ch.12. Field and Eady question the long-held assertion of common lawyers that the adversarial system is good at truth-finding, discussed in Ch.12.

3. EROSION OF THE ADVERSARIAL PROCESS

9–007 From the last quarter of the twentieth century onwards we have seen an erosion of this archetype at work in the English legal system:

- In criminal cases, there has been increased use of statutory powers to admit uncontentious witness evidence via a statement, instead of calling the witness to court. In civil cases, case managing judges will readily use their powers to curtail the number of witnesses, or ask for their evidence to be given in writing and each witness's evidence in chief is submitted in a written statement, with very limited opportunities to add to this orally.
- The RCCJ considered whether the court should have an investigative role before and during the criminal trial. They examined continental trial systems. They did not recommend this but urged that:

> "Wherever practicable in complex cases judges should take on responsibility for managing the progress of a case, securing its passage through the various stages

of pre-trial discussion to preparatory hearing and trial and making sure that the parties have fulfilled their obligations both to each other and to the court" (p.10, recommendation 254).

- The 1995 Practice Direction on Plea and Directions Hearings in the Crown Court went some way towards this aim and, as explained in Ch.12, judges' trial management powers in criminal cases have been emphasised and significantly enhanced by the Criminal Procedure Rules from 2005.
- The Heilbron–Hodge Committee (1993) and Lord Woolf (1996) recommended an interventionist role for the civil trial judge, and active case management is now the hallmark of civil procedure, with the judge controlling the speed and length of the civil case, limiting the evidence presented. For an excellent and entertaining analysis of the implications of this change in the judicial role see Lightman (1999). Since 1999, the judge's role has become so much more proactive because of civil procedure reforms and active case management that Lord Neuberger, President of the Supreme Court said:

> "From having been a detached umpire who gave a view on the law and the facts at the end of a case and held the ring in the meantime, a judge is now a case manager, a time-tabler, a time-keeper, a rules enforcer, a mediation facilitator, a mediator, a chairman of a meeting, and a costs assessor before and after the event. First instance judges have been, if you like, converted from guard dogs, who sat on the sidelines and only barked occasionally to warn, into sheep dogs, who continually worry away at the parties to ensure that they fall into line." (2015)

- The interim report of the *Civil Justice Review* (1986) prompted the courts to require, by Practice Directions, that the parties exchanged witness statements, forcing them to lay some of their cards on the table. Openness was massively enhanced by the requirement for skeleton arguments and document bundles to be exchanged pre-trial and presented to the court.
- Since the 1990s, skeleton arguments, bundles and use of witness statements have made a significant shift from oral case argument to arguments on paper with the judges and opposition reading them, pre-trial. No longer can a student observe court proceedings and expect to be entertained to a full story unfolding in the courtroom. Oral argument has been limited in the USA since 1849 but until the 1990s, advocates in England and Wales dictated the length of trials by simply giving an estimate to the court. The CA first introduced a requirement for skeleton arguments in 1989. See the comparative account by Leggatt LJ and the horror of the American, Martinau, at the primitive nature of unreformed, oral civil appeals in the 1980s.
- In civil cases, since the Civil Procedure Rules 1998 have been in force, parties have been encouraged to share a single expert. Nevertheless, in a criminal case, a jury or magistrates will routinely find themselves having to decide between two experts (for example, on psychiatric or forensic evidence).

- Jolowicz considered that most judges wanted to do substantive justice in the case (get to the truth), not just procedural justice, and that the Woolf reforms would help them to realise that objective, which is to be welcomed. (1996)
- Small claims in the county court have always been an exception to the adversarial stereotype. Research by Applebey (1978) showed some registrars (now called district judges) employed an inquisitorial technique. Many of those who appear are unrepresented and, therefore, the progress of the case depends on the district judge's being somewhat interventionist. This was explored and confirmed by Baldwin's research. These research findings are cited in Ch.10 on civil procedure. The *Civil Justice Review* (1998) recommended that judges adopt a more standardised inquisitorial role in small claims.
- There is now a very high incidence of litigants in person in the civil courts, right up to the Court of Appeal, as demonstrated in Darbyshire, *Sitting in Judgment*. This has increased from 2013, thanks to cutbacks in legal aid. As the Senior President of Tribunals pointed out in his annual report for 2014, the courts have a lot to learn from tribunals. As legal aid has never been available in most tribunals, many applicants and respondents have represented themselves. Lord Chief Justice Thomas has said in out of court speeches that thanks to cutbacks in legal aid, there are many more litigants in person and they would benefit from the judge taking on an inquisitorial role.
- In family cases relating to children's care, control and/or residence, judges sometimes say they take an inquisitorial role. The cases are multi-party and multi-issue. The child is both the object of the dispute and a party. They may have both a guardian and a legal representative. The judge must focus on the best interests of the child and sometimes comes up with a solution no-one has argued for. See research by Darbyshire, 2011, Ch.12.
- Academic scholars have drawn attention to the fact that recent reforms have brought English (adversarial) and European criminal justice systems closer because of some external and some internal influences, notably the European Convention on Human Rights. See Colson and Field.
- Following the 2016 *Transforming Our Justice System* vision paper, and "digital by default", the unified courts and tribunals judiciary will be expected to take a more inquisitorial and problem-solving approach, as described in the tribunals chapter by Ryder LJ in a 2016 speech.

Bibliography, further reading and sources for updating this chapter

9–008 Free updates of this book are available on the Sweet & Maxwell website: *http://uklawstudent.thomsonreuters.com*.

Summary and revision: P. Darbyshire, *Nutshells English Legal System*, 10th edn (London: Sweet & Maxwell, 2016).

Appleby and Baldwin, *The Civil Justice Review*, Heilbron and Woolf are cited in Ch.10 on civil procedure.

P. Carlen, *Magistrates' Justice* (Oxford: Wiley Blackwell, 1976).

R. Colson and S. Field, *The Transformation of Criminal Justice: Comparing France with England and Wales* (Paris: Éditions L'Harmattan, 2011).

M. Damaska, "Evidentiary Barriers to Conviction and Two Models of Criminal Procedure" (1973) 121 University of Pennsylvania Law Review 507.

P. Darbyshire, *The Magistrates' Clerk* (Chichester: Barry Rose, 1984); *Sitting in Judgment: The Working Lives of Judges* (Oxford: Hart Publishing, 2011).

S. Dell, *Silent in Court* (London: Bell [for the Social Administration Research Trust], 1971).

J.A. Jolowicz, "The Woolf Report and the Adversary System (1996) 15 C.J.Q. 198.

J.H. Langbein, *Comparative Criminal Procedure: Germany* (St Paul, Minn.: West Publishing, 1977), p.1; *The Origins of Adversary Criminal Trial* (Oxford: Oxford University Press, 2003).

Leggatt LJ, "The Future of the Oral Tradition in the Court of Appeal" (1995) 14 C.J.Q. 1. (*Westlaw*).

Lightman J, at (1999) 149 N.L.J. 1819; Sir Gavin Lightman's 2003 lecture at Sheffield University is reproduced as Lightman LJ, "The Civil Justice System and Legal Profession—The Challenges Ahead" (2003) 22 C.J.Q. 235.

J. Jackson, "The Adversary Trial and Trial by Judge Alone", in M. McConville and G. Wilson, *The Handbook of The Criminal Justice Process* (Oxford: Oxford University Press, 2002).

R. Martineau, *Appellate Justice in England and the United States: A Comparative Analysis* (Getzville, NY: William S. Hein & Co., Inc., 1990).

Lord Neuberger, "Some thoughts on the post-LASPO civil judge's role before and during trial", speech, January 2015, UKSC website.

P. Rock, *The Social World of an English Crown Court* (Oxford: Oxford University Press, 1993) and see the material he cites therein.

The Royal Commission on Criminal Procedure 1993 is cited in Ch.12.

M. Zander, *Cases and Materials on the English Legal System (Law in Context)*, 10th edn (Cambridge: Cambridge University Press, 2007), Ch.4.

CHAPTER 10

Civil Procedure

"English institutions have tended to reflect the traditions and values of upper class England. . .civil procedure has always reflected. . .the English sport of cricket most markedly in the adversary system of justice, and not only in the sense that both are slow and boring. . . each side prepares its team for the contest. One side in turn goes into bat (i.e. address the court and call its witnesses) and faces the bowling of the other side (i.e. the cross-examination of its witnesses); then the other side takes its turn at the wicket, calling its witnesses. Each side then has the opportunity in final speeches to make its case and unmake that of its opponent. Throughout, an independent third party umpire, selected on grounds of his relative expertise and experience, watches, listens, and enforces the rules, and at the end of the game gives his decision to the winner ... The adversary system has a number of disturbing features for those who are more interested in the achievement of justice than in the playing of the game." (Lightman J 2003).

"The judiciary should have modern, flexible, digital tools and problem solving techniques to help them get to the heart of their cases quickly; resolving wrong decisions, or weeding out the hopeless case...justice can be delivered in many ways – by the most appropriate decision-maker; in modern hearing rooms, or in mental health hospital units, community halls or remote locations; by video links, on laptops, tablets and smartphones, and online with the citizen and decision maker coming together virtually...Justice, and access to it, should lie at the heart of the community...This will be a justice system where many sizes fits all; not one size for all. A much simpler system of justice, with the judiciary at its heart, citizens empowered to access it, using innovation and digital tools to resolve these cases quickly, authoritatively and efficiently...To serve the needs of a 21st Century society, the justice system must be digital by default and design...The creation of online justice cannot therefore simply be a matter of digitising what might be called the frontline processes. It must go further than that. It must properly embrace what is described as Online Dispute Resolution... Digitisation presents an opportunity to break with processes that are no longer optimal or relevant [and deliver something more accessible, including]...the 'one stop shop'. If a litigant, party or user has a problem, they should be able to come to the system to have that problem resolved." (Sir Earnest Ryder, 2016, describing the current courts and tribunals reform programme, which he called *"the largest programme of change in any justice system in the world"*).

In the last chapter, we saw what is meant by adversarial procedure in civil and criminal cases. This chapter explains civil procedure, normally activated when one private citizen or enterprise seeks redress for a civil wrong, such as a breach of contract, or a tort. In Ch.1 we saw that it is up to the claimant to bring a civil case, not the State. The State has no interest in the outcome, unless it is one of the litigants. It just provides the courts, described in Ch.6, to enable resolution of a private dispute. On the subject of "access to justice", this chapter must be read in conjunction with Ch.11, on alternative dispute resolution (ADR) and Ch.17 on legal aid, because to enforce the civil law and civil rights, people need access to affordable, user-friendly dispute resolution. For an in-depth portrait from empirical research of the real world of civil litigation in 2002–2010, see Darbyshire (2011) Chs 11, 13 and 14.

The vast majority of people who could obtain a civil law remedy to their problem do not take it to court or an alternative forum. They resolve disputes between themselves, or give up. Even if they see a lawyer, lawyers negotiate settlements on behalf of most of their rational clients because, as a Lord Justice of Appeal remarked during my research, "You'd never do it yourself, would you?", meaning, take a case to court, knowing how much it costs to litigate. Even in that tiny proportion of cases where civil proceedings are issued, almost all settle pre-trial. All this was well known before its confirmation by Genn's research in *Paths to Justice* (1999). Zander concluded that most people cannot be bothered to go to court, however much you simplify procedure and make the courts more accessible:

> "When a dispute occurs, most people are prepared to complain and many are prepared to go so far as to take advice, but on the whole ... they show little interest in using any of the forms of civil justice. I believe that this is not to be regarded as necessarily a bad thing, there is probably very little that can be done to change the situation." (2000, p.38.)

In this chapter we (critically) examine the seemingly simple system envisaged by the Woolf Reforms, then the Jackson reforms, then we enter the brave new world of online courts, via a digital revolution from 2017, each reform promising to enhance "access to justice".

1. CIVIL PROCEDURE NOW, AFTER "THE WOOLF REFORMS"

10–002

> "There was a time when there was a premium on ambush and taking your opponent by surprise: litigation was a sport and the outcome turned very much on who you could afford to instruct as your advocate and champion." (Lightman J, 1999.)

After centuries of complaint that English civil litigation was conducted as a lawyers' Dickensian game—slow, expensive and complex, the Civil Procedure Rules 1998 (CPR) were passed, in the hope that one simplified set of plain-English rules for the High Court and County Court, introducing mandatory judicial case management, would eliminate these problems. The Rules followed the recommendations of Lord Woolf's 1996 report, *Access to Justice*. The CPR and Practice Directions replaced two sets of rules for the High Court and County Court, in 1999. They embodied a radical new approach. The background to the "Woolf reforms" is explained below. One major problem with the pre-Woolf setup is that an adversarial system, where the parties are left to battle it out, uncontrolled by the court, is unfair, where the parties are not equally matched in terms of resources, information or wealth, such as where a patient sues a health authority or a consumer sues a large company, or an employee sues an employer.

Section 1 of the Civil Procedure Act 1997 provided for one set of rules, "with a view to securing that the civil justice system is accessible, fair and efficient". Section 2 provided for a Civil Court Rule Committee to include people "with experience in and knowledge of" consumer affairs and lay advice so that rules were not drafted just by judges. Section 6 established a Civil Justice Council to keep the system, including ADR (alternative dispute resolution), under review.

2. THE CIVIL PROCEDURE RULES 1998 (CPR)

The Overriding Objective

This is set out in CPR r.1.1. Amendments during the Jackson reforms 2013–2014 are in italics: **10–003**

> "These Rules are a new procedural code with the overriding objective of enabling the court to deal with a case justly *and at proportionate cost*
> (2) …
> a.   ensuring the parties are on an equal footing;
> b.   saving expense;
> c.   dealing with the case in a way which is proportionate:
>   (i)   to the amount of money involved;
>   (ii)   to the importance of the case;
>   (iii)   to the complexity of the issues;
>   (iv)   to the financial position of each party;
> d.   ensuring that it is dealt with expeditiously and fairly; and
> e.   allotting to it an appropriate share of the court's resources, *while taking account of the need to allot resources to other cases*; and
> f.   *enforcing compliance with rules, directions and orders*." (My emphasis.)

The court must apply the overriding objective in interpreting the rules and exercising power. It is not waffly sentiment. It was immediately applied by the Court of Appeal, as soon as the rules were implemented. There is no need to refer to art.6 of the European Convention on Human Rights (fair trial) because of the court's obligation in the Rules to deal with cases justly: *Daniels v Walker* (2000).

> *"To the outsider these objectives of a civilised legal system would appear self-evident, and the surprise lies, not in their statement in the CPR, but in the need to state them and their absence prior to implementation of the reforms"* (Lightman J, 2003).

Pre-action protocols

These are statements of best practice during negotiation, encouraging exchange of information and putting the parties into a position to settle fairly. Fair negotiation is very important because only a small fraction of civil disputes are ever brought to court (Genn, 1999; Zander, 2000). If one party behaves obstructively, they can be penalised in costs, if the action later comes to court. Protocols have been issued for many topics. A 2009 Practice Direction (PD) on **10–004**

"Pre-action behaviour" introduced a more robust stance on pre-action negotiation. It tries to help parties to settle and avoid litigation. The parties *must* exchange information in reasonable time, disclose relevant documents, minimise the cost of experts, and attempt ADR, though they cannot be forced to do so. If the case comes to court, it *must* take account of compliance.

Starting proceedings (Pt 7 CPR)

10–005   As we saw in Ch.6, most claims are made in the County Court. The claimant applies on a claim form. This must include particulars of the claim (statement of case) or they must be served within four months. They may include points of law, witness lists and documents and the form must include statements of truth and value, and specify the remedy sought. From 2014, because of the "Jackson reforms", the statement of truth certifies that the costs budget is fair, accurate and proportionate. Money claims up to £100,000 can be issued online. All forms are meant to be in plain English. From 2014, claims under £100,000 or personal injury claims under £50,000 may not normally be issued in the High Court. Defamation claims must generally be in the High Court. The claim may be issued at any County Court hearing centre. In 2015, 1.5 million claims were made in the County Court. 1.2 million of these were money claims. Most are bulk debt claims by banks and credit card companies and they are handled at a centralised County Court Business Centre. Proceedings start when the court issues a claim on the defendant.

The defendant must, within 14 days, admit the claim or file a defence (statement of case) or acknowledge the claim. If he files a defence, the case is normally transferred to his home court. If not, the claimant may request a default judgment (Pt 12) asking the court to grant his claim. *Most cases end at this point* (over 90 per cent in 2015). With undefended bulk claims, judgment is automatically issued, without the involvement of a judge. Most are then enforced by warrants issued centrally. If the defendant is one of the 10 per cent who defends himself, he may issue a claim against a co-defendant or third party or make a counterclaim (Pt 20). The claimant may reply and defend. The parties may write direct to others requesting further information (Pt 18).

Procedural judges and allocation (CPR 26.5–26.11)

10–006   Judges manage cases: masters in the Royal Courts of Justice and district judges in the County Court and High Court district registries, outside London. Most case management is done on paper or electronically, in district judge's chambers, described in Darbyshire (2011), Ch.11. Hearings may be by telephone. If the Briggs recommendations 2016 work, all claims under £25,000 will be managed digitally. Commercial Court judges manage their own cases. Defended claims are allocated to one of three tracks, as follows, once the parties have completed their directions questionnaires.

Small claims

For most actions under £10,000, with exceptions. The limit was £5000, before the   **10–007**
Jackson reforms 2013–2014.

Fast track

For most cases £10–£25,000, which can be tried in a day. Oral expert evidence is   **10–008**
limited to two fields; one expert per field.

Multi-track

Claims over £25,000, or over one day's trial. These will normally be transferred   **10–009**
to a County Court Civil Trial Centre.

Claims with no monetary value

Such as applications for injunctions, are allocated where the judge considers they   **10–010**
will be dealt with most justly.

Discretionary factors

The procedural judge *must* have regard to the: **10–011**

- nature of the remedy sought;
- complexity of facts, law and evidence;
- number of parties;
- value of the claim and counterclaim;
- oral evidence;
- importance of the claim to non-parties;
- parties' views and circumstances;

The Woolf Report 1996 suggested the following cases for the multi-track:

- those of public importance;
- test cases: an example was successful negligence litigation by ex-miners, suffering from respiratory diseases, which encouraged many others to claim compensation, in 1998;
- clinical disputes and cases with a right to jury trial.

District judges hear almost all small claims and many fast track. Multi-track trials are shared between district, circuit and HC judges, depending on value, complexity and importance.

The court's duty to manage cases (CPR r.1.4)

10–012 All judges have always had an inherent common law *power* to manage cases. This *duty* had already been introduced, as a matter of good practice (rather than law), from 1994 in Practice Directions. It includes timetabling, the requirement for skeleton arguments and limitation of oral argument. In the CPR, the *duty* to further the overriding objective by actively manage cases now includes:

- encouraging parties to co-operate;
- identifying issues at an early stage;
- deciding promptly which can be disposed of summarily;
- deciding the order of issues;
- encouraging alternative dispute resolution;
- helping parties settle all or part of the case;
- fixing timetables;
- considering cost benefit;
- grouping issues;
- dealing with the case without the parties having to attend;
- making use of IT; and
- directing the trial process quickly and efficiently.

Sanctions for failure to comply with case management

10–013 These include striking out (meaning dismissing the case), cost penalties and debarring part of a case or evidence. Trials will only be postponed as a last resort. Sanctions should be designed to prevent rather than punish non-compliance with rules and timetables.

Interim Orders

10–014 Parties may apply for the orders below but the Rules permit the court to act on its own initiative. There is an obligation to apply early.

- Pre-action remedies if urgent.
- Applications without notice (formerly "ex parte").
- Extensions or shortening of time.
- Requiring attendance.
- Separating, consolidating or excluding issues.
- Deciding the order of issues.
- Staying (pausing) all or part of the case, hoping for settlement.
- Interim injunctions/declarations.
- Freezing injunctions, which can also be made against a third party, and search orders. They may only be ordered by a HC or authorised judge. The effect is draconian. The former freezes a party's financial assets, such as bank accounts.
- Pre-action disclosure of evidence or inspection, including against non-parties.
- Interim payments and offers to settle.

- A costs management order.

Other points

Summary judgment (Pt 14)

This may be initiated by the claimant, defendant or court, where the claim or   10–015
defence "has no real prospect of success". The court may enter judgment, dismiss
the case, strike out a claim, or make a conditional order.

District judges

They have unlimited jurisdiction to assess damages, unless otherwise directed.   10–016
They should not deal with complex cases. There is a Practice Direction on case
allocation to judges.

A group litigation order (Pt 19)

This may be made to allow for case management in multi-party actions. An   10–017
example is *Deep Vein Thrombosis and Air Travel Group Litigation* (2005).

RTA claims

A streamlined procedure was introduced in 2010 for road traffic accident personal   10–018
injury claims of £1,000–£10,000, with fixed fees. In 2013, this was extended to
employer and public liability personal injury claims under £25,000.

Basic procedure in defended cases

Small claims (Pt 27)

Most claimants are unrepresented. The procedure is meant to be simple enough   10–019
for people to use without a lawyer. Madge, an experienced district judge, reported
(2004) that unrepresented "litigants in person" had little difficulty in preparing.
After allocation, standard directions, such as requiring the exchange of
documents, are issued. Hearings are meant to be in public (European Convention
on HR art.6, fair trial) but are normally held in the judges' chambers. The public
very rarely observe these proceedings and are probably unaware that they are
open. Costs are low and fixed so, however much the litigant spends on her side of
the case, she cannot expect to recoup extravagant expenses. Keeping costs down
is meant to enhance access to justice by encouraging people to use small claims
to enforce their rights. The parties are required to help the court in furthering the
overriding objective. It is rare for evidence to be taken on oath.

The judge may adopt any procedure she considers fair, including hearing lay
representatives. Baldwin's research indicated different judicial preferences.
Judges may follow traditional adversarial procedure, with speeches and
examination of witnesses, or a more inquisitorial approach. Madge observed "An
interventionist approach ... is effective in eliciting evidence from litigants in

person. It is seen by unrepresented parties as a 'helping hand' … By discussing the facts of the case, judges find what common ground does exist between the parties … ." The key judicial skills were maintaining a balance between informality and fairness, and ensuring a level playing field. Judges give formal judgments, applying the law, and state their reasons orally.

10–020 Small claims courts were developed outside the court system, in London and Manchester, in 1971, to deal with small consumer complaints, for which County Court procedure was too elaborate and expensive. They proved so popular that they were absorbed into the County Court system in 1973.

In 1997, Baldwin found that three quarters of small claimants were contented with the handling of their case, whereas, of those involved in formal trials, 40 per cent considered them inappropriate and disproportionately expensive. Small claims tended to be used by professionals or businesses and had not provided the poor with an avenue for redress. Madge presented a snapshot of the types of case he heard in 2002: 44 per cent were business debts, 22 per cent landlord and tenant, 16 per cent road traffic claims and 10 per cent were complaints about services, such as work by builders or plumbers. 42 per cent were for less than £1,000. Half the litigants were companies. Four fifths were unrepresented. The time between claim and final hearing was less than six months, in 70 per cent of cases. Permission to appeal was sought in 6 per cent but not granted. Small claims may be referred to the SC Mediation Service, if the parties consent (26.4A).

Fast track (Pt 28)

10–021 The intention is for the court to maintain "proportionality", which means limiting the costs recoverable from the unsuccessful party. The aim is to increase access to justice by removing uncertainty. The court directs the timetable and fixes the trial date no more than 30 weeks ahead. Lord Woolf said it was important for the court to protect the weaker party against oppressive or unreasonable behaviour by a powerful party. Standard directions include disclosure and the exchange of witness statements and expert evidence. Parties are encouraged to use a single or a court-appointed expert. The judge pre-reads the bundle and case summary which must be delivered pre-trial.

Multi-track (Pt 29)

10–022 This varies. Simple cases are treated like fast track ones. Complex ones may have several directions hearings:

1. a case and/or costs management conference;
2. a pre-trial review of the statement of issues;
3. other directions hearings.

Practice Directions make more detailed requirements. They may require the submission and exchange of skeleton arguments and document bundles pre-trial.

Disclosure (formerly "discovery") (Pt 31)

Lord Woolf thought one of two major generators of unnecessary cost was   **10–023**
uncontrolled discovery so standard disclosure requires only documents on which
a party relies and documents which:

- adversely affect his case;
- adversely affect another party's case;
- support another party's case;
- or are required by a Practice Direction.

The court's power to control evidence (Pts 32 and 33)

The court has power to control the issues, the nature of the evidence and its   **10–024**
delivery: whether it is prepared to hear oral, video-link, hearsay, or written
evidence, and so on.

Expert witnesses (Pt 35)

The 1990s saw the massive growth in the use of "experts" and they used to act as   **10–025**
"hired guns", giving evidence for the party who paid them. Lord Woolf found this
had made litigation costly and unduly adversarial. He denounced the development of the "large litigation support industry ... This goes against all principles of
proportionality and access to justice." (1996). The assumption is now that one
expert will do, in small claims and fast track cases (re-emphasised from 2009).
The expert's overriding duty is to help the court. No party may call an expert or
use a report without permission. The court has a duty to restrict expert evidence
and can make a costs order against an expert who has caused significant expense:
Phillips v Symes (2004). Problems remain. After the "Jackson reforms",
2013–2014, the aim is to further limit their role. Parties applying to use an expert
must list the issues to be addressed, and provide a costs estimate.

Offers to settle (Pt 36)

This procedure encourages the parties to settle by financial incentive. Under the   **10–026**
old rules, the defendant could make a payment into court and force the plaintiff to
take a gamble: take the money or proceed to trial and risk paying both sides' costs
since the time of the payment in, which could be a Pyrrhic victory for a winning
plaintiff. This happened to Albert Reynolds, former Irish Prime Minister, in 1996,
when he won a libel action against the *Sunday Times* and was awarded one penny
in damages but had to pay over £1 million in costs. The intention of Pt 36 is that
allowing the *claimant* to make an offer to settle, as well as the defendant, alters
the balance of power. Where the offer is the same as or better than that ordered by
the judge, the offeror is rewarded by having the judge order that the other side
will pay both sides' costs since the date of expiry of the offer, including interest,
plus an additional amount. Traditionally, the trial judge knew nothing of the offer,
otherwise the gamble would not work. Since 2015, the judge can be told of the

offer but not the contents, at a preliminary hearing. Where the offer is not a genuine attempt to settle, the court can refuse costs.

Basic trial procedure

10–027   The Woolf reforms were intended to cut trial length. Suitable cases may be disposed of without a hearing (r.1.4(2)). The statutory right to jury trial was unaffected in deceit, libel, slander, malicious prosecution and false imprisonment (but, since 2014, parties have to *apply* for a jury trial in libel and slander). Generally, hearings must be in open court. There are exceptions, such as mortgage possession cases and proceedings involving children. In fast and multi-track trials, procedure is as follows.

1.   The claimant/claimant's advocate makes her opening speech.
2.   Traditionally, the claimant's first witness was examined by the claimant or advocate and then cross-examined by the defendant or her advocate but pre-trial witness statements, including expert reports, now count as evidence-in-chief in the trial so the witnesses are only cross-examined, to save time. Supplementary questions may be asked only for "good reason". If there is a single joint expert, whose evidence is agreed, it may not be necessary to call them to court. Witnesses may appear via video link.
3.   This is repeated for each subsequent claimant witness.
4.   At the end of the claimant's case, the defendant may submit that there is "no case to answer", where he considers the claimant's case has no real prospect of success. If the court agrees, it may dismiss the case. Appeal lies to the CA from a circuit judge's finding of "no case".
5.   The defendant or defence advocate makes her opening speech.
6.   Each defence witness is (examined and) cross-examined, as above.
7.   Closing speeches are made by the claimant, or her advocate, and defendant, or advocate.
8.   Unless a jury is present, the judge decides whether the claimant has proven the case to her satisfaction. The standard of proof is "proof on the balance of probabilities", which is a much lower standard than in a criminal case, which has to be proven "beyond reasonable doubt".
9.   The judge delivers judgment, or, if a jury is present, she sums up the evidence to them and they deliver their verdict. The judge makes an order. The CA has said that the judge has a duty to give reasons, which is a function of due process. Parties should know why they have won or lost; the losing party will know whether there is a ground of appeal; giving reasons concentrates the mind so the decision is more likely to be soundly based on the evidence: *Flannery v Halifax Estate Agencies Ltd* (2000).
10.   The judge hears arguments on costs then makes an order as to costs.
11.   The judge hears any application for permission to appeal.
12.   The whole trial will have been recorded so that a transcript may be requested.

Costs and Costs Management (Pts 3 and 44–48)

Under the pre-1999 regime, in most cases costs would "follow" the event so the **10–028** outcome would amount to "winner takes all". Under the 1998 rules, the judge must assess costs in accordance with which party won different issues and the judge's view as to how reasonably the parties behaved. The court may make a wasted costs order against a representative if she has acted improperly, unreasonably or negligently and her conduct has caused unnecessary costs to the other party. Throughout the proceedings, costs should be kept down to a proportionate level but this has not happened, hence the 2014 "Jackson reforms" on costs, explored below. Courts have been granting costs capping orders for years, limiting the amount of costs a party can recover. It is incumbent on everyone to take all steps to reduce costs: *Pastouna v Black* (2005), reiterating their duty under CPR rr.1.1 and 1.3. Brooke LJ castigated solicitors and counsel for coming to London from Liverpool at taxpayers' expense, when the brief hearing could have been conducted by video conference. The major outcome of the Jackson reforms was the requirement, from 2014, for all parties except litigants in person to file and exchange *pre-trial costs budgets* as part of case management, in all multi-track claims, with certain exceptions and unless the court orders otherwise. Cases over £10 million are exempted. Pre-2014, the court had a *power* to make a costs management order but CPR r.3.15 is designed to enforce Jackson's emphasis on *proportionality* and requires that

> "the court *will* make a costs management order unless it is satisfied that the litigation can be conducted justly and at proportionate cost in accordance with the overriding objective without such an order being made". (My emphasis)

In managing the case, the court and parties must abide by the amended, stricter overriding objective of dealing with the case at proportionate cost. Lawyers in general have been very resistant to pre-trial costs-budgeting, which is why is has taken from 1996 till 2014 to enforce it. As Rowley (2013) remarked "Costs budgeting is seen by many practitioners as an extended form of fixed fee torture", time consuming, requiring predicting the other side's tactics and giving away strategic information.

General points

Judicial bias is a ground of appeal. Judicial independence is examined in Ch.14. **10–029** If a judge interferes too much in the presentation of the case, he risks breaching the common law rules of "natural justice", or fairness and, consequently, art.6 of the European Convention. The CA considered what level of intervention was tolerable, in *Alpha Lettings Ltd v Neptune Research* (2003). The trial judge was irritable with the defendant's witnesses and counsel and made numerous interventions. The CA remarked that part of the trial had been "depressing to hear on the tape". They rejected the defendant's argument, however, because the judge had not prevented the witnesses from giving evidence, nor had he prevented the advocates from eliciting that evidence. They approved Bingham MR in *Arab Monetary Fund v Hashim (No.7)* (1993):

"In some jurisdictions the forensic tradition is that judges sit mute, listening to the advocates without interruption, asking no question, voicing no opinion ... it is not ours ... The English tradition sanctions and even encourages a measure of disclosure by the judge of his current thinking ... An expression of scepticism is not suggestive of bias unless the judge conveys an unwillingness to be persuaded of a factual proposition whatever the evidence may be."

10–030   An *advocate to the court*, formerly known as an amicus curiae, may be appointed by the Attorney General, at the court's request, where there is a danger of an important and difficult point of law being decided without the court hearing relevant argument. The advocate represents no-one and will not normally lead evidence, cross-examine witnesses or investigate the facts. They are sometimes instructed by the Treasury Solicitor where the court wants to hear specialist argument by a neutral lawyer. This often happens in chancery cases about pensions where the appellant is unrepresented: *Secretary of State for Work and Pensions v Morina* (2007).

All *advocates* have a common law duty not to mislead the court: *Vernon v Bosley (No.1)* (1997) and a duty to keep up-to-date with recent law reports: *Copeland v Smith* (2000).

3. APPEALS

10–031   In *Access to Justice*, 1996, Lord Woolf said:

"Appeals serve two purposes: the private purpose, which is to do justice in particular cases by correcting wrong decisions, and the public purpose, which is to ensure public confidence in the administration of justice by making such corrections and to clarify and develop the law and to set precedents." (p.153.)

Procedure is contained in the Access to Justice Act 1999, the CPR and in Practice Directions. The regime was set out by the CA (Civil Division) in *Tanfern Ltd v Cameron-Macdonald* (2000). The Government planned to achieve proportionality and efficiency by diverting from the CA those cases which did not require the attention of the most senior judges, and by reforming methods. The guiding principles are as follows, from 2000.

● Permission is always required and will only be given where the court considers that an appeal would have a real prospect of success.
● In normal circumstances, more than one appeal cannot be justified.

Jurisdiction

10–032   ● In fast track cases heard by a district judge, appeal lies to a circuit judge. Grounds are not restricted. There is a guarantee of an oral hearing, which is a review, not a rehearing.
● In fast track cases heard by a circuit judge, appeal lies to a HC judge.
● In multi-track cases, appeals against final orders lie to the CA, regardless of the original judge, though Briggs LJ in his 2016 Review said that cases should be routed to the HC, to stop overloading the CA.

- In multi-track cases, appeals against a procedural decision lie to a judge immediately higher in the hierarchy.
- Exceptional cases involving important points of principle or which affect a number of litigants may "leapfrog" straight to the CA, from the County Court. A case may leapfrog from the HC to the Supreme Court if (from 2015) the trial judge thinks it involves matters of national importance or the benefits of consideration by the UKSC outweigh the benefits of consideration by the CA.

Composition

Under the 1999 Act, the CA can consist of one, two or three judges, according to the importance and complexity of the case. They rarely sit in pairs because if they cannot agree, the case may have to be re-argued before a new court of three, which is expensive for the parties. Briggs LJ recommended that they sit in pairs in most cases, though, in order to reduce the backlog of civil appeals in 2016.   **10–033**

Procedure (in Practice Directions)

If the trial judge is unsure whether the appeal would have a real prospect of success or involves a general point of principle, she should decline permission and let the litigant seek it from the CA. Permission can be granted without a real prospect of success, if there is a public interest issue. Appeals on points of law should only be granted if the CA is likely to come to a different conclusion, on principle, and this would affect the outcome. Appeals on law include lack of evidence. On appeals on fact, the CA will rarely interfere with a trial judge's assessment of the oral evidence but will consider challenges to the judge's inference from primary facts, or where the judge has not benefited from seeing witnesses.   **10–034**

The CA has been attempting to cut down delays and the length of hearings since 1994. The judges work at a very fast rate, as I reported in 2011, from observational research. They have vast amounts of papers to read, in preparation. They normally sit in court four days a week, so have to fit in judgment-writing and preparatory reading into one "reading day", plus evenings and weekends. They do not have the time to read irrelevant material or to deal with skeleton arguments or document bundles which come in late. (I regularly saw evidence bundles delivered at 10.15am for a 10.30am hearing.) Exasperated with practitioners who do not seem to understand this, they amended the appeal Practice Direction (CPR PD 52) in 2004. In *Scribes West Ltd v Relsa Anstalt (No.1)* (2004), the CA complained bitterly of a "proliferation of bundles ... (and) widespread ignorance of provisions ... which were designed to assist the court but did not succeed in their object". The Direction requires the exclusion of all extraneous documents, with a costs penalty for unnecessary copying or incomplete bundles. The appellant must file a skeleton argument 14 days in advance and the respondent a week in advance, or the court may refuse to hear an argument. The Direction is strict. Its purpose is to support the CA's determination to streamline its work and prevent this being defeated by inefficient lawyers. The problem persists. The CA has made repeated warnings about massive bundles and repetitive, lengthy skeletons. In *Midgulf* (2010), there were 15 lever arch files of bundles, five containing 100 authorities, and a 132 page skeleton. Lawyers have still not learned their lesson: *Standard Bank* (2013) and *Revenue and Customs Commissioners v Ben Nevis* (2013). One of the main findings of the 2016 Briggs Review was that the CA overload was unsustainable and appeal routes and procedures must change.

Grounds

10–035 Appeals will only be allowed where the lower court was wrong or where it was unjust because of a serious procedural or other irregularity. Under the post-2000 procedure, the decision of the lower court attracts a much greater significance so decisions must be recorded accurately.

Admitting fresh evidence

10–036 The leading case is *Ladd v Marshall* (1954), which requires that the evidence could not have been obtained with reasonable diligence at the trial; it would probably have an important influence on the result and it must be apparently credible, reiterated in *Riyad Bank v United Bank* (2005).

Approach and powers

10–037 Every appeal is limited to a *review* of the decision of the lower court, unless Practice Direction provides otherwise, or the court considers that it would be in the interests of justice to hold a rehearing. Generally, an appeal court has all the powers of the lower court. It can also affirm, set aside or vary any order or judgment, or refer any claim or issue for determination by the lower court, or order a new trial or hearing and order costs. The CA is very reluctant to overturn a trial judge's findings of fact, because, unlike them, she has seen the witnesses and/or their statements. They are even more reluctant to overturn a jury's decision. As we can see from the quotation from *R. v McIlkenny*, in the Criminal Division, discussed in Ch.12, this is mainly because judges accord juries a special constitutional position. Also, as juries do not give detailed reasons, that makes it all the more difficult to draft an appeal or reconsider their findings of fact.

The leading case (worth reading for comedy entertainment) on the conditions in which the CA will overturn a civil jury's decision is *Grobbelaar v News Group Newspapers* (2001). The CA overturned an £85,000 damages award to a former Liverpool goalkeeper for a defamation action in which the jury were persuaded that he had been falsely accused of match fixing, despite strong video and audio-taped evidence (repeatedly shown on TV) of his taking bribes (he was handed an envelope) and boasting of a previous conspiracy. Simon Brown LJ warned, in the CA: "the court must inevitably be reluctant to find a jury's verdict perverse and anxious not to usurp their function" but he was satisfied that the CA had the jurisdiction to entertain an appeal on the ground of perversity, if the verdict, on all the evidence, was not properly and reasonably open to the jury. A detailed examination of the facts led the CA "inexorably to the view that Mr Grobbelaar's story is, quite simply, incredible. All logic, common sense and reason compel one to that conclusion." Mr Grobbelaar appealed to the law lords. They allowed his appeal because they *could* find a rational explanation for the jury's verdict, on an examination of the facts, but they agreed with Simon Brown's reasoning on appellate courts' reluctance to overturn a jury verdict: (2002). Lord Bingham set out the position of an appellate court:

> "The oracular utterance of the jury contains no reasoning, no elaboration. But it is not immune from review…While speculation about the jury's reasoning and train of thought is impermissible, the drawing of inevitable or proper inferences from the jury's decision is not, and is indeed inherent in the process of review … it is a very serious thing to stigmatise as perverse the unanimous finding of jurors who have solemnly sworn to return a true verdict according to the evidence. A jury may, of course, from time to time act in a wholly irrational way, but that is not a conclusion to be reached lightly or if any alternative explanation not involving perversity presents itself." (para.7).

The House nevertheless reduced the damages to a nominal £1, or "derisory damages" as Lord Millett called them, Lord Bingham explaining that the appellant "acted in a way in which no decent or honest footballer would act".

In exceptional cases, the CA has power to re-open an appeal. This was done on grounds of alleged bias, in *Taylor v Lawrence* (2001).

4. BACKGROUND TO THE WOOLF REFORMS

The problems have been notorious for centuries. Prior to the *Civil Justice Review* 1988, there had been 63 reports since 1900. With frustrating repetition, they all identified the same core defects, articulated by Woolf in 1995: "The process is too expensive, too slow and too complex". People were unable to enforce their rights. The very title of the 1996 Woolf report, *Access to Justice*, seemed like an ironic cliché.   **10–038**

The 1988 Review resulted in the Courts and Legal Services Act 1990 and delegated legislation. It recommended merging the jurisdiction of the County Court and HC and enabling the Lord Chancellor to make rules allowing for flexible distribution of the caseload between them. This was done, as was the radical shifting down into the County Court of most cases, leaving the HC for procedurally or evidentially complex cases and judicial review. Yet, despite the fact that its reforms were potentially the most radical since the Judicature Acts of 1873–1875, they did not satisfy critics. The two sides of the legal profession (barristers and solicitors) swiftly produced the 1993 Heilbron–Hodge Report identifying the problems in procedure and proposing solutions, prompting the Lord Chancellor to commission Woolf to carry out yet another scrutiny. In the meantime, the Heads of Division (Master of the Rolls, Lord Chief Justice and Vice-Chancellor) took matters into their own hands by issuing radical Practice Directions for the conduct of litigation in the HC. Described below are some reviews and reforms which pre-empted Woolf.

The Heilbron–Hodge Report 1993

10–039   The report, published by the Bar Council and Law Society, was entitled "Civil Justice on Trial—The Case for Change". They complained that:

- "An air of Dickensian antiquity pervades the civil process";
- "Procedures are unnecessarily technical, inflexible, rule-ridden, formalistic and often incomprehensible to the ordinary litigant...";
- lawyers and judges were reluctant to change;
- progress of actions lay with the parties rather than the courts, causing avoidable delay;
- fear of cost deterred people from using the courts;
- most people wanted their dispute resolved rather than their "day in court".

The principles underlying their recommendations were:

- litigation should encourage early settlement;
- litigants should have to follow sensible time-frames;
- judges should adopt a more interventionist role to ensure that issues were limited, delays reduced and court time was not wasted;
- since court time was costly, a balance should be struck between the written and oral word and what could be achieved out of court rather than in court;
- justice should, where possible, be brought to the people;
- a widespread introduction of technology was urgently required;
- facilities urgently need improving;
- additional resources should be found to improve the system.

Here are some of their main recommendations. Some reforms were effected by the 1994/95 Practice Directions. My comments are bracketed:

1.   HC listing should be computerised (done).
3.   Common procedural rules for the HC and County Court (done by the CPR 1998).
4.   Judicial review cases to be heard on circuit (done).
5.   Revival of an ethos of public service amongst court staff and assistance to litigants.
6.   Plain English court documents (done).
7.   A more interventionist approach by judges at trial and on appeal (done: the CPR *duty* to manage cases).
8.   Limits on discovery of documents; requirements for skeleton arguments and bundles to be delivered to the court and to opposing parties (done: Practice Directions 1994–1995, then CPR).
9.   Judicial intervention at trial to avoid time wasting (done: CPR).
10. Promotion of ADR (done: CPR).

The 1994/95 HC Practice Directions

Heilbron–Hodge prompted these and the 1994 establishment of Woolf's scrutiny. **10–040** The Directions emphasised the importance of reducing cost and delay, threatening costs sanctions for non-compliance. The court was encouraged to limit documents, oral submissions, examination of witnesses, the issues on which it wished to be addressed, and reading aloud from documents and authorities. Witness statements would generally stand as evidence-in-chief. Bundled documents and skeleton arguments were to be lodged in court pre-trial. Opening speeches were to be succinct and, where appropriate, lawyers had to verify that they had considered the possibility of ADR with their client. These Directions had a significant impact on the shape of the civil trial. The parties and the judge now read most of the arguments and documentation in advance, thus departing radically from the oral tradition which characterised common law adversarial procedure. The Directions encouraged the judge to control the nature and content of the cases presented, again departing from the traditional common law role (see Ch.9) as a non-interfering umpire, who allowed the parties to dictate the shape and pace of the case. The expectation that judges would pre-read was revolutionary. In 1990, a judge would generally walk into a courtroom knowing nothing of the case. The advocates would relate the whole evidential story, and the law, orally, cross-referring to documents and law reports. Testimony would normally be adduced from live witnesses, in examination and cross-examination. The exception was the Commercial Court, where judges had been proactively managing cases and demanding exchange of witness statements and skeleton arguments pre-trial since 1978 or before.

The Interim Woolf Report 1995 and *Access to Justice* 1996

Woolf repeated many of the recommendations of the *Civil Justice Review* and the **10–041** Heilbron–Hodge Report in his 1995 interim report. He sought:

1. An effective system of case management by the court, instead of allowing the parties to flout rules and run the cases.
2. An expanded small claims jurisdiction and a fast track for cases above this.
3. Judicial, tailored case management for cases above the fast-track.
4. Encouragement of early settlement and enabling either party to make an offer to settle.
5. The creation of a Head of Civil Justice.
6. A single set of High Court/County Court rules.
7. Court appointment of single, neutral expert witnesses.
8. Promotion of the use of IT for case management by judges; use of video and telephone conferencing.

Almost all of this was repeated in the final report, *Access to Justice*, in 1996, then translated into the law, in the CPR 1998 explained above. There were some amendments. For example, on point 7 above, the court does not appoint experts but normally requires the parties to agree on a single joint expert. Crucially, point

8 of Woolf's plan has still not been fulfilled by 2017 and was reiterated in the 2016 Briggs Review. Progress on IT, especially case management software, in the civil courts is worse than dismal.

5. REACTIONS TO THE WOOLF REPORT

10–042 Professor Zander (1995/1996/1997) was highly critical. He said the overwhelming majority of cases settled, so did not need management; "we have virtually no information about either delays or costs" and Woolf had not commissioned research; they had been trying to reform the system in the USA for 20 years without success. Increasing judicial discretionary powers would create inconsistency. Lawyers would be unable to stick to time-limits. Case management was a common theme throughout Canada, the USA and Australia. He cited a study of 10,000 US cases by the Rand Corporation which found that some US judges believed case management emphasised speed and efficiency at the expense of justice and added to costs because lawyers spent an extra 20 hours responding to court directions, even in cases which would have settled anyway. Costs would become front-loaded. Woolf responded that Zander's criticisms were "strident . . . misleading and inaccurate" (1997). Zander defended himself many times (2000) but his warning on "front-loading" of costs came back to haunt Woolf and everyone else involved in civil litigation.

6. EVALUATING THE WOOLF REFORMS: RESEARCH, SURVEYS AND COMMENTS

Research and surveys

10–043 There is little research and lots of surveys. A 2001 national consumer satisfaction survey of court users found 79 per cent satisfied with the overall level of service. A survey of legal departments of UK companies by Eversheds, found 54 per cent of respondents considered civil litigation improved in 1999–2000; 52 per cent found litigation quicker but only 22 per cent considered it cheaper; 43 per cent were settling cases earlier. Clients no longer sought aggressive, uncompromising lawyers. 41 per cent had used ADR. Only 24 per cent thought litigants were getting better justice. Costs had risen, according to 19 per cent.

A 2000 MORI survey of 180 firms found that 76 per cent said there had been faster settlements and less litigation, although most respondents thought the outcome would have been the same under the old system. The early-settlement offer, bringing heavy penalties to those refusing to settle, had had the biggest impact on litigation, according to 66 per cent. Mediation had increased. The Civil Justice Audit found 80 per cent of lawyers were satisfied with the Rules; 36 per cent believed litigation had decreased; 47 per cent reported settling cases faster; 60 per cent thought judges should initiate settlement discussion; 58 per cent thought cases should be stayed for mediation and 78 per cent of in-house lawyers thought mediation should be required before a business dispute went to court (2000). A Wragge survey of in-house commercial lawyers found: 81 per cent thought courts did not have enough resources; 89 per cent liked the changes and found litigation quicker; 41 per cent found costs cut; and 80 per cent found ADR had proved popular (2000). A 2001 Law Society survey of 130 solicitors showed they were concerned that the assessment of costs was arbitrary and unpredictable, often causing them to make a loss over litigation. They thought judges were unwilling to apply sanctions and lacked consistency. New procedures making more work at the beginning of litigation ("front loading") were not cheaper for clients and led to more work, as Zander, above, had warned. Most considered the use of joint experts inappropriate in multi-track cases.

In 2002, the Lord Chancellor's Department published an evaluation of the **10–044** reforms, confirming their "broad success". The use of pre-action protocols and offers to settle had diverted cases from litigation. About 8 per cent settled at the court door and 70 per cent settled earlier. Time from claim to trial had dropped from 639 days in 1997, to 498 in 2000–2001. There had been a levelling off in the use of ADR. A 2002 Court Service users survey showed 20 per cent of lawyers found procedures difficult to understand but 45 per cent thought the reforms had simplified procedures. In 2002, Lord Phillips MR said case management had reduced the average length of time for a case to come to trial from 600 to 520 days and for claims over £5,000 from 750 to 450 days. Nevertheless, there was a lot of anecdotal evidence that the Woolf Reforms had increased the cost of litigation for cases going the whole way.

A 2002 report by Goriely and others reported the results of the first detailed piece of *research*. They examined the impact on pre-action behaviour. They concluded that the Woolf reforms had enhanced access to justice. Early disclosure had led to more settlements at the pre-action stage and they were based on better information. Most practitioners regarded the reforms as a success, citing clearer structure and greater certainty in the fast track. They praised the invention of claimants' Pt 36 offers and considered that pre-action protocols enabled informed settlement. They complained of a lack of sanctions for breach, however. Expert evidence continued to be problematic, although the instruction of agreed experts had almost eradicated the concept of an expert owned by one side. Many felt that the courts were inefficient in listing. Problems caused by lack of IT were well known. In a 2005 Department of Constitutional Affairs Research Report, the researchers concluded that the litigation culture had changed for the better, noting the drop in civil cases since 1997, from 2.2 million to 1.5 million in 2003. Costs per case had increased, though, and were front-loaded. In a 2010 research report, the Ministry of Justice published findings that in most cases, the rules were followed, questionnaires were completed on time and guidelines on trial scheduling were followed. In my research, work-shadowing judges (2011), I asked those with civil experience what they thought of the Woolf reforms. Eleven of twelve district judges rated them as a success, four in strong terms: "brilliant", "amazing", "incredibly successful" but the circuit judges were less enthusiastic, with only ten commenting positively. Sixteen of the thirty-three expressed concern about wildly disproportionate costs.

Comments

10–045 In 2000, Robert Turner, Senior Master (case manager) in the HC, welcomed the new rules. The adversarial approach had been replaced by co-operation. Settlements were achieved earlier, procedures were defining the real issues between the parties, and solicitors would find the quicker disposal rate allowed them to do more work. In the short term, however, the new rules had not succeeded in attacking cost, delay and complexity because the new system was costly at the commencement of the action ("front loaded"); the new procedures with pre-action protocols, allocation and listing questionnaires and case management conferences were more complex. Another master, John Leslie commented on "a new spirit of co-operation abroad". He found around 50 per cent of cases stayed (suspended) for a settlement attempt did settle. He too complained of a lack of IT, though. Zander, in 2000, described the Woolf reforms in a more tempered way than before, praising some elements, but he reiterated his criticism of front-loading of costs, in the manner of "I told you so".

Suzanne Burn, an experienced civil litigator, wrote a very useful article in 2003, summarising many evaluations of Woolf and adding comments from her experiences. There had been very limited research into the impact of the reforms. Lightman J (2003) drew the following conclusions, from his 32 years at the Bar and nine as a HC judge:

1. Although the pre-action protocols had front-loaded costs they had substantially reduced the number of claims.
2. Summary orders for costs had led to parties "feeling the pain" earlier and so they were more cautious. Unnecessary cases were avoided.
3. Full case management powers enabled the court to ensure delay was minimised.
4. The limitation on expert witnesses had removed a drain on resources and court time.
5. Small claims provided a public service of inestimable value.

Nevertheless, in 2007, Sir Anthony Clarke, Master of the Rolls and Head of Civil Justice told the American Bar Association that he was unhappy with the continuing "evils of delay, inefficiency and costs". In 2009, Professor Dame Hazel Genn was heavily critical of the poverty of resources in the civil courts and the passion for ADR:

> "We are witnessing the decline of civil justice—the downgrading of the importance of civil justice, the degradation of court facilities, and the diversion of civil cases to private dispute resolution, accompanied by the anti-litigation/anti-adjudication rhetoric that interprets these developments as socially positive … The anti-law story suggests that society is in the grip of a litigation explosion or compensation culture … the civil justice system has few friends in government, since it is through civil cases that the government is directly challenged."

The tenth anniversary of the CPRules' operation, in 2009, saw the publication of many opinions. Lord Justice Jackson, below, had already published his critical preliminary report. Lord Woolf acknowledged that one of his aims, cost reduction, had not been achieved. This was partly not of his making. The government had replaced most legal aid with conditional fee (no-win no-fee) agreements (CFAs). The related insurance premiums had increased costs. Court costs had soared. "This has been a very retrograde step ... I was relying on the client controlling the costs. They have not exercised sufficient control." He would have liked to have introduced a docketing system, with each case always being managed by just one judge. Zander, Woolf's constant critic, said most of his fears had been justified. He again pointed to the front-loading of costs. The trouble was, this applied to all cases, not just the 10 per cent that went to trial but also the other 90 per cent, which would have settled anyway. He felt delay had remained the same. Goriely's 2002 research showed that while the post-claim stage had become quicker, the pre-issue stage was slower. District Judge Hill, a member of the CPR Committee considered the fast track "Hugely successful ... I have tried many fast-track cases. None has ever gone over the one-day allowed". He felt the most successful change effected by the CPR was in expert evidence. Experts used to be "hired guns". Now, the rules emphasised their duty to the court and all fair experts welcomed this, causing huge savings. "I can think of many cases, typically modest building disputes, where a single joint expert's report has been the key to unlocking the case."

The total volume of litigation

This has fallen since 1999 but this is the continuation of a previous trend, from 1990. The rate of settlement pre-trial has increased. One of Woolf's aims was to encourage early, fair settlements by placing the parties on an equal footing. Whether settlements are for fair amounts of damages is almost impossible to quantify. Qureshi pointed out that Woolf considered that individuals had a constitutional right to an accessible and effective system of civil litigation, via the courts, yet, in 1998–2002, there had been a 500 per cent reduction of proceedings commenced in the Queen's Bench Division. My reaction is as follows. Parties may be resorting to ADR. We can never measure this, because ADR is unquantifiable. It is mostly unregulated and operated as a multitude of private enterprises, whose statistics are not made public. If ADR is increasing, it is surely a success of the Woolf reforms, not a failure, since Woolf wanted to encourage ADR. The case law reinforces this by costs. The mischief of the Courts and Legal Services Act 1990 was to shift the civil case load downwards onto the County Court, reserving the HC for complex or unusual cases and the 1998 Rules continued this aspiration, so if the QBD has lost work that too is a success. One needs to take account of the total civil case load. Examining County Court business as well, we can see that its case load diminished too, from about 2,245,000 in 1998, to 1,879,000 in 2009. That this is a continuation of a previous trend is disclosed by the statistics, as in 1990 there were over 3,311,000 claims, compared with 1.5 million County Court claims in 2015.

Making the process simpler?

It is arguable whether this has been achieved. While the Rules and forms are simple and in plain English, Burn said there were over 500 forms and the Rules

10–046

10–047

and Practice Directions were (and are) longer than the old rules. Amendments are frequent. In 2009, Thompson, general editor of *The Civil Court Practice*, said the 391 pages of the old *The County Court Practice* were replaced with 2,301 pages, "a 550% increase! ...The aims of simplification and unification of procedures were admirable but they have not been achieved".

Has there been a culture change among lawyers?

10–048 Woolf hoped for a significant shift from adversarialism, the battle approach. Burn considered that lawyers were now more careful about sending deliberately aggressive letters to the opposition and "tactical" applications were less frequent but the "costs war" on conditional fees (see below) indicated adversarialism. Zander (2009) acknowledged that there had been a diminution in the adversary culture. Allen (2009), a director of the Centre for Effective Dispute resolution, described the massive shift in lawyers' behaviour:

> "When I train mediators in ... Ireland, Scotland, Pakistan, India and South Africa, it always jolts me that, except in England and Wales, it is still largely true that not to ambush is negligent. Trials can still start with undisclosed documents, witness statements and expert reports ... Suddenly hundreds if not thousands of applications for particulars or further discovery vanished from the chambers' lists of masters and district judges, and the Bear Garden was translated to its current status as a haven of peace."

There are some exceptions, though. Litigation taking 12 years over the collapse of the BCCI bank in 1991 scandalised the business world and led to criticism that the reforms were not working as intended. The BCCI bank was set up in Pakistan in 1972. Many British Asians deposited money. It became a money laundry for drug smugglers and defrauded its clients. Deloitte, the liquidators, decided to litigate against the Bank of England for letting BCCI go on for so long. The BoE refused repeated offers to settle. The case was hopeless as Deloitte could not prove negligence or misfeasance and they dropped it after 12 years. There were several pre-trial hearings and a case went up to the law lords as to whether the claim should proceed. In court, the lawyers' opening statements took 86 days and 119 days. The parties spent 256 days in court. The bank sought £73.5 million in legal costs (not damages), plus £8 million in interest. The Commercial Court judge, Tomlinson J, said he had warned Lord Woolf CJ that the case was a farce, and it could "damage the reputation of our legal system". He criticised Gordon Pollock QC, Deloitte's barrister, for "sustained rudeness". Lord Woolf himself had criticised the length of HC cases, saying that judges had failed to stop them spiralling out of control: Chong.

Pre-action protocols as a culture change

10–049 In personal injury cases, over 85 per cent settle at the protocol stage. Burn said concerns had been expressed in all surveys that these front-loaded costs, because they require a lot of work from solicitors *before* a claim is issued, in investigating their client's case and disclosing information to the other side, affirmed by judges interviewed in Darbyshire (2011). Another complaint was that the courts rarely penalised parties for non-compliance.

Case management

Burn concluded that "There seems to be no consensus about the value of judicial case management". Plotnikoff and Woolfson's research found that judges were comfortable in the role of case manager but some practitioners, said Burn, complained that judges did not read the case papers in advance. Case management conferences varied considerably from court to court. Burn remarked that

> "the one great advantage of CPR case management over the old-style laissez-faire approach is that cases no longer drift—there is always a return date to ensure judges keep an eye on progress ... Many practitioners, sadly, are their own worst enemies if they wish to minimize judicial 'interference'."

She remarked on failure to complete forms correctly and disproportionate costs estimates and "a casual attitude to case management". From spending several weeks during my empirical research in 2002–2003, looking over the shoulders of eight district judges, I can verify this. They frequently showed me that papers sent in to them by solicitors were a "dog's breakfast". They routinely referred cases back to solicitors for forms to be correctly completed (2011, Ch.11) and see District Judge John.

Sanctions and cost penalties

Burn said that relatively few cases were struck out for non-compliance with court directions and orders. She concluded that dealing with cases "justly", rather than by the rule book was working well.

7. CONTINUING PROBLEMS AND THE JACKSON REVIEW OF COSTS

Disproportionate costs, the "costs war" and the "chilling effect" of CFAs

Conditional fee agreements (CFAs) were Irvine LC's alternative solution for claimants who could not afford to litigate, after he withdrew legal aid from many of them, in the Access to Justice Act 1999, explained in Ch.17. A CFA means a "no win no fee" contract between a private client and a solicitor. The client can take out insurance against losing, as he would then be liable to pay the winner's costs. He may agree to pay a success fee to the solicitor, a percentage of the costs, if he should win. Until 2011, this has to be repaid by the loser. The success fee enables the solicitor to build up funds to finance the cases he loses. The clients do not care what level of success fee they agree to, because they know they will pay

10–050

10–051

10–052

nothing at all, whether they win or lose. A problem arose because litigants who lost cases, often insurance companies, felt solicitors were profiteering by charging unreasonable percentages as success fees. Also, satellite litigation, arguing about these amounts, bedevilled the civil courts after 2000. In *Callery v Gray* (2002), the law lords said that regulating civil litigation was the CA's business. Defendant insurers continued to bring technical challenges to CFAs and the CA ran out of patience. They awarded costs against the defendants and said such litigants should "stop all this nonsense". The Civil Justice Council commissioned research, in 2003, on how to calculate the reasonableness of a success fee and the Master of the Rolls decided to mediate a settlement between the two sides in the costs war. In the 2002 Annual Report of the Civil Justice Council, he complained that costs were the "Achilles heel" of the Woolf reforms. In 2004, 13 media organisations complained that high fees in CFAs were severely damaging press freedom in privacy and libel cases. They were forced to settle even weak claims. Claimants' lawyers were encouraging defamation suits and charging disproportionate fees. Naomi Campbell took a case against the *Daily Mirror* to the House of Lords under a "no win no fee" contract, described in Ch.4. Alastair Brett, of News International complained of "a revolting state of affairs with some lawyers displaying a greed unparalleled in any other profession". The total costs were over £1 million, including a success fee of over £250,000 and the law lords ordered MGN to pay her costs in the CA and HL, yet she had been awarded just £3,500 in damages at first instance. MGN lost their argument that such a success fee inhibited freedom of expression and was thus a breach of art.10 of the European Convention on HR but they *won* on this point in the European Court of Human Rights, in *MGN v UK* (2011). The Strasbourg court held that the recovery of success fees was disproportionate. CFAs were under new regulations after 2005.

10–053   In the meantime, there were many examples of disproportionate costs, usually caused by success fees. In 2007, Peter Bassano, conductor of the Oxford University Sinfonietta, was ordered to pay £185,000 costs after a case over an unpaid builder's bill of £16,000. In *Baigent v Random House Group* (2007), a case about *The Da Vinci Code*, the costs were over £3 million. *Douglas v Hello!* (2007), the fight about the wedding photos of Catherine Zeta-Jones and Michael Douglas, ended in the House of Lords, after six years, having incurred estimated costs of £8 million. In *Peakman v Linbrooke* (2008), three CA judges criticised the case. The dispute was about a £2,232 small claim but the lawyers' fees were over £100,000. The district judge had allocated it to the multi-track because of a spurious counterclaim. The judge should have taken control and struck out the counterclaim much earlier so the claim could have reverted to the small claims track.

Finally, there came the straw that broke the camel's back. One farcical case prompted the Jackson Review of Costs from 2009 and costs reform from 2011. This was *Multiplex Constructions UK Ltd v Cleveland Bridge* (2008), in a four-year dispute about the construction of Wembley Stadium. It absorbed £22 million in lawyers' costs, including £1 million on photocopying. Multiplex claimed £25 million in damages but Jackson J ordered only £6.1 million, observing that each party had thrown away golden opportunities to settle. He considered the costs outrageous and complained bitterly and publicly. As a consequence, he was tasked by the judiciary with conducting a fundamental review of costs in civil litigation, described below, and resulting in "the Jackson reforms", ongoing since 2011. In 2016, the pressure group Civitas called for the abolition of CFAs and the damages based agreements that were designed to replace them from 2014 because they have "corrupted the legal profession and permitted a vast increase in lawyer-driven litigation".

Do we have a compensation culture?

Teachers, businesses, insurers, local authorities and public bodies, notably the NHS, complained from the 1990s that they were suffering from a compensation culture, fuelled by potential claimants' ability to obtain CFAs from solicitors and claims handling companies. Pre-1992, UK citizens considered themselves culturally allergic to litigation, compared with Americans and Germans, who the UK considered to be overly litigious. Any civil justice system needs to balance the competing interests of access to justice and combating social exclusion on the one hand and greed and profiteering on the other. In 2003, The Law Society and the Federation of Small Businesses sought action from the Lord Chancellor to curb the growth of "ambulance chasers", blamed for increasing insurance liability premiums by encouraging employees to sue for accidents in the workplace. They called for regulation of claims farmers.

10–054

The government-commissioned Better Regulation Task Force published *Better Routes to Redress* in 2004. It concluded that there was no compensation culture but the *perception* that there was caused a fear of litigation. One highway authority spent £2 million of its £22 million budget settling claims. The news media were fond of reporting outlandish claims but neglected to report their outcome—that they often got nowhere. They acknowledged that the emergence of CFAs and claims farmers had encouraged more claims but some were well-founded and made public authorities and others better at managing risk. On the negative side, the "have a go" culture drained public resources, made organisations cautious, contributed to higher insurance premiums and clogged up the system for meritorious claimants. They recommended:

- better regulation;
- consumer advice;
- restrictions on advertising in hospitals and surgeries;
- raising the small claims limit in personal injuries;
- examining the overlap between ombudsmen;
- more encouragement of mediation;
- researching the possibility of contingency fees;
- promoting NHS rehabilitation and risk management.

In a 2005 speech Tony Blair PM said:

> "Public bodies, in fear of litigation, act in highly risk-averse and peculiar ways. We have had a local authority removing hanging baskets for fear that they might fall on someone's head, even though no such accident has occurred in the 18 years that they have been hanging there."

The Government sponsored the Compensation Bill, now Act of 2006. Part 1 is about the law of negligence and seeks to address misperceptions that encourage a disproportionate fear of litigation and thus risk-averse behaviour (such as schools declining to organise field-trips for children). The Act makes clear that when considering a claim in negligence, a court is able to consider the wider social value of the activity in the context of which the injury or damage occurred. This was further reaffirmed by the Social Action, Responsibility and Heroism Act 2015.

Part 2 provides for the regulation of claims management services. A regulator is responsible for ensuring that they abide by clear rules and a code of practice. They are required to give consumers clear advice about the validity of their claim and options for funding the costs. In 2007–2011, the Ministry of Justice closed 200 rogue firms. 700 closed in 2012–2013. In 2013 it expanded its enforcement staff. Also, the Government, courts and insurers have at long last started to tackle fraudulent personal injury claims. *Summers v Fairclough Homes* (2012) was a typical case of exaggerated injuries. A claimant demanding £800,000 was caught on camera. The UKSC said such claimants could expect imprisonment for contempt and for crime. Johnson (2013) said there was a trend for courts to award exemplary damages in cases where fraud was proven. In 2013, the Ministry of Justice proposed an independent medical panel to assess whiplash claimants. These measures are long overdue. Whiplash claims were copied from scams in the USA that were prevalent when I worked there in 1992–1993 and were imported here in the mid-1990s. The Forum of Insurance Lawyers welcomed this crackdown. Whiplash fraud cost UK insurers £2bn in 2012. The Criminal Justice and Courts Act 2015 s.57 *requires* courts to dismiss dishonestly inflated injury claims and s.58 bans firms offering inducements to potential claimants.

10–055   In 2016, HM Treasury published an *Independent Review of Claims Management Regulation*, as there was still perceived to be widespread misconduct by claims management companies and most interested parties thought the Claims Management Regulation Unit lacked powers and resources.

Senior judges have been robust in stifling a compensation culture. In *Cole v Davies-Gilbert* (2007), the CA dismissed Cole's claim against the British legion for £150,000. She broke her leg falling into a hole left by a maypole on a village green. Scott Baker LJ said if they upheld the claim "There would be no fetes, no maypole dancing and no activities that have come to be a part of the English village green". For an excellent demystification of false stories and examples of real cases see Dyson MR's Magna Carta lecture 2015.

In 2010, another government-commissioned report was produced by Lord Young, *Common Sense, Common Safety*. He suggested referral fees (paid by solicitors to claims farmers) should be scrapped, like Jackson LJ below, and agreed that success fees should not be recoverable. He said the opportunity to reform clinical negligence claims had been missed. In 2009–2010, the NHS paid out £279 million in damages and £163.7 million in costs, 75 per cent of which went to pay claimants' solicitors.

The Jackson Review of Costs—and Outcomes

Now promoted to the Court of Appeal, after widely expressing his disgust at costs **10–056** in his Wembley Stadium case, above, Jackson LJ did a lot of comparative research, finding out how other countries solved the problem of high litigation costs. Jackson's *Review of Civil Litigation Costs: Final Report 2009* (judiciary website) made these recommendations. The quotations are from the press release. Many were implemented in the Legal Aid, Sentencing and Punishment of Offenders (LASPO) Act 2012.

He re-emphasised proportionality. Costs in "no-win, no fee" cases were wildly disproportionate, indeed were 158–200 per cent of the damages awarded. *Outcome*: some judges have now adopted fairly draconian policies, which Lord Woolf was probably expecting would have happened after his 1998 reforms. A new costs management scheme commenced for multi-track cases in 2013. Parties are obliged to meet and confer. The judge must approve each party's planned budget. When applying to use an expert's report, a party must estimate the costs and list the issues to be addressed. Some judges have been specially trained and costs-manage all cases in their courts. Pilot studies showed that clients appreciated costs control (Brown 2012).

There should be fixed costs in the fast track. Lord Woolf had recommended this, nothing had happened and this was a major reason why his reforms never reduced costs. *Outcome*: From 2013, there are fixed costs for personal injury claims up to £25,000. There are fixed costs in the Intellectual Property Enterprise Court for claims up to £500,000. Lawyers have always opposed fixed costs because they think fees will be too low to reflect the work done.

Success fees and "after the event" insurance premiums should cease to be **10–057** recoverable by the winner from the loser in "no-win no-fee" cases ... "as these are the greatest contributors to disproportionate costs", and while these are congenial for lawyers, the costs have to be borne by taxpayers, council tax payers, insurance premium payers and uninsured defendants. No other jurisdiction allows success fees to be recoverable. In no-win no-fee cases, costs were no less than 158–200 per cent of damages awarded. In other cases, costs were 47–55 per cent. In 2011, his disgust was echoed by the European Court of Human Rights, who ruled in the Naomi Campbell case that success fees breached the Convention. *Outcome*: under ss.44 and 46 of the LASPO Act 2012, courts are now banned from ordering the loser to pay the winner's lawyer's success fee or insurance premium.

Lawyers' success fees, which were set at a maximum of 100 per cent, should be limited to 25 per cent. *Outcome*: under s.44 of the Act and delegated legislation, success fees in personal injury cases are limited to 25 per cent.

"To offset the effects ... general damages awards for personal injuries and other civil wrongs should be increased by 10 per cent." *Outcome*: in *Simmons v Castle* (2012), the LCJ confirmed that general damages would rise by 10 per cent from 2013.

"Referral fees should be scrapped." *Outcome:* they are banned in claims for personal injury by s.56 of the LASPO Act 2012.

There should be "Qualified 'one way costs shifting'—claimants will only make a small contribution to defendant's costs if a claim is unsuccessful ...

removing the need for after the event insurance". *Outcome*: Under Pt 2 of the LASPO Act 2012, personal injury claimants who lose their cases no longer have to pay all of their opponent's costs. Unsurprisingly, this is controversial.

10–058 "Establish a Costs Council to review fixed costs and lawyers' hourly rates annually." Allow lawyers to enter into CFAs, where lawyers are only paid if a claim is successful, normally receiving a percentage of actual damages won but clients must be independently advised. Underwood welcomed this. He spent a lot of time working for US law firms and said that commercial clients loved them and it was common to get a higher fee for a speedy settlement, with the lawyers doing less work—"deeply counterintuitive to UK lawyers". The English have always considered these American inventions (contingency fees) to be the work of the Devil, though they have long been permitted in Scotland. Moorhead (2010) critically analysed the idea that they caused a claims explosion in the USA and might cause one here. *Outcome*: these are permitted in the LASPO Act 2012, as "damages based agreements", in all areas of civil litigation, with a 50 per cent cap, and a 25 per cent cap in personal injury cases and a 30 per cent cap in employment cases. If the client loses, the lawyer gets nothing.

"Before the event" legal insurance should be promoted, for instance as part of household insurance.

ADR should be promoted. *Outcome*: Jackson commissioned a book on ADR, to be given to all judges.

Costs management should be included in continuing professional development training for lawyers and judges. *Outcome*: judges are now trained, as above.

He was concerned about the huge cost of clinical negligence to the National Health Service. After his report, in 2010, Penningtons Solicitors reported a 12.2 per cent rise in these claims in 2009. Damages payments made were £769.2 million, with a further £13.3 billion potential liabilities. Clinicians continued to refuse to apologise, despite the fact that research showed this lessened the chance of being sued.

He recommended "concurrent evidence" of experts, known as *"hot tubbing"* in Australia and Canada. They prepare a joint statement. The judge controls the proceeding and she and the lawyers can question the experts and they can challenge one another's evidence. *Outcome*: the procedure is explained in Practice Direction 35. Commercial Court judges that I interviewed for my research (2011) claimed that they had already been using this procedure.

Disclosure ramped up costs so should be controlled. *Outcome*: from 2013, parties in multi-track cases must produce a disclosure report, including descriptions of possibly relevant documents, the costs of standard disclosure and proposed directions. The court can make a variety of orders.

Jackson sought a "culture change" towards strict compliance with rules and case management orders. *Outcome: Mitchell*, below.

The Minister launched a consultation, *Solving disputes in the County Courts: creating a simpler, quicker and more proportionate system.* This re-emphasised proportionality and proposed raising small claims to £15,000. The HC would be limited to cases over £100,000 and housing equity cases over £300,000. The simple, speedy online system for road accidents would be expanded to personal injury. All of these were put in place by 2014, though the small claims limit is still £10,000.

Reactions to the Jackson Reforms

The Court of Appeal, headed by Lord Dyson MR, in *Mitchell v News Group*   **10–059**
Newspapers (2013) established the new, tough approach the courts should take.
This defamation action arose out of the "plebgate" affair, a spat between police
officers and a minister on a bike, in Downing Street. Former minister Andrew
Mitchell's lawyers failed to lodge their costs budget seven days before the
hearing. The case managing master held that the rule was mandatory and the
budget would be deemed to be for court fees only, ignoring the claimant's
£589,000 costs. Mitchell applied for relief from sanctions under r.3.9, newly
re-drafted and emphasising compliance. The CA said there had been a shift in
emphasis. In each case, the court should consider the nature of non-compliance.
If it was trivial, the court would usually grant relief but the new, more robust
approach meant that relief from sanctions would be granted more sparingly.
Jackson had made everything clear. No lawyer could have been in any doubt. The
case was followed by *Durrant* (2013) and *Thevarajah* (2014), and a rash of High
Court cases in 2014, though it was tempered by *Denton v TH White Ltd* (2014).

In a 2014 speech, Jackson said "almost no-one" ever enters into a damages
based agreement. He was appointed in 2017 to conduct a new review of fixed
recoverable costs, as he is in favour of fixed costs in the fast track. In a 2015
lecture reviewing costs management he said it worked. "When an experienced
judge or master costs manages litigation with competent practitioners on both
sides, the costs of the litigation are controlled from an early stage." On disclosure,
Jackson remarked in a 2016 lecture that it would be to the public benefit if all
involved addressed their minds to what disclosure was needed rather than
defaulting to standard disclosure.

Litigants in person, McKenzie friends, lay representatives, litigation friends and vexatious litigants

Litigants in person (LIPs) are not inherently problematic but judges think they   **10–060**
slow case progress (although research by Genn and Balmer, commissioned for
the Bridge Review 2016 showed that this was not the case in the Court of Appeal)
and thanks to radical cutbacks in legal aid and the doubling of the small claims
limit in 2013, there are now many more of them in the civil and family courts.
Every civil judge, including those of the CA, frequently has LIPs appearing
before them. See research examples in Darbyshire (2011). If the case is factually
and/or legally complex and there are LIPs on both sides, then the judge has to
work extremely hard to help them and this does not sit well with the traditional
adversarial model of judge as non-interfering, non-researching umpire. Much
judicial time and energy is spent in helping them to argue their cases. See *Wright
v Michael Wright Supplies Ltd* (2013). Outside the courtroom, time and resources
of court staff and volunteers is devoted to helping them. LIPs are at a
disadvantage in our adversarial system, which requires each party to bring all
relevant argument and information to the court and requires the adduction of
evidence through examination and cross-examination, as explained in Ch.9. Very

few lay people can cope with this and they become dependent on the court to help them. In 1997, Applebey remarked on the "explosion" of LIPs but numbers have risen dramatically because:

1.   The 1980s and 90s saw legal aid decline to the extent that even those on state benefits were above the financial limit for eligibility and a 2012 Act almost extinguished it (see Ch.17).
2.   The small claims limit has increased from £100 in 1973 to £10,000.
3.   Lawyers are very expensive in the UK. Often people go to court to recover money, or defend themselves over money claims, or appear because they have been made bankrupt and they can ill afford the court fees, let alone legal representation.
4.   There are many appellants who, although they were represented in the lower court, have had their legal aid withdrawn after losing their case.
5.   Some LIPs choose to represent themselves, even though they could afford a lawyer.

   The 1990s saw England's longest trial, "the McLibel Trial" described in Ch.4. The defendants were unrepresented. Trials such as this caused the Judges' Council to establish a working party, chaired by Otton LJ, reporting in 1995. It concluded that LIPs in the Royal Courts of Justice (RCJ) were occupying a disproportionate amount of time, resources and staff. LIPs could be "seriously disadvantaged", compared with those who were represented. Some had no case; others could not cope with the complexity of proceedings. They lacked objectivity and advocacy skills. The report recommended strengthening the Citizens' Advice Bureau in the RCJ for legal advice. HC judges were given a pool of judicial assistants for legal research, where one or both parties were incapable of researching the law.
   Lord Woolf (1996) thought that courts should be more pro-active in helping LIPs with information and advice. Judges should be interventionist, in helping LIPs to understand procedure, present their case and test the evidence. They should treat them with respect and not give priority to lawyers. Much of what Woolf and Otton recommended has been achieved. The 1998 Rules are simplified, in plain English; Latin has been eliminated; the courts have developed user guides, simplified forms and multi-lingual leaflets. Advice and support remains patchy outside of the RCJ, though. Thanks to cutbacks in public spending, we have gone into reverse since 2010. County Court counters, the frontline helpers for most LIPs, are barely open and, in my experience from 2014, some courts never answer the phone. District Judge Richard Chapman said judges' work was hampered because people had not been able to get help in completing the forms correctly.

10–061   The Citizens' Advice Bureau (CAB) in the Royal Courts of Justice employs lawyers and hundreds of volunteers, from almost 60 city law firms. It helps about 12,000 people a year. In some cases, the CAB can arrange specialist advice or free representation from the Bar Pro Bono Unit. It is supplemented by the Personal Support Unit (PSU). Its 550 volunteers accompany people in court to provide emotional support. In 2015–2016 there were 16 sites across the country, helping 3,700 people per month. They remarked in their 2003 report that LIPs are usually stressed. Frequently, their behaviour causes stress in court staff and judges. See further Burke.

The Department of Constitutional Affairs published a report by Moorhead and Sefton, in 2005. It provided a detailed picture of their prevalence, nature and impact:

1. LIPs were common, usually as defendants. Obsessive or difficult litigants were a very small minority but posed considerable problems.
2. A large part of the reason for non-representation was non-participation. Some were partially represented. Significant numbers had some advice but this help was ad hoc.
3. Cases where both parties were LIPs were rare. Some were vulnerable.
4. The issues at stake were significant for the LIPs. There was a range of reasons for non-representation, including the lack of free or affordable representation.
5. Cases with LIPs could involve more court-based activity than those without.
6. Most participation took place in the court office not the courtroom.
7. LIPs made more mistakes than represented parties. They struggled with law and procedure.
8. There was modest evidence that their cases took longer. They were less likely to settle.
9. Some courts were better at helping. They were not confident in directing LIPs to alternative help.
10. Judges responded with varying degrees of intervention. Court staff recognised LIPs' needs but were unsure of what help was permissible because of a "no advice" rule.

Love and Hunter (2011) remarked that the increase in LIPs came at a time   **10–062**
when many court staff had been removed, whose job it was to help LIPs. They quoted Lord Dyson: "There are some very good litigants in person but there are an awful lot who, understandably, don't know what they are doing. They feel frustrated, angry. They ... take masses of bad points." In 2011, the Civil Justice Council reported on Access to Justice for Litigants in Person. They recommended a review of all court forms and leaflets, increasing the number of Personal Support Units, and promoting public legal education. "The ... legal aid reductions will take away routes to...early advice ... and leave intervention too late or denied altogether ... we will find more cases started [by LIPs] ... that need not have been started." LIPs had a strong emotional attachment to their case, "which can result in a subjective assessment of their claim and a reluctance to settle".

Court guides show that judges expect advocates to adjust their tactics. In some cases the court has to assist the LIP because there may be an argument that they have not raised: *Feltham v Commissioners for HM Revenue and Customs* (2011). Love and Hunter advised solicitors that LIPs are often very reluctant to settle their claim, leading to an escalation of costs. They suggested ADR was a good idea. For a useful literature review by the Ministry of Justice, see Williams (2011).

Judges have to be very patient and sensitive in handling LIPs and they must take care to ensure that their rights to a fair trial are upheld. The law provides them with some rights to help in court:

1. A "litigation friend" may represent a child or mental patient, under Pt 21 of the CPR.
2. A "McKenzie Friend" may accompany the LIP in court, to support and take notes but has no right to speak.
3. A lay representative is permitted to represent an LIP in a small claim, under s.27 of the Courts and Legal Services Act 1990 but the LIP must be present. The court has a general discretion to hear anyone.
4. A lawyer with appropriate rights of audience may represent the individual without charging (pro bono).

In *O (Children), Re* (2005), the CA held that in family cases there was a very strong presumption permitting representation by a McKenzie friend. LIPs were entitled to be treated courteously. They were often nervous, anxious or upset. A McKenzie friend, unless they are a lawyer with rights of audience, or appearing in a small claim, has no *right* to speak but the court has *discretion* to permit them to do so.

Judges and staff in the Royal Courts of Justice (HC and CA) are well aware that there is a growing industry of people who are prepared to act as paid lay representatives. There are competing values and uneven results here, as Moorhead observed. On the one hand, the judges sympathise with LIPs who cannot obtain legal aid. On the other hand, they have to protect the legal profession's rights of audience. Some courts have observed in their judgments how useful a lay representative can be: *Izzo v Philip Ross* (2002). In other cases, incompetent McKenzie friends can be a nuisance. Moorhead described the cases of *Paragon Finance v Noueiri* (2001). In this group of cases, the McKenzie friend was an experienced LIP. He submitted futile appeals and told the LIP he would win £250,000 and he wanted 20 per cent of that. The CA was satisfied that he was practising advocacy in the RCJ as an unqualified person and that he must be stopped, in the public interest. The CA made an order banning him acting except with a judge's permission, and they gave general guidance on McKenzie friends, now revised. Kennedy, a non-practising solicitor who worked for a charity training McKenzie friends, praised their interventions in magistrates' courts. See research on McKenzie friends, conducted by Leanne Smith and others for the Bar Council (2017).

10–063   For some LIPs, their litigation becomes a fulltime pursuit. I spent many research days, shadowing judges in the RCJ in 2004 and was told by judges' clerks and judges about litigants who virtually "live" in the Royal Courts of Justice. When LIPs become obsessive, attempting to persecute one or more parties or making multiple hopeless applications, they may be classed as "vexatious litigants" and can be banned from initiating proceedings. In the cases of *Bhamjee v Forsdick* (2003) and *R. (on the application of Mahajan) v*

Department for Constitutional Affairs (2004), the CA set out guidelines as to the court's duties and power when faced with such pests. The first LIP had acted against a number of defendants and was attempting to sue five barristers. The second LIP was involved in numerous claims in the County Court, HC and CA. In a third case, *HM Att Gen v Chitolie* (2004), Mr Chitolie was found to be a vexatious litigant after involvement in eighteen actions. These cases were followed, in 2004, by a new rule (3.11) setting out the courts' powers to make a civil restraint order (CRO) against a vexatious litigant. In *Douglas v Ministry of Justice* (2013), the High Court said litigants who made unmeritorious claims caused costs to others with no loss to themselves because they had time on their hands and no means of paying litigation costs so a costs order against them would be no deterrent. There was a strong public interest in placing additional restraints on them. The courts are still amazingly tolerant. In *Agarwala v Agarwala* (2016), the CA remarked "This litigation has been running...for seven years. It has taken up countless court and judge hours as both parties, incapable of compromise, have bombarded the court with endless applications...[both sides were the subject of restraining orders] and... court staff and judge have been inundated with emails..."

For some, vexatious litigation is a disease, known elsewhere in Europe as De Clerambault's syndrome. Naturally, vexatious litigants often try to sue their lawyers, the judges and the courts. In the period 1997–2003, the Lord Chancellor's Department (now Ministry of Justice) spent £3 million defending itself from such actions. Lord Clarke MR said in a 2006 speech that vexatious litigants denied other people access to justice because they wasted precious time that should be used on genuine litigants. See the fascinating article by Mahendra. He mentioned *AG v Benton* (2004). Benton had issued 32 separate proceedings in 25 months. He was suffering from a fixed delusional syndrome.

Unregulated experts

Wealthy litigants would line up an array, pre-Woolf. All that is now gone. The outstanding problem is the unregulated "industry". Anyone can claim to be an expert. The two bodies representing experts have failed to agree on regulation. The system is open to fraud. In 2005, Barain Baluchi was convicted. An ex-taxi driver, he had gained registration as a doctor in 1998, by stealing the identity of a Madrid psychiatrist. He bought a PhD from a "distance learning" college and gave evidence on over 2,000 asylum seekers, 1,000 of whom were allowed to stay in the UK. His name appeared in the Expert Witness Directory, endorsed by the Law Society. In 2004, the Legal Services Commission proposed that experts regularly providing forensic services should be quality-assured and hired on fixed fees. In 2005, a new Practice Direction was issued. The Civil Justice Council launched a new protocol. It reminds experts that they do not serve the interests of those who retain them and they should not act as mediators. See, however, Levy. In *Jones v Kaney* (2011), the UKSC abolished expert witnesses' immunity from being sued for breach of contract or negligence. In *R (Y) v Croydon LBC* (2016) the CA reaffirmed the fundamental right of a defendant to choose what witnesses they thought fit.

10–064

The failure to enforce judgments

10–065 If people cannot get their damages from defendants, there is no point in having gone to court. They will have expended money in court fees and costs and will be even worse off. In 2003, Baldwin published research examining civil claims ending in a "default judgment". Only a small proportion of claimants received full payment within the time ordered by the court. Baldwin and Cunnington found in their research (2004) that "Very many defendants were highly elusive". Only 13.3 per cent of HC claimants surveyed had received full payment and some had had to go to considerable lengths to get it. The more money was at stake, the less likely claimants were to be paid. The futility of the court process led to feelings of "bitterness, frustration, cynicism, anger, disenchantment and power-lessness". Some ensured that recalcitrant defendants were bankrupted or blacklisted for credit, by being entered on the register of County Court judgments. The courts, they argued, could not be expected to assume responsibility for debt recovery that fell on lenders and "Since the interests of creditors and debtors are often quite irreconcilable, no system of enforcement could be devised that would achieve even a satisfactory balance between them".

IT

10–066 The Woolf reforms were launched without the supporting IT systems. The Court Service published a consultation in 2001, *Modernising the Civil Courts*, envisaging the "virtual court". This was never achieved.

Lack of IT has caused frustration to judges, problems for the court staff and annoyance to court users who could not email large documents into the Commercial Court, or even email most courts before 2005. Only then was progress commencing on the sort of e-communication between parties and courts that was envisaged by Woolf. Civil courts took second place behind the LINK communication and case management system installed in the criminal courts and criminal justice agencies from 2012. In his *Annual Review of the Administration of Justice* 2008, the Lord Chief Justice listed all the IT deficiencies caused by "the continued lack of funding for a modern case-management system… promised almost ten years ago". District Judge Oldham (2009) said e-filing and document management had been abandoned, except for the Commercial Court. Paper files got lost regularly and there were fewer staff to manage them. In 2012, a major project to introduce e-working in the new Rolls Building in London, which houses the business courts, was shelved. £9.5 million had been spent since 2008. The scope of remedial work was too big. A £5 million contract started in 2015.

8.   JUDICIAL REVIEW

10–067 Historically, a person aggrieved with an error of law or the procedure of a lower court could petition the monarch to refer the proceedings for examination in the High Court. The HC now exercises this residuary monarchical prerogative, in judicial review proceedings. Procedure is determined by CPR Pt 54 and a

Practice Direction. The claim is made in the Administrative Court, or the Upper Tribunal. Permission is normally considered without a hearing. At the hearing, the court or tribunal examines the legality and procedural correctness of the decision of the lower court or tribunal and whether the body has exceeded its powers (acted ultra vires). The court may impose a quashing order on a defective decision, or make a mandatory order that a public body carry out its duty, or order an injunction, preventing an illegality. An applicant may ask the court or tribunal to declare what the law is, where it is uncertain. The judge has no concern with substituting a new finding of fact. Guidance was given by Lord Steyn in *R. v Secretary of State for the Home Department Ex p. Daly* (2001). He emphasised the difference between proportionality, under the European Convention on Human Rights, and traditional grounds for review, despite the overlap. He said

> "the doctrine of proportionality may require the reviewing court to assess the balance which the decision maker has struck, not merely whether it is in the range of rational or reasonable decisions ... The proportionality test may go further than the traditional grounds of review in as much as it may require attention to be directed to the relative weight accorded to interests and considerations."

Since the 1960s and especially since the procedure was made easier in 1981, there has been an enormous growth in judicial review cases and most of these have been challenges to the legality of public bodies' decisions, mostly local or central government. Challenges have been made to a broad list of such decisions: planning, hospital closure, policing tactics, benefits which apply differently to men and women, decisions relating to the National Lottery and so on. In the Criminal Justice and Courts Act 2015, the Government sought to curb the number of applications and of challenges in planning cases. Part 4 increases control and restrict costs payments to interveners. The Act provides that the court *must* refuse an application "if it appears to the court to be highly likely that the outcome for the applicant would not have been substantially different if the conduct complained of had not occurred", with a public interest exception. The Government said this was "designed to tackle the large and growing number of unmeritorious judicial review applications" because the volume of applications in 2012 (12,600) was nearly three times that of 2000. These measures were criticised because judicial review is a very important element of the constitution, a mechanism by which executive government is made accountable. Lawyers said the restrictions lacked an evidence base.

9. FAMILY PROCEDURE

Family procedure is outside of the scope of this book. The unified Family Court was established by the Crime and Courts Act 2013, from 2014. The Family Procedure Rules apply. Also in 2014, parts of the Children and Families Act were brought into force. See S. Gold's articles in the 2014 N.L.J. The Act requires applicants for private law children's orders and financial remedies to attend mediation information and assessment meetings, as described in the next chapter. Children's "residence" and "contact" orders are replaced with "child arrangements" orders. There are very strict time limits on public law proceedings where

10–068

an authority is applying to take a child into care and severe restrictions on experts, who used to appear in multiples. This results from the scandalous delays over care proceedings, recognised in the 2011 *Family Justice Review*, by David Norgrove. I described the pitiful progress of care cases dominated by multiple experts, and the working lives of all types of family judges in *Sitting in Judgment* (2011). Norgrove said the family justice system was not a system. It was characterised by mutual distrust and a lack of leadership.

10. THE BRAVE NEW WORLD OF THE ONLINE COURT

10–069   Before we examine the future, we should examine current reforms. During consultations on the new Financial List, court users called for "shorter and more flexible trial options for business litigation" described by the LCJ in his 2016 *Report*.

> "The Shorter Trials Scheme involves tight control of the litigation process by the court...disclosure is limited by proportionality and oral evidence is kept to the minimum... trials are limited to four days and costs are assessed summarily...inspiration for this scheme comes from the success of the Intellectual Property Enterprise Court... The Flexible Trials Scheme...enables parties, by agreement, to adapt procedure to suit their particular case, and...enables cases to proceed in a similar manner to arbitrations."

The Financial List also introduced a market test-case procedure to resolve issues and benefit financial markets. Also, insolvency express trials were introduced in 2016.

In 2015, the Online Dispute Resolution Advisory Group to the Civil Justice Council recommended three tier ODR for low value claims and also in 2015 the lawyers' pressure group JUSTICE produced *Delivering Justice in An Age of Austerity*, in which they recommended a streamlined dispute resolution system facilitated by a registrar but these models were rapidly eclipsed by Briggs LJ's *Civil Courts Structure Review: Final Report* in 2016. In Ch.6 of this book, on the civil courts, we also encountered the 2016 vision paper by the Lord Chancellor, Lord Chief Justice and Senior President of Tribunals, *Transforming Our Justice System*, which, in very vague terms, dreams of

> "developing a single online system for starting and managing cases across the criminal, civil, family and tribunal jurisdictions. This will help people understand their rights and what options are open to them...[with] a new, highly simplified procedural code. An online form will guide people through their application and the progress of their case."

As we saw in Chs 6 and 7, 86 more court buildings will close as they will be redundant. "In the civil courts, we will automate and digitise the entire process of civil money claims by 2020." In a September 2016 lecture the LCJ explained

> "Procedure...must be based on digital technology...simpler and more efficient to operate...and also the means to match process to claims more effectively in at least three ways –

(1)   Process should be "digital by default

(2)   ...simpler and cheaper [and] be matched to the nature and value of disputes.

(3)   Process should provide options for litigants as to both the type of process they desire as well as the amount of process they require.....digitalisation is a starting point. It is simply the means to achieve this radical change. It must be underpinned by clear principles. It must be designed to secure both the private interest of individuals and the public interest, in a manner as economical and efficient as is consistent with that aim. What then is the fundamental principle that should underpin a common basic procedural system based on a single IT system? The answer is, in my view, a single generic code applicable to all cases, whether civil, family or administrative and, possibly, criminal."

My imagination simply cannot stretch as far as a single procedural code that also includes *criminal* procedure. The criminal justice system aims to do something entirely different from the civil justice system, as we saw in Ch.1 of this book. Also, as we can also see from Chs 5 and 10, criminal procedure is ludicrously complex. People have been striving to simplify and fully codify procedure of all types for centuries.

Unlike the vision paper, *Transforming Our Justice System*, The Briggs Review 2016 is not vague but highly detailed.

Civil Courts Structure Review, The Briggs Review

Briggs LJ was commissioned to report on the civil courts structure but his recommendations were on procedure, like those of Woolf and Jackson. He identified five weaknesses (p.115). I have italicised key words: 10–070

- Lack of access to justice caused by *cost*, and "*lawyerish culture and procedure*".
- "[T]he inefficiencies arising from the continuing *tyranny of paper*, coupled with...obsolete and inadequate *IT*".
- *Delays in the CA* caused by excessive workload.
- Under-investment in justice *outside London*.
- Poor *enforcement* of judgments and orders.

This is depressing. The first two were identified by Woolf in 1996. Briggs' main recommendations were as follows and I have added in my comments.

An unprecedented compulsory *Online Solutions Court, separate from the County Court*, for claims up to £25,000, operable by unrepresented litigants, with assistance for those who need it, rather than a paper alternative. Voluntary agencies should be funded to offer support. Housing possession would be excluded, as would professional negligence, intellectual property and landlord repairs. This would remove the bulk of claims from the County Court.

Comment: this and the vision paper raise enormous issues of access to justice. Note that this will be compulsory. £25,000 is a significant amount of money to most people. This recommendation is predicated on the idea that people can bring or defend a claim without a lawyer *and* that they can do it online. I was shocked to find in my own empirical research, over a 10-year period (2011), that County Courts are not full of rich people asserting their property rights but the dispossessed: poor people, people with mental or physical ill-health, substance abusers, the homeless, asylum seekers, bankrupts, people lacking capacity and so on. Happily, Briggs has excluded housing possession and landlord repairs but many if not most other people will need help. If people are too reliant on "voluntary agencies", this is grossly inadequate. As can be seen from Ch.17 of this book, on legal aid, thanks to the extinguishing of most legal aid, since 2012, voluntary agencies such as Citizens' Advice are overwhelmed with people seeking help and at the same time, some not-for-profit agencies, such as law centres, have suffered overwhelming losses of legal aid income. History has shown that governments cannot be trusted to provide and maintain funding for either legal aid or voluntary agencies as a substitute. Also this is a flawed model. Why devise a new state agency, an online court, without providing *state* funds to ensure that it runs properly, via *state* employees, paid to help people? Also, even if users can cope with the IT, they will need to be signposted immediately to adequate IT helplines, where someone can be relied on to give them timely and adequate telephone help and they will need to be signposted adequately to affordable legal help. The experience of lawyers and judges and not-for-profit agencies over the last four decades provides no confidence at all that all of this will be put in place and be maintained by successive governments. Indeed, all of the evidence is to the contrary, as can be seen from my discussion of Court Management and IT in Ch.6 and as can be seen from Ch.17 on legal aid.

10–071   The *Transforming Our Justice System* vision paper dreams of "assisted digital" for those people who cannot cope online. This conjures ghastly scenes like the one in the Job Centre in the film *I, Daniel Blake*, where the protagonist struggles and fails to register online. The simple fact is that many people involved in court or tribunal proceedings are exactly those people who cannot be expected to function online. This point was put less forcefully, incidentally, in the Civil Justice Council's response to the *Transforming Our Justice System* consultation (on their website). On this topic, by February 2017, the government had consulted on their plans for "assisted digital" and responded to the consultation responses but although they provide more information, it is not reassuring. For example, they say that users will have the same access to legal advice that they now have which Ch.17 of this book demonstrates is grossly inadequate.

Secondly, government departments and public bodies have decades of history of failing to acquire adequate software systems, hardware that can indeed run the software, and both hardware and software that can link all relevant agencies and all end-users together. Court administration is no exception. Indeed, millions if not billions has been wasted on inadequate IT in the courts and related agencies, since the 1980s and much of that is illustrated in my own research (2011). Most obviously, in 1996, Lord Woolf envisioned judges relying on IT in case management, yet in my research with district judges in 2003–2005, I observed two courts piloting experimental case management software. As reported in my book, one district judge showed me that it took nine minutes just to open one electronic case file, whereas he could deal with an entire paper file, identify the issues and make the required order on the case management question in the file within a few minutes, indeed less than five minutes in some cases. The system will only work if adequate software is acquired and if the whole system is user-friendly enough for people with very limited IT skills to operate. While all those recommending ODR, such as the Civil Justice Council, point to eBay ODR as a beacon to copy, I would respond that eBay users are, by definition, fairly competent IT users.

Procedure would be in stages. There would be "an automated online triage **10–072** stage designed to help litigants without lawyers articulate their claim in a form which the court could resolve, and to upload their key documents and evidence." (Briggs 6.4). Stage 2 would mean *case management* by legally *qualified case officers* identifying and recommending to parties "*the conciliation method best suited* to their case, which may include ODR, both telephone and face to face mediation, and judicial Early Neutral Evaluation... Conciliation measures available to users at Stage 2 of the Online Court should not be limited to short telephone mediations."

Comment: Professor Dame Hazel Genn might well react here that this is not about just settlement but just about settlement (2010, p.117), that a presumption is operating that people will settle their case by some form of ADR and that this model presumes that settlement by trial in a court is pathological. I, on the other hand would argue that the overwhelming bulk of civil claims do settle by negotiation between the parties. The experience of judges shows that many small claimants come to court without having discussed the issue with the other side, indeed some parties think this is forbidden. At least this model, if it works as Briggs intends, will signpost people to ADR and help them.

Determination of legal rights and duties which cannot be settled at stage 2 should be done by a district judge at *stage 3 by a traditional trial, video hearing or conference call*, whichever is the most suitable.

Comment: there is no problem with this, on the face of it. District judges have been conducting case management conference calls for decades. On the other hand, all of the technology will have to be in place and be reliable, and court staff will have to be adequately trained to use it. Adequate systems were not yet in place in the youth courts that I observed in 2016.

- The case officers would be supervised by judges and answerable to the LCJ.
- There would be *fixed recoverable costs*, modelled on the small claims track, allowing for "*early, bespoke, affordable advice* to would-be litigants on the merits of their case (including defence) from a qualified lawyer".
- *Online* material should *inform* court *users* that "*litigation* should be regarded as a *last resort*, after using all available means of *pre-issue ADR*."
- Court *users* should be *alerted* online *to alternative forms of resolution*, free or affordable *advice* and basic legal guidance, designed to help ascertain whether there is a dispute or whether the claim is for the enforcement of undisputed rights.
- Corporate or represented litigants would by-pass the Stage 1 triage process.
- *New IT systems* should harvest management information about judicial time-use.
- We should re-establish court-based out of hours private mediation.
- Provide public legal *education*.

- Provision for *HC cases* in the *regions*, including circuit judges, should be strengthened and no case should be regarded as too big to be decided outside London.
- County Court financial limits should be removed. HC minimum should be £500,000.
- The default court for *enforcement* should be the County Court, *centralised*. Enforcement needs a *separate review*. This is a good idea. One big weakness of the current system is that so many successful claimants never receive their damages.
- "The decision of HMCTS to approach the provision of IT solutions and LiP friendly language development for online courts on a cross jurisdictional basis is welcomed and recommended."

Reactions 2017

10–073   There are some very obvious comments to make before we examine others' reactions. First, this is a really extreme set of recommendations and as is obvious from *Transforming Our Justice System*, that what is required is a complete rethink of the nature of procedure, not just a change in the method of delivery of the civil justice system—and indeed the criminal and family systems. The Briggs Review contains only the recommendations of a single judge, though looking at judicial speeches throughout 2016, the Review clearly has strong support by the Lord Chief Justice and Senior President of Tribunals and is in full accord with the plans of the Ministry of Justice and HM Courts and Tribunals Service. These recommendations will require extensive consultation and primary legislation, therefore much of this will then have to be scrutinised by Parliament. MPs and peers may have strong views on how all of this impinges on openness and access to justice. Having said that, the first Bill that would have facilitated part of the "digital by default" vision paper was before Parliament in 2017 but was dropped: the Prisons and Courts Bill.

These proposals and those in *Transforming Our Justice System* also raise very big issues of open justice too, as discussed in Ch.6 on civil courts. The government response so far appears in the press release on the Prisons and Courts Bill 2017, which was designed to facilitate some of these plans:

"To ensure justice is also open and seen to be done, video booths will be installed in courts across England and Wales to allow members of the media and public to observe virtual hearings from court buildings anywhere in the country. Lists and results of cases that have taken place online, as well as those concluded in a physical courtroom, will also be available digitally."

I commented on this in Ch.6.

The first section of the 2017 volume (vol.36) of the *Civil Justice Quarterly* is dedicated to learned articles on Briggs. Ahmed noted that Briggs had rejected keeping the *pre-action protocols* and indeed Jackson has found that businesses said they add to costs. The Civil Justice Council report and JUSTICE had said that courts must extend their reach beyond dispute settlement to dispute avoidance and containment. This depended on public legal education. It must be made clear to parties that they are expected to engage constructively at Stage 1, that their behaviour will be scrutinised and may be penalised in costs if the matter comes to trial.

Judge Bird considered *open justice*. Lord Bingham emphasised that it was central to the rule of law (see Ch.1 of this book). Article 6 of the European Convention requires a public hearing in the *determination* of rights and obligations but the common law principle is wider, requiring openness at all hearings. It is currently written into the CPR, requiring video and phone hearings to be open. Some applications have a hearing. Some final decisions may be in private, such as judicial review. The public can see statements of case, public judgments and orders and other documents with permission. Lord Dyson pointed out that while it is fine for mediation to occur in private, we must not allow the IT to develop so that court proceedings become secret. Briggs LJ said that securing openness was still being worked on.

McCloud, a QBD Master, examined the *knowledge engineering* that will be needed to construct the Stage 1 automated online interactive triage (diagnostic) stage. She examined the two less ambitious systems overseas and commented on the real accessibility likely to be provided, and openness to abuse.

Assy questioned whether the court would *compromise the quality* of its judgments, examining the feasibility of procedure and the £25,000 ceiling, remarking that case value does not indicate complexity. Is a simple and informal process legitimate just because the claim value is low?

Of course there are and will be in future many more reactions on the websites of The Bar Council, The Law Society, The Legal Action Group and in many law journals and the newspapers, and some are extracted in *Westlaw's* current awareness, such as this one:

> "...Briggs has said that the Bar had nothing to fear from his proposal for an online court, but it must take 'direct access' seriously. Briggs LJ said the online court was not...designed to exclude lawyers but to encourage litigants to get early advice and then more specialist advice, if needed...the Bar was 'uniquely well placed to provide bespoke advice' but...barristers would have to embrace direct access."
> *Legal Futures* 18 October 2016, *Westlaw* abstract.

Readers of this textbook will need to keep abreast of developments in civil, family, criminal and tribunal procedure, as all of this is an extremely radical set of interlinked plans and the digital by default theme continues now, across the next two chapters of this book, into tribunals and ADR, and criminal procedure.

Bibliography

Articles by M. Ahmed, Judge N. Bird, Master V. McCloud and R. Assy appear at (2017) 36 (1) C.J.Q. 12, 23, 34 and 70.

G. Applebey, "The Growth of Litigants in Person in English Civil Proceedings" (1997) 16 C.J.Q. 127.

P. Allen, "In a fix" (2013) N.L.J. 27 September, p.10.

T. Allen, "A few home truths" (2009) 159 N.L.J. 489, responding to Zander's 2009 article.

J. Baldwin, "Monitoring the Rise of the Small Claims Limit: Litigants' Experiences of Different Forms of Adjudication", LCD Research Series 1/97,

10–074

DCA archived website; *Small Claims in the County Court in England and Wales: The Bargain Basement of Civil Justice* (1997); "Small Claims Hearings: The 'Interventionist' Role Played by District Judges" (1998) 17 C.J.Q. 20; "Increasing the Small Claims Limit" (1998) 148 N.L.J. 274; "Lay and judicial perspectives on the expansion of the small claims regime" LCD Research Series 8/02; "Evaluating the Effectiveness of Enforcement Procedures in Undefended Claims in the Civil Courts" DCA Research Study 3/03 (2003).
J. Baldwin and R. Cunnington, "The Crisis in Enforcement of Civil Judgments in England and Wales" (2004) 23 C.J.Q. 305.
Briggs LJ, *Civil Courts Structure Review: Interim Report* (December 2015) and *Civil Courts Structure Review: Final Report* (July 2016), Judiciary website.
HH Judge S. Brown, on costs budgeting (2012) 162 N.L.J. 498, 773.
J. Burke, "A helping hand" *Counsel*, March 2011, p.30.
S. Burn, "The Woolf Reforms in Retrospect", *Legal Action*, July 2003, p.8.
R. Chapman, "Shutting up Shop" (2012) 162 N.L.J. 637.
The Civil Justice Audit was summarised at (2000) 150 N.L.J. 531.
Civil Justice Council Online Dispute Resolution Advisory Group, *Online Dispute Resolution for Low Value Claims*, February 2016, Judiciary website.
Civitas, "Abolish contingency fees and conditional fee agreements" (An extract from *Democratic Civilisation or Judicial Supremacy? A discussion of parliamentary sovereignty and the reform of human rights laws* by David G. Green, 11 March 2016).
L. Chong, "Deloitte's 12-year case puts Woolf reforms in question", *The Times*, 13 April 2006.
Civil Justice Council, *Access to Justice for Litigants in Person* (2011).
Civil Justice Review: Report of the Review Body on Civil Justice, Cm.394 (1988).
Sir Anthony Clarke MR, "Vexatious litigants & access to justice: past, present, future", speech, June 2006; "A UK Perspective on EU Civil Justice—Impact on Domestic Dispute Resolution," speech, 25 October 2007.
Editorial "Civil Litigation: A Public Service for the Enforcement of Civil Rights" (2007) *Civil Justice Quarterly* Vol.26, 1–9.
P. Darbyshire, *Sitting in Judgment: The Working Lives of Judges* (Oxford: Hart Publishing, 2011).
Department of Constitutional Affairs Research Report 09/2005 *The Management of Civil Cases: the courts and the post-Woolf landscape.*
Lord Dyson, "Magna Carta and the Compensation Culture", speech, 13 October 2015.
General Council of the Bar and Law Society, "Civil Justice on Trial—The Case for Change" (Heilbron–Hodge) (1993).
H. Genn, *Paths to Justice* (Oxford: Hart Publishing, 1999); *Judging Civil Justice* (Cambridge: Cambridge University Press, 2010).
F. Gibb, "How pruning dispute grew into an £80,000 legal bill", *The Times*, 4 May 2007.
District Judge S. Gold, "Civil Way" (2014) N.L.J. 18 and 25 April, p.19.
T. Goriely, R. Moorhead and P. Abrams, *More Civil Justice? The impact of the Woolf reforms on pre-action behaviour*, Civil Justice Council and Law Society (2002).

R. Gosling, "Survey of Litigants' Experiences and Satisfaction with the Small Claims Process" DCA research report 9/2006.

DJ Robert Hill, "10 years on—a personal view" Association of HMDJs *Law Bulletin*, Winter 2008/9 20 (1), p.6.

A. Jack, "Court fees: the new stealth tax?" (2004) 154 N.L.J. 909.

Jackson LJ, *Review of Civil Litigation Costs: Final Report* 2009, Judiciary website; Keynote speech, Law Society Conference on Commercial Litigation: "The Post Jackson World", 20 October 2014; "Confronting Costs Management", Harbour Lecture, 13 May 2015; "Disclosure", lecture, 10 October 2016.

T. John, "The District Judge as scrutineer" (2006) 156 N.L.J. 569.

A. Johnson, "A sword & a shield" (2013) N.L.J. 6, p.18.

JUSTICE, *Delivering Justice in an Age of Austerity* (2015), JUSTICE website.

J. Kennedy, "McKenzie Friends Re-United" (2011) 161 N.L.J. 416.

Lightman J, "The case for judicial intervention" (1999) 149 N.L.J. 1819 (an excellent account of how civil litigation used to be, pre-1999); "The Civil Justice System and Legal Profession—The Challenges Ahead" (2003) 22 C.J.Q. 235.

Lord Chancellor, Lord Chief Justice and Senior President of Tribunals, *Transforming Our Justice System*, September 2016, Judiciary website.

S. Love and T. Hunter, "Going it alone" (2011) 161 N.L.J. 1639.

N. Madge, "Small Claims in the County Court" (2004) 23 C.J.Q. 201.

B. Mahendra, "A law unto themselves" (2008) 158 N.L.J. 1278.

Master John Leslie was cited in *Counsel* (2000).

Ministry of Justice, *Monetary Claims in the County Courts (1996–2003)*, research summary 1/10 (2010); "Solving disputes in the county courts: creating a simpler, quicker and more proportionate system—a consultation on reforming civil justice in England and Wales", Cm.8045 CP6/2011 (2011); press release on the Prisons and Courts Bill 2017, "Prisons and Courts Bill to improve access to justice and better protect the vulnerable", 20 March 2017, Ministry website; "Transforming our justice system: assisted digital strategy, automatic online conviction and statutory standard penalty, and panel composition in tribunals – Government Response", February 2017, MoJ website.

R. Moorhead, "Access or Aggravation? Litigants in Person, McKenzie Friends and Lay Representation" (2003) 22 C.J.Q. 133; "An American Future? Contingency Fees, Claims Explosions and Evidence from Employment Tribunals" (2010) 75 (3) M.L.R. 752; R. Moorhead and M. Sefton, Research Report 2005/2, *Litigants in person—Unrepresented litigants in first instance proceedings*.

D. Oldham, "Online justice" (2009) 159 N.L.J. 615; (2009) 159 N.L.J. 1223.

J. Plotnikoff and R. Woolfson "Judges' Case Management Perspectives: the Views of Opinion Formers and Case Managers" LCD Research Series 3/02, DCA archived website.

J. Rowley, "Grappling with the cost" (2013) N.L.J. 13 December, p.18.

Sir Ernest Ryder, "The Modernisation of Access to Justice in Times of Austerity", lecture, 3 March 2016.

L. Smith, E. Hitchings and M. Sefton, "A study of fee-charging McKenzie Friends and their work in private family law cases" (2017) Bar Council website.

Thomas LCJ, "Cutting the Cloth to Fit the Dispute: Steps Towards Better Procedures Across the Jurisdictions", September 2016, Judiciary website; *The Lord Chief Justice's Report 2016*, Judiciary website.

P. Thompson, "Woolf's litigants" (2009) 159 N.L.J. 293.

L. Trinder et al, *Litigants in Person in Private Family Law Cases*, Ministry of Justice 2014.

Senior Master Turner was quoted at (2000) 150 N.L.J. 49.

K. Underwood, "Contingency Matters" 160 (2010) N.L.J. 387 (in praise of American contingency fees).

The Wragge Survey was summarised in *The Times*, 2 May 2000.

Lord Chancellor's Department, "Civil Justice Reform Evaluation—Further Findings" (2002).

Lord Woolf "Cutting costs and delays: why we are doing well but can do better" *The Times*, 11 June 2009.

K. Williams, "State of fear; Britain's 'compensation culture' reviewed" (2005) 25 (3) *Legal Studies* 499; *Litigants in person: a literature review*, Ministry of Justice Research Summary 2/11 (2011).

Lord Young, *Common Sense, Common Safety*, HM Government, 2010, Health and Safety Executive website.

M. Zander on the Woolf report: (1995) 145 N.L.J. 154; (1996) 146 N.L.J. 1590; (1997) 147 N.L.J. 353 and 539; Woolf on Zander (1997) 147 N.L.J. 751; Zander defends himself: (1997) 147 N.L.J. 768 and *Civil Justice Quarterly*. See responses to Zander and other critics by Greenslade at (1996) 146 N.L.J. 1147. Zander had the last word in *The State of Justice* (London: Sweet & Maxwell, 2000), Ch.2. See also his tenth anniversary article "Zander on Woolf" (2009) 159 N.L.J. 367.

Further reading and sources for updating this chapter

10–075   Free updates of this book are available on the Sweet & Maxwell website: *http://uklawstudent.thomsonreuters.com*.

Summary and revision: P. Darbyshire, *Nutshells English Legal System*, 10th edn (London: Sweet & Maxwell, 2016).

Civil Procedure Rules.

Civil Justice Council website: *https://www.judiciary.gov.uk/related-offices-and-bodies/advisory-bodies/cjc/*.

Civil Justice Quarterly on *Westlaw*.

HM Courts & Tribunals Service.

Judges' speeches, Judiciary website.

Ministry of Justice.

Legal Action; *New Law Journal*; *The Guardian* and *The Times*.

TRIBUNAL STRUCTURE UNDER DEVELOPMENT (2010 – 2017)

Employment is not part of the new structure.

Appeals on point of law or judicial review

UK UPPER TRIBUNAL

Senior President (LJ) and Deputy (HC judge)

Immigration & Asylum Chamber	Lands Chamber	Administrative Appeals Chamber	Tax & Chancery Chamber
Immigration & asylum appeals and judicial reviews.	Valuation; compensation for compulsory acquisition; rights of light; restrictive covenants.	Appeals from the chambers below, on points of law; judicial review of criminal decisions comp and procedural decisions; appeals from Traffic Commissioners.	Appeals from Tax Chamber; charity appeals: pension regulation; financial services; judicial review, consumer credit.
President, Vice President (HC judges), other HC judges, circuit judges, UT immigration judges	President, Vice President, (HC judges), other HC judges, circuit judges, UT judges	President, VP, HC judges, circuit judges, UT judges	President, VP, HC and circuit chancery judges, Upper Tribunal judges, non- legal members

FIRST TIER TRIBUNAL

Immigration & Asylum Chamber	War Pensions & Armed Forces Compensation Chamber	Social Entitlement Chamber	Health, Education & Social Care Chamber	Property Chamber	General Regulatory Chamber	Tax Chamber
Immigration and asylum	War pensions and armed forces compensation	Asylum support; social security and child support; criminal injuries compensation; housing benefit; council tax benefit, etc.	Care standards; mental health review; special educational needs and disability; primary health lists.	Land registrations; agricultural land and drainage; residential property.	Charities; consumer credit; estate agents; transport gambling; claims management services; information; environment; food; prof regulation immigration services.	Tax, VAT and duties; MPs' expenses.
President, Deputies (circuit judges), First Tier immigration judges, non-legal members	President, Deputies (circuit judges), First Tier tribunal judges, members of armed forces	President, Deputies, First Tier tribunal judges	President, Deputies, lay members, doctors, psychiatrists, etc.	President, judges, farmers, landowners, valuers, experts.	President, etc.	President, non- legal members, etc.

Most first instance appeals will be heard in the First Tier Tribunal. The Upper Tribunal is a Superior Court of Record, like the High Court. Appeals from the UT on important points of law lie to the Court of Appeal. Non-legal members sit in some UT and some FTT cases (in accordance with the tribunals they replaced). Court of Appeal judges may sit in the UT.

CHAPTER 11

Alternatives to the Civil Courts: Institutions and Procedures

"an end to the parallel existence of courts and tribunals and the parallel courts and tribunals' judiciaries. The creation of a single judiciary in a single system - a system that combines the best qualities and processes of the present courts and tribunals systems" (Thomas LCJ, speech, October 2016, explaining the joint vision statement, *Transforming Our Justice System*).

"Having spent years in court reading the papers for cases only to be told at the last minute that the parties have come to terms I am persuaded that alternative dispute resolution is something that people ought to try first." (Lord Browne-Wilkinson, former law lord turned mediator, 2005).

"It avoids the trauma of court proceedings ... Any sensible person who finds himself party to a dispute will wish to resolve it if possible by negotiation. Over 90% of actions that are commenced in England end in a negotiated settlement before trial. One reason for this is the cost of litigating under the adversarial process." (Lord Phillips CJ 2008).

This chapter deals with alternative hearings for civil disputes, outside the court system. Note the big difference between them, however. With tribunals, Parliament has decided that certain disputes will not go to court but to an alternative forum. *The litigant has no choice*. With arbitration and Alternative Dispute Resolution (ADR), it is generally the litigants who have chosen to use a private alternative because they have the sense to realise what all judges know: it is an incomparably cheaper, simpler and more civilised means of resolving a disagreement.

1. TRIBUNALS

The Special Commissioners of Income Tax celebrated their 200th birthday in 2005. Income tax, intended as a temporary measure, was introduced by Pitt the Younger to raise funds to fight the Napoleonic wars. (*Counsel*, February 2005.)

11–002

Function

Outside the court system, over 130 types of specialist civil dispute are determined by statutory tribunals, which dispose of over 300,000 cases per year (annual tribunal statistics, every March). This constituted 130 separate systems. Since 2010, many have been restructured and streamlined into a single First Tier

11–003

Tribunal, with appeals routed to an Upper Tribunal, as depicted in the diagram here. They were sometimes referred to as "administrative tribunals", because almost all of them hear appeals by the citizen against an administrative decision.

As the State grew throughout the twentieth century so it devised statutory schemes to confer benefits or regulate people's activities in more and more ways. Those Acts created individual systems of tribunals to adjudicate consequent disputes arising between citizen and State. The variety of subjects can be seen from the diagram. There are many more outside the unified structure. Some determine disputes between private citizens. Employment tribunals, outside the structure, hear employees' claims against employers relating to unfair dismissal, redundancy and discrimination. These are more like court-substitutes and there is no logical reason why the County Court should not have been given this work, indeed Briggs LJ considered overlaps in his 2016 Review.

Characteristics

Creation

11–004   All tribunals are creatures of separate statutes but the Tribunals, Courts and Enforcement Act 2007 prescribed the new unified structure. They were decided by the Franks Committee (1957) to be "machinery for adjudication", in other words, court-like bodies, not part of the administrative set-up. The Franks Report said they should be run according to the principles of "openness, fairness and impartiality". Some appellate bodies are superior courts of record, on a level with the High Court, such as the Upper Tribunal, the Employment Appeal Tribunal and the controversial Special Immigration Appeals Commission.

Composition

11–005   Some are composed of a lawyer acting as a solo judge and some have a lawyer chair and two laypeople. Where laypeople are used, they are normally representative of certain groups, such as employer-representatives (business-people) and employee-representatives (often trade-unionists) in the employment tribunals; or they provide expertise, such as doctors and psychiatrists in the mental health review section of the First Tier Tribunal, or accountants in the Tax and Duties Chamber of the First Tier Tribunal. Indeed, as with lay magistrates and jurors, this is another significant way in which the legal system makes use of non-lawyers as adjudicators. In his 2010 Review, Lord Judge CJ acknowledged their importance.

> "After the magistracy, the next largest group of judiciary is the tribunals' judiciary, of whom there are around 7,000. These are a mixture of salaried and fee-paid judiciary, many of whom are legally qualified but who also include a wide variety of other specialists, from doctors and other medical professionals to chartered surveyors and those with experience of life in the armed forces."

But in 2017, as we shall see, there are plans to drastically cut the use of laypeople on panels, and resolve issues digitally by default, which will radically change the character of most tribunals.

Appointments are now mostly made by the Judicial Appointments Commission, following the Constitutional Reform Act 2005. The Judicial College provides training. Some HC judges sit in the Upper Tribunal. All Chancery Division judges are members of its Tax and Chancery Chamber.

Procedure

The Council on Tribunals, then the Administrative Justice & Tribunals Council (now abolished) published model procedural rules. When tribunals were reformed under the new structure, the intention was that they would have uniform procedure rules but as can be seen from HM Courts and Tribunals Service (HMCTS) website, this did not come to fruition and the different chambers have specialist rules. From 2008, early dispute resolution for many tribunal cases was being piloted. Case loads vary enormously.   **11–006**

Organisation

The Ministry of Justice administers the mainstream ones. They were run by separate government departments but the HMCTS took over responsibility for the major tribunals from 2006, following the Leggatt recommendations. Some sit nationwide, such as those dealing with tax, employment, benefits, and so on, and some sit centrally. From 2008, multi-jurisdictional hearing centres were being created in some locations. Some tribunals have never been constituted.   **11–007**

Appeal and judicial review

From most tribunals, there is no appeal on *fact*, except from those with an appellate level. For instance, appeal lies from employment tribunals to the Employment Appeal Tribunal. The Court of Appeal (CA) held, in *P v Secretary of State for the Home Department* (2004) that an appellate tribunal should not determine the facts afresh. They should accept the facts found by the lower tribunal unless it was shown that the evidence did not support the findings made, or the findings were clearly wrong. Within the unified structure, appeal on a point of *law* lies, with permission, to the Upper Tribunal (UT), as indicated in the diagram, or, for tribunals outside the new structure, to the High Court or CA. The UT deals with some judicial review cases that have been transferred from the Administrative Court, such as mental health, immigration and asylum and tax. It is not constrained in its approach in the same way as an appellate court. Contrary to *P v Secretary of State for the Home Department* above, it has been held that the Upper Tribunal comes to its own decision on the evidence and it can receive further evidence: *Pensions Regulator v Michel van de Wiele NV* (2011). In terms of *precedent*, The Upper Tribunal and Administrative Court should follow one another's decisions, because of judicial comity (reciprocity) and the common law method, despite the fact that HC judges do not normally bind one another: *R. (on the application of B) v Islington LBD* (2010). Decisions of the Upper Tribunal (if not judicial reviews themselves) are amenable to judicial review by the HC: *R. (on the application of Cart) v The Upper Tribunal* (2010). Losers may seek permission from the UT or CA to appeal to the CA, where either court considers   **11–008** it would raise some important point of principle or practice. There is no appeal to the CA from a refusal of the UT to review its decision to refuse permission to appeal: *Samuda v Secretary of State for Work and Pensions* (2014).

The Administrative Justice & Tribunals Council

11–009 This supervisory body was created by the Tribunals, Courts and Enforcement Act 2007 s.44, to replace the Council on Tribunals. Its purpose was to help keep tribunals accessible, fair and effective by promoting coherent principles and good practice, and emphasising the needs of users, but, despite protestations from the Parliamentary Justice Committee, it was abolished in the Coalition Government's "bonfire of the quangos", in the Public Bodies Act 2011. This was a huge loss, as the Council was very active as an independent scrutineer of government and of tribunals, as can be seen from its archived website and newsletter, safeguarding the interests of tribunal users and researching tribunal work and promulgating reform.

Advantages and disadvantages of tribunals

11–010 The early tribunal systems were established by Labour and Liberal governments to keep disputes out of the courts and the grasp of Conservative or conservative judges who they distrusted. Since then, new tribunals were frequently created by governments of all parties.

H.W.R. Wade, in his authoritative text *Administrative Law*, claimed they were cheap, speedier and more accessible than the courts. Harlow, 2001, challenged this. More specifically, benefits were said to be: low cost—there are no court fees and people can supposedly manage without lawyers; informal procedure and tribunal members can assist the parties; limited jurisdiction so members become specialists, compared with a civil judge, who is a "Jack-of-all-trades"; and they involve laypeople as adjudicators. They are not bound by precedent but those tribunals with an appeal level (which is most of them, now) developed their own specialist sets of law reports, which effectively act as precedents.

Critics of tribunals point to their informality, lack of visibility, lack of precedent and consequent unpredictability as endangering a fair hearing. Worse, legal aid was only made available for applicants to four tribunals until 2000, so in all but a handful of cases, people have to pay for a lawyer or represent themselves. It is still not available before most tribunals, though under the LASPO Act 2012, it can be provided: see Ch.17. Absence of or refusal of legal aid is unfair in those tribunals which have become very like courts, because of the frequent use of private lawyers by those who can afford them, and because they have developed their own case law, such as employment tribunals. Research (e.g. Genn and Genn, 1989) showed that being represented at a tribunal by anybody enhanced the appellant's chances of success. Conversely, employers now see tribunals as biased against them. A 2005 CBI survey showed that employers lacked confidence in the system, often settling weak or vexatious claims to avoid using it. A survey of 40 employers showed that all firms sampled with under 50 staff settled every claim, despite advice that they could win half. 45 per cent believed the system was ineffective and 50 per cent reported a rise in vexatious claims in the previous 12 months.

In 1995, the Citizens' Advice Bureaux complained that tribunals were neither speedy nor free from technicality. The Human Rights Act 1998 prompted Irvine LC to authorise the extension of legal aid in 2000, to hearings before the immigration tribunals (now Immigration and Asylum Chamber of the First Tier Tribunal) and in 2001, to proceedings on VAT and income tax and any other tribunal dealing with criminal type penalties.

Ironically, some tribunals have become so court-like that they have lost any advantage, especially after civil court procedure was radically simplified by the Woolf Reforms of 1998–1999. Therefore, ADR is now offered as an alternative to tribunals. For instance, from 2001, parties could opt out of the overcrowded employment tribunals and into an ACAS arbitration scheme for simple unfair dismissal claims. This was copied with an early dispute resolution process in other types of tribunal. In response to some of these concerns, the employment tribunal rules were changed in 2001, with the insertion of the overriding objective, the extension of case management powers, and power to penalise an advocate with a costs order, all ideas borrowed from the Woolf reforms. From 2014, applicants cannot launch proceedings in the employment tribunal without making contact beforehand with ACAS. **11–011**

It was often pointed out that tribunals were administered and clerked by the department whose decision was being appealed against so they appeared to lack independence. This is why the independent Tribunals Service (now HMCTS) was created.

Many condemned as cost-saving measures the reorganisation of social security tribunals in the Social Security Act 1998. Oral hearings were reduced, despite government statistics which showed they enhanced the applicant's chances of success. Three-person tribunals were cut down, meaning the elimination of laypeople (see Adler). Under plans made in 2016–2017 this will go much further, as we shall see.

The Leggatt Review of Tribunals 2001—background to the unified structure

Tribunals developed piecemeal. Numbers increased significantly in the twentieth century. Their growth was questioned by the Committee on Ministers' Powers (1932) and the Franks Committee on Administrative Tribunals and Enquiries (1957) and they were under review in 2000–2001 by the Review of Tribunals (Leggatt Committee). The Franks Report, having concluded that tribunals were judicial bodies, recommended judicial safeguards of openness, fairness and impartiality. Consequently, the Tribunals and Inquiries Act 1958 provided for procedural rules, reasoned decisions, appeals on points of law to the High Court, lawyers in the chair and the establishment of the Council on Tribunals, the predecessor of the AJTC. **11–012**

The Leggatt Review was prompted by what Lord Irvine LC called the "haphazard growth of tribunals, complex routes of appeal and the need for mechanisms to ensure coherent development of the law". The Review body proposed standards of fairness: independence from government departments; accessible and supportive systems; suitable jurisdiction; simple procedures; effective and suitable decision-making process; proportionate remedies; speed; authority, expertise and cost effectiveness. They invited comments.

Adler and Bradley (in Partington, 2001) examined the Australian Administrative Review Tribunal, two-tiered, with the first comprising a number of specialist review tribunals and the second being a panel to review first tier decisions raising substantial questions of law or mixed fact and law. They also examined the Quebec system. They proposed a Unified Appeal Tribunal (UAT) with 10 specialist divisions. There would be a right of appeal from all government discretionary decisions. Procedure and training would be standardised. The UAT would be able to commission research. Appeals on law would go from the upper tier to the courts. Existing tribunals would be brought into this unified structure:

> "...consider what the state of the ordinary courts would be like if there were as many specialised courts as there are tribunals and if, every time Parliament created some new private law rights or new regulatory offences, a new civil or criminal court were to be created."

Leggatt recommendations

11–013 Sir Andrew Leggatt's Review of tribunals, 2001, concentrated on 70 "statutory bodies which provide a specialised machinery for the adjudication of cases that would otherwise be decided by the civil courts".

Identifiable problems

11–014 "The most striking feature of tribunals is their isolation ... narrowness of outlook ... duplication of effort. Each tribunal invents its own IT ... internal processes, and ... standards. There is under-investment in training ... The bigger tribunals have good accommodation ...; the smaller ones are scratching around for ... venues ... Most ... IT is primitive and is years behind the systems we found in Australia. Most tribunals find it difficult to retain suitable staff." (para.1.18)

The relationship with government departments

11–015 "There [is] ... an uneasy relationship ... the chairmen and members feel that they cannot be seen as independent ... paradoxically, many tribunals do not enter into the appropriate dialogue which would enable departments to learn from adverse tribunal decisions and thereby to improve their primary decision-making." (para.1.19)

The relationship with users

11–016 There were unacceptable delays, because of inefficient document-handling, poor listing and too many adjournments. Users were frequently "left in the dark" (para.1.22).

Procedures

> "In some tribunals, proceedings are informal. In others, they are at least as formal as those of the courts ... approaches sometimes differ within the same tribunal ... the biggest challenge ... is to enable users ... to come to the tribunal without undue apprehension, and to leave feeling that they have been given a fair opportunity to put their case." (paras.1.24–1.25)

11–017

A more independent system

Most consultation respondents thought tribunals were not perceived to be independent from government departments. Although Leggatt examined the separate system of administrative *courts* in the major European systems, he concluded that establishing these would be wholly disproportionate. On the European Convention, he concluded that art.6(1) (fair trial) did not apply to some tribunals but the "equality of arms" principle had implications for Mental Health Review Tribunals and immigration tribunals. He interpreted the Convention case law as requiring "institutional and structural impartiality", like courts. (para.2.25). Users thought tribunals were on the government's side. (para.2.16). Tribunals should be formed into a coherent system to sit alongside the ordinary courts, administered by the Lord Chancellor (para.2.27).

11–018

A more coherent system

There should be a single system, enabling the citizen to submit an appeal in the knowledge that it would be allocated to the correct tribunal. It would provide a clearer and simpler system for developing the law. The Woolf reforms should be quickly adapted for tribunals, to ensure that procedures were speedy, proportionate and cheap. On land, property and housing, there were confusing overlaps between courts and tribunals as well as between tribunals (Ch.3).

11–019

More user-friendly

Users should be given information on how to present a case, compliant with the European Convention on HR. Decision-makers should provide information on what the appellant's statutory entitlement was, what had been decided, the reasons, and whether there was a right of appeal. Legal aid should be provided on a case-by-case basis (Ch.4).

11–020

Structure and powers

The proposed Tribunals System should be divided by subject-matter into divisions, one of which should deal with disputes between citizens and the rest with disputes between citizen and state. Appeals should be as they are now, described above (paras 6.1–6.15).

11–021

Precedent

11–022 "First tier tribunals should continue to consider each case on its merits... Their decisions should not set binding precedents (para.6.19) but a system of designating binding cases should be adopted throughout the appellate division."

Judicial review

11–023 Second tier tribunals should be statutorily excluded from judicial review (JR) and JR from first-tier tribunals should be precluded unless all rights of appeal had been exhausted. The aim of the new appellate Division would be to develop a coherent approach to precedent and the law. The Senior President and other Presidents would be High Court judges so it would be inappropriate to subject them to JR by another equal status judge.

Presidents

11–024 The Tribunals System should be headed by a Senior President, who should be a HC judge. Some of the Division Presidents should be HC judges. They should co-ordinate consistency in decision-making and uniformity of practice and procedure and should hear the most difficult, novel or complex cases (Chs 6 and 7).

Conduct

11–025 Tribunal members should take an "enabling" approach, "giving the parties confidence in their ability to participate" (para.7.5). Recruitment and training should emphasise the need for interpersonal skills to help users to overcome communication difficulties (Ch.7).

Active case management

11–026 Copying case management under the Civil Procedure Rules 1998 (Ch.8).

Relationship with departments

11–027 Government departments should introduce internal review procedures to establish that their side of the case is correct in fact and law and that contesting the appeal was the only realistic action and a justifiable use of public funds. Departments should adopt a central capacity for scrutinising tribunal decisions and disseminating lessons learned. Tribunals should be able to identify systemic problems and suggest remedies (Ch.9).

Outcomes: the Tribunals, Courts & Enforcement Act 2007

In 2003, The LC announced the launch of the Tribunals Service (now HMCTS) **11–028** and a policy to increase tribunal accessibility, raise service standards, and improve administration. In 2004, he published a White Paper, *Transforming Public Services: Complaints, Redress and Tribunals*. The summary claimed that the programme of reform

> "goes further than just looking at tribunals—it sets out proposals to improve the whole ... dispute resolution process ... This means helping to improve standards of decision making across government and ... promoting quicker and more effective means of dispute resolution, so that fewer cases come before tribunals ... the new [Service] will be more than just a federation of existing tribunals ... Its mission will be to help prevent and resolve disputes, using any appropriate method".

Notice the language here and the breadth of vision. Government recognised the need *to prevent disputes arising in the first place* and that the whole handling system for citizens' complaints about government needed restructuring. It is also a formal acknowledgement of the irony I pointed out above, that tribunals, originally established as informal, cheap and quick alternatives to the courts, had themselves become so elaborate and complex that ADR was needed to avoid a tribunal hearing. The paper's main points were as follows, with the outcomes bracketed.

1.   The creation of a Senior President of Tribunals. (TCE Act s.2. He has a similar role to the Lord Chief Justice with the mainstream judiciary—training, guidance, welfare and so on.)
2.   A unified and cohesive system of deployment for those sitting in first-tier tribunals and another for those sitting in appellate tribunals (TCE Act ss.4–8).
3.   The renaming of legal members of tribunals as "Tribunal Judge" and "Tribunal Appellate Judge" respectively (done, 2007.)
4.   Simplifying the arrangements whereby panel members can sit in more than one jurisdiction while safeguarding necessary expertise (outcome as in 2).
5.   Further improving arrangements for training and appraisal. (Training is fairly integrated with that of the mainstream judiciary.)
6.   Structural changes include a statutory tribunals rule committee (rules are made under TCE Act s.22); a more coherent structure of appeals and reviews (TCE Act s.2 provides for a First Tier Tribunal and Upper Tribunal (UT). The UT is a superior court of record, equivalent to the Administrative Court in the HC and divided into four chambers. It may be and indeed has been granted a (limited) judicial review jurisdiction, under the 2007 Act, exercised by HC judges only. The first tier is divided into Chambers with Presidents, as in the diagram).

Most of this took until 2010 to achieve but the full tribunal system is still under development. The Judicial Appointments Commission, created in 2006, took over the recruitment process for tribunal members. The property chamber was added in 2013. In 2013, some of the Upper Tribunal chambers gained judicial review powers and took over parts of the case load from the over-worked Administrative Court, such as immigration and asylum reviews. In 2013, the Ministry of Justice consulted on creating a planning chamber in the Upper Tribunal, to enable the transfer of planning reviews out of the Administrative Court.

The current system and work of the tribunals system is outlined on HMCTS web-pages and further detail is contained in their annual report, the tribunal statistics and the very useful annual report of the Senior President of Tribunals, on the judiciary website. In 2015–2016, there were 408,000 applications to tribunals, compared with 1.5 million applications to the County Court.

Research

11–029   There is far too little research in the UK, compared with that in other jurisdictions (see Cane, 2009). The AJTC, described above, now abolished, was proactive in commissioning research and disseminating results to those who needed to learn lessons. This was usually very specific. For instance, in 2011, they published a report on the experiences of patients appealing against detention to the First Tier Tribunal (Mental Health). They identified complaints about defects in representation, distress caused by delay and lack of communication, concern about limits to case-presentation and lack of information about appeal rights.

The "Vision"

11–030   The 2016 "vision statement", *Transforming our Justice System*, by the Lord Chancellor, Lord Chief Justice and Senior President of Tribunals expressed these dreams. I have italicised the main points.

> "...our judges and members to adopt *a more inquisitorial and problem-solving approach*, focused around the needs of individuals ... underpinned by...*one system, one judiciary*, and better quality outcomes.
> Innovative '*problem-solving*' opportunities will be created to improve the determination of a range of issues which have historically been spread across courts and tribunals. This '*one stop shop*' approach is being piloted with property disputes which can be dealt with before one specialist Judge, giving claimants a speedier and conclusive resolution [as recommended by the Civil Justice Council in 2015, because elements of some property disputes were spilt between courts and tribunals]...
> ...*digital by default*, with easy to use...online processes...to help people lodge a claim more easily, but with the right levels of help... Once a claim is made, automatic sharing of digital documents with relevant government departments will mean that the tribunals and the parties will have all the right information to allow them to deal with claims promptly and effectively, saving time for both tribunal panels and claimants...*access to specialist judicial expertise using* tools and *technology* that they use routinely in other parts of their lives. This will allow the nub of a case to be identified quickly, wrong decisions resolved, and hopeless causes weeded out.
> In the next 18 months, *online dispute resolution* will be tested in Social Security & Child Support hearings...

By 2020, tribunals will be part of a *single justice system with a single judiciary*. They will offer a range of choices… from virtual hearings, online decision making, early evaluation, mediation and conciliation to the traditional face-to-face hearing." (Part 6)

Further detail was announced in the accompanying consultation.

"…over time [*tribunals*] have become *complicated* and *slow* to deal with, *burdened with paper* and unnecessary *bureaucracy… straightforward* tribunal *decisions do not require full physical hearings*, so where appropriate, judges will be making decisions based on written representations, hearings will be held over telephone or video conference and specially trained case officers will help cases progress through the system." (p.10)

By 2016, case management powers had already been delegated to registrars and authorised staff, in mental health cases.

"…*we want to move away from…using non-legal members* regardless of whether their specialist expertise and knowledge is relevant or required…they should only be part of the panel where their presence is relevant to the case. Their expertise and knowledge may also be used in innovative ways, with a greater focus on online engagement and ongoing conversation outside of traditional hearings…" (p.18)

"Some change has already been introduced [in practice]…cases in the First-Tier Tribunal (Immigration and Asylum) are now usually heard by a *single judge*…in the Employment Tribunal, the Government has reduced panel members in most unfair dismissal claims…"

"We therefore propose to give the SPT [Senior President of Tribunals] greater freedom [to provide that] a tribunal panel in the First-tier Tribunal is to consist of a single member unless otherwise determined by the SPT…Where specialist expertise or knowledge is required, it will still be provided…For example, *[lay members] could be used as a pool of specialist experts* who could be deployed across various Chambers and jurisdictions who would benefit from their expertise, answering specific queries from judges or helping people work through the process by sharing their skills and knowledge…The use of multiple panel members in the unified tribunals currently costs the taxpayer around £21m per year in fees alone, with daily fees for each member ranging from £200 – £500, plus additional costs for travel and subsistence, training, appraisal and general administration." (pp.18–19)

For a more complete "vision" of the digital future, see the speech by Sir Ernest Ryder, the SPT. He described the "online continuous hearings" to be piloted for state benefits claimants.

"It works like this. Change your view of litigation from an adversarial dispute to a problem to be solved. All participants, the appellant, the respondent Government department…and the tribunal judge, are able to iterate and comment upon the basic case papers online, over a reasonable window of time, so that the issues in dispute can be clarified and explored. There is no need for all the parties to be together in a court or building at the same time. There is no single trial or hearing in the traditional sense. We will have a single, digital hearing that is continuous over an extended period of time…[As with] the traditional approach of the tribunals, the judge will take an inquisitorial and problem-solving approach, guiding the parties to explain and understand their respective positions. Once concluded, this iterative approach may allow the judge to make a decision there and then."

Conclusion

11–031　Almost all of Leggatt's recommendations were implemented, with very little alteration. There was a fundamental streamlining of the hotch-potch of tribunals, or at least the main ones. This is to be welcomed and copies the model laid down in other countries decades ago. Nevertheless, dozens of tribunals still lie outside this new structure, notably the busy employment appeal tribunals; legal aid is still not available for representation in the vast majority of hearings and abolishing the AJTC was a truly retrograde step, taking us back to 1956. Fees were introduced for employment tribunal claims in 2013. While there is an argument that this is a denial of access to justice, this may deter vexatious litigants, who have in the past bedevilled the employment tribunals and some employers. The Ministry of Justice said fees would save expense to taxpayers and encourage people to look for alternatives such as mediation, or use the free ACAS service.

Respondents to the consultation on the radical "vision" of digital by default were very worried about the capacity of users to operate the procedure and about the removal of lay people from most adjudications, because of the loss their expertise. Many people who appeal to tribunal over state benefit are the least able of all citizens to cope with IT. The Government responded in 2017 that it would drop the default assumption that all hearings would be by judge-alone unless otherwise specified. Nevertheless, the vision paper's recommendation of dropping lay people to save money is brutal and unprincipled. It barely acknowledges the value of lay decision-making, especially expert lay decision-making, and the second value that they have as creating a tribunal of three rather than one. This is astonishingly provocative and a bit sad. Imagine if the same thing happened in magistrates' courts and it was suddenly suggested that the default position was that district judges would sit alone, disposing of most lay justices.

2.　ARBITRATION

11–032　Arbitration was well known as the nineteenth century merchants' alternative to the expense and delay of the High Court. It is classified by some as a form of ADR but, as it is more formal and results in a legally binding decision, most specialist ADR writers exclude it. It means the reference of a dispute to a third party or parties to decide according to law but outside the confines of normal courtrooms or procedure. The parties pay privately for the arbitration. It may arise in one of three ways.

1.　By reference from a court. A judge of the Commercial Court, or one of the other business courts, may refer a suitable case to arbitration or herself act as arbitrator. Commercial Court judges have always been extremely keen on arbitration and if they can cut out part of one of their complex cases and send it to arbitration, they will do. The Lands Chamber of the Upper Tribunal (formerly lands tribunal) has a statutory power to act as arbitrator by consent.

2.   By agreement after a dispute has arisen. For instance, if a contract has broken down, the parties might agree to refer their dispute to an arbitrator.

3.   By contract. Contracting parties may agree that, in the event of a dispute arising under the contract, they will refer it to an arbitrator to be appointed by, say, the Chartered Institute of Arbitrators, or the Bar Council, or the International Chamber of Commerce. Such clauses are common in commercial contracts and insurance. Examine your own household or vehicle insurance policy if you want to see an example of an arbitration clause to which you are, unwittingly, a party.

Where a business contracts with a consumer, they must fully explain any arbitration clause. It is unfair if it creates a significant imbalance in parties' rights and obligations, detrimental to the consumer.

Arbitrations are usually conducted by one or three people. An arbitrator may be a specialist lawyer or, more likely, a technical expert in the subject in dispute. Some are doubly qualified. The Chartered Institute of Arbitrators (CIArb) has over 14,000 members, in 133 countries. It provides training leading to qualification. Arbitrations are governed by the Arbitration Act 1996. Section 1(a) states that the object of arbitration is "the fair resolution of disputes by an impartial tribunal without unnecessary delay or expense". Section 1(b) continues that "the parties should be free to agree how their disputes are resolved, subject only to such safeguards as are necessary in the public interest". The arbitrator has both the right and the duty to devise and adopt suitable procedures to minimise delay and expense. Section 34 gives her absolute power over procedure. An arbitration will normally follow essentially the same stages as civil litigation: exchanging documents, factual and expert evidence and then a hearing, but frequently issues are dealt with by written submissions and then a telephone or video hearing. Often, there is not a general duty of disclosure, as in the courts, but only an obligation to identify the documents relied on by the party. The Act provides that the arbitration is not bound by the strict rules of evidence. Unlike civil litigation, where the court is bound to decide according to the law, the arbitrator may decide the dispute in accordance with "such other considerations as are agreed by (the parties) or determined by the tribunal" (s.46). This means that an equity clause may be agreed, requiring the arbitrator to decide according to equity and good conscience.

Once parties have voluntarily submitted to arbitration, the courts will not normally entertain one party if they try and ignore this agreement and make a court claim. The court will normally order a stay or stop of proceedings, under s.9. There is a major exception to this in relation to EU courts, however. In *Allianz SpA v West Tankers Inc* (2009), the ECJ ruled that a court in one EU Member State had no power to rule that a party should drop a case in another EU state on the ground that the parties had agreed to refer any dispute to arbitration. While some lawyers feared this would allow people to avoid arbitrating in London and persuade others to arbitrate in countries where there is power to award anti-suit injunctions, such as New York or Singapore, thus robbing

11–033

England of work, others disagreed. Peter Clough, head of disputes at Osborne Clarke, said London still has its appeal "founded on its respected framework for arbitration, legal expertise and English law being the law of choice in many commercial sectors". See Friel and Jones and see further Qureshi (2009).

In the UK, the arbitrator gives a reasoned decision which is enforceable in court. Under the 1996 Act, there are three grounds on which an award may be challenged in court: jurisdiction, serious irregularity or a point of law. The question must be one of general public importance and the decision of the arbitrators should be at least open to serious doubt: *CMA v Beteiligungs-Kommanditgesellschaft* (2002). The Act has been subject to considerable interpretation in case law. The courts can act as an appointing authority of last resort, where the parties cannot agree on an arbitrator. They can compel the production of evidence and enforce an arbitration award. Because many foreign arbitrations are conducted in London, difficult issues of private international law can arise. In *Lesotho Highlands Development Authority v Impregilo SpA* (2005), the House of Lords reminded us that the philosophy and ethos of the Arbitration Act 1996 was to alter the relationship between arbitration and the courts. Lord Steyn said "A major purpose of the new Act was to reduce drastically the extent of intervention of courts in the arbitral process". He looked at the debate on the Bill and a departmental advisory committee report and concluded that the UK was subject to international criticism that the courts interfered too much.

Most disputes in shipping or aviation are referred to arbitration, as are those of multinational corporations. They are common in oil, gas, banking, commodities, insurance and securities and international trade. Arbitrations are very big, lucrative business to London's lawyers and are a product of London's prominence as an international commercial centre and stable law and legal system. Many cross-border disputes arose through the construction of the channel tunnel, for instance a £1 billion claim by Eurotunnel against Trans Manche Link, but they were often resolved by arbitration conducted through the International Chamber of Commerce in Paris. Other international arbitration bodies include the London Court of International Arbitration, the London Maritime Arbitrators Association and centres in New York, Geneva, Stockholm and Hong Kong. It is estimated that Paris has the most international arbitrations but, since the nature of arbitration is private, there are no statistics of the total.

11–034   In the UK, a number of specialist schemes exist, such as Professional Arbitration on Court Terms, run by the Law Society and Royal Institute of Chartered Surveyors as an alternative to courts determining lease renewal terms and commercial rents. Some barristers are trained as arbitrators. CIArb runs a business arbitration scheme.

Arbitration became popular because it had the advantages of being quick, arranged at a date to suit the parties, cheaper than court proceedings and private. Obviously, this is desirable where time is of the essence, (e.g. a dispute about liability for damage to a perishable cargo) or the parties do not want their commercial secrets exposed in the courtroom. Sampson (1997), however, argued that, because of lawyer-domination, arbitration had become "a mirror image of litigation", with complex parallel procedures to civil litigation. He quoted Sir Thomas Bingham MR:

"the arbitration process, by mimicking the processes of the courts and becoming over-legalistic and overlawyered has betrayed its birthright by allowing itself to become as slow, as expensive and almost as formal as the court proceedings from which it was intended to offer escape".

The 1996 Act was meant to reverse this process, by enabling arbitrators to force the pace of arbitration. The advantages offered by civil litigation in the courts are: if one party believes the other's case has no substance, she can ask for summary judgment; further parties can be added if necessary; the arbitrator has no power to consolidate arbitrations in a multi-party action. In the 2016 Bailii lecture, Thomas LCJ examined in great depth the relationship between the courts and arbitration, in commercial disputes. He emphasised the benefits of the new business courts, with their new and fast procedures. Courts, he said, play a vital role in developing the law in the light of reasoned argument; enabling debate and public scrutiny of the law. An issue can be brought back to the courts and parliament if necessary. The result of the strict tests under the 1996 Act were to reduce the number of appeals to the courts. The promotion of arbitration had undermined the means by which the common law's strength, its excellence, was developed. Lack of openness could reduce the degree of certainty in the law. There was now a lack of case law on construction, engineering, shipping, insurance and commodities, because too many disputes had moved into arbitration. The UK had gone too far in favouring the perceived advantages of arbitration.

3. ALTERNATIVE DISPUTE RESOLUTION

This was reinvented in the USA in the 1970s and became the fashionable **11–035** development in England and Wales from 1990, though mediation was common in England in the 11th century, or earlier, according to Lord Neuberger's speech (2015). Many UK lawyers, notably the Lord Chancellors Mackay (Conservative) then Irvine (Labour) took a very active interest in this US import, ADR, as a means of avoiding public and private expense and the private pain of litigation. If current plans for the online court just described above in Ch.10 come to fruition, there will be a massive diversion of civil problems away from the courts and into ADR.

ADR can be defined as any method of resolving a legal problem without resorting to the legal process. Experts consider that any subject can be referred to ADR but advisability depends on the parties' attitudes. McIntyre explained that there are two types of dispute resolution. In adjudicative methods, such as arbitration, adjudication, binding reference and dispute resolution boards, the decision-maker(s) impose a decision on the parties. In consensual methods such as negotiation and mediation, the parties resolve the matter by agreement.

Types of ADR

ACAS   The Advisory, Conciliation and Arbitration Service was established in   **11–036** 1974 to trouble-shoot employment disputes and keep potential complaints out of employment tribunals.

Adjudication   A quick dispute resolution process designed for the construction industry, to make sure work is not unduly delayed. It was created by the Housing Grants, Construction and Regeneration Act 1996. There is a statutory right to adjudication at any time and decisions are enforceable in the courts.

Conciliation   The conciliator communicates with both parties, determining what is important to them and operates in a flexible manner. Mediation and conciliation have been used in China for centuries. The United Nations Commission on International Trade Law provides a set of model rules.

Early neutral evaluation   A neutral professional, often a lawyer or judge, hears a summary of each party's case and gives a non-binding assessment of the merits, which can be used as a basis for settlement or negotiation. Since a 1996 Practice Statement, the Commercial Court judges can offer this to parties appearing before them. Under the proposed courts and tribunals reforms, this is one type of resolution into which civil disputes might be guided. Like much of ADR, it developed transatlantically, (Thomas LCJ, 2016). It started in London's ship-chartering and insurance markets in the 1950s, then became part of the formalised judicial process in California in the 1980s.

Expert determination   An independent expert is appointed to reach a binding decision. It is not caught by the Arbitration Act and thus is not elaborate and has no right of appeal. An example is the use of a surveyor at a rent review.

Formalised settlement conference   These were described in 1995, in the *New Law Journal*. In 2016, they were being trialled in some areas in 2016–2017. The Family Judge takes an inquisitorial approach.

Mediation   A mediator helps both sides to come to an agreement which they can accept. It can be evaluative, where the mediator assesses the legal strength of a case, or facilitative, where the mediator concentrates on assisting the parties to define the issues. If an agreement is reached it can be written down and forms a legally binding contract, unless the parties state otherwise. If not, traditional civil litigation is still open, so proponents consider it a "no lose" option for a lawyer. Usually, the mediator acts as a go-between, negotiating with each party in their separate private rooms.

Med-arb   This is a combination of mediation and arbitration, where the parties agree to mediate but if no settlement is reached, the dispute is referred to arbitration. The mediator may turn into an arbitrator.

Mini trial   The hiring of an independent person to give a non-binding decision on the issue. Hiring retired judges to do this is common in the USA.

Neutral fact finding   This is a non-binding procedure used for complex technical issues. A neutral expert is appointed to investigate the facts and evaluate the merits of the dispute. It can form the basis of settlement or negotiation.

Online dispute resolution   There are a number of websites offering this, usually used for low-value disputes. See Ortolani on Bitcoin, for example.

Limitations of ADR

ADR is not suitable for every claim. For instance, where the parties refuse to speak to one another, or where, as in most civil cases, the defendant is silent and judgment is ordered in default to the claimant. It is not suitable where there is little room for compromise, such as in housing possession proceedings. If a case turns on a point of law and both parties want the law clarified or one wants to change the law, then ADR will be unsuitable. Similarly, this applies where only a court order will suffice, such as a court-sanctioned settlement in family law or an injunction to stop an illegal act. ADR is ideal where the parties must continue in a relationship, such as neighbours or businesses. Also, it can save years of nit-picking argument, generating thousands of pounds of costs, in multi-party commercial disputes. Neuberger (2015) examined in depth the advantages and disadvantages of mediation.

11–037

Examples of ADR

Family mediation and conciliation

This began with the 1974 Finer Report, which referred to family conciliation. Mediation became much more fashionable in the 1990s. Hundreds of lawyers trained as mediators. Under the Family Law Act 1996, attending a mediation information meeting was made compulsory for the legally aided, in certain circumstances. A family judge could order mediation but there were no sanctions for failing to attend. Monitoring showed disappointing results, as often only one side attended. Public funding (legal aid) is available for mediation. The problem with the 1996 Act was its hopeless lop-sidedness. Frequently, one party was not legally aided. They were paying for their own representation and, as the law stood, they could not be compelled to co-operate, so the Minister of Justice announced that anyone wishing to contest the terms of a divorce must attend a mediation awareness session. The MoJ said:

11–038

> "National Audit Office figures on legally-aided mediation show that the average time for a mediated case to be completed is 110 days, compared to 435 days for court cases on similar issues. Mediation is also often cheaper than going to court—data from Legal Aid cases show the average cost per client of mediation is £535 compared to £2,823 for cases going to court." (News release, 23 February 2011.)

In the meantime, family resolution pilots were commenced in three locations, to try to keep child contact disputes out of court. A Green Paper was published in 2004, proposing to put this type of ADR on a statutory footing, giving judges power to direct parents to in-court conciliation and mediation, although it would not be compulsory, as research had shown compulsion would breed resentment. The Family Mediation Council (meaning Resolution (lawyers), the Law Society and others) recommended compulsory mediation assessment meetings for all parents who wanted to go to court over children's contact and residence and parents arguing about money. Under the Children and Families Act 2014, a person is now required to attend a mediation information and assessment meeting, MIAM, with a trained mediator, before making an application for certain court orders, such as child arrangements, parental responsibility and financial maintenance. The respondent is expected to attend the meeting. The mediator assesses whether mediation is appropriate. The court has a general power to adjourn proceedings for non-court resolution to be attempted. Parties are exempted from this requirement in cases of domestic violence. In 2013, Resolution said that cuts in legal aid had reduced awareness of mediation because fewer people had access to free legal advice, even though legal aid for mediation itself has increased. In 2017, the Government at last admitted legal aid cuts had caused the sharp fall in MIAMs. In a June 2013 press release, the Ministry of Justice claimed that the cost of mediating separating couples' financial disputes was £500 compared with £4,000 in court.

In-court conciliation schemes conducted by family judges have been used for years. Trinder and Kellett, in a 2007 research report for the Ministry of Justice drew mixed conclusions on the success of "The longer-term outcomes of in-court conciliation". By 2005, more than 250 family lawyers had been trained in "collaborative law", a no-court divorce scheme that originated in the USA. Parties get a signed guarantee that lawyers will not let things escalate or insist on going to court. Resolution lawyers said the use of collaborative law in divorce had increased by 87 per cent in 2006–2007.

Court schemes

11–039   Commercial Court judges are very keen on ADR. They established a working party to examine the scope for applying pressure on litigants to use ADR. Coleman J enforced a mediation clause in a commercial contract in *Cable & Wireless Plc v IBM* (2002). In the Technology and Construction Court, judges who have received extra training in dispute resolution techniques may use a court settlement process at the request of the parties where it is felt such a procedure could achieve an amicable settlement. The Court of Appeal has offered a mediation scheme since 2003. It was broadened in 2012. As for small claims, in 2012, the MoJ announced that up to 80,000 more cases per year would be referred to a small claims mediation service, which is available under CPR Pt 26. It gives people the option of a telephone mediation service. Ministers claimed that 98 per cent of existing users were satisfied; 95 per cent of mediations were conducted by phone and mediation took 5–6 weeks to arrange, compared with 13–14 weeks for a court hearing. "In the 12 months to the end of April 2010, the service settled 73 per cent of the 10,000 mediations it conducted" (press release, 9 February 2011). Marshall pointed out that even if a claimant does win in court, it is notoriously difficult to enforce the court's order but where both parties have chosen mediation, they are more likely to engage in how the settlement will be implemented. See further below.

NHS

After reports by the National Audit Office that clinical disputes could cost £4.4   **11–040**
billion per year, the NHS set up a pilot project to help resolve claims quickly. An
example of a large group mediation was that involving the parents of children
whose organs were wrongly retained, after death, at the Alder Hey Children's
Hospital. After the mediation, in 2003, each set of parents received a sum of
money, an apology and a pledge to erect a plaque to commemorate the children.
£100,000 was donated to charity. In 2005, a Speedy Resolution Scheme for some
publicly funded clinical disputes involving Welsh NHS trusts was piloted. The
Trusts set out an accident plan in each case, to prevent future accidents, as well as
offering an apology and explanation, where appropriate. The NHS Redress Act
2006 introduced a scheme for claims up to £20,000 in England. It encourages
staff to report mistakes. Patients have a right to an investigation, explanation,
apology or remedial care, if compensation is inappropriate. An example of how
ADR can save cost occurred when the NHS and a number of claimant firms
entered into an ADR protocol to manage over 200 claims over a suspended
urogynaecologist. Had they been litigated, it would have taken 12.5 years to
obtain 400 expert reports, costing £500,000; the claims would have cost £126,000
to issue; other costs would have been about £2.5 million. See Locke. In late 2016,
the NHS litigation authority increased its use of mediation in an attempt to stop
"compensation culture". It paid out £1.4 billion in 2015–2016.

Government contractual disputes

The Government announced, in 2001, that it would be using ADR in its disputes.   **11–041**
Departments now include ADR clauses in their standard procurement contracts
and all relevant literature and new schemes promote ADR, such as in the tribunal
restructuring, described above. In 2011 the Government published a new Dispute
Resolution Commitment, meaning all departments must consider ADR first. A
press release, on 23 June 2011, claimed they had already saved £360 million in
the previous decade.

EU cross-border disputes

The EU Directive on mediation in civil and commercial matters was implemented   **11–042**
in 2011. Member states should encourage mediator training and a code of
conduct; provide judicial powers to invite parties to mediate; ensure mediated
settlements are enforceable like court judgments; ensure confidentiality and
suspend limitation periods during mediation.

Legal aid for ADR

Legal aid is discussed in Ch.17. It is available for early neutral evaluation,   **11–043**
mediation and arbitration. In 2005, the Government announced a restructuring of
aid to promote the resolution of disputes out of court. It also launched a National
Mediation Helpline, to put callers in touch with an accredited independent
mediator. That was closed in 2011 and replaced with a Civil Mediation Online

Directory. The costs are fixed and very low. Aided clients are able to claim reasonable costs. To discourage unnecessary litigation, in clinical negligence cases and actions against the police, most applicants are now expected to pursue any available complaints system before they make a claim. Coalition Minister of Justice Ken Clarke was determined to shift most civil disputes, especially family disputes, into ADR and his radical plans for legal aid, in 2010–2011, in force from 2013–2014, were geared to encourage it.

Will the courts enforce ADR?

11–044   In *Frank Cowl v Plymouth City Council* (2001), Lord Woolf CJ said

> "insufficient attention is paid to the paramount importance of avoiding litigation whenever this is possible … both sides must by now be acutely aware of the contribution alternative dispute resolution can make to resolving disputes in a manner which both meets the needs of the parties and the public and saves expense and stress" (at [1]).

This case involved a judicial review of the closure of a care home, with residents complaining that there had been insufficient consultation and a violation of their Convention rights, under arts 2, 3 and 8. Under pressure from the CA, the parties agreed to an ADR process. Lord Woolf said courts should take a pro-active approach to ADR. Parties should be asked why a complaints procedure had not been used. The courts should not permit judicial review proceedings, except for good reason, where a significant part of the issues could be resolved outside the litigation process. Lord Woolf asked the legal aid providers to co-operate in this approach and they have done so, expecting applicants to give details of alternatives to litigation. The issue is whether a private paying client would go to court rather than seeking to pursue alternatives, taking into account the likely effectiveness of alternatives, the attitude of the opponent and all other circumstances.

The CA held, in *Dunnett v Railtrack* (2002) that a party to litigation who turned down ADR, when it was suggested by the court, might suffer uncomfortable consequences in costs. Brooke LJ reminded the parties that they had a duty to further the overriding objective of the Civil Procedure Rules (set out in Ch.11 of this book). There have been a number of cases since then where this precedent has been applied and successful parties have had their costs refused or reduced. The Commercial Court gave a strong endorsement to ADR six months later in *Cable & Wireless Plc v IBM UK Ltd* (2002), above. Colman J held that a contractual term providing for mandatory ADR should not generally be held void for uncertainty. For the courts to decline to enforce contractual references to ADR on the grounds of intrinsic uncertainty would be to fly in the face of public policy. Even where there was an unqualified reference to ADR, a sufficiently certain and definable minimum duty of participation should not be hard to find. Further, an ADR clause was analogous to an arbitration agreement ancillary to the main contract and enforceable by a stay (pause) of proceedings or by an injunction. He remarked that the making of an ADR order in the Commercial Court had become commonplace, even where one or both parties objected. This case was applied by Blackburne J in *Shirayama Shokusan Co Ltd v Danovo Ltd* (2003). He decided he had the power to order ADR in the face of repeated refusals by the claimants to accept the defendants' offers to mediate. He was persuaded by the defendants that the parties had a shared interest in mediating as they were likely to continue in a long-term relationship.

The courts backtracked, however, on their view that unwilling parties could be forced into ADR, in a very important CA ruling. In *Halsey v Milton Keynes General NHS Trust* (2004), the CA produced a definitive set of guidelines on two points: the court's powers to order ADR and whether a party who refuses to participate in ADR should be penalised in costs:

> "It is one thing to encourage the parties to agree to mediation, even to encourage them in the strongest terms. It is another to order them to do so ... It seems to us likely that compulsion of ADR would be regarded as an unacceptable constraint on the right of access to the court and, therefore, a violation of article 6 ... the court's role is to encourage, not to compel. The form of encouragement may be robust ... mediation and other ADR processes do not offer a panacea, and can have disadvantages as well as advantages ..." (at [9]).

The question whether a party has acted unreasonably in refusing ADR must be **11–045** determined having regard to all the circumstances of the particular case: (a) the nature of the dispute; (b) the merits of the case; (c) the extent to which other settlement methods have been attempted; (d) whether the costs of the ADR would be disproportionately high; (e) whether any delay in setting up and attending the ADR would have been prejudicial; and (f) whether the ADR had a reasonable prospect of success. These factors should not be regarded as an exhaustive check-list. This precedent was applied in *Reed Executive Plc v Reed Business Information Ltd* (2004), *McMillan Williams v Range* (2004) and *Burchell v Bullard* (2005). See discussion by Sautter. In *Hickman v Blake Lapthorn* (2006), the costs were £435,000 and the award was £130,000 (incidentally, proportionality had clearly flown out of the window in this case). Had the defendants accepted the claimant's offer to settle for £150,000, they would have saved £205,000 in costs. They refused to mediate because, although their solicitor agreed to it, their barrister did not. Jack J thought this was reasonable, however. The parties should not be forced to settle. Criticising the case, Prince pointed out that the barrister was *not* being forced to settle but simply asked to attend a mediation. She noted the reluctance to order mediation, as part of case management, since *Halsey*. Sir Gavin Lightman was highly critical of *Halsey* in a June 2007 speech. In a May 2008 speech, the Master of the Rolls acknowledged that *Halsey* might have been over-cautious. Compulsory ADR did not appear to breach art.6 of the European Convention on Human Rights and indeed was referred to in the EC Directive on Mediation. Compulsory ADR had been introduced in a number of US jurisdictions, demonstrating that compulsion did not breach fair trial rights in common law or European jurisdictions. *Halsey*, he said, "may be open to review". The statement suggesting that compelling ADR was unlawful was, in any event, obiter, and should not stop district judges requiring parties to mediate. He pointed to powers of compulsion available in the Civil Procedure Rules. That was not to say, however, that the courts should penalise parties for refusing to take part in mediation, unless the refusal was unreasonable. This does not affect the enforceability of a contractual ADR clause.

It was accepted by the CA in *Sunrock v SAS* (2007) that damages could be awarded for breach, where a party refused ADR. In *PGF II SA v OMFS Co 1 Ltd* (2013), the CA held that failure to reply to an invitation to mediate was unreasonable and might result in cost sanctions. Shipman examined the conflict between compulsory mediation and the individual's rights under arts 5 and 6 of the European Convention on HR. Examining the case law of the ECtHR, she concluded that while there appeared to be little potential for conflict in the use of penalties such as imprisonment for contempt for refusal to comply with a mediation order, the automatic use of draconian penalties would be likely to violate the applicant's Convention rights. Below, we return to the issue of whether ADR ought to be compulsory.

The slow growth of ADR

11–046   The slow development of ADR in the last 27 years shows that judges, courts and government departments were much faster to learn about it and promote it than practising lawyers and the quotations from the case law above express judges' frustration with lawyers. By 1989, ADR was highly developed in the USA. By 1992, the Law Society (representing solicitors) announced it was a priority in their continuing education scheme and it was favoured in the 1993 Heilbron–Hodge report on civil litigation, discussed in the previous chapter, and the Woolf Report 1996 and was promoted by Mackay LC in all his speeches and plans on legal aid in 1995–1996.

Lawyers

11–047   Nevertheless, although it was discussed in law journals from 1989 and law firms started offering it commercially, many lawyers had still not heard of it by 1997. Also, lawyers were hostile to it, (Shapiro, 1997 and Genn, 1998). The biggest commercial solicitors' firms were the first lawyers to catch on to ADR, with a 1997 survey of the 200 top property law firms showing that 70 per cent regarded mediation as effective. In a 1999 survey of the top 500 companies in the North West, 52 per cent of respondents said their solicitors had not discussed with them the possibility of resolving a dispute through mediation (Goriely and Williams, 1997). The same year, concerned at the lack of uptake of ADR, the Lord Chancellor's Department (now Ministry of Justice) published a discussion paper to try and ascertain why. Respondents said it was not easy to find out about different ADR services. There was no central register. Levels of awareness of ADR were low but 51 per cent of respondents had found benefits of ADR in time, cost or convenience. Benefits cited were: preserving or rebuilding relationships between disputants, privacy, flexibility, informality, stress reduction, the enabling of a win-win scenario, innovative solutions, greater client participation and the ownership of the process. Most thought that government should do more to promote ADR but that it should not be obligatory. The Civil Justice Council responded, warning that art.6 of the Convention meant that access to the courts could not be excluded. They urged "a major educational push" to attract a wider public to the benefits of ADR.

At last, by the late 1990s a critical core of big law firms had been attracted to mediation, the most popular form of ADR, in non-family cases. S.J. Berwin offered ADR to their clients from 1997. A breakthrough came in 1998, when a case funded by the Law Society and ADR Group successfully challenged the Legal Aid Board's refusal to fund non-family mediation. Nevertheless, the biggest boost to ADR, especially mediation, came from its promotion by r.1 of the Civil Procedure Rules 1998. A 2000 MORI survey of 180 law firms showed that, since the rules had come into force the previous year, 54 per cent said they were more likely to have been involved in mediation.

ADR trainers found that most people wishing to be trained as mediators were lawyers but they had to drop the adversarial habit of aggressive confrontation (*Gazette*, 1997). In May 2008, Clarke MR said

> "[e]ven now ... far too many people know far too little about mediation. I think we can all agree that this has to change. ADR ... must become an integral part of our litigation culture."

Judges

Since lawyers were slow to use ADR, it was left to the judges to devise schemes **11–048** for it but even then, they struggled and have had to resort to the case law above to emphasise its desirability. A 1993 Practice Note announced that Commercial Court judges would encourage ADR in suitable cases and from 1996 a judge could grant a stay (suspend) a case to enable the parties to try ADR. From 1995, High Court Practice Directions required the parties' solicitors to certify whether they had considered resolving the dispute by ADR and discussed this with their client. From 1996, the London Patents County Court offered litigants the alternatives of expert arbitration or fast-track mediation. A mediation scheme was offered, virtually cost-free, at Central London County Court from 1996. Genn evaluated it after two years. She found that in only about five per cent of cases both parties accepted mediation. The joint demand for mediation was lowest where both parties were legally represented. Interviews with solicitors revealed widespread ignorance of mediation, apprehension about showing weakness and litigant resistance to compromise. Of those who mediated, 62 per cent settled and the settlement rate was highest where neither party was legally represented. Average settlement amounts were £2,000 lower than non-mediated settlements. Solicitors felt mediation had saved time but there was a common view that failure to settle at mediation increased costs. Some of the most successful mediators were barristers. From 1997, legal aid was available for the Central London scheme and another court-linked mediation scheme was commenced in Bristol. Following the Woolf Report 1996, the Civil Procedure Rules 1998 r.1, placed a duty on the court, as part of its active case management, to encourage the parties to use ADR, if the court considered it appropriate. The CA set up an ADR scheme, whereby invitations to participate in the scheme were sent out in almost all final appeals. Acceptance of voluntary, court-annexed schemes was initially disappointing. From November 1998 to March 1999, parties in 250 CA cases were offered mediation but both sides agreed to mediate in only 12.

The courts were keen to establish more court-based mediation schemes and many County Courts renamed themselves "Civil Justice Centres" to reflect the fact that they offer ADR as well as litigation. A 2004 evaluation of a small claims mediation scheme at Exeter showed that a high proportion of small claims referred to mediation settled. Parties generally found mediation useful. They thought the proceeding was more informal and the mediator a better listener than a judge. It was more likely to be successful between business parties than those in personal relationships or emotionally-charged disputes, with 90 per cent saying they thought they would use mediation again. A major advantage was that, even if the case failed, parties benefited from hearing the other side and receiving directions from the judge.

In 2004–2007, the Central London County Court started a new scheme of automatic referral, copied from Ontario. Under this, about 20 random cases per week were automatically referred to mediation. This applied to personal injury, trade, or housing debts above the small claims limit. If one or both of the parties objected to mediation, they had to give reasons. A district judge decided whether the case should be referred to mediation, or proceed through court. If a party still declined to mediate, for reasons unsatisfactory to the judge, they risked being liable to pay costs. If mediation was unsuccessful, or only partially successful, they were free to continue with court proceedings. Manchester County Court (Civil Justice Centre) introduced a free mediation adviser in 2004. From 2007, all County Court mediation was organised through the National Mediation Helpline. The Lord Chancellor said in 2007:

> "We are providing a simpler and quicker service in the County Courts through dealing with all but the most complex small claims through mediation. During a one year pilot here in Manchester, 86% of the mediations conducted were settled on the day, not one of which required any follow up."

The London scheme was researched by Hazel Genn in 1998 and 2007.

11–049   Another report by Genn (2002) reviewed the Commercial Court's ADR scheme and the voluntary Court of Appeal ADR scheme, in 1996–2000. She concluded that voluntary take-up of ADR remained "at a modest level" and, outside commercial practice, "the profession remains very cautious about the use of ADR". In 2002, Lord Woolf CJ said he felt we had not gone "nearly far enough" with ADR. The fact that it was not compulsory was delaying things.

Statistics from private ADR firms showed show a big rise in mediation by 2004. The Centre for Effective Dispute Resolution(CEDR) statistics demonstrated a significant increase in mediation after the Civil Procedure Rules came into force in 1999. There was then a slight decline until 2002, when the case of *Dunnett v Railtrack* (above) showed that the courts were prepared to penalise even winning parties in costs if they refused to mediate. Their 2004 statistics disclosed an overall increase of 35 per cent in mediation in 2003, and 8 per cent in 2004. Most mediations lasted just one day with 75 per cent of cases settling on the day or shortly after. CEDR perform regular audits. The 2007 audit claimed that the market had grown 33 per cent in the previous two years and by 2015–16 they reported 10,000 *commercial* mediations, an increase of 5 per cent.

A 2003 article by Lewis gave an interesting insight into why solicitors in big law firms used ADR by then. One observed that clients were now thinking about it as a first option and there was much more awareness of it. Another attributed the growth of ADR to the civil procedure pre-action protocols in his field, construction and engineering. These require the parties to state why they do not consider ADR appropriate in their case.

Turning to public and welfare law, by way of contrast, social welfare lawyers remained remarkably resistant to ADR. In 2002, Carr addressed this. She said they were concerned at the imbalance of power between their clients and the opposite party, whether a private employer or the State. Mediation could disguise the fundamental causes of social welfare problems and some, such as racial harassment or domestic violence, were not amenable to mediation.

In a 2004 conference organised by the Public Law Project, Maurice Kay LJ   **11–050**
said ADR had the greatest potential in housing, community care and education cases where there was an ongoing relationship between the claimant and a public body. The Administrative Court was trying to promote use of ADR. While lawyers acting for the socially disadvantaged in public law judicial review cases had been wary of ADR, experienced mediators pointed out the advantages. ADR could increase parties' sense of ownership of the case and the solution, in contrast with the limited remedies available in judicial review that did not address the real grievance. The grievance could be addressed directly. This reduced acrimony and promoted a continuing working relationship. It got away from the idea of winners and losers and focused on practical solutions. Lord Woolf on his retirement as Lord Chief Justice took up a post with the CEDR. He trained as a mediator and arbitrator. Since writing his report on civil justice, *Access to Justice*, 1996 (The Woolf Report), he had been a very strong advocate of ADR. Judges remained frustrated at the low use of ADR.

As I write in 2017, it remains difficult to collect statistics on ADR because by its nature it is private, yet annual statistics are published on court business. The CEDR website remains a good source for statistics, research and discussion, but its biennial mediation audit (May 2016) can only give part of the ADR picture. Sir Rupert Jackson, in his review of litigation costs, discussed in Ch.10, considered ADR under-used. He said all litigation lawyers and judges, the public and small businesses should be informed about the benefits of ADR. The President of HM Association of District Judges called for all DJs to be trained in mediation: N.L.J. news, April 2010 and was supported in a speech by Lord Neuberger. Given their obligation under the CPR 1998, it is alarming that DJ training in ADR has only become routine from 2011.

On the other hand, Foggo and Ahmed were more optimistic, pointing out that the top 20 law firms promote their litigation practices as "dispute resolution". They felt the pro-ADR culture change that Jackson LJ had called for had already happened for commercial litigators. Qureshi, chairman of The CityUK's Legal Services and Dispute Resolution Group, said 2010 research by his organisation showed ADR had been a major growth area in 2008–2010, with over 34,000 disputes resolved through arbitration and mediation in 2009. He reiterated that London is in a pre-eminent position for international business disputes. Research by the School of International Arbitration, QMUL, in October 2010, *Choices in International Arbitration*, found London was the preferred seat of arbitration for 203 corporate counsel surveyed: N.L.J. news, 15 October 2010. In 2016, the CIArb produced a paper on ADR commissioned by the Ministry of Justice. It concluded that there was room for an expansion of commercial ADR to complement the online court of the future.

Should ADR be compulsory?

11–051 In her 2008 Hamlyn lectures (2010), Genn argued very forcefully that the anti-litigation pressure, especially from judges, had already gone too far.

> "I want to focus on the decline of civil justice ... the diversion of civil cases to private dispute resolution, accompanied by an anti-litigation/anti-adjudication rhetoric that interprets these developments as socially positive (p.4) ... The anti-law story suggests that society is in the grip of a litigation explosion or compensation culture. (p.32) ... The outcome of mediation is not about *just* settlement, it is *just about settlement*" (p.117)

She argued that civil justice reviews around the world had been conducted in the absence of research or principled discussion. They were all about efficiency, reducing civil case loads and diverting cases into alternatives, to save money. While evaluation of court-annexed mediation schemes showed high levels of satisfaction among those who volunteered, there was little demand from the parties. She said her 2007 research, *Twisting Arms*, had shown that people did not like being pressured to settle. Brunsdon-Tully argued that the advantages of ADR—consensuality, informality, cost and speed, were lost when ADR was coerced. Sir Rupert Jackson in his review of civil costs, discussed in Ch.10, was not in favour of compulsory ADR.

On the other hand, in two interesting articles, mediator Paul Randolph asked why litigation is so often preferred to mediation and whether mediation should be compulsory.

> "Mandatory ADR is accepted globally, from the US, through Scandinavia and China, to Australia and New Zealand. Furthermore, there is no constitutional bar in the UK to mandatory mediation ... Protracted litigation can be one of the most destructive elements in society: it destroys businesses, breaks up marriages and damages health ... [ADR] cannot offer the degree of vindication that parties crave, nor the measure of public humiliation of the opponent they seek." (2010 and 2011)

Bibliography and further reading

Tribunals
11–052 Adler (1999) 6 *Journal of Social Security Law* 99 and *Legal Action*, September 1997.
Briggs LJ, *Civil Courts Structure Review: Interim Report* (December 2015) and *Civil Courts Structure Review: Final Report* (July 2016), Judiciary website.
Lord Browne-Wilkinson was quoted in *The Times*, 16 March 2005.
P. Cane, *Administrative Tribunals and Adjudication* (Oxford: Hart Publishing, 2009).
H. Genn and Y. Genn, *The Effectiveness of Representation at Tribunals* (1989).
H. Genn, B. Lever and L. Gray, *Tribunals for Diverse Users,* DCA Research Report 1/2006.

Lord Judge CJ, *The Lord Chief Justice's Review of the Administration of Justice in the Courts*, February 2010.

Sir Andrew Leggatt, *Report of the Review of Tribunals, Tribunals for Users One System, One Service*, National Archives.

Lord Chancellor, Lord Chief Justice and Senior President of Tribunals, *Transforming Our Justice System*, vision paper, September 2016, Judiciary website.

Ministry of Justice, *Transforming our justice system: assisted digital strategy, automatic online conviction and statutory standard penalty, and panel composition in tribunals – Government Response*, February 2017.

G. Richardson and H. Genn, "Tribunals in Transition—Resolution or Adjudication" (2007) *Public Law* 116–141.

M. Partington (ed.), *The Leggatt Review of Tribunals: Academic Seminar Papers* (University of Bristol, 2001).

M. Partington, N. Kirton-Darling and F. McClenaghan, *Empirical Research on Tribunals—An Annotated Review of Research Published between 1992 and 2007*, 2007, on the AJTC archived website, National Archives.

Lord Phillips CJ, "Alternative Dispute Resolution: An English Viewpoint" speech, 29 March, 2008.

Sir Ernest Ryder, "The Modernisation of Access to Justice in Times of Austerity", lecture, University of Bolton, 3 March 2016, Judiciary website.

Thomas LCJ, "Building the Best Court Forum for Commercial Dispute Resolution", speech, 21 October 2016, Judiciary website.

Further reading and updating
Administrative Justice and Tribunals Council archived website.   **11–053**
HM Courts and Tribunals Service.

Ministry of Justice, especially consultation paper, *Transforming Tribunals*, November 2007, including list of research and academic work.

Tribunals journal, on *Westlaw*.

Tribunal statistics: the annual statistics are published in the March quarter. *https://www.gov.uk/government/collections/tribunals-statistics*.

On Arbitration
There are many books on arbitration and dedicated journals such as *Arbitration*,   **11–054**
on *Westlaw*.

Chartered Institute of Arbitrators *http://www.ciarb.org*.

S. Friel and C. Jones, "London Waiting" (2009) N.L.J. 247.

T. Sampson, "Arbitration Act 1996—a fresh start?" (1997) 147 N.L.J. 261.

M. Smulian, "City feels the heat", Law Society's *Gazette*, 19 June 2003.

Thomas LCJ, "Developing commercial law through the courts: rebalancing the relationship between the courts and arbitration, The Bailii Lecture 2016", 9 March 2016, Judiciary website.

K. Qureshi, N.L.J. news, 24 September 2010; "Absolute power" (2009) 149 N.L.J. 1393.

On ADR

11–055   T. Allen and K. Mackie "Higher resolution" (2010) 160 N.L.J. 1143.

V Bondy, "Who Needs ADR?" *Legal Action*, September 2004, p.6.

M. Brunsdon-Tully, "There is an A in ADR but does anyone know what it means any more?" (2009) 28 C.J.Q. 218–237.

H. Carr, "Alternative routes to justice", *Legal Action*, March 2002, p.1.

Civil Mediation online directory, Ministry of Justice: *https://civilmediation. justice.gov.uk/*.

Sir Anthony Clarke MR, *The Future of Civil Mediation*, speech, 12 May 2008.

Formalised settlement conferences were described at (1995) 145 N.L.J. 383.

G. Foggo and M. Ahmed, in "What's the alternative" (2010) 160 N.L.J. 1194.

The Finer Report – *Report of the Committee on One-Parent Families* (1969), National Archives.

H. Genn, "The Central London County Court Pilot Mediation Scheme Evaluation Report", LCD Research Report 5/98 (1998) and "Court-Based ADR Initiatives for Non-Family Civil Disputes: the Commercial Court and the CA", LCD Research Report 1/02 (2002); *Twisting Arms: Court Referred and Court Linked Mediation Under Judicial Pressure*, Ministry of Justice Research Series 1/07 (2007); *Judging Civil Justice* (Cambridge: Cambridge University Press, 2010).

T. Goriely and T. Williams, "Resolving Civil Disputes: Choosing Between Out-of-Court Schemes and Litigation—A Review of the Literature", LCD Research Report 3/97 (1997).

J. Lewis, "Meet the Middleman", Law Society's *Gazette*, 9 May 2003.

Lightman J, "Mediation: An Approximation to Justice", speech, 31 July 2007.

D. Marshall, "Branching out", (2013) N.L.J., 11 October 2013.

D. McIntyre, "We can work it out" (2013) 163 N.L.J. 23.

J. Michaelson, "The A–Z of ADR" (2003) 153 N.L.J. 101, 146, 181, 232, and see the 2013–2014 series in the N.L.J.

Lord Neuberger, "Has mediation had its day?" speech, November 11, 2010, judiciary website; "Keynote address: A View from On High", Civil Mediation Conference, 12 May 2015, UK Supreme Court website.

P. Ortolani, "Self-enforcing ADR: lessons from Bitcoin" (2016) 36 OJLS (3) 395.

S. Prince "Negotiating mediation" (2006) 156 N.L.J. 262.

K. Qureshi, "Money walks?" (2010) 160 N.L.J. 1361.

P. Randolph, "Compulsory mediation?" (2010) 160 N.L.J. 499 and "The mediation conundrum" (2011) 161 N.L.J. 207.

E. Sautter, "*Halsey*—mediation one year on" (2005) I55 N.L.J. 730.

S. Shipman, "Compulsory mediation: the elephant in the room" (2011) 30(2) C.J.Q. 163–191.

Thomas LCJ, "Commercial Justice in the Global Village: the Role of Commercial Courts", speech, Dubai, 1 February 2016, Judiciary website.

L. Trinder and J. Kellett, *The longer-term outcomes of in-court conciliation*, Ministry of Justice Research Report 15/07 (2007).

Further reading and updating

11–056   Centre for Effective Dispute Resolution website.

Articles on specialist ADR are in specialist journals; articles on family mediation are in *Family Law* and similar journals; articles on construction dispute resolution are in construction law journals and so on.

General sources for further reading and updating this chapter

Free updates of this book are available on the Sweet & Maxwell website: **11–057**
http://uklawstudent.thomsonreuters.com.
Summary and revision: P. Darbyshire, *Nutshells English Legal System*, 10th edn (London: Sweet & Maxwell, 2016).
Limited items from the Law Society's *Gazette* and *Legal Action*.
Civil Justice Quarterly.
Public Law (on *Westlaw*).
The *New Law Journal* (on *Lexis*).
Law journals: search *Lexis* and *Westlaw*.
Judges' speeches on the Judiciary website and UK Supreme Court website.
Ministry of Justice research reports on its website.

CHAPTER 12

Criminal Procedure

"Having a Criminal Justice Bill before Parliament is like having a skip outside your house overnight. People take your rejected junk and other people stuff their junk into it." (Professor John Spencer, 1996, quoting a contributor to the Justices' Clerks' Society Conference that year.)

"The criminal justice system included the old Assizes. On my Circuit, the High Court judge would travel from Aylesbury to Bedford then to Northampton, Leicester with a possible stop off in Oakham, then on to Lincoln, finally back to Nottingham, delivering the jails. We no longer have Assizes nor, and this is an important consideration, a system in which every case was concluded—that is from the very start to a verdict—in a day or less." (Lord Judge CJ speech 5 November 2008.)

"The criminal justice system is close to breaking point. Lack of shared accountability and resource pressures mean that costs are being shunted from one part of the system to another and the system suffers from too many delays and inefficiencies. There is insufficient focus on victims, who face a postcode lottery in their access to justice... The system is already overstretched and we consider that the Ministry of Justice has exhausted the scope to make more cuts without further detriment to performance." (House of Commons Committee of Public Accounts, May 2016.)

Since the 1980s, criminal procedure and courts have been under continual **12-001** review and major restructuring. Much has been well thought through and long overdue. Additionally though, each government cannot resist making statutory alterations *every* year. There were over 100 Criminal Justice Acts and 4,000 new criminal offences in 1989–2009 (Leveson, 2015, p.5). As explained in Chs 6 and 7, governments have closed hundreds of local courts since 2010. They have altered the sentencing structure (yet again) and dismantled the legal aid system. In 2009, former Director of Public Prosecutions, Ken Macdonald, said that government departments were so keen on gimmicky changes that they would telephone him asking for "this month's idea". The result is a mish-mash mesh of legislation, layered over by later legislation, which is a nightmare to apply for judges, magistrates' legal advisers and lawyers. Apart from the challenge of ascertaining which sections of new and old statutes are in force, there is the problem that one provision has barely, or never, been implemented before another supersedes it. Magistrates' advisers work at the chalk face, their courts dealing with the bulk of criminal cases. They are the first to discover that a new bit of "junk" does not fit in, as they struggle to make sense of the latest initiative. Circuit judges in the Crown Court, determined to assert their independence, simply ignore many of the changes that they disapprove of, provided that they can get away with it. This is typified by attitudes towards the Criminal Procedure Rules (CrimPR), which many circuit judges simply ignored (Darbyshire, 2014).

The 2005 Rules were hailed as a consolidation of multiple sets of rules, in plain language. This was a hollow promise. New statutes and rules have been passed. As Professor Spencer said in 2010:

> "When laws are made like this, how is anybody supposed to keep abreast of them? … In most other countries, the task of keeping up with changes in criminal procedure is made much easier because the rules of criminal procedure are contained within a single document—a Criminal Procedure Code, of which consolidated versions are published in hard copy at regular intervals …" (*Archbold Review*).

Procedure has been scrutinised by the Royal Commission on Criminal Procedure 1981, resulting in the Police and Criminal Evidence Act 1984 (PACE) and the creation of the Crown Prosecution Service; then the Royal Commission on Criminal Justice 1993 (Runciman Commission), generating the Criminal Justice and Public Order Act 1994, the Criminal Appeal Act 1995 and the Criminal Procedure and Investigations Act 1996; then the Narey Report 1997, generating the Crime and Disorder Act 1998, creating a new youth justice scheme. Since 2000, the Human Rights Act (HRA) 1998 has affected criminal procedure more than any other area of the law. Then Auld published his *Review of the Criminal Courts in England and Wales* 2001, making sweeping proposals, some of which were enacted in the Courts Act and the Criminal Justice Act 2003 (CJA 2003). Added to these major overhauls, there has been a battery of statutes on specific aspects of procedure. Spencer called for a unified Code of Criminal Procedure. The first unified set of CrimPR was published in 2005, now regularly amended, but the centuries-old plan to codify statutes has been abandoned, because the law is far too complex, as explained in Ch.5. We are currently living through massive practice reforms recommended by Leveson LJ, in his *Review of Efficiency in Criminal Proceedings* 2015. Afficionados can keep up to date with "Better Case Management" newsletters, online. Much more dramatically, as explained in previous chapters, we are promised a future of "digital by default", heralded in the 2016 vision paper, *Transforming our Justice System*, launched by the Minister of Justice, the Lord Chief Justice and the Senior President of Tribunals. Leveson himself found that people were suffering from "transformation exhaustion".

1. SOURCES AND PRINCIPLES

The common law

12–002 The oldest principles are contained in English common law and the unwritten UK constitution. They are articulated in instruments ranging from Magna Carta 1215, to books of ancient authority, listed in Ch.2, plus statute and case law. Since UK lawyers drafted the European Convention on Human Rights, they not surprisingly modelled much of it on common law principles. For instance, the writ of habeas corpus to challenge unlawful imprisonment dates back to the fifteenth century, replacing earlier civil actions (Baker) and it is clearly the basis of art.5. Lord Bingham said "It has been widely recognized as the most effective remedy against executive lawlessness that the world has ever seen" (2010, p.14). Coke (1628, see Ch.2 of this book) and others discussed the rules of natural justice at length. By the twentieth century they were articulated in clear rules of fair trial, now repeated in art.6 of the Convention. The ancient English rule against torture clearly forms the basis of art.3. Because the UK constitution is unwritten, the ancient principles of the English legal system tend to be treated by governments as mere rhetorical devices rather than practical constraints on law-makers and law enforcers so it is left to the judiciary to apply them to restrain politicians' natural tendency to grab and centralise power. Many significant human rights challenges have been brought before the top courts but the judges have often found solutions in these ancient common law rules, instead, as we saw in Ch.4.

Toulson LJ's judgment below is an example. In *TTM v LB of Hackney* (2011), the Court of Appeal found that detaining someone in breach of the requirements of the Mental Health Act 1983 was unlawful at common law.

"Magna Carta 1297 provides:

'No freeman shall be taken or imprisoned, or be disseised of his freehold, or liberties, or free customs, or be outlawed, or exiled, or any other wise destroyed; nor will we not pass upon him, nor condemn him, but by lawful judgment of his peers, or by the law of the land.'

The right to freedom enshrined in Magna Carta is a fundamental constitutional right. From ancient times two writs were fashioned for its enforcement—the writ of habeas corpus for obtaining release and the writ of trespass to the person for obtaining compensation where the right has been infringed. Trespass to the person can take different forms, one being false imprisonment...: Clerk and Lindsell on Torts (2010) 20th ed, para 15-01" (paras 32–33)

He said the common law had developed the writ of trespass to the person so the unlawful detention was actionable for damages, as it was under art.5 of the Convention.

The rule of law

This was discussed in Ch.1. State agents must be able to point to a legal basis for their action. No-one is above the law, derived from common law principles, well established before Magna Carta cl.39 (above) encapsulated them, as explained by Lord Bingham in *The Rule of Law*. Modern writers have traced the concept back to authorities such as Aristotle.   **12–003**

The presumption of innocence

The burden of proving guilt is on the prosecutor. It should not be up to the defendant to prove his innocence. Critics highlight the increasing number of evidential "reverse" burdens on the defendant. See Ashworth and Blake (1996). Their fairness was considered in *Sheldrake v DPP* (2004). An evidential burden is not a burden of proof. It is a burden of raising an issue on the evidence for the consideration of the tribunal of fact. It is then for the prosecutor to prove beyond reasonable doubt that it does not avail the defendant. In *Grayson v UK* (2009), the   **12–004**

European Court of Human Rights decided the reverse burden in the Drug Trafficking Act 1994 did not breach art.6: the presumption of innocence is part of the right to a fair trial that applies throughout criminal proceedings but it is not absolute and presumptions of fact or law are not prohibited so long as they remain within limits. Ashworth commented (2009) that it was high time the ECtHR spelled out exactly what content it is intended to give to the presumption of innocence. In 2016, the EU passed a Directive requiring member states to apply the presumption.

The right to speedy trial

12–005   This is prescribed in Magna Carta 1215, cl.40 and later versions:

"(40)   To no one will we sell, to no one deny or delay right or justice" (British Library website).

and now reflected in art.5, below. On English law, see Ashworth and Redmayne, Ch.8.

The quantum or degree of proof

12–006   Guilt must be proven beyond reasonable doubt. This is a much higher burden on the prosecutor than the claimant's burden in a civil case, proof on the balance of probabilities. It dates back to the seventeenth century and is applied throughout the common law world. Shapiro examined its fascinating history.

The double jeopardy rule

12–007   A person cannot be tried twice on the same facts. See Friedland, cited by Dennis (2014). It is one of the oldest principles, consisting of "autrefois acquit" and "autrefois convict", plus the doctrine of abuse of process. It is "founded on the desirability of finality in litigation, fairness to the defendant, of efficiency in the investigation and prosecution of crime, and of maintaining a constitutional check on the power of the state to harass its citizens by repeated prosecutions" (p.247). DPP Kier Starmer (2012) said the rule could be traced back to Roman times and was established in English common law by the twelfth century. The Criminal Justice Act 2003 made an exception, permitting the Court of Appeal to quash an acquittal and order a retrial on new and compelling evidence, in serious cases. See below, on appeals from the Crown Court.

Procedure is adversarial

12–008   As explained in Chs 1 and 9, the common law court is an unbiased umpire. It takes no part in directing the gathering of evidence, or shaping the case. This does not mean that judges cannot take a very robust stance in case management. Common lawyers have traditionally boasted that adversarial processes are better at exposing the truth than "inquisitorial" European systems but in a very powerful article, using evidence from a new project investigating allegations of wrongful conviction, Field and Eady (2017) demonstrate the fundamental theoretical and practical flaws in this idea. As they say, one of the aims of the criminal process, articulated in the overriding objective of the CrimPR, is accuracy of outcomes: convicting the guilty and acquitting the innocent. As I explained in Ch.9, the adversarial model is predicated on the idea that there is "equality of arms". Both sides in a case are unaided by the court and it is their responsibility to bring to it all the evidence and legal argument. This causes problems in most civil cases, where the parties are unevenly matched, in evidence and resources. In criminal cases, the scales of justice are even more unbalanced: the lone defendant, meagrely equipped with an underfunded legal aid lawyer, or no legal aid, faces the might of the all-powerful state, holding the "keys" to much of the evidence and equipped with the police service, prosecutors and forensic services, all constructing the prosecution case. Field and Eady raise questions about the willingness of the police and the capacity of defence lawyers to expose exculpatory evidence. They question whether the powers of the Court of Appeal and Criminal Cases Review Commission equip them to investigate effectively. We return to them in the section on causes of miscarriages of justice.

The rules of natural justice = fair trial

Nemo judex in causa sua (the judge must be impartial) and *audi alteram partem*   **12–009**
(hear the other side) are reflected in art.6 below and confirmed by Magna Carta 1215. Nevertheless, Auld (2001) reminded everyone that "a criminal trial is not a game under which a guilty defendant should be provided with a sporting chance. It is a search for the truth in accordance with the twin principles that the prosecution must prove its case and that a defendant is not obliged to inculpate himself..." (cited in *CPS v C* (2017), a typical drink driving case, where the defence tried every imaginable defence. The Senior District Judge emphasised the duty of all parties, under the CrimPR, including the defence, to limit summary trial to the real contested issues).

The right to confront accusing witnesses

Oral cross-examination in public was compared favourably by Blackstone (1769)   **12–010**
with the Continental inquisitorial procedure, where depositions were taken in private and thus subject to the danger of "mendacity, falsehood and partiality", cited by Dennis (2010). He said it is a rule ancillary to the presumption of innocence, arising from the state's obligation to prove its case (p.261). The right is now reflected in art.6 and we return to it below.

The rule against torture

Its 500 year history was explored by the law lords in *A v Secretary of State for the*   **12–011**
Home Department (No.2) (2005), which Keir Starmer QC called the leading judgment in the world on torture. It is one hallmark of the difference between the English legal system and European civil law (Roman law) systems. See Langbein. The common law set its face against judicial torture in the fifteenth century but it did not disappear until Star Chamber was abolished in 1640

(Bingham, 2010, p.16). Incidentally, the UK, like the USA, is not without spectacular hypocrisy in modern armed conflict, outside their territorial jurisdictions. Armed forces and other state agents seem to forget the rule against torture when it comes to extracting information from detainees perceived to be enemy combatants. We examined the rule in Ch.4.

Cruel and unusual punishments

12–012   These were prohibited by the Bill of Rights 1689 and proportionate penalties were repeatedly prescribed in Magna Carta 1215.

The right to legal advice and representation

12–013   As explained in Ch.17, this is not an ancient right. It was only in 1836 that defence counsel were given the right to address the jury. In 2009, the Recorder of London said there was no right to a McKenzie friend in a criminal trial.

The right to jury trial

12–014   Magna Carta 1215 is not the source, because at that time, the jury was a group of oath-swearing compurgators, local witnesses. The right is prescribed in the Bill of Rights 1689. In indictable offences, I have argued that it is difficult to conceptualise this as a right, because the defendant has to be tried by jury and cannot opt for trial by judge alone: see Ch.16.

The right of silence

12–015   This is not ancient. The defendant only became a competent witness in his own defence in 1898. Until the Criminal Justice and Public Order Act 1994, the defendant had a virtually unqualified three stage right to silence: on the street, in the police station and at trial. In court, this extends to the right not to be asked questions: the accused can choose simply to stay in the dock. Formerly, the judge could comment on a defendant's exercise of the right but not adversely. The right was considered by the Criminal Law Revision Committee 1972, the Royal Commission on Criminal Procedure 1981, and the Royal Commission on Criminal Justice 1993 (RCCJ), and it has long been a subject of controversy.

Proponents hail it as a major safeguard of the English legal system that the defendant cannot be expected to convict himself out of his own mouth. It leaves the burden of proof on the prosecution. Opponents criticise it as a rule protecting the guilty. Some allege it encourages the police to intimidate suspects into confessing. Some have said that it is sentimental to argue that the accused should not be allowed to convict himself.

The RCCJ 1993 recommended that adverse inferences should *not* be drawn from silence at the police station. Only when the prosecution's case had been fully disclosed should the defendant be required to offer an answer to the charges made against him, at the risk of adverse comment at trial on any new defence he then disclosed, or any departure from a previously disclosed defence (in other words, in the event of an "ambush defence").

The 1994 Act went much further than this and, critics would say, effectively vitiates the right of silence. Sections 34–39 allow the court to draw "such inferences as appear proper" from the accused's failure to mention, under police questioning, any fact which he could have been expected to mention, or failure, under questioning, to account for any objects, marks or substances, or failure, under questioning, to account for his presence at a particular place, or failure to give evidence or answer questions at trial.

12–016

The sections caused many appeals. It is said that they offer no protection to the mentally disordered suspect and that the re-drafted police caution is too lengthy and complex for suspects to understand. The CA ruled that the trial judge was required to remind the jury of certain rules still protecting the defendant, for instance, that the burden of proof lay on the prosecution and that the defendant was entitled to remain silent. They ruled that an inference drawn from silence could not on its own prove guilt, that the jury had to be satisfied that the prosecution had established a case to answer before drawing any inferences from silence and, finally, that if the jury concluded that his silence could only sensibly be attributed to the defendant's having no answer or none that would stand up to cross-examination, they *could* then draw an adverse inference. The silence rules and case law have become impossibly complex. By 2017, the new *Crown Court Compendium* supplies judges with a farcical 15 pages of complex instructions on how to direct juries in the event that a defendant does not mention something. In my research with judges (Darbyshire, 2011), I found that all those who presided over jury trials simply avoided this minefield by not mentioning such a failure to the jury (Chs 9 and 10).

Those who considered these sections to be a breach of art.6 of the Convention were disappointed by *Murray v UK* (1996), in which the ECtHR ruled that there was no such thing as an absolute right of silence and it was only a matter of common sense to permit the drawing of adverse inferences where a defendant said nothing in the face of overwhelming evidence. The ECtHR, nevertheless, considered legal advice crucial to a defendant who exercised his right to silence so the Youth Justice and Criminal Evidence Act 1999 disapplies s.34 (adverse inferences) in cases where the suspect has not been allowed the opportunity to consult a solicitor prior to questioning. In *Condron v UK* (2001), on the advice of their solicitor, the defendants did not respond to questioning as they were suffering from withdrawal symptoms. The court found a violation of art.6(1) because the judge had left the jury at liberty to draw an adverse inference, even if they had been satisfied that the applicants remained silent for good reason on the advice of their solicitor. The CA has struggled to interpret the 1994 Act, amid a mass of appeals and case law, as can be seen from the *Crown Court Compendium*.

The constant stream of appeals arises because the sections are so difficult for judges to apply. In 1999, Birch argued that on a cost-benefit analysis, s.34 should be repealed. It consumed too much judicial time at trial and on appeal. If the law was wrongly applied, it could result in the quashing of an otherwise respectable conviction. Despite Birch's article, nothing has been done. In most relevant cases, there is a "partial failure" by the accused: he answers some questions under interrogation and not others. This makes it very difficult for the judge to instruct the jury. Waller LJ said in *Bresa* (2005):

12–017

"It is a matter of some anxiety that, even in the simplest and most straightforward of cases, where a direction is to be given under section 34 it seems to require a direction of such length and detail that it seems to promote the adverse inference question to a height it does not merit".

I would add this comment: magistrates and juries will surely draw what inferences they see fit from the silence of the accused, regardless of instructions. Section 34 is *so* problematic that the CA has called it a "minefield" and warned that it should be used sparingly. Legal advisers are faced with a complex and risky decision in advising their clients whether to remain silent under interrogation. For a penetrating critique of the law in action, see Quirk's 2016 book. She found that the biggest impact of the 1994 Act was to compromise the lawyer-client relationship, eroding the safeguards for the accused and further tipping the scales of justice.

The privilege against self-incrimination

12–018   The right of silence at trial was said by Ashworth and Redmayne (Ch.5) to be the most fundamental application of the English common law privilege against self-incrimination. It was recognised by the ECtHR as part of the fair trial requirement of art.6 in *Funke v France* (1993). In *Saunders v UK* (1997), the ECtHR held that English law breached the privilege by requiring a fraud suspect to answer questions and produce documents. His refusal could be punished as a contempt of court and evidence gleaned could be used at his trial. As a result of this case, the Youth Justice and Criminal Evidence Act 1999 s.59 and Sch.3 amended a spectrum of legislation to prevent evidence obtained in this way from being used at trial. In *O'Halloran v UK* (2008) and *Francis v UK* (2008) the ECtHR ruled that there was no violation in the requirement to disclose driver details when cars were caught on speed cameras. Car owners were aware of the regulatory regime imposed on them because car use could cause serious injury. People who drive cars could be taken to have accepted certain responsibilities. They adopted this reasoning from Lord Bingham in *Brown v Stott* (2001).

European Convention on Human Rights arts 5 and 6

12–019   The Human Rights Act 1998 restated the Convention rights as part of English law, as explained in Ch.4. Article 5, based on the rule of law, the principles of Magna Carta and the common law on habeas corpus, and art.6, based on the common law rules of natural justice, have become the secondary yardstick against which all statute and case law must now be measured, in addition to the common law.

Right to a fair trial (art.6)

12–020   "1.   In the determination of his civil rights and obligations and of any criminal charge against him, everyone is entitled to a fair and public hearing within a reasonable time by an independent and impartial tribunal established by law. Judgment shall be pronounced publicly but the press and public may be excluded from all or part of the trial in the interests of morals, public order or national security in a democratic society, where the interests of juveniles or the private life of the parties so require, or to the extent strictly necessary in the opinion of the court in special circumstances where publicity would prejudice the interests of justice.

2.   Everyone charged with a criminal offence shall be presumed innocent until proved guilty according to the law.

3.   Everyone charged with a criminal offence has the following minimum rights:

    a.   to be informed promptly, in a language which he understands and in detail, of the nature and cause of the accusation against him;

    b.   to have adequate time and facilities for the preparation of his defence;

    c.   to defend himself in person or through legal assistance of his own choosing or, if he has not sufficient means to pay for legal assistance, to be given it free if the interests of justice so require;

    d.   to examine or have examined witnesses against him and to obtain the attendance and examination of witnesses on his behalf under the same conditions as witnesses against him;

    e.   to have the free assistance of an interpreter if he cannot understand or speak the language used in court."

There is a substantial case law on fair trial, at common law, on the rules of natural justice, and from the Strasbourg court, on art.6. See Hoyano (2014). In *Al-Khawaja v UK* (2012) the Grand Chamber said that art.6(3)(d) emphasised the principle that all evidence against the accused must be presented in his presence with a view to adversarial argument. In *Schatschaschwili v Germany* (2015), the approach they took was to assess the overall fairness of the trial. See useful commentary by Laird (2017).

Right to liberty and security (art.5, paraphrased)

1.   Everyone has the right to liberty and security of person. No-one shall be deprived of his liberty save in the following cases and in accordance with a procedure prescribed by law: **12–021**

- lawful detention after conviction;

- lawful arrest or detention for non-compliance with a court order or to secure fulfilment of a legal obligation;

- lawful arrest or detention, effected to bring someone before a competent legal authority on reasonable suspicion of having committed an offence or when it is reasonably considered necessary to prevent his committing an offence or fleeing after having done so;

- detention of a minor by lawful order for the purpose of educational supervision or lawful detention to bring him before a competent legal authority;

- lawful detention to prevent spread of infectious diseases, of persons of unsound mind, alcoholics or drug addicts or vagrants;

- lawful arrest or detention to prevent unauthorised entry into the country, or for extradition or deportation.

2.   Everyone who is arrested shall be informed promptly, in a language which he understands, of the reasons for his arrest and of any charge against him.

3.   Everyone arrested ... shall be brought before a judge or other authorised officer to exercise judicial power and shall be entitled to trial within a reasonable time or to release pending trial. Release may be conditioned by guarantees to appear for trial.

4.   Everyone who is deprived of his liberty by arrest or detention shall be entitled to take proceedings by which the lawfulness of his detention shall be decided speedily by a court and his release ordered if the detention is not lawful.

5.   Everyone who has been the victim of arrest or detention in contravention of the provisions of this Article shall have an enforceable right to compensation.

The Criminal Procedure Rules 2005 and later versions

12–022 Auld (2001) agreed with Spencer (2000), about developing a code: a concise, simple, consolidated statement of statutory and common law procedural rules that were easy to amend. The Rules were to be amended twice a year. They are drafted by a committee. Their task was to reduce into 50 parts the chaos that was (and is) English criminal procedure and to review the old rules to check that they were accessible, fair and efficient and rewrite them so they were "simple and simply expressed", as required by the Criminal Justice Act 2003. Accompanying them is a set of Practice Directions, which are not law. The Rules introduced a novel overriding objective and detailed regulations about case management. Judges were given a *duty* to manage cases, supplementing their existing common law and statutory *powers* to do so. The rules imposed duties even on defence lawyers and aimed to bring about "a culture change", according to Lord Woolf CJ and Falconer LC.

The overriding objective

12–023 Rule 1.1

> "The overriding objective of this procedural code is that criminal cases be dealt with justly."

[This includes (1.2)]

"(a)   acquitting the innocent and convicting the guilty;
(b)   dealing with the prosecution and the defence fairly;
(c)   recognising the rights of a defendant, particularly under Article 6 of the European Convention on Human Rights;
(d)   respecting the interests of witnesses, victims and jurors and keeping them informed of the progress of the case;
(e)   dealing with the case efficiently and expeditiously;
(f)   ensuring that appropriate information is available to the court when bail and sentence are considered; and
(g)   dealing with the case in ways that take into account—
      (i)   the gravity of the offence alleged,
      (ii)   the complexity of what is in issue,

(iii)   the severity of the consequences for the defendant and others affected, and

(iv)   the needs of other cases".

Critique

This overriding objective was undoubtedly prompted by the Civil Procedure Rules 1998. That one was uncontroversial and has been a successful waymark for civil trial judges and the appeal courts but this one is more problematic. Consider:

    12–024

1.   Under (a), is convicting the guilty meant to be as important as acquitting the innocent? The rhetoric of the English legal system has traditionally asserted that convicting the innocent is a much graver fault than acquitting the guilty. Ancient writers have made repeated claims that we are prepared to acquit some guilty people in the endeavour to protect the accused's due process rights and minimise the risk of convicting an innocent. Blackstone (1769) set the ratio of risk as 1:10, but other writers have set it as 1:20 or as high as 1:100, in Bentham's case. Given the power of Blackstone's rhetoric over our thinking in the English legal system, we mostly seem to have settled for his 1:10 ratio. Auld gave considerable thought to the principles underlying the criminal justice system, in his Review, Ch.1.

2.   The last subsection seems to import the civil procedural concept of proportionality but is that appropriate in criminal cases? Does it mean trivial cases should be accorded less time and attention? That may suit the system and recognise how most cases are speeded through the magistrates' court following a guilty plea but does it recognise the seriousness to the accused of even a minor conviction of, say, theft?

3.   Every case participant is under a duty to further the overriding objective but is this appropriate in criminal proceedings? Whereas the law assumes civil litigants to be on an equal footing, the defence in a criminal case can never be on an equal footing with the prosecutor where, as in most cases, the prosecutor is the Crown, representing the full might of the State, with all the resources of the police and prosecuting authorities, so there is an inherent imbalance, which English law has traditionally recognised by giving many protective rules to the defendant. At common law, while the prosecutor's duty is to the court, the defence lawyer's duty is to his client. Is (g) compatible with this and, if not, is this satisfied by (c)?

Active case management under Pt 3

From 2005, criminal courts were placed under a *duty* to further the overriding objective by actively managing the case (3.2), in addition to their management *powers*. This includes (paraphrased):

    12–025

1.   early identification of issues;
2.   early identification of the needs of witnesses;
3.   achieving certainty as to who is to do what, by timetabling;
4.   monitoring progress and compliance with directions;
5.   ensuring evidence is presented in the shortest and clearest way;

6.   discouraging delay and avoiding unnecessary hearings;
7.   encouraging co-operation;
8.   making use of technology.

Case progression

12–026   Rule 3.4 requires a "case progression officer", to monitor compliance with directions and keep the court informed. (They were not new.) Under r.3.5 the court may nominate a judge, magistrate or legal adviser to manage a case. Directions can be made by the court without a hearing. Communication can be made by telephone or electronic means. A magistrates' court may give directions as to how the case is to proceed in the Crown Court. Under r.3.9, at every court hearing, if the case cannot be concluded then, the court is under a duty to give directions on timetabling, witnesses, translation, "ground rules" for the conduct of questioning, the presentation of evidence and so on, so that the case can be concluded at the next hearing or as soon as possible.

Penalties

12–027   In r.3.5 the court is given powers where a party fails to comply with a rule or direction. These include making costs orders. These were not new but before the Rules were in force, defence lawyers feared they would suffer losses. Some judges were disturbed at the prospect of being expected to fine lawyers. Rule 3.10 permits the court to require a certificate of readiness from the parties. The progress of criminal proceedings is always chaotic, as any court observer can see. Defence solicitors in magistrates' courts are routinely delayed by their disorganised clients' failure to turn up to appointments. Delays are frequently caused by court technology failing, or prison vans being late, or, in London, by reports not being ready because the probation service is overworked and underfunded. (See research by Darbyshire, 2011; 2014.)

Results

12–028   Judges, the Attorney General and the Ministry expressed enthusiasm over the results of the pilots of the Effective Trial Management Programme, which commenced in 2003. By 2004, it was reported that at one Crown Court alone, 700 witnesses had been spared attendance and ineffective trials had been cut to 12.8 per cent. This efficiency drive continues but we seem to be going backwards now, thanks to cutbacks in spending. Ineffective Crown Court trials had been reduced from 23 per cent in 2002 to 12 per cent in 2007. This is very deceptive though. To update these statistics, in 2015, *cracked* trials in Crown Court were 35 per cent, which was down from 42 per cent in 2007. *Ineffective* trials were 15 per cent, up from 12 per cent in 2007 (Annual Court Statistics, March 2016). An ineffective trial is usually caused by prosecution or defence not being ready but a cracked trial is caused by the defendant pleading guilty at the last minute, or the prosecution offering no evidence. Either way, court time and judge time has been wasted and witnesses have turned up needlessly. Ineffective trials are a bigger waste of resources because the trial has to be rescheduled. Lord Judge CJ said, in his 2010 *Review of the Administration of Justice*, "I am troubled that the Rules are honoured more in the breach than in compliance. This needs to change." Thanks to massive cutbacks in the Ministry of Justice budget from 2010, case progression in general became much worse. A March 2016 report by the Audit Commission, *Efficiency in the Criminal Justice System* found that only one third of trials were effective, in 2014-2015. £21.5 million was wasted on cases that did not go to trial, with unquantifiable extra costs. The case backlog had increased by 33 per cent in two years. Trials were increasingly lengthy, so, even though there were 11 per cent fewer trials than in 2010-2011, trials cost £44 million more, because of their increasing length.

Background

The background to proactive, judicial case management, apart from the Auld **12–029** Review 2001, is a 2002 Audit Commission Report, *Route to Justice*. It identified reforms necessary to make the criminal process more efficient, including the co-ordination of agencies, better information management and more logical incentives. Ministers said a culture change was needed and there should be no advantage for lawyers "in stretching things out for long enough so that their client's case might slip through the cracks".

Evaluative comments and research

Denyer (2008) said: **12–030**

> "The search for sanctions remains elusive. The situation will only improve as the culture changes and all lawyer participants regard it as their professional duty to comply..."

He said that, in reality, prosecution failures were seldom sanctioned because the state had an interest in ensuring that suspects did not escape because of prosecutors' mistakes. On the other hand, non-compliance by the defence could not be allowed to jeopardise the defendant's fair trial. Judges who tried serious fraud said management techniques had worked (Julian, 2008) but these specialist judges keep a very tight rein over the advocates and insist that they prepare very carefully for such trials, at lengthy preparatory hearings. My empirical research in ten Crown Courts in 2012 showed a very wide divergence in judicial case management regimes. Many judges who had invented strict management regimes before 2005 simply ignored the CrimPR and new practice initiatives, because they considered their practices to be superior. There was widespread ignorance of the rules among the legal profession and even among some judges. Most judges did not impose sanctions on lawyers who failed to comply with orders or the rules. Instead, most courts had discovered that special extra court hearings were extremely effective, because they were inconvenient to lawyers: Darbyshire (2014). This research was presented to the Lord Chief Justice and Senior Presiding Judge in December 2013. In February 2014, the LCJ asked Leveson LJ to conduct a *Review of Efficiency in Criminal Proceedings* (2015).

Leveson Reforms – "Better Case Management"

12-031   He was asked to review practices and procedure, especially pre-trial, to recommend ways in which hearings could be further reduced or streamlined, with an improved use of technology. He was to review the Rules to ensure that maximum efficiency was required from every participant. He made 56 recommendations in his 2015 Review. They bore a depressing similarity to those of the Runciman Commission 1993 and the Auld Review 2001, which had clearly not been heeded. Here are the main ones.

- In charging the suspect and disclosing an appropriate amount of evidence, the police and prosecutors should "get it right first time".
- The police, prosecution and defence should identify one person who "owns" the case and they should have a duty to engage with one another.
- Judicial case management should be robust and consistent, with all parties under a duty to comply with the rules and a single HMCTS case progression officer engaging with the parties.
- High quality IT should provide for video links from prisons and shifting pre-trial hearings out of court and the smooth presentation of digital evidence.

The rest of his recommendations appear in the summary online and relevant sections of the text below. In order to monitor implementation at long last, Leveson's successor as Senior Presiding Judge, Fulford LJ, was in charge of "Better Case Management" (BCM), until 2017. He monitored compliance and was then replaced by Lady Justice Macur. See Judiciary web-page on BCM for the information pack, newsletters, documents and links.

2.   AGENCIES AND PARTICIPANTS

Government and independent agencies

12-032   The Ministry of Justice was created in 2007, headed by the Lord Chancellor (Justice Secretary). It took over responsibility for criminal procedure. The Courts Act 2003 Pt 1 sets out his duties. He is responsible for the courts (run by HMCTS), the administration of justice, judges' numbers, pay and resources, legal services and the regulation of the legal profession. The Criminal Justice Board comprises the Minister of Justice, Home Secretary, DPP, senior judges, and representatives of other agencies, such as the police and prisons. The Sentencing Council (formerly Sentencing Guidelines Council) is independent and resulted from Auld's 2001 recommendations. The Youth Justice Board is a non-departmental body, established by the 1998 Act. They advise the Justice Secretary on and monitor performance in the youth justice system. The Act created multi-agency Youth Offending Teams in each local authority.

The prosecutors

The Attorney General is an MP or member of the House of Lords and a **12–033** Government minister in charge of the prosecution policy in England and Wales. He is answerable to Parliament for all his decisions. He is appointed by the Prime Minister and will change when the Government changes. He and his deputy, the Solicitor General, are the Law Officers. The most serious offences, such as those under the Official Secrets Act, may only be prosecuted by the AG but it is rare for him to appear in court. There are over 500 offences which require consent to prosecution. He authorises jury vetting in terrorist and top security trials. He may stop any prosecution with a *nolle prosequi*. He issues prosecution-related guidelines (see webpages). He refers prosecution appeals on points of law and unduly lenient sentences to the Court of Appeal and considers allegations of contempt of court. He runs panels of lawyers who represent the government. The Attorney superintends the Government Legal Department, Government Legal Services, the Crown Prosecution Service (CPS) and its Inspectorate and the Serious Fraud Office. His full list of jobs is so long it seems to be a recipe for conflicts of interest. He has civil jobs too. He is meant to act in the public interest but this raises the question of whether the public interest is determined objectively or in his political capacity. The AG has wide *executive* and *quasi-judicial* powers and, as an MP, is a member of the *legislature*. He is the legal adviser to the Cabinet and House of Commons. This obvious breach of the separation of powers and consequent conflicts of interest led to public concern in 2007, especially sparked by Labour AG, Lord Goldsmith's activities. The AG attends Cabinet meetings to give advice but is not a Cabinet member and it is a constitutional convention that Cabinet do not interfere in his decisions. But, quite apart from years of criticism over lack of clarity on Goldsmith's advice to Prime Minister Tony Blair on the legality of the Iraq war, he was also attacked for not prosecuting BAE systems. This was alleged to be a political decision. Slapper complained that the office of the AG was a "conspicuous anachronism" (and see discussion in other media in 2007). In 2007, the HL Constitutional Affairs Select Committee examined the role of the AG. The Labour government promised reform, in 2008, in the Draft Constitutional Renewal Bill. Two further independent commentaries were published in 2008, a report of the Justice parliamentary select committee and a joint parliamentary committee report on the draft Bill, but the process stalled. The Bill was dropped. All that remains is a 2009 Protocol (not a law) on the Attorney's website, setting out the relationship between the Attorney and the Director of the prosecuting authorities for which he is responsible. It says:

> "4 (a)2. It is a constitutional principle that when taking a decision whether to consent to a prosecution, the Attorney General acts independently of government, applying well established prosecution principles of evidential sufficiency and public interest."

It confirms that the AG may direct that a prosecution is not started or continued on the grounds of national security but if he does so, he must report to Parliament. It sets out guidelines for the involvement of the AG in "sensitive" cases and deals with the possibility of the AG consulting ministers when deciding what is in the public interest. It deals with the close liaison on policy development that is obviously necessary, between the AG and DPP and Director of the SFO.

12–034   The Director of Public Prosecutions (DPP) is in charge of the Crown Prosecution Service (CPS) and some prosecutions require her consent. Her appointment is non-political. The protocol says the Attorney is responsible for safeguarding the DPP's and other prosecutors' independence. Prosecution policy must be agreed with the AG. The DPP issues a Code for Crown Prosecutors. The DPP and the SFO Director report annually and the reports are laid before Parliament by the AG. The AG may issue guidance to prosecutors. 2009 saw the appointment of Keir Starmer QC. The appointment of this internationally eminent human rights lawyer was very heartening, as was the appointment of his predecessor, Ken Macdonald, a defence lawyer. There was no danger of their becoming "prosecution-minded". For instance, Sir Ken opposed the government's plans for 42 day detention for terrorist suspects. In his first press conference, Kier Starmer said he said he wanted a transparent prosecution service, firm and fair, renowned for high quality casework and high ethical standards. He left office in 2013. He published decision-making criteria, explained how decisions had been reached and through the internal victims' review procedure, he provided a mechanism for victims to challenge decisions. See his 2013 speech.

The CPS is a national but not universal prosecution service, created by the Prosecution of Offences Act 1985 and it now undertakes most prosecutions, including those formerly taken by HM Revenue and Customs. Many others are initiated by those government departments (central or local) and government agencies with statutory powers of prosecution. These include the Civil Aviation Authority, Department for Business, Innovation and Skills, Department of Work and Pensions, Environment Agency, Financial Services Agency, Food Standards Agency, Gambling Commission, Health and Safety Executive, Maritime and Coastguard Agency, Office of Fair Trading, Office of Rail Regulation, and Service Prosecuting Authority. Private citizens retain their right to prosecute, unlike in Scotland. In 2017, a woman accused of causing the death of a cyclist in London is due to stand trial in a prosecution crowd-funded by a charity, Cycling UK.

The Crown Prosecution Service

12–035   The CPS is responsible for advising the police on potential prosecutions, reviewing cases submitted by the police and preparing and prosecuting them in court. Ever since the CPS was created, there have been allegations that it is underfunded and that Crown Prosecutors are overworked and too many cases are dropped or lost through lack of preparation. A 2010 CPS Inspectorate report said that in the London CPS area, which handled almost one fifth of prosecutions in England and Wales, failings allowed lots of defendants to go free, through poor case preparation, with 15.4 per cent of cases being dropped before trial. The CPS was bombarded with initiatives and prosecutors were struggling with caseloads, just "firefighting". Hammersmith had seven chief prosecutors in a year. See Gibb (2010). Nevertheless, *The Five Year Review and Annual Report 2014–2015* was much more positive. CPS caseloads had fallen sharply in the previous five years, by 31 per cent in the magistrates' courts and 17 per cent in the Crown Court. Charging decisions had improved. Effective trial rates had improved. Conviction rates had risen. Inspections, reviews and audits had helped the CPS improve performance.

> "The Service now complies better with judges' orders, has improved its handling of custody time limits, made significant changes for the better in its management of disclosure in large and complex cases and amended the Graduated Fee Scheme for counsel's fees to improve value for money. At the Area level, close working... has helped management teams to turn things around...and assisted the largest Area (London) to put itself on a more resilient footing."

Sanders provided a more penetrating critique in 2016, examining whether the CPS had achieved its original objectives of securing consistency in prosecution and diversion policy and practice; reducing the number of weak cases prosecuted and counter-balancing extra powers to be given to the police from 1993. He pointed out that it is not a national prosecution agency but only a police agency and other statutory prosecutors are much more likely not to prosecute. They prefer to educate businesses and others on how not to break the law. They only had a one per cent prosecution rate, whereas the CPS had and has a pro-prosecution policy. He said that the CPS mindset had not changed much since his 1992 research. He gave examples of their prosecuting trivial cases. The failure to give the CPS statutory powers over the disposal of all cases meant that penalty notices for disorder were created, allowing police disposal and a consequent scandal about their overuse, described below. He agreed with the House of Commons Justice Committee 2009 that the CPS lacked strategic direction and its roles and policies had developed piecemeal, imposed by statute, case law and other external influences.

The Crime and Disorder Act 1998 s.53 provides that a member of the CPS staff who is not a Crown Prosecutor may prosecute guilty pleas in the magistrates' court, and The Criminal Justice and Immigration Act 2008 permits designated CPS case workers to conduct summary *trials* and conduct contested bail applications in serious cases. DPP Ken Macdonald initiated a policy of expanding in-house prosecutions by barristers employed by the CPS and by paralegals in the magistrates' courts. See Gibb, 2008. This was condemned by the Law Society and the Bar Council. An internal CPS survey revealed that only half the 400 CPS paralegals felt that they had had enough training for this. A third felt under pressure to do court work well beyond their abilities. There are two concerns: **12–036**

1.   The quality of some prosecutors leaves a lot to be desired. Also, the expansion of non-lawyers appearing before lay justices, who are also non-lawyers, is worrying. The quality of performance by some independent barristers, often briefed with little notice, is even worse.
2.   Some lawyers and judges are alarmed at the diminution in independent barristers available to prosecute.

The CPS has a highly-informative, user-friendly website. The Code for Crown Prosecutors is written simply, in 13 languages.

Other participants

12-037   For a wonderful, evocative and very rare insight into the real world of the Crown Court from the viewpoint of victims, witnesses and defendants, in their own words, I recommend the 2015 book by Jacobson, Hunter and Kirby, *Inside Crown Court*. This type of penetrating empirical research was much more common in the 1970s. It is especially valuable to read quotations from defendants.

Victims and witnesses

12-038   Like the AG, the DPP is empowered to stop a prosecution. Victims can ask for judicial review of a decision to discontinue: *R. (on the application of Joseph) v DPP* (2000) but the courts are loath to interfere. In 2013, the CPS launched a Victims' Right to Review Scheme, making it easier for a victim to ask for an internal review of a decision not to prosecute. The Code emphasises that the CPS does not act for victims but prosecutors should take account of their wishes in deciding whether it is in the public interest to prosecute and should abide by the Victims' Code. A Practice Direction provides for the victim to make a personal statement, which may be read out in court. It should be taken into account in sentencing. Victims can track the progress of their case online at many courts. The Domestic Violence, Crime and Victims Act 2004 s.32 requires the minister to produce a *Code of Practice for Victims of Crime* and appoint a Commissioner for Victims and Witnesses. All criminal justice agencies have a duty to keep victims informed and those who consider they have been mistreated may complain to the Parliamentary Commissioner for Administration (Ombudsman). An independent charity, Victim Support, provides advice and support. From 2010, there is a National Victims Service. There is a Witness Charter and information on the Ministry of Justice YouTube Channel. Nevertheless, Hall (2010) challenged the rhetoric claiming that victims were at the heart of the criminal justice system. See further Ormerod (2012). The 2016 Parliamentary Public Accounts Committee report above said an underfunded criminal justice system was letting down witnesses and victims. There was a big case backlog and two thirds of Crown Court trials did not go ahead or were delayed.

There has traditionally been a ban on prosecutors interviewing their witnesses prior to their court appearance. English law has frowned on the US practice of coaching witnesses. This means the CPS has no means of testing their reliability. In 2002, the AG proposed that prosecutors should interview all witnesses (not just the vulnerable) face to face, instead of relying on signed witness statements. Until the 1970s, the DPP used to be able to test the reliability of prosecution witnesses by requesting an old style full committal in the magistrates' court. The whole of the prosecution case would be presented to the examining magistrates and prosecution witnesses would be examined and cross-examined in the same way as they would later, in the Crown Court trial. Roberts and Saunders (2008) assessed the benefits of pre-trial interviewing: sifting out weak cases and improving witness care, thus saving resources. It has become popular to hire private training companies to prepare prosecution witnesses. The CA set out in *R. v Momodou* (2005) what is permitted for prosecution and defence: coaching is prohibited. There should be no discussion of the proceedings. It is permissible to engage in witness familiarisation so that witnesses understand the layout of the courtroom and likely sequence of events. It is lawyers' professional duty to inform the trial judge if any familiarisation process had taken place, using outside agencies. Hungerford-Welch argued that prosecution interviews of *defence* witnesses, permitted by the CJA 2003, from 2010, provided insufficient safeguards for the accused. The provision was enacted to stop ambush defences and help "rebalance the justice system". He said it diluted the burden of proof.

Under Pt 18 of the CrimPR, where children give evidence in criminal **12–039** proceedings alleging violence or sex offences, "special measures" may be provided, on the order of the case managing judge. They are interviewed in advance of the trial, on film, by specialists, then, in some cases, examined from the courtroom on video link, while they wait in a witness suite. Under the Youth Justice and Criminal Evidence Act 1999, rules provide for the same facility for adult vulnerable adult witnesses, or screens around the witness box. Trials may be conducted without wigs and gowns, and without people in the public gallery. Pilot projects commenced in 2002, to examine the possibility of allowing intermediaries to assist witnesses with communication difficulties, and the use of video recorded pre-trial cross-examination, and these measures are now in place since 2009. From 2014, *pre-recorded* cross-examinations for the most vulnerable adults and all child victims were being piloted and are now, in 2017, being extended to adult victims. This is called "Achieving Best Evidence" and can be used for all alleged victims of sex offences. Leveson (2015) said around 40 per cent of Crown Court trials were now on sex offences and usually used ABE interviews. He said they were too long and recommended a second interview, short and focussed, to be used in court. A judge may order witness anonymity.

All measures to protect witnesses are a response to the concern that many prosecutions failed because witnesses failed to turn up to court or failed to perform as expected in the witness box. More than 30,000 cases were abandoned in 2001, as witnesses and victims refused or failed to give evidence: Langdon-Dow; Home Office 2002; NSPCC/Witness Support 2004 and Audit Commission 2003. The Criminal Justice Act 2003 s.116 allows admission of statements from witnesses who are too frightened to testify. In 2010, Ellison and Wheatcroft concluded that witness familiarisation allowed witnesses "to maintain greater control over their own testimony" (p.836), bearing in mind it is the advocate's aim to take control over the witness, but they observed, rather alarmingly, that "most adult witnesses ... enter the witness box with the barest pre-trial preparation" (p.824).

Of course, when prosecution witnesses are heavily protected, defence lawyers will allege that the accused has suffered an unfair trial, in breach of art.6. In a 2005 murder trial, two young victims, Charlene Ellis and Letitia Shakespeare, had been killed in cross-fire in a gangland revenge attack and it proved extremely difficult to persuade witnesses to come forward. Prosecution witnesses were given false names and various protective devices in court. The DPP said it was the only way the case could be brought to trial. The House of Lords held that the trial was unfair: *Davis (Iain)* (2008). The Criminal Evidence (Witness

Anonymity) Act 2008 was swiftly enacted, replacing common law powers to protect witnesses with a statutory regime of measures to protect identity. There is a growing problem of witness intimidation but trials must be fair. Four test cases came before a five-judge CA. See reports on *R v Mayers* and joined cases and comment by Ormerod (2009). The court said the Act sought to preserve the delicate balance between the art.6 rights of D and the witness's art.2 (life), art.3 (security) and art.8 (privacy) rights. See now the Coroners and Justice Act 2009 Pt 3, which replaced the 2008 Act. The DPP and the AG issued guidance on anonymous witness applications.

12–040   Judges and all lawyers need educating in how to treat vulnerable witnesses and in the role of the intermediary in helping a witness who, for instance, has learning difficulties. The Advocate's Gateway was launched by academics and researchers with charitable support, in 2012. It provides "toolkits" and training films for lawyers, judges and others to help them prepare to interact in and out of court with vulnerable witnesses and defendants. See very interesting empirical research by Henderson (2016) which suggests that at least judges, if not advocates, now understand the importance of pre-trial "ground rules" meetings and controlling advocates' cross-examinations of vulnerable witnesses.

Concern about the unsuitability of cross-examination as a process of confronting vulnerable witnesses has been ramped up in recent years. In 2014, Henderson called it "the most despised and vilified practice within the criminal trial". She reviewed recent Court of Appeal case law, *Barker* (2010), *E* (2011), *W and M* (2010) which appeared to redefine the rules for cross-examining vulnerable people. For further reading, see her footnotes. At last, in 2016, new guidelines were issued to prevent overly harsh questioning of vulnerable witnesses and free training was offered to lawyers by the Bar Council, Law Society and CPS.

Restorative justice, a popular development of the early 1990s in Australia, NZ and the USA has belatedly attracted attention in the UK and the Ministry of Justice produced an action plan on it in 2014 and it is referred to now in the Victims' Code and there are various schemes. Where the offender admits guilt, it gives the victim an opportunity to communicate with or meet him. In 2016, the Parliamentary Justice Committee reported on it. See Epstein (2016).

Expert witnesses are discussed below, in the section on miscarriages of justice.

Defendants

12–041   There has been a tendency to neglect the obvious point (from anyone regularly observing courts and/or police stations), that a lot of *defendants* are also vulnerable. Defendants are far from being a cross-section of the public at large. Articles recognising their needs are P. Cooper and D. Wurtzel (2013), McEwan (2013) and P. Cooper et al (2016). In 2016, the charity *Transform Justice* published *Justice denied? The experience of unrepresented defendants in the criminal courts*. Using interviews, observations and survey data, they found that judges and lawyers believed there was an increase in unrepresented defendants in magistrates' courts and that they were at a disadvantage. If numbers have increased, it is in part due to cutbacks in legal aid. Under the plan to digitise criminal case management, unrepresented defendants will not be able to access information. Concern was expressed in 2016, in a joint report by HM CPS Inspectorate and HM Inspectorate of Constabulary. Given the progress that has been made with the provision of intermediaries since 1999, Hoyano and Rafferty (2017) regret that they are now severely rationed for defendants, by the Criminal Practice Direction 2016, which says their appointment should be "rare" for defendants. Not only is this a striking inequality of arms with prosecution witnesses but the authors point out just how vulnerable most defendants are. They cite research which demonstrates an extremely high level of mental illness, communication difficulties, substance misuse, low IQ, special educational needs, and abuse or neglect among child defendants. The 2014 Carlile Report on the youth justice system showed that up to 75 per cent of children in custody had had a traumatic brain injury and up to 78 per cent had missed school. Hoyano and Rafferty provide heart-rending and barbaric examples from real cases. See further Wurtzel (2017) on the rationing of defence intermediaries and the lack of training for lawyers.

At the time of writing, 2017, David Lammy MP is conducting a review of race in the criminal justice system, due to be published in Summer 2017. Emerging findings confirm previous academic research and statistics that minority defendants are more likely to be remanded in custody, plead not guilty in the Crown Court and be sentenced to imprisonment.

Defence lawyers

The defence lawyer's duty is to their client. This is reaffirmed in PACE (Police and Criminal Evidence Act) Code C and PACE gives a statutory right to legal advice at the police station. From 2005 they have a duty to further the overriding objective of the CrimPR. Edwards and Hardcastle (2016) argue that the 1994 qualification of the right to silence, explained below, has increased the status of the defence solicitor but in a context where some prosecutions are still not reviewed by the CPS as they should be, solicitors have to be all the more vigilant to ensure that they give the defendant the correct advice as to plea. 12–042

3. STAGES OF THE CRIMINAL PROCESS

This book does not deal with police powers. 12–043

Bail

Police detainees may be released with no further action or officially cautioned if they admit their offence. They are normally released unconditionally but conditional cautions may now be administered. Most offenders who are arrested by the police are bailed by them for a court appearance at the next available court sitting of the magistrates' court. The police may grant bail at the police station and the Criminal Justice Act 2003 permits "street bail" from the scene of the arrest. This pre-charge bail has been over-used in unfair circumstances so it has been severely restricted by the Policing and Crime Act 2017 because suspects were being bailed for months. It introduces a presumption that suspects will be 12–044 released without bail, unless bail is necessary and proportionate and authorised by a senior officer, only renewable beyond three months by a magistrate. Bail may include conditions, such as a curfew, or specified residence, or exclusion from the environs of the victim's home, or surrendering of a passport, and a surety (money guarantee) may be required. Bail may be renewed by the clerk or magistrates, if the defendant is not dealt with at the first court appearance. The offender has a right to bail under the Bail Act 1976, which reversed the common law presumption *against* bail so, if the police oppose bail and the suspect contests this, a bail hearing will take place at the magistrates' court. At each appearance, the court (magistrates' or Crown Court) must consider whether bail should be granted. The defendant accused or convicted of an imprisonable offence need not be granted bail if the court is satisfied that there are substantial grounds for believing that the defendant, if released on bail, would fail to surrender to custody, or commit an offence, or interfere with witnesses.

The defendant need not be granted bail if the offence is indictable or triable either way and he was already on bail for another offence, or if the court is satisfied he should be kept in custody for his own protection or (child) welfare, or he is serving a custodial sentence, or if there has not been time to obtain sufficient information to decided on bail, or if he has been arrested whilst on bail, or he is being remanded for a report and it would be impractical to make inquiries without keeping him in custody. The CJA 2003 introduced a presumption against bail for an offender who had previously failed to surrender to custody ("jumped bail"). There is also a presumption against bail for certain class A drug users. Where the defendant is accused of a non-imprisonable offence, acceptable reasons for refusing bail are more limited. The Legal Aid, Sentencing and Punishment of Offenders Act 2012 Sch.11 introduced a number of restrictions on the courts' powers to remand adults and children in custody where there is no real prospect that they would be sentenced to custody if convicted. This is a new cost-saving measure.

12-045   Those convicted of or charged with manslaughter, murder, attempted murder, rape or attempted rape lost their right to bail under the Criminal Justice and Public Order Act 1994 but this was amended in 1998, in order to satisfy the requirements of art.5 so defendants in this category must have their individual case considered.

The defendant may renew his application, if the magistrates refuse it, or appeal to a judge in chambers. Under the Bail Amendment Act 1993, the *prosecution* may appeal against a grant of bail by magistrates, to a judge in the Crown Court. The Legal Aid, Sentencing and Punishment of Offenders Act 2012 also gives prosecutors the right to appeal against Crown Court bail decisions when they think the defendant could be dangerous, or might flee the country. Contested bail hearings can be heard by audio or video link.

The decision to charge

12-046   The Criminal Justice Act (CJA) 2003 gave the CPS a new power to charge suspects and they do the charging in about 25 per cent of cases. This was justified on the basis that the police, not being lawyers, made mistakes as to charge (Auld Review 2001). This change was criticised, on the ground that it put CPS prosecutors into police stations, when the very reason for creating the CPS was to create independent prosecutors. The police can now call the CPS on a 24 hour phone line to take advice. It is important to understand, however, that unlike some of their Continental European counterparts, English and Welsh prosecutors do not have the power to direct police investigations. This charging scheme was introduced in 2004 after pilot schemes resulted in a 40 per cent increase in early guilty pleas and a decrease of up to 90 per cent in discontinued, ineffective or changed cases. The Code for Crown Prosecutors sets out a "Threshold test" for charging before there is sufficient evidence. The Crown Prosecutor decides whether there is a reasonable suspicion but not all the evidence is available by the time they must be released or charged, and the suspect poses a bail risk. The 2003 Act gave the police custody officer power to bail a person, without charge, to enable the DPP to decide whether to charge: pre-charge bail, described above. The Leveson Review found that too many trivial cases were going to the Crown Court and in many cases, charges were reduced straight before the trial, resulting in a collapsed, "cracked" trial. The solution, he recommended, to "get it right first time", was that charging decisions should only be made by those who were properly trained in the law. There should be a mechanism for review and the DPP should be accountable. By November 2016, HM CPS Inspectorate reported on compliance and the CPS responded on their website:

> "…the Inspectorate has commented positively on the principles of BCM [Better Case Management] and the CPS contribution to…implementation…The report notes that there are sound governance arrangements in place and that significant resource materials and training for CPS staff has been provided. There is a high level of engagement from our members of staff, particularly in relation to the DCS [Digital Case System], and early data indicates an excellent level of decision making, with 99.4% of CPS decisions to charge being compliant with the Code for Crown Prosecutors."

The decision to prosecute

There is no obligation on a prosecutor to prosecute all offences. Common law   12–047
countries have "opportunity" systems not "legality" systems, such as that in Germany. This is classically expressed in Lord Shawcross's 1951 statement in the House of Commons, repeated in the *Code for Crown Prosecutors*:

> "It never has been the rule in this country—I hope it never will be—that criminal offences must automatically be the subject of prosecution."

For instance, many young offenders (10–17) are completely diverted from the system or cautioned for the offences they admit. The practice of official cautioning for juveniles was developed and administered in different ways by police forces during the twentieth century and only placed on a statutory basis of reprimands and final warnings, in the Crime and Disorder Act 1998, now replaced with a system of "youth cautions" and "youth conditional cautions", under the Legal Aid, Sentencing and Punishment of Offenders Act 2012. Since 1998, the scheme and guidance on its operation are very detailed and prescriptive, clearly designed to minimise the police discretion that had resulted in a degree of variation. The child must admit the offence; there must be sufficient evidence to charge; an appropriate adult must be present and the child must be referred to the Youth Offending Team to be placed in a rehabilitation programme. This was extended to adults, following a recommendation in the Auld Review. They may be given a simple or conditional caution by the police, following a decision by a prosecutor that it is in the public interest to divert the offender from prosecution. The CJA 2003 permits the CPS to issue a conditional caution, where there is sufficient evidence to charge a suspect with an offence which he or she admits, and the suspect agrees. If the suspect fails to comply with the conditions, he may be prosecuted for the offence.

A restorative justice process has been developed. Offenders and victims agree on what reparations the offender should make to the victim or the wider community, instead of being prosecuted. Following concern about the over-use of cautions, discussed below, the Minister of Justice reviewed and consulted on adult cautions in 2013 and new guidelines were issued. They are now included in the Criminal Justice and Courts Act 2015, s.17. Simple cautions are no longer normally available for indictable (serious) offences and some "either-way" offences, or where an offender has been cautioned or convicted for a similar offence within the last two years. Hynes and Elkins (2013) suggested that, for the sake of consistency and transparency, cautions could be discussed in the police station even before an admission of guilt. Edwards, an eminent defence solicitor, said many defendants do not understand that a caution gives them a criminal record (2012).

In deciding whether to prosecute, CPS prosecutors review the file of evidence they receive from the police and apply the Code for Crown Prosecutors, which requires a two-stage test, the evidential stage and the public interest stage. The prosecutor must first decide on the sufficiency of the evidence to provide a realistic prospect of conviction and then, only if that test is satisfied, ask whether it is in the public interest to go ahead with the prosecution.

The evidential stage

12–048   The Crown Prosecutor must be satisfied that there is enough evidence to provide a realistic prospect of conviction, meaning a court is more likely than not to convict. They need to be satisfied that the evidence is legally admissible, reliable and credible. The Code instructs that they must "swiftly" drop cases that do not satisfy this test and cannot be strengthened.

The public interest stage

12–049   Once the evidential test is satisfied, prosecutors must take account of public interest factors for and against prosecution but there is a *presumption in favour of prosecution*, criticised by Sanders, as discussed above. The more serious the offence and the greater the level of the suspect's culpability, the more likely it is to be prosecuted. Prosecutors must consider the circumstances of the offence, harm to the victim, age of the suspect, impact on the community, whether a prosecution is a proportionate response and whether a prosecution might expose evidence that could damage national security, international relations or sources of information. The prosecutor must keep the decision under review. DPP Keir

Starmer made prosecution much more transparent by placing sets of guidelines online. The public interest in prosecuting young people involved in sexual activity is a grey area. For instance, there may be no public interest in prosecuting two 15-year-olds for having consensual sex. In the case of a 12-year-old who uploaded indecent video of herself and young sisters onto the internet, the police viewed her as a paedophile but other agencies disagreed. See Spencer (2012).

Background: concern about fixed penalty notices (FPNs) and cautions

A decision not to prosecute is not ordinarily judicially reviewable. In *R. v DPP Ex p. Kebilene* (1999), the law lords confirmed that, "absent mala fides or an exceptional circumstance, the decision of the Director (to consent to a prosecution) is not amenable to judicial review" (per Lord Steyn). A decision to prosecute can be challenged before the trial judge as an abuse of process, or form a ground of appeal. By 2004 it seemed that the Administrative Court was weary of wasting time dismissing fruitless applications for judicial review of decisions to prosecute: *R. (on the application of Pepushi) v CPS* (2004). The ECtHR has held, in a group of cases heard against the UK in 2001, that in certain exceptional instances, where parties might reasonably expect a prosecution, that the DPP must give reasons for not prosecuting: *McKerr v UK* (2002). Keir Starmer DPP wrote a very useful analysis in 2012. He examined the "substantial body" of case law.

12–050

> "Whichever way you come at it, whether from the perspective of victims' rights or from a more traditional public law perspective, it seems to me that finality has to yield ... to the need to reach the right decision on the facts of the case" (p.530).

The 2013 version of the Code for Crown Prosecutors now states that it will re-start a prosecution, "particularly if the case is serious" where the previous decision was wrong, or where a case is stopped pending the likelihood of soon obtaining new evidence (and the defendant will be so warned), or where the case is stopped through lack of evidence but significant evidence is discovered later, or cases where there was a death and the post-inquest review concludes that a prosecution should be brought. Any alleged victim can request a review, or bring a private prosecution, explained above.

In 2009, the Home Secretary, Lord Chancellor and AG launched a review of out-of-court disposals, such as cautions and on-the-spot fines (fixed penalty notices issued on the street by the police and introduced in 2008). This was doubtless prompted by the horrific BBC1 *Panorama* programme, *Assault on Justice*, in November 2009, on people committing hideous crimes such as violent burglary and "getting off" with a caution. The DPP himself also condemned the over-use of cautions and called for a review. See Gibb, November 2009. Her article mentioned 40,000 on-the-spot cautions per year for assault, including a man who smashed a beer glass into a pub landlady's face. BBC Radio 4's *Law in Action* carried an interview with the outgoing DPP, Ken Macdonald, saying the same thing.

The programme included Mr Guest. He obtained a judicial review of the decision not to prosecute: *R. (on the application of Guest) v DPP* (2009). He was asleep in bed when attacked at home. Goldring J held the decision was "fundamentally flawed". Both prosecution tests had been satisfied. The DPP's guidelines on cautioning did not permit cautioning for actual bodily harm. The victim had not been involved in the decision to caution, in breach of the guidelines. Indeed, it was clear he did not agree. (He had written letters indicating this.) Goldring J said, per curiam,

> "By a decision to offer a conditional caution ... the court is effectively bypassed. It means that someone who is guilty ... is not prosecuted, does not appear before the court and is not sentenced by the court. The effect on the victim and the damage to the criminal justice system is self-evident if such a decision is taken without proper regard to the relevant guidance ... It seems to me astonishing ... that the Crown Prosecution Service could seriously contemplate not prosecuting someone who, it was alleged, deliberately went to a person's house at night [and] attacked him inside that house with some ferocity ..." (paras 56 and 57)."

The court distinguished *Jones v Whalley* (2006) where the law lords said a private prosecution following a formal caution for the very same offence arising from the same facts was an abuse of process.

12–051   In *R. v Gore; R. v Maher* (2009), G was issued with a fixed penalty notice for a drunken altercation and M for a public order offence. Later, having reviewed the CCTV footage, both were charged with inflicting grievous bodily harm. The Home Secretary's guidelines permitted charging in these circumstances. The CA held it was abundantly clear that the Criminal Justice and Police Act 2001 only precluded prosecution for the same offence as that in the FPN. Again, *Jones v Whalley* was distinguished. *R. (on the application of Lowden) v Gateshead Magistrates' Court* (2016) reaffirmed that a caution did not preclude a private prosecution where D had been warned that he might face further action. Lawyers, judges and the public remained concerned about the increased use of FPNs and cautions. As Leveson LJ said, in a November 2010 speech

> "just to take penalty notices for disorder and cautions, were over 450,000 cases truly appropriate? Further, when we consider issues such as transparency and open justice the picture becomes a little more blurred. In issuing an out of court disposal the police are essentially acting as prosecutor and judge, outside the environment of an open court."

In 2011, HM Inspectorate of Constabulary and HMCPS Inspectorate published a joint study. They called for a national strategy in using out-of-court disposals, because:

> "In 2009, 38 per cent of the 1.29 million offences 'solved' by police were dealt with outside of the court system. We found that the use of out-of-court disposals has evolved in a piecemeal and largely uncontrolled way ... public support ebbs away when they are used for persistent offenders ... We found wide variations in practice across police force areas in the proportion and types of offences handled out of court." (Summary)

In 2011, Judge LJ said out-of-court disposals had increased 135 per cent since 2003. In 2013, the Justice Minister launched a new review which resulted in the restrictions on adult cautions from 2014 and the 2015 Act, explained above. Probably as a result of all this concern and the current restrictions, out of court disposals have declined 69 per cent since 2007, according to the Criminal Justice Statistics 2015–2016 (March 2016) and the cautioning rate has declined from 31 per cent to 14 per cent. The statisticians' commented that "community resolutions", available to the police since 2008, are another reason.

Getting the case into court (in the virtual world)

Following the issue of a written charge by the police or prosecutor, the defendant is issued with a requisition to appear in court, under s.29 of the CJA 2003, or a summons, or a warrant (CrimPR Pt 7). Had the Prisons and Courts Bill 2017 been enacted, indictable only cases would have gone straight to the Crown Court, without a preliminary hearing in the magistrates' court. Also, thousands of hearings may not have been heard in court but in the virtual legal system.

12–052

> "...a further 60,000 pre-trial hearings in the magistrates' court and 17,000 contested bail hearings can also take place by video, along with 30,000 pre-trial hearings in the crown court. This will save around 34,000 hours of courtroom time...online convictions for some limited offences will also benefit the courts...around 8,000 offences – including 7,000 cases of people travelling without a train and tram ticket, and a further 1,300 cases of people fishing without a licence – could be handled online...[also]...around 420,000 summary and triable either way offences can be progressed without the need for administrative hearings...For example, offenders will be able to enter a plea online reducing the need to go to court until they need to attend trial or a hearing where they can be sentenced. Discussions between the court and legal representatives...will be able to take place via email or telephone or video conferencing, instead of being in a courtroom." (Press release, March 2017)

Duties of prosecution and defence

In *Randall v R.* (2002), the Privy Council set out clear guidelines for fair trial, including a reiteration of the rule that the duty of prosecuting counsel was not to obtain a conviction at all costs but to act as a "minister for justice" and the jury's attention must not be distracted from its central task of deciding on guilt, to the required standard. Under the CrimPR, Part 1, all trial participants are under a duty to further the overriding objective. Under Part 3.3 they are under a duty to "actively assist the court". Following Leveson's recommendation (2015), this now includes communicating with one another and the court about the plea, the information needed and who is doing what. It is shocking that this has to be put into a legal rule but my research in *Sitting in Judgment* (2011) and on Crown Court case management (2014) demonstrated that all trials I observed either started late or were interrupted and there was a culture of failure to take responsibility for unproduced evidence or failure to communicate. Following Leveson, Rule 3.10 now spells out parties' duty to comply with the court's directions, ensure that documents and witnesses are in court and inform the court of problems.

12–053

Pre-trial disclosure of evidence

The rules governing the disclosure of evidence are complex. They are contained in the Criminal Procedure and Investigations Act 1996, as amended by the CJA

12–054

2003, the CrimPR, the European Convention, arts 5 and 6, considerable ECtHR and English case law, the AG's *Guidelines on Disclosure*, CPS manuals and guidelines and a judicial protocol (2013). In 2011, Gross LJ, in his *Review of Disclosure in Criminal Proceedings* said virtually all his consultees had complained of the plethora of guidance. Principles of the current post-Leveson regime are spelled out by Leveson LJ himself in *R. v R.* (2015).

When or *before* the accused first appears before the magistrates' court, the prosecutor must serve on the court Initial Details of the Prosecution Case (IDPC), under Pt 8 of the CrimPR.

Controversially, the 1996 Act introduced a requirement for pre-trial disclosure by the accused, with defaulters risking the court's drawing an adverse inference. It was condemned as a breach of the presumption of innocence and an unacceptable derogation from the right of silence. The government were concerned by the findings of the Runciman Commission 1993, that the defence were gaining an unfair advantage over the prosecution by disclosure requirements which had become unduly onerous in the wake of serious miscarriages of justice, such as the Birmingham Six case. Defence lawyers could delay trial and put obstacles in the way of a prosecution by requiring the disclosure of more and more evidence, yet the accused was still in the position of being able to ambush them with a surprise defence, at trial.

The Act was immediately attacked as unfair. Defence lawyers made repeated challenges to it and there were widespread allegations of prosecution non-disclosure and an increasing number of prosecutions stopped by judges. Corker (2004) commented that eight years after its introduction, the disclosure regime was a failure. Prosecutors, starved of resources and wary of becoming the scapegoat for wrongful convictions, chose to permit the defence access to all non-sensitive material. Judges, keen to secure fair trials, were reluctant to penalise defendants for not providing statements.

The Criminal Justice Act 2003 Pt 5 reorganised procedure, following Auld 2001. It introduced a single objective test, requiring the prosecutor to disclose prosecution material that might reasonably be considered capable of undermining the case for the prosecution against the accused, or of assisting the case for the accused. It places a continuing duty on the prosecutor to disclose material that meets this test. The prosecutor is required to review the material on receipt of the defence statement and to make further disclosure, if required.

12–055   The 2003 Act also amended defence disclosure, requiring the accused to provide a more detailed defence statement, setting out the nature of his defence, including any particular defences on which he intends to rely and indicating any points of law he wishes to take, including any points as to the admissibility of evidence or abuse of process. This is because the 1996 Act had not persuaded defendants to be forthcoming. Defence statements usually amounted to a couple of useless lines and judges were reluctant to penalise defence non-disclosure. Lord Judge CJ, in a 2008 speech, explained how one particular case, on the "7/7 bombers" prompted the change.

> "A stark example arose in the case tried by Fulford J of the 21st July bombers ... The judge was sure that some of the defendants had 'tried to mould their defences to the

scientific evidence ... rather than providing information that would enable useful tests to be undertaken at the outset' ... As a result of his observations the law has been amended."

An updated defence statement may be required, to assist the management of the trial, requiring the accused to serve details of his witnesses and experts, giving the police a new power to interview defence witnesses prior to trial. The judge has the discretion to disclose the defence statement to the jury. If the defence fails to comply, the court or any other party can make such comments as appear appropriate and the court or jury can "draw such inferences as appear proper", in other words, adverse inferences (1996 Act s.11, as substituted by the CJA 2003). In the leading case of *Rowe and Davis v UK* (2000), the ECtHR said:

"The right to an adversarial trial means, in a criminal case, that both prosecution and defence must be given the opportunity to have knowledge of and comment on the observations filed and the evidence adduced by the other party ... In addition, Article 6(1) requires, as indeed does English law ... that the prosecution authorities should disclose to the defence all material evidence in their possession for or against the accused."

The court warned, however, that "entitlement to disclosure of relevant evidence is not an absolute right". There are three competing interests that might lead to the withholding of evidence—national security, protection of witnesses and preserving secrecy in police investigations. Problems have arisen in relation to claims of public interest immunity (PII) by the prosecution, where they seek the judge's permission to withhold evidence from the defence on the grounds of its sensitivity, such as the national interest or, more usually, that they sought to protect the identity of a police informer. Where this application is made there is a pre-trial hearing by the judge, and special counsel may be appointed to represent the interests of the accused. In *R. v H, R. v C* (2004) the law lords held that this should be a course of last resort.

The 2006 protocol on disclosure of unused material, issued by the Court of Appeal (now replaced with a 2013 judicial protocol) demonstrated exasperation with lawyers for ignoring legal requirements. In the introduction the judges complained "Disclosure is one of the most important—as well as the most abused—of the procedures relating to criminal trials." Lawyers' applications and judges' decisions had been based on misconceptions or a general laxity of approach. This was costly and had obstructed justice.

"In the past, the prosecution and the court have too often been faced with a defence statement that is little more than an assertion that the Defendant is not guilty ... There must be a complete change in the culture. The defence must serve the defence case statement by the due date. Judges should then examine the defence case to ensure that it complies."

Demanding a culture change will not necessarily achieve it, given the underfunding of the CPS and the poor remuneration of defence solicitors, the caseloads they suffer and an ingrained culture of cynicism of and disregard for the disclosure regime. Research on disclosure was published by Quirk (2006), **12–056** demonstrating that the protocol was "unlikely to succeed". Identifying prosecution material that needs to be disclosed takes time and effort. Neither police nor prosecution have sufficient personnel. Police officers are "ill-equipped by purpose, training and occupational culture". They find the job "onerous, time consuming and unpopular". Naturally, as non-lawyers, the police officers she interviewed had little understanding of what was required of them and some were prepared to admit that they were reluctant to give the defence exculpatory evidence. Many of the defence lawyers she interviewed and one third of Crown prosecutors were concerned that important material was omitted from the schedules. Astonishingly, Quirk's research, reported in 2016, showed that 43 per cent of police officers interviewed would not give unrepresented suspects an outline of the case against them and 56 per cent would not read the main points from statements. Hardly any would let suspects have copies of the evidence. In 2011, the Ministry of Justice yet again reviewed the prosecution's duty of disclosure "in cases which generate large volumes of investigative material, where a disproportionate part of the disclosure cost burden lies" (Ch.6 of their legal aid reform consultation, 2010). For a fuller examination of disclosure, see Darbyshire (2014). My research conducted in 10 Crown Courts in 2012 found that CPS failures to disclose evidence in accordance with judges' orders or required deadlines was one of the biggest handicaps to judicial case management. Judges expressed exasperation in extreme terms: "The CPS depresses me", "The CPS frightens me", "We've gone backwards". The 2015 five year review of the CPS observed that disclosure of unused material was rated good or excellent in only 23 per cent of cases. In July 2017, a joint inspection by HM CPS Inspectorate and HM Inspectorate of Constabulary identified the causes of widespread failures and set out a timetable for reform. Leveson (2015) recommended that the previous disclosure review recommendations be implemented, that initial disclosure should be made early, to a named defence lawyer and that legal aid remuneration should be altered to encourage defence lawyers to engage with their clients and identify the issues early. This last change has just been done in 2017, having been recommended by the Runciman Commission in 1993.

The plea

12–057   In common law countries, once the accused has pleaded guilty, this relieves the prosecutor from proving the case by bringing evidence. There is no trial. The guilty plea procedure was considered and approved by the ECtHR on at least two occasions. In *DPP v Revitt* (2006) the Lord Chief Justice said the correct analysis was as follows. Where a defendant made an unequivocal plea of guilty which the court accepted, the defendant was thereupon "proved guilty according to law" within the meaning of art.6(2). The presumption of innocence ceased to apply and he could be sentenced on the basis that he had been proven guilty. Where a plea was equivocal, it had to be treated as a plea of not guilty. Where he was unrepresented, it was the duty of the court to make sure the nature of the offence was made clear to him before a plea of guilty was accepted. If the Prisons and Courts Bill 2017 had been enacted, defendants to some charges would have been able to plead guilty online. The Bill was dropped in June 2017. The Bar Council warned that online pleas risked trivialising the serious consequences to the accused.

Plea bargaining and sentencing discounts

At any time prior to or during a criminal trial, it is very common for a defendant to change his plea from "not guilty" to "guilty" on one or more counts. This results in what has become known as a "cracked trial". This wastes court time and public resources and, in relation to trial on indictment, was one of the concerns of the Runciman Commission 1993. It usually results from plea negotiations between prosecution and defence, which may be initiated by either, commonly known as "plea bargaining". This means that the defendant agrees to plead guilty in exchange for a concession by the prosecutor, such as a reduced charge (charge-bargaining) or a concession that the facts of the crime were not so serious as originally alleged (fact-bargaining). The defendant may also plead guilty in the hope of a reduced sentence. The CA has long sanctioned a system of a 25–33 per cent "sentence discount", rewarding the defendant for pleading guilty but the case of *Turner* (1972) prohibited the trial judge becoming involved in a plea bargain to assure the defendant of a specific sentence discount. This prevented the development of a full-blown system of legally enforceable plea bargains, conducted in special hearings, before a judge, which exists in most of the USA. There is an interesting US/English comparison and a critique of the *AG's Plea Negotiation Framework for Fraud Cases*; Vamos (2009). It is important to understand that plea bargaining in the UK cannot work in the fully entrenched way it does in the USA because prosecutors do not have the same powers to recommend sentence. 12–058

The Runciman Commission said nothing about pre-trial negotiations involving the judge but, in order to try and reduce cracked trials, recommended a "sentencing canvass", offering the defendant a graduated system of sentencing discounts: the earlier the plea, the greater the discount. Whilst acknowledging the danger that this might induce innocent people to plead guilty, the Commission, heavily influenced by the Bar Council's Seabrook Report (1992), concluded that this risk would not be increased by "clearer articulation of the long accepted principle". Section 48 of the Criminal Justice and Public Order Act 1994 and later legislation gave statutory recognition to the system of informal sentencing discounts and, indeed, made it mandatory, by requiring the sentencing judge to take into account the timing and circumstances of a guilty plea and, if the punishment is accordingly reduced, to state so in open court. According to *Turner*, advocates were not meant to pressurise clients into pleading guilty and judges were not meant to offer specific discounts but cases decided by the CA exposed the frequency of breaches of these rules by judges and counsel doing secret pre-trial deals in chambers.

In cases from the late 1990s, the courts moved towards enforcing promises held out to defendants. In *R. v Ricky Jackson* (2000) the judge had promised a sentence discount so the CA felt obliged to enforce it, despite the defendant's "appalling" driving record. This was swiftly followed by the *Attorney General's Guidelines on the Acceptance of Pleas* (2000), in which the Attorney reminded 12–059 prosecutors that justice should be transparent. It was the duty of the advocate to remind the judge of the CA's decisions and disassociate himself from sentence discussions. This reflects concern over the number of Crown Court judges who flouted *Turner.* See now the latest guidelines on the AG's website, the Code for Crown Prosecutors and *R. v Cairns* (2013). These say that the basis of plea must not be on a misleading or untrue set of facts. It must take proper account of the victim's interests, be scrutinised by the prosecutor, and the judge must be told of differences between the basis of plea and the prosecution's case.

The Bar has long advocated the formalisation of the system of plea bargaining, by offering graduated sentencing discounts, and they spelled out this "sentencing canvass" in their 1992 Seabrook Report. My view is diametrically opposed. I do not want to see the English legal system going down this American route. I set out a long list of reasons, in 2000. Not least of my objections are these.

1. Every piece of research into defendants discloses a subset who plead guilty while maintaining innocence, often induced to do so by the temptation of a lighter sentence. C. Yarnley, in a letter to *The Times*, 14 June 2010, said "A great many defendants can be described as of limited intellect and strength of character. The temptation to yield to the offer 'plead now and you can go home and we promise you lenient sentencing' could be overwhelming."

2. Rewarding someone for pleading guilty is morally repugnant and hypocritical, since it punishes those who exercise their right to trial.

3. Before the 1994 Act, magistrates, who do most sentencing, managed without discounts so I cannot see why they should be expected to give them now.

4. Scottish judges traditionally considered sentencing discounts immoral and inappropriate and spoke out against them.

5. Research by Henham found that the application of the discount was erratic in both the Crown Court and in magistrates' courts.

For an analysis of the arguments for and against discounts and a comparison with the Scottish system, see Leverick (2014). In his 2001 Review, Auld reiterated the Royal Commission's call for a formalised canvass, coupled with a system of advanced indication of sentence. The Government responded that it intended to introduce a clearer tariff. This is not incorporated in the CJA 2003. Section 144 requires the sentencing court to take account of the timing and circumstances of the guilty plea. Where the accused has been given an indication of sentence by magistrates, no court may impose a custodial sentence, but apart from this, a sentence indication is *not* binding on a court and will not provide grounds of appeal.

In accordance with Auld's recommendations, the newly created Sentencing Guidelines Council (now Sentencing Council) published guidance on its website, on a graduated discount structure for guilty pleas, to be applied by all courts from 2005 (s.172 of the CJA 2003).

12–060   In *R. v Goodyear (Practice Note)* (2005), a five-judge CA laid down guidelines on what judges should do in the light of this "different culture". Re-emphasising the principle that the defendant's plea must be made voluntarily, they said a defendant *could* seek an advance indication of sentence. The judge should confine himself to indicating the maximum sentence for a guilty plea at that point and could only act at the request of the defendant. The judge could refuse an indication but, once given, it was binding on him or any other judge. The judge should never be invited to give an indication on the basis of a plea bargain. He should not be asked to indicate levels of sentence dependent on different pleas. The defence advocate was personally responsible for ensuring that his client fully appreciated that he should not plead guilty unless he was guilty, and that any indication remained subject to the AG's right to appeal against an unduly lenient sentence. Any agreed basis of plea should be reduced into writing before an indication was sought. If there were no agreement, there should be a hearing on the disputed facts, in front of the judge (called a *Newton* hearing). Any sentence indication should normally be given at a case management hearing and should be in open court and recorded. It would be wise to see how these new arrangements settled in at the Crown Court before copying the procedure in the magistrates' court. (See further Darbyshire 2006.)

Although the guidelines warn Crown Court judges against taking part in any apparent plea bargain, these graduated sentencing discounts are designed to encourage early guilty pleas and will promote bargaining between prosecution and defence. Those of us who oppose plea bargaining have irretrievably lost the battle. In support of the system, discounts at least have the virtue of transparency—to offenders, judges, magistrates, victims and the public—on the Sentencing Council website. The scheme is highly unlikely, however, to produce consistency in sentencing, because sentencers will differ, as research shows they have done, in deciding on the starting point: the appropriate full, undiscounted sentence. The CA has warned judges that it is incumbent on the sentencing judge to explain why he is not following it, if he chooses not to follow a guideline: *R. v Bowering* (2005); *R. v Gisborne* (2005). Research in 10 Crown Courts in 2012 found that it was surprisingly rare for a defendant to request a *Goodyear* sentence indication: Darbyshire (2014).

In 2006, a case where a man had raped a baby but was given the automatic one **12–061** third sentence discount, despite being caught in the act, caused a public outcry and the *Sun* newspaper waged a campaign against judges. The AG referred the case to the CA as unduly lenient. The CA said that the trial judge had been correct: *Att Gen's Reference (Nos 14 and 15 of 2006) (Tanya French and Alan Robert Webster)* (2006). Following consultation, the Sentencing Guidelines Council amended the guidelines. They emphasised that reductions are recommendations not maximums and where the evidence was overwhelming, only a 20 per cent discount need be given. See now *R. v Wilson* (2012). Even in an overwhelming case, the CA said the guilty plea had a distinct public benefit, in this case preventing further suffering to the victim and sparing a jury from viewing paedophile images.

Justice Minister Ken Clarke caused a public outcry in 2011 by repeating a proposal for a 50 per cent discount for defendants (rapists) who plead guilty and suggesting that some rapes were not "proper rapes". He had said in his 2010 legal aid consultation paper, referred to in Ch.17, below:

> "[W]e have already asked the Sentencing Council to consider how sentence discounts might form part of a package of measures to encourage those who acknowledge their guilt to do so at the earliest opportunity. The earlier the guilty

plea, the less trauma likely to be suffered by victims and witnesses at the prospect of giving evidence in court; and the lower the costs to the courts and other agencies".

The proposal was withdrawn in 2011 but his legal aid consultation paper 2010, discussed in Ch.17, proposed a restructuring of advocates fees to encourage early guilty pleas and in his 2010 Review, Lord Judge CJ said "the criminal justice system must do all it can to encourage those who are guilty to plead at the earliest opportunity". In 2012–2013, the Early Guilty Plea (EGP) scheme was launched, to encourage defendants to plead guilty at the earliest possible opportunity to receive the maximum discount. The idea is to reduce the number of guilty pleas on the day of trial (three quarters) by offering the defendant destined for the Crown Court another opportunity to get a discount and a speedy procedure by pleading guilty at an EGP hearing. The "earliest possible opportunity" is not always the police station, though a guilty plea at the plea and trial preparation hearing in the Crown Court is not normally the first opportunity and may only attract a 25 per cent discount: *Caley* (2012). Leveson (2015) recommended that magistrates' seek the plea at the first hearing and that if D pleaded not guilty in the magistrates' court then pleaded guilty at the Crown Court, the court should be entitled to reduce the discount. Following consultation, the Sentencing Council has amended the guideline, in force from 2017, as follows.

- The maximum discount is one third, normally granted at the first hearing where a plea is sought.
- After this, the maximum reduction is one quarter, reducing on a sliding scale to one tenth on the first day of trial (meaning at the point of pre-recorded cross-examination.
- No discount need be given for a plea during trial.
- Where the court is satisfied that D's ability to understand the allegation was significantly reduced, or it was otherwise unreasonable to expect a plea, they can still grant a one third discount.

The last point is a response to concerns that vulnerable defendants, defendants who had not had legal advice and those without the benefit of useful prosecution disclosure would be disadvantaged. Both the House of Commons Justice Committee and the Minister of Justice expressed serious concerns about these guidelines in draft form. I have already criticised plea bargaining and sentence discounts (2000). There is a further concern about these guidelines. Given that the Sentencing Council's own research demonstrated that defendants plead guilty mainly because of the weight of evidence against them, why is it necessary to offer anyone a discount? Secondly, the guidelines state: "Nothing in the guideline should be used to put pressure on a defendant to plead guilty." But the discount will necessarily induce some people to plead guilty. That is its aim.

Extreme bargaining

12–062 Prosecutors have up their sleeves an even bigger incentive to offer to defendants than the astonishing one third discount available for a guilty plea. At common law, the prosecutor has always had power to grant immunity to a suspect against whom there is sufficient evidence to prosecute. This occurs where a *defence* witness or defendant offers to "turn Queen's evidence" and testify on behalf of the Crown against a co-accused, in exchange for total or partial immunity from prosecution. English law gives enormous discretion to the police and to prosecutors. In 2006, the English and Welsh legal system took an alarming leap by introducing formalised American-style plea bargaining, in organised crime. As a result of its *Fraud Review—Final Report*, the Government announced plans to introduce statutory binding pre-trial bargains. Witness immunity or short sentences may be offered to minor defendants in exchange for evidence against key defendants. This was supported by the Financial Services Authority, because of concern over the high level of city fraud but Lake warned that English law came unstuck previously, with the use of the "supergrass" system in Northern Ireland, by making similar offers to alleged terrorists in order to obtain evidence against their co-conspirators. Hundreds of IRA convictions had to be overturned because the system was perceived to be open to abuse. Unsurprisingly, appellants successfully argued that their convictions were unfairly obtained and unreliable because they were obtained by relying on witnesses who had benefited from massive incentives to give evidence against them. See now Martin (2013). Nevertheless, by 2008, the Attorney General was consulting on a framework for plea negotiation in fraud. This smacked of desperation. The consultation paper overtly acknowledged concern about the cost of running fraud trials, the collapse of many expensive jury trials, described in Ch.16, and the low guilty plea rate compared with other common law countries. In 2009, the Attorney General published guidelines on *Plea discussions in cases of serious or complex fraud*. These enable the prosecution and defence to discuss acceptable pleas before charges are brought, to sign a written plea agreement and to make joint submissions to the court as to the appropriate sentence and applicable sentencing ranges.

Also, the Serious Organised Crime and Police Act 2005 ss.71–75 introduced a type of statutory formalised extreme plea bargaining. Prosecutors can give *contractual immunity* from prosecution, undertakings about the use of evidence, and offer reduced sentences in exchange for assistance with investigations. In *R. v P; R. v Blackburn* (2007) the CA gave guidelines on applying ss.71–75. In 2009, Corker and others noted that "there is no desire to utilise ss.71 or 72 in preference to the common law regime" but de Grazia and Hyland, in 2011, a former US prosecutor and a CPS prosecutor strongly advocated greater use of ss.73 and 74 and explained a detailed USA blueprint of "golden rules" developed by prosecutors. They argued these should be copied by the UK in using the evidence of such "assisting offenders", as they are called, to safeguard against a repeat performance of the "disastrous" collapse of the Northern Irish supergrass system. They support the system as a prosecuting tool, citing cases such as the defendant who enjoyed immunity in exchange for testimony against gang members who had killed 11-year-old Rhys Jones in Liverpool in 2007, and *Bevens* (2009), a gangland murderer who received a five year discount from a life sentence, for inculpating a corrupt police officer. Of course, they pointed out that it must be born in mind that if a witness is at risk, "co-operation triggers a life-long obligation to provide protection".

In *R. v D* (2010), after being sentenced for importing drugs and given a 20 per cent discount, D entered into an agreement under the SOC and Police Act 2005, to provide details of 32 other drug traffickers. He did not agree to give evidence and did not provide full admissions of all his criminal activities. He applied to the Crown Court for his sentence to be reviewed. The judge considered that a *further* 25 per cent discount was appropriate but D considered this insufficient. He thought he was due the "normal" discount of 50–66 per cent. The CA said that, as a matter of principle, any discount must be based on the value to the administration of justice, not on whether D had carried out his agreement, which was "much less comprehensive than it might have been". The risk to D from his former gangland colleagues was less than it would have been had he given evidence, as in *Blackburn* (2008). The judge should go back to the original starting point: the sentence that reflected his criminality.

12–063   It has been common practice to offer common law immunity or sentence discounts to those who have given evidence against other offenders and the courts have upheld their part of the bargain by giving astonishingly generous discounts, typified by *R. v A* (2006) where the CA said the courts were prepared to assist the authorities by giving discounts up to *two thirds*, depending on the quality of the material. These deals will continue, in addition to those under the statutory scheme. In *R. v Daniels* (2010), D was offered a massive reduction in culpability in exchange for giving evidence against a co-accused. Roberts (2011), commenting on this case, said "It hardly needs stating that the prospect of a substantial reduction in sentence might lead to a witness to tailor his or her evidence to meet the expectations of the prosecutor".

In one case though, the train hurtling down the track into US-style plea deals was derailed. In *R. v Innospec Ltd* (2010) the sentencing judge was Thomas LJ, who later became Lord Chief Justice. An Anglo-American company pleaded guilty to corruption. The British subsidiary entered into a plea agreement with the Serious Fraud Office to pay a confiscation order of $6.7 million and a civil recovery order of $6 million and the US company entered into a plea agreement with federal prosecutors, to pay $14 million in fines. Thomas LJ determined that there was a problem with the plea agreement. Under the law of England and Wales, the prosecutor (SFO) could not enter into an agreement as to penalty. Sentencing submissions could not include a specific sentence or agreed range and that was made clear by the Consolidated Criminal Practice Direction and AG's guidelines on plea discussions in serious or complex fraud. The Practice Direction reflected the *constitutional principle* that, save in matters such as motoring offences, the imposition of a sentence was a matter for the judiciary. For transparency, a court must rigorously examine the basis of plea in open court to see whether it reflected the public interest. Judges who specialise in trying serious fraud were agreed that there was a place for plea bargaining in England and Wales. They were reluctant to develop a fully fledged US system but Julian (2008) commented that the pre-trial management system would accommodate it.

A novelty form of extreme bargaining for corporate white collar criminals is now available from 2014, under the Crime and Courts Act 2013, copied from the USA. The UK loses £73 billion per year in fraud. Policing it is very difficult, as corporations grow and become more global and complex. Prosecution often relies on self-reporting or whistle blowing. Companies need to avoid prosecution if they are to avoid share-price damage and being excluded from tendering for government contracts. "Deferred prosecution agreements" can now be offered by the DPP or Serious Fraud Office to commercial organisations in economic crimes such as money laundering and fraud. Unlike in the USA, they are subject to judicial supervision, with Crown Court proceedings commenced on a suspended bill of indictment, with a judge determining whether the interests of justice are served and the terms are fair, reasonable and proportionate. The terms will be pronounced in public and published. All of this is far more transparent than normal plea bargaining and judicial supervision is a welcome novelty. Dyer and Hopmeier (2013) give interesting American examples. Siemens agreed to pay a $800 million fine to settle a bribery and corruption scandal. They appointed an anti-corruption adviser and 500 compliance officers, suspended their applications to the World Bank, and agreed to pay $100 million to organisations fighting corruption. They disciplined or sacked 900 personnel. All this cost Siemens 2.5 billion Euros but it meant that the USA was prepared to offer them federal contracts. The first English DPA was approved by Leveson LJ in 2015. Standard Bank was alleged to have had inadequate systems to prevent "associated persons" committing bribery. The bank agreed to pay $7 million in compensation, plus a penalty of $16 million, pay for an independent review of its anti-bribery and corruption controls and pay the SFO's costs. The judge had to be satisfied that this was in the interests of justice and was fair, reasonable and proportionate (Padfield 2016). In 2017, the SFO and Tesco reached a DPA, with Tesco paying a £129 million penalty plus costs, to be approved in the Crown Court.

Cases heard in the magistrates' court

The Criminal Law Act 1977 divided offences into three categories: offences triable on indictment in the Crown Court; offences triable only summarily in the magistrates' court; and between those two, offences triable either way ("either way offences"). The Criminal Justice Act 1988 added a fourth category, summary offences triable on indictment. As I pointed out in 1997, in the twentieth century Parliament repeatedly downgraded indictable offences to "triable either way", and "either way" offences to summary offences, thus shifting criminal business down onto the shoulders of the magistrates. Also, when new offences are created they tend to be summary or triable either way, thus guaranteeing that all of the first category and most of the second will be heard by magistrates. The number of people proceeded against has been declining since 2007 and was 1.7 million in 2015-2016. 1.46 million were prosecuted at magistrates' courts. 6 per cent of these were sent for trial at the Crown Court. 81 per cent were tried at the magistrates' court. (13 per cent were stopped) (Criminal Justice Statistics to March 2016, containing the annual statistics).) It should be obvious from that statistic that magistrates' work is not trivial, contrary to many people's perceptions.

The most obvious summary offences are almost all Road Traffic Act offences; assaults such as common assault; minor criminal damage and cases prosecuted by government departments or agencies. Procedure in the magistrates' court is called summary procedure. Any case is now commenced by a written charge issued by the prosecutor and a requisition/summons requiring them to appear in the magistrates' court (CJA 2003 Pt 4). The Road Traffic Act allows defendants to motoring offences to plead guilty by post, avoiding a court appearance. Duty

12-064

solicitors, private practitioners funded under the legal aid scheme, are meant to be available, at each magistrates' court. Governments are continually thinking of money-saving devices. The Criminal Justice and Courts Act 2015 provides for summary, non-imprisonable offences, such as some road traffic offences and TV licence non-payment, to be heard by a single justice (with a legal adviser), on the papers, not in open court and without the prosecutor if there is a guilty plea. And in future, as explained above many more offences will be processed following an online plea.

Speeding cases through the magistrates' court—the guilty plea

12–065   Under a 2015 amendment to the Rules, courts are under a duty to conduct pre-trial proceedings by live link or telephone where possible. When the accused first appears in court, he is asked if he pleads guilty or not guilty, unless he has done so online, which is supposed to be in place by 2019. The vast majority of offenders plead guilty. If he pleads guilty, he may be convicted and sentenced immediately, unless the magistrates require more information on the defendant, in which case they will adjourn for the preparation of a medical or psychiatric report, or a pre-sentence report, prepared by a probation officer or social worker. Leveson (2015) said these should be discouraged unless really necessary.

The 1997 Narey Report on delay recommended various measures to speed criminal cases through the courts, responding to a concern that an "adjournment culture" pervaded most magistrates' courts. Sections of the Crime and Disorder Act 1998 are designed as time-saving measures. Under s.43, time-limits may be set. Section 46 provides that where a person is bailed (by the police) to appear before a magistrates' court, his appearance should be set for the next available court sitting so someone arrested on a Thursday night should appear before the court on Friday morning. If they plead guilty, they should normally be sentenced there and then.

An experiment with virtual courts commenced in 2009. Once a person is charged with an offence at a police station, they appear on a video link to a magistrates' court within two hours. The legal framework is the Police and Justice Act 2006. The government says that defendants are able to opt for real court hearings but Keogh (2009) objected that research showed that they often did not know their rights. He said 50 per cent of police station detainees were not represented. The pilot evaluation report was published in 2010. The decision to expand this system was criticised in the *New Law Journal* because of the cost.

> "The findings indicate that the pilot was successful in reducing the average time from charge to first hearing, failure to appear rates and prisoner transportation and police cell costs. However, these savings were exceeded by costs of the pilot, particularly those associated with the technology used" (Ministry of Justice).

12–066   The number of adjournments and hearings was more than the comparator; it was harder for prosecution and defence to communicate; the 15-minute time slots were perceived by magistrates and district judges to cause hasty justice; some magistrates and judges thought it was more difficult to impose authority remotely and so the defendant did not take it seriously and the representation rate was lower. Leveson (2016) said he supported the 2015 Transforming Summary

Justice principles which are designed to maximise efficiency. This scheme was mentioned above. It requires the prosecution to review the case file prior to the first court appearance. Anticipated guilty plea cases are listed 14 days after charge in Guilty Anticipated Plea (GAP) courts, with the aim of concluding all stages at one hearing, including sentencing. Cases where a not guilty plea is expected are listed 28 days after charge in Not Guilty Anticipated Plea (NGAP) courts, allowing time for review and preparation before the first hearing, and early contact with the defence.

In 2016, the CPS Inspectorate said it appeared to be a success, as 81 per cent of first hearings were effective. Leveson (2015) recommended that lawyers' details be exchanged early so as to enable speedy "Initial Disclosure of the Prosecution Case", and this is now required by the CrimPR. He also recommended that legal aid fees be amended so as to incentivise early engagement. This appears to have been done at last, in 2017, 24 years after it was recommended by the Runciman Commission.

In 2014, the Minister of Justice launched the Digital Business Model, to be used in all magistrates' courts. It included plans for:

> "... police contact the Crown Prosecution Service (CPS) directly for a charging decision ... Defendants in custody to appear in court via prison to court video links for pre-trial hearings ...
>
> Criminal prosecutors and defence lawyers in magistrates' courts to work digitally, presenting cases from mobile digital devices in court instead of bundles of paper files.
>
> Case information to be viewed digitally by magistrates on digital devices...
>
> Digital in-court presentation equipment to display evidence like CCTV, photos or 999 calls" (Press release 11 April 2014).

Nevertheless, while prison video links have been in place in some Crown Courts for many years and they use digital in-court presentation, all criminal courts have been bedevilled by equipment that does not work or digital media that are incompatible. See *Sitting in Judgment* (2011) and things had not improved when I observed courts in 2016. Lord Woolf's 1996 vision of fully digital *civil* courts has never been realised. As part of the above plan, CPS prosecutors were given tablet computers but unfortunately they did not work as required. In the 2016 vision paper *Transforming Our Justice System*, the Minister and judges acknowledged that "there is still too much evidence being carted around the country on CDs and CCTV tapes, and too many 'digital' ways of working rely on people scanning in pieces of paper" but they promised a fully digitised criminal justice system by 2019.   **12–067**

In 2012 2013, flexible working was piloted at 42 magistrates' courts, with mixed results. Sunday courts were unsurprisingly unpopular with staff and other agencies. Saturday courts were popular with defendants but depended on sufficient case volumes and staffing. Experiments in weekend and evening courts were made in the 1970s and since then but were abandoned as they depended on all other agencies and lawyers being prepared to cooperate. In March 2017, the Bar Council objected to plans to have magistrates' courts (and others) sitting until 20.00 because it would disadvantage barristers with children and offend against the cab rank rule wherein barristers were obliged to accept cases without knowing listing details.

The not guilty plea and summary trial in the magistrates' court

12–068   If they plead *not* guilty to a summary offence, the defendant's first appearance may take the form of an early administrative hearing, under the Crime and Disorder Act 1998 s.50, at which their eligibility for legal aid may be determined (If not already in place and dealt with online, which is meant to be in place by 2019). Under the criminal practice directions, the court should complete a preparation for effective trial form, as part of its case management duty. Such hearings may be conducted by a single magistrate or a justices' clerk, or a legal adviser (court clerk), including a lot of judicial trial management powers which are likely to be exercised at a later hearing. For instance, a clerk may renew bail on conditions previously imposed. I have expressed concern about giving these judicial powers to legal advisers (see Ch.15). The Courts Act 2003 s.45 places on a statutory basis pre-trial case management hearings which have been held since the 1970s.

If a plea of not guilty is entered there will be a trial. At trial the prosecutor will outline the case against the accused, then the court may invite the defence to identify the issues in the case, following a recommendation by Leveson (2015). Then the prosecution call witnesses to substantiate that accusation. They may be cross-examined by the defence. Any witness may now give evidence by live video link from anywhere in the UK, provided that the court considers it to be in the best interests of efficient and effective administration of justice: CrimPR Pt 29. Any witness with communication difficulties (prosecution and defence) may be assisted by an intermediary and/or an interpreter and children and vulnerable witnesses' evidence, including cross-examination, may be pre-recorded, as explained above.

No case to answer

12–069   As the onus of proving guilt is on the prosecution, it follows that at the conclusion of the prosecution case, the defence may submit to the magistrates that there is "no case to answer". This means, simply, that the evidence produced by the prosecution does not prove that the defendant has committed the offence. If the magistrates uphold that submission, the case is dismissed. If not, the case for the defence is then presented. The defendant may choose to enter the witness box, give evidence and be cross-examined; defence witnesses will be called; the prosecutor may cross-examine them and the magistrates will decide whether or not the evidence is sufficient for them to convict. If so, they may sentence the defendant. If they are considering custody or one of the alternatives, they will adjourn for a pre-sentence report. If they decide to acquit, the case is dismissed.

Legal advice/magistrates' powers

12–070   Magistrates can call for the assistance of their legal adviser if the case raises issues of law or mixed fact and law and they can ask her advice on sentencing. This is explained in the chapter on magistrates. The maximum penalty open to the magistrates is six months' imprisonment, and/or a fine. If a defendant is convicted of two or more offences at the same hearing the magistrates can imprison for 12 months. They may send a convicted defendant to the Crown Court for sentencing, if they feel their powers are inadequate. Had the CJA 2003 s.282 come into force, it would have doubled the magistrates' sentencing power to one year's custody for a single offence. Magistrates who were the subject of research by Herbert were opposed to this change. Many felt they were already being asked to handle cases at the extreme of their ability.

Young offenders 10–17

These are explained in Ch.7. Most young offenders are tried in the youth court, which is a separate part of the magistrates' court. The courtroom is informal, normally with all participants on the same level and the accused sitting next to his appropriate adult and addressed by his first name. Magistrates' and judges are trained to "engage" with the young person and will speak directly to him. They must sit as a mixed-gender bench, although a district judge will sit alone. When Juvenile Courts were introduced in 1908, the intention was that they would be housed in a separate building, but this has not been achieved, other than in big cities (see Ch.7). The public are excluded and press-reporting restrictions may be imposed.   **12 071**

Offences triable either way, allocation and sending for trial, CrimPR Part 9

Where an adult accused is charged with an "either way" offence, a decision must be taken whether to allocate it to summary trial in the magistrates' court or trial on indictment in the Crown Court. Under the Prisons and Courts Bill 2017, had it been enacted, this decision would have been handled online. Under the Magistrates' Courts Act 1980, the magistrates can send the case up to the Crown Court if they consider it too serious or complex for them (with case management directions) but in most instances, they are content to accept jurisdiction. In this event, the accused is then given the choice as to mode of trial. The CJA 2003 Sch.3 introduced provisions to make magistrates' and the accused's decision-making on mode of trial better informed, following the recommendations of Auld (2001). Before deciding on mode of trial, the magistrates should be told of the accused's previous convictions. They must give prosecution and defence a chance to air their views and take account of the allocation guidelines issued by the Sentencing Council. If the court decides the case is suitable for summary trial, they must explain so, in ordinary language, to the accused and tell him he can choose a Crown Court trial but that, if the charge is of a certain violent or sexual offence, they can still commit him to the Crown Court for sentence if, having tried the case, they think their sentencing powers are too low.   **12–072**

The accused can then request an indication of the sentence he might get if he were to plead guilty in the magistrates' court, but the court is not obliged to provide this. If they do, they must allow the accused an opportunity to reconsider his plea, which he will have entered before, or online. If the accused does not change his plea, the CJA 2003 makes it clear that any sentence indication is not binding on a later court. In cases involving child witnesses or complex fraud, the prosecutor may require magistrates to send the case up. If the value is below

£5,000, the magistrates must keep the case even if the accused pleads not guilty but the accused can nonetheless override them and require jury trial in the Crown Court. In any case, the prosecutor can *request* that the case is sent up to the Crown Court.

The vast majority of defendants who have an option choose to have the case tried by magistrates and the 2003 amendments to the allocation procedure were designed to provide more information to the magistrates and the accused, in the hope of persuading magistrates to keep more cases in their court and persuading even more defendants to choose summary trial in the magistrates' court. In Ch.16 on juries, the story is told of attempts to remove the accused's choice as to mode of trial. Reflecting identical concerns voiced by governments since 1965, the Minister of Justice said, in his 2010 legal aid consultation (paraphrased):

> "Too many criminal cases that could adequately be dealt with in the magistrates' court are going to the Crown Court. Increasing numbers of those cases go on to plead guilty, often at a late stage in the proceedings. This is inefficient and ineffective for the criminal justice system as a whole and does not represent best value in legal aid expenditure (Chapter 6). In 2006–09, the number of cases received for trial in the Crown Court increased by 26% and the number of guilty pleas rose by 35%. Most were either way cases. 73% of either way cases at the Crown Court pleaded guilty, costing £1,700 average, or just over £3,200 for a cracked trial, compared with £295 at the magistrates' court. 60% of sentenced either way cases were within magistrates' eligibility limits. The number of defendants proceeded with at the magistrates' courts fell by 13%." (The paper is discussed in Ch.17.)

Lord Judge CJ voiced the same concern in his February 2010 Review. In 2013, Justice Minister Damien Green made the same point in a series of speeches to magistrates. He said over 4,000 defendants were sent to the Crown Court for sentencing each year yet given sentences within the magistrates' powers "costing valuable money and time" (press release 14 August). This issue was considered yet again by Leveson (2015). Apart from recommending that prosecutors and police should get the charge "right first time", he also recommended that the defence be invited at the outset of the case to say whether the accused intends to elect Crown Court trial. This would save lengthy speeches about the suitability of the court. He thought magistrates should be more robust in the application of the allocation guideline, which says that they should only send cases to the Crown Court if it was *likely* that their sentencing powers would be insufficient. Crown Court judges should engage with magistrates and give them feedback. The Sentencing Council should re-emphasise the guideline. The following month, a new strongly worded guideline was issued:

> "In general, either way offences should be tried summarily unless:
>   the outcome would clearly be a sentence in excess of the court's powers for the offence(s) concerned after taking into account personal mitigation and any potential reduction for a guilty plea; or
>   for reasons of unusual legal, procedural or factual complexity, the case should be tried in the Crown Court…".

Request for plea

Section 49 of the Criminal Procedure and Investigations Act 1996 and CrimPR   **12–073**
9.8 require the magistrates, before determining mode of trial in triable either way
cases, to ascertain the accused's plea. Where he indicates a guilty plea, they must
proceed to deal with the case summarily. Where the accused pleads not guilty, as
explained above, they may choose to send the case up to the Crown Court or,
where they decline to do so, they must still give the defendant the option of
summary trial or trial on indictment at the Crown Court. In other words, if the
defendant expresses an intention to plead guilty, he loses the right to opt for the
Crown Court. The magistrates must hear the case but retain the right to send it up
to the Crown Court for sentence, where they feel their own sentencing powers are
too low. There is, of course, nothing to prevent the accused from indicating a not
guilty plea at this stage, then changing his plea to guilty at the Crown Court. In
such cases, the section fails to achieve its desired objective, hence the
introduction of the graduated sentencing discount to induce early guilty pleas,
described above.

Sending young offenders to the Crown Court

Young offenders will only be sent to the Crown Court for trial if certain   **12–074**
conditions are satisfied under Sch.3 of the CJA 2003, or other statutes. D.A.
Thomas endeavoured to explain the complex rules applicable from 2005. He
commented "It might be possible to devise a more convoluted scheme than this,
but only with great difficulty."

1. A defendant under 18 must be sent to the Crown Court if he is charged with
   murder or manslaughter, or has committed certain firearms offences.
2. He must be sent if charged jointly with an adult or if called as a witness and
   so on.
3. If none of these conditions is satisfied but the offence is one to which s.91
   of the Powers of the Criminal Courts (Sentencing) Act 2000 applies, the
   court must follow the plea before venue procedure. If he pleads not guilty
   and the court considers that, if convicted, it ought to be possible to sentence
   him to detention under s.91, or if the offence is a specified offence and he
   may be given a sentence to protect the public or an extended sentence, then
   he should be sent to the Crown Court. In all other cases he must be tried
   summarily.
4. If he has pleaded guilty and been convicted in the magistrates' court, he
   may be sent to the Crown Court for sentencing under certain circumstances
   and if the court feels the Crown Court has the power to sentence to
   detention. This power does not apply to a young person who has been
   found guilty after trial.
5. He should be sent to the Crown Court if he has committed a "specified
   offence" and the court considers he qualifies for a sentence of detention for
   public protection or an extended sentence of detention.

When magistrates tried to apply the criteria, derived from old and new statutes, their legal advisers realised that the statutes gave them clashing obligations. In an appeal to the Divisional Court, Rose LJ, by now running out of patience with the avalanche of new legislation on criminal procedure that he had been obliged to interpret since 1997, was sympathetic:

> "The provisions are not merely labyrinthine, they are manifestly inconsistent with each other. The most inviting course for the court ... is to hold up their hands and say 'the Holy Grail of rational interpretation is impossible to find'".

See useful, critical comment on the current law and practice in sending young people to the Crown Court: Thompson (2012). He said that personal factors were being taken account of in, and distorting, the magistrates' decision as to whether to send a defendant up. Decisions are subjective and inconsistent. The result is that too many young people end up in the Crown Court, when it should be reserved for grave crimes, as originally intended.

The abolition of committal proceedings

12–075   After previous failed attempts, the Crime and Disorder Act 1998 s.51 removed committal proceedings for indictable offences, from 2001. There is a simple preliminary hearing in the magistrates' court. Its purpose is to decide the defendant's remand status and deal with legal representation and the defendant may indicate a guilty plea and be fast-tracked under the early guilty plea scheme. Magistrates will usually hear a full bail application at such a hearing and may adjourn the hearing if there is insufficient information. Committals in either way cases were abolished by the CJA 2003, from 2013. Under the Prisons and Courts Bill 2017, had it been enacted, defendants charged with indictable offences would have gone straight to the Crown Court, without an initial appearance in the magistrates' court.

Crown Court: plea and trial preparation hearing

12–076   A defendant sent to a Crown Court is arraigned on a written or digital indictment. Under a Rule amendment made in 2015, the court is under a duty to conduct pre-trial proceedings by live link or telephone, where possible. For all defendants at the Crown Court (except in cases of fraud which have a special procedure under the CrimPR, Pt 15) they have been required, since the mid 1990s, to appear at a proceeding designed to prepare for trial and fix the date. In all class one or serious or complex cases, the prosecution provides a summary, identifying issues of law and fact and estimating trial length. The arraignment takes place at the hearing: the defendant enters a plea to each of the charges. Following a not guilty plea, the parties are expected to inform the court of such matters as: witnesses, defence witnesses whose written statements are accepted, admitted facts, alibi, points of law and special requirements for the trial (for example, live video links for vulnerable witnesses) and these requirements are now embodied in the case management and progression rules of the CrimPR, Pt 3. The Practice Directions require the completion of a PTPH form.

If the plea is "guilty", the judge should, if possible, proceed to sentence the defendant, after hearing his plea in mitigation. This is a plea for leniency, allowing the defendant to argue any partial excuses or explanation for his admitted offences. If the judge or recorder is considering imposing a custodial sentence or non-custodial alternative, she may require a pre-sentence report to be prepared, or, where appropriate, a medical or psychiatric report. Auld (2001) recommended a move away from pre-trial hearings towards standard timetables and co-operation between the parties. That did not happen, which is why Leveson repeated it in 2015.

Fitness to plead

Where there is doubt as to the accused's mental capacity to understand and participate effectively in the trial, the issue of fitness to plead is now determined by the court, sitting without a jury, since the Domestic Violence, Crime and Victims Act 2004 ss.22–25, amended the Criminal Procedure (Insanity) Act 1964.

12–077

Trial on indictment at the Crown Court

Judges terminating trials; appeals against judges' terminating rulings

One of the big advantages to the defendant of a trial in the Crown Court is that the pre-trial legal argument stage provides a realistic opportunity for the case to be dismissed on the order of the trial judge, in an ordered or directed acquittal. When the prosecution appear at court and offer no evidence, the judge *orders* an acquittal and one of the biggest factors causing this was the non-appearance of a crucial witness, or their retraction of evidence. Baldwin found that this was foreseeable in many such collapsed cases and the prosecution could have been withdrawn at an earlier stage. It was doubtless research such as this which prompted the new special measures for vulnerable witnesses, described at length above. The current Court Statistics do not disclose how many acquittals were judge-ordered or judge-directed but, as explained above, a 2016 report by the National Audit Office on *Efficiency in the Criminal Justice System* found that only one third of trials were effective, in 2014-2015. £21.5 million was wasted on cases that did not go to trial, with unquantifiable extra costs. The case backlog had increased by 33 per cent in two years. The proportion of cracked trials (collapsed on the day), had reduced from 30 per cent in 2011 to 24 per cent.

A judge may *direct* an acquittal during the trial. Mostly, this happens at the close of the prosecution case when the defence have successfully invited the judge to find that there is not a sufficient case to convict the defendant, in a submission of "no case to answer". This may be decided on a point of law, or an assessment of the sufficiency of the evidence. Also, legal argument may take place at any time in the trial, where the judge is asked to rule on a point of law or evidence in the absence of the jury, in a "voir dire" hearing (a trial within a trial). When the prosecution depends on poor quality, unsupported identification evidence, the judge must direct an acquittal. Otherwise, the judge's task is to consider, without usurping the jury's function, whether there is evidence upon which a reasonable jury could convict. Directed acquittals were caused mainly by

12–078

inadequate or untrustworthy witnesses but also by legal problems and evidential insufficiency (Baldwin). In *R. v Brown* (2001), the CA held that the judge may not prevent the prosecution bringing their case because he thinks the defence is likely to be believed: *Attorney General's Ref No.2 of 2000* (2001).

If the judge upholds the defence submission and directs an acquittal, the prosecution did not, in the past, have the power to appeal. Pattenden powerfully argued that this meant that any wrongfully directed acquittal by the judge had to go unchallenged, which was unfair for the victim, witnesses and public. Prosecutors had much more extensive rights in some common law and European jurisdictions. The Law Commission's Report, *Double Jeopardy and Prosecution Appeals* (No.267, 2001) recommended that where the judge acquitted on a point of law, the prosecution ought to have a right of appeal against an acquittal. This was accepted by the Government. Consequently the CJA 2003 Pt 9 introduced a prosecution right of appeal, in certain offences, against a judge's evidentiary ruling which has terminated the trial before a jury has been convened or during the prosecution case, or as a result of a defence submission of "no case to answer". The Act also introduced a prosecution right to appeal against a judge's ruling which has been made at any time before the close of the prosecution case. The CA may affirm the ruling and acquit the defendant, remit the case to the trial court, or order a retrial, where they think it is in the interests of justice to do so. The grounds for overturning a trial judge's ruling are if it was wrong in law, involved an error of law or principle, or was unreasonable. See Pattenden (2009) and Ormerod et al (2010). They examined prosecution appeals on rulings made in Crown Court trials. They found that, although this created an unintentionally wide route of appeal, there was little danger of this exacerbating the CACD's "already unhealthy workload".

Jury trial

12–079   If the plea is "not guilty" the court swears in 12 jurors, who will be responsible at the end of the trial for deciding whether the accused is guilty or not guilty. Once the jury is sworn in, the prosecution will open by outlining their case. The court may then invite the defence to identify what is in issue. I originally recommended this in my (2001) paper on juries for Auld LJ, discussed in the jury chapter. He copied the recommendation. It was copied by Leveson in 2015 and has at last gone into the CrimPR. The prosecution then call their witnesses to give evidence to prove those facts. The defence can cross-examine all such witnesses. Undisputed evidence can be admitted by written statement. As explained above, any witness with communication difficulties may be assisted by an intermediary, and/or an interpreter and vulnerable and child witnesses may be accorded special measures, including the admission of their evidence by pre-recorded cross-examination (achieving best evidence). At the close of the prosecution case the defence counsel has the right to submit "no case to answer", i.e. to argue that there is insufficient evidence upon which the jury can convict. Only the judge can invite the jury to acquit at this point: *R. v Speechley* (2004).

Unless such a submission is successful, the defence advocate presents the defence case and calls witnesses for the defence, possibly including the defendant. These witnesses too can be cross-examined on their evidence, by the prosecution. The accused is not required to give evidence, or be examined. This right of silence is explained above.

The judge has a duty to ensure that the trial is conducted fairly and that inadmissible or irrelevant evidence is excluded. The CA has held that the judge had a duty to impose time-limits where counsel indulged in prolix or repetitious questioning on matters which were not really in issue: *R. v B* (2005). In 2005, one judge provided a training exercise in how not to conduct a trial fairly, through three highly publicised CA decisions. In one case he demonstrated his preference for the prosecution case by rolling his eyes, throwing down his pen during the defence and treating prosecution witnesses much more politely: *R. v Patrick Bryant.* See also *R. v Lashley* and *R. v. Dickens.* Later, another judge in *R. v Cordingley* (2007) provided a horrendous example of bad behaviour, in which the CA said the judge "should be ashamed" of his rudeness and discourtesy. Pre-trial, he queried several times why a trial estimate of three days was necessary and warned he would require an explanation for the waste of court time at the end of the trial. Counsel was refused 10 minutes to marshal his papers after transfer from another courtroom. Although D was of previous good character and had been on bail, bail was withdrawn. The judge refused to direct that D should be given the clean clothes that had been brought for him. The defendant consequently remained in the same clothes until the afternoon of the third day and broke down in tears in the witness box because he had not been allowed to shower or change. He was convicted. The CA quashed the conviction, saying the safety of the conviction did not depend just upon the safety of the evidence but on the observance of due process. In *R. v Tedjame-Mortty* (2011), the trial judge was rude to the defendant: "shut your mouth and listen" and sarcastic, and he revoked D's bail over a weekend without giving counsel a chance to make representations.

When the final speeches by the prosecution and defence advocate have been **12–080** made, the judge "sums up" the evidence for the benefit of the jury. This summing-up and the judge's direction on law is the last speech which the jury hear before they retire to consider their verdict. In it, the judge has to balance the arguments of the prosecution and the defence, but leave the jury to decide on the issue of guilt, beyond reasonable doubt, of the accused. In complex cases and in many murder cases, the judge will give the jury written directions, approved by the advocates. The use of these has grown in recent years and Leveson recommended that they should be standard. He also said that the summing up should not recount all the evidence but explain and concentrate on the relevant issues. This is now embodied in the Criminal Practice Direction 26K. The judges' directions can be split up. Early directions can be given and some directions can be given before the advocates' closing speeches, to save repetition. Juries are discussed in Ch.15.

As a result of the abolition of the requirement for a unanimous verdict, by the Criminal Justice Act 1967, it is possible for the judge to accept a majority verdict of the jury, provided that there are not more than two in the minority. If there are three or more in the minority this is known as a "hung jury" and the trial is abandoned. It is then up to the prosecution whether to request a retrial. The judge will only stop this if she considers it an abuse of process. Normally prosecutions are abandoned after two juries have hung but there is nothing in law stopping a retrial.

If the jury has dropped to 11 or 10 in number, there can be a majority verdict if there is not more than one dissenter. The jury must have been out for at least two hours before the judge is able to accept a majority verdict. If the verdict is "not guilty" the accused is immediately discharged; if the verdict is "guilty", then after a plea in mitigation by his counsel, and, usually, pre-sentence reports, he will be sentenced by the judge. A sentencing hearing may be conducted by video link from prison.

Trial by judge alone

12–081 Section 44 of the 2003 Act allows the judge to direct a judge-only trial where there is a danger of jury tampering. The judge must be satisfied that there is a "real and present danger that jury tampering would take place". The second condition is that, notwithstanding any steps that could be taken, such as police protection, the likelihood of tampering is so great as to make it necessary in the interests of justice for the trial to be conducted without a jury. The section gives examples of cases where there is a real and present danger of jury tampering: where the trial is a retrial because of a previous case involving jury tampering; where the defendant or defendants have previously been involved in a case where there has been jury tampering, or where there has been intimidation or attempted intimidation of witnesses.

In 2009, the CA ruled that the requirements of the section were satisfied in the case of four defendants for a 2004 bungled armed robbery at Heathrow: *R. v T* (2010). The robbery had already resulted in three trials costing £22 million. At the first trial, Twomey suffered a heart attack in prison and was severed from the indictment. At the second trial the jury were reduced to nine and failed to reach a verdict. The third collapsed after a "serious attempt at jury tampering", according to the trial judge. The prosecution had applied under s.44 but the judge was satisfied that the jury trial *could* go ahead, spending up to £6 million and using 82 police officers on jury protection, then the CA reversed the decision in 2009 and ordered a non-jury trial under s.44. The CA gave guidance on such cases, including that, when a judge dismissed a jury on a tampering allegation, he should normally order that he should conduct the trial alone, even if he had considered "public interest immunity" protected material. They held that dispensing with a jury did not offend against D's fair trial rights. See case and comment by Taylor (2010). Taylor suggested that jury sequestration could have been used as an alternative—on a four month trial. Marcel Berlins, in the *Guardian* criticised the fact that the cost of an alternative jury trial was taken into account. Twomey was on trial in the Royal Courts of Justice and told the *Guardian* he felt the police had born a grudge against him after he gave evidence in a 1982 police anti-corruption inquiry. See Gibb (2010). In *R. v KS* (2009), the CA quashed a judge's decision to proceed to trial without a jury. He had sentenced co-conspirators in previous trials and some of the judge's observations in sentencing the others were specific to and critical of the appellant.

Section 13 of the Domestic Violence, Crime and Victims Act 2004 permits the prosecution to apply for trial by jury of sample counts on an indictment where there are so many counts that trial by jury of all of them would be impracticable. If the jury convicts on a sample count, the other counts may be tried by judge alone. This measure is controversial, in eroding jury trial, but commentators appeared to fail to notice its passage through Parliament. It was created on the suggestion of the Law Commission, because of the difficulty of successfully running fraud trials.

Trial of young defendants in the Crown Court

In *T and V v UK* (2000), the ECtHR agreed that the formality and ritual of the   **12–082**
Crown Court trial must have been intimidating and incomprehensible to 11-year-old children in their murder trial (for the murder of two-year old Jamie Bulger) and so their art.6 rights had been violated. Consequently, in 2000, the Lord Chief Justice issued a Practice Direction requiring that youth trials should take account of the age, maturity and development of the defendant. For instance, robes, wigs and police uniform should not normally be worn; participants should be on the same level; the young defendant should be able to sit near their family or guardians and they should be given regular breaks. The court is not open to members of the public. The victim may wish to attend. See further *SC v UK* (2005), where an 11-year-old child with learning difficulties had had little understanding of the trial. The same publicity restrictions apply as described above in the youth court. The Children and Young Persons Act 1933, as amended, provides that nothing may be published which is likely to lead members of the public to identify a person (victim/witness/defendant) under 18. This may require preventing the naming of adults involved.

Appeals and judicial review from the magistrates' court

The whole appeal structure in criminal proceedings is a completely confusing   **12–083**
mess. Spencer (2006), argued that it is illogical and contained in 10 different statutes. In 2007, the Law Commission published a consultation paper. Nothing came of it. Dennis (2010) reported that the Law Commission said it would not proceed with its proposals on sorting out rights of appeal to the HC because of opposition but, he commented, there was a strong case for rethinking and review of the appeal system, though it is unlikely to happen at the moment unless cost savings are guaranteed. This was apparent from Auld's thorough examination of appeals in his 2001 Review.

The convicted defendant has an unqualified *right* to appeal to the Crown Court on fact and/or sentence. The appeal will be heard by a circuit judge or a recorder accompanied by two lay magistrates who must accept the judge's rulings on law. They conduct a complete rehearing of the case. The witnesses give their evidence again. The Crown Court has a duty to give reasons: *R. v Kingston Crown Court Ex p. Bell* (2000). If a point of law has been argued before the court, they may agree to state a case for the consideration of the Queen's Bench Divisional Court.

Alternatively, either side (prosecution following an acquittal or the defendant following a conviction) may appeal to the Divisional Court of the Queen's Bench

Division by way of "case stated", on the grounds of error of law and/or insufficient evidence. This means asking the magistrates to state a case for the consideration of the High Court. This case is then prepared in writing by the magistrates' legal adviser setting out the point of law which was raised, the decision of the magistrates and the reason why they decided it as they did. If the Divisional Court decides that the magistrates were wrong, it has three options: (i) it may reverse, affirm or amend the magistrates' decision; (ii) remit the case to the magistrates requiring them either to continue hearing the case, or to discharge or convict the accused, as appropriate; (iii) or it may make such order as it thinks fit. If the prosecution succeed in such an appeal, the case may be sent back for the magistrates with a direction to convict.

The Queen's Bench Divisional Court also exercises the High Court's supervisory jurisdiction over the functioning of magistrates' courts and the Crown Court when dealing with summary cases. The proceedings may be reviewed for procedural impropriety, unfairness or bias. The QBD has stated that it would prefer that convictions were challenged by way of case stated than by judicial review: *R. v Gloucester Crown Court Ex p. Chester* (1998). A further appeal, subject to leave being obtained, is possible to the UKSC. Such cases are rare.

Post Appeal

12–084   The Criminal Appeal Act 1995 gives the Criminal Cases Review Commission (described below) an unconditional power to refer a conviction or sentence imposed by magistrates to the Crown Court, to be treated as an appeal.

Appeals from the Crown Court

12–085   Prosecution appeals from terminating rulings are discussed above.

Appeals by the convicted defendant

12–086   A convicted person may appeal from the Crown Court to the CA (Criminal Division) with leave of the CA, or if the trial judge grants a certificate that the case is fit for appeal: Criminal Appeal Act 1968 s.1 as simplified by the Criminal Appeal Act 1995 s.1. He may appeal against sentence, with leave of the CA: ss.9–11. Applications for leave to the CA are considered on paper, by a High Court judge. If the judge refuses leave, the application may be re-heard by the CA in open court. An appeal by way of case stated on a point of law may be made to the Divisional Court. An application for judicial review is precluded "in matters relating to trial on indictment" but not in relation to other matters: Senior Courts Act 1981 s.29(3).

Prosecution applications for retrial following acquittal

12–087   The CJA 2003 Pt 10 made a controversial exception to the double jeopardy rule, which protects a person from being tried twice for the same offence. With the DPP's consent, a prosecutor may apply to the CA to quash an acquittal and order a retrial. This can be done following trial on indictment or a successful appeal. If the CA is satisfied that there is "new and compelling evidence" ("reliable" and "substantial") against the person, in relation to the offence and that it is in the interests of justice to do so, the court must quash the acquittal and order a retrial. In determining the interests of justice, the CA must take into account, among other things, whether a fair retrial is likely and the length of time since the alleged offence was committed. The provision applies only to serious offences such as kidnapping, terrorist offences, rape, armed robbery, certain Class A drugs offences and murder and manslaughter. This enactment follows a recommendation of Auld (Review, Ch.12). He was influenced by this suggestion in the Macpherson Report on the Stephen Lawrence Inquiry, a recommendation of the House of Commons Home Affairs Select Committee and a Law Commission Report. *R. v Dunlop* (2006) was the first time the CA exercised this new power, quashing Dunlop's 1991 acquittal for the murder of Julie Hogg. He confessed to the murder in 1999. Dunlop pleaded guilty at his retrial in 2006. In 2012, two of Stephen Lawrence's killers, Gary Dobson and David Norris, were tried and convicted of murder. Tiny bloodstains on their clothing had been found to be a DNA match to Stephen Lawrence. DNA analysis had not been so sophisticated when Dobson was tried in 1996. The 2003 Act was used to retry him. See fascinating insight by the then Director of Public Prosecutions, Keir Starmer (2012). Dennis (2014) showed that by 2014, there had been 13 applications to the CA. Nine had resulted in a retrial, with eight defendants being convicted.

Powers of the CA in appeals against conviction by the Crown Court

Grounds

Section 2(1) of the Criminal Appeal Act 1995 amends the Criminal Appeal Act 1968 to set out simplified grounds upon which the CA may allow a criminal appeal. "The Court of Appeal: (a) shall allow an appeal against conviction if they think that the conviction is unsafe; and (b) shall dismiss such an appeal in any other case". The 1995 amendments resulted from the recommendations of the Runciman Commission 1993, Ch.10. These were a culmination of years of criticism from JUSTICE (1989), the House of Commons Select Committee on Home Affairs (1981), academics, MPs and others. The grounds of appeal in the 1968 Act were narrow and ambiguous. The CA interpreted their powers too narrowly. They were too ready to uphold a conviction, even where they accepted there had been an irregularity at trial. They were too reluctant to admit fresh evidence. The Act was designed to simplify the grounds of appeal so, for instance, it was decided to make the s.2 ground for quashing an appeal simply a determination that it was "unsafe", as it was thought that "unsafe" was a comprehensive enough term to cover all types of miscarriage of justice which should be quashed. It was left undefined, to the regret of Sir John Smith (1995). The CA sometimes quashes a conviction on the rather vague common law ground that they have a "lurking doubt" about its safety. See Leigh (2006) and Pattenden (2009) but this criterion is rarely used. Appeal courts stick closely to the wording of the statute. Negligent advice is not a ground of appeal if the conviction is safe, confirmed in *R. v Good (Alfie)* (2016).

12-088

Receiving fresh evidence

12–089   The CA may "receive any evidence which was not adduced in the proceedings from which the appeal lies" where it is necessary or expedient in the interests of justice to do so. The court must, in considering whether to receive any evidence, have regard in particular to:

1.   whether the evidence appears to the court to be capable of belief;
2.   whether it appears to the court that the evidence may afford any ground for allowing the appeal;
3.   whether the evidence would have been admissible at the trial; and
4.   whether there is a reasonable explanation for the failure to adduce the evidence at trial. (Criminal Appeal Act 1968 s.23(2), as amended by s.4 of the 1995 Act, paraphrased.)

The court is free to admit evidence irrespective of these criteria, however: *Bowler* (1997). In *Craven* (2001) the CA held that, empowered as it was to receive fresh evidence and taking account of all the evidence before it, including evidence to which the jury might not have had access, they should uphold a conviction if they considered it safe. Thus a defect at trial, rendering it unfair, could be cured by a fair and proper consideration of the evidence on appeal. They applied the ECtHR case of *Edwards v UK* (1993). The same principle was applied in *Hanratty* (2002) where the CA heard an appeal that put an end to one of the longest "miscarriage of justice" sagas in English legal history. Hanratty had been hanged for the "A6 murders" in the 1960s. Generations had grown up assuming him to be innocent. Campaigners took it for granted that once the CA admitted DNA evidence from Hanratty's exhumed body this would prove his innocence. To their horror, the DNA results confirmed his guilt. The CA held that the overriding consideration for the court in deciding whether fresh evidence should be admitted was whether the evidence would assist the court to achieve justice. Justice could equally be achieved by upholding a conviction if it was safe or setting it aside if it was unsafe. Accordingly, fresh evidence could be admitted when tendered by the prosecution, even where it was not relevant to a specific ground of appeal, but rather to the guilt or innocence of the appellant at large.

As Duff (below) pointed out, a common reason for non-referral by the CCRC of a case to the CA was that, although fresh evidence had come to light, there was no reasonable explanation why it was not adduced at trial. The prosecution are entitled to take account of new evidence at trial and can change their allegations: *Mercer* (2001). In *Pendleton* (2001), the House of Lords confirmed that the correct test for the CA to apply in determining an appeal related to the effect of the fresh evidence on the minds of the members of the court, not the effect it would have had on a jury. The question was whether the conviction was unsafe, not whether the accused was guilty. The CA

> "is not and never should become the primary decision-maker ... The Court of Appeal can make its assessment of the evidence it has heard, but save in a clear case it is at a disadvantage in seeking to relate that evidence to the rest of the evidence which the jury heard ... it will usually be wise for the Court of Appeal, in a case of any difficulty, to test their own provisional view by asking whether the evidence, if

given at trial, might reasonably have affected the decision of the trial jury to convict. If it might, the conviction must be thought to be unsafe."

Where an appellant seeks to rely on a new witness not called by D's lawyer at trial, the CA will not admit the new evidence unless there is a lurking doubt that injustice was caused by flagrantly incompetent advocacy: *R. v Gautier* (2007).

Referral to the CCRC

Section 5 of the 1995 Act gives the CA a power to direct the Criminal Cases   **12–090**
Review Commission to investigate and report on any specified matter relevant to
the determination of an appeal against conviction, where such an investigation is
likely to result in the court being able to resolve the appeal and where the matter
cannot be resolved by the court without such a reference.

The nature of an appeal to the Court of Appeal

The CA does not provide a rehearing, unlike an appeal from a magistrates' court   **12–091**
to the Crown Court. Its limited powers were spelt out in the successful appeal of
the Birmingham Six, *R. v McIlkenny* (1992).

> "Nothing in section 2 of the Act, or anywhere else obliges or entitles us to say
> whether we think that the appellant is innocent. This is a point of great
> constitutional importance. The task of deciding whether a man is innocent or guilty
> falls on the jury. We are concerned solely with the question whether the verdict of
> the jury can stand. The Criminal Division [of the CA] is perhaps more accurately
> described as a court of review."

Further, the CA may substitute a conviction for an alternative offence, or order
a retrial, where it feels this is required by the interests of justice.

Retrials

There are arguments for and against retrials. A retrial is preferable for the accused   **12–092**
over an outright dismissal of his appeal. At least he gets another chance. On the
other hand it is said retrials may be tainted by publicity, as the jury may have
developed their own opinions about the first trial or appeal in a highly publicised
case. This was unsuccessfully argued as inherently unsafe, in *Stone* (2001). The
CA held that the question as to whether a retrial should be ordered where there
had been extensive publicity had to be decided on a balance of probabilities:
whether he would suffer serious prejudice to the extent that no fair trial could be
held. Also, the witnesses' memories will have faded and the element of surprise in
cross-examination will be lost, as all witnesses will have become familiar with all
the evidence. A retrial gives both prosecution and defence the opportunity to
strengthen their case.

Attorney General's References

12–093   The AG may refer a point of law to the CA, on behalf of the prosecution, following an acquittal: Criminal Justice Act 1972. The CA simply clarifies the law for the future, leaving the acquittal verdict untouched. The point may then be referred to the House of Lords.

Appeals on sentence

12–094   The defendant may appeal against the sentence to the CA who may substitute any other sentence or order, provided it is not more severe than originally. The Criminal Justice Act 1988 s.36 gives the AG a prosecutorial power to refer any "unduly lenient" Crown Court sentence to the CA, who then have the power to quash it and substitute any sentence within the Crown Court's powers. This applies to indictable and some either-way offences.

CA's workload

12–095   The court regularly complains of being swamped with material, in the way that cases are argued, because lawyers cite too many precedents. Its workload is extremely high and advocates do not make life easy for the judges. In *R. v Erskine; R. v Williams* (2009), Lord Judge cited Viscount Falkland in 1641: if it was not necessary to refer to a previous decision, it was necessary not to refer to it. Advocates should expect to be required to justify every citation. Anyway, appeals on fresh evidence all turned on their own facts. The CA also had strong words in *R. v Fortean* (2009) about meritless applications. The court said it was "coping" with 6,000 applications a year and applications "without any vestige of merit" hampered its work, which was why the application form contained a warning in bold letters that the court could, under the 1968 Act, order that time spent in custody as an appellant should not count towards sentence. For a portrait of the CA at work see *Sitting in Judgment* (2011). See Ch.7 of this book on the current overload of the Court of Appeal, especially with a glut of cases where solicitors had failed to advise asylum seekers of a statutory defence to illegal entry to the UK if they could show good cause. This was typified by *R. v Zaredar* (2017). The CACD said there was no excuse for continuing professional failures to advise clients of their defence. Happily, this problem has been acted on by the CCRC, below. In 2015-2016 alone, there were 33 referrals on these cases from the CCRC. In the past, the CCRC has not used its powers to feed back into the system to improve it but in this instance, the CCRC raised awareness in the media and wrote to the CPS and UK Border Agency. The Solicitors Regulation Authority examined the quality of legal advice: Sato et al (2017).

Appeals to the UKSC

12–096   A further appeal to the UKSC is possible by the prosecution or the defence but only if the CA certifies that the case reveals a point of law of general public importance and either that court or the UKSC grants leave (permission).

Post-appeal: resolving miscarriages of justice

The work of the Criminal Cases Review Commission

Until 1996, the Home Secretary had power to refer cases to the CA but would **12–097** only do this where all avenues of appeal had been exhausted and there was fresh evidence upon which the CA might decide that the conviction was unsafe and unsatisfactory. Following widespread criticism of this restrictive approach and the fact that a convict had to petition a member of the executive government who was always reluctant to overturn a judicial decision, the Runciman Commission 1993 recommended the creation of an independent Criminal Cases Review Commission (CCRC). Consisting mainly of non-lawyers, it was created by the Criminal Appeal Act 1995 ss.8–25.

They have power to refer to the CA any conviction or sentence at any time after an unsuccessful appeal or a refusal of leave, where they "consider there is a real possibility that the conviction, verdict, finding or sentence would not be upheld" because of an argument or evidence not raised in the convicting court, or an argument, point of law or information not raised prior to sentence: s.9. Section 13(2) provides an even wider power to refer any other case, in exceptional circumstances. They have a duty to take account of representations made to them and they have wide investigatory powers. They may seek the CA's opinion, direct an investigation by the police or any other relevant public body, require the production of documents, reports or opinions or undertake any inquiry they consider appropriate. The Administrative Court gave guidance on the CCRC's exercise of its powers, in *R. v CCRC Ex p. Pearson* (1999). They emphasised the uniqueness of the CCRC's predictive function and stressed the broad discretion accorded to it by Parliament. They considered that, in new evidence cases, the CCRC was correct to try and predict whether the CA would be likely to exercise its powers to admit fresh evidence. As we will see, there are continuing concerns that this approach and that of the CACD are too restrictive. In *R. v Cottrell; R. v Fletcher* (2007), the CA held that the CCRC should not normally refer a conviction back to the CA just because the criminal law has changed and this is now a statutory restriction, under the Criminal Justice and Immigration Act 2008 s.42.

The 1995 Act preserves the Home Secretary's prerogative power to *pardon* a convicted individual. Jack Straw did this in 2000, where a prisoner in transit saved a life in a road accident. This power has existed since the seventh century. See Quirk (2009). Section 16 gives him the power to refer any case to the Commission.

Critiques of the CCRC

Concern was at first expressed that the CCRC uses police to investigate **12–098** miscarriages of justice, some of which would have been caused by police malpractice, but there is no evidence that this has caused a problem. There has always been a backlog of pending cases. The Commission has to consider about 980 cases a year and only refers about 32 back to the CA: see web pages on the

MoJ website. Nobles and Schiff analysed the CCRC's performance in 2005. They and others made some of the criticisms in the numbered list below.

A common critique of its powers is that it is limited to referring cases where there is a "real possibility" the CA will find the conviction unsafe. This seems to place the Commission in "an essentially dependent position" (Duff, 2001) and to require them to apply "a parasitic standard" (Nobles/Schiff, 2005). This is demonstrated in *R. v Criminal Cases Review Commission Ex p. Pearson* (1999). The applicant sought judicial review of a determination by the CCRC not to refer her case to the CA because they considered it unlikely the court would admit fresh evidence or quash her murder conviction. She argued that the Commission had sought to usurp the CA's functions. The Divisional Court refused her application, because applications to call fresh evidence depended on their peculiar facts and the CCRC had given detailed reasons for its view. Duff said this case showed the Commission was diverted from its principal task of investigating alleged miscarriages of justice into detailed analysis of the jurisprudence of the CA to second guess its likely determination of a case. Duff, a member of the Scottish CCRC, demonstrated just how difficult it could be for the Commission to decide on a reference. He was concerned at the over-legalistic approach of the English Commission. He suggested, for example, that where there is convincing *inadmissible* evidence of a miscarriage of justice, the CCRC should readily refer a case to the Home Secretary in the hope that he would apply the prerogative of mercy.

The CCRC's interaction with the CA is usefully examined by Nobles and Schiff, in 2005. Some of the points they make are summarised below. Critics consider that the CCRC fails to refer sufficient numbers of cases to the CA. The chairman of the CCRC, then Graham Zellick, defended them, saying they had to take account of the CA's approach. To refer too many cases would raise expectations and cause confusion and would not serve the public interest: interview with Gibb, 2004. He said the CA quashed 70 per cent of CCRC referrals, which he considered about right. Nobles and Schiff also made the following points:

1. The task of second guessing what the CA might do is made more difficult by the need for both bodies to take account of exceptional circumstances.
2. The CCRC's caseload represents a potential threat to the workload of the CA so the CA has expressed some concerns over the approach of the CCRC.
3. The CA has suggested the CCRC should not re-interview witnesses in some cases. Nobles and Schiff were concerned that this might cause injustice.
4. The CA has criticised the CCRC for referring cases out of time where there has been no appeal and the court has used the difficulties in assessing the safety of old convictions as a reason for declining to examine them.

Zellick replied in 2005. Richard Foster, the next chair of the Criminal Cases Review Commission, said that before he took over in 2008, the referral rate to the CA had fallen to an all-time low and he was encouraging staff to be much more bold in referring to the CA, in an interview on Radio 4's *Today* programme, 5 January 2009.

Cooper revisited the relationship between the CA and the CCRC. He pointed **12–099** out that the new s.16C of the Criminal Appeal Act 1995, inserted by the Criminal Justice and Immigration Act 2008, explained above, was aimed at referrals by the CCRC to the CA based on a change in the law and aimed to stop these where the CA itself would not have granted a time-extension for such an appeal. Cooper said the mischief that this Act was aimed at was "more imagined than real". It was not surprising that if someone was convicted on an interpretation of the law that had now been declared incorrect, they wished to appeal. They would feel just as much injustice as someone in a case where new evidence established they did not commit a crime. The CA, said Cooper, had always been fearful of "floodgates" but, for example, there had not been even a single appeal from someone convicted under the *Caldwell* interpretation of recklessness, since *G* (2003) said it was wrong. Anyway, the CA had never granted appeals just because the law had changed. They always required evidence of a "substantial injustice". Also on this subject, Taylor, commenting on the case of *Stock* (2008) felt that the CA had interpreted "exceptional circumstances" justifying a referral, too narrowly.

> "If the CCRC is to seek to mirror the approach of the Court of Appeal and therefore only refer those cases in which there is a genuine 'real possibility' of the conviction being overturned based on the Court of Appeal's self-imposed restrictions, then the meaning of 'lurking doubt' will be virtually empty. This was not the intention behind the 1995 legislation."

In 2015, the House of Commons Justice Committee reported on the CCRC. They considered the strong criticisms of the "real possibility" test, concluding that there was room for the CCRC to be less cautious. On complaints of the CACD's powers being too restricted, and the reluctance to interfere without fresh evidence, they concluded that the Law Commission should review the court's grounds of appeal. They recommended extra funding to help reduce the CCRC's backlog and legislation to extend and strengthen the CCRC's investigatory powers: to require disclosure from private bodies and to sanction public bodies for disclosure failures. This was done in the tiny Criminal Cases Review Commission (Information) Act 2016. Having taken advice from the CACD, the Government declined to alter its powers.

Compensating miscarriages of justice

Since 2006, the only means of securing compensation is through the statutory **12–100** scheme, under s.133 of the Criminal Justice Act 1988. Restrictions were made in the Criminal Justice and Immigration Act 2008 s.61. Alarmed at the cost of compensation (£38 million per year), the Government abolished an old ex gratia scheme in 2006 and developed a policy of restricting claimants to the statutory right to compensation. The assessor will make bigger discounts in awards based on his view of the applicant's conduct leading to the conviction. Similar detailed restrictions have been made by the 2008 Act. The law lords approved deducting cost of living expenses from compensation awards: *R. (on the application of O'Brien) v Independent Assessor* (2007). The 2008 Act restricts the amount to a total of £5 million, or £1 million for those who have been wrongly detained for

10 years. The appellant has to prove a new or newly discovered fact. Incompetence of counsel in deploying the facts at trial was not sufficient to constitute a "miscarriage of justice": *Adams v Secretary of State for Justice* (2011), upholding the CA. This is a very old rule but is appallingly harsh. The Anti-social Behaviour, Crime and Policing Act 2014 s.175 specifies that there has been a miscarriage of justice only if the new or newly discovered fact shows beyond reasonable doubt that the person did not commit the offence. See the miserable result in Victor Nealon's case (2014).

Spencer's articles are always informative and powerfully argued. In 2010, he addressed the question of when compensation ought (morally) to be paid and concluded that the English rules, compared with the French and German rules, are "harsh and arbitrary ... devoid of intelligent justification". He pointed out that the House of Lords failed to agree a definition of "miscarriage of justice" in *Mullen* (2004). He listed a number of "demonstrably innocent" applicants, such as victims of mistaken identity, who would now not be compensated, such as Colin Stagg, the Cardiff Three and so on. He advocated copying the moral basis of French and German law: if blameless people are forced to suffer for the public good, they should be compensated.

Note that when people like those described below were released following appeal, they were given none of the help or rehabilitation of other released prisoners. Nicholls was freed with £85 in cash and a holdall of personal possessions. He was not allowed to take with him the medication he needed as a stroke victim, nor his squeeze ball which aided recuperation. This was prison property. He was put alone in a taxi and left to catch the Isle of Wight ferry for the mainland. When Paddy Hill met him there, he was shaking, confused and blue around the lips. When Robert Brown was freed, he was given £40, a train ticket to his native Glasgow and a box of legal documents marked HMP (Her Majesty's Prisons). Both were eligible for compensation but this takes some time to secure and is not available to everyone who has been wrongfully convicted, as explained below. By the time of Sean Hodgson's successful appeal, in 2009, he was able to rely on the CA's miscarriage of justice unit, which provided healthcare, managed his medication and made sure that he was suitably housed. Nevertheless, victims of decades of wrongful imprisonment seldom recover. Six months after his successful appeal, *The Times* reported that "Mr Hodgson has struggled with everyday life, spending periods in homeless hostels and wandering the streets of London ... In poor mental and physical health, he needs regular medication and psychiatric care." Sally Clark never recovered from her ordeal, described below. In 2007 she died, aged 42. Stephan Kisko, below, died one year after release.

The causes of wrongful convictions; the work of the CCRC

12–101   There is a big literature on miscarriages of justice and patterns emerge in identifying common causes. The latest article, by Field and Eady (2017), is well worth reading because it is so revealing of modern causes of miscarriages of justice and the incapacity of the CCRC to investigate them. The work is a brilliant exposition of what handicaps truth-finding in the adversarial system. There are these inherent problems: the Runciman Commission said that it was the duty of the police to investigate fairly both exculpatory and inculpatory evidence but they operate "confirmation bias" looking for evidence to construct the case against their preferred suspect. There are barriers to the defence in investigating exculpatory evidence or even in finding out that it exists: defence lawyers lack the time, resources and legal powers to review the evidence, investigate the case and pursue alternative arguments, evidence and witnesses. Also, it is tactically dangerous to accuse the police of hiding material or failing to keep proper records. The CCRC showed that it did not disapprove of targeted case construction by the police. They did not consider further investigating a case to establish the truth. Unless it could be demonstrated that there was fresh evidence that substantially undermined the prosecution case, it could not be persuaded to investigate. Fact finding was a one-shot investigation. If facts could theoretically have been found by the defence before trial, the CCRC would not act. These are the same criticisms that have been raised for decades.

Historic cases

Given the enormous backlog, it was a matter of concern to some that precious resources have been prioritised towards clearing up wrongful hangings of those long dead, such as Derek Bentley, hanged in 1952, while possible innocents still live in prison for years. In some capital cases where convictions were upheld by the CA, the court doubted the value of the CCRC's efforts: *R. v Ellis* (2003), the case involving the last woman to be hanged in Britain, in 1955, and *Knighton* (2002). In its annual reports, the CCRC defended this practice. Three cases from the 1950s where the convicted person had been hanged were quashed by the CA: *Mattan* (1998) and *Kelly* (2003), both on new evidence and non-disclosure, and *Bentley* (2001), on the grounds of an unfair trial. In 2004, the CCRC decided not to refer the case of Timothy Evans, wrongly hanged in 1950 for murdering his baby daughter. John Christie later confessed to this and other murders and was hanged. The case, like Bentley's, had been one of the most notorious miscarriages of justice in English legal history. It had been the subject of a book, *Ten Rillington Place* and a film. The CCRC declined to refer the case to the CA as Evans had been given a posthumous royal pardon in 1966. In judicial review proceedings, the High Court upheld the CCRC's refusal but publicly declared Evans to be innocent. One notorious case referred by the Board was that of the A6 murderer *Hanratty* (2002), mentioned above. He was hanged in 1962, and his body was exhumed in 2000 for DNA tests.

Some other references by the CCRC involved very old convictions, which took place before the Police and Criminal Evidence Act 1984 offered protection to the accused and rendered confessions obtained in oppressive circumstances inadmissible. One such case was that of Stephen *Downing* (2002). In this group of cases, defects identified by the CCRC include oppressive questioning, failure to protect mentally vulnerable suspects, like Downing, failure to caution, or "verballing", meaning the police attribution of false statements to the accused.

Also in this old group are cases involving police malpractice, reminiscent of the famous miscarriages of justice, such as the Birmingham Six and Guildford Four, the first of which prompted the establishment of the Royal Commission on Criminal Justice, whose recommendations led to the establishment of the CCRC. One such case was that of Robert Brown, freed on appeal in 2002, after serving

12–102

25 years in prison. On his arrest in 1977, Brown was a 19-year-old, with one conviction for stealing a pair of shoes, who was arrested for non-payment of his fine. He was questioned over the death of a woman near his home, despite eyewitness evidence of a suspect in his thirties. In the police station, he was interrogated by two police officers, Butler and Bethell. Neither took notes. Butler punched him. They took his clothes and, while he was naked, they made him do step-ups and assaulted him. After two days' humiliation and abuse, he signed a confession. He refused to plead guilty, despite the offer of a plea bargain for a guilty plea to manslaughter. Two appeals failed before the CCRC examined the case and reported to the CA that Bethell had rewritten forensic evidence that might have established Brown's innocence. What makes this story all the more cruel, is that because Brown was an unco-operative prisoner, who went on hunger strikes and refused to work, he was ineligible for parole and so, like Stephen Downing, he spent many extra years in prison (see the account by Petty). People who do not acknowledge their guilt have often found themselves denied parole and/or remission and have spent many extra years in prison, as a result. Sean Hodgson, below, falls into this category.

Non-disclosure

12–103 Yet another man who was refused parole for protesting his innocence was the second long-serving victim of wrongful imprisonment, Patrick Nicholls, freed with an apology by the CA in 1998, 23 years after being wrongfully convicted of the murder of a woman who almost certainly died of natural causes. Nicholls had found the body of the 74-year-old, Gladys Heath, at the bottom of her stairs and was convicted on flawed pathology evidence. The CA found that medical and police notes that raised the possibility that no murder had taken place had not been passed to prosecuting counsel or to Nicholls.

Elks usefully commented that, although it was widely predicted that there would be a flood of applications to the CCRC resulting from the disclosure regime in the CPIA 1996, described above, this did not occur. Critics of the Act feared that prosecutors would wrongly withhold significant material, causing miscarriages of justice. This supports Corker's comment, above, on disclosure under the 1996 Act, that prosecutors did not have the time or resources to sift evidence into that required for primary and secondary disclosure so they gave *everything* to the defence, rather than too little. Incidentally, Sally Clark's second and successful appeal rested on non-disclosure by a prosecution witness, her babies' pathologist, as explained below, but this was not a failure to disclose on the part of the CPS under the 1996 Act. See further examples by Field and Eady.

Expert evidence

12–104 Nicholls' case, above, is also an example of a conviction obtained by expert evidence which was later proven to be flawed. Two pathologists, both dead by the time of his appeal, had concluded that Mrs Heath had been suffocated and beaten about the face. The CA heard new evidence from an Irish state pathologist that her facial injuries were trivial and probably caused by a fall.

A stunning case of a wrongful conviction involving a litany of flawed expert evidence was that of solicitor Sally Clark, who was convicted and given two life sentences, in 1999, for murdering her babies, who she claimed were victims of cot deaths. She lost her first appeal but her husband, Stephen, and others waged a high-publicity campaign, supported by the Law Society. An eminent paediatrics professor, Sir Roy Meadow, had given evidence to her trial jury that there was a one in 73 million chance of both of her sons dying in cot deaths. At that time, he was famous for "Meadow's law", that "one cot death is a tragedy, two is suspicious and three is murder". He reiterated this to Sally Clark's jury and to the jury at Angela Cannings' trial, below. By the time of Sally Clark's second appeal, in 2003, his theory was discredited, with other experts asserting that the chances of two cot deaths were more like one in sixty, and Sir Roy had admitted his statistics were mistaken. Many statisticians had pointed out that he was not a statistician and his calculations were wrong.

The success of Sally Clark's second appeal however, rested on the discovery **12–105** of misconduct by yet another expert at her trial, the pathologist of her two dead babies, Alan Williams. In 1998, he received evidence of a potentially fatal infection in the second baby, Harry's spinal fluid but had failed to disclose it. It was found by the vigilance of Sally Clark's husband, hidden in the file on the *other* baby. Dr Williams had initially concluded that Harry had died from being shaken, then changed his mind to claim smothering. Two years earlier, a manslaughter trial (quite unconnected) had ended when Williams admitted making an error. By 2005, Dr Williams was appearing before a General Medical Council disciplinary panel, on a charge of serious professional misconduct. Astonishingly, despite criticism by the CA in the *Sally Clark* case, and widespread attacks in the media, Williams won his appeal against removal from the Home Office register of forensic pathologists.

As if two unreliable experts were not enough, it almost defies belief that a third decided to involve himself in falsely accusing Stephen Clark of being the real murderer. Professor David Southall, then regarded as one of the country's foremost paediatricians, made the accusation *after watching a TV programme* showing Stephen Clark describing the baby's illness. Without having even examined the medical files on the babies, he contacted the police and told them Stephen Clark should be investigated for murder. He said their third and remaining child should be taken into care and, given Professor Southall's eminence, the local authority seriously considered doing this. He was later found guilty of serious professional misconduct by the GMC who recommended striking him off the medical register in December 2007, but this was overturned on appeal.

Following Sally Clark's successful appeal, in January 2003, the evidence of Professor Sir Roy Meadow became suspicious. He had been one of the first UK experts to write about Munchausen's syndrome by proxy, wherein parents injure their children in order to draw attention to themselves. Parents have been filmed doing this but Sir Roy was too ready to offer this explanation in cases of multiple infant deaths, thus effectively reversing the burden of proof, obliging the parents to find an innocent explanation for their children's deaths.

In this context, it became predictable that the CA would overturn the **12–106** conviction of Angela Cannings, in 2004, as she had also been convicted on his evidence, and his "Meadows' Law", of murdering her two sons, in 2002. Note that the 2004 appeal was Cannings' first appeal, not a reference from the CCRC, so does not meet most definitions of "miscarriage of justice". The CA took the opportunity to lay down guidelines in such cases: where there were two or more unexplained infant deaths in a family, no cogent evidence and serious disagreement between expert witnesses, then the parents should not be prosecuted for murder. They said experts should be more open-minded, less dogmatic and where there is disagreement among reputable experts, prosecutors should be cautious. The CA added, in *R. v Kai-Whitewind* (2005) that this did not automatically mean a prosecution should not be brought. It was for the jury to decide in a dispute between experts. There was ample evidence here to justify the guilty verdict. See also *Bowman* (2006).

Of course medical experts are also used in civil cases of alleged child abuse, where a local authority applies to the family courts to take a child or children into care, for their own protection. Sir Roy Meadow and those who followed his theories had given evidence at hundreds of such hearings, which were held in private, out of the scrutiny of reporters.

After *Clark*, the Attorney General announced a review of 258 convictions in the previous 10 years, priority being given to 50 cases where the parent was still in prison. As a result of this, 28 people had their convictions referred to the CCRC and six of these asked for their convictions to be referred back to the CA. Civil care cases were also reviewed, since there were many where Professor Meadows had given evidence, after which a child was taken into local authority care. Only one care order was changed on review, however. Also as a result of the widespread concern prompted by these cases, a group of agencies involved in sudden infant deaths established a working group, chaired by Baroness Kennedy. Its recommendations had a wider impact than on infant deaths alone.

1. Prosecution medical experts must disclose scientific data favourable to the defence.
2. They have a duty to ensure their evidence is sound and based on peer reviewed research. Medical experts should not use the courtroom to "fly their personal kites".
3. They must ensure they are independent and doctors should not give expert evidence on their own patients.
4. Doctors should be trained in the principles applied by the courts and the difference between civil and criminal courts.
5. Care should be taken in selecting the correct expert.
6. Doctors should be willing to say "I don't know".
7. Judges have a proactive duty to ensure these high standards are followed.
8. There should be a pre-trial meeting of experts.

12–107   For further detail, see the Royal College of Pathologists report, updated in 2016, and the article by Rowe.

Naturally, the public were scandalised by the fact that these convictions rested on the dogmatic and sometimes controversial beliefs of experts who were regarded as eminent in their field and who were later exposed as over-zealously applying their own over-generalised theories. Uncontrolled use of expert evidence had resulted in restrictions on its use in *civil* cases, as we have seen in the civil procedure chapter, by the Woolf reforms. Auld, in the 2001 *Review of the Criminal Courts* was also critical of experts. He had expressed concern that there was no single system of accreditation of expert witnesses and no requirement for them to have any qualifications. He thought there should be a single body with the following attributes: independence; verifiable standards of current competence; a code of conduct; and disciplinary powers of removal. Keogh commented that, by 2004, the Council for the Registration of Forensic Practitioners seemed to be satisfying these needs. The House of Commons Science & Technology Committee attributed Angela Cannings' wrongful conviction to systemic failures and recommended that judges should have a gate-keeping role, ensuring that evidence presented to juries is sufficiently reliable, as in the US Federal Rules of Evidence and US Supreme Court case law. Roberts (2009) said that the principal weakness concerning the reception of expert evidence was that its development had been based on pragmatism rather than principle. He called for a judicial statement of principle, which may depend on acknowledging that we have to use fundamentally different procedures from those used for normal testimony. The Law Commission wanted primary legislation on a "reliability test" to regulate the use of experts. In 2013, the Government announced its decision not to take forward the Commission's recommendations. Instead, they invited the Rule Committee to amend the CrimPR, from 2014, to require more information from those wishing to adduce expert evidence, placing judges in a better position to refuse to admit evidence which is irrelevant or not credible. (Law Commission implementation report 2014.)

False confessions

In addition to the many old pre-PACE miscarriages of justice caused by false   **12–108**
confession, such as Downing, above, there have been successful appeals of post-PACE convictions, where confessions have been obtained from unprotected vulnerable suspects. In 2009, Sean Hodgson was freed after 27 years of false imprisonment. While in prison for theft, he falsely confessed to the 1979 murder of Teresa de Simone. He retracted this confession. At his 1982 trial, his defence that he was a compulsive liar was not believed by the jury, though he had confessed to two nonexistent murders and other fictitious crimes. His 1983 application for leave to appeal was refused. Many confessions have been exposed as false by Professor Gisli Gudjonsson, the world expert in the phenomenon of false confessions: see his 2003 *Handbook*.

New techniques

Thankfully, exhibits from old trials are normally kept. Retesting them with new   **12–109**
DNA techniques has provided exculpatory evidence in a number of cases, not forgetting that in Hanratty's case it confirmed his *guilt*, of course. In November 2007, Ronald Castree was convicted of the 1975 murder of 11-year-old Lesley Molseed, after a DNA sample taken in connection with an unrelated offence was matched with a sperm sample on Lesley's underwear. Stephan Kisko had served 16 years of wrongful imprisonment for the murder, to which he falsely confessed

in 1976, after two days of questioning without a solicitor. Kisko had the mental and emotional age of a 12-year-old. In prison, he was beaten up and kept in solitary confinement for his own protection. His conviction was quashed, on evidence that he was infertile. He died in 1993, one year after returning home. Though Lesley's clothes were destroyed in 1985, the Forensic Science Service preserved sperm samples on adhesive tape. In 1994, two police officers were summoned on charges relating to non-disclosure of evidence but were not brought to trial. Sean Hodgson, above, was exculpated by DNA testing in 2008 that showed he could not be linked to 20 exhibits preserved from the 1979 crime scene. After his successful appeal, in 2009, an inquiry was launched. The DNA proved to be that of David Lace, who killed himself in 1988. His body was exhumed. He had also confessed to the 1979 murder but was not believed because he was one of seven men who confessed to it.

In addition to the many old pre-PACE miscarriages of justice caused by false confession, such as Downing, above, there have been successful appeals of post-PACE convictions, where confessions have been obtained from unprotected vulnerable suspects.

Laurence Elks, in his overview of the first ten years of the CCRC, commented that some causes of wrongful convictions have faded away, such as oppressive interviews, but some persist, such as late-returned briefs, where barristers receive too little notice of the case and provide an ineffective defence. There are new factors, such as rapid developments in expert evidence: see the review of his book.

Bibliography

12–110   Most important: *Westlaw* Current Awareness and *The Criminal Law Review* on Westlaw: articles AND case comments.

Archbold (Westlaw).

Archbold News.

A. Ashworth and M. Blake, "The Presumption of Innocence in English Criminal Law" [1996] Crim. L.R. 306; comment on *Grayson and Barnham v UK* [2009] Crim. L.R. 200 at [202].

A. Ashworth and M. Redmayne, *The Criminal Process* (4th edn. 2010).

Auld, *Review of the Criminal Courts of England and Wales* (2001), National Archives.

J. Baldwin, "Understanding Judge Ordered and Judge Directed Acquittals" [1997] Crim. L.R. 536.

J. Baker, *An Introduction to English Legal History* (Oxford: Oxford University Press, 2002).

D. Birch, "Suffering in Silence: A Cost–Benefit Analysis of s.34 of the Criminal Justice and Public Order Act 1994" [1999] Crim. L.R. 769.

W. Blackstone, *Commentaries on the Laws of England*, Vol. IV, *Of Public Wrongs*, originally 1769, facsimile edition (1979).

P. Cooper and D. Wurtzel, "A Day Late and a Dollar Short: In Search of an Intermediary Scheme for Vulnerable Defendants in England and Wales" [2013] Crim. L.R. 4; P. Cooper, C. Barryessa and C. Allely, "Understanding What the Defendant With Asperger's Syndrome Understood" (2016) 180 J.P.N. 795.

S. Cooper, "Appeals, Referrals and Substantial Injustice" [2009] Crim. L.R. 152.

D. Corker, "Disclosure Stripped Bare", *Archbold News*, Issue 9, 11 November 2004, p.6; D. Corker, G. Tombs and T. Chisholm. "Sections 71 and 72 of the Serious Organised Crime and Police Act 2005..." [2009] Crim. L.R. 261.

Criminal Court Statistics Quarterly.

Criminal Justice Statistics are issued quarterly by National Statistics for the Ministry of Justice: *https://www.gov.uk/government/collections/criminal-justice-statistics*.

The Crown Court Compendium (2017), Judiciary website.

P. Darbyshire, "An Essay on the Importance and Neglect of the Magistracy" [1997] Crim. L.R. 627; "The Mischief of Plea Bargaining and Sentencing Rewards" [2000] Crim. L.R. 895; "Transparency in Getting the Accused to Plead Guilty Early" [2006] C.L.J. 48; *Sitting in Judgment: The Working Lives of Judges* (Oxford: Hart Publishing, 2011); "Judicial Case Management in Ten Crown Courts" [2014] Crim. L.R. 30.

J. de Grazia and K. Hyland, "Mainstreaming the Use of Assisting Offenders: How to make SOCPA 2005 section 23 and section 24 work" [2011] Crim. L.R. 357.

I. Dennis, "Reverse Onuses and the Presumption of Innocence..." [2005] Crim. L.R. 901; "The Right to Confront Witnesses...[2010] Crim. L.R. 255; comment on the Law Commission paper on appeals [2010] Crim. L.R. 669; "Quashing Acquittals..." [2014] Crim L.R. 247.

R.L. Denyer QC, "Non-Compliance with Case Management..." [2008] Crim. L.R. 784.

P. Duff, "CCRC and Deference to the Courts..." [2001] Crim L.R 341, examining Nobles and Schiff (1995) 58 M.L.R. 299.

P. Dyer and HHJ M. Hopmeier, "Time to Agree Terms?" N.L.J., 13 September 2013, online.

A. Edwards, "LASPO Act..." [2012] Crim. L.R. 584; "Legal Update..." (2013) L.S. Gaz. 21 Jan, 18; A. Edwards and M. Hardcastle, "The Changing Status of the Defence Solicitor" [2016] Crim. L.R. 830.

L. Elks, "The CCRC—Lessons from Experience" Archbold News, 8 March 2004; book review of M. Naughton (ed.) *The Criminal Cases Review Commission: hope for the innocent?* (2010) Archbold News (1), p.5; *Righting Miscarriages of Justice? Ten Years of the Criminal Cases Review Commission*, published by JUSTICE and reviewed at [2009] Crim. L.R. 52.

L. Ellison and J. Wheatcroft, "'Could You Ask Me That in a Different Way Please?' [2010] Crim. L.R. 823.

R. Epstein, "Restorative Justice: The Parliamentary Report" (2016) 180 J.P.N. 775.

S. Field and D. Eady, "Truth Finding and the Adversarial Tradition..." [2017] Crim. L.R. 292.

M.L. Friedland, *Double Jeopardy* (Oxford: Clarendon Press, 1969).

F. Gibb, "Justice's quality controller" on the CCRC, *The Times*, 23 November 2004; "We are determined to do more ourselves", *The Times*, 8 April 2008; "Chief prosecutor demands curb on police cautions", *The Times*, 8 November 2009; "First criminal trial without a jury for 400 years starts", *The Times*, 13 January 2010; "Shortfalls in CPS leads to hundreds of defendants avoiding trial", *The Times*, 16 March 2010.

G. Gudjonsson, *The Psychology of Interrogations & Confessions: A Handbook* (Chichester: Wiley, 2002).

E. Henderson, "All the Proper Protections—The Court of Appeal Rewrites the Rules for the Cross-Examination of Vulnerable Witnesses" [2014] Crim. L.R. 93; "Taking Conrol of Cross-examination...of Vulnerable People" [2016] Crim. L.R. 181.

A. Herbert, "Mode of Trial and Magistrates' Sentencing Powers" [2003] Crim. L.R. 314.

Home Office, *Review of Delay in the Criminal Justice System*, 1997 (The Narey Report); *Narrowing the Justice Gap*, 2002.

House of Commons Justice Committee, *Criminal Cases Review Commission Twelfth Report of Session 2014–15*, 17 March 2015.

House of Commons Public Accounts Committee, *Efficiency in the Criminal Justice System, First Report of Session 2016–17*, HC 72, May 2016.

L.C. Hoyano, "What is Balanced on the Scales of Justice? In Search of the Essence of the Right to a Fair Trial" [2014] Crim. L.R. 4; L. Hoyano and A. Rafferty, "Rationing Defence Intermediaries..." [2017] Crim. L.R. 93.

P. Hungerford-Welch, "Prosecution Interviews of Defence Witnesses" [2010] Crim. L.R. 690.

P. Hynes and M. Elkins, "Suggestions for Reform to the Simple Cautioning Procedure" [2013] Crim. L.R. 966.

J. Jacobson, G. Hunter and A. Kirby, *Inside Crown Court* (Bristol: Policy Press, 2015).

Lord Judge CJ, "The Criminal Justice System in England and Wales—Time for Change?" speech, 5 November 2008; *Review of the Administration of Justice* (2010).

R.F. Julian, "Judicial Perspectives in Serious Fraud Cases . . ." [2008] Crim. L.R. 764.

JUSTICE, *Miscarriages of Justice* (1989).

Andrew Keogh, "Experts in the dock" (2004) 154 N.L.J. 1762; "Police state or proportionate response" (2006) 156 N.L.J. 81; "Witness anonymity—balancing rights" (2006) 156 N.L.J. 1337; "Lights, camera, action!" (2009) 159 N.L.J. 9.

Law Commission Consultation Paper *The High Court's Jurisdiction in Relation to Criminal Proceedings* (2007 Law Com. CP 184). See editorial comment at [2008] Crim. L.R. 175.

K. Laird, commentary on *Schatschaschwili* at [2017] Crim. L.R. 140.

M. Lake, "Retreat from due process" (2006) 156 N.L.J. 86; "The supergrass system—a metamorphosis" (2006) 156 N.L.J. 908.

J.H. Langbein, *Torture and the Law of Proof* (Chicago: University of Chicago Press, 1977).

G. Langdon-Down, "A voice for the weak in court trials", *The Times*, 16 July 2002.

L. Leigh, "Lurking Doubt and the Safety of Convictions" [2006] Crim. L.R. 809.

F. Leverick, "Sentence Discounting for Guilty Pleas..." [2014] Crim. L.R. 338.

Leveson LJ, "The Roscoe Lecture, Criminal justice in the 21st century," 29 November 2010; Speech on expert evidence, 18 November 2010; as President of the QBD, *Review of Efficiency in Criminal Proceedings*, January 2015, Judiciary website.

Magna Carta, British library website; several judicial lectures and speeches in 2015, on the UKSC and Judiciary websites.

J. McEwan, "Vulnerable Defendants and the Fairness of Trials" [2013] Crim. L.R. 100.

R. Martin, "The Recent Supergrass Controversy…" [2013] Crim. L.R. 273.

M. Narey, *Review of Delay in the Criminal Justice System*, Home Office (1997) National Archives.

R. Nobles and D. Schiff, "The Criminal Cases Review Commission…" [2005] Crim. L.R. 173.

NSPCC and Witness Support, *In their Own Words* (2004).

D. Ormerod, comment on *Mayers* [2009] Crim. L.R. 272. D. Ormerod, A. Waterman and R. Forston, "Prosecution Appeals—Too Much of a Good Thing?" [2010] Crim. L.R. 169; D. Ormerod, A.L.T. Choo and R.L. Easter, "The "Witness Anonymity" and "Investigation Anonymity" provisions" [2010] Crim. L.R. 368; editorial [2012] Crim. L.R. 317.

N. Padfield, "Deferred Prosecution Agreements" [2016] Crim. L.R. 449.

R. Pattenden, "Prosecution Appeals Against Judges' Rulings" [2000] Crim. L.R. 971; "Pre-verdict judicial fact-finding in criminal trials with juries" (2009) 29(1) O.J.L.S. 1–24; "The Standards of Review for Mistake of Fact in the Court of Appeal, Criminal Division" [2009] Crim. L.R. 15.

H. Quirk, "The significance of culture in criminal procedure reform: Why the revised disclosure scheme cannot work" (2006) 10 *International Journal of Evidence and Proof* 42; "Prisoners, Pardons and Politics" [2009] Crim. L.R. 648; *The Rise and Fall of the Right to Silence: Principle, Politics and Policy* (Abingdon: Routledge, 2016).

A. Roberts, "Rejecting General Acceptance, Confounding the Gate-keeper: the Law Commission and Expert Evidence" [2009] Crim. L.R. 551; comment on *R. v Daniels* [2011] Crim. L.R. 556 at p.560.

P. Roberts and C. Saunders, "Introducing Pre-Trial Witness Interviews…" [2008] Crim. L.R. 831.

J. Rowe, "Expert Evidence and sudden infant deaths: where next?" (2004) 154 N.L.J. 1757.

Royal College of Pathologists, *Sudden unexpected death in infancy and childhood: Multi-agency guidelines for care and investigation* (2nd edn. November 2016).

The Royal Commission on Criminal Justice Report, Cm.2263 (1993), National Archives.

A. Sanders, R. Young and M. Burton, *Criminal Justice*, 4th edn (Oxford: Oxford University Press, 2010).

A. Sanders "The CPS – 30 Years On" [2016] Crim. L.R. 82.

M. Sato, C. Hoyle and N. Speechley, "Wrongful Convictions of Refugees and Asylum Seekers…" [2017] Crim. L.R. 106.

Sentencing Council, *Allocation Guideline*, effective 1 March 2016.

B. Shapiro, *Beyond Reasonable Doubt and Probable Cause* (California: University of California Press, 1991).

Lord Shawcross's statement is taken from *Hansard* and quoted in the *Code for Crown Prosecutors*.

G. Slapper, "You may not be prejudiced, my Lord, but you look it", *The Times,* 25 April 2007.
J.C. Smith, "The Criminal Appeal Act 1995: (1) Appeals Against Conviction" [1995] Crim. L.R. 920.
J.R. Spencer QC, "The Case for a Code of Criminal Procedure" [2000] Crim. L.R. 519; "Does Our Present Criminal Appeal System Make Sense?" [2006] Crim. L.R. 677; "Compensation for Wrongful Imprisonment" [2010] Crim. L.R. 803; "Farewell to the surprise witness" (2010) 4 Arch. Rev 4; "Controlling the Discretion to Prosecute" 71 (2012) *Cambridge Law Journal* 27.
K. Starmer, on *A v Secretary of State for the Home Department*: (2005) 155 N.L.J. 1911; "Finality in Criminal Justice...?" [2012] Crim. L.R. 526, speech to the Bingham Centre on the Rule of Law, 16 July 2013.
Taylor's comment on Stock [2009] Crim. L.R. 188, at 190.
D.A. Thomas, comment on *R. (on the application of H, A and O) v Southampton Youth Court* [2005] Crim. L.R. 398.
R. Thompson, "Grave Crimes—Now It's Personal" [2012] Crim. L.R. 30.
N. Vamos, "Please Don't Call it 'Plea Bargaining'" [2009] Crim. L.R. 617.
D. Wurtzel, "Intermediaries for Defendants: Recent Developments" [2017] Crim. L.R. 463.
G. Zellick, "The Criminal Cases Review Commission and the Court of Appeal: The Commission's Perspective" [2005] Crim. L.R. 937.

Individual miscarriages of justice

12-111 On Derek Bentley: D. Pannick, *The Times*, 11 February 1997.
The Birmingham Six: *Counsel*, April 1991, p.8; (1990) 140 N.L.J. 160.
The Bridgewater Three: *The Times*, 22 February 1997; *R. v Home Secretary Ex p. Hickey* (1997).
On Robert Brown: M. Petty, "They Took my Life ...", *The Times*, 22 July 2004.
On Angela Cannings: J. Bale, "Mother who killed sons...", *The Times*, 17 April 2002.
Sally Clark, news reports, 30 January 2003; J. Batt, *Stolen Innocence* (2004).
Stephen Downing, (2000) 164 J.P.N. 909; news in 2000; on Ronald Castree, the real killer: "Justice at last as DNA traps girl's murderer 32 years on", *The Times*, 13 November 2007.
Guildford Four: (1989) 139 N.L.J. 1441 and news media.
Hanratty: Law Report, above; news, week beginning 15 April 2002.
Sean Hodgson: S. O'Neill, *The Times*, 19 March 2009. On the real killer: S. O'Neill, "Barmaid's killer...", *The Times*, 18 September 2009.
The Maguires: *The Times*, 17 July 1990.
Stephan Kisko: *The Times*, 18 February 1992; D. Sanderson, "Man arrested over 1975 murder", *The Times*, 6 November 2006.
Victor Nealon: BBC News website, 18 June 2014.
Patrick Nicholls: D. Kennedy, "Court clears man of murder after 23 years in jail", *The Times*, 13 June 1998.
The Winchester Three: (1990) 140 N.L.J. 164.

Further reading and sources for updating this chapter

Free updates of this book are available on the Sweet & Maxwell website: **12–112**
http://uklawstudent.thomsonreuters.com.

Summary and revision: P. Darbyshire, *Nutshells English Legal System*, 10th edn (London: Sweet & Maxwell, 2016).

Attorney General's Office web-pages.

Audit Commission *http://www.audit-commission.gov.uk.*

Crown Prosecution Service.

HM Courts and Tribunals Service.

Home Office.

Judiciary website: "Better Case Management" pages; judges' speeches; Judicial College and publications.

Law Commission.

Ministry of Justice, especially CrimPR and directions web-pages.

Parliament website: bills; reports of the Justice Committee and Public Accounts Committee.

Sentencing Council: *https://www.sentencingcouncil.org.uk/.*

Victim Support *http://www.victimsupport.org.uk.*

Youth Justice Board.

On miscarriages of justice generally

Criminal Cases Review Commission.   **12–113**

INNOCENT: *http://www.innocent.org.uk.*

R. Buxton, "Miscarriages of Justice and the Court of Appeal" (1993) 109 L.Q.R. 66.

J.J. Eddleston, *Blind Justice* (Santa Barbara, CA.: ABC-CLIO, 2000).

B. Forst, *Errors of Justice* (Cambridge: Cambridge University Press, 2004).

D. Jessel, *Trial and Error* (Headline Book Publishing, 1994).

JUSTICE, *Miscarriages of Justice* (1989); *Remedying Miscarriages of Justice.*

R. Kee, *Trial and Error* (London: Penguin Books Ltd, 1989).

R. Nobles and D. Schiff, *Understanding Miscarriages of Justice* (Oxford: Oxford University Press, 2001).

M. Naughton, *The Innocent and the Criminal Justice System* (Basingstoke: Palgrave Macmillan, 2013).

B. Woffinden, *Miscarriages of Justice* (Philadelphia, PA.: Coronet Books, 1989).

PART 4

PROFESSIONALS IN THE LAW

CHAPTER 13

Lawyers

"The quality of solicitors and counsel varies as does the quality of wine from 'unfit to drink' to vintage. Vintage tends to be very expensive beyond the means of the ordinary litigant. Most must be satisfied with 'plonk'" (Lightman J, 2003).

"I was called to the Bar in 1963 . . . It was a privilege to have been a barrister. In 25 years in practice in what is a very competitive profession only one dirty trick was played on me by another advocate. But . . . some of those who started with me made careers as advocates in criminal courts but a large number who wanted to did not. It was then as it is now a cruel profession" (Lord Judge CJ, 2009).

1. BARRISTERS AND SOLICITORS

The odd characteristic of the English legal profession is that it is divided into two **13-001** main branches, barristers and solicitors. This makes it very unusual but not unique, world-wide. For centuries, each side has enjoyed certain protected monopolies and restrictive practices but, since 1985, most of these have been abolished by degrees. This and the aim of the Legal Services Act 2007 to liberate lawyers' business structures, have the potential to blur the division. At the end of the chapter, we turn to examine the arguments for and against fusing the divided profession. To complicate the picture, the progressive demolition of those monopolies and restrictive practices has permitted the very significant development of competing types of lawyer, such as licensed conveyancers, legal executives, patent agents and paralegals, plus firms of non-lawyers such as claims handlers.

The barrister is usually thought of as an advocate. Until 1990, barristers had virtually exclusive rights of audience before all the senior courts (Crown Court and above). They are known as "counsel" (singular and plural, like sheep). In 2015 there were 15,899 barristers with practising certificates, of whom 12,757 (80.2 per cent) were self-employed.

The solicitor has a right to appear as an advocate in the magistrates' court and County Court and may, since the Courts and Legal Services Act 1990 (CLSA), qualify for rights of audience at all levels, but she is traditionally more familiar to the public in her role as a general legal adviser. In February 2017, there were almost 179,647 solicitors, of whom around 136,596 held practising certificates. Members of the public are able to call at a solicitor's office (or go online) and seek advice, whereas a barrister could, until 2004, only be consulted indirectly through a solicitor, except by specified clients, and most clients still access a barrister via a solicitor. The solicitor is sometimes likened to a general practitioner doctor and the barrister to a consultant. The analogy must not be taken too far, since the legal knowledge of the newly qualified barrister will not equal that of the senior partners of a firm of solicitors. Often, the solicitor is more of a specialist than the barrister.

Apart from the independent barristers and solicitors in private practice, a large number of other lawyers are employed in solicitors' firms or law firms: barristers, legal executives and paralegals. Many are also employed in the public sector, such as central and local government, in the CPS, and in private sector commerce, banking, industry and education. As the practising rules have been progressively relaxed, so more barristers do not work in the independent Bar. For instance, in 2015, there were 2,897 employed barristers (18.2 per cent of practising barristers). Since 2011, when the Legal Services Act permitted alternative business structures, there are more firms with all types of lawyer in partnership together, or employed by, or in partnership with other non-lawyers, or owned by commercial organisations. The breakdown of firms is on the Solicitors Regulation Authority (SRA) website. As of February 2017, there were 10,387 solicitor firms: 2,582 sole practitioners, 1,921 partnerships, 4,290 incorporated companies, 1,552 LLPs (limited liability partnerships) and 42 others.

2.   TRAINING, ENTRY AND DIVERSITY

13–002   The Solicitors Regulation Authority and the Bar Standards Board regulate the training for solicitors and barristers. Both must undertake an academic stage (*qualifying* law degree or equivalent, covering the seven foundations of legal knowledge) and a vocational (professional) stage of qualification and training. A Legal Education and Training Review (LETR) was published in 2013, after extensive research and consultation. At the time of writing, 2017, training requirements are in transition and still under consultation but the basic pattern will not change.

The LETR website lists their detailed findings and recommendations but here are some highlights. They found insufficient assurance of consistent quality of outcomes and standards of assessment; knowledge and skills gaps in ethics, communication, management and equality and diversity awareness and limits on horizontal and vertical mobility for lawyers, which would hamper them in the increasingly fluid marketplace that I describe below. The recommendations were mainly about setting a common framework (across the professions) of appropriate learning outcomes, matched to an occupational analysis of the knowledge, skills and attributes that lawyers need, and publishing guidance and standards alongside them. They recommended professional standards for internships and work experience so that these complied with requirements for access and diversity. They noted the increasing number of paralegals (explored below) and recommended further work on developing licensed paralegal schemes. They encouraged development of apprenticeships for non-graduates as a means of promoting diversity. Some apprenticeships have now been launched. The LETR found lawyers' continuing professional development arrangements were out of line with modern professional requirements and "leading edge" training in other jurisdictions.

Barristers

In March 2017 the Bar Standards Board (BSB) authorised future training routes 13–003 for barristers. They will retain the three stages: academic, vocational and work-based learning. A would-be barrister must register as a student member of one of the Inns of Court, Gray's Inn, Lincoln's Inn, Inner Temple and Middle Temple, who have the exclusive power to call a person to the Bar. Students must normally obtain a qualifying law degree, as the academic stage, and then complete the one-year Bar Professional Training Course (BPTC) or complete it over two years, part-time, as the vocational stage. They are then called to the Bar in their Inn. Those without a law degree have to pass a one-year course, the Common Professional Examination (CPE) or Graduate Diploma in Law (GDL), before passing a Bar Course Aptitude Test (resulting from the LETR) to be allowed to enter the BPTC course (still in place but under review in 2017). Assessments are centrally organised. The BPTC may be combined with a master's degree. (It is proposed that in future, the BPTC *may* be in 2 stages, with a knowledge-based learning stage which must be passed before proceeding to a practical skill-based stage). The student may then be called to the Bar at their Inn of Court, provided they have attended 12 dining or educational sessions in their Inn. This quaint requirement to dine in one's Inn is a relic of the Inns' history. They were residential educational colleges that provided legal education in the common law, practised in the courts, in the era when the universities only provided an education in Roman law. After call, the student has to undergo vocational training known as pupillage. This involves understudying a barrister or work in another approved organisation, in day-to-day practice, for 12 months. In the first six months they must pass an advocacy course. Pupils must be paid a minimum wage of £12,000 (2017) and may practise and appear as an advocate in the second six months. They cannot enter the second six months unless they have been called to the Bar and they must attend a practice management course. Students entering employment may undergo pupillage as an employee. All barristers are required to obtain and renew a practising certificate and all are required to complete a forensic accountancy course during the first three years of practice. All are required to undertake continuing professional development. Following LETR, this must now be outcomes-based. The new CPD scheme commenced in January 2017 and is on the Bar Standards Board (BSB) website.

Solicitors

The usual method of entry is a qualifying law degree and then a one-year Legal 13–004 Practice Course (LPC), or by taking a four-year law degree. The LPC is more flexible from 2009. It is split into two parts and may be taken in stages, with different providers. The first part covers essential practice areas and the second contains vocational electives. Evaluation of achievement is by a statement of outcomes. Students can tailor their course to suit their needs. Non-law graduates, or those with foreign degrees or non-standard qualifications complete a one-year conversion course (CPE or GDL, as above) before the LPC. In 2004, approval was given to the first courses geared to the needs of individual big firms, such as Linklaters and Clifford Chance. Block exemptions from parts of qualification or training have been granted to groups such as legal executives and magistrates' legal advisers. Under the new regime, "knowledge and skills outcomes" can be recognised as having been achieved through assessed learning and work-based learning. At the time of writing, 2017, the Solicitors Regulation Authority is proposing introducing an independent assessment, the Solicitors Qualifying Examination. It is opposed by the Association of Law Teachers and Junior Lawyers.

Having completed both academic and vocational qualification stages, the student must serve as a trainee in a firm of solicitors, or alternative organisation, such as a local authority, or an in-house legal department for two years full-time or four years part-time. The trainee must be closely supervised by a training principal (barrister or solicitor) and ought to be paid a recommended minimum salary of £20,913 in London and £18,547 outside (2016–2017). Trainees must attend a professional skills course during their training. It is again "outcomes based" and includes advocacy and oral presentation and case and transaction management, client care, communication, drafting, legal research, negotiation and so on. There is now a "part-time study" training contract, for those who are completing a law degree, CPE or LPC. When the student has completed the training contract, or alternative, she may be "admitted" to the roll of solicitors. The solicitor may not practise without an annual practising certificate individually issued by the Solicitors Regulation Authority (SRA). All solicitors must undergo regular continuing professional development. A new self-certification scheme came into force in November 2016, following the LET Review.

Entering the legal profession and career progress: numbers, diversity and cost

13–005   Numbers of lawyers escalated from about 1960. Since the 1990s, the growth in law graduates outstripped the growth in the profession, as can be seen from the 2015 statistics. In 2015, 15,431 people graduated in law in England and Wales. In 2015 5,457 entered trainee solicitor contracts and 6,077 new solicitors were admitted to the roll, representing a decline from 8,491 in 2008–2009 (Law Society statistics).

Entry to the Bar is *much* more difficult. The workload of the criminal Bar (half the Bar, at that time) declined in the 1990s. Since then and especially since 2012 there have been massive cuts in legally aided work. The Bar Standards Board website contains a "health warning", that about 3,000 people apply for pupillage each year and only about 433 pupillages are offered. In 2014-2015, 1,184 people were called to the Bar, representing a downturn from 1,629, in 2010-2011, and only 422 people entered pupillage. Bearing in mind that there were about 17,500 law graduates in 2012, *only 270 new barrister "tenants" were registered*, in 2014-2015. In other words, only 270 new barristers entered independent practice in chambers (Bar Standards Board statistics). All graduates in England and Wales face stiff competition from lawyers already qualified overseas. A very high proportion of new entrants each year transfer from overseas.

Women and non-whites

Entry to the profession is expensive and, historically, has been difficult for **13–006** disadvantaged groups. By the twenty-first century, however, non-whites represented over 10 per cent of solicitors and barristers, a greater proportion than was then in the general population of England and Wales. Women represented about a third of practising barristers and almost half of practising solicitors. Women have been the majority of law graduates since 1993.

In the 1980s and 1990s, many research studies demonstrated a bias in entering and progressing in the solicitors' profession, against women, ethnic minority applicants, those from new universities and from less privileged backgrounds, irrespective of academic performance, detailed in previous editions of this book. Non-whites had to make more applications than their white counterparts. Attitudes of the profession were exposed by Thomas in *Discriminating Lawyers* (2000). In 2002, the Law Society launched an Equality and Diversity Framework for Action, followed by more schemes, to provide scholarships to law students from disadvantaged backgrounds. By 2015, 15.5 per cent of solicitors with practising certificates were BME, compared with 5.5 per cent in 1999 and 3.1 per cent in 1993.

The Law Society conducted three surveys in 2010, on issues and barriers faced by minorities. They concluded there was a need for more role models and mentors. A disproportionate number of referrals to the Solicitors Regulation Authority (SRA) for discipline involve BME solicitors. The SRA said it was because they were more likely to be in smaller firms. BME groups are still disadvantaged in progressing within the profession, according to *Ethnic diversity in law firms: Understanding the barriers* (Law Society, 2010). A 2008 salary survey found a pay disparity between BME and white solicitors. Focus groups showed BME solicitors felt they had been ill-informed when embarking on their career and therefore felt they had made the wrong choices and missed career opportunities. "For many, finding a training contract involved several years and hundreds of applications." BMEs felt they had been channelled towards immigration, family, legally aided and personal injury work, which were less lucrative than company and commercial work. They felt they did not progress satisfactorily to partnerships within firms and that fact explained why disproportionate numbers of BMEs set up their own firms. Solicitors are meant to have used equality codes since the 1980s but, as earlier editions of this book recorded, did not make fast progress in eliminating discrimination in the 1980s or 1990s. Since 2011, the SRA has elevated equality and diversity to a mandatory principle for all solicitors: "You must run your business or carry out your role in a way that encourages equality of opportunity and respect for diversity".

Women as a percentage of solicitors are still increasing year on year and by **13–007** 2015 they accounted for two thirds of solicitors under 35 years old, 57 per cent of BME solicitors with practising certificates and 48 per cent of whites with practising certificates, compared with 1993, when women accounted for 27.6 per cent of solicitors. In 2017, the Law Society estimated that about one third of law firms were majority owned by women but only 33 per cent of partners are women, and they represent only 19 per cent of partners in the top 10 law firms. Partly because of this and partly because of the Judicial Diversity Task Force, described in the next chapter, many top law firms have set themselves targets of 30 per cent female partnerships in the near future. In 2016, women lawyers were paid 10.3 per cent on average less than males (Office for National Statistics pay gap tracker). In 2015, female commerce and industry in-house lawyers earned £75,000 on average, and males £100,000 on average (Law Society).

Half of 800 women solicitors surveyed by The Law Society and Association of Women Solicitors in 2010 feared their career prospects would suffer if they made use of family friendly policies: "Obstacles and barriers to the career development of women solicitors". The summary says:

"The survey … revealed that organisational culture, outdated perceptions of women, resistance to contemporary management practices such as flexible working, and perceptions of client expectations meant the legal sector was still very male dominated causing real issues for the retention and advancement of top female talent. Crucially, respondents felt that female solicitors achieving partner status had often sacrificed personal and family relationships and this was not considered to be a positive, beneficial or attractive aspect of career development for women in city firms. It resulted in women pursuing in-house or public sector positions in a bid to maintain a reasonable work-life balance."

13–008   In 2012, LexisNexis and the Law Society commissioned an international survey of women lawyers, *Women in the Law*. Women called for a culture change using new performance measures and abandoning male routes to promotion, and a proper acceptance of flexible working. The survey found an unconscious bias towards men. Many firms acknowledge that it is bad management not to tap into talent. See comment by Fiona Woolf, then President of the Law Society (2012).

Of the practising bar in 2016, 36.5 per cent were women and 12.7 per cent were BME. Women as a percentage of practising barristers have increased throughout the last five decades. They were 25 per cent in 1997. In 2016, 10 per cent of barristers (1,609) were Queen's Counsel ("silks", the elite of the Bar). Only 13.7 per cent were women and 10 per cent BME. Of the 113 QCs appointed in 2017, 31 were women and 16 were BME. *QC Appointments* immediately announced that it was commissioning research to see what deters women from applying for silk. Important empirical research by Blackwell (2015) showed that the 2004 reforms in the QC appointment system, explored below, had not improved the pattern of appointments but that could be because of lower rates of applicants. Since almost all senior judges and about a third of circuit judges are QCs, we return to these important statistics in the next chapter, because this is very detrimental to the judicial diversity.

Previous editions of this book detailed the sad and sometimes shocking history of discrimination at the Bar in the 1990s. In 2002, the Council of the Inns of Court agreed to measures to try to eliminate sex and race discrimination. The Inns' benchers were overwhelmingly white and male. There was a systematic bias in favour of whites in the award of scholarships and bursaries by the Inns.

As with solicitors, there is a large attrition rate of women barristers from practice. The Bar Council has been launching equality strategies since the 1980s. In 2012, the Bar Standards Board launched new equality and diversity rules but decided to write to all chambers in 2016, after they surveyed women barristers and found that two thirds of respondents reported having suffered harassment. Only a fifth reported it, fearing impact on their career. There were similar findings in gender discrimination. Four months later, the Minister of Justice said she was going to force the pace of change in diversifying the legal profession and the judiciary. In 2016, the Bar Standards Board said it may have to counter unconscious bias, as pupillage statistics show that whites and males as more likely to succeed in applications.

Cost and educational background: social exclusion

In 2014, Lord Neuberger, President of the Supreme Court, said the advancement of those with a less privileged economic, social and educational background was "the biggest diversity deficit and the most difficult inclusivity problem for the legal profession". In 2017, the fee for the BPTC (Bar Finals) was £13,500–18,000 and in 2016, the Chair of the Bar Council said the cost of qualifying, including living costs, could go up to £127,000. Many lawyers carry large debts by the time they qualify. Ironically, the 2000 report of the Policy Studies Institute Cohort study found that professional sponsorship was most likely to go to those from well-off families, with 74 per cent of Oxbridge graduates receiving LPC funding, compared with three per cent from new universities. Of trainees, 60 per cent were paid below the Law Society minimum, with the disabled, non-Oxbridge graduates and those from state schools paid the least. In 2016, the Sutton Trust said more than half the top partners in magic circle law firms were Oxbridge graduates and 43 per cent went to the most highly selective universities. Only 17 per cent of 100 QCs went to state school. Statistics compiled by Chambers Student Guide showed that 80 per cent of trainee solicitors in the top 124 law firms went to Russell Group (top 24) universities. In 2016, the first study on the Inns of Court and social mobility found that students from non-traditional backgrounds faced a lot of challenges, like not understanding the profession, as well as lack of money, which hampered them in getting work experience. It was suggested that the Bar could do more to help, such as funding mini-pupillages. In 2017 an all-party Parliamentary group on social mobility called for a ban on unpaid internships. In 2016, government statistics showed that lawyers who were Oxford graduates had median earnings of £61,500 five years after graduation, compared to £17,500 for graduates of Bradford.

In 2014, veteran Oxford graduate Geoffrey Bindman was struck by the generosity of law firms in sponsoring Oxford but asked "why the concentration on Oxbridge?" He said

> "they get the bulk of the funding and their graduates are favoured in the competition for traineeships. That prejudice is on the increase, at least so far as the Bar is concerned … 34.5% of new pupils in 2010–11 were from Oxbridge, whereas in the previous year the proportion was 23.7% … Dr. Louise Ashley of the Cass Business School recently carried out a study of prominent London law firms … they did not recruit from 'less prestigious' universities because they believed they were less academically gifted…They ignore the need for social inclusion".

Local authority discretionary grants, which used to fund many through the Bar exams (80 per cent of students in 1987) ceased decades ago. One grant recipient from a poor background was Cherie Booth QC, wife of Tony Blair PM who said the expense of going to the Bar discriminated against the poor (1997 Bar

13–009

Conference). In 2003, the Bar Council established a task force on funding entry to the Bar. Many new barristers cannot survive, because their earnings are less than their chambers rent. Hence, many drop out of the Bar within the first five years, with large debts. Until 2001, pupillage was unpaid.

The education bias extends further back than favouring Oxbridge graduates, to independent schooling. In June 2005, the Sutton Trust published a survey of senior judges, barristers at top chambers and partners in leading law firms. While seven per cent of schoolchildren in England and Wales attend private schools, two thirds of barristers sampled, three quarters of judges and half the solicitors had attended independent schools. Responding to such concerns, "Diversity in the Legal Services", published in 2005 by the DCA (now Ministry of Justice), encouraged leading firms and chambers to monitor diversity and to publish the details and urged them to look for recruits from a wider range of universities. The College of Law and the Sutton Trust funded a five-year *Pathways to Law* project to fund children from state schools whose parents were not professionals. In 2016, it was extended from sixth formers to years 10 and 11.

13–010 In 2007, the Bar Council published a report by Lord Neuberger, then a law lord, *Entry to the Bar Working Party Final Report*. He considered too many of the wrong people were attracted to the Bar and the image of the Bar put off the right people. He wanted to attract able people from state schools who did not think of the Bar as a career and did not meet professional people. His report made a number of recommendations, including a professional training loan scheme and training in selection procedures for all those selecting pupils and tenants. The Bar then announced a new package, including a placement programme to enable state school gifted children to learn about the Bar and courts.

Law apprenticeships were invented recently, to promote social mobility. They have been set up in law firms but only in 2017 did the BSB announce that it would start thinking about a Bar apprenticeship route. An example is the six year apprenticeship route leading to an LLB in legal practice and qualification as a solicitor, set up by City University and law firms. Similar programmes have been established by BPP and the University of Law. At the time of writing, 2017, the Inns of Court are conducting a feasibility study on launching a new law school, to provide a more affordable Bar Professional Training Course.

Obviously, disadvantaged groups progress poorly in other professions too. In 2009, the Labour Cabinet Office published *Unleashing Aspiration*, which disclosed that half of professional occupations are dominated by those from independent schools, who represent only seven per cent of the population. There is less social mobility now than post-war. The Coalition Cabinet published a report in 2010 on social exclusion, by Iain Duncan-Smith, making the same point. I dealt with this issue at length in 2011. I pointed out that most of the judges in my research sample were "baby boomers". Some came from very humble backgrounds and benefited from the huge growth of the legal profession, from 1960, and the upward social mobility of their generation. I pointed out that lawyers and the judiciary in the future could be *less* socially diverse than they are now.

Are we over-lawyered?

Between 1980 and 2011, the number of solicitors with practising certificates rose   **13–011**
by 210 per cent. Professor Mayson of the Legal Services Institute said in 2010
that we were over-lawyered, with 17,000 law graduates per year for 50 million
people, compared with 12,000 in Germany for 80 million people. In addition to
the thousands of home-grown lawyers in England and Wales, no fewer than an
astonishing quarter or so of admissions to the roll of solicitors came through the
Qualified Lawyers Transfer Scheme, especially because of City firms attracting
talent from overseas. In 2013, the Legal Services Board, contrary to Mayson, said
limits should not be placed on numbers entering the profession. The liberalised
legal services market would function best with a more flexible labour market.
There is a strong counter-argument that we are not over-lawyered. In a 2010
College of Law Podcast, the chief executive of Freshfields said demand for UK
qualified lawyers would not dissipate, because English law, along with NY law,
remained the law of choice for most global transactions. Many are made in
London and lawyers can move around the world and practise English law.

3. ORGANISATION AND REGULATION

The organisation of the two main branches of the legal profession is the   **13–012**
responsibility of two separate sets of governing bodies. Since 2010, they are
overseen by a new super-regulator, the Legal Services Board, created by the
Legal Services Act 2007, explained below, in section 7.

Barristers

The Inns of Court are administered by their senior members, Benchers. They are   **13–013**
close to the Royal Courts of Justice. The Inns originated around the fourteenth
century as residential colleges teaching the common law to advocates, when the
universities of Oxford and Cambridge only taught Roman law. They own and
administer valuable property in the Temple area from which most of London's
practising barristers rent their chambers. Every Bar student and barrister must
belong to an Inn. Students dine in their Inn on a few occasions and are called to
the Bar there.

The Bar Standards Board is the independent regulatory board of the Bar
Council, created in 2006, following the Clementi recommendations, explained
below. It sets training and entry standards and prescribes and enforces the Bar
Code of Conduct. The General Council of the Bar, known as "The Bar Council",
is the trade union of the Bar. Among its objectives are to develop and promote the
work of the Bar, to combat discrimination and disadvantage at the Bar, to
promote the Bar's interests with Government, international Bars and so on, and to
provide services for barristers, such as publications and conferences and practice
guidance. In addition, the six court circuits have their own Bar Associations, as
do specialist barristers. All practising barristers, however old, are called "junior
counsel" unless they have been appointed Queen's Counsel (QC). An elite group
of barristers, known as Treasury Counsel, plus the Attorney General's specialist

panels, are briefed to appear for the Government in public law cases and for the prosecution in top criminal cases. In the past, this system suffered two accusations. The first was a complaint that the selection system was secretive and discriminatory, favouring white males from a limited background, and the second was that Treasury Counsel were overpaid. A former circuit judge, in a report to the Attorney General in 2000, said they were often paid twice as much as the judges before whom they appeared and there was a second independent inquiry, in 2006, established by the Attorney. In response, the system has been reformed and the panels are recruited by open competition, detailed on the Attorney's web-pages.

It is normal for a "set" of independent barristers in chambers to share a clerk as a business manager and it is said that the clerk, or practice manager, can make or break the barrister. The barrister's clerk arranges work and negotiates the fee unless it is a legally aided case. An Institute of Barristers' Clerks represents clerks' interests. In 2000, the *Independent* reported that some clerks earned up to £350,000, far more than most barristers.

Solicitors

13–014   The Solicitors Regulation Authority was created in 2007, following the Clementi recommendations. It says its purpose is to protect the public by ensuring that solicitors meet high standards. They draft the entry standards and rules of professional conduct. The Law Society used to be the statutory regulator and disciplinary body for solicitors but, thanks to the 2007 Act, its only remaining function is as the solicitors' trade union, promoting their interests.

Legal executives and paralegals

13–015   The routine work of a solicitor's office is largely carried out by 22,000 trainee and practising legal executives plus hundreds of paralegals and they are significant fee earners in many practices. About 40 per cent of fee-earners in firms regulated by the Solicitors Regulation Authority are not solicitors or barristers. When most people go to a solicitor's office, they may think they see a solicitor but many are interviewed by a legal executive. Their regulatory and examining body is the Chartered Institute of Legal Executives. In 2016, they had a record number of graduates, 275, including fellows and advocates.

Recent decades have seen the rise of the paralegal. The Institute of Paralegals estimates that there are 300,000 employed in the UK. Small solicitors' firms have been "quietly facing tough competition from non-solicitor i.e., paralegal, law firms (PLFs) for years now", according to James O'Connell, solicitor and CEO of the Institute of Paralegals. He drew attention to the 6,500 paralegal firms that had developed over the previous 15 years.

> "Solicitors are losing market share to PLFs in numerous areas, eg uncontested divorces, will-writing, immigration advice, landlord repossessions, debt enforcement, and small and medium enterprise employment law advice." (2011)

The National Association of Licensed Paralegals has introduced a qualification process, detailed on their website. In 2013, Newcastle College launched a foundation degree in paralegal studies, the first UK course to be endorsed by them. There is an Institute of Professional Will Writers and in 2016, the Professional Paralegal Register was launched.

Increasing regulatory control over lawyers: the complaints system

The Law Society's hopeless struggle to regulate solicitors and respond to consumer complaints satisfactorily is almost too painful to describe and is the reason why the Legal Services Act 2007 was passed to restructure the regulation of all lawyers. Since the 1979 Royal Commission on Legal Services (RCLS) Report, there was growing governmental concern. Independent surveys exposed poor quality work, in 1995, 2000 and 2004. The Law Society, which used to be the solicitors' regulator as well as trade union, was failing to cope with a mounting backlog of complaints. The Practice Rules required solicitors' firms to provide an in-house complaints procedure. Research by Bristol University in 1998 found 80 per cent of clients sampled had not been told of such a procedure. There were highly publicised reports and TV documentaries throughout the 1990s that demonstrated solicitors' incapacity and unwillingness to respond to complaints. In 1999, the Legal Services Ombudsman, appointed under the Courts and Legal Services Act 1990 to oversee the complaints process, described it as "spiralling out of control". In 1998, Irvine LC warned the Society that he would ask Parliament for statutory power to take over regulation from the Society and this was granted in the Access to Justice Act 1999.

    In 2001, Minister David Lock gave a final written warning to the Society that it would lose its "privilege" of self-regulation if it did not radically improve matters but the Legal Services Ombudsman repeated this warning. She was satisfied with complaints handling in only 57 per cent of cases. In 2003, she again reported that the situation was "unacceptable". In 2004, Falconer LC gave her the additional job of Legal Services Complaints Commissioner and the power to fine the Law Society £1 million if it failed to deal adequately with complaints. A 2004 Consumers Association survey showed that almost all complainants were dissatisfied with complaints handling. One person described the Law Society as "a body drinking at the same waterhole as the legal hyenas it purports to be checking up on". In 2005, Ombudsman Zahida Mansoor reported that the Law Society "appears to struggle to maintain the basic quality standards that it should". The Society would be fined unless it drastically improved complaints handling. Despite the development of an independent regulatory section of the Law Society, the SRA, in her 2007 annual report, Mansoor said that complaints had still not been handled in accordance with her instructions. In 2007, an SRA survey found consumers considered solicitors to be under-regulated. The main complaints were communication, cost and delay. The SRA decided to publicise on its website details of solicitors found guilty of misconduct. Under the 2007 Act, the compensation limit went up.

Clementi on complaints and regulation

Through exasperation with solicitors' legendary arrogance and inability to regulate themselves, but also because of the attacks on the profession by the

13–016

13–017

Office of Fair Trading, Falconer LC established *The Review of the Regulatory Framework for Legal Services in England and Wales*, carried out in 2003–2004 by David Clementi. He was appointed to examine what form of regulation would be best to promote competition and innovation, serve consumer interests and make lawyers more accountable. In his 2004 Review, he remarked that existing arrangements did not prioritise the public interest. He complained of the "absolute cat's cradle" of 22 existing regulatory bodies for lawyers. Unsurprisingly, he suggested abolishing lawyers' right to self-regulation. There should be a new super-regulator, a Legal Services Board, chaired by a non-lawyer and accountable to Parliament. Its statutory objectives would include upholding the rule of law, promoting access to justice, protecting consumer interests and promoting competition. It would have the power to exercise all regulatory functions but would normally delegate these to the professional bodies. It would assess their rules, in consultation with the Office of Fair Trading. The Bar and Law Society would have to separate their regulatory functions from their trade union functions. All complaints would be made to an independent Office for Legal Complaints, to provide "quick and fair redress to consumers". It would have the power to investigate complaints, mediate between client and lawyers and make binding orders for redress. It would not get involved with discipline, as executed by the Solicitors' Disciplinary Tribunal. The Government accepted Clementi's recommendations and they were generally enacted in the Legal Services Act 2007, as described below, in section 7 of this chapter.

13–018   Following Clementi's recommendation, the Law Society quickly established an independent Legal Complaints Service and separated off their regulatory functions to the Solicitors Regulation Authority (SRA), as mentioned above. The Bar Standards Board was also introduced, to oversee the Bar Council's former regulatory functions. Under the Legal Services Act 2007 Pts 6 and 7, the Office for Legal Complaints came into operation in 2010. It covers all parts of the profession authorised under the 2007 Act. An Ombudsman scheme investigates and resolves complaints about legal services. The Ministry of Justice published a Baseline survey to assess the impact of legal services reform. The research found:

> "Thirty-four per cent of people in England and Wales aged 16+ were found to have used legal services in the last three years. Legal service users were generally content with their legal service providers and the services they provided. For example, 91% of users felt that they received a good service, 92% felt that their provider acted in their best interests and 92% were satisfied with the outcome of their matter." (Research Series 3/10, March 2010)

About a quarter felt the work had taken too long and a quarter thought it was too expensive. Depressingly, a 2011 survey by the Legal Services Board, the super-regulator, found that half of the dissatisfied clients surveyed had not been told about their service provider's complaints system, as they should have been, and a number had even been charged a fee to handle their complaints.

The Legal Ombudsman's office opened in 2010, not to be confused with the former Legal Services Ombudsman. It is a *lay* organisation with 350 staff, and replaces eight former bodies, generally composed of lawyers. Lawyers have eight weeks to resolve a complaint. The Ombudsman may order fees to be repaid, work to be re-done or compensation of up to £50,000 paid. In April 2017, the Solicitors

Regulation Authority announced that it is going to investigate how law firms deal with complaints. We return to the Clementi Review below in section 7, on its other topic, business structures.

4. WORK OF BARRISTERS AND SOLICITORS

The 2015 survey of *Innovation in Legal Services*, commissioned by the SRA and BSB found solicitors and barristers' work was as follows:

13–019

> "Among Solicitors…22.5 per cent of organisations described their 'main legal activity' as residential property/conveyancing. The next largest categories were criminal (9.0 per cent) and family and matrimonial (8.5 per cent) and litigation (8.1 per cent). Personal injury, commercial property and immigration and commercial and corporate work were slightly less commonly cited as organisations' main activity. Among Barristers' chambers criminal (22.4 per cent), family and matrimonial (15.4 per cent) and personal injury (9.0 per cent) dominated." (Enterprise Research Centre)

As we shall see later in section 7, legislation dismantling lawyer's monopolies and permitting new business structures has opened up new ways of working, as has new technology. In 2017, accountants Heywoods said that at least 800 lawyers are working for virtual firms, and city estate agents say that city law firms are shrinking their floor space. Legal news is full of examples of different types of lawyer teaming up to provide new services in new business models. We shall see in section 7, new "alternative business structures", permitted by the 2007 Act, are the most innovative firms.

Some barristers and solicitors have always been employed as in-house lawyers. In 2016, HSBC had the biggest team in the FTSE 100, with 1,109 lawyers.

Barristers

Most barristers are independent specialist advocates, capable of objectively prosecuting in a criminal case one day and defending the next; or working for a civil claimant one day and a defendant the next. Trial advocacy requires much office research and preparation of documents and skeleton arguments. Additionally, barristers are routinely asked to give a solicitor's client a written opinion or provide it direct to the client, as permitted recently. Some who specialise in planning, tax or employment may do most of their work from their offices (chambers), or home, almost never appearing in court. Over half of practising barristers work in London. The remainder operate from around 60 provincial centres, or purely online.

13–020

Until 2008, when forced to change their practice rules by the 2007 Act, barristers were not allowed to form partnerships, other than overseas. Those in independent practice normally shared (and still share) a set of chambers and normally share the clerk and team. When court hearings overlap, another barrister usually in the same chambers has to take the case at short notice. This is called a "late brief". From a low point of 1,919 barristers in 1960, the Bar has increased annually and, until recent years, had not lost business to solicitor advocates, because so few solicitors chose to qualify. Barristers' work has diversified in parallel with solicitors' work. The Access to Justice Act 1999, while seen as threatening some publicly funded work, permitted quality civil rights chambers to gain legal aid contracts for the first time, in the same way as firms of solicitors. Very significantly, the 1999 Act allowed *employed* barristers to appear in court and made it much easier for solicitor advocates to qualify. Like solicitors, the Bar have developed their own pro bono (free legal services) scheme, some of which is directed to working with volunteers on welfare law advice. The 2007 Act permits alternative business structures. These are at the forefront of innovation and are described in section 7. As with all lawyers, new technology has facilitated innovation. From 2017, the national direct access chambers, Clerksroom, will offer "pay as you go" video conferences with clients.

Solicitors

13–021   The trend of the 1980s and 1990s was towards having multiple solicitors in partnership or incorporated companies, and towards larger firms or consortia and this trend increased, partly because of legal aid contracts, which do not favour small firms. This forced solicitors to specialise. Sole practitioners declined by 22 per cent in 2012-2016, because of regulation and many have joined virtual law firms. Large London firms have hundreds of highly specialised partners. In 2016, Eversheds merged with an Atlanta firm to form a 2,700 lawyer partnership.

City solicitors advise on company formation and organisation, taxation, insolvency, intellectual property, pensions, insurance and financial regulation. Most large London firms are now multi-national. Many serve exclusively foreign clients, contributing £25.7 billion to the UK economy. The CityUK's 2016 report said the UK accounts for ten per cent of global legal services and was the most international market for legal services. Two of the four biggest global law firms are based there, as are 200 foreign law firms from 40 jurisdictions.

Many UK lawyers practice internationally, either from the UK or established overseas. English firms have offices in over 40 foreign countries. While the UK is still in the EU, the Rights of Establishment Directive 98/5/EC (implemented in 2000 and explained on the SRA and Europa websites) makes it easy for lawyers to open up offices in other EU states. Also, in 2011, in judgments against Belgium, Luxembourg, France, Germany, Greece and Austria, the Court of Justice of the EU reaffirmed that it is illegal for a member state to prohibit non-nationals from becoming notaries.

Solicitors all have rights of audience before magistrates' courts and the County Court. Additionally, since 1994 they may qualify for an advocacy certificate in the higher courts.

The rest of this chapter provides many examples of lawyers work.

5. PROFESSIONAL HIERARCHY

It is well worth reading Hazell's 1978 book, *The Bar on Trial*, to understand the   **13–022**
fusty profession that the pupil barrister entered in the 1970s and 1980s. This
explains everything about the Dickensian culture and career background of any
lawyer or judge who graduated and practised in that era. It also explains a great
deal about the entrenched quality of the divide in the legal profession. The
judiciary and the legal profession is organised in a hierarchy, symbolised in the
layout of the courtroom and historically supported by the professions'
monopolies and rules of etiquette and dress. In the courtroom, the judge, usually
an ex-barrister, sits on a raised dais. In old courtrooms such as Chester, this is
many feet above the Bar. Until 2008, High Court judges had five different sets of
gowns and two types of wig, for ceremony, different types of case and red letter
days (saints' days). Even in the 1980s, advocates addressed them in grovelling
language and some still do "May it please your lordship ...". A court observer
will still spot some grovellers. Queen's Counsel sit nearest to the judge, on the
front row. They wear a special wig, a long court coat and a silk gown. Lesser
barristers, 90 per cent of the Bar, known as junior barristers, sit behind them,
wearing a different horsehair wig and stuff gown. On the back of their gown is a
pocket, where, historically, the barrister's fee, a gift for services rendered
(honorarium), would be inserted by a grateful client, as this "gentlemen's
profession" could not be seen to soil their hands with money. If a solicitor
qualified to sit in these rows, as she could from 1994, as a solicitor-advocate, she
was not permitted to wear a wig, until 2007, and this was a great source of
annoyance. Solicitor advocates wear a different gown from barristers. Behind the
barristers and solicitor advocates sit the solicitors or, more likely, representatives,
traditionally called "outdoor clerks". Barristers still address one another in court
as "my learned friend" and solicitors as "my friend". An outsider could be still
forgiven for thinking that barristers are the superior profession, more learned
people who have passed more difficult exams, and that QCs are the very crème of
the intellectual crème of the law.

Barristers and solicitors are closely restricted in their professional conduct by   **13–023**
their practice rules. Generally, until direct access was permitted in 1994, a client
had to see a solicitor with their legal problem; they could not go direct to a
barrister. Historically, a barrister only met the lay client when the solicitor, or
solicitor's representative, was present, thus emphasising the isolation, as well as
the objectivity, of the barrister. In order to prevent barristers gaining unfair
advantage by cultivating the friendship of solicitors, there used to be a rule which
prevented a solicitor and barrister in a case from having lunch together. Separate
dining rooms were created even in the court buildings of the 1980s.

In a 2000 vote, most barristers chose to retain wigs, as enhancing the dignity
and solemnity of court proceedings and a formal sign of the advocate's status and
importance in the courtroom. This is despite the fact that Lord Woolf CJ thought
they were outmoded, Irvine LC expressed his distaste for wigs in civil disputes
and Lord Phillips CJ abolished judges' wigs in civil cases and dispensed with
most HC gowns from 2008. Solicitors, of course, regard all this as so much
snobbery. They expressed disappointment at Lord Falconer's 2004 decision not to

abolish QCs. Even employed barristers complained to Sir David Clementi that they felt like second class citizens compared with the independent Bar.

There used to be a rule, articulated in the 1969 case of *Rondel v Worsley* (1969) that barristers could not be sued for negligent work in court, or in preparation of court work. In *Arthur JS Hall & Co v Simons* (2002), the House of Lords abolished this protection as no longer in accord with public policy and being out of line with the liability of other professions, such as doctors, and with lawyers in other EU states. A corollary of this immunity was the rule that barristers did not sue for their fees. Historically, barristers were not contractually bound to solicitors but were paid an honorarium, or gift for services rendered. The Courts and Legal Services Act 1990 s.61, permitted barristers to enter into binding contracts. Finally, one result of the division of the legal profession is that no-one can practise as both a barrister and a solicitor at the same time although it is now possible to be doubly qualified. Since the Access to Justice Act 1999, however, it has become progressively easier to transfer.

6. DISMANTLING LAWYERS' MONOPOLIES AND RESTRICTIVE PRACTICES: BAR WARS

13–024   Since the mid-1970s, people questioned the desirability of allowing the legal profession to preserve its ancient monopolies, perceived as restrictive practices, limiting competition and consumer choice and allowing lawyers to overcharge. Margaret Thatcher, PM from 1979, assumed all monopolies and restrictive practices to be anti-competitive. New Labour, from 1997, shared that view. In 2003, European Commissioner Mario Monti warned that states would be taken to the European Court of Justice if they permitted unjustified restraints on competition. Notice, from the following elongated tale, what a slow struggle it has been to dismantle lawyers' restrictive practices and how both sides of the profession have passionately defended them on the ground that they best serve the public interest.

Abolishing solicitors' conveyancing monopoly

13–025   The Royal Commission on Legal Services 1979 found most solicitors' practices derived 40 to 60 per cent of their gross fee income from their legally protected conveyancing monopoly. Critics complained that it allowed solicitors to overcharge. They operated a scale of fees which meant that, for conveying an expensive property, however simple the work, they charged a large amount. Solicitors claimed that their training, professional ethics and compulsory indemnity insurance all protected the public.

The Commission disappointed critics by siding with solicitors but Thatcher's Farrand Committee recommended abolition. A system of licensed conveyancers was enacted in the Administration of Justice Act 1985. Solicitors perceived a much greater threat from conveyancing by banks and building societies, though. The Building Societies Act 1986 gave the Lord Chancellor the power to permit this but it remained unimplemented. A 1989 consultation paper proposed a simplified framework. Solicitors argued that the public would suffer from conflicts of interest, being persuaded to have their conveyancing done by their mortgage lender, who probably also sold them their house. They claimed that "unfair competition" from banks and building societies would extinguish most high street solicitors, thus denying the public easy access to legal services. The Government ignored them, promoting the Courts and Legal Services Act 1990 ss.34–53, which permits a system of licensed conveyancers. Most importantly, s.17(1) articulated the philosophy that you serve the consumer by widening choice.

> "The development of legal services in England and Wales (and in particular the development of advocacy, litigation, conveyancing and probate services) by making provision for new or better ways of providing such services and a wider choice of persons providing them, while maintaining the proper and efficient administration of justice."

Solicitors relaxed their advertising ban. Conveyancing costs fell dramatically. Solicitors began selling houses and found new areas of work. The profession has expanded each year. Solicitors retaliated, however, by attacking the Bar's monopoly over higher court audience rights, as we shall see.

Direct access to barristers and the abolition of solicitors' probate and litigation monopolies

Solicitors' statutory monopolies over probate and litigation work (negotiation and case management prior to trial) were abolished by the 1990 Act but this had no impact for decades, until these rights were granted to competing groups of lawyers. From 2014, legal executives, patent attorneys and trade mark attorneys and costs lawyers can be entered on the court record because they are all categories of lawyer who may now conduct litigation, under the LSA 2007.   **13–026**

The Bar had been contemplating for decades whether clients should be permitted direct access to barristers. It was permitted on a very limited basis in 1994, and has now been extended to advice, negotiation and drafting, as well as advocacy. There is a Direct Access Portal run by the Bar Council and many groups of barristers have their own portals. The Access to Justice Act 1999 permitted the Bar Council to authorise litigation so the only barrier was barristers' own practice rules. The BSB now authorises some barristers to litigate provided they satisfy training and other requirements. Westminster Law School carried out research in 2008. 90 per cent of users found that instructing a barrister direct provided better value for money. By 2016, there had been a six-fold increase in direct client work since 2011.

Abolishing the Bar's monopoly over higher court advocacy

Since County Courts were created by the County Courts Act 1846, solicitors have had rights of audience before them. In magistrates' courts, the vast majority of advocates are solicitors. Solicitors may appear in tribunals. Solicitors are by far the most numerous advocates but the public's image has always been the robed and bewigged barrister because, until 1994, they had a legally protected monopoly over rights of audience in the Crown Court and all senior courts, with   **13–027** certain exceptions. Senior court cases are generally more complex, time consuming and, importantly, lucrative. As barristers claimed to be superior advocates, one would expect that they would be trained in advocacy but this is not the case, until surprisingly recently, around 1990. In 2011, in *Sitting in Judgment*, I told some stories of poor advocacy, based on observational research. Anyone can test this for themselves by observing courts. An Advocacy Training Council was established in 2004.

Solicitors asked the Royal Commission on Legal Services 1976-1979 to extend their rights of audience to the Crown Court (at the very least). The Commission concluded that this would be against the public interest. Note their reasons because they are being re-argued in 2017 in the new row about quality of advocacy and in defence of a separate Bar, in the argument about fusion, below in section 8.

- Solicitors would destroy the livelihood of the junior Bar (90 per cent of the Bar), who derived 30–50 per cent of their income from criminal work. Also, the "offender requires the highest possible standard of representation which can only be provided by a specialist advocate".
- If it resulted in prosecuting or defending firms, this would lead to the loss of independence.
- It might lead to the development of large, specialist firms, which would be against the public interest.
- County Court trials, which solicitors were used to conducting, could not be compared with Crown Court jury trials, which required the skills of public speaking, a detailed knowledge of the law of evidence and the ability to cross-examine.
- Most solicitors' practices were not geared to providing advocacy services.
- Most solicitors could not absent themselves from their offices for most of the working day, sometimes for days on end.
- Such a change would be a step nearer to a fused legal profession, which the Royal Commission did not favour.

13–028   In the very week that the Government announced a review of solicitors' conveyancing monopoly, their trade union, the Law Society, retaliated by launching an attack on the Bar's audience rights. The two sides of the profession waged a bitter and farcical public debate, in the 1980s. To take the heat out of the atmosphere, the two sides established the *Committee on the Future of the Legal Profession*, (Marre Committee) in 1986. Lady Marre recommended extending solicitors' audience rights to the Crown Court.

The next watershed was the 1989 Lord Chancellor's consultation paper, *The Work and Organisation of the Legal Profession*. It acknowledged the Bar's arguments:

- Judges work without legal assistance, therefore rely on the strength and adequacy of advocacy.
- Judges need to trust advocates not to mislead the court.

- Judgments create precedents. Judges look to advocates to cite all relevant authorities. "The presentation of cogent legal argument is a highly skilled task requiring not only a knowledge of the law but also constant practice in advocacy."

It concluded that this did imply that rights of audience should be restricted to those who are properly trained, suitably experienced and subject to codes of conduct which maintain standards. Then Lord Mackay LC dropped his bombshell:

> "The basic premise is that the satisfaction of such requirements should, for the future, alone be the test for granting rights of audience; and not whether an advocate happened by initial qualification to be a lawyer, whether a barrister or a solicitor, and whether in private practice or employed." (para.5.8)

He said a system of advocacy certificates would be established, with professional bodies determining whether candidates had satisfied the requirements, such as exams. The LC, after consulting the judges, would determine which bodies would grant audience rights.

The judiciary, almost all ex-barristers, exploded with rage. They were deeply affronted, considering it was their exclusive prerogative to decide who could appear before them. The Bar Chairman warned of "grave constitutional dangers". Top judges were hysterical (in both senses). Lord Lane CJ called the consultation "one of the most sinister documents ever to emanate from government". He warned, famously, "Oppression does not stand on the doorstep with a toothbrush moustache and a swastika armband". Lord Donaldson MR added, "Get your tanks off my lawn!" Judges threatened a one-day strike. Solicitors retorted that judges were using a double standard, forgetting that solicitors were already advocates in the lower courts.

A watered-down version was enacted in the Courts and Legal Services Act **13–029** 1990. While s.27 provided that "appropriate authorised bodies" could grant advocacy rights, s.29 required them to be subjected to such a cumbersome machinery for approval as to be almost unworkable. By 1998, there were only 624 solicitor-advocates, out of 70,000 solicitors. This was partly because of the cost and the palaver of taking the course and exams. Some solicitors, with many years' advocacy experience in the magistrates' court, could see little point in making this effort which would place them in no better position than a newly qualified barrister.

In the meantime, by 1993, work for the youngest barristers was dropping, because of a reduction in criminal cases and competition in magistrates' courts from freelance solicitors who acted as agents for other solicitors. Solicitors preferred to use them because, unlike the Bar, they were prepared to guarantee an appearance and would not return a brief at the last moment. Experienced solicitors were more skilful than new barristers. Surprisingly, given the judicial backlash above, not much fuss was made when the Crime and Disorder Act 1998 granted audience rights to *non-lawyers* employed by the Crown Prosecution Service (CPS) in the magistrates' courts, which handle the bulk of criminal cases.

The "sorry saga" of employed lawyers—"a mouse of reform"

13–030   The 1990s saw the Law Society and the Crown Prosecution Service in a frustrating struggle to gain higher court audience rights for employed solicitors and for CPS employed barristers. To cut a six-year long story short, proponents argued that it was bizarre to deny audience rights to someone like the Director of Public Prosecutions, who had formerly been an eminent QC. CPS employees and employed solicitors were acceptable advocates in the lower courts so why not allow them higher court rights? The Bar argued that the interest of justice benefited from the use of private practice solicitors and counsel, hired ad hoc by the CPS, because they took independent decisions, unconstrained by CPS instructions. CPS in-house lawyers would strive to enhance their conviction rates.

In June 1998, the new Labour Lord Chancellor, Lord Irvine, produced a rocket of a consultation, *Rights of Audience and Rights to Conduct Litigation in England and Wales*, designed to propel the Dickensian Bar into the modern era. His language betrayed exasperation.

> "there remain features of the way the [legal] profession is organised which ... stifle innovation and maintain rigid structures, limiting consumer choice and increasing the expense of going to law ... members of the public often complain that they are required to hire two lawyers, where one would do ... The 1990 Act was intended to allow solicitors to obtain the right to appear in any court, thus increasing the public's choice of advocate; it was also intended to allow employed lawyers, such as Crown Prosecutors, to appear in the higher courts. However, there has been continuing opposition to these changes ... with the result that the Act has achieved virtually nothing. Eight years on, nearly all advocates in the higher courts are barristers in private practice.
>
> The failure of the Act's good intentions and the inadequacy of the mechanisms it put in place to extend rights of audience are best illustrated by the sorry saga of the Law Society's attempt to obtain rights of audience in the higher courts for employed solicitors ... After a prolonged gestation of six years to-ing and fro-ing ... a Byzantine procedure produced a mouse of reform: employed solicitors were allowed to appear in substantive proceedings in the higher courts, provided they were led by a lawyer in private practice... Our view is that all qualified barristers and qualified solicitors should in principle have the right to appear in any court."

13–031   Additional arguments in his paper were:

- Audience rights needed to be restricted because the consequence of using an untrained advocate might adversely affect the client, any other party and the tax payer.
- It was irrational that barristers lost audience rights on becoming employed and regained them when they returned to private practice.
- As for their argument that barristers provided high quality advocacy, there were concerns about standards. The Public Accounts Committee showed that, at some Crown Court Centres, 75 per cent of CPS instructions (briefs to barristers) had been returned. In a third of these cases, there was concern about the experience level of the new barrister who handled the case.
- The argument that junior barristers must be allowed to cut their teeth prosecuting in the Crown Court was inconsistent with arguments that the independent Bar provided uniformly high quality advocacy.

- Barristers should be employed because of their merits, not because they had a monopoly.
- Audience rights should be portable. Once a person had qualified, she should carry that qualification to any other branch of the profession.

The LC crystallised his plans in his 1998 White Paper, *Modernising Justice*, which accompanied the Access to Justice Bill and explained its background. The Bar and judges were stuck in a time-warp, again arguing that to allow a minister to decide audience rights breached the separation of powers and this was a judicial prerogative dating back to 1280. David Pannick QC, the eminent *Times* columnist, dismissed this:

> "[P]arliament can and does intervene to regulate the administration of justice in all other respects...because the public interest is most effectively, and democratically assessed by those we elect... rather than by barristers who have been appointed to the bench ... The special pleading of judges and barristers has had no persuasive effect on laypeople, save to reinforce their low opinion of the legal profession."
> (*The Times*, 1998)

The Access to Justice Act 1999

Backed by the Office of Fair Trading, Lord Irvine promoted the 1999 Act. Part III **13-032** granted audience rights to every barrister and solicitor in all proceedings, subject only to the qualification regulations and rules of conduct imposed by their professional bodies, and prohibited any restriction on the audience rights of all employed advocates. It made advocacy rights portable.

The Law Society and the Bar Council were forced to change their rules by 2000, to comply with the Act and permit higher court audience rights to employed barristers. The Law Society produced a new scheme designed to make it much easier for solicitors to train. By March 2017, 6,690 solicitors have higher court audience rights, which poses a significant threat to those barristers who depend on legal aid, as do barristers employed by the Crown Prosecution Service.

Bar Wars V – The Empire Strikes Back

From 2008, the Bar started attacking solicitor advocates' quality of advocacy and **13-033** some judges joined in. At the Bar Conference 2008, the chairman of the Criminal Bar Association said there had been a "huge rise" in the number of solicitors with higher court advocacy certificates and some were "truly appalling". Also, some CPS advocates who were leading murder prosecutions were barristers who left the Bar because they could not make more than a modest living. He said it was "upsetting" to watch "the destruction of the system" by "cheap and inadequate labour". In 2010, an independent review commissioned by the Law Society said that solicitor advocates' training was "not fit for purpose". A new accreditation scheme was developed. In 2011, an advisory group was established, to advise on what has become the Quality Assurance Scheme for Advocates (QASA), which requires all advocates, including QCs, to undergo compulsory re-accreditation every five years. Barristers were horrified when they realised that they too would be subjected to this scheme and they did everything possible to obstruct or boycott it. The scheme was challenged by judicial review but the High Court found that it was justified in the public interest and did not contravene the requirement for independent advocates: *Lumsdon v Legal Services Board* (2014).

Another new layer of quality control was added. From 2011, the CPS would only brief advocates who had satisfied its own quality assurance scheme and been admitted to its Advocates Panel. Their in-house employed advocates were also quality assessed. For a fascinating examination of how a barrister's working life has changed and a description of the *six* competency frameworks for advocates in 2009, see Lord Judge's 2009 Kalisher lecture, cited at the top of this chapter. By 2013, the Jeffrey review of independent criminal advocacy was established. The Legal Services Board responded that there was no need for Government intervention to protect the Bar. Unemployed barristers should be helped out of the profession or diversify. To make matters worse for the criminal Bar, they were rendered extremely insecure in 2013–2014 by large reductions or threatened reductions in their legal aid fees, by the Ministry of Justice. This is discussed in Ch.17. Sir Bill Jeffrey found as follows in his 2014 review:

- In the previous seven years, solicitor defence advocacy in contested trials had gone from 4% to 24% of contested trials and from 6% to 40% of guilty pleas. CPS in-house lawyers prosecuted in Crown Court trials.
- There was no hard evidence but consistent strong disquiet by judges.
- Barristers had 120 days of advocacy training before call; solicitors could appear in the Crown Court after 22 hours' training.
- The Legal Aid Agency could be more of a guarantor of quality.
- If only barristers would establish legal entities, they could compete for legal aid contracts.
- The number of practising advocates had increased as magistrates' business had dwindled.
- All Crown Court advocates should have a common training and continuation training.
- There should be a list of approved defence advocates.
- There should be research on the advocacy market and on quality.

13–034   In a 2014 lecture, Green J provided an interesting analysis: There was a schism at the Bar. Those doing privately funded work were thriving and that part of the Bar was recruiting. The legally aided Bar were in peril. There were falling advocacy standards, in both the Crown Court and magistrates' court, with criminal advocates taking on cases beyond their competence. Remuneration was poor and advocates were unprepared. The problem was systemic in the way legal aid was distributed. Solicitors' firms, instead of sending out their advocacy work to a trusted advocate were keeping it in-house to save money. As Jeffrey put it:

> "As it exists now, the market could scarcely be argued to be operating competitively or in such a way as to optimise quality. The group of providers who are manifestly better trained as specialist advocates are taking a diminishing share of the work, and are being beaten neither on price nor on quality."

There were other perverse incentives, for instance

"...selling litigation rights. Contract holding solicitor firms...will instruct an outside advocate but upon the basis that a portion of the advocacy fee is remitted to the client or the solicitor or split between the two."

So solicitors chose advocates who were prepared to split the fee, rather than according to their quality of advocacy. Also, fees had been cut. There was no solicitor to sit behind an advocate in court and report back to their firm on the quality of the advocacy. There had been highly publicised, horrific sex trials where advocates had subjected complainants to "quasi-gladiatorial" cross-examination. One judge had failed to stop this. There was regulatory inertia, with a failure to agree on the QASA scheme. The future of the self-employed Bar was unclear. There had been no help from Government on standards. A good job, then that academics and practitioners had developed the training and resources portal, The Advocates' Gateway, free to all.

This beggars belief but by 2017, QASA, meant to be implemented in December 2011, is still not in operation because different groups of lawyers cannot agree on how it will work and the Ministry of Justice is now deciding whether to set up an overlapping scheme of quality assurance for publicly funded work. In the meantime, in 2017, the Bar Standards Board introduced measures to improve youth court advocacy, including compulsory registration. This followed research by Wigzell, Kirby and Jacobson that exposed a "highly variable" quality of advocacy.

Queen's counsel "silks"

"[I]n the public perception the grant of silk is a licence to print money ... informed advisers wisely recommend prospective litigants ... to sue on the Continent ... In those countries at least equal justice is obtainable at a fraction of the cost" (The Hon. Mr Justice Lightman, 2003).

13–035

The status, first recognised in the sixteenth century, is bestowed by the Queen, exercising her prerogative power on the advice of the Lord Chancellor (LC). Until 2003, the LC held an annual competition. The change of status is, financially, something of a speculation. Once appointed, the QC is expected to appear only in the most complex and/or important cases. She is known as a "leader" because she is often accompanied by one, and sometimes two, junior counsel. There used to be a rule called the Two Counsel Rule whereby a QC had to pay a junior to appear as an assistant in court. This was abolished in 1977, following criticism by the Monopolies and Mergers Commission but it is still widely followed in practice. Becoming a QC is called "taking silk", since the status entitles the barrister to wear a silk gown, rather than a junior's "stuff" gown. QCs enjoy other privileges. Apart from being paid significantly higher fees, even in legally aided cases, they are entitled to sit in the front row of the courtroom. Indeed, in the old courtrooms in the Royal Courts of Justice, a gate separates that row from those behind. Apart from sitting closest to the judge, they also have the formal right to address her before any other advocate.

The appointment system for silks was again under scrutiny by Falconer LC in 2003–2004. The old criteria required candidates to have practised for 10 years, with at least five years' advocacy experience in the higher courts. This meant that solicitor advocates were not considered suitable until about 1999. The LC's criteria included outstanding ability as an advocate; high professional standing and respect; a high quality practice based on demanding cases, and demonstrably high earnings. The LC made "consultations" with the judiciary and the profession. Very few women and ethnic minorities applied. The Adam Smith Institute published a strong attack on the silk system, in Reeves' 1998 report, *Silk Cut*. They recommended abolition, for these reasons:

- The term "junior" for other barristers was misleading.
- Barristers employed in local authorities, the CPS and industry were not eligible.
- Very competent barristers might seldom appear before the consultant judges.
- Silks were (and are) about 10 per cent of the Bar. This kept out able juniors.
- Clients were lured into extra expense because they thought it would enhance their chances of success.
- Judges had criticised the waste of public money in using silks.
- Despite the abolition of the Two Counsel Rule, silks rarely appeared alone.
- Although silks were meant to be selected for their outstanding competence as advocates, the European Court of Justice had criticised the written submissions of British lawyers as unduly long and repetitive.
- Without silk, a free market in advocacy would prevail, with reputations dependent on competence.
- An archaic and misleading title was bestowed upon relatively few practitioners, which did nothing to enhance legal services.

In 1999, over 100 MPs, led by Andrew Dismore, started campaigning for abolition. Lord Irvine LC defended the award of silk as "the kite-mark of quality", enabling lawyers and clients to identify the leading members of the profession and to identify likely candidates for the judges' Bench. In 2000, the Law Society President condemned the rank as a perk for barristers. Unexpectedly, in the Bar's 2000 annual conference, they voted to reform it. From 1995, there had been increasing concern expressed in the press over the earnings of silks, especially legally aided for criminal defence, as "fat cats", with a number being paid millions of pounds a year in fees from the Legal Aid Fund. (See Ch.17.)

13–036   In 2002, the Lord Chancellor's Department published a consultation paper, *In the public interest?* This was provoked by a 2001 Office of Fair Trading report, *Competition in the Professions*. The OFT insisted that the QC system was anti-competitive, lacked quality control and was of little use to customers. The earning power and competitive position of barristers was enhanced but little extra value was offered to clients. It lacked quality control because the title QC was not removed from a barrister if standards dropped. The Law Society considered it inappropriate for the Queen to confer on members of a single private profession a public honour and rank which accorded them precedence. There was no logical reason why outstanding doctors or dentists should not be so honoured. Solicitors did not find the QC rank of use in selecting an advocate of guaranteed quality. They objected to the rank's being a reward for advocacy, when in litigation nowadays there was an emphasis on seeking an early *settlement*, usually engineered by solicitors. (This argument is all the more persuasive in 2017, incidentally.) They also objected to the selection process, which was then based on consultations with judges and lawyers, "the old boy network", rather than evidence.

In 2003, Lord Falconer LC (himself a QC, married to a QC) published yet another consultation, *Constitutional reform: the future of Queen's Counsel*. Two thirds of respondents were barristers or judges. Lord Falconer did not abolish the system but instead, he asked the Bar and Law Society to develop new schemes. The disappointed Law Society and the Bar agreed on a new scheme, from 2006, designed to improve fairness and transparency. "Secret soundings" with judges were replaced by a system with structured references from judges, practitioners and clients and self-assessment of required competencies. Selection is made by a panel of judges, lawyers and lay people. Poorly performing silks may have their title revoked.

The controversy over the QC system continues. In a 2008 survey of solicitors by the Law Society, over half considered that the rank "should become a broader mark of excellence among lawyers" and that the Law Society should withdraw its support if the rank was not open to a wider range of lawyers. Only one person regarded the new system as an improvement. The rank is restricted to advocates so solicitors have always felt niggled that it does not serve to promote the vast majority of them in any way. They feel it is yet another way in which the Bar asserts claims to be the superior profession.

7. LAWYERS' BUSINESS STRUCTURES: THE CLEMENTI REPORT, "TESCO LAW" AND THE LEGAL SERVICES ACT 2007

From 2004, Lord Falconer allowed banks, building societies and insurance companies to handle probate. He suggested supermarkets and other retailers should be able to provide legal services and appointed Sir David Clementi to conduct his review of regulation (discussed above) and lawyers' business structures. Commentators branded this as "Tesco law". In 2004, Clementi produced his report: *Review of the Regulatory Framework for Legal Services in England and Wales*. Above, we have already seen how his recommendations resulted in a new system of regulation and complaints handling. "The review," said Clementi, "favours a regulatory framework which permits a high degree of choice: choice both for the consumer, in where he goes for legal services, and for the lawyer, in the type of economic unit he works for." He recommended: 13–037

1. Lawyers of any kind should be allowed to practice together in Legal Disciplinary Practices. Managers could include non-lawyers. There would be a Head of Legal Practice and a Head of Finance and Administration. Non-lawyers would have to sign up to a code of practice prioritising clients. There should be a majority of lawyers in the management group but these could include any lawyers, including legal executives and licensed conveyancers.

2. Investment in LDPs could come from outside owners (e.g. Tesco/RAC) but they would need to be "fit to own" and there should be no conflict of interest. An insurance company could not own, say, a personal injury firm. The benefit of such investors would include fresh ideas, better attention to customer service than lawyers gave, and competition, and thus lower prices.
3. Multi Disciplinary Partnerships (MDPs) might be considered, once LDPs had been tested.

Consumer Bodies like the Office of Fair Trading were enthusiastic. The government promised legislation. The Law Society welcomed the proposals, especially for LDPs. They said Tesco law was not a threat. Statistics showed that many solicitors already found private practice a decreasingly attractive option. For most consumers, supermarkets were a good thing. The Bar welcomed competition but said they were concerned about the ethics of non-lawyers running a legal practice. Tesco law could encourage a compensation culture. They were very hostile to MDPs, fearing conflicts of interest. They said lawyers belonged to a profession yet Clementi had spoken of "the legal service *industry*". There was a danger of over-commercialising the law. A lawyer owed a duty not simply to his client but to the court. No country in the world favoured MDPs. The Legal Services Commission (the then legal aid regulator and funder) welcomed the proposals for regulation, saying a single independent regulator would better serve the needs of the vulnerable and the socially excluded. Tesco, in the meantime, had started offering DIY kits on some areas of the law.

A survey of 50 of the UK's top 100 commercial law firms found that one in five expected to take advantage of the multi-disciplinary partnership model and seek outside investment. One in 10 said they were likely to be floated on the stock exchange. In its 2005 White Paper, the Government broadly accepted Clementi's proposals: *The Future of Legal Services—Putting Consumers First*.

The Legal Services Act 2007 and its results

The Act

13–038 The resultant Legal Services Bill 2006–2007 was published in draft, to maximise consultation. The National Consumers Council lobbied parliamentarians to try to ensure that it was not watered down. Concern was expressed by some critics that the new setup would threaten the independence of the legal profession. The Legal Aid Practitioners Group argued the very important point that the proposed Legal Services Board's powers to direct the Law Society to take certain steps breached the UN Basic Principles of the Role of Lawyers, which stated:

> "Lawyers shall be entitled to form and join self-governing professional associations to represent their interests, promote their continuing education and training and protect their professional integrity. The executive body of the professional association shall be elected by its members and shall exercise its functions without external interference."

They also quoted The Council of Bars and Law Societies in Europe which said there were "overriding reasons for not permitting forms of integrated cooperation between lawyers and non-lawyers with relevantly different professional duties" (meaning multi-disciplinary practices): see Miller. Scrutiny of the draft bill by a joint committee of the Lords and Commons ensured that the Bill was substantially amended. The committee re-introduced public interest. By 2008, critics seemed content that their concerns over independence of the legal profession had been addressed in the 2007 Act: see Young (2008) and Ludlow (2007). Here are the concessions and main points:

- The LC can only make appointments to the Legal Services Board (LSB) after consulting the Lord Chief Justice.
- The LSB chair must be a lay person.
- The independence of the profession is an objective of the Act: s.1(1)(f).
- A legal disciplinary practice must have 75 per cent legally qualified managers.
- 75 per cent of shares must be held by lawyers.
- Other managers must be approved by the Law Society.
- Alternative business structures would be available from 2011 but in licensing them, account must be taken of the regulatory objective of improving access to justice. It is possible to limit percentage ownership by non-lawyers so there will be no 100 per cent Tesco Law.

Under the 2007 Act, "alternative business structures" were permitted from October 2011. This means any business performing "reserved legal services", unless all interests are held by lawyers and all managers are lawyers. "Reserved legal services" are: rights of audience, litigation, reserved instrument activities, probate, notarial activities and the administration of oaths. The Solicitors Regulation Authority and Bar Standards Board introduced "outcomes focused regulation". There were new Codes of Conduct.

Comments and outcomes

McConnell (2009) considered that firms that practiced internationally were not likely to transform into ABSs or accept outside ownership because both were banned by the American Bar Association and there were similar problems in Europe, for instance in Germany. As for High Street firms, they would be affected because Tesco etc. would sell commoditised, standardised legal products. The Legal Services Policy Institute considered that smaller firms would lose out. The Law Society said, in 2009, that over-regulation might discourage barristers and solicitors from forming partnerships. In 2010, Professor Stephen Mayson found that about 80 per cent of what most law firms do is *un*reserved work, such as legal advice, tribunal work, making wills and pre-litigation negotiation. The category of "reserved legal services" was criticised. In 2010, Robins said that they were haphazard and historic. The chair of the Solicitors Regulation Authority considered them a "nonsense" and suggested that consumer protection should be extended to all solicitor activities. The Legal Services Consumer Panel considered whether will-writing should be regulated because, oddly, it is not a

13–039

regulated activity. In 2009, Lord Hunt, reporting for the Law Society, said that the public would be taken aback to learn that anyone could set themselves up as a will-writer (Gibb, 2009). The Minister of Justice, however, announced in 2013 that will-writing would not be made a reserved activity and that has been confirmed in 2016.

Underwood, solicitor, argued that firms like his might become tempted to deregulate and spare themselves the cost of indemnity insurance and practising certificate fees and all the straightjacket of regulation. He said lawyers could be competing with a tranche of unqualified entrants to the market, in ABSs, probably 5,000 organisations, such as claims management companies, universities and so on. In January 2011, the Legal Services Consumer Panel (an independent section of the LSB) said ABSs ought not to be able to avoid regulation by setting up separate businesses to do unreserved work but they would do just that. "The government has learned nothing from pension and endowment mis-selling."

In 2009, the Bar Standards Board approved of barristers joining LDPs. It had no choice, because of the 2007 Act. Barristers are permitted to practise as both LDP managers and independent practitioners. They were then permitted to form barrister-only partnerships. In 2011, the BSB confirmed that it would be prepared to regulate advocacy-focussed ABSs, Legal Disciplinary Practices (LDPs) and barrister-only *entities*, but not MDPs. The entities it regulates may not be externally owned (so no Tesco law) and, unlike solicitors, may not hold client money but *may* apply to conduct litigation. A majority of owners must be barristers or advocates with higher court audience rights. Barristers are free to manage or work for ABSs. For barristers to be able to form partnerships, own and manage law firms and conduct litigation is revolutionary. This swiftly developed, as barristers felt the competition. From 2014, self-employed barristers were now allowed to form associations with non-barristers. Baroness Deech said all superfluous rules had been stripped away. A 2012 survey by the Bar Standards Board found that two-thirds of self-employed barristers would consider working in an ABS. From April 2017, the Bar Standards Board is at last empowered to licence ABSs.

Examples of new business structures

13–040 The Co-op aimed to create one of the first ABSs. By 2011, it was offering legal services through three branches of its high street banks. Co-op Legal Services offers help and advice on personal injury, wills, probate, conveyancing and employment law. By 2016, it reported operating profits of £2.2 million.

ABSs include the Buckinghamshire County Council, the AA (Automobile Association), SAGA; a charity set up by a community advice and law service and Knights Solicitors, who have hired a team of town planners to offer a one-stop shop to property developers. Another example of a new type of legal structure is Riverview Law, a fixed-priced provider, backed by an international law firm, DLA Piper. It is a team of solicitors and barristers, including 12 silks, delivering legal advice to small businesses through Riverview Chambers and Riverview Solicitors. It merely has a customer services centre in the Wirral and a small London office. The silks will remain in their existing chambers. A listed company, Quindell, has bought a personal injury firm, Silverbeck Rymer. Slater & Gordon, a personal injury firm in Australia, quoted on their stock exchange, has taken over the solicitors, Russell Jones and Walker. Insurance companies are talking of forming ABSs. Price Bailey was the first accountancy firm to acquire an ABS licence, in 2013. It took on a second licence in 2016, to do probate work. In 2016, a specialist paralegal firm, Wills & Legal Services, took on an ABS to allow it to undertake reserved work. In 2016, Jonathan Fisher QC launched Bright Line Law, a corporate entity to bring together his financial crime work and teaching and consultancy. An ABS, Lawyers Inc, aims to recruit 1000 lawyers and act as an "umbrella" firm. In 2017, Norfolk Public Law, a shared legal service run by four Norfolk Councils set up an ABS to increase its revenue and client base.

The biggest ever survey of *Innovation in legal services* was published in 2015, for the Legal Services Board and Solicitors Regulation Authority. 1500 organisations were surveyed. It found that ABSs had promoted innovation and diversity in legal services, as intended. Barristers appear to be a little more cautious. A 2017 report by the BSB revealed that barristers still preferred to be in chambers and new delivery models were not widespread.

In March 2017, according to the SRA, there were 2,573 sole practitioner solicitors, 1,915 partnerships (but some of these are massive), 1,556 LLPs, 4,328 incorporated companies and 41 "other" firms. The SRA has complained to both the Government and Parliament that the Law Society is unfit to perform any regulatory function and it wants to be free of the Society. In July 2016, the Ministry of Justice consulted on amending the LSA 2007 to relax the regulation of ABSs because there are now over 600 ABSs. They have not caused problems and they are far more regulated than traditional law firms. Curiously, though, by July 2017, this seemed to have been dropped.

Is the Act serving consumers?

In July 2016, the Legal Services Board, the super-regulator, published a market **13–041** evaluation of how the 2007 Act was performing, mainly a meta-analysis of all research and statistics since 2006–2007. Its summary reports the following.

> "The sector has grown substantially since 2007 and new business models...have established significant market shares. Changes to regulation have acted as drivers for procompetitive changes in the market. ...ABS are more innovative... [BUT] Levels of shopping around by consumers have only marginally improved. Limited price transparency, little advertising and an absence of high profile comparison website services inhibit faster improvement. There is some evidence that prices have risen ...but... fixed fee deals... offer consumers greater certainty on price.
> ...more people are handling legal issues alone and fewer are obtaining professional advice; however the proportion of those who do nothing when faced with a legal issue [unmet legal need] appears unchanged...the trend to handle issues alone is driven by better technology (e.g. online probate applications and commercial DIY services) and legal aid reform (e.g. increase in litigants-in-person) [and]...People tend to handle things alone as they believe the matter is relatively straightforward and should not require lawyers, but a perception that lawyers are high cost is a barrier for some. Small businesses...still do not view lawyers as cost-effective...

Levels of satisfaction with service have remained above 2009 levels. While the volume of complaints …has increased, more are being resolved at the first-tier – this trend is driven by new business models which have better complaint resolution ratios. The Legal Ombudsman's caseload has also fallen. Misconduct cases appear to be falling over time…The international standing of UK law has been maintained: over time the reputation of the UK legal sector has improved, while in 2014 net exports of legal services were 33% higher than in 2007…

…more progress needs to be made and the pace of change needs to increase. We need to continue to break down regulatory barriers to competition, innovation and growth, empower consumers and enable the need for legal services to be met more effectively. In the longer-term we consider that legislative reform is necessary to complete the liberalisation of the legal services market."

BUT, in December 2016, the government's Competition and Markets Authority (CMA) concluded, after a year-long study, that

"competition in legal services for individual consumers and small businesses is not working well. In particular, there is not enough information available on price, quality and service to help those who need legal support choose the best option" (press release 15 December).

Research showed that fees varied considerably. Research by the LSB had found massive pricing differences. For instance, fees varied between £3,200 and £250 for selling the same property. Fees for an uncontested divorce involving children varied from £150 to £17,000. Working with the eight lawyers' regulators and the LSB, the CMA have drawn up a package of measures. They recommended that providers (lawyers) be obliged to display prices and other information, including some pricing online, which only 17 per cent of providers now do; revamping the Legal Choices website, as an informative consumer entry point, and facilitating price comparison sites, because now only 22 per cent of consumers compare prices first. Providers should be encouraged to engage with feedback and consumer review-platforms. Following consultation in 2017, the Solicitors Regulation Authority now supports obliging certain firms to publish their prices online and has asked the CMA for advice on how it can stimulate more legal services price comparison websites.

8.   FUSION: DO WE NEED TWO PROFESSIONS?

13–042   Because the monopolies and restrictive practices of the two sides of the mainstream profession have been torn down since 1985 and lawyers business structures are now extremely fluid, as described above, this raises the question of whether the two will eventually merge and, if so whether a fused profession would better serve the public interest. Barristers have always argued that giving rights of audience to solicitors would sound the death knell to the Bar but numbers of independently practising barristers have increased every year since the Courts and Legal Services Act 1990, as they did every year since the 1960s. The Royal Commission on Legal Services 1976–1979 (RCLS) and many other individuals discussed the feasibility and desirability of a fused profession. Here are the pros and cons, famously argued by Zander in 1968 and F.A. Mann in 1997 but these points are obviously supplemented by the facts and arguments examined above, so the reader will recognise some of the points below and this whole chapter is relevant.

Arguments against a divided profession

Expense to the client

Why should the client pay for one or two barristers to argue his case in court, accompanied by a solicitor's representative? Why not just let the client hire one lawyer to do everything, instead of paying for three "taxi meters" clocking up a huge bill, hour by hour? Zander provoked the establishment of the RCLS in 1976 by famously making this argument, fully explored in his book, *Lawyers and the Public Interest* (1968). By 2017, Zander has got his way in most cases, because of all the reforms described above. For instance, things have changed in the County Court. As District Judge Monty Trent said, in 2010, "judges are expected to condemn as disproportionate anybody who sits in the second row, scribbling in their notebooks" and in criminal appeals in the CACD nowadays, solo barristers normally appear unaccompanied.   **13–043**

Inefficiency, failures in communication

Some witnesses suggested to the RCLS that the present structure caused this because of the distance between barristers and solicitors. Written instructions sent to counsel were often inadequate.   **13–044**

Returned briefs

Very frequently, a solicitor sends a brief to chambers marked for a named barrister. At the last minute, the brief is returned because the barrister is otherwise occupied and this is still a big problem. The solicitor then has to find another barrister or permit the brief to be passed on to another barrister in the same chambers, who may be a stranger to him or the client. This causes frustration to the solicitor, denied the choice of original barrister, and may destroy the client's confidence (see Mackenzie, 1990). The solicitor may have reassured the client of the best of service from the named barrister yet the client is faced with a stranger at the doors of the court. Many defendants complained of the shoddy service they received after meeting their barrister on the morning of trial, in Bottoms and McClean's *Defendants in the Criminal Process* (1976) and *Standing Accused* (1994) by McConville et al.   **13–045**

Zander and Henderson's *Crown Court Study* for the Royal Commission on Criminal Justice (RCCJ) 1993 provided statistics which illustrated how bad the problem was. In 66 per cent of contested cases, the CPS said the barrister who appeared at trial was not the barrister originally instructed by the prosecution. In most cases, the CPS learned of the change of barrister at the last minute. In eight per cent of cases where there was a change of barrister it was said to cause a problem. As for defence barristers, in 48 per cent of cases, the barrister at trial was not the one originally instructed and in the majority of such cases, the solicitor was informed on the day before, or on the day of hearing. In 60 per cent of cases, the defendant either saw no barrister or a different one before trial. In 17 per cent of cases, the solicitor said the original barrister would have been better than the substitute.

In 1997, research by the National Audit Office showed that CPS briefs had been returned in 75 per cent of the cases sampled and new counsel was judged to be inappropriate in almost a third of these. In 1998, the CPS Inspectorate published a report on child witnesses, heavily critical that briefs were returned in half of all child abuse cases. The Legal Action Group, in evidence to the RCCJ 1993, argued that the "detachment" which the Bar claims to be an advantage is seen by the client as ignorance of his case and circumstances. Public confidence in the legal system suffers.

Arguments against fusion

Free from interruptions by clients

13–046   Barristers can concentrate on the specialist matters, benefiting from the fact that another lawyer has already identified the issues and sifted out the relevant facts.

Advocacy

13–047   In a fused system, there would be a drop in quality of advocacy, which would damage not just the interests of the client but the administration of justice. Standards would decline because the specialist knowledge of the Bar would be diluted. Specialisms need regular practice. The Bar can fairly claim to be specialist advocates. This was the traditional argument, as we have seen. As we have also seen, however, liberating the advocacy market to employed barristers and solicitors has not been accompanied by suitable regulation and training requirements, apparently. The quality of advocacy is said to be very poor now in some instances, clients and trial preparation are said to be suffering and the professions, the regulators and Government seem to be paralysed in resolving this problem.

Jury advocacy

13–048   This is a specialist type of advocacy, requiring special skills akin to those involved in public speaking. These skills require regular practice. There may be grave consequences to the client. Emotions run high. The barrister is accustomed to this environment and can provide the necessary detachment.

Loss of choice

13–049   If the profession were fused, leading barristers would join large firms of solicitors and so the ability to brief them would be lost to all other solicitors. Under the old split system, clients in the remotest areas or with the most complex problems still have access to the best barristers. Solicitors under a fused profession would not readily refer a client to another firm. Access to advocates would be reduced. Most firms of solicitors have few partners. They could not absent themselves from the office for days on end appearing in court. It is therefore important that solicitors have access to barristers to provide services which they could not.

Cost effectiveness

The separate system is more cost effective. Under a fused system, it would be more expensive to have a solicitor to represent the client as solicitors' law firm overheads are far larger than barristers' chambers overheads, because solicitors' firms are geared up to provide all types of legal service, including advice, negotiation, litigation and non-litigious services.

13–050

Orality

English practice rests on the principle of oral hearing, which demands well prepared, experienced practitioners. This point was made by Mann and is no longer as valid as it then was. Since 1994, skeleton arguments must be prepared in all civil cases and most appeals.

13–051

Procedure

English procedure requires a single and continuous hearing, which requires time and undivided attention that few solicitors could afford.

13–052

Judicial unpreparedness

In England and Wales the principle of curia novit legem applies. This means that the advocate submits the law to the court, which is assumed to know nothing. Counsel has a duty not to mislead the court. Such a system requires specialist knowledge and experience, intensive preparation and much training. If we required judges to research and prepare the law in each case, we would need many more judges (as they have in Continental jurisdictions).

13–053

Comment

These are good points in relation to advocacy in the higher courts but firstly, they ignore the fact that most lower court advocates are solicitors and, since Mann wrote, the County Court deals with some very important civil cases, where solicitors have rights of audience. Really Mann's arguments support the existence of specialist advocates, not a divided profession, bolstered by all the monopolies and restrictive practices lawyers enjoyed in his day. Further, the notion that solicitors generally choose the best advocate for the job, from amongst the pool of barristers, sounds great in theory but, as we have seen, in the routine of the Crown Court, in very serious criminal cases, both prosecution and defence briefs end up, more often than not, with a barrister who was not the one originally selected. Sir Geoffrey Bindman QC, a distinguished veteran solicitor and writer, produced compelling articles in 2010 calling for the unification of solicitors and barristers. He said there was no obvious rationale for the division. Like many

13–054

solicitors, he had "sometimes felt aggrieved at being cast in the role of second-class citizen". There used to be a general perception that the Bar was the glamorous choice of career, "Solicitors were the pettifogging ranks who did the boring legwork". He felt that now that all the restrictive practices had largely been dismantled, "the survival of the Bar … depends on a mixture of mythology and practical convenience". Bindman's comments should be set in the context of the statistical trend demonstrated in *Bar Barometer Trends in the Profile of the Bar* (2011 and 2014) which drew attention to a decline in the growth rate of the Bar. While Bar numbers have grown every year since the 1960s, the rate of growth has slowed in the last few years and the slowest growth rate was in 2009–2010.

A report published by Jomati Consultants LLP in September 2010 said that the golden age of the Bar was over. They will dwindle in numbers and many will earn less, because public and corporate bodies are reducing their advocacy spending, solicitor advocates are increasing and larger firms may seek to do more in-house. The number of referring law firms in family and crime will decline and Bar tenancies will decrease. The Bar Council and BSB have responded by permitting new business structures (as described above), allowing barristers to obtain work directly from clients and join with solicitors to bid for work. Baroness Deech, then head of the BSB, said the independent Bar must be kept going, to defend the rule of law and human rights and stand up to government (Gibb, 2011). See further, Flood (2009).

Now that the Bar can approve alternative business structures from 2017 and barristers can form entities, some barristers and solicitors think that the two sides of the profession are moving towards fusion. The fact that so many solicitors and barristers are rapidly joining ABSs indicates that many of them are creating fused businesses, in practice. This is clearly also encouraged by the Bar's "entity" model.

Bibliography

13–055 Bar Standards Board, statistics in media centre.

G. Bindman QC, "All Bar none", (2010) 160 N.L.J. 711; "End of an era?" (2010) 160 N.L.J. 1428; "Wig not included" (2011) 161 N.L.J. 611; "Spread the wealth" (2014) 164 N.L.J. 22.

M. Blackwell, "Taking Silk: An Empirical Study of the Award of Queen's Counsel Status 1981-2015" (2015) 78(6) M.L.R. 971.

A.E. Bottoms and J.D. McClean, *Defendants in the Criminal Process* (1976).

P. Darbyshire, *Sitting in Judgment: The Working Lives of Judges* (Oxford: Hart Publishing, 2011).

Sir David Clementi, *Review of the Regulatory Framework for Legal Services in England and Wales*, 2004: *http://www.legal-services-review.org.uk* (National Archives).

Department of Constitutional Affairs, *Constitutional reform: the future of Queen's Counsel*, 2003, on the DCA archived website.

J. Flood and A. Whyte, "Straight there, no detours: direct access to barristers" (2009) 16 (2–3) *International Journal of the Legal Profession* 131.

F. Gibb, "Too many legal 'experts' putting consumers at risk", *The Times*, 5 October 2009; "It is the independent Bar who will stand up for the rule of law", *The Times*, 17 February 2011.

Green J, "Advocacy in Peril", speech, 2014, Judiciary website.

R. Hazell, *The Bar on Trial* (London: Quartet Books, 1978).

Sir Bill Jeffrey, *Independent criminal advocacy in England and Wales* (2014).

Judge LJ, The Kalisher Lecture 2009, "Developments in Crown Court advocacy", 12 October 2009, judiciary website, "speeches". This is a really interesting account of life at the Bar in the twentieth century, and discussion of advocacy.

The Law Society, *Ethnic diversity in law firms: Understanding the barriers* (2010); *Annual Statistics Report*, published each June.

Legal Services Board, *Evaluation: Changes in the legal services market 2006/07—2014/15 – Summary*, July 2016.

Lightman, "The Civil Justice System and Legal Profession—The Challenges Ahead" (2003) 22 C.J.Q. 235.

J. Ludlow, "A Class Act" (2007) 157 N.L.J. 1553.

Mackenzie (1990) 150 N.L.J. 512.

F.A. Mann (1977) 98 L.Q.R. 367.

M. McConville et al., *Standing Accused* (Oxford: Oxford University Press, 1994).

C. McConnell, "A profession in transition" (2009) 159 N.L.J. 1069.

R. Miller, "Cross-purpose competition" (2006) 156 N.L.J. 1113.

J. O'Connell, (2011) 161 N.L.J. 1453.

Lord Neuberger, Rainbow Lecture, House of Commons, 12 March 2014, UKSC website.

D. Pannick, "Will lawyers become reformed characters?" *The Times*, 3 November 1998, p.41.

P. Reeves, *Silk Cut* (London: Adam Smith Institute, 1998) criticising the system of Queen's Counsel.

J. Robins, "An unfair divide?" (2010) 160 N.L.J. 1662.

Solicitors Regulation Authority.

P. Thomas, *Discriminating Lawyers* (London: Routledge-Cavendish, 2000).

District Judge M. Trent, "The old days" (2010) 160 N.L.J. 476.

K. Underwood, "Alternative business structures mean consumers will lose out", *Guardian*, 26 January 2011.

Westminster Law School, *Straight There, No Detours: Direct Access to Barristers* (2008).

A. Wigzell, A. Kirby and J. Jacobson, *The Youth Proceedings Advocacy Review: Final Report* (2015), Institute for Criminal Policy Research, commissioned by the BSB and CILEX.

F. Woolf, "Gender agenda", (2012) L.S. Gaz., 23 February.

S. Young, "A class Act" (2008) 158 N.L.J. 10.

M. Zander and P. Henderson, *Crown Court Study* (1993).

Additional materials are cited within the text.

Further reading and sources for updating this chapter

13–056   Aside from Ministry of Justice email updates and the website below, the most useful research tool I used for updating this chapter was *Westlaw* Current Awareness. It provides abstracts and hyperlinks. Most updating material is in the public domain, or accessible via *Lexis* and/or *Westlaw* or other databases subscribed to by university libraries.

Free updates of this book are available on the Sweet & Maxwell website: *http://uklawstudent.thomsonreuters.com*.

Summary and revision: P. Darbyshire, *Nutshells English Legal System*, 10th edn (London: Sweet & Maxwell, 2016).

Bar Council.

Bar Standards Board.

Counsel, the Bar's in-house magazine.

The Chartered Institute of Legal Executives.

The *Guardian* online.

The Law Society.

The Law Society's *Gazette*.

Legal Services Board.

Legal Action.

Ministry of Justice.

The New Law Journal on *Lexis*.

Solicitors Regulation Authority.

CHAPTER 14

Judges

PD *"Are you at the Bar then?"*
LH *"No I'm a Law Lord."*
PD *"Ooh sorry!"*
LH *"That's OK. I'm one of the old white male geezers."*
(The author bumps into Lennie Hoffman at a party, 1996.)

"It's a very jolly life not being a judge. Getting loads of money, making jokes and doing really interesting work. You do really unusual, fascinating things working with people you like. There is lots of flexibility, long holidays, no bureaucracy. Why would you stop?" (Female QC explaining why she would not consider applying to be a judge, from Genn's 2008 research).

"If the worst they can say about you is you're an OPENLY GAY EX-OLYMPIC FENCER TOP JUDGE, you've basically won life." (J.K. Rowling, Twitter, 3 November 2016, mocking the *Daily Mail*'s "exposé" of the backgrounds of the judges in the High Court "Brexit" ruling earlier that day, under its banner headline ENEMIES OF THE PEOPLE.)

This chapter starts by telling the story of the new constitutional setup under the **14–001** Constitutional Reform Act 2005, under which the Lord Chancellor's complex role was dismantled, because he was too powerful in all three organs of government, breaching the separation of powers. The Lord Chief Justice became top judge for England and Wales and he and his Court of Appeal colleagues now manage the rest of the judiciary but the Lord Chancellor, now also the Minister of Justice, remains the minister in charge of the judges, lawyers, legal aid and courts so he still has a number of judiciary-related functions, described here. After examining the constitutional concept of judicial independence, most of the chapter is spent on the highly controversial subject of the past and present recruitment systems and lack of diversity in the judiciary—who can apply to be a judge; how the process of appointment now works since the 2005 Act; an in-depth critique of what was wrong with the old system and an assessment of whether the new system is working to diversify the bench. Training and appraisal are briefly examined towards the end of the chapter.

1. THE CONSTITUTIONAL REFORM ACT 2005—A NEW CONSTITUTIONAL FRAMEWORK

The Lord Chancellor

The dramatic effect of art.6: repositioning the judiciary in the UK constitution

14–002 The most radical impact of art.6 of the European Convention on Human Rights was significant constitutional reform to the role of Lord Chancellor (LC), the top court and the rest of the judiciary, effected by the Constitutional Reform Act 2005. The Act originated in a 2003 announcement by the Labour Government that they intended to make sweeping changes. They proposed to abolish the 1,400 year old office of Lord Chancellor, convert the law lords into a Supreme Court, reform the system of judicial appointments and consider abolishing Queen's Counsel. Affected parties were shocked, because these were presented as decisions, as a fait accompli, without consultation or forewarning. The architect of previous constitutional reforms including the Human Rights Act itself, Irvine LC, had dismissed suggestions for these further reforms so he had to go. On the same day as the reforms were announced, Cabinet was reshuffled and Lord Falconer replaced him.

The background to the 2005 Act is explained in the Supreme Court section of Ch.6 and explored further below. Lord Falconer LC said the government's aim was to "put the relationship between Parliament, the Government and judges on a modern footing. We will have a proper separation of powers and we will further strengthen the independence of the judiciary". It had become apparent that the LC's tripartite role, as an extremely prominent member of all three organs of government: legislature (as speaker in the House of Lords), executive government (as a minister) and head of judiciary, was unacceptable under art.6 of the European Convention on Human Rights. It requires that a judge must be independent of the government. The Council of Europe (the organ enforcing the HR Convention) also made it clear to the UK Government that the law lords' position breached the separation of powers, because, as judges, they were also peers in Parliament, entitled to speak in debate and sit on committees. Accordingly, under the 2005 Act, the LC ceased to be head of the judiciary. The Lord Chief Justice of England and Wales (LCJ) is now head. It created a new Judicial Appointments Commission (JAC) and a UK Supreme Court. It divided judiciary related functions between the LCJ and the reformed LC, now also called Minister of Justice.

14–003 The Act places great emphasis on judicial independence. It requires the LC to be qualified by experience. He is not required to be a judge or a member of the House of Lords, or even a lawyer any more. Indeed, the present LC and Minister of Justice is a member of the House of Commons. The LC and *all* ministers are now under a statutory duty to uphold judicial independence. They must not seek to influence judicial decisions, through any "special access". The LC must "have regard to" the support judges need to carry out their functions and to the need for the public interest to be represented in matters relating to the judiciary or administration of justice. This (s.3) should be read in conjunction with the Courts

Act 2003, which sets out the duty of the LC to ensure that there is an efficient and effective system to support court business.

The 2005 Act provided for the LC's judicial appointment functions to be transferred to the monarch and for many others to be disposed of. These remain the responsibility of the LC:

- The framework of the courts, including jurisdictional and geographical boundaries, and allocating business between them.
- Providing and allocating money and resources for the administration of justice.
- Judges' pay, terms, conditions and training resources.
- Determining the number of judges.

> "*I do swear that in the office of Lord High Chancellor of Great Britain I will respect the rule of law, defend the independence of the judiciary and discharge my duty to ensure the provision of resources for the efficient and effective support of the courts for which I am responsible. So help me God.*" (The 2005 Act requires a new Lord Chancellor to swear this oath and its wording became extremely important in 2016–2017.)

Lord Chief Justice

The Act declares that the LCJ holds office as President of the Courts and Head of the Judiciary for England and Wales. He has the responsibility of representing judges' views to Parliament and government; for judicial welfare, training and guidance and for deployment of judges and allocation of work within the courts. He is entitled to lay before Parliament a written representation on any matter of importance to the judiciary or administration of justice. The following responsibilities were transferred from the LC to the LCJ: **14–004**

- Allocating jobs for individual judges and authorisation to do particular work (known as "ticketing").
- Making rules for deploying magistrates.
- Allocating work within courts of one level.
- Appointing judges to specific posts, committees and boards.

Accordingly, when he took over as head of the judiciary in 2006, 60 civil servants were installed in the Royal Courts of Justice, to run the Judicial Office for England and Wales and the Judicial Communications Office. He runs the judiciary with the help of the Heads of Division, who now comprise a Judicial Executive Board. The Judges' Council represents all judges and helps the LCJ develop policy and react to outside events such as government policy and Parliamentary activity. (See Judiciary website.)

The LCJ became Head of Criminal Justice. The Act created a Head of Family Justice, a post to be held by the President of the Family Division. These copy the statutory post of Head of Civil Justice, established by the Courts Act 2003. The LCJ may delegate to them power to make practice directions. The Vice-Chancellor of the Chancery Division became the "Chancellor of the High Court". A post of President of the Queen's Bench Division was created.

The background to this part of the Act—the unacceptable role of the Lord Chancellor in all three organs of government

14–005   The UK has never had a real separation of powers but the LC's role constituted the most spectacular breach, as he was a key member of all three organs of government. As mentioned above, he was not just a judge but the *head* of the judiciary and he sat in the top UK court as a law lord. He was not just a minister but a most important Cabinet minister, in Irvine's case, on nine crucial Cabinet committees and chairing four of them. He was not just a member of the legislature but the very *speaker* of the House of Lords and, unlike the Commons speaker, free to participate in political debate.

In Ch.6 I explained why, by 2003, the Government were embarrassed by the criticisms made by the Strasbourg court and the Council of Europe into dismantling the LC's role and removing the law lords from Parliament. I explained that the government's decision was preceded by attacks on the status quo by two law lords, Bingham and Steyn. I quoted Steyn's 2002 speech advocating a proper Supreme Court to replace the law lords. Most of his speech was a strident attack on the office of Lord Chancellor. He listed all the ways in which it breached the separation of powers and he demolished, one by one, the arguments raised in its defence, especially by Irvine LC. This was the problem:

> "nowhere outside Britain is the independence of the judiciary potentially compromised in the eyes of citizens by permitting a serving politician to sit as a judge at any level, let alone in the highest court which fulfils constitutional functions ... [this] no longer serves a useful purpose and is contrary to the public interest ... The fog surrounding the figure of the Lord Chancellor, so vividly described in 1853 by Dickens in Bleak House, has not entirely lifted ... By convention the Lord Chancellor is a Cabinet Minister, and he is in charge of a large spending government department. For a long time the Lord Chancellor's predominantly political role has raised questions about the propriety of his subsidiary judicial role ... He is responsible for formulating and implementing policies affecting the administration of justice, which are often a matter of party political debate. In addition he chairs Cabinet committees over a large range of policy issues beyond his departmental responsibility. He is at the centre of political power in a party political sense. In all these respects he is bound by the doctrine of collective responsibility."

It would be unthinkable, said Steyn, for him to sit in any of the major cases coming before the law lords on constitutional law, devolution, or human rights. He concluded:

> "The practice of the Lord Chancellor and his predecessors of sitting in the Appellate Committee is not consistent with even the weakest principle of separation of powers or the most tolerant interpretation of the constitutional principles of judicial independence or rule of law ... In no other constitutional democracy does the judiciary have a 'representative' in cabinet ...".

Attacks on the role of LC were not new. The lawyers' pressure group, JUSTICE, had called for reform for more than 20 years. Academics had frequently drawn attention to the anomalous role. Real pressure was ultimately placed directly on the Government in May 2001, when the Parliamentary Assembly of the Council of Europe called on the UK Government to review the office of LC.

Nevertheless, there was a furore when the Government made its dramatic announcements in June 2003. Given the extent of the reforms and the fact that they were announced as a *decision*, commentators criticised the Government's failure to inform the Queen, and some members of the judiciary were aggrieved that they had not been consulted. Most importantly, Lord Woolf CJ voiced his disquiet at the determination to abolish the LC. Charlie Falconer was introduced as "the last" Lord Chancellor (though ultimately the government did not succeed in abolishing the LC, as can be seen). Falconer was also appointed Secretary of State for Constitutional Affairs and the Lord Chancellor's Department was renamed the Department for Constitutional Affairs (DCA). In 2007, it became the Ministry of Justice.

The anxious Lord Woolf CJ postponed his retirement to fight for judicial independence because of the loss of the LC, who he saw as the defender of the judiciary in the Cabinet. He could only be appeased by a 2004 "Concordat", an agreement between him and the Government, guaranteeing judicial independence, making the Lord Chief Justice the Head of the Judiciary, guaranteeing that judicial appointments would be free from political interference and detailing how responsibilities for appointments and the administration of justice were to be shared between the LCJ and government ministers. The guarantees he secured were all spelled out in the Constitutional Reform Act. In the meantime, in 2003, the Government published several consultation papers: on judicial and QC appointments, the Supreme Court and the LC's non-judicial functions. They were consulting not on *whether* these massive constitutional reforms were to take place but *how.* Another consultation paper was published, curiously late, in 2004, on the judiciary-related functions of the LC. **14–006**

Many others shared the LCJ's concern. "If the Lord Chancellor goes, who will fight the Treasury for legal aid, which carries few votes? Who will have ultimate authority over the legal profession?" asked the eminent lawyer, Lord Alexander. Radical QC Baroness Helena Kennedy was not the only person to point out that Irvine had clung onto office not out of stubbornness but out of a genuine anxiety to defend the rule of law and judicial independence against the increasingly unrestrained attacks of his Cabinet colleague, Home Secretary Blunkett. I return to this point, under judicial independence.

The Government gave in to a demand that the Bill be referred to a select committee. It made no fewer than 400 amendments and voted to retain the title of Lord Chancellor. In all the heated debate in 2003–2005, it was left to the eminent academic Robert B. Stevens, below, to quietly remind us that the LC had only become the champion of judicial independence in 1880 and in any event, the separation of powers and independence of the judiciary were, in the UK context, considerably flaky concepts.

2. WHAT IS MEANT BY THE INDEPENDENCE OF THE JUDICIARY?

14-007

> *"With the Executive sitting in the legislature, English discussions of the separation of powers and judicial independence have a slightly unreal quality."* (Robert B. Stevens, 2004.)

The independence of the judiciary and the separation of powers

14-008   Constitutional theorists, notably the Englishman Locke in the seventeenth century and the Frenchman Montesquieu in the eighteenth, praised the separation of powers as a guarantee of democracy. The concentration of governmental power of more than one type—legislative, executive and judicial—in the hands of one person or body is considered dangerous. It is notable that when a dictator or an extreme regime takes power, they dismiss judges who will not do their bidding. This happened in 2003 in Malaysia and in Pakistan in 2007, not to mention the detention of over 1,600 judges and prosecutors in Turkey in 2016. Some written constitutions try to guard against this. In the British constitution there is no point in looking for a separation of powers. All we can hope for in the UK is a system of checks and balances that allows one organ of government to be kept in check by the others.

Stevens, in *The Independence of the Judiciary* (1993) attributed to Blackstone (*Commentaries*, 1765) the concept of the judiciary as one of the three organs of government which needed independence from the other elements, though he reminded us that from 1701 to 1832, the judges were an integral part of the ruling oligarchy. "Nothing underlines the atheoretical nature of the British Constitution more than the casualness with which it approaches the separation of powers" (1993). It is a constitutional myth, Stevens has often said, that there is independence of the judiciary in England (1994). All the Act of Settlement 1701 provided for was independence for individual judges, not for the independence of the judiciary as a whole, as a co-equal branch of government, in Montesquieu's sense, as the judiciary is meant to be in the USA. Our judges simply moved from being "lions under the throne" to lions under the Parliamentary mace.

By this he meant, as Dicey pointed out in the nineteenth century, the rule of law was dependent on the supremacy of Parliament so the task of judges was and is to carry out the will of Parliament. UK judges do not have the power to judicially review primary legislation and declare it to be unconstitutional, as does the US Supreme Court. The only exceptions have come in the European Communities Act 1972, which gave the judges power to declare a UK Act to be incompatible with EU law (see Ch.3) and the Human Rights Act 1998 (see Ch.4), permitting them to reinterpret primary legislation, where possible.

14-009   Nor did our judges have control over an independent budget and court service. As Professor Scott pointed out, since the Beeching reforms in the Courts Act 1971, until 2006, judicial administration in England was not "judiciary-based" but "executive-based", unlike the US and the Australian Federal courts (though magistrates controlled their budget till 2005). Increasingly, UK governments have sought to increase executive control over court management and expenditure. Judges objected to this, often in hysterical terms, throughout the late 1980s and

1990s. They were fond of quoting early American constitutionalist, Alexander Hamilton, writing in *The Federalist* (No.78), who described the judiciary as the weakest and least dangerous department of government. Professor Scott argued that there was the opportunity for strengthening the separation of powers by making the senior courts "judiciary-based". The 2005 Act did that in part. It allowed judges much more autonomy to manage the courts and much of the time of CA judges is now spent on managing the judiciary. Judges do not have control over the courts or judiciary budget, or real control over how to spend it, though.

For the sake of balance, it is important to point out that judges had not made a brilliant job of running the courts, judging from the archaic and bizarre practices of the assizes and quarter sessions until 1972. Similarly, the power of magistrates to run their own courts until 2005 had many negative consequences. Researching in the 1970s, I found that magistrates' training varied radically, depending on the views of the local magistrates' courts committee, as did the quality and qualifications of the clerks (legal advisers) they hired (1984). Throughout the 1980s, many magistrates' courts were closed (see Ch.6), destroying local justice, and such closures were often the decisions of the magistrates. By 1998, courts had all acquired different computer hardware and software systems which could not communicate with one another or with other criminal justice agencies. Two failed attempts to co-ordinate all these systems then ultimately replace them was an enormous waste of public money.

Lord Phillips, President of the UKSC, gave a speech in February 2011, concerned about the means of funding the UKSC and the danger to independence. Lord Falconer had assured Parliament that it would be paid for direct by the Treasury. The 2005 Act did not provide for that but for the cost to be spread through the civil courts of the three jurisdictions. This did not work out. There was no money from England and Wales so the LC made up the difference. Thus, the UKSC was not independent. The budget was cut. They had managed with 11 judges for years. That did not matter but there were serious ramifications in the lack of independence of the UKSC. Many of its cases are public law. Human rights cases like the 2004 Belmarsh case irritate governments and render the court vulnerable to attacks by ministers. I return to this point, below.

In its case law activity, however, the UK judiciary has grown in review power **14–010** and independence since 1960 and this has re-adjusted the balance of power between the three organs of government. Stevens pointed out that judicial review of executive (government) action had grown out of all recognition. This, I would add, was escalated by simplifying the procedure from 1981 and review powers have been developed on the judges' own initiative, in very significantly broadening the concept of what is "unreasonable", when striking down subordinate legislation (made by ministers) and governmental decisions. Then the Human Rights Act 1998 has added new grounds to their tool kit of review. Whenever a Government has tried to oust the power of the courts to review executive action, the courts have circumvented it. An extreme example of the struggle between the judiciary and government over what judges saw as an authoritarian piece of primary legislation was the law lords' declaration of human rights incompatibility of anti-terrorism legislation in December 2004 in *A (FC) v Secretary of State for the Home Department*, the Belmarsh case, which is what Lord Phillips was referring to above, in 2011. It is discussed in Ch.4. The judges, in cases like this, see themselves as upholding the rule of law and civil liberties established centuries ago in the ancient unwritten British constitution, and as giving force to the will of Parliament. Helena Kennedy, below, was writing in February 2004 but her words could have been about the Belmarsh case, 10 months later.

> *"Populist governments can get all manner of laws through Parliament; the whole purpose of human rights principles is that in their application they provide standards against which all law must be measured ... A common mistake is that MPs come to equate a party political majority with 'Parliament' ... They seem to think that, as long as a Commons majority approves of what a minister does, nothing more need be said about the legality of his or her behaviour ...The judges are in fact asserting the supremacy of parliament rather than their own ... If they fulfil their function properly, judges will at times upset public opinion and governments because they will protect the interests of unpopular minorities—those accused of crime, asylum-seekers, paedophiles, prisoners and probably fox-hunters".* (Baroness Helena Kennedy QC, 2004.)

Cases like this have frustrated ministers and prompted them to complain, publicly. In 2004, Stevens said that history had just repeated itself. Judges were nervous at the threatened abolition of the LC because they feared a non-lawyer replacement could not protect them from the increasingly bitter and personal attacks of a powerful minister like Home Secretary David Blunkett. This struggle between judges and government rumbled on, as described below. Governments see themselves as having a democratic mandate that the "irresponsible" judges lack. Michael Howard, former Home Secretary said:

> "The power of the judges, as opposed to the power of elected politicians, has increased, is increasing and ought to be diminished. More and more decisions are being made by unelected, unaccountable judges, instead of accountable, elected Members of Parliament who have to answer to the electorate for what has happened." (quoted by Lord Phillips, 2011)

This type of concern, over judges' growing review powers, led to calls for candidates to the UKSC be publicly examined, a point addressed below. In 2011 Lord Sumption famously criticised the "judicial resolution of inherently political issues", in his F.A. Mann lecture. He was challenged by Sir Stephen Sedley.

The surprise creation of a Ministry of Justice

14–011   The idea of a ministry of justice was mooted in the nineteenth century and it was judicial panic about that prospect which led to the LC becoming head of the judiciary in the Cabinet government at that time. Then the Labour party revived the idea of a Ministry, in opposition, in the 1990s. Some believed that it would provide a counterweight to the power of the Home Office. Many other countries have such a ministry. Its astonishing, unannounced creation in May 2007 made judges think that the government ministers had not understood their own duty to protect judicial independence, under the 2005 Act, because they did not even tell the judges, let alone consult them. The LCJ learned about it in a Sunday newspaper. Senior judges were very concerned to ensure that judicial independence was maintained and that HM Courts Service did not suffer cuts resulting from sharing a budget with the over-stretched prison service. Note the strongly worded castigation in 2006–2007 in the House of Commons Constitution Committee's Report on *Relations between the executive, the judiciary and Parliament*, 2007.

> "We are disappointed that the Government seem to have learnt little or nothing from the debacle surrounding the constitutional reforms initiated in 2003. The creation of the Ministry of Justice clearly has important implications for the judiciary. The new dispensation created by the Constitutional Reform Act and the Concordat requires the Government to treat the judiciary as partners, not merely as subjects of change." (para.175)

3. INDIVIDUAL JUDICIAL INDEPENDENCE

While the UK does not have an independent judiciary with a power equal to that of Parliament, it does protect the independence of individual judges. In modern times, independence and impartiality are fundamental principles of the United Nations Basic Principles on the Independence of the Judiciary and the European Convention on HR art.6, as enacted into UK law in The Human Rights Act 1998. Judicial independence seems to contain these elements: 14–012

1. Security of tenure

Making them easily removable would subject them to political interference. Senior judges enjoy a formidable security of tenure. Under the Act of Settlement 1701, they may only be removed following a motion by both Houses of Parliament. No English judge has been removed in this way. Until 2005, removing and disciplining the lower judiciary (meaning circuit judge and below) was the LC's job. In the 2005 Act, power of discipline was transferred to the LCJ. With the agreement of the LC, he may advise, warn or reprimand any judge. Under the Courts Act 1971, the LC can remove a circuit judge from office on the ground of incapacity or misbehaviour. Under the 2005 Act this can only be done with the LCJ's consent. The Judicial Conduct Investigations Office is discussed below.   14–013

Concern arose that short term judicial appointments, which the English legal system relied on, breached art.6 of the Convention. This arose from the Scottish case of *Starrs v Ruxton* (2000). It was held that a temporary sheriff in Scotland was insufficiently secure in his judicial role to satisfy art.6. Immediately, the LC abolished the post of assistant recorder.

2. High salaries

These are fixed by a non-governmental body, the Senior Salaries Review Body. A high salary was meant to protect them from corruption. Relative to 1825, when judicial salaries were fixed at £5,500, and relative to modern barristers' earnings, judges are not very highly paid, now, however. Most senior judges and many circuit judges are appointed from the ranks of Queen's Counsel, whose average   14–014 earnings are over £250,000 per year. Several earn millions. In 2017, a High Court judge is paid £179,768, and a circuit judge £133,506 which is less than the highest earning primary head teacher, at £330,000 (*Daily Mail*, 4 November 2016). Currently, there is a serious shortage of High Court judges.

3.   Judges cannot be MPs and should not engage in politics

14–015   It was very common in the early twentieth century for judges to have been MPs and a political career was seen as a good background for life on the bench. This died out in the latter half of the century. Lawyers were heavily represented in Parliament, throughout history. Indeed, Parliament's hours were organised around court sittings so a lawyer could appear in court in the morning and in the House in the afternoon. Stevens (2004) observed that even in 1960, a third of judges had been MPs or Parliamentary candidates.

It is important to acknowledge, though, that a few members of the lower judiciary have been local councillors, some senior judges have been high profile "political animals" and no attempt has ever been made to separate lay magistrates from politics. Many of them are local councillors. In the 1970s, in some towns, most councillors were also magistrates.

Out of court, judges are meant to refrain from controversial and outspoken speeches but the rule has frequently been broken, said Stevens (1993), giving the example of Lord Goddard CJ's enthusiasm for hanging and flogging, in the 1950s. Lord Denning frequently courted controversy in the 1970s and 1980s. He gave speeches in law schools, even during an election campaign, attacking secondary picketing. A reprimand was famously delivered by the LC to Melford Stevenson J for describing the Sexual Offences Act 1967, legalising private homosexual acts, as "a buggers' charter".

In 1988, Mackay LC suspended the Kilmuir Rules, which had prevented judges speaking out in public. This was taken advantage of by Judge James Pickles, who invited media attention at every opportunity, culminating in the development of his own chat show. He once held a press conference in a pub, at which he called the LC an "aged dinosaur". After his retirement, in 1991, Pickles became the *Sun's* star columnist, styling himself "Judge Pickles", a title he was no longer permitted to use. Pickles' books tell the story of his cat and mouse games with two Lord Chancellors.

In his campaign for the Chancellorship of Oxford in 2003, Lord Bingham "call me Tom" of Cornhill, then senior law lord, was very outspoken and set up his own website. He called for the legalisation of cannabis, stating it "is stupid to have a law which is not doing what it is there for". He wanted all wigs and gowns banned and better pay for judges. In 2013, Mr Justice Coleridge was disciplined for giving newspaper interviews in favour of traditional marriage.

One controversial practice that critics say forced judges into the political arena in an undesirable manner is the use of judges to chair public inquiries. This is an enormous waste of judicial time. Masterman (2004) gave the example of Lord Saville who had been hearing the Bloody Sunday inquiry since 1999. This deprived us of one of 12 Law Lords for almost 10 years. See Beatson's extensive examination.

Like many law students, I read J.A.G. Griffiths' *The Politics of the Judiciary*, which taught us how Labour governments were suspicious of judges, because of their reputation for conservatism and for undermining Labour legislation. I never thought I would see judges opposing governments from the *left* but from 1996 to 2010, the two main political parties tried to outdo one another on being tough on crime and terrorism and asylum seekers. *Judges are consistently the voice of the liberal left, of human rights and the rule of law.* The litmus test for this is that attacks on judges now come from the right wing press.

4. Judges cannot be sued for remarks in court

This is the same as the protection parliamentarians enjoy, when speaking in Parliament, as a matter of Parliamentary privilege. Court users frequently complain about judges and magistrates, though. Nowadays, court buildings are festooned with notices of how to complain to the Judicial Conduct Investigations Office.

14–016

5. Parliamentarians do not criticise judicial decisions

Stevens pointed out that this convention is set down in *Erskine May, Parliamentary Practice* but remarked that, while the rule about not commenting on cases sub judice (in progress) seemed to have remained intact, criticism of judges has been more acceptable in recent decades. In evidence to the House of Lords Select Committee on the Constitution in 2007, the judiciary argued that individual judges should not be asked to explain their decisions because they were accountable via the media and they are "institutionally accountable". Judges are sometimes criticised in Parliament, as they were in 2011 for granting super-injunctions to protect public figures such as footballers, but Lord Judge CJ said judges were only trying to enforce the Human Rights Act that Parliament itself had passed.

14–017

6. Politicians should refrain from criticising judges out of court

Thanks to former Home Secretary David Blunkett, this rule seemed to have flown out of the window in 2000–2005. In *R. (on the application of Q) v Secretary of State for the Home Department* (2003), Andrew Collins J ruled that the Government's policy of requiring asylum seekers to register on arrival in the UK was unfair. Blunkett launched into a vendetta, supported by the *Daily Mail*, which showed no appreciation of the separation of powers. He complained of being "frankly fed up" with judges overturning measures Parliament had debated. The LCJ and other judges defended Collins J as upholding the will of Parliament. Things went from bad to worse in 2003. A retired judge, Sir Oliver Popplewell, accused Blunkett of being a "whiner" and Blunkett said judges were out of touch with public views on sentencing, in a speech to the police. "I just want judges that live in the same real world as the rest of us. I just like judges who help us and help you to do the job," Blunkett grumbled when the courts took away his power to determine life prisoners' release dates, because of the Human Rights Act (see Ch.4).

14–018

As it turned out, judges were right to be anxious in the 2003 debate to ensure that the Constitutional Reform Act should require ministers to respect their independence. The very next year, when Lord Bingham refused to "discuss" the Belmarsh case with him, Home Secretary Charles Clarke complained: "The judiciary bears not the slightest responsibility for protecting the public and sometimes seems utterly unaware of the implications of their decisions for our society" (quoted by Lord Phillips, 2011). Stevens, the academic commentator, considered the guarantee of judicial independence in the 2005 Act to be meaningless and as far as some ministers are concerned, it has proven to be ineffective. Prime Minister Blair showed a lack of appreciation of independence, as guaranteed by his own Constitutional Reform Act, in July 2005, when he expressed the hope that judges would now change their hostility toward terrorist legislation after the suicide bombings of July 7 (7/7). Retired judges, Lords Ackner and Donaldson defended the judiciary. Blair was also irritated by the Belmarsh case, below. His wife, Cherie Booth QC, was swift to defend the judges' human rights record. JUSTICE launched a *Manifesto for the Rule of Law*. In it, they asked governments to refrain from criticising judges in a way that would diminish public confidence.

In 2006, Vera Baird, junior minister for the Department of Constitutional Affairs, joined in the *Sun's* campaign against judges, described below, making mistakes of fact, and forgetting the Lord Chancellor's (her senior minister's) and her own statutory duty to defend the independence of the judiciary. She had to apologise. The main target of the attack was a judge who had announced to a paedophile (Sweeney) that he would be eligible for parole after five years of his sentence. Critics did not understand that he was *obliged* to read this out, and that it was the law and government ministers themselves who prescribed the parole regime. The House of Lords Constitutional Affairs Committee were severely critical, in their 2007 report, mentioned above:

> "The Sweeney case was the first big test of whether the new relationship between the Lord Chancellor and the judiciary was working properly, and it is clear that there was a systemic failure. Ensuring that ministers do not impugn individual judges, and restraining and reprimanding those who do, is one of the most important duties of the Lord Chancellor. In this case, Lord Falconer did not fulfil this duty in a satisfactory manner."

7. The media should refrain from criticising judges

14–019 Looking at news media reporting over the centuries, I doubt that this was ever a convention. Stevens said that the idea that criticising a judge was a contempt of court was invented by the CA in 1900 to protect Darling J. It is clear that by now, judge-bashing is a hobby of the *Daily Mail* and a fairly frequent indulgence of other "red top" newspapers. When Lord Woolf spoke up for asylum seekers and the rule of law, he was met with "loutish pummelling" by certain papers, as *The Times* columnist Anthony Howard put it. Lord Woolf CJ made speeches deprecating this behaviour but it never had any impact. At long last the LCJ established a press office in 2005. As described above, in June 2006 the *Sun* started a "name and shame" campaign against judges it considered to be over-lenient. The latest hilarity was the personal attacks on the judges who delivered the Brexit High Court ruling, *R. (on the application of Miller) v Secretary of State for Exiting the European Union* in 2016, Thomas LCJ, Etherton MR and Sales LJ. The *Mail* headline shrieked:

> "ENEMIES OF THE PEOPLE: Fury over 'out of touch' judges who have 'declared war on democracy' by defying 17.4m Brexit voters and who could trigger constitutional crisis."(3 November 2016)

J.K. Rowling made fun of it (see top of this chapter) and liberal news media were swift to attack the *Mail* for undermining the rule of law. The *Mail* followed this up on 2 December, by giving all 11 UKSC Justices star ratings based on information about their supposed pro-EU activities and those of their families, before the UKSC ruling. The top court delivered judgment on 24 January and Liz Truss LC issued this press release:

> "Our independent judiciary is the cornerstone of the rule of law and is vital to our constitution and our freedoms. The reputation of our judiciary is unrivalled the world over, and our Supreme Court justices are people of integrity and impartiality."

For Lord Chief Justice Thomas, this was far too late. Appearing before the House of Lords Constitution Committee in March 2017, he was highly critical of her for refusing to defend the judges after the HC Brexit decision was attacked. The following week, Lord Neuberger, President of the UKSC, reminded the Committee of the LC's duty under the 2005 Act to correct and criticise the newspapers.

8. Freedom from interference with decision making

It is a hallmark of undemocratic regimes that the government tells the judges how to judge. Judicial freedom in this sense includes the discretion to conduct procedures as they see fit. A lengthy spat went on in 2003–2004 between Lord Woolf CJ and David Blunkett, over sentencing and whether the judiciary or the executive should decide the minimum sentence for murder, for example, and who should decide when to release prisoners. The Home Secretary suffered a series of defeats before the European Court of Human Rights and the House of Lords, under art.6 of the Convention, which prescribes that judges, not government ministers, should exercise judicial powers. The UK was the only country in the Council of Europe that permitted executive control over sentencing, something that Blunkett could never understand was unacceptable under art.6. Blunkett retaliated by amending the Criminal Justice Bill 2003 to introduce statutory minimum sentences. Lord Woolf was very outspoken in criticising this. Lord Donaldson, a former Master of the Rolls, said the Bill's provisions on sentencing revealed the Home Secretary's total misunderstanding of the judiciary in the British unwritten constitution. He explained this element of individual judicial independence, as he saw it.

14–020

> "Parliament can limit the powers of judges, can indicate its view of what should be the appropriate sentences for the normal sort of offence. What it cannot do, either

directly or through guideline-making bodies, is to dictate what should be the proper sentence in individual cases, the circumstances of which are infinitely variable." (House of Lords chamber, 17 June 2003)

9. The rule against bias

14–021   Individual judges are meant to conduct proceedings in a fair and unbiased manner, without interfering in the presentation of the case. If they "step down into the arena" of the court (metaphorically) the result may be appealed or judicially reviewed. Similarly, judges must recuse themselves (stand down) if they have a connection with any of the parties or the issues. In *Pinochet Ugarte (No.2), Re* (2000) the House of Lords extended the rule that a judge was automatically disqualified from a hearing in which he had a pecuniary interest, to cases where the judge was involved personally, or as a director of a company, in promoting some cause. In this case, the law lords had to re-hear a case in which Lord Hoffman had failed to declare his connections with Amnesty International. In 2000, following *Locabail* (2000), the Lord Chancellor published guidance to judges on outside interests, on his website. The bias test is now set out in *Medicaments and Related Classes of Goods (No.2), Re* (2001), by Lord Phillips MR (as paraphrased in The *Times* law report, 2 February 2001):

> "The Court first had to ascertain all the circumstances which had a bearing on the suggestion that the judge was biased. It then had to ask whether those circumstances would lead a fair-minded and informed observer to conclude that there was a real possibility, or a real danger, the two being the same, that the tribunal was biased. The material circumstances would include any explanation given by the judge under review as to his knowledge or appreciation of those circumstances."

Helow v Secretary of State for the Home Department (2008) added that the question is one of law, to be answered in the light of the relevant facts. This may include a statement from the judge as to what he knew at the time but there was no question of cross-examining the judge.

In 2004, the Judges' Council produced a *Guide to Judicial Conduct*, now on the judiciary website (2013, revised 2016), explaining to judges the practical implications of the need for independence, impartiality, propriety, equality of treatment, competence and diligence. These requirements were laid down in the Bangalore Principles of Judicial Conduct, initiated by the United Nations in 2001. The current version includes guidance on blogging. All judges receive equal treatment training and *The Equal Treatment Bench Book*. If judges behave discourteously or partially in court, they will rapidly find they may be the subject of complaint or an appeal. Toe-curling examples are given in Ch.12.

In *Howell v Lees Millais* (2007) the CA heavily criticised Peter Smith J. The judge was negotiating with a firm of solicitors for a consultancy, if he were to retire from the bench. It ended with an acrimonious email from the judge. Shortly after this, a hotly contested trust case came before him, involving a partner in the same firm. The QC asked the judge, by letter, to recuse himself and he refused to do so. This application was renewed in court, with a partner from the firm appearing as a witness. There was then an astonishing exchange between the judge and the QC. The judge remarked that the QC's application was nonsense, that he ought to grow up and that he lived on another planet. He threatened the

QC with "professional consequences". The judge still refused to stand down so the claimants applied to the CA and the hearing occurred three days later. The Master of the Rolls, leading the court, said the transcript "did not make happy reading". The judge was referred to the Office for Judicial Complaints for his failure to recuse himself and was reprimanded. This is a sad case. The judge was the darling of the press a few months earlier, portrayed in a very favourable light, when he wrote his own code within his judgment in the case on the book *The Da Vinci Code*. Just as cringe worthy was the story behind *El Farargy v El Farargy* (2007). In a preliminary hearing, the HC judge, Singer J, commented on the uncooperative behaviour of H, an Egyptian Muslim, and asked "What good would that do if he chose to depart on his flying carpet?" He asked counsel if H's evidence was "a bit gelatinous . . . like Turkish delight?" He suggested that maybe he should not take the case and then, remarkably, refused to recuse himself. (The racist interchange was indeed worse, as can be seen from the transcript.) The CA called his remarks "regrettable and unacceptable".

10. A politically independent appointments system

For many decades, the system was in the hands of one person, the LC, a politician, and was criticised as an affront to judicial independence and open to political abuse. Stevens' 1993 book gives examples of political appointments. Most notably in modern times, Lord Donaldson was appointed Master of the Rolls by Margaret Thatcher after many controversial years chairing the National Industrial Relations Court, the scourge of trade unions. He languished unpromoted during the interim Labour governments. It does not follow, however, that Prime Ministers will always select judges according to party political bias. Famously, Conservative John Major appointed Sedley J, a sometime member of the Communist Party, and some of his other senior appointments were of fairly outspoken radicals. The danger of allowing politicians to appoint judges is illustrated by a story told in 2004 by Keene LJ: **14-022**

> "When Margaret Thatcher was Prime Minister, she had a conversation with one of her back benchers, who told her that the then Lord Chief Justice, Geoffrey Lane, had said something critical of government policy. Her response, as I have been told by the backbencher in question was 'What, my Lord Chief Justice?' That is emphatically not how the system should be."

Below, we examine the arguments for and against public selection hearings.

11. Impartiality

This is a close relation of independence. Individual judges are meant to be impartial, hence the rule against bias, but from the 1970s critics have attacked the appointment system and rules of eligibility for the judiciary on the grounds that it produces a judiciary of "old, white, male geezers" as Lord Hoffman called himself, in the quotation heading this chapter. Some critics have long argued that judges who are so demographically imbalanced cannot possibly be impartial in their judgments over a diverse population. This brings us neatly to the appointments system.   **14-023**

4.   WHO CAN APPLY TO BE A JUDGE?

14–024   Qualifications for being a judge are all set out in statute but the statutes have been amended and a number of conditions for appointment have been added, as a matter of policy. Historically, most judicial appointments were restricted to barristers, the exception being registrars in the County Court. Since solicitors have always had rights of audience (rights to appear as an advocate) in County Courts, they have always been eligible for appointment as County Court registrars, now called district judges. The Courts and Legal Services Act 1990 based eligibility on rights of audience. As part of the Government's attempt to diversify the judiciary, described below, the Tribunals, Courts and Enforcement Act 2007 amended this. Part 2 changed the minimum eligibility requirements to stipulate that an applicant must satisfy the "judicial-appointment eligibility condition". In almost all instances, this means the applicant must be a barrister or solicitor and must have had relevant experience in law for the qualifying period, meaning if a person was a legal adviser, or law lecturer, say, for five years, whilst qualified as a solicitor or barrister, they would satisfy the five year judicial appointment eligibility condition. Section 52 specifies what is meant by gaining suitable experience in law. It includes working as a paralegal, teaching and researching law, acting as an arbitrator and so on. Section 50 permits the LC to extend qualification to legal executives and members of other designated bodies and by 2010, this had been done. In respect of many judicial offices, the number of years for which a person must have held qualification before they become eligible for judicial office was also reduced. All those ranks which now require five-years post-qualification experience used to require seven.

Justices of the Supreme Court, e.g. Lady Hale, The Right Honourable the Baroness Hale of Richmond

14–025   When the Supreme Court replaced the House of Lords Appellate Committee in 2009, (see Ch.6), the first Justices were the existing law lords and their qualification was the same, as prescribed by the Constitutional Reform Act 2005. They were appointed by the Queen by letters patent. They must satisfy the judicial-appointment eligibility condition on a 15 year basis, or have been a qualifying practitioner for 15 years. The PM still recommends appointments but under the 2005 Act, he or she has no discretion. He or she must pass on the recommendation made to him by the LC. The new selection system is described below. The Act creates posts of President and Deputy President. The first President was selected in 2008, Lord Phillips of Worth Matravers, who was LCJ at that time. New Justices are now given the courtesy title "My Lord" or "My Lady". Note the alleged scandal of judges forcing Jonathan Sumption QC out of the recruitment race in Summer 2009, before the new appointment system came into force: Gibb (2010). He had the last laugh when he was appointed direct to the UKSC from the Bar in 2011. This is unusual but not unique. Though almost all members of the top court are former appeal judges, at least two law lords were recruited direct from the Bar and Lord Slynn was a judge in the European Court of Justice. As with the law lords, there is always one Justice from Northern Ireland and two from Scotland.

The Heads of Division: Master of the Rolls, Lord Chief Justice, Chancellor, and Presidents of the Family Division and Q.B.D., e.g. The Right Honourable Sir Terence Etherton, Master of the Rolls and Head of Civil Justice, or Etherton MR

These are appointed by the Monarch on the advice of the Prime Minister. The Queen takes no part in the choice and the PM is advised by the Lord Chancellor. Recruits must be Lords Justices of Appeal (and most are) or qualified as such. The Judicial Appointments Commission (JAC) selects just one candidate and that person's name must be passed onto the PM from the LC. They have lost the discretion in the selection process that they had before the 2005 Act was passed. The LC may only reject a candidate or ask the selection panel to reconsider if he considers the selected candidate unsuitable. **14–026**

Lords Justices of Appeal, e.g. The Right Honourable Sir Gary Robert Hickinbottom, Lord Justice Hickinbottom, or Hickinbottom LJ

These judges sit in the CA. They are appointed by the Monarch on the advice of the PM, who receives a recommendation from the LC who, in turn, will be given just one name by the JAC. Candidates must satisfy a seven-year "judicial appointment eligibility condition" or be judges of the HC, which is the normal route. **14–027**

High Court judges, e.g. The Honourable Dame Sarah Jane Asplin DBE, or Asplin J, or Mrs Justice Asplin

These are appointed by the Queen on the advice of the LC. They need to satisfy a seven-year "judicial-appointment eligibility condition", or to have been a circuit judge for at least two years. A few appointments are made from circuit judges and the rest are mainly barristers who have practised for 20 to 30 years and are QCs. The Courts and Legal Services Act 1990 made solicitor-advocates eligible for appointment. **14–028**

Deputy High Court judges

These are appointed by the Lord Chancellor, under the Senior Courts Act 1981 s.9(4) but the system was made more open and transparent by the Crime and Courts Act 2013 so that the Judicial Appointments Commission now determines the selection process. There is a policy of testing out potential HC judges by appointing them to sit part-time, as deputies. Circuit judges, recorders and some tribunal judges may apply, as may practising lawyers. **14–029**

Retired judges

The LC has power to authorise retired senior judges to sit part-time until their 75th birthday. **14–030**

Circuit judges, e.g. Her Honour Judge Baxter

14-031 These are appointed by the Queen on the recommendation of the LCJ, under the Courts Act 1971, as amended. They are selected by the JAC. They must satisfy the judicial appointment eligibility condition on a seven year basis, meaning solicitor with a Crown Court advocacy certificate, or barrister, or be a recorder or have been in fulltime office in another judicial capacity, such as a district judge. The LCJ will normally consider only applicants who have sat as recorders (part-timers) for at least two years, or 30 sitting days. Once appointed, circuit judges may sit at the Crown Court or County Court, or Family Court, or a combination. Some sit in the specialised jurisdictions, such as chancery or mercantile courts. Experienced circuit judges may be authorised to hear HC cases. Some senior circuit judges sit occasionally in the Criminal Division of the CA.

Deputy circuit judges

14-032 These are appointed by the LCJ from among retired judges.

Recorders, e.g. Cherie Booth QC

14-033 These are part-timers appointed by the Queen, on the recommendation of the LCJ for a renewable period of five years. They are selected by the Judicial Appointments Commission. Appointees must satisfy the judicial-appointment eligibility condition on a seven year basis. Some district judges (magistrates' courts) sit as recorders. They sit in the Crown Court and/or the County Court, handling less serious matters than a circuit judge. They are required to sit for at least 15 days per year.

District judges, e.g. District Judge Deborah Wylie

14-034 These are appointed by the Queen, under the 2005 Act. They sit full-time in the County Court. The statutory qualification is to satisfy the judicial-appointment eligibility condition on a five year basis. The LCJ normally only considers applicants who have been serving deputy district judges for two years. They are selected by the JAC and appointed on the recommendation of the LCJ.

Deputy district judges

14-035 They are normally practising solicitors, barristers or legal executives sitting part-time, normally for 20–50 days per year. Their performance is appraised and helps inform the selection process of those who apply for full time posts.

Registrars and masters of the High Court

These mainly deal with HC case management. Costs judges manage costs. They are normally appointed aged 40–60, from the ranks of deputy masters. They must satisfy the judicial-appointment eligibility condition on a five year basis. They are appointed by the Queen, on the recommendation of the LCJ but selected by the JAC.   **14–036**

District judges (magistrates' courts)

They sit full-time in the magistrates' court and must normally have served as a deputy. They must satisfy the judicial-appointment eligibility condition on a five-year basis.   **14–037**

Tribunal judges, e.g. Judge Zucker

They are described and listed on the on the Judiciary website, like all other courts and tribunals judges.   **14–038**

5. THE JUDICIAL APPOINTMENTS SYSTEM FROM 2006

This section examines the current system and the consultation that preceded it, before analysing in greater detail the arguments that provoked this reform.   **14–039**

The Constitutional Reform Act 2005

The Act radically altered the system of appointments to meet mounting criticism of the old system, whereby most appointments were effectively in the gift of the Lord Chancellor, who consulted with the judiciary. In this section, I examine the new statutory framework and below, the background consultation and arguments. The wording of these sections and schedules of the Act is complex so I have relied heavily on the explanatory memorandum accompanying the Act.   **14–040**

Selecting and appointing UK Supreme Court (UKSC) Justices

When a Justice is needed, a special Selection Commission is appointed. It consists of a lay chairperson, thanks to the Crime and Courts Act 2013, the Deputy President and one member from each of three Judicial Appointments Commissions, Scotland, Northern Ireland and England and Wales. At least one must be a non-lawyer. Once the LC has accepted the selection made, the Commission is dissolved. Selection must be on merit. The Commission must consult senior judges and ministers from each jurisdiction. Once a selection has been made, the LC can accept it or ask the Commission to reconsider, or reject their selection but the Act severely curtails his discretion in doing this and limits the acceptable grounds for rejection. When the creation of the UKSC was announced in 2003, law lord, Lord Steyn commented that a small appointing commission, like this, would be appropriate   **14–041** "the new system will have to be more open and transparent than has so far been the case … it should be a neutral and impartial body. It must therefore be in no way identified with the government or civil service. On the other hand it should not be entirely dominated by judges." (2003)

The Act provides for "acting", supplementary judges, where the president or deputy requests it. They must be drawn from the Supplementary Panel or Courts of Appeal of the three UK jurisdictions. The Panel consists of retired UKSC Justices. The background discussion to all of this is contained in the 2003 consultation paper, *Constitutional Reform: a Supreme Court for the United Kingdom*. The Supreme Court was also the subject of law lords' speeches and many academic articles, which are discussed and listed in Ch.6 and above.

The growth in judicial reviewing power, referred to above, is what prompted Stevens (back in 1994) and others to argue that the views of the judges are a matter of public interest so maybe candidates for the top court should be carefully publicly examined before appointment, as they are in the USA and South Africa, because judges' decisions frequently have political repercussions. Furthermore, in enforcing the HR Convention, the courts have effectively become constitutional watchdogs and the extreme argument is that the UKSC Justices now effectively constitute a constitutional court. For this reason, John Patten (1999), a former Conservative Home Office Minister, argued in favour of public hearings, similar to those when a new US Supreme Court Justice is appointed. Professor Oliver examined these oft-repeated arguments in 2003 but emphasised the problems. She questioned what criteria such a confirmation hearing would apply. A Parliamentary Committee would be less qualified than an appointments commission to make a decision on a candidate's suitability. A hearing was likely to be concerned with a judge's beliefs and politics, which ought not to be relevant in the UK. Ultimately it could lead to a reduction in security of tenure. The UK system assumed judges were open minded and would not let their prejudices influence them and this had generally worked. The idea was revived in Gordon Brown's Cabinet's consultation paper, *The Governance of Britain: Appointing Judges*. Professor Zander called it "A waste of space". Coming just a year after the establishment of the Judicial Appointments Commission, it was "ridiculous". He attacked the implicit suggestion that the judiciary should change to reflect "the communities of Britain", as judges do not serve communities. They serve the law, the administration of justice and, in a vague sense, the community and "The very idea that Parliament should exercise a role in the making of judicial appointments sends shivers down the spine of lawyers".

14–042   The politicised selection system for US Supreme Court Justices is well publicised in England and lawyers and judges do tend to find it repugnant or hilarious, because of the undignified spectacle of US candidates making all manner of meaningless assertions to try to get selected. US Justice Sonya Sotomayer had to retract five speeches containing the assertion that "a wise Latina woman with the richness of her experiences would, more often than not, reach a better conclusion", once adding "… than a white male who hasn't lived that life". In her confirmation hearings, she also asserted, like some of her predecessors, that a judge's job was to apply law, not make it (see Smith, 2009). This is a farcical notion in a common law country and all the more so in the US Supreme Court. The HL Select Committee on the Constitution embarked on an inquiry into judicial appointments in 2011. See Gibb (2011). The committee said it was interested in whether there should be a role for parliamentarians in the selection process. Professors Hazell and Malleson advised the Committee that Parliament should have a role in appointing judges to the UKSC and CA. They suggested that three names, not one, should be put forward to the LC by the JAC. Judges are strongly against Parliamentary involvement, as is Professor Bogdanor, historian. He said it would be a step backwards. The Constitutional Reform Act 2005 insulated the judiciary from politics. "Parliamentary confirmation hearings would be a backward step. It would bring the appointment of judges into the political arena, and allow politicians to get their sticky fingers on the appointments process." The argument for public hearings was revived by *The Daily Mail*, in November 2016, after the High Court's decision that the Prime Minister was not empowered to trigger Article 50, Brexit, without Parliament. As explained above, *The Mail* published details of the judges' backgrounds, and then gave all the UKSC Justices an EU star rating prior to their hearing the case. It did not specify what the result of Parliamentary public hearings would be, though.

Other judges—the Judicial Appointments Commission

The Act (now amended by the Crime and Courts Act 2013) created a new 14–043 independent Judicial Appointments Commission (JAC), which, in 2006, assumed responsibility for the judicial appointment selection process in England and Wales and for tribunal appointments made by the LC. It is confined to making *selections*. It does not *appoint* judges. The JAC selects one candidate for each vacancy, or several candidates where multiple vacancies arise, and reports that selection to the LC, or, below the High Court, to the Lord Chief Justice or Senior President of Tribunals (this change was made in 2013). The Commission makes selections for appointment of the Lord Chief Justice, Heads of Division, Lords Justices of Appeal and HC judges, and Sch.12 to the Act lists the offices below the High Court for which the Commission will make selections (with tribunal members being the largest group of appointments).

The LC or LCJ or SPT appoints or recommends for appointment the selected candidate, or rejects a candidate, once, or may ask the Commission to reconsider, once. Having exhausted these options of rejection and reconsideration, the LC or LCJ or SPT *must* appoint or recommend for appointment whichever candidate is selected. The Act makes special provision for the appointment of the LCJ and Heads of Division and of Lords Justices of Appeal; in these cases the Commission will establish a selection panel of four members, consisting of two senior judges (normally including the LCJ) and two lay members of the Commission. Since 2013, the chair of the panel appointing the LCJ must be a lay person. The appointments of Lords Justices and above continue to be made by The Queen formally on the advice of the Prime Minister after the Commission has made a recommendation to the LC.

The Act requires the Commission to encourage diversity and specifies that "selection must be solely on merit" and that appointees must be of good character. Under the 2013 Act, the LC and LCJ are also under a statutory diversity duty. This is the first time that this has been a statutory requirement.

Under the pre-2006 system, the LC's informal criteria specified that appointments must be made solely on merit. Since the 2013 Act, there is a tie-break provision. Where two candidates are of equal merit, the JAC should select the candidate on the basis of improving diversity. The LC is able to issue guidance to the Commission, to which they must have regard, but it is for them to determine the detailed appointments procedures they follow. Guidance can only be issued after consultation with the LCJ and after being approved in draft by both Houses of Parliament. The Commission must report on its selections and methods to the LC and he can, in consultation with the LCJ, require them to make specific reports.

Schedule 12 sets out the membership of the JAC and its powers and responsibilities, which reflect its status as an executive non-departmental public body. There is a lay chairman with five other lay members, five judicial members (including a senior tribunal judge, since 2013), two legal professionals (which could include a legal executive, since 2013), the holder of an office listed in Sch.12 and a Justice of the Peace or lay tribunal member. Commissioners are appointed for five years and can hold appointment for a maximum of ten. Lord Kakkar was appointed Chair of the Commission in 2016. He is a professor of surgery at UCL and has been a peer since 2010 and chaired the House of Lords Appointments Commission. The other commissioners work for three days per month. The details of the way the JAC operates are on its website, as are its reports on its progress in diversifying the judiciary. It advertises each new competition. As well as requiring a written self-assessment application form and references, it administers assessment days or selection days and, for some posts, written qualifying tests which are designed to assess legal reasoning, forensic judgment and ability to explain decisions. Aspiring judges can subject themselves to practice tests. Selection exercises are tailored to the posts for which the JAC is recruiting. The written tests were discussed by Sumption (2011). Toulson LJ (2010) explained senior circuit judge selection.

Removal of judges, discipline and complaints

14–044   The LC has statutory powers to remove judicial office holders below the HC (including tribunal members and lay magistrates) for incapacity or misbehaviour. These powers can be exercised only with the agreement of the LCJ. Part 4 of the 2005 Act makes statutory provision for a disciplinary system in relation to judges, in cases falling short of removal, in which the Lord Chief Justice is given power to advise, warn or reprimand, following disciplinary proceedings, with the agreement of the LC. This does not affect the LCJ's general ability to speak informally to any judge on any matter which concerns him, without having to inform or obtain the agreement of the LC. In 2017, Judge Patricia Lynch QC was given informal advice when ten people complained that she had called an aggressive defendant a cunt because he called her a cunt. The LCJ may suspend judges from sitting, with the agreement of the LC. The LCJ has the power to make regulations and rules governing disciplinary cases, with the agreement of the LC. The Judicial Appointments and Conduct Ombudsman, who must be a lawyer, is able to consider complaints about the handling of disciplinary cases.

Under previous legislation, a Liverpool County Court judge, William Ramshay, was removed, following endless complaints and an unseemly battle with the press. Judge Keith Bruce Campbell was removed, in 1983, following his conviction for smuggling 125 litres of whisky and 9,000 cigarettes. Judges often resign before they can be removed. Circuit Judge Angus MacArthur resigned from the Bench in 1997, shortly before being convicted for his third drink-driving offence and jailed for 28 days. In 1998, commentators were critical when Butler-Sloss LJ was offered retraining instead of prosecution for careless driving after a crash which left a passenger with facial injuries. The problem with cases where judges receive lenient treatment is that the public may perceive them to be above the law.

There is no statutory definition of "misbehaviour" so it was up to the interpretation of the LC of the time, although this has become much clearer, now the Judges' Council has published the *Guide to Judicial Conduct*. Appended to it is guidance to the judiciary on reporting their minor offences, agreed by the LC and LCJ. The reports of the Judicial Conduct Investigations Office give general details of complaints about judges, and outcomes. It is not unusual to remove part-time judges. For instance, in 2012–2013, a recorder was removed for failing to declare he was the subject of civil proceedings and had been declared bankrupt. Another was removed for practising as a barrister without a Bar Council Practising certificate, which is a criminal offence. Constance Briscoe, a well-known recorder, was imprisoned for 16 months in 2014, for conspiring to pervert the course of justice, when she spun an elaborate web of lies as a witness in a criminal trial. In 2016, an immigration judge, a district judge and a deputy were removed for using their judicial computers to view porn.

There are two problems with the media reporting of judicial misconduct. The first is that its scandalous tenor and relentless repetition means that people remember reporting of daft remarks in court or "porn-judge" for decades afterwards, whereas in reporting of ordinary judges behaving well or commendably in court, the judge is normally not even named. The second is that when a lawyer sitting part-time as a judge misbehaves he is always referred to as a "judge", as if he were a real judge, as in "Judge and former lover face prison sentences for £1m theft" (*Times*, 2017). I examined in depth the public image of the judiciary in my research into the working lives of judges (2011, Ch.2). Indeed, it was the mismatch between the appalling public image of judges and the hard-working, down to earth judges who came to speak to my students which partly prompted the research.

Judges who leave office

In 2005, Laddie J announced that he was leaving the HC out of boredom and **14–045** because he would prefer teamwork in a solicitor's firm to the isolation of his judicial role. Michael Cook, a former circuit judge, also announced that he was to join a firm of solicitors. In 2007, following consultation, the Government concluded that the convention that former judges should not return to practice should remain in place. It had been suggested that permitting judges to return to practice might encourage more applicants but there was insufficient evidence that lifting it would increase diversity. It is not strictly true that there is a ban on judges resigning and returning to practice, as has sometimes been said. In 1970, Sir Henry Fisher left the HC after two years, to work in the City. Like Laddie J, he found the job boring. He also despised the snobbery of some other HC judges. It is very common for retired senior judges to take on independent work. Many have trained as mediators. Dyson MR returned to his Bar chambers in 2016.

Immediate background to the new appointments scheme: the 2003 consultation paper *Constitutional Reform: a new way of appointing judges* and responses

14–046

"*We are fortunate to have a judiciary that is politically neutral, incorrupt, and of the highest calibre, with an international standing second to none. However we intend that a Judicial Appointments Commission will insulate more the appointment of judges from politicians. It will also promote opening up appointments to some of those groups of lawyers which are under-represented in the judiciary at the moment, including women, ethnic minorities and, at the higher levels, solicitors.*" (Lord Chancellor Falconer, announcing the consultation papers on constitutional reform, July 2003, DCA Press Release 296/03.)

Since the 1970s, criticism had mounted that the appointments system was unfair and drew from too narrow a pool of potential candidates and this is explored in depth, below. Most judges were chosen by just one man, the LC, a politician. He appointed all lay justices, on the recommendation of local advisory committees. He selected all of the lower judiciary (circuit judges and below) and he put forward names for the senior judiciary, to be considered by the PM. Pre-2006, he consulted widely among the existing judiciary, seeking their opinions on candidates for the judiciary. Lord Chancellors made progressive reforms, from 1994, but these did not satisfy the critics. The Bench was said to be too narrow, in terms of class, education, age, gender and ethnic background. The old scheme was repeatedly criticised by academics, politicians, the pressure group JUSTICE, the Law Society and women and minority lawyers' groups. The most thorough exposure of these views was collected in the House of Commons Home Affairs Committee, third report for the session 1995–1996, *Judicial Appointments Procedures Volume II, Minutes of Evidence and Appendices* (1996), abbreviated here to "JAP".

As part of the package of constitutional reforms announced in 2003, the Government consulted on their declared intent to create a new, independent commission for selecting and/or appointing judges to replace the Lord Chancellor because:

"In a modern democratic society it is no longer acceptable for judicial appointments to be entirely in the hands of a Government Minister ... the appointments system must be ... transparent ... accountable ... inspire public confidence ... the current judiciary is overwhelmingly white, male and from a narrow social and educational background ... the Government is committed to opening up the system of appointments ... from a wider range of social backgrounds and from a wider range of legal practice." (Foreword to the 2004 consultation paper, *Increasing Diversity in the Judiciary*, by Falconer LC)

The Government did not believe in a continental style career judiciary "but they do believe that new career paths should be looked at to promote other opportunities and diversity in appointments." The paper described three possible models: an appointing Commission; a Commission which would make recommendations to a Minister or a hybrid Commission which made junior appointments and recommended senior appointments. The Government favoured a recommending commission, with appointments made by a Minister. A judicial ombudsman would deal with complaints about appointments.

The Commission for Judicial Appointments, the then watchdog, had a critical influence. It considered that the majority of the proposed Commission (JAC) should be lay persons, applying best practice on human resources. The Law Society said appointment to the senior judiciary must be by open competition only. "The absence of any appearance of cronyism is vital to establishing a positive public perception". Tackling the discriminatory aspects of the then current process, such as automatic consultation of a homogeneous pool of senior judges, should be a priority. The Bar Council thought the Minister should have a statutory duty to protect judicial independence. The Judges' Council wanted the LCJ to head the judiciary. **14–047**

On 26 January 2004, Lord Falconer LC and Lord Woolf CJ announced the details of the proposed new statutory framework. These principles became known as The Concordat. The judges were clearly annoyed that the reforms had been announced without informing them so after 2003 there had then been extensive negotiations between the judiciary and the LC. Crucially, Lord Falconer LC understood the importance of judicial independence:

> "The reforms seek to clarify and embed in statute the principle of judicial independence. Judges must enforce, impartially, the law made by Parliament. The executive must continue to guarantee security of judicial tenure and remuneration, and ensure that the judiciary is supported by an efficient and effective system of court administration ... there should be a general statutory duty [to uphold] ... judicial independence ... there should be a separate specific duty falling on the Secretary of State for Constitutional Affairs to defend and uphold the continuing independence of the judiciary." (*Hansard*, Column 13)

As can be seen from the contents of the Act, above, the Government agreed to embody all of the above comments in the Bill. The JAC's responsibilities now extend to tribunal members and were *meant* to extend to lay justices. By 2017, this has not happened and the old system remains in place, described in the next chapter, on magistrates.

Notice that the JAC's discretion is severely curtailed. It is a *recommending* commission, despite the fact that the majority of respondents favoured an *appointing* commission, to guarantee judicial independence, or a hybrid commission. Almost all judges are now appointed following open competition and this even applies to specific jobs, such as resident judge in the Crown Court and judges who undertake training, and the small number of circuit judges who sit in the Court of Appeal. As for heads of division appointments, notice the involvement of the most senior judges, since many respondents to the consultation felt their views were especially valuable.

6. DEEPER BACKGROUND: PROBLEMS WITH THE PRE-2006 SYSTEM OF APPOINTING JUDGES

14–048   "The system demonstrably ensured that those who were appointed were good; it did not however demonstrably ensure that those who were good were appointed. It was criticised as being a system under which white Oxbridge males selected white Oxbridge males." (Lord Phillips CJ referring to the pre-2006 system of appointing judges, speech, 2007)

I can hardly bear to relate the story below. It recounts the pathetically slow progress in getting rid of the old selection system. It was the epitome of the worst kind of old boys' network: not only blatantly sexist, racist, classist, homophobic and elitist but wholly unprofessional. It disfavoured *all* sections of lawyers who did not appear as advocates in front of "the right" judges. It used to disgust me when I was a 1970s student.

The roles of the Lord Chancellor and Prime Minister

14–049   As Griffith said, in successive editions of *The Politics of the Judiciary*, "The most remarkable fact about the appointment of judges is that it is wholly in the hands of politicians". Some bodies had expressed concern about this long ago, such as a JUSTICE sub-committee in 1972 and the Bar in 1989. This point has been discussed under the heading of "Judicial Independence", above. As Drewry pointed out, however, by 1998

> "even the sternest critics ... would surely have to concede that any vestige of the old party political 'spoils' system that prevailed until the early part of this century has been eradicated".

Critics remained concerned about the *potential* for political appointments, as can be seen from Keene LJ's comment on Margaret Thatcher, above. Rodney Brazier, in evidence to the 1995 Parliamentary Select Committee, voiced the concerns of many:

- The concentration of power in the hands of one person, without the benefit of a structured system of advice, was unsatisfactory. The system lacked openness, relied on unstructured questions to advisers of unknown identity. There was no accountability to Parliament.
- The increased size of both branches of the profession meant the Lord Chancellor could not have adequate knowledge of all potential candidates. (The 1992 JUSTICE report said that, some 50 years earlier, with a Bar of 1,500 and under 100 judges, the Lord Chancellor was personally involved in choosing judges, because he *knew* the candidates.)

Some modern commentators still advocate removing the role of the Prime Minister. In 2005, the PM's role in judicial appointments was the subject of a different type of criticism. Tony Blair was attacked for "cronyism", not for the first time. He selected Potter LJ to be the new President of the Family Division, with little experience of the family courts. Potter had been the Bar pupil-master of

Charlie Falconer, Blair's flatmate. This followed a pattern: Blair had appointed Falconer LC to replace Lord Irvine, who happened to be Blair's pupil-master and who introduced Blair to his wife, Cherie Booth. Frances Gibb, Legal Editor of *The Times* commented that "The appointment [of Potter] caused disbelief among senior judges, who had tipped Lord Justice Thorpe". Thorpe LJ had dedicated his judicial life and much of his spare time to promoting the reform and development of family law and procedure on an international scale. He was the Deputy President of the Family Division. Professor Cretney, the leading academic family lawyer, remarked on the irony that this appointment was made at the very time when the Constitutional Reform Bill was before Parliament, designed to replace cronyism with an appointment system that was fair, open and transparent. In 2008, Justice Minister Jack Straw introduced a draft bill to remove the PM from the appointment system but it was dropped.

The call for sweeping reform—a Judicial Appointments Commission

The suggestion for an advisory or appointing commission had been made by JUSTICE, in 1972 and 1992. Visible and real independence from the executive and judiciary would be crucial. The proposal was designed to secure a more diverse bench. The Law Society strongly supported this, in evidence to the House of Commons Home Affairs Committee, in 1996. The Judges' Council disagreed. The Labour party, then in opposition, set out its plans for a Commission in 1995–1997, although the proposal did not appear in its 1997 election manifesto. Instead, the new Labour Lord Chancellor, Lord Irvine, announced some reforms of the system and promised to consider establishing an ombudsman, for those aggrieved by the appointments process, and a system of performance appraisal. He appointed Sir Leonard Peach to examine the appointments system. Peach reported in 1999.

14–050

In the meantime, two papers, by Thomas and Malleson, had been commissioned by the Lord Chancellor's Department, on European and North American judicial appointment commissions (1997). Malleson reviewed US and Canadian models and found there was no strong evidence to suggest that the use of commissions as opposed to other appointment methods had any significant effect on the make-up of the judiciary in terms of competence or representativeness. She found that public confidence in the use of commissions was generally very high. Thomas showed that the very different European recruitment systems resulted in radically different judiciaries. Women made up a significant proportion of the judiciary in most of the countries examined and at least *half* of incoming judges in France, the Netherlands, Germany and Italy. As recruitment was through public examination based on university-level knowledge of the law, women normally fared better than men. She concluded:

> "Recruitment of judges later in their professional career, as occurs in common law countries, tends to bring into play social forces which reduce women's chances: family commitments and professional discrimination. Civil law, bureaucratic-style judiciaries have favourable employment conditions for women (maternity leave, flexible working hours, etc.,) and the judiciary is seen as a positive career choice for women law graduates." (p.21)

14–051   She suggested that the continental practice of involving lower ranking judges in judicial appointments commissions might also encourage an increase in the appointment of women judges, minorities and other less traditional types. It shifted the criteria for appointment and lessened the influence of legal elites who tended to favour the status quo.

In Peach's 1999 report, he recommended a Commission for Judicial Appointments and this was done in 2001. This was *not* the model suggested by JUSTICE. It was simply a reviewing watchdog, which published an annual report. In 2000, Lord Steyn became the first law lord to call for a commission. The Law Society pointed to Genn's study, *Paths to Justice*, 1999, which found that the public thought that judges were old and out of touch.

The head of this new CJA was Sir Colin Campbell, a non-lawyer. He and the other commissioners had broad recruitment experience in commerce and industry. From their standpoint of outsiders, the commissioners clearly found some aspects of the old appointment system shocking and indefensible and their annual reports carried highly publicised and strident criticisms which doubtless embarrassed the Government, as can be seen from their contents. In 2003 they commented that the system of appointing judges and Queen's Counsel was rife with wide "systemic bias" against minorities, women and solicitors that infected the way the legal profession and judiciary operated. See more below.

The pre-2006 system of "secret soundings"—"comment collection"

14–052   Prior to the 1990s, aspirants did not apply for a fulltime job as a judge. They were invited to join the bench by the metaphorical "tap on the shoulder" by the LC, whose civil servants gathered files of fact and opinion on potential judges and kept candidates under constant review. Until 1960, the Bar was around 1,000, so the LC was presumed to know all the candidates personally. By 1990, this could not work. Many candidates for recorderships and the circuit judiciary applied for the job but some were still invited. There was no standard application form, other than for district judges. In empirical research on the judiciary reported in 2011, I interviewed judges who claimed that there was a system of seniority in certain barristers' chambers in the 1980s. When each barrister achieved sufficient seniority in chambers, the LC would ask if they were interested in becoming a QC or, for those less talented, a circuit judge, so they knew to expect that their "turn" would come. I found this story so far-fetched it made me laugh out loud and I had to check it with a number of judges. In some of the Crown Courts and County Courts I visited in the provinces, in 2003–2009, many judges had been barristers in the same city so they had just tip-toed up, as it were, from the bar to the bench.

Hailsham LC published his selection criteria in the 1980s. Mackay LC made countless speeches urging more women and ethnic minorities to put themselves forward. In 1994–1995 he at last opened up the recruitment and selection system by advertising lower judicial posts (circuit judge and below) on the internet, with detailed job specifications, and introducing interview panels. There were still two major problems. All senior judges were still recruited by the "tap on the shoulder" till 1998 and, despite many reforms made by Lords Mackay and Irvine, the LC was still heavily reliant on "consultations" with existing judges. They were referred to by critics, such as solicitors, as "secret soundings". The Judges' Council, in their 1996 evidence to the Parliamentary Home Affairs Committee defended the system:

> "judges see and hear most of the potential candidates before them, day in, day out, from a position in which they are uniquely well placed to assess their professional competence and personal qualities, and to compare them with competitors in the field" (JAP, p.219).

The Equal Opportunities Commission, in their evidence, expressed "a major concern":

> "Selection for appointment should depend on an objective assessment of the applicant's skills and abilities. Given the predominance of men in the senior ranks of the judiciary, the bar and the solicitor's profession, there is an increased risk of stereotypical assumptions being made with regard to 'female' as opposed to 'male' qualities and aptitudes" (JAP, p.211).

Most critics giving evidence made the simple point that any system which relied on the say-so of a limited group was inevitably vulnerable to members of that group selecting people like themselves. As Chris Mullin MP retorted:

> "... it appears to be self-perpetuating does it not? They all know each other, many of them went to school together, most of them were at university together and they have no doubt known each other all the time dining in their various Inns of Court. They are males aged between 55 and 66 on average ... and they appear to move in very limited circles" (JAP, p.5).

The Law Centres Federation, the Association of Women Barristers and the Law Society, representing solicitors, told the Parliamentary Home Affairs Committee that the system disadvantaged those who were not from the standard background for judges and perpetuated the weight given to advocacy skills. It disadvantaged women and solicitors who were unlikely to appear before serving members of the judiciary. They wanted "soundings" replaced with a system of objective tests and interviews, such as is used in civil service recruitment (JAP, p.229). The Bar Association for Commerce, Finance and Industry (employed barristers) called the system "wholly indefensible" (JAP, p.204). The African, Caribbean and Asian Lawyers' Association said, in their evidence, that the composition of the judiciary reflected neither the British population nor the legal profession.

The accusation that the system perpetuated a clique was strikingly illustrated **14–053** by research undertaken on behalf of the Association of Women Barristers. Examining 104 High Court appointments made during 1986–1996, 70 (67.3 per cent) came from a set of chambers of which at least one ex-member was a judge. Only 58 of 227 sets of London chambers produced judges, of which seven sets produced an astonishing 30 appointees. Of the 131 sets outside London, they produced only seven judges. The 104 appointees, from a pool of 8,800 barristers, replaced over two thirds of the judges, yet came from roughly the same chambers as those they replaced (Hayes, 1997).

Peach (1999) suggested that each candidate should nominate three referees and this change was made. The problem was, however, that this extensive "soundings" system carried on alongside that. Many judges were sent the list of candidates applying for various judicial posts and each judge chose upon whom to comment (I observed judges doing this in 2004, in my empirical research cited above). This disappointed all critics, especially the Law Society, who repeated their condemnation of the "old boys' network". Peach recommended that consultations be supplemented with alternative methods of evaluating an applicant's suitability, such as one-day assessment centres and psychometric and competence testing (Malleson, 2000). In 2000, Malleson and Banda reported to the LC on *Factors affecting the decision to apply for silk and judicial office*. They exposed widespread dissatisfaction.

Assessment Centres were piloted in 2002 for deputy district judges and HC masters. They were used instead of traditional interviews, to identify whether the approach encouraged more applications from under-represented groups. Candidates had to show political correctness, awareness of other cultures, proficiency in relating to people from a diverse society and "empathy and sensitivity" in the building of positive relationships with litigants, witnesses, advocates and colleagues. The assessments included practical exercises and role-play, an interview and written examination. In 2003, they were extended to recorder selection. Judges caused the first selection process used by the JAC to be re-run, because it did not take account of their views and Malleson argued that judges' opinions are indeed a useful resource.

> "The creation of a system of open selection is not, however, inherently incompatible with the consultations process which still has strong defenders. In common with all peer-based appointments, promotions, or performance review systems, it allows decisions to be based on the knowledge and views of those who best know the work and characteristics of the candidates." (2009)

In the 2015 book she co-authored with Gee, Hazell and O'Brien, *The Politics of Judicial Independence*, they concluded that judges were still influential:

> "As repeat players...senior judges are adept at using additional selection criteria and statutory consultation to ensure that weight is attached to their viewpoints...judicial influence remains particularly high at the top levels."

The Commission for Judicial Appointments savages the old boys' network

14–054 The comments of the CJA demonstrated how its members, experienced recruiters and employers from the real world, were horrified at what they found. Some of their sensible prescriptions for reform are still not in place, as far as I can see. Their 2003 report was highly condemnatory. They uncovered some vague and subjective comments about applicants, by judges and lawyers, which bore little relation to the professed selection criteria, such as:

- "She's too primly spinsterish".
- "She's off-puttingly headmistressy".

- "She does not always dress appropriately".
- "Smug and self-satisfied and pompous".
- "Down and out scruffy".

The commissioners had not come across comments like them, in 20 years of experience in commerce and industry, said Sir Colin Campbell, their outspoken chair. Such comments were symptomatic of a "wider systemic bias in the way that the judiciary and the legal profession operate, that affects the position of women, ethnic minority candidates and solicitors in relation to silk and judicial appointments". He also felt that HC appointments, which were still mainly made by the "tap on the shoulder" method, should all be filled by application and interview.

In 2004, their recommendations were even more forceful. Consultations disfavoured solicitors and should be replaced with a more structured and accountable method of collecting views on candidates' suitability. "We call for much fuller audit trails of how selection decisions have been reached." All candidates must have an equal opportunity to demonstrate their suitability. All relevant evidence must be evaluated against known competencies and appropriate criteria. Judicial opinions could be taken account of but gleaned in a much more organised and restricted manner. They welcomed the extension of appraisal of part-time office holders, as that could provide useful information in selecting for full-time posts.

The system was also institutionally biased against full-time judges applying **14–055** for higher posts, who were not visible to the consultees. The appointment process did not recognise skills demonstrated by other judges, such as tribunal chairs, who dealt with cases at least as demanding as those heard by circuit judges. This disproportionately affected women, since they accounted for 24 per cent of tribunal chairs.

They were especially critical of the High Court competition, which had started in 1998. The parallel system whereby senior judges could nominate people for consideration for the HC (tap on the shoulder) was unfair because this meant different information was available for nominees and applicants. This led to "serious inequalities" in their treatment. There was no information on how the Heads of Division arrived at their shortlist. Under a reformed system, head hunting would be acceptable but all candidates should apply through the same route. In response, in 2005, all HC candidates were required to apply in writing and include a 1,500 word self-assessment. The CJA's 2004 report is well worth reading, as it exposes the shortcomings of the old appointment process and gives practical examples of how it prejudiced the chances of some applicants. It made frustrating reading for those of us who were writing student essays containing identical criticisms back in the 1970s. In *Sitting in Judgment* (2011), I explored in depth judges' stories of how they were recruited to the bench through the evolving process, from the 1970s to 2003.

Restricting appointments to those with rights of audience: the emphasis on advocacy

14–056   The gist of the above criticism, that those who did not appear before the "right" judges would not be selected, was compounded by the law itself, the Courts and Legal Services Act 1990, which based all judicial appointments on audience rights. It should be noted that this problem was *not* cured by the Constitutional Reform Act 2005. The system in 2017 still excludes most solicitors (and there are 10 times as many of them as barristers, as we saw in the last chapter) from most appointments and all those with purely academic qualifications from *all* judicial appointments. The Judges' Council defended this restriction, in their 1996 evidence to the Parliamentary Home Affairs Committee:

> "Successful advocates must develop and exhibit the ability, founded upon sound judgment, to evaluate the strengths and weaknesses of their opponent's case as thoroughly as their own ... In addition, the administration of justice in England and Wales depends upon lawyers who appear before the court owing their paramount duty to the interest of justice, and not advancing arguments or evidence which are improper, mendacious or corrupt." (JAP, p.219)

Groups like JUSTICE have long argued that prowess as an advocate, standing in court arguing one side of a case, does not demonstrate the skills needed of a judge, to sit quiet and give an impartial hearing to both sides and exercise fair judgment.

> "The best drama producers may not be the best critics; the best players do not necessarily become the best referees. In particular the strong combative or competitive streak present in many successful advocates is out of place on the bench." (JUSTICE, *The Judiciary in England and Wales*, 1992)

14–057   The Law Society, representing solicitors, argued that the emphasis on advocacy "actually impairs the selection of the best candidates". Fulltime advocates suffered the disadvantage of a lack of experience of dealing with clients directly, or of conducting litigation, which could lead to "a rather unworldly approach" (JAP, pp.234–235). Other jurisdictions do not limit the judiciary to practising advocates and use is made of academics as judges in the highest courts. Thinking of the qualities needed of judges in the CA and the UKSC, they spend most of their time considering and developing points of law. Academic lawyers devote their whole careers to developing expertise in specialist areas of the law.

Lord Irvine accepted some of these criticisms. As a result of the Peach Report and Banda and Malleson's research, he re-wrote the appointment criteria to emphasise that he did not regard advocacy experience as an essential requirement for appointment to judicial office, from 1999. The Constitutional Reform Act 2005 did not alter the legal requirement that candidates have rights of audience as a barrister or solicitor, however. Most respondents to the 2003 DCA consultation paper on judicial appointments favoured perpetuating the restriction. This is hardly a surprise, since most respondents were barristers, solicitors, judges or their representative organisations. Nevertheless, the Tribunals, Courts and

Enforcement Act 2007 made some inroads into the restrictiveness of the law, as explained above, in Part 4. This was an overt attempt to widen the recruitment pool.

7. THE REMAINING PROBLEM IN 2017—LACK OF DIVERSITY

So the old recruitment system was blamed for producing the current lack of diversity but it seems to me that the problem lies deeper than this, in the law itself, restricting the judiciary to those with rights of audience, and in the legal professions, themselves pathetically unrepresentative, as seen in Ch.13. As I pointed out there, in practice almost all senior judges (HC and above) and a large proportion of circuit judges are recruited from QCs, who are wildly imbalanced, in gender and ethnicity. In 2004, Falconer LC published a DCA consultation paper, *Increasing Diversity in the Judiciary*. It is the statutory job of the Judicial Appointments Commission to devise methods of securing greater diversity but Lord Falconer did not wait around until 2006. Thanks to the efforts of Lord Chancellors Mackay and Irvine, since 1994, above, the lower sections of the judiciary have become more diverse but this was not enough for Lord Falconer.

14–058

Composition in 2017—the continuing problem of lack of diversity

Statistics are on the judiciary website. In 2017, this was the pattern of judges sitting in courts (not tribunals). Incidentally, 51 per cent of the general population of England and Wales were female and 12 per cent were BMF.

14–059

- All judges are barristers or solicitors, except two deputy DJs, who are legal executives. The vast majority of recorders, circuit judges and senior judges are barristers. Solicitors are at the bottom of the hierarchy. Most district judges and deputies are solicitors yet there are 10 times as many solicitors in practice as there are barristers.
- In 2017, there are 11 white UKSC Justices, one of whom is a woman, Baroness Hale of Richmond, the first woman to be appointed as a law lord, in October 2003. All are barristers or advocates (Scottish equivalent).
- In 2016, of the 39 all-white judges in the CA, all were barristers. Eight were women.
- Of the 106 High Court judges, 105 were barristers. Five were non-white. 22 were women.
- Of the 626 circuit judges, 557 were barristers. 23 were non-white. 160 were women.
- Of the 430 County Court district judges, 338 were solicitors. 34 were non-white. 153 were women.
- Of the 133 district judges (magistrates' courts), 87 were solicitors. Seven were non-white. 44 were women.

Arden LJ drew attention to the absence of women in HC appointments in 2005–2008, in a very powerful and informative speech.

"The value of women has been accepted in many other walks of life. For instance, 17% of ambassadors, 19% of Members of Parliament, 23% of permanent secretaries and 61% of the Government Legal Service are women ... women judges account for 17% of the judges of the European Court of Justice; 18% of the judges of the High Court of New Delhi, India; 19% of the judges of the Federal Constitutional Court of Germany; 27% of the judges of the Constitutional Court of South Africa, 29% of the judges of the High Court of Australia; 30% of the judges of the Court of Appeal of New South Wales; 31% of the judges of the European Court of Human Rights; 44% of the judges of the Supreme Court of Canada and so on." (AWB, June 2008)

Lack of social diversity

14–060   The 2004 consultation paper barely mentioned the lack of social and educational diversity but this has been criticised for decades. It was famously attacked by Griffith in *The Politics of the Judiciary* (5th edn, 1997, p.18). The *senior* judiciary (HC, CA and UKSC) was (and is) is dominated by Oxbridge graduates, educated at independent schools. The Labour Research Department published regular surveys of the judiciary and in 2002, they reported that Labour had failed to make the judiciary any more diverse in this respect, since they came to power in 1997. The survey found that 67 per cent went to public school and 60 per cent attended Oxford or Cambridge universities. Under Labour, those in the senior courts were *more* likely to have been public school educated; the average age of the judges was over 60.

It goes without saying that judges will always be middle class, by definition, because they are recruited from lawyers, but judges' lack of educational diversity is extreme. I have argued that the criticism of *senior* judges for being predominantly Oxbridge educated is misplaced, however. Judges in the senior courts need to be exceptionally clever and highly educated. Top judges in other jurisdictions are graduates of elite universities. Oxbridge graduates are predominant in other power elites in the UK, such as politics and commerce. Criticism should be directed instead at the historic class divisiveness of entry to Oxford and Cambridge, which, until the 1970s, favoured applicants from independent schools, who still form a disproportionately high proportion of entrants. (See Darbyshire, 2007 and 2011 for unique interview material from 77 judges, describing their backgrounds.)

Why is lack of diversity a problem?

14–061   Lord Mackay did not think it was. "It is not the function of the judiciary to reflect particular sections of the community, as it is of the democratically elected legislature" (JAP, 1996, p.130). He expected composition would broaden over time. Griffith attacked this sentiment as "weasel words" (JAP, p.261). Lord Irvine (Labour) appeared to take a different view from his Conservative predecessor: "I believe that the judiciary should be a microcosm of the community that it serves" (1999) and clearly Lord Falconer considered it to be an urgent problem, in 2004.

Many have argued that an imbalance in the judiciary warps the administration of justice itself. For instance, Pannick argued "the quality of judicial performance would be improved if more of the bench enjoyed the experience peculiar to more than half the members of our society" (1996). Hewson (1996; 1997), of the

Association of Women Barristers, listed examples of gender bias in judicial and tribunal decisions and advocated the research and educational work of gender bias task forces, such as existed in the USA, where the National Judicial Education Program identified three types of gender bias: stereotypical thinking about the nature and roles of men and women, how society values women and men, and myths about the social and economic realities of women's lives.

On her appointment as the first female law lord, Baroness Hale spelled out why the judiciary needed more women. Quoting Canadian Chief Justice Beverley McLachlin, she argued it would promote public confidence; be symbolic, as the judiciary are required to promote equality and fairness; and be a sound use of human resources, tapping the intellectual qualities of the missing half of the population and bring a different perspective to judgments.

She acknowledged that the last point was controversial and that most of her **14-062** judgments could have been written by a man. Nevertheless she agreed with McLachlin that jurists were informed by their background and experience. For cultural, biological, social and historic reasons, women's experience was different. She concluded: "The present judiciary is disadvantaged but means well. Few if any are actively misogynist or racist but they have a lamentable lack of experience of having female or ethnic minority colleagues of equal status" (Hale, 2003). In 2014, Lady Hale said:

> "I can think of a few judgments where my experience and perceptions of life made a difference to my view of the law, often but not always a view which my brethren were then persuaded (not necessarily by me) to share: the nature of the damage done to a woman by an unwanted pregnancy; the definition of violence to include more than simply hitting people; the importance of seeing children as individual human beings rather than adjuncts of their parents; the realities of owning a family home jointly."

Hunter, McGlynn and Rackley would agree with academic colleagues, Feenan and Moran that some judgments would be different if they were not written by white, heterosexual males. The authors of the collection *Feminist Judgments* (2010) demonstrate the potential difference, by writing "missing" judgments in key cases in the ELS. Professor Hunter argues that we need affirmative action to broaden our judiciary, like some Australian states. See further, Malleson (2006), who challenged the traditional UK hostility to affirmative action in judicial selection. She thought it was not incompatible with the merit principle.

US Supreme Court Justice Sandra Day O'Connor used to say the question of whether more women judges would make a difference was "dangerous and unanswerable". It was dangerous to assert, without research evidence, that changing the composition of the judiciary would automatically change the nature of decision-making. That it *would* do so seemed to be the tacit assumption of Vera Baird QC, speaking for the Fawcett Society in 2005. She thought that introducing more women into the judiciary would result in more rape convictions, perhaps not realising that there is very strong evidence that female jurors and female dominated juries are more likely to acquit. Letters to *The Times* in reply made some wise comments, on 11 October 2005. As explained above, Sonia Sotomayer used to make speeches claiming that a wise Latina woman (like her) with a richness of experience would "reach a better conclusion" but she had to retract that sentiment in order to get appointed onto the US Supreme Court, as explained above. In 2005, the LC started a recruitment drive, saying " … over time, if the group of people who are judges are 50 per cent men, 50 per cent women, that will have a significant effect on the sort of discretionary decisions judges make all the time". Malleson (2004) warned, however, that "The idea that a judge can represent the interests of a group from which he or she is drawn is clearly incompatible with the notion of impartial justice." There was no empirical evidence that women more effectively represented the views of women. American research disclosed little difference between male and female judicial decision-making (reiterated by Genn, 2010, at p.153). In 2013, Durham University students participated in an experiment to see if they could tell the difference between male and female judgments. They were wrong about half of the time. Reacting to the results, Baroness Hale commented "Women sometimes decide cases differently from men but that is not a very frequent occurrence because we are judges and lawyers first and men and women second". Professor Rackley, who helped organise the experiment, said the argument for greater diversity was not that women and men would judge in different ways but the insights of both would be fed into the law and lead to better decision-making (Rackley, 2013). (See further Schultz and Shaw (2013) and Kenney (2013).) Malleson said that one might hope that diversifying the judiciary would increase their range of skills and experience which would enhance decision-making in general but the real reason for including under-represented groups was that "the corrosive impact of their absence on the legitimacy of the judiciary is now too great to ignore." Falconer LC's 2004 DCA consultation paper said:

> "Society must have confidence in that the judiciary has a real understanding of the problems facing people from all sectors of society with whom they come into contact … We must ensure that our judicial system benefits from the talents of the widest possible range of individuals in fairness to all potential applicants and to ensure that talent, wherever it is, is able to be appointed." (*Increasing Diversity in the Judiciary*)

It said the media portrayed judges as elderly, male and of a narrow social class and they and the public concluded that judges were out of touch (see further *Sitting in Judgment*, Ch.2).

I cannot say whether diversifying the judiciary would make a difference to their decisions. Indeed, I saw nothing to indicate that it would, throughout my research years (2002–2012, including both research projects), sitting next to judges, though that was not the topic of my inquiry. I did point out, however, that previous researchers and writers had shown that the composition of the top court, in terms of personalities, does determine the outcome of cases. I found that UKSC Justices acknowledged this fact and were keen to sit in bigger benches more often, to eliminate the lottery effect. I argued that since this is a law-making court, confining itself to points of law of general public importance, it is essentially a political court, especially now it is fuelled by the Human Rights Act. It is not *party* political but clearly its composition matters, practically and symbolically.

14–063   My own view on this issue is that, regardless of whether bench composition affects decision-making, *the visible lack of diversity in our judiciary is, quite* *simply, an international embarrassment.* In my opinion, it is one of the pernicious outcomes of our divided and divisive legal profession, described in the last chapter, where the rank of QC, and jobs as judges have been perceived as a perk of the Bar. Few critics make the most obvious point that solicitors constitute 90 per cent of the legal profession, yet they are concentrated at the bottom of the judiciary, as can be seen from the statistics above. I describe in some detail in *Sitting in Judgment*, how the judicial hierarchy reflects the hierarchy of the legal profession, with most senior judges drawn from the QC rank, most circuit judges recruited from the Bar and most district judges being solicitors. The book is laced with stories from solicitor judges of how they suffered from the snobbery of barristers and of how they were steered *down* to the district bench when they applied to be a judge. Nevertheless, while it is said that lack of diversity in our legal profession has *caused* lack of diversity in our judiciary, this cannot fully explain the narrow makeup of our top courts compared with other countries. As Malleson has pointed out, the argument that underrepresented groups will eventually "trickle up" to our top courts, notably the UKSC, is "weakened by the fact that many other top courts in common law countries around the world had succeeded in diversifying their membership despite being similarly drawn from those who have first had a career of some kind in legal practice". She pointed to the number of women in the Canadian and Israeli Supreme Courts and the South African Constitutional Court, "the rainbow court". She said most other top courts draw from a wider range of career backgrounds. For instance, the year after Malleson wrote this, Elena Kagan, who had never served as a judge, was appointed to the US Supreme Court. Since then, Jonathan Sumption was appointed direct to the UKSC from the Bar, so this is now a more obvious route into diversifying the UK's top court and the courts of England and Wales.

Why specific groups are underrepresented or overrepresented

The exclusion of solicitors

They were the most persistent critics of the old system. As the 1990 Act confined judicial posts to those with rights of audience, this excluded them from much of the bench. Their route onto it was to become a recorder or district judge and seek promotion, or, from 1994, to gain rights of audience as a solicitor-advocate, in the Crown Court or above, which few solicitors have done. Prior to the 1990 Act, solicitors could not be promoted above circuit level. This provoked the criticisms that the system was unfair and produced too narrow a pool of candidates. In 2017, there is still only one solicitor in the entire senior judiciary. **14–064**

Solicitors complained that the published criteria, pre-2006, still placed too much emphasis on career success and income. The requirement for part-time sitting, prior to fulltime appointment, was too lengthy. Short blocks of sitting were disruptive of solicitors' practices. In *Sitting in Judgment*, I quoted solicitors who said their colleagues had resented their sitting as part-time judges. Other minor judicial appointments, such as tribunal chairman, did not seem to be a stepping stone to the circuit bench, since few were promoted. This problem has only been addressed recently, in the Crime and Courts Act 2013, which introduces flexible deployment between courts and tribunals, with the stated aim of enhancing career development. As long ago as 1999, solicitors had become exasperated over the lack of reform and the Law Society announced they were boycotting the "consultations" system. In other words, if solicitors were consulted about potential candidates, they would not offer an opinion. There has not been an enormous amount of progress here, a point which I address below.

The emphasis on silk

14–065 Most senior judges now in office were recruited from QCs, as were many circuit judges. Solicitors, women and ethnic minorities alleged that this was unfair, because the selection system for silks disadvantaged them, because of the emphasis on advocacy and because the method of recruitment to silk pre-2006 was via the same "consultations" system as was used to select judges, effectively an old-boys network. Baroness Hale kept pointing out that only 10 per cent of silks were women. This criticism is still valid, because almost all silks are recruited from advocates and almost all are barristers. Blackwell (2012) supported this argument, by examining statistics on Queen's Counsel and senior judicial appointment since 1995. He showed that, looking at statistical trends, while the solicitors' branch of the profession might achieve gender parity within five years, the Bar would not achieve gender parity for 26 years. The increase in numbers of women QCs was so slow that it would take until the end of the century to achieve gender parity. Therefore, the emphasis on recruiting High Court judges from among QCs means that almost all solicitors are excluded and it is still *very* discriminatory against women, in 2017.

Race—was the old appointments system discriminatory?

14–066 In a provocative 1991 article, Bindman suggested that the pre-2006 system was indirectly discriminatory and thus illegal. He cited the Commission for Racial Equality's code of practice for employers, which discouraged recruitment through the recommendations of the existing workforce where the workforce was predominantly from one ethnic group and the labour market multi-racial. Recruitment by word of mouth was a common cause of discrimination. Lord Mackay retorted that he was struggling to attract sufficient numbers of women and BME candidates to apply.

His successor, Lord Irvine, appeared equally frustrated at the low numbers of minorities applying. At the Minority Lawyers' Association Conference in 1997, he reiterated Prime Minister Tony Blair's embarrassment that there were so few BME judges at that time. He explained that only about one per cent of barristers of 15 years' call, the group eligible for HC appointments, were minority, at that time. The root cause was long-term discrimination in the legal profession: "I cannot solve all the problems by myself. The professions need to ensure their houses are in order." As we shall see, below, to add to the challenge of recruiting a diverse bench, women and BME groups were *still* less likely to apply to be a judge than white males, in 2017.

The exclusion of women

The statistics are quoted above. As for the circuit bench, recruitment was examined by Hughes in 1991, in *The Circuit Bench—A Woman's Place?* She challenged the excuse made by Mackay LC that the numbers of women on the Bench would naturally increase as the number in legal practice increased. Examining two cohorts of barristers, she found that women took longer than men to be appointed to the Bench and were recruited from a much narrower age range. Their late appointments could not be accounted for by maternity leave. Of the 173 circuit judges appointed during 1986–1990, only 4.6 per cent were women. The majority of women judges surveyed thought that, although some had suffered discrimination early in their legal careers, the judicial appointments system did not discriminate against women. Nevertheless, many women had had low career expectations and one third had been *invited* to apply to the bench, without having put themselves forward. This was consistent, said Hughes, with employment research which showed that women were less likely to apply for promotion and more inclined to accept initial rejection than men. The Association of Women Solicitors complained that the requirement to sit as a judge part-time for several years was a double bind for women solicitors. They might annoy their business partners by disrupting their practice and reducing their earning capacity shortly after taking a career break or maternity leave. The judicial atmosphere was unwelcoming to women. Women were disadvantaged by the existence of male clubs, where judges and barristers lunched. The Inns of Court and freemasonry provided opportunities for male barristers to fraternise with judges.

14–067

Some of their recommendations, and those of other parties have since been followed, such as open advertising and reformed selection criteria (partly satisfied in 1995) and the removal of obstacles to employed barristers (in the Access to Justice Act 1999). Malleson and Banda (2000) found that white female barristers felt the demands of practice put them off applying for judicial office, as did a lack of confidence in being taken seriously. The quotation below, from the UK Association of Women Judges, spells out the problem.

Gays and lesbians

Martin Bowley, then President of the Bar Lesbian and Gay Group, had a sorry personal tale of prejudice to tell the Parliamentary Home Affairs Committee, in 1995 (JAP 1996). He had been informed that he was not appointed to the Bench because this was against Lord Mackay LC's policy "since [homosexuals] were particularly vulnerable to public and private pressures". This rule was dropped in 1994. The Lord Chancellor staged the first special recruitment event at the Lesbian and Gay Law Conference in 2000.

14–068

What was the government response to such criticisms, in 1994–2004?

As described above, various reforms took place from 1994. A working party on equal opportunities in judicial appointments and silk was set up in 1997, consisting of representatives of the Bar Council, Law Society, and minority

14–069

lawyers' groups. It reported to the LC in 1999, making 42 recommendations aimed at increasing numbers of women and ethnic minorities applying for silk and judicial appointment. Many were implemented immediately, or following the 1999 Peach report. A work-shadowing scheme was established, to allow lawyers to sit with judges in court. All the 1990s reforms resulted in some success and the number of applicants increased, not just because of reforms but because of the downturn in some areas of lawyers' work.

Attempts to increase diversity from 2006—can they ever fully diversify the judiciary?

14–070   Falconer LC's 2004 consultation paper examined what other tactics might be used to enhance recruitment, in addition to the 2005 Act. While acknowledging that the shortcomings in the old process had been a major factor, the paper rightly said that there were other problems. There was a lack of diversity in the legal profession. Statistics showed that "trickle-up" *was* working, since the numbers of women and minorities entering the profession was now much greater, but was very slow. There was indeed a "trickle out" rate, with women dropping out of the legal profession. The Law Society has been researching the causes of this since the 1980s, as seen in the previous chapter and on their website. Crucially, the 2004 paper pointed out that male and female applicants delayed applying for a judicial post until many years after becoming eligible to be a judge. It explored how to improve communication to lawyers on what judicial appointment offered as a career option; the requirements for judicial office; the working practices of the judiciary and opportunities for progression, and what more might be done by the legal profession to diversify the applicant pool.

Requirements for appointment

14–071   The 2004 paper noted that academics and researchers were experts on the law but were excluded by statute, because of the requirement for audience-rights, unless they were also barristers or solicitors. Similarly, the requirement for several years of post-qualification experience (seven for a district judge or ten for a recorder) conflicted with an appointments process that claimed to be merit-based. Requiring a HC judge to have 20 years experience was indirectly discriminatory, because only 14 per cent of practitioners with that length of experience were women.

The paper articulated the rationale behind the policy of requiring people to sit part-time before appointing them full-time:

1.   Full-time judicial office was unique, a job for life. It was essential to appoint people who were and would continue to be capable of doing a good job. Part-time service allowed them to demonstrate that.
2.   It allowed part-timers to see if they wanted to become a judge.
3.   It allowed them to build their skills and experience. This was essential for non-practitioners like academics.
4.   It afforded an opportunity to appraise them.

5. It was a way of ensuring a high and consistent standard of fulltime appointments.

On the other hand it posed a problem for people with caring responsibilities and for solicitors whose firms banned them from part-time judicial office or who were hostile to it. The 2007 Act and delegated legislation made a wider range of lawyers eligible for the judiciary, including legal executives and patent agents. Selection under the 2007 Act is based on *post-qualification experience* not just rights of audience and time in practice. This still does not address the problem that statutory requirements are based on rights of audience, so a professor with a doctorate in law, thirty years research and teaching experience and profound expertise cannot apply for *any* judicial post if she is not professionally legally qualified. Also, non-barristers enter the fulltime judiciary at the very bottom. It is very rare for a solicitor or a barrister who is not a QC to apply for, or be considered for a High Court post and even then they would be expected to have served as a recorder of deputy HC judge.

Judicial working practices

The 2004 paper pointed out that *salaried part-time* judicial work had been introduced in 2001 for those who could not do a full-time job. This is different from a fee-paid deputy or recorder appointment. It is a salaried fractional appointment as a professional judge. By 2004, 40 judges worked like this, on a flexible basis. Some judges job-share (Bertodono 2009). At long last, the Crime and Courts Act 2013 and delegated legislation extended flexible working to senior judges.   **14–072**

The legal profession

The paper noted the attrition rate of women from the legal profession. Women tended to leave before the point at which they might be expected to apply to be a judge. There was a lack of support from the profession to those who sought judicial appointment. This was especially acute for solicitors, some of whom were forced to choose between partnership in their firm and applying to be a deputy district judge or recorder. The paper complained of the cost of entering the legal profession, the cost of university tuition fees and a sense of bias against degrees from certain universities. In their response to the 2004 paper, The UK Association of Women Judges perfectly encapsulated the problem for women: **14–073**

"The vast majority of successful candidates to the High Court Bench are drawn from the most successful members of the Bar. The majority of candidates to the Circuit Bench are drawn from practising members of the Bar. Yet the Bar is a profession in which is ... extremely difficult to excel if there are home commitments. A successful practice at the Bar, particularly in London, is not a job, it is a way of life. It involves being available, often at short notice, to take on an urgent matter, perhaps with travel away from home, working late in the evenings and at weekends. It involves uncertainty over which days are going to be committed, and holidays being forfeit for the sake of work. There is the uncertainty of being self-employed, with the consequential lack of employment rights. There are no regular hours, or days, or places of work. It is a job which is very self-reliant (rather than being team related) and involves selfless and selfish dedication ... Many talented women give up the Bar and many allow themselves to be 'sidetracked' in chambers ... Many women feel that the price paid is too high."

Even if women did manage to keep a busy practice afloat they could not afford the time for "networking" at evenings and weekends. They suggested that one solution was that all women lawyers should be trawled for judicial appointments, including employed lawyers and academics.

Progress from 2006 seems very slow indeed, the main hurdle being the failure to attract applicants from underrepresented groups. In a 2007 speech, Mrs Justice Dobbs, the first black HC judge, pointed out that she was 0.06 per cent of the senior judiciary and no women had been appointed since 2005. A judicial diversification strategy was launched in 2007. A five-point plan to encourage more solicitors to apply for judicial office was launched by the minister for judicial diversity, in 2007, including publicising the benefits to the individual and their law firm.

In 2008, the new Judicial Appointments Commission was criticised by academics for not using affirmative action, as other judiciaries have done. (Malleson and Russell made an international collection of critical perspectives, 2006.)

14–074   In 2008, the Judiciary commissioned independent research to find out what attracted people to or put them off applying to the senior judiciary. Professor Dame Hazel Genn interviewed recent HC appointees and 29 highly qualified barristers and solicitors and she cited some of the (hilarious) responses in her Hamlyn lectures on civil justice (2010). The review report is on the UCL website and is worth reading.

> "It's a very jolly life not being a judge... ." (female silk; the rest of the quotation opens this chapter)

> "I have no interest in full-time appointment ... Five-fold reduction in income. Less control over professional life and I would feel bound to go on Circuit ... I have young children ... I like to have dinner with my husband and friends rather than talk to a load of High Court judges ... The hours of service ... 60–70 hours ... judges have a huge workload and other activities. I can take a week off if I want to. The loss of autonomy and flexibility is an issue ... The idea of spending the next 15 years of my life being a High Court judge doing rubbish work is frankly too depressing to contemplate ... ."

As the JAC has a statutory duty to promote diversity under the 2005 Act, it had a Diversity Forum. Its 2008–2009 research reports indicated that the following factors discouraged potential applicants and these are outside the control of the JAC:

• the policy of requiring applicants to have served part-time (in fee paid work);
• lack of availability of *salaried* part-time working;
• a lack of diversity among lawyers; and
• working conditions within the judiciary (2008–2009 *Annual Report*).

Research published by the JAC in June 2009 showed that "unfounded myths" were deterring solicitors from applying for judicial appointments. The press release on *Barriers to Application* summarised the findings:

> "For example:
> - One third … believe that they cannot apply unless they know a High Court judge who will act as a referee.
> - It is still widely believed that to become a judge one needs to be a barrister, have the right kind of education, be part of the right social network and know the top judges.
> - It is believed that being under 40 or working class is a disadvantage.
> - Many still do not see the appointments process as based solely on merit. For example, women think men have an advantage and men think women are favoured."

Nevertheless, over half said they would consider applying if they could work part time. Baroness Neuberger headed a 2010 committee preparing *The Report of the Advisory Panel on Judicial Diversity.* The main points were:

- We lack a coherent, comprehensive strategy and there is no quick fix.
- We need to address everything, from the legal career to appointments at the top level, also addressing retention and promotion. The JAC should revise its merit assessment criteria, to clarify its commitment to diversity.
- Heads of the legal profession need to be included in the effort.
- We need a "mythbusting" campaign.

By 2017, it is still an uphill battle to recruit solicitors, women, BME lawyers **14–075** and disabled people. The JAC's 2009 report *Barriers to Application for Judicial Appointment Research* found that for barristers and solicitors there was a massive aspiration gap in terms of how likely they were to apply in the future. The Law Society set up a mentoring group to encourage more solicitors to apply and the JAC and Law Society launched a joint plan to support solicitor applicants, in 2011. The proportion of solicitor recorders in three circuits rose from five per cent to nine per cent and this was claimed to be a success. As we saw in the last chapter, many of the fee earners in solicitors' offices are legal executives. In 2010, for the first time, fellows of the Institute of Legal Executives were able to apply for part-time employment as immigration and asylum judges and the first one to be a DJ was appointed. In 2010, senior paralegals were invited to apply to become judges in the first tier tribunals.

In 2013, the JAC repeated the *Barriers to Application for Judicial Appointment Research*, with 4,051 eligible lawyers. The results showed that fewer lawyers were put off, in 2013, than those interviewed in 2008.
97% thought the work would be interesting (up from 92%, in 2008).
87% thought the job would be enjoyable (up from 74%).
46% considered applying (up from 32%).
73% thought they had the right skills and experience (up from 66%).
The most unappealing aspects of the job were: isolation, travel and judicial culture.
People had not applied because they thought they would not be appointed (51%), or were too young.

Women, solicitors and legal executives were less confident that they had sufficient skills and experience and had insufficient information.

> "Women, solicitors and CILEx are less confident in their abilities in comparison to men and barristers—66% of women; 70% of solicitors and 62% of CILEx believe they have the skills and experience to make a good judge (males 78%; barristers 87%)."

Women, minorities and disabled people strongly believed you needed good contacts. BAME and disabled people were concerned about the fairness of the selection process and how welcoming the judicial culture would be.

In 2013, for the first time, women outnumbered men among newly-appointed judges. In the 2016 JAC annual appointment statistics women made up 45 per cent of those recommended for appointment overall. BAME were 16 per cent of applicants and 9 per cent of appointees. Disappointingly, solicitors were only 13 per cent of those recommended, which entirely supports my argument throughout the sections above. Lesbians, gays and bisexuals were four per cent of applicants and five per cent of those recommended. In 2012–2015, women were 12 per cent of applicants for jobs above HC and 19 per cent of those recommended.

14–076   Introducing the 2016 judicial diversity statistics (not the same thing, as they cover the whole judiciary, not new appointees), the LCJ pointed to the fact that 49 per cent of tribunal judges are women. In 2016, The Senior President of Tribunals and the Lord Chief Justice at last came up with the plan of deploying the courts and tribunals judiciary in a more flexible way, using the 2013 Act, which already provides for a unified judiciary. This would not only achieve a more appropriate and flexible use of their skills, so that a property expert could sit in the County Court and the property chamber of the tribunals structure for instance, but it would also be a great way to facilitate "upskilling" (Ryder LJ, 2016). Clearly, the agenda here is to help members of the diverse tribunals judiciary to became "real" judges in the courts so that the courts judiciary becomes more diverse.

The Judicial Diversity Taskforce reported annually on how many of the 53 Baroness Neuberger Report (2010) tasks have been done. In the Final Report (2015), the legal professions, JAC and judiciary reported what they had achieved to promote diversity, which was a long list. For instance, The Bar Council reported on extending its Bar Placement week targeted at students from non-traditional backgrounds, and its mock trials competition in 170 state schools. The judiciary pointed to its 112 "diversity and community relations judges" who do outreach work, and many other schemes: work-shadowing, mentoring and so on. The Law Society reported that it had encouraged top firms to declare commitment to supporting applicants for the judiciary and networking events with solicitor-judges. The JAC said it had made significant efforts towards all the goals set for it in 2010. It had introduced webinars to outreach to underrepresented groups, constantly monitored and modified its online tests with the help of an occupational psychologist; it had introduced "situational questioning" suitable for candidates without judicial experience applying for fulltime posts and provided generic and individual feedback.

In 2013, the Judges Council established a diversity committee to support the LCJ in his duty to encourage diversity. As it represents roughly the same groups, it has replaced the diversity taskforce. The judiciary's activities and achievements are on the judiciary website, including outreach work in schools and colleges and to various sections of the legal profession. There is already a judicial work-shadowing scheme and a judicial mentoring scheme and these, and the judicial role-models scheme, are explained in detail on the JAC website and the judiciary website. As can be seen from their 2017-2018 action plan, judges are making huge efforts to persuade people to apply.

In 2017, the judiciary offered a "High Court support programme" reserved for 30 candidates in the female, or BAME or less advantaged backgrounds, to provide intensive help to those potential applicants. In 2015 and 2016 the JAC ran a fast track scheme for underrepresented applicants for deputy HC judge. No judicial experience was required, whereas candidates would normally be expected to have sat as a recorder. Following training and sitting part-time, they would be expected to be ready for the 2017 and 2018 HC selection exercises. In 2017, Thomas LCJ persuaded the President of the Law Society to co-author a letter to law firms, asking them to encourage their most senior partners to consider applying for these deputy HC posts. In a March 2017 speech, he pleaded with City solicitors "we can get nowhere without your support and, in particular, the help of each and every firm... it is not only in the interest of our nation for you to do this but it is in your own interests ...

> "...I hope that we can persuade firms to consider their partners sitting as judges as part of their commitment to public service...[and] the law firm benefits from the continued pre-eminent status of English Common Law and from having a workforce with additional skills and experience. Similarly, the individual lawyer benefits from honing existing skills and developing new ones."

If you browse the JAC website, as if you were applying to be a judge, you will find every sort of support and assistance to applicants, including guidance on preparation, coaching videos, tips from successful candidates, not to mention all the workshops, and the mass of outreach events, mentoring opportunities and so on. None of this exists if you want to apply for a job as an academic. Some of this smacks of desperation. According to a March 2017 "Law in Action" programme on BBC Radio 4, there were about 25 unfilled HC vacancies and 120 or more on the circuit bench, because they failed to fill vacancies in 2016. **14–077**

From its inception in 2009, the UKSC has been visibly and provocatively lacking in diversity, to the concern of Lady Hale and its President, Lord Neuberger. As he pointed out, in 2016, they were 10 white men and one white woman. Only two were state schooled and none were from underprivileged backgrounds. In 2015, the outgoing Chief Executive, Jenny Rowe, published a review of the UKSC Selection Commissions' processes. She made 13 recommendations, including job description, structured questions for referees, mentoring, consulting the Society of Legal Scholars about how to attract academics and develop the best form of diversity training for the recruiters. In 2017, the court offered insight visits to applicants, as they need to recruit a number of Justices. In 2015, Lord Sumption said, in a provocative *Evening Standard* interview, that it could take 50 years to achieve gender balance in the senior judiciary. "It takes time. You've got to be patient." He said:

"The Bar and the solicitors' profession are incredibly demanding in the hours of work and the working conditions are frankly appalling. There are more women than men who are not prepared to put up with that. As a lifestyle choice, it's very hard to quarrel with it... ."

Within weeks, Baroness Hale gave a speech which was seen as a riposte. She said the UKSC should be ashamed of itself if it did not radically improve itself in the next round of recruitment. There had been 13 new judges appointed since her, in 2004. All were white males. "All but two went to independent fee-paying schools. All but three went to boys' boarding schools. All but two went to Oxford or Cambridge. All were successful QCs in private practice, although one was a solicitor rather than a barrister". Most specialised in commercial, property or planning law.

14-078   There is still a very long way to go, as the judicial diversity statistics demonstrate. A 2016 report from the Council of Europe, on the 47 contracting states of the European Convention on Human Rights, showed that the number of women in the judiciary of England and Wales, 30 per cent overall, was one of the lowest of Europe, where the average is 51 per cent. The report explained that this partly reflects the recent feminisation of some judiciaries. For example, women became the majority of judges in Italy in 2015, yet they were only allowed to apply for judicial posts from 1965.

The leading writer on the judiciary is Professor Kate Malleson. In a pessimistic 2011 article co-authored with Barmes, they comment:

"[T]his brief critical interrogation of how judicial recruitment pools are constructed shows that access to the judiciary cannot be fairly opened to all until group segmentation and stratification in the legal profession is broken down and/or the appointments system becomes significantly less deferential to the legal professions' (skewed) internal hierarchies and ascriptions of value. In current conditions it is clear that however neutral and meritocratic the judicial appointments process, diversity will remain elusive while the demonstrably false premise obtains that appointments are from an equally neutral, meritocratic legal profession."

In other words, the post-2006 recruitment and selection process has not changed and cannot change the fact that judges are still recruited from the same types of lawyer as always, because of systematic group-based inequality in the legal profession and in professional and public life. Public bodies like the JAC have a statutory duty to pursue equality and diversity aims which they have a limited capacity to bring about.

A more radical suggestion—a career judiciary

14-079   Most continental countries have developed a career judiciary. Descriptions are given in Thomas's 1997 discussion paper (see further Bell, 2006). Most judges are recruited soon after graduating in law. They are selected like civil servants, by competitive examinations, which sometimes include psychological and fitness testing, as well as legal knowledge, which results in women being the majority of recruits. The new recruit must attend courses at judicial college and then starts off at the bottom of the ladder and may, if successful, be promoted through the ranks to the senior judiciary. It is common to require continuing education and further examinations. Few judges are selected from amongst practising lawyers. A portrait of judges in France was drawn in an article by Sage (1998), who claimed that judges were young, radical and middle-class.

From time to time, it has been fashionable to suggest a career judiciary in England and Wales. Most witnesses giving evidence to the 1995 Home Affairs Committee did not mention such a radical plan. The Judges' Council rejected the suggestion on the basis of profound differences between common law systems and the legal systems of continental Europe. The Home Affairs Committee agreed with Brazier's opinion, in evidence, that the judiciary was already a career, in the sense that a career path of a judge may involve sitting in courts of a progressively higher rank. Nevertheless, the Committee firmly rejected any move to a career judiciary in this country. Dawn Oliver, in 2003, examined arguments in favour of a career judiciary but pointed out that it is not on the active agenda in the UK at present, or that of any common law jurisdiction. The habit of recruiting judges from legal practice was "deeply embedded". The high status that our judges enjoyed and respect for the rule of law in the UK relied to an extent on the seniority and successful prior careers of those appointed.

Proponents of a career judiciary generally point out that this would significantly lower the age of the judiciary and inevitably make it much more diverse. Not everyone considers the youthfulness of European career judges to be an asset. Stephen Jakobi, then Director of *Fair Trials Abroad* had more experience than any lawyer in the comparative merits and shortcomings of the lower judiciary around Europe:

> "Countries that seek to attract young people to the bench at an early age but also insist on prolonged professional training and the existence of either experienced colleagues sitting with them or lay assessors until they reach maturity (e.g. Germany and the Netherlands) seem to deliver a quality of justice commensurate with international standards. Those where judges start young but where one or more of these other factors are missing (e.g. Spain and France) do badly." (2003)

He thought the British system worked well. Malleson (1997) argued that, since 1970, the judiciary had undergone a process of formalisation which had resulted in the creation of a *form* of career judiciary for the following reasons: the judiciary had expanded massively; the majority of work in the criminal courts (she meant the Crown Court) was carried out by part-time recorders, many of whom were seeking promotion. This must have strongly influenced their behaviour. Significantly, performance appraisal had only been introduced to monitor the suitability of part-time judges for promotion.

8. TRAINING AND APPRAISAL

We lack the systematic form of judicial training and examinations which are a **14–080** universal requirement for continental judges. It has been said that our system of recruitment direct from practising professional advocates is the antithesis of training.

The fear of undermining judicial independence

14–081 For centuries, judges resisted the suggestion that they undergo training, on the ground that it might undermine their independence. One of the most famous books written by a judge about judging is Lord Devlin's *The Judge* (1978). In it, he delivered a 20-page tirade against a 1976 Home Office Consultative Working Paper suggesting the introduction of training. Here are some extracts:

> "when in 1948 I was appointed to the High Court ... I had never exercised any criminal jurisdiction and not since my early days at the Bar had I appeared in a criminal court. I had never been inside a prison except once in an interviewing room. Two days after I had been sworn in, I was trying crime at Newcastle Assizes ... for centuries judicial appointments have been made on the basis that experience at the Bar is what gives a man the necessary judicial equipment ... where the independence of the judges may be touched or appear to be touched, it is a good thing to have a protocol. Protocol should, I think, decree that in the acquisition of background information a judge should be left to his own devices." (pp.34–35)

The sentiments were typical of judges of that era. He thought training belonged on the continent. Nevertheless, the Judicial Studies Board was established in 1979.

Malleson challenged the claim that judicial training and performance appraisal posed a threat to independence (1997). She commented that judges used the objection of threat to their independence as a sort of trump card to play when opposing any innovation in the judiciary but they failed to explain what they meant by independence. Certainly, in opposing the establishment of the Board, judges insisted on freedom from control by the executive, or interference by any outsider, such as an academic director of studies. For this reason, the College, as it is now called, is still run by judges. Its independence is now guaranteed because the 2005 Act passed responsibility for training to the LCJ and he exercises this via an Executive Board and an Advisory Council.

Malleson pointed out, however, that judges perform a dual function: a constitutional role as one branch of the State counterbalancing the interest of the executive and Parliament and a distinct social service role carried out in their day-to-day work in the courts. Training and performance appraisal were not matters which affected the constitutional position of the judges, "they are concerned with the way in which legal services are provided to the public" (p.660). Training and performance appraisal, she concluded, did not pose any threat, if they were confined to updating the law and questions of how judges handled cases before them.

The current training regime

14–082 New recorder recruits attend a frightening skills-based residential course, requiring a performance before an unpredictable mock jury (of their fellow trainees) before they sit. Judges I interviewed in *Sitting in Judgment* considered it to be a brilliant but gruelling baptism of fire. Deputy DJs must attend civil training before sitting. Following a training review by Professor Dame Hazel Genn, in 2011, the JSB became a virtual Judicial College. It has very little training accommodation. Its current strategy is in general terms, on the Judiciary website, along with outline information and an annual *Activities Report*. It acknowledges the difficulty of evaluating the success of training. The development of a prospectus, from 2010, aims to offer judges a choice of continuation seminars, instead of standardised ones, and to move away from black letter law to the acquisition of judicial skills. Nevertheless, as can be seen from the stories about training in *Sitting in Judgment*, the new recorders' mock trial was ahead of its time as a challenging, skills-based session. Delivery of law updates is shifting to e-learning, with a learning management system launched in 2013. Circuit and district judges are required to attend one national residential seminar a year (cut to two days in 2014 because of a budget cut), plus usually one day on circuit.

Training for handling litigants in person is embedded in a variety of training exercises. In 2008, the JSB published a Judicial Skills Framework. It is meant to be a self-help guide. It emphasises fair treatment in every aspect of judging and explains how this is to be integrated into training. All judges have been expected to refer to a comprehensive *Equal Treatment Bench Book* since the 1980s. It is designed to educate them and alert them to about twelve equality issues, including social exclusion, minorities such as travellers and gender reassignment.

Until very recently, there was a gap in judicial training as new HC judges had none. In 2009, the JSB's senior judiciary committee proposed that new HC judges have five days' training in their first year and two days thereafter and that was agreed. It piloted a three-day serious crime seminar for them in 2010, and the prospectus also contains HC seminars in civil and family cases. From 2014, national seminars are offered in QBD work and a seminar on administrative law. My research in *Sitting in Judgment* demonstrated the extreme necessity of this, because of the demand for judges to sit in the Administrative Court and the lack of judges with experience in administrative law. There is at last a HC Director of Training. Deputy district judges have had the benefit of mentoring and appraisal since 2002, as have lay magistrates before them. A mentoring scheme was introduced for recorders in 2009 and another has been developed for HC judges. They are given an information pack. New HC judges are offered a flexible programme of sitting-in and visits, devised with their Head of Division and they may, as before, attend continuation seminars geared for circuit judges and evening seminars in the Royal Courts of Justice, and they have access to online learning and written material. The seminars are normally chaired by a CA judge and are attended by CA and HC judges. They cover topical issues, for example, new statutes.

The call for judicial performance appraisal

Critics have called for some form of performance appraisal for full-timers, possibly linked with training. For instance, the Royal Commission on Criminal Justice, 1993, said: "We ...find it surprising that full-time judges seldom if ever observe trials conducted by their colleagues" (para.98). Judge Holden, who had headed the independent tribunal service, advocated it in 1993, as it was in use throughout the tribunal system.   **14–083**

It was part of Labour policy prior to their election to power in 1997. It was extended from tribunals to the lay magistracy, in 1998, then extended to deputy district judges and, following the Peach recommendations, it was extended to all part-time appointments. Peach also advocated self-appraisal. Auld LJ (2001) was in favour of extending it to all fulltimers. Most solicitors were well used to appraisal systems. "A trial judge's job is a solitary one", he observed. "The only judge he sees in action is himself" (Ch.6). For the Lord Chief Justice and Senior President of Tribunals, "Quality Assurance", was one of their new buzz-phrases, in 2016-2017, in their plans for a unified courts and tribunals judiciary, in their 2016 vision paper, *Transforming Our Justice System*, discussed in earlier chapters, and their speeches. Tribunal judges were used to appraisal. It and it would be an important tool for career progression (Ryder 2016, para.51).

9.   RESEARCH

14–084   Except for the top court, about whom there was nothing we did not know, thanks to a string of books, the latest being Paterson (2013), there is very little research on judges in England and Wales, as explained in *Sitting in Judgment* (2011). This is partly caused by historic judicial hostility and partly by academic laziness or lack of interest. In her 2008 Hamlyn lectures (2009) Professor Dame Hazel Genn rightly said that there is an "information black hole":

> "There is virtually nothing to be read on styles of judging, court behaviour, influences on decision making, managing the routine, managing the complex, the realities of life in court in the post-Woolf era, what approaches are effective for fact gathering, how credibility is assessed, what styles of communication work best with unrepresented parties." (p.131)

The UCL Judicial Studies Institute was launched in November 2010, directed by Genn and Professor Cheryl Thomas. It says it is "the country's first and only centre of excellence in research, teaching, policy engagement and scholarship on the judiciary", though no events were scheduled for 2016 or 2017.

In my research, I work-shadowed a very broad sample of 40 judges and interviewed 77, at every level of the ELS, in all six circuits, with a view to finding out what judges did and what they were like. I enjoyed unprecedented help from the judiciary, thanks to the support of Igor Judge, who was the Lord Chief Justice of England and Wales. I was even permitted to observe and report on the deliberations of the CA. My main findings were that the public image of judges as out of touch is grossly unfair, given that the most disturbing and disturbed of people fill their courts; a surprising number of judges are from humble origins; most are not self-important; some, especially family and senior judges, work ridiculously hard, over long hours, on cases that require the analysis of a mass of documentation, which is often highly technical. Their working conditions are often appalling, with courts that are badly designed or in need of repair, staff that are an underpaid, poorly trained, scarce resource and scandalously poor IT. They are hard pressed to progress the cases through their lists because the agencies that appear before them are all underfunded so cases are not properly prepared. Nevertheless, all but 3 of the 77 sampled loved their job. They saw themselves as giving something back to society. In 2009, Genn referred to them as "heroic". An example of recent empirical research, which is part of this encouraging new trend because it uses interview material, is Fielding's 2011 article, in which he compares the attitudes of English and American judges to selection, training and sentencing.

When the July 2017 statistics were released, the LCJ complained that recruitment of BAME judges was too slow. The statistics support my point about the exclusion of solicitors, very starkly. Of the 746 solicitor applicants, only 14 were successful. For the latest analysis of judicial diversity, see the 2017 JUSTICE report.

Bibliography

Arden LJ D.B.E., address to the Association of Women Barristers AGM, 3 June 2008, on her disappointment at the lack of women HC judges. Includes interesting statistical comparisons.   **14–085**

Auld LJ, *Review of the Criminal Courts in England and Wales* (2001), Ch.6, National Archives.

V. Baird QC, "Judges are chosen from too small a gene pool", *The Times*, 20 September 2005.

BBC Radio 4, "Top Dogs", 8 September 2009.

J. Beatson, "Should Judges Conduct Public Inquiries?" (2005) 121 L.Q.R. 221–252.

J. Bell, *Judiciaries Within Europe: A Comparative Review* (Cambridge: Cambridge University Press, 2006).

M. Bentham, "Rush for gender equality with top judges 'could have appalling consequences for justice'", interview with Jonathan Sumption, *Evening Standard Online*, 1 September 2015.

G. Bindman, "Is the system of judicial appointments illegal?" Law Society's *Gazette*, 27 February 1991, p.24.

T. Bingham, "The Old Order Changeth" (2006) 122 L.Q.R. 211–223.

M. Blackwell, "Old boys' networks, family connections and the English legal profession", [2012] P.L. 426.

O. Bowcott, "Proportion of female judges in UK among lowest in Europe", *The Guardian Online*, 6 October 2016.

Commission for Judicial Appointments, website archived in 2007: *http://www. webarchive.org.uk/pan/15580/20070220/www.cja.gov.uk/index.html*.

The Concordat between the Lord Chancellor and Lord Chief Justice, January 2004, is properly known as "Constitutional Reform—The Lord Chancellor's judiciary-related functions: Proposals", on the archived Department for Constitutional Affairs website: *http://webarchive.nationalarchives.gov.uk/ 20100512160448/http://www.dca.gov.uk/index.htm*.

The Constitutional Reform Act 2005 and explanatory notes.

S. Cretney, "He may be an eminent man, but is he right for the job?" *The Times*, 21 February 2005.

P. Darbyshire, "Where do English and Welsh Judges Come From?" (2007) 66 *Cambridge Law Journal* 365–388; *Sitting in Judgment: The Working Lives of Judges* (Oxford: Hart Publishing, 2011).

S. de Bertodano, "I hope my new role will encourage others", *The Times*, 4 June 2009.

DCA, *Increasing Diversity in the Judiciary*, 2004, CP 25/04: (DCA archived website, in the consultation papers, National Archives).

G. Drewry, Comment [1998] P.L. 1.

D. Feenan, "Women judges: gendering judging, justifying diversity", (2008) (35) (4) J.L.S.

N.G. Fielding, "Judges and their work" (2011) 20(1) *Social and Legal Studies* 97–115.

G. Gee, R. Hazell, K. Malleson and P. O'Brien, *The Politics of Independence in the UK's Changing Constitution* (Cambridge: Cambridge University Press, 2016).

Professor Dame Hazel Genn, *The attractiveness of senior judicial appointment to highly qualified practitioners* (Directorate of Judicial Offices for England and Wales, 2008, Judiciary website); *Judging Civil Justice The Hamlyn Lectures 2008* (Cambridge: Cambridge University Press, 2010).

F. Gibb, "Crony taunts return with job for friend of Falconer" *The Times*, 13 January 2005; "Convictions are quashed following trial judge's bad temper" *The Times*, 22 July 2005; "Why diversity is still proving difficult" *The Times*, 13 March 2007; "Is this an unseemly rush to change?" *The Times*, 1 May 2007 (on the Ministry of Justice); "Supreme ambition, jealousy and outrage" *The Times*, 4 February 2010.

House of Commons Home Affairs Committee, Third Report, Session 1995–1996, *Judicial Appointments Procedures Vol.II* (HMSO, 1996) (abbreviated in the text to JAP).

J.A.G. Griffith, *The Politics of the Judiciary*, 5th edn (London: Fontana, 1997).

Dame Brenda Hale, "Equality and the Judiciary: why should we want more women judges?" [2001] P.L. 489; "Welcome to the white men's club" *The Guardian*, 30 October 2003; "Women in the judiciary", speech, 27 June 2014; "Appointments to the Supreme Court", speech, 6 November 2015 and see more speeches, UKSC website.

J. Hayes, "Appointment by invitation" (1997) 147 N.L.J. 520.

B. Hewson, on gender bias in judicial decisions, *The Times*, 17 September 1996 and (1997) 147 N.L.J. 537 and see C. McGlynn at (1998) 148 N.L.J. 813.

A. Howard, "Lord Woolf v The Home Secretary" *The Times*, 9 March 2004.

R. Hunter, C. McGlynn and E. Rackley (eds), *Feminist Judgments: From Theory to Practice* (Oxford: Hart Publishing, 2010).

S. Jakobi, "Younger judges", letter, *The Times*, 10 July 2003.

Sir Igor Judge, "Heroes and Villains", speech, 13 October 2003, archived judges' speeches, National Archives.

Lord Judge CJ, speech, "Judicial Independence and Responsibilities", 5 May 2009, National Archives.

Judicial Appointments—Balancing Independence, Accountability and Legitimacy (2010), a collection of essays published jointly by ILEX, The Bar Council, The Law Society and the JAC.

JUSTICE, *Increasing Judicial Diversity* (2017).

Keene LJ, "Changing the Constitution: the Executive, the Judiciary and the John Adams Problem", the 80 Club Lecture, Liberal Democrat Lawyers Association, 23 June 2004, reproduced in *The Legal Democrat* 2004.

Baroness Helena Kennedy, "A good brand: is that all the Lord Chancellor is?" *The Times*, 24 February 2004.

S. Kenney, *Gender and Justice: why women in the judiciary really matter* (Abingdon: Routledge, 2013).

C. Kinch QC, "Judicial Maladies" (on recent examples of "cantankerous and difficult" judicial behaviour), *Counsel*, November 2010, p.20.

Labour Research Department Press Release, December 2002 and later material *http://www.lrd.org.uk*.

Legal Studies (special issue on the 2005 constitutional reforms, especially judicial appointments) Vol.24, Issues 1 and 2, March 2004.

K. Malleson, *The New Judiciary* (Aldershot: Ashgate Publishing, 1999); "Judicial Training and Performance Appraisal: the problem of judicial independence" (1997) 60 M.L.R. 655; "The Peach Report on Silk and Judicial Appointments" (2000) 150 N.L.J. 8; "Creating a Judicial Appointments Commission: Which Model Works Best?" [2004] P.L. 102; "Rethinking the merit principle in judicial selection" (2006) 33(1) JLS 126–140; "Appointments to the House of Lords: Who Goes Upstairs", in L. Blom-Cooper, B. Dickson and G. Drewry, *The Judicial House of Lords 1876–2009* (Oxford: Oxford University Press, 2009). Professor Malleson is the leading UK writer on the judiciary. For a list of her publications, see *http://www.researchpublications.qmul.ac.uk/publications/staff/20655.html*.

K. Malleson and F. Banda, *Factors affecting the decision to apply for silk and judicial office* LCD Research Report No.2/2000 (2000), DCA archived website, National Archives.

K. Malleson and P.H. Russell (eds), *Appointing Judges in an Age of Judicial Power* (Toronto: University of Toronto Press, 2006).

R. Masterman, "A Supreme Court for the United Kingdom: two steps forward but one step back on judicial independence" [2004] *Public Law* 48.

Lord Neuberger MR, "Who are the masters now?" (on judicial supremacy v parliamentary sovereignty), speech, 6 April 2011, archived judges' speeches, National Archives.

D. Oliver, *Constitutional Reform in the UK* (Oxford: Oxford University Press, 2003), Ch.18.

D. Pannick, "Preventing the Ministry of Justice causing injustice" *The Times*, 8 May 2007.

A. Paterson, *Final Judgment: The Last Law Lords and the Supreme Court* (Oxford: Hart Publishing, 2013).

L. Peach, *An Independent Scrutiny of the Appointment Process of Judges and Queen's Counsel in England and Wales: A Report by Sir Leonard Peach* (1999), National Archives.

E. Rackley, *Women, Judging and the Judiciary* (Abingdon: Routledge, 2013); "The Neuberger Experiment" (2013) 163 N.L.J., August 16, p.13.

The Report of the Advisory Panel on Judicial Diversity (Ministry of Justice, 2010), "The Neuberger Report", and *Improving Judicial Diversity—Progress towards delivery of the "Report of the Advisory Panel on Judicial Diversity 2010"*, 2011 and annually, JAC website. The final (2014) report was published in

June 2015, "Improving Judicial Diversity", on the Judiciary website. News of the Judges Council Diversity Committee, which took over from the Diversity Task Force, is on the Judiciary website.

The Rt. Hon. Sir Ernest Ryder, Senior President of Tribunals, "The Modernisation of Access to Justice in Times of Austerity", speech, 3 March 2016, Judiciary website.

A. Sage, on French judges, *The Times*, 1 December 1998.

I.R. Scott, "A Supreme Court for the United Kingdom" (2003) 22 C.J.Q. 318.

U. Schultz and G. Shaw (eds.) *Gender and Judging* (Oxford: Hart Publishing, 2014) (essays by 30 authors from 15 countries).

S. Sedley, "Judicial Politics" (challenging Sumption), *London Review of Books*, Vol.34 No.4. 23 February 2012, online.

R. Smith, "Judging the Judges" (2009) 159 N.L.J. 1154.

R. Stevens, *The Independence of the Judiciary* (Oxford: Oxford University Press, 1993); "On being nicer to James and the children" (on independence, countering attacks on Mackay LC) (1994) 144 N.L.J. 1620; "Reform in haste and repent at leisure: Iolanthe, the Lord High Executioner and Brave New World" (2004) 24 *Legal Studies* 1.

(Lord) J. Steyn, "The Case for a Supreme Court" (2002) 118 L.Q.R. 392; "Creating a Supreme Court", *Counsel*, October 2003, p.14.

J. Sumption QC, "Making the Grade", *Counsel*, April 2011, p.18; F.A. Mann, Lecture 2011, "Judicial and Political Decision-Making: The Uncertain Boundary", Pembroke College, Cambridge University website, *http://www.pem.cam. ac.uk/wp-content/uploads/2012/07/1C-Sumption-article.pdf*.

The Governance of Britain—Judicial Appointments, Cm.7210 (2007).

C. Thomas and K. Malleson, "Judicial Appointments Commissions: The European and North American Experience and the possible implications for the United Kingdom" (1997) L.C.D. Discussion Paper 6/97, summarised on the DCA archived website, National Archives.

Toulson LJ, "Stepping up to the Bench", *Counsel*, November 2010, p.27.

The United Nations website.

D. Woodhouse, *The Office of Lord Chancellor* (London: Bloomsbury, 2001).

Lord Woolf CJ, Squire Centenary Lecture, "The Rule of Law and a Change in the Constitution", Cambridge, 3 March 2004, judges' speeches, National Archives.

M. Zander, "A waste of space" (2007) 157 N.L.J. 1649.

Further reading and sources for updating this chapter

14–086 Free updates of this book are available on the Sweet & Maxwell website: *http://uklawstudent.thomsonreuters.com*.

Summary and revision: P. Darbyshire, *Nutshells English Legal System*, 10th edn (London: Sweet & Maxwell, 2016).

Guardian Online.

Judiciary of England and Wales website, including judges' speeches. Speeches before 2013 are in the archived website in the National Archives.

The Judicial College is on the Judiciary website.

The Judicial Appointments Commission website, especially general information on the appointments process and research and publications, under "About the JAC".

Lexis.

The Judicial Complaints and Investigation Office.

The Ministry of Justice.

Parliament, especially the Constitution Committee and the Justice Committee.

The Department of Constitutional Affairs archived website, National Archives, as the DCA was replaced by the Ministry of Justice in 2007.

UCL Judicial Studies Institute: *http://www.ucl.ac.uk/laws/judicial-institute.*

Counsel.

International Journal of the Legal Profession.

The New Law Journal.

Westlaw Current Awareness and Journals.

PART 5

LAYPEOPLE IN THE LAW

CHAPTER 15

Magistrates

"for 1% of the court service's operating budget, [the magistracy] deals with over 90% of the criminal cases, with an appeal rate of less than 1%". (Chair of the Magistrates' Association, appearing before the House of Commons Justice Committee, 7 June 2016).

"Lord Bingham, a senior law lord, calls them 'a democratic jewel beyond price'" (Lord Andrew Phillips, solicitor and Liberal Democrat Peer, 2001).

Magistrates' courts are described in Chs 6 and 7. There, we saw that many have been closed since 2011 and many more are scheduled to close from 2017, thus destroying the concept of local justice by local people. Lay magistrates' numbers have diminished from almost 30,000 in 2011, to under 18,000 in 2017 so some of them feel under threat. The role of magistrates was the subject of a rare and overdue review by the House of Commons Justice Committee in October 2016, which exposed how demoralised some of them feel, unsurprisingly, since they have been fighting a losing battle for years.   **15–001**

1. LAYPEOPLE IN THE LEGAL SYSTEM

The English legal system is unique, in worldwide terms, in making such extensive use of laypeople as decision-makers: as magistrates, jurors and tribunal members. This is partly the product of history but is now justified as keeping the law in touch with the public affected by it. In 2011, magistrates celebrated their 650 year history. They were recognised by statute in 1361. There are 17,552 lay justices (2016). They are the most important judges in the legal system, in the sense that, along with professional magistrates called district judges (magistrates' courts) (DJMCs), they deal with over 80 per cent of criminal charges, from start to finish, and most sentencing. They hear almost all prosecutions of young offenders, in the unseen youth court. Furthermore, they have a very significant civil workload, including family cases, which have shifted into the Family Court, from 2014. Their jurisdiction in children's family cases is as powerful as that of the circuit judge. Magistrates also sit in the Crown Court, alongside a circuit judge, hearing criminal appeals from the magistrates' court. For most people, a criminal court appearance, real or virtual, means an appearance before the magistrates. People are remarkably ignorant about magistrates. The 2001 MORI poll cited below found a third of the public did not know that the majority of magistrates were laypeople and hugely underestimated the proportion of cases they heard. Criminal procedure and the law of evidence have been developed   **15–002** around judges' and Parliament's false assumption that most criminal cases are dealt with by judge and jury. This is a big mistake (Darbyshire, "Neglect", 1997).

2. APPOINTMENT AND REMOVAL

15-003 Both lay justices and DJMCs are Justices of the Peace. The Senior Presiding Judge appoints lay magistrates, on behalf of the Lord Chief Justice. Magistrates are recruited locally and were required to live near their bench. The Courts Act 2003 abolished this rule. The SPJ receives recommendations for appointment from 45 advisory committees, mostly chaired by the Lord-Lieutenant of the county and comprising mostly of magistrates, though one third must be non-magistrates. The Judicial Appointments Commission was meant to be taking over responsibility for selecting magistrates, Under the Constitutional Reform Act 2005 but this has never been implemented. Advisory Committees are non-statutory, composed mainly of magistrates, and directed by the Lord Chancellor, who is responsible for recruitment and selection.

Any adult aged 18–65 can apply. UK nationality is not a condition, under the Act of Settlement 1701. Qualities required are good character, understanding and communication, social awareness, maturity and sound temperament, sound judgment, commitment and reliability. Some people's jobs preclude them from consideration: anyone working in the criminal justice system. Partners or spouses of prison officers are ineligible. Some criminal offences, bankruptcy and recent bans from driving *may* be a barrier to recruitment. Applicants should usually be able to serve for at least five years. They must observe court sittings before applying. Candidates undergo a two-stage interviewing process. Lay justices are unpaid volunteers. They are entitled to travelling expenses, subsistence payments and a loss of earnings allowance but this by no means compensates business owners. Few justices claim allowances (Morgan and Russell, 2000).

Criticism

15-004 The persistent problem with the magistracy was (and is) its lack of diversity. Some said that this was partly caused by the fact that magistrates select new magistrates. Even the Magistrates' Association called this system a "self-perpetuating oligarchy", in evidence to the House of Commons Home Affairs Select Committee in its report on *Judicial Appointments Procedures* (1995), although the 2000 report of the Lord Chancellor's Equality Working Group refuted this. Advisory Committees are given no advertising budget (Darbyshire, "Concern", 1997). The LC ran the first national recruitment campaign for a month in 1999. It aimed to destroy the stereotype that magistrates were white and middle class. Magistrates' courts sometimes organise open days. The Magistrates' Association runs a "Magistrates in the Community" campaign addressing schools, employers and local groups, in an endeavour to demystify the magistracy and attract applicants, though in the House of Commons Justice Committee's 2016 report, they noted that it is underfunded.

The report also noted the lack of advertising and they heard evidence from Luke Rigg, a very young magistrate, that people do not know what magistrates do and whether they are paid or working voluntarily. I have been making this point for years and it has been supported by research. In evidence, the Staffordshire Advisory Committee reported that they had launched a successful major publicity campaign, using local newspapers and TV and radio, and putting advertisements in libraries, leisure centres, supermarkets and parish noticeboards.

The problem of achieving a balanced bench

Successive Lord Chancellors have boasted that the magistracy represents the community. This is not true. Like many before me, I argued, using the support of statistics and research, that it was then predominantly Conservative, white and middle class (see "Concern", 1997). It has at last been acknowledged in the current recruitment literature that certain groups are underrepresented and those people are especially encouraged to apply: BMEs, young, disabled, non-managerial and non-professional people. Information on party politics is not collected nowadays. I was and still am concerned that magistrates are too old. Since I made that argument in 1997, their age profile has become significantly older. Later, Lord Chancellors appeared to be trying to address some of these problems on a national level. Lord Falconer launched a National Strategy for the Recruitment of Magistrates in 2003. It responded to complaints of lack of diversity and recommendations made by Auld, in his 2001 *Review of the Criminal Courts*. Recruiting more young magistrates was a key diversity objective of the Ministry of Justice. Since 2011, however, recruitment has stopped in half the advisory committee areas and the numbers have shrunk. The exception in 2017 is London, which needs to recruit 350 new magistrates, owing to retirements and resignations over bench closures.

15–005

Age

"The Lord Chief Justice has expressed the need for magistrates of fatherly rather than grandfatherly age." (R.M. Jackson, in *The Machinery of Justice* (1st edn, 1940))

15–006

"In theory, you can become a magistrate at 21. In practice nobody is ever appointed before 27" (Rosemary Thomson, chairman of the Magistrates' Association in evidence to the House of Commons Home Affairs Committee, 1995). In 1997 ("Concern"), I complained that, since the peak age of offending is around 18 for males and 15 for females, magistrates' age profile makes a double generational difference between the bench and the accused. This did not bother Lord Chancellor Irvine. Indeed, he raised the maximum age for new magistrates from 60 to 65, in the hope of achieving a more *socially* balanced bench. I complained in 1997 that only 22 per cent of lay justices were under 40. By 2016, the situation was much worse. 4 per cent were under 40, and 86 per cent were over 60. A 21 year old magistrate, Luke Rigg, gave evidence to the Parliamentary Justice Committee in 2016 (below) but young appointments are exceptional.

Social class and politics

15–007 Successive studies, cited in my 1997 article, demonstrated over-representation of the middle classes and certain occupational groups and this was confirmed by Morgan and Russell (2000), who found the magistracy to be "overwhelmingly drawn from managerial and professional ranks". A Magistrates' Recruitment Strategy was launched in 2003, admitting "There is a general difficulty in attracting applications from the working public". Various reasons have been identified, since the mid-twentieth century. People who travel in their jobs are unavailable. Those running small businesses may find the loss of earnings allowance inadequate. Insufficient blue collar workers are attracted to apply, according to evidence of the Magistrates' Association and others to the Parliamentary Home Affairs Committee, in 1995. Despite the fact that their jobs are protected by the Employment Rights Act 1996, people may fear they will be sacked for taking time off to be a magistrate, or will irritate colleagues, or hamper their chances of promotion. The 2003 Strategy acknowledged that employers needed the message that magistrates acquire marketable transferable skills. These were listed on the magistrates' recruitment website and applicants were given a DVD to explain to their employers the benefit of employing a magistrate. The Recruitment Strategy added that some single parents could not spare the time to undertake voluntary work and many people could not afford to undertake voluntary unpaid work. There are no publicly available statistics on magistrates' occupational backgrounds, in 2017. Yet again, in 2016, the Parliamentary Justice Committee tried to address the problem of persuading employers to support their employees sitting as magistrates and received a battery of suggestions, including an idea that employers who supported employees to be magistrates should be recognise by a Kitemark.

In 2003, Falconer LC announced that voting patterns would no longer be used as indicators of balance and would be replaced with new indicators to determine how far the local bench represented the community: occupational, industrial and social groupings, matched against the census data. This followed the same trend in the full-time professional judiciary, of distancing the bench further from party politics because, for most of the twentieth century, party politics had been a big issue on the bench. In the 1970s, in some towns most of the magistrates were local councillors. Going further back, magistrates *were* the local government until councils were created by the Local Government Act 1888. A 2010 consultation paper on advisory committees reminded us that they were established in 1911, following complaints of political selection:

> "The position of Magistrates was seen as a reward for political services. This was highlighted by the large variation…appointed under different Governments either side of the 1906 elections." (para.2)

Clearly we have shifted to a position where the bench is supposedly so independent of party politics that it is taboo even to ask a candidate what party they support. This directly reflects the position in the fulltime judiciary. There is no reason to suppose that magistrates represent the Conservative party, as they did in 1997.

Race

Historically, the lay magistracy has under-recruited minorities. It used to be difficult to attract applications. The contrast is visible in court, where non-whites are over-represented among defendants and victims. This was especially acute in areas of minority population concentration ("Concern", 1997). Recognising this, Lord Chancellors Mackay (Conservative), then Irvine, then Falconer (Labour), tried to compensate by appointing proportionately more non-whites than there were in the population at large. Recruitment of non-whites was above 8 per cent every year 1999–2010. This doubtless reflects the success of various recruitment drives, including the Operation Black Vote shadowing scheme, described below. In 2016 10 per cent of lay justices were non-white, below the 14 per cent non-white population of England and Wales, according to the 2011 census. In 1997, I commented that the worst visible differences, though, were in areas of large non-white populations. As can be seen from the 2003–2016 statistics, however, and the 2015–2016 recruitment statistics in the government response to the Parliamentary Justice Committee report, below, a great effort had been made to recruit non-whites in areas of high minority populations but it is still not enough, in my opinion. For instance, of the 2,549 magistrates in London, in 2016, there were 599 non-white magistrates (in a general population of 40 per cent non-white). In Birmingham and the Black Country, 144 of the 702 magistrates were non-white (general population 46 per cent non-white). Of course, that makes for a stark difference between predominantly white benches and the population appearing before them in court, in which non-whites are visibly over-represented. **15–008**

In 2004, the Department of Constitutional Affairs (now Ministry of Justice) published research by Vennard and others, *Ethnic minority magistrates' experience of the role and of the court environment*. It aimed to explore whether minority magistrates had experienced racism and whether they complained of this; what was the impact of perceived discrimination and racism upon their satisfaction with the role and what levels of responsibility minority magistrates achieved. 128 magistrates from 14 benches were interviewed.

1. Most respondents considered racism endemic in this country.
2. They were motivated to become magistrates from a sense of civic responsibility and a desire to put something back into the community. Others derived personal satisfaction. Some wanted to make a positive contribution in cases with minority defendants.
3. 70 per cent had wholly favourable initial impressions and were as fully integrated as they wished to be. 30 per cent initially felt uneasy or marginalised.
4. 72 per cent had not encountered racist attitudes or behaviour among magistrates. For 28 per cent, some felt they had been excluded or marginalised by a white chairman in court but they enjoyed a good relationship with most white colleagues.
5. Four believed they had been subjected to unequal treatment.

6. Most praised their justices' clerk and her team. 8 per cent found staff had displayed racist attitudes towards others. Some recalled racist behaviour by lawyers, police or defendants.

7. Most were impressed by the efforts made by their court to be fair. 21 per cent had observed magistrates displaying racist attitudes towards defendants.

8. Magistrates identified a number of obstacles to recruiting minorities: financial disincentives; employers' reluctance to allow time off; the white, middle class image of the magistracy and the misperception that only educated, professional people could be magistrates.

9. 20 per cent fewer minority magistrates had become bench chairmen. There was an underrepresentation of minorities in the family court.

Disability

15–009 The Equality Working Group (below) reported a shortage of applications from disabled people so the recruitment web-pages now encourage applications. This problem was also recognised by the Parliamentary Justice Committee in 2016.

Gender

15–010 Many commentators complained in the past that the magistracy was overwhelmingly male. This was not true, as I pointed out in 1997, nor is it true now. The 2016 statistics show that 53 per cent are women so, in this respect, they are far more gender balanced than the mainstream judiciary.

Enhancing diversity

15–011 In response to the report of the Stephen Lawrence Inquiry (1999), the Lord Chancellor's Department (now MoJ) audited its procedures to assess whether they provided equality of opportunity and supported diversity. An Equality Working Group was established to seek ways of diversifying the bench. A 2000 report praised the efforts of Irvine LC but recommended the following:

- Attract media attention to raise the magistracy's profile among underrepresented groups.
- Train advisory committees to distinguish between positive action and positive discrimination.
- Communicate zero tolerance of discrimination.
- Copy the Territorial Army model of presenting awards to employers who allowed staff time off to be magistrates.
- Consider how to change people's attitudes to colleagues who take time off to serve.
- Develop an integrated national strategy to replace the present piecemeal one.
- Make court buildings more accessible for disabled magistrates.
- Find out why justices resign. It seemed to be because they could not fulfil the sittings required.

- Ensure dress codes were not culturally biased.

Auld emphasised the value of the lay magistracy in his 2001 Review but commented that there was "scope for improvement ... [in] recruitment, so as to achieve a better reflection, nationally and locally, of the community" (p.98). He recommended:

- Reviewing community relations and educational initiatives to inform the public better.
- Supporting local advisory committees with a National Recruitment Strategy (done in 2003).
- Equipping advisory committees with local and national demographic data.
- Reviewing ways to make service as a magistrate more attractive to a wider range of the community.

In 2001, the Lord Chancellor's Department and Operation Black Vote piloted the magistrates' shadowing scheme, encouraging members of minority ethnic communities to sit with justices, in the hope of recruiting some of them (implemented nationwide 2004). In 2003, Falconer LC launched the National Strategy for the Recruitment of Lay Magistrates. The Government wanted to increase recruitment and retention of a diverse spectrum of the population; raise the profile of the magistracy and dispel misconceptions; encourage younger people; target ethnic minorities and the disabled and make sitting days more flexible. Recruitment campaigns were targeted at underrepresented groups. Some plans were simple, such as developing a recruitment leaflet, and others more complex, such as educating employers that magistrates could import useful transferable skills. They promised an extensive advertising campaign using a variety of channels.

Three recent reports are concerned that attempts to diversify the judiciary have stopped. The Policy Exchange, a "right-wing think-tank" published two reports in 2013 and 2014. Transform Justice, another pressure group, published a report in 2014. They, the Magistrates' Association and many others suggested recruitment and appointment reforms in their evidence to the Justice Select Committee inquiry 2016, which is all available on the Parliament website. In their 2013 report, The Policy Exchange said:

> "'Diversity' as currently measured, in terms of gender, ethnicity and disability is too narrow. Whilst these are central and essential dimensions of diversity, this focus distracts from other crucial dimensions such as occupational and socioeconomic diversity." (p 7)

Their research analysed magistrates from Manchester, Salford and Oxford- **15–012** shire. They found that almost 90 per cent were from "higher managerial, administrative and professional occupations". They recommended extending the OBV scheme to working class people, to attract them to public appointments. They praised a bus company which encouraged drivers to become magistrates (p.66). The driver-magistrates had a "special loyalty" to their firm. Employee morale was boosted. In their 2014 report they suggested that diversification might be encouraged by introducing evening and weekend courts. Magistrates should be recruited for a 10-year tenure period. Ex-offenders would be useful as magistrates. Some should be trained as "problem solving" specialists in drug and alcohol addiction. Transform Justice were concerned that

> "magistrates are becoming less diverse: older and less representative of black and minority ethnic groups. This trend, unless reversed, threatens the support they currently enjoy and the very purpose of having a lay magistracy—judgement by peers." (p.2)

"[N]umbers of magistrates have declined from 29,841 in 2007 to 23,401 in 2013—a drop of 6,440 or 22%" (p.9). There was no research to show whether the diversity campaigns 2000–2009 worked. They criticised the application process. In many areas, there might be a narrow appointment window, as little as three weeks, once every two years. (This is still true, according to the March 2017 recruitment information.) Only the first 20–40 forms were considered (also still true in most areas). Magistrates of Asian origin were under-represented. There was a 16.8 per cent gap between the percentage of BME magistrates and the BME population in London and a similar gap in age proportions. There was poor data on socio-economic profile. There was no current diversity drive. They recommended that, since magistrates' work is declining, there should be a freeze on recruitment of (professional) district judges. More Crown Court work should be delegated, by increasing magistrates' sentencing powers. Like the Policy Exchange, they called for a 10-year fixed tenure for magistrates, though fixed tenure appointment were opposed by some who gave evidence to the Justice Committee in 2016 so they declined to recommend this.

The Parliamentary Justice Committee recommended proactive advertising and continuous recruitment, with a swift and streamlined selection system. Note especially the suggestions for much more professional and targeted recruitment in Riley Smith's evidence. with proactive recruitment of minorities, including the unemployed. (See all recommendations in evidence on the Parliament website, on the same page as the report). In its 2016 response the government said "Appointment data...shows that this picture is improving: in 2015/16, 22% of the 668 new magistrates were from BAME backgrounds and 40% were under 50 years of age (compared to just 14% of magistrates overall)". The Justice Committee also recommended making the appraisal scheme more robust, in order to weed out magistrates who had become "insufficiently committed to their role". This could make room for more diverse recruits. The Government agreed that appraisal should be more robust and said that this was provided for under the Justices of the Peace Rules 2016 (below). The Justice Committee also recommended a "Kitemark" and reward for employers who support the magistracy. The Government responded that it was considering that suggestion.

Removal

15–013 The Lord Chancellor (with the LCJ) can remove any magistrate from the Commission, under the Courts Act 2003. This is rarely done, usually because a magistrate refuses to enforce a particular law, or for personal indiscretion, such as conducting an obvious extra-marital affair with another magistrate. Under the Constitutional Reform Act 2005, complaints are now the responsibility of the

Judicial Conduct Investigations Office. The *Annual Report 2015–2016* discloses that 15 magistrates were removed and 15 advised, warned or reprimanded. More resigned during proceedings and more were investigated by local advisory committees. Reasons for complaints and removal included failure to fulfil judicial duties, inappropriate comments on Twitter, rudeness to staff, criminal convictions and poor conduct in handling cases.

3. TRAINING

Lay justices are non-lawyers. They need to understand basic elements of procedure, evidence, and the law they commonly apply and appropriate court behaviour. Until 2005, training was the responsibility of local Magistrates' Courts Committees (MCCs) and justices' clerks. Consequently, its quality differed from court to court, dependent on local attitudes and how much the Committee was prepared to spend: *The Magistrates' Clerk* (1984).   **15–014**

The Courts Act 2003 s.19 provided for rules about lay justices' training and appraisal, which is now the responsibility of the Lord Chief Justice. Following the recommendation of Auld (2001), the Government promised that the Judicial College would have a much stronger role in magistrates' training, to ensure more consistency in standards across the country. It is responsible for advising on, developing and monitoring training, which is still delivered locally. The training regime is on the Magistrates Association website. Magistrates are trained to achieve competences. Their knowledge and observed court behaviour are assessed. They are mentored for 18 months. They are trained before and during their first year. They sit with experienced magistrates and visit penal institutions. They are appraised every three years and receive update and continuation training. There is further training for presiding in court, chairing the bench and sitting in the youth and family courts. (The Justice Committee recommended continuing professional development but the government rejected this). The Judicial College develops training materials, syllibi and good practice guidance and it trains court trainers. Training is delivered locally by justices' clerks, legal advisers, magistrates and sometimes district judges. The Magistrates' Association was established to provide local training when there was none, in 1921. The College now influences training content nationally and offers some training. The Justices of the Peace Rules 2016 Pt 4 introduced stricter rules on compulsory training and appraisal. There are new committees, the JTAAAC and FTAAAC. They organise and supervise training and appraisal locally for justices in the adult and youth courts and in the family court. They supervise authorisations to sit as bench chair, or in the youth or family courts. They must review justices' competence and can revoke approvals and authorisations for incompetent justices or those who have not fulfilled sitting or training requirements. In 2016, the Parliamentary Justice Committee received some stark evidence of training being run on extremely diminished budgets and they recommended a comprehensive review of training needs. They also recommended a more robust appraisal scheme, including reviewing the future of magistrates who had become insufficiently committed, and linked to continuing professional development.

4. ORGANISATION

15–015   Until 2005, magistrates' courts were administered by local magistrates' courts committees (MCCs), consisting of magistrates. One of their hallmarks was their idiosyncratic differences. In 2001 Auld recommended they be replaced by local courts boards and a central executive agency, administering all courts. This was done from 2005 but they were abolished in 2012. HM Courts and Tribunals Service runs all courts. Local judicial business groups comprising staff, a justices' clerk, judges and magistrates deal with case distribution, policy and performance.

Lay justices sit in pairs or threes. District judges (magistrates' courts) normally sit alone. In the Youth Court, three justices of mixed gender sit, or one district judge, or a mixed bench. Collectively, magistrates are known as "the Bench". The Chairman of the Bench is annually elected.

5. DISTRICT JUDGES (MAGISTRATES' COURTS), FORMERLY STIPENDIARY MAGISTRATES

15–016   DJMCs are full-time professionals, described in the chapter on judges. Applicants will normally have sat as deputies, part time. In 2016, there were 133 DJMCs (33 per cent female; 6 per cent BME) and 101 deputies. DJMCs are younger, on average, than lay justices. Historically, although most cases in Outer London and the provinces are heard by lay justices, most cases in Inner London have, for the last three centuries, been dealt with by these professionals, stipendiary magistrates or "stipes" as they used to be known. Later, professionals were appointed in some provincial cities, to meet increased caseloads, because they deal with cases more speedily than justices. The Runciman Commission 1993 recommended that there should be a more systematic approach to the role of stipendiaries so a unified stipendiary bench was created by the Access to Justice Act 1999 when they were renamed.

6. MAGISTRATES' CLERKS

15–017   "In many ways the most important person in the whole set-up of the administration of justice" (Lord Parker CJ, in the House of Lords debate on the Justices of the Peace Bill 1968).

The importance of magistrates' clerks, legal advisers, should not be underestimated. Lay justices and DJMCs are arbiters of both fact and law so, in criminal cases, they perform the same functions as both judge and jury in the Crown Court. Both lay justices and DJMCs are advised by magistrates' clerks and since the lay justices are appointed because they are not, generally, lawyers, they are wholly dependent on their clerks for advice on law and practice. Remember that this is in the context of magistrates handling over 80 per cent of criminal business and a substantial amount of family business. Section 28 of the Courts Act 2003 states:

"(4)   The functions of a justices' clerk include giving advice to any or all of the justices of the peace to whom he is clerk about matters of law (including procedure and practice) on questions arising in connection with the discharge of their functions, including questions arising when the clerk is not personally attending on them.

(5)   The powers of a justices' clerk include, at any time when he thinks he should do so, bringing to the attention of any or all of the justices of the peace to whom he is clerk any point of law (including procedure and practice) that is or may be involved in any question so arising."

Section 29 emphasises the independence of the clerks in their advisory functions. In 1955, Glanville Williams said that, "If legal argument takes place in court, the argument is addressed to the justices, who may hardly follow a word of it; in reality, however, it is intended for the ears of the clerk". This is still the case. Indeed, the High Court warned magistrates that they should follow their clerk's advice, in *Jones v Nicks* (1977). Williams said that the danger arising from this was that clerks could be tempted to interfere in proceedings in a way that is "theoretically unwarrantable." The only significant piece of empirical research on magistrates' clerks was conducted in the 1970s and reported in *The Magistrates' Clerk* and thus too old to be of any practical application. In this research, I found examples of clerks effectively taking decision-making out of the justices' hands, especially in relation to the admissibility of evidence and sentencing. I also found significant differences in approach, from clerk to clerk and court to court. Since the 1970s, magistrates and legal advisors are much better trained and most advisors are now professionally qualified.

As Glanville Williams pointed out in 1955, if clerks or legal advisers retire (behind the courtroom, with the justices) to give advice to the justices, as they often did, it might give the impression that the clerk could exercise undue domination over the justices. He suggested that clerks give their advice in open court. In 2000, when I was asked to advise Auld on the implications of the Human Rights Act 1998 in magistrates' courts, I expressed the same opinion, drawing attention to art.6 of the Convention, on fair trial. Since the 1990s, all clerks and legal advisers have been trained to give their advice in open court, where possible, and that, where they give advice in the retiring room, that this should be repeated in open court. This has now been spelled out in The Criminal Procedure Rules Pt 37.14, below, which clarifies the legal adviser's role and specifies that an adviser is not necessary where the court includes a DJ, below. (Duties in the new family court are prescribed in The Justices' Clerks and Assistants Rules 2014.)

Duty of justices' legal adviser

"**Duty of justices' legal adviser**   **15–018**

37.14(2) A justices' legal adviser must—
(a)   before the hearing begins…draw the court's attention to—
(i)   what the prosecutor alleges,
(ii)   what the parties say is agreed,
(iii)   what the parties say is in dispute, and
(iv)   what the parties say about…timetabling;
(b)   whenever necessary, give the court legal advice and—
(i)   if necessary, attend the members of the court outside the courtroom to give such advice, but

          (ii)   inform the parties of any such advice given outside the courtroom; and

   (c)   assist the court, where appropriate, in the formulation of its reasons and the recording of those reasons.

(3)   A justices' legal adviser must—

   (a)   assist an unrepresented defendant;

   (b)   assist the court by—

          (i)   making a note...[of evidence] to help the court recall ...

          (ii)   ...

          (iii)   ensuring that an adequate record is kept of the court's decisions and the reasons for them, and

          (iv)   making any announcement, other than of the verdict or sentence..."

The chief clerk at each court is called the justices' clerk, normally in charge of more than one Bench. The nationwide trend of the last four decades has been to amalgamate clerkships. In the 1970s, there were over 400 justices' clerks. There are now under 30. They expressed concern that they would lose their pastoral and personal working relationship with magistrates. Since they are now in charge of whole counties, the person advising the bench in court will be a legal adviser, not a JC. Had the Bill been enacted, they would have ceased to have had a separate statutory function but would have been put into a pool of legally qualified HMCTS managerial staff.

Assistants are legal advisors (court clerks). Since 2010, they must be professionally legally qualified, thanks to legislation introduced in 1999. Delegated legislation in 1980 required that, if not professionally qualified, court clerks should be law graduates or equivalent, or possess a special Home Office diploma in magisterial law, or be qualified by five years' experience before 1980. This led to the curious situation where, in some provincial courtrooms, the court clerk advising the lay justices was/is not professionally qualified. More anomalous is the fact that in Inner London, where most cases are heard by DJMCs, they are often advised by professionally qualified clerks, barristers or solicitors. The nationwide situation remains patchy. Disappointingly, the over 40s were exempted from the Justices' Clerks (Qualifications of Assistants) (Amendment) Rules 1999, because some areas were so dependent on unqualified clerks that they would not all be able to qualify in time. More disappointingly, those who were in post in 1998 were also exempted from qualification. The Ministry apparently does not keep statistics on legal advisers' qualifications now.

The justices' clerk and staff used to be recruited and paid by the local MCCs. Since they may exercise judicial functions and these are routinely delegated to other legal advisers, they were anxious when it was proposed they become part of HMCTS in 2005. They felt it was anomalous and a breach of the separation of powers for them to become civil servants like the clerks of other courts, who do not give legal advice or exercise judicial functions. Justices' clerks and their staff are now appointed by the Lord Chancellor under s.27 of the Courts Act 2003 but their independence in giving advice is emphasised in s.29.

Concern over clerks' powers

In 1999, I raised the following concerns. Under the Crime and Disorder Act 1998, extensive pre-trial judicial powers could be delegated to a single justice or justices' clerk, exercisable in an early or pre-trial hearing, as suggested by the Narey Report, *Review of Delay in the Criminal Justice System* (1997). In reality this is delegated to court clerks (legal advisers). In the Lords' debate on the Bill, Lord Bingham CJ expressed the same concern: pre-trial management powers are judicial and clerks are not judges. Magistrates should be doing the judging. As a result of this intervention, fewer management powers were given to clerks than they wanted. Case management powers are now set out in general terms in the Criminal Procedure Rules but these cross-refer to the existing legislation. Justices' clerks and legal advisers are, of course, listed as potential case managers and had the Bill been enacted, their management powers would have been enhanced.

15–019

7. HISTORY

Most people consider that a royal proclamation in 1195, which set up keepers of the peace to assist the sheriff in the maintenance of law and order, was the origin of the justice of the peace. Clearer evidence comes from statutes in 1327 and 1361 under which "good and lawful men" were to be "assigned to keep the peace", holding administrative rather than judicial authority and, like the present-day justice, not legally qualified and acting part-time. The title Justice of the Peace was first used in the 1361 statute. In 1363, a statute required four quarter sessions to be held annually, and gradually the power to deal with criminal cases was added to the administrative work. From 1496, justices were permitted to try the minor (summary) criminal cases locally at petty sessions, instead of at quarter sessions, so giving rise to magistrates' courts as courts of summary jurisdiction, as they now are. When quarter sessions were replaced by the Crown Court in 1972, magistrates retained their role, hearing appeals alongside a circuit judge. Magistrates were the local government until elected authorities were created under the Local Government Acts of 1888 and 1894.

15–020

8. SHOULD LAY JUSTICES BE REPLACED BY PROFESSIONALS?

Lay justices' conspiracy theory

Despite repeated assurances to the contrary by successive Lord Chancellors and then by Auld, many lay justices have a theory that there is a conspiracy to replace them with professionals. This is typified by Robson's article. In 2002, she warned that this could be the point "where the lay magistracy may be launched on a long farewell".

Some lay justices' anxiety has not abated, despite the fact that the Criminal Justice Act 2003 potentially doubled their sentencing powers (not brought into

15–021

force, though the government is considering it in 2017) and the £5,000 ceiling on their fining powers has been removed. For instance, in 2011, Robson repeated the same allegation that there was a plot to professionalise the magistracy. I have found examples of the theory dating back to the 1970s and earlier. The problem arises because modern magistrates are ignorant of their own history. I tried to explain the true position in a 2002 essay. They are correct to point out that professionals have increased since 1950. They have not acknowledged that lay justice numbers have increased too. Lay justices also sit far more often than they did previously. In 1948, over 65 per cent of justices sat less than 26 times and 10 per cent did not sit at all. Nowadays, lay justices are required to sit on 26 occasions per year but some sit over 50 days per year. Morgan and Russell, below, found they sat, on average 41 times a year. Most importantly, as I was at pains to point out in 1997, "Neglect", magistrates' jurisdiction has increased out of all recognition in the last few centuries, as more and more criminal business has shifted down from the assizes, now Crown Court, onto the shoulders of the magistracy. Offences are regularly reclassified downwards, from indictable to either-way, or from either-way to summary only. When new offences are created they are usually summary only or either-way, thus guaranteeing that they will all or mostly be tried by magistrates. Since 2008, the Crown Court has shifted almost all child defendants into the youth court. Much of this comprises serious sex offences with trials lasting several days so lay justices should not be alarmed that this new work is given to district judges.

It is true, however, that magistrates' courts' criminal caseload for *petty* offences has declined since 2008 because of the creation of fixed penalty notices and penalty notices for disorder, as well as adult cautions. Parking and licensing have been shifted into other forums. Anti-social behaviour and petty crime can now be resolved by community resolution (see Sentencing Council website). Single justices are now empowered to handle a lot of work that had to be done by two or three. All criminal offences going through the courts have diminished significantly. There is no sinister plot to do away with lay justices but I agree with the concern that bench closures have completely destroyed "local" justice and made it more difficult for magistrates to get to their bench and for all parties to get to court so some have resigned over that (evidence to the Parliamentary Justice Committee, 2016).

The curious position of London

15–022   In Inner London, for the best part of three centuries, most cases in the magistrates' courts have been heard by stipendiaries, now DJMCs, whereas in outer London and the provinces, most cases were and are heard by lay justices. The position is rendered odder by the fact that Inner London was the first to professionalise its clerks so by the 1970s we had the anomalous position where cases in Inner London were routinely tried by a professional magistrate, advised by a lawyer, whereas elsewhere most cases were decided by lay justices, advised by court clerks who were not lawyers. There is no logic to this difference. It arises from history. Professional magistrates were appointed from the eighteenth century in London in response to concern about corruption among local lay justices. When stipendiary numbers increased in the provinces, they were installed at the request of the local benches, usually to help out with a large workload. Since 1999, when the professional bench was organised on a national basis, a district judge can be appointed anywhere and moved around. There are many DJMCs who sit in different courts on a rota basis or are brought in to handle long and/or complex trials.

The lack of logic in our current distribution of criminal cases

As I pointed out in "Neglect" (1997), there is no logic in the way in which we currently allocate criminal cases. This is still the case. While DJMCs may do more of the serious work of the magistrates' courts, they are not confined to that. In the courts where they sit alongside lay justices, parties may not be able to predict in advance whether they will be heard by a lay bench or a DJMC, because if one court finishes early, the clerk is sent to fetch work to relieve the list of a busier bench. A defendant may find himself tried by a judge alone, a DJMC, but he has no choice. If he is tried in the Crown Court, having pleaded not guilty, again he has no choice. He must be tried by judge and jury. Yet in other common law jurisdictions (North America for instance) he could choose a non-jury trial before a single judge, called a "bench trial", discussed in the chapter on juries.

15–023

The value of lay justices

The last body to consider this, prior to Auld in 2001, was the 1948 Royal Commission on Justices of the Peace. This passage illustrates the principled reasons for keeping lay justices.

15–024

> "(L)ike that of trial by jury, it gives the citizen a part to play in the administration of the law. It emphasizes the fact that the principles of the common law, and even the language of statutes, ought to be ... comprehensible by any intelligent person without specialized training. Its continuance prevents the growth of a suspicion in the ordinary man's mind that the law is a mystery which must be left to a professional caste and has little in common with justice as the layman understands it. Further, the cases in which decisions on questions of fact in criminal cases are left to one man ought to be, as they now are, exceptional." (p.7)

Doran and Glenn (2000), commissioned to examine *Lay Involvement in Adjudication* for the review of the criminal justice system in Northern Ireland, provided a very useful survey of issues raised in debate between supporters and detractors of the principle of lay participation, as below.

The right of participation in the adjudicative process

Every person has an equal right to participate in matters of general concern. Lay participants are more representative of the local community and establish a link between the courts and local affairs. On the other hand, in reality, some members of the community are excluded from participation and lay adjudicators are a social elite.

15–025

The personality of the participants

15–026 Lay participants possess an informal and experiential body of knowledge gleaned from the local environs, whereas professionals possess formal technical knowledge. The problems with this are whether participants are truly local, whether "local knowledge" sits happily with the concept of acting as a neutral arbiter and whether participants will encounter defendants outside the courtroom in an embarrassing or dangerous context. The argument that the professionals' training makes them superior can be countered by training lay participants but that might destroy the "layness" for which they are valued.

The process of participation

15–027 It is said to be safe to entrust minor matters to lay participants because they are legally advised and because the guilty plea rate is high. The problem with this argument, however, is that it trivialises the work of the lower courts and, as I have just pointed out above, English and Welsh magistrates are not confined to trivia, as are lay magistrates in other jurisdictions. It is also argued that lay involvement injects realism and popular values into decision-making so that law and legal procedure become less mysterious. Further, lay people are said to be cheaper, more flexible and less case-hardened and their reasoning based on reasonableness, equity and fairness. There are problems with these arguments. There is no evidence that the law is kept less complex by the presence of lay persons on the bench. Those who sit regularly may become just as case-hardened as professionals. The vague form of reasoning of laypeople can produce inconsistent decisions and regional disparities that are less susceptible to review, create uncertainty and diminish public confidence. Professionals are said to be more consistent and procedurally correct. On the other hand, some say that professionals can be inflexible, legalistic, detached from the community and less sympathetic with arguments raised before them. Bearing in mind that magistrates are volunteers, giving up lots of spare time for training and making life harder for themselves if they have a full-time job, their morale can be adversely affected and they feel undervalued when courts are closed, as they are being from 2011.

Several pieces of research have allowed us to reach a better informed opinion on the practical differences between lay and professional magistrates, to test the assumptions underlying the arguments of principle. In 1990, Shari Diamond's research affirmed lawyers' long held anecdotal assumption that professional magistrates are harsher in sentencing than lay justices. In research reported in *The Role and Appointment of Stipendiary Magistrates* (1995) Seago, Walker and Wall aimed to examine the function of stipendiaries. They found that:

- Very few courts had rules for allocating work to stipendiaries.
- There was a striking difference between the work of stipendiaries and acting (deputy) stipendiaries, who were kept away from more legally and evidentially complex cases.
- Metropolitan stipendiaries appeared to be almost twice as quick to hear contested cases as provincial stipendiaries.

- Most of their judicial work was general list cases but they also heard long trials (especially those lasting more than a day), or complex or highly publicised trials and they had a heavier caseload than lay justices.
- Stipendiaries dealt with all types of work more speedily than lay justices. One provincial stipendiary could replace 32 justices and one metropolitan stipendiary could replace 24 justices.

In discussing the future role of stipendiaries, the authors suggested that pressure on the Crown Court could be relieved. "Consideration could be given to an enhanced jurisdiction (up to two to three years' imprisonment) for a trial tribunal consisting of a stipendiary and two lay magistrates". In 2000, a major research project was undertaken for the Home Office and Lord Chancellor's Department. It is reported in *The Judiciary in Magistrates' Courts* by Morgan and Russell. Its aims were to investigate the balance of lay and professional magistrates and the arguments in favour of that balance. Apart from the findings on composition, above, they concluded: **15–028**

- Lay justices sat on 41.4 occasions per year, on average. Additionally, they spent a working week on training and other duties. They sat in threes, in 84 per cent of cases.
- Professionals sat in court around four days a week, rarely with lay justices.
- Stipendiaries' work allocation was the same as found by Seago, Walker and Wall. Stipendiaries' time was concentrated on either-way cases.
- Stipendiaries heard 22 per cent more appearances than lay justices. If their caseloads were identical, they could deal with 30 per cent more appearances.
- Stipendiary hearings generally involved more questioning and challenging.
- Stipendiaries showed more command over proceedings and would challenge parties responsible for delay. People applied for fewer adjournments and were less likely to be granted them.
- Lay justices were less likely to refuse bail or use immediate custody as a sentence.
- Court users had more confidence in stipendiaries. They were seen as more efficient, consistent in decisions, questioning appropriately and as giving clear reasons. Lawyers admitted to preparing better for stipendiaries.
- Court users considered lay justices better at showing courtesy, using simple language and showing concern to distressed victims.
- Few members of the public had heard there were different types of magistrate.
- One stipendiary could replace 30 lay justices. Doubling stipendiary numbers would cut down court appearances but increase the prison population. The net cost would be about £23 million per year.

In 2013, the Ministry of Justice published another comparison, based on interview and observational research by Ipsos MORI, *The Strengths and Skills of the Judiciary in the Magistrates' Courts*. They found that magistrates were perceived as having a greater connection with the local community, being fair, less "case hardened" or fatigued and more open-minded. Some associated a   **15–029** bench of three with "a greater degree of democracy". Some noted their cost-effectiveness, as they are unpaid. DJs were speedier and considered more adept at case management. Legal advisers provided more support for lay magistrates. Lawyers said they adjusted their case presentation according to the type of bench. There was no consistent approach to listing practices in the 44 courts but policies suggested that complex, lengthy or serious cases should be listed before DJs. (A 2012 protocol says DJMCs should be given long or complex cases, plus their share of more routine cases.) 30 per cent of DJ cases were "either-way" whereas 18 per cent of lay magistrates' cases were either-way. Nevertheless, the differences in case profiles were not clear cut and differences not as significant as suggested in the interviews. DJs were more costly per case, because they were salaried. DJs were more likely to impose custody, disqualify defendants from driving and impose bail. Most respondents supported the extension of magistrates' sentencing powers, especially DJs, who pointed to the anomaly of higher sentences being available in the youth court. People highlighted cost savings but justices' clerks were concerned about the increased workload in magistrates' courts and an increase in the prison population as magistrates would impose more custody than Crown Court judges. Some defence solicitors also highlighted the need for appropriate training. Most interviewees were not in favour of mixed benches of a DJ and two lay justices. DJs said it would slow them down.

15–030   The Institute for Public Policy Research commissioned a MORI public opinion poll on the magistracy in 2001. It (with A. Sanders) reported that a third of the public polled did not know that the majority of magistrates were laypeople and hugely under-estimated the proportion of cases heard by magistrates.

In 2014, Donoghue published the ultimate penetrating examination of the theory of lay justices, in a highly informative article.

> "I argue that the laity is an intrinsically valuable institution because the role of magistrates is an embodiment of society in the legal process which exists as a direct democratisation of that process. Moreover, lay magistrates possess distinct technocratic advantages as well as providing an important check on professional power…I contend that the relative financial merits of the lay magistracy, taken together with democratic arguments, provide the combination of elements most worthy of consideration in the conceptual framework of the value of magistrates' participation in summary justice. In the second part of the article, I examine the ways in which the delivery of magistrates' 'local justice' has progressively been undermined by protracted processes of reform over several decades… I conclude that current policy proposals collectively fail to recognise that rapidly declining magistrate numbers together with continuous (and continuing) programs of court closures are irreconcilable with the future viability of the lay magistracy. The government's proposed reforms will do little to strengthen the role of magistrates if they take place in a policy vacuum."

As can be seen above, I consider that this fails to take account of the fact that magistrates have gained a lot more serious work at the same time as losing the trivial work. In a 2016 report on the role of the magistracy by the House of Commons Justice Committee, a Magistrates Association survey showed that, while 88 per cent were satisfied or very satisfied with their work, most felt they were not consulted on changes. The magistracy had dropped by a third in less than a decade. The Committee's main recommendations were as follows.

> "to develop an over-arching strategy for the magistracy—to incude workforce planning ... and the wider promotion of [the] role ... take into account the impact of court closures and consider whether the role of magistrates could be expanded, in particular with any proposals for problem-solving courts. "

They recommended implementing s.154 of the CJ Act 2003, thus doubling magistrates' sentencing powers to a year.

Mixed benches

In 1948, the Bar recommended that peripatetic stipendiaries be created, to travel **15–031** around and sit with local lay justices and that was done in some areas. I briefly discussed mixed benches in 1997, as did Seago, Walker and Wall in 1995. I mentioned that this pattern was common in Eastern Europe. As I pointed out in 1997, the obvious danger here is that the professional will dominate the lay participants and some of the research on the Eastern European models verifies this, as Vogler was swift to point out in 2001. Sanders (2001), above, concluded that the skills of both professional and lay magistrates, sitting as a mixed bench, are needed in deciding complex cases: legal skills to apply the relevant law to the facts; social skills to assess character and judge honesty and managerial and administrative skills. Panel decision-making was preferable to sole decision-making. Justice should be transparent and accountable. This was promoted by lay participation. Public confidence needed to be safeguarded and increased. A 2012 protocol suggests that DJMCs should sometimes sit with lay magistrates, to teach the latter about case management and to promote collegiality.

The Civil Liberties Trust, in its 2002 report, "Magistrates' Courts and Public Confidence—a proposal for fair and effective reform of the magistracy", called for reform of the magistracy to inspire public confidence. They recommended mixed tribunals, with the lay justices and professionals separately responsible for the fact-finding and the law. Magistrates should be drawn randomly from the population and required to sit for a specified period of time. Alternatively, the current lay magistracy should be expanded.

My response to Vogler was to argue, in 2002, that he was not comparing like with like. In all the European examples he gave, the lay participants were and are more like jurors. Lay justices are appointed to sit frequently for many decades and are trained and experienced in fact finding and sentencing. Further, as I had already pointed out in 1997, this danger could be averted by training the professionals not to dominate the lay justices and training the lay justices not to defer to the professional. Besides, as I have also pointed out before, we have many examples of mixed tribunals in England and Wales, dealing with civil cases, as described in Ch.11. The mixing of lay and professionals there does not seem to have caused problems.

Auld (2001) considered all these arguments of principle and the research above and made some controversial recommendations, which I will not deal with in great depth, because they were rejected by the government. In brief, he recommended the creation of a middle tier of his proposed unified criminal court, called the "district court", with lay justices sitting together with one DJMC. The lay justices would participate in fact finding but the DJMC would do the sentencing. Many commentators were opposed to this. The Law Society thought the cost of running a middle tier would outweigh the benefit. I criticised the proposed mixed bench because the lay justices would be relegated to the position of jurors; the DJMC would do the sentencing alone. I can see no logic in this suggestion, given that justices are experienced sentencers and given that the justices are there to represent the community including, presumably, local attitudes to the relative gravity of local crimes.

Having rejected Auld's proposal for a middle tier criminal court, the government opted instead to double magistrates' sentencing powers. This was done in the Criminal Justice Act 2003 s.154. This has not come into force. If it does, the potential effect will be to significantly increase the criminal case load of the magistrates' courts, which simply continues the trend of the last two centuries of shifting work down onto the shoulders of the magistracy.

Bibliography and further reading

15–032 Auld LJ, *Review of the Criminal Courts of England and Wales* (2001).

C. Barnett JP, speech at MA AGM 19 November 2008.

The Civil Liberties Trust: Liberty.

P. Darbyshire, *The Magistrates' Clerk* (Chichester: Barry Rose, 1984); "The Lamp That Shows That Freedom Lives—is it worth the candle?" [1991] Crim. L.R. 740; "An Essay on the Importance and Neglect of the Magistracy" [1997] Crim. L.R. 627; "For the New Lord Chancellor—Some Causes of Concern About Magistrates" [1997] Crim. L.R. 861; "A Comment on the Powers of Magistrates' Clerks" [1999] Crim. L.R. 377; "Magistrates", in *The Handbook of the Criminal Justice Process* (McConville and Wilson (eds.) (Oxford: Oxford University Press, 2002).

J. Donoghue, "Reforming the Role of Magistrates: Implications for Summary Justice in England and Wales" (2014) 77(6) M.L.R. 928.

S. Doran and R. Glenn, *Lay Involvement in Adjudication*, Criminal Justice Review Group (N Ire.) (2000).

Department of Constitutional Affairs, *National Strategy for the Recruitment of Magistrates*, 2003, National Archives.

S. Diamond, "Revising Images of Public Punitiveness..." (1990) L.S.I. 191.

The Home Office, *Review of Delay in the Criminal Justice System*, 1997 (The Narey Report), National Archives.

House of Commons Home Affairs Committee, Third Report, Session 1995–1996, *Judicial Appointments Procedures, Vol.II* (HMSO, 1996).

House of Commons Justice Committee *Role of the Magistracy Inquiry*, including all the evidence and reform suggestions by interested parties, the Committee's 2016 report, below, and the government response (all highly informative), Parliament website.

House of Commons Justice Committee *The role of the magistracy Sixth Report of Session 2016–17*, 11 October 2016.

Ipsos MORI, *The Strength and Skills of the Judiciary in the Magistrates Court* (Ministry of Justice, revised 2013).

Judiciary website: *Becoming a Magistrate in England and Wales* (2015); statistics.

Lord Chancellor and Secretary of State's Directions for Advisory Committees on Justices of the Peace, Ministry of Justice (2015).

H. McLaughlin, "Court Clerks: Advisers or Decision-Makers?" (1990) 30 *British Journal of Criminology* 358.

R. Morgan and N. Russell, *The Judiciary in the Magistrates' Courts* (2000), Home Office.

A. Phillips (Lord Andrew Phillips of Sudbury), "We must hold on to local justice", *The Guardian*, 2 December 2001.

The Policy Exchange, *Reforming Public Appointments* (2013); *Future Courts* (2014).

G. Robson, "The Lay Magistracy: No Time for Complacency" (2002) 166 *Justice of the Peace* 624; "A clouded future?" (2011) 175(20) *Criminal Law & Justice Weekly* 288.

A. Sanders, *Community Justice* (2000) IPPR.

P. Seago, C. Walker and D. Wall, *The Role and Appointment of Stipendiary Magistrates* (Leeds: Centre for Criminal Justice Studies, 1995).

Seago et al., "The Development of the Professional Magistracy in England and Wales" [2000] Crim. L.R. 631.

Transform Justice, *Magistrates: representatives of the public* (2014); *The Role of the Magistrate?* (2016) and other publications.

J. Vennard, G. Davies, J. Baldwin and J. Pearce, "Ethnic minority magistrates' experience..." DCA Research Report 3/2004, archived DCA website.

G. Williams, *The Proof of Guilt* (London: Stevens & Sons, 1955).

R. Vogler, "Mixed Messages on the Mixed Bench", *Legal Action*, May 2001, p.8.

Sources for updating this chapter

Free updates of this book are available on the Sweet & Maxwell website: **15–033** *http://uklawstudent.thomsonreuters.com*.

Summary and revision: P. Darbyshire, *Nutshells English Legal System*, 10th edn (London: Sweet & Maxwell, 2016).

Criminal Law and Justice Weekly, on *Lexis*.

The Magistrates' Association.

Westlaw Current Awareness and *Lexis*.

CHAPTER 16

The Jury

"Each jury is a little parliament ... The first object of any tyrant in Whitehall would be to make Parliament utterly subservient to his will; and the next to overthrow or diminish trial by jury for no tyrant could afford to leave a subject's freedom in the hands of twelve of his countrymen. So that trial by jury is more than an instrument of justice and more than one wheel of the constitution: it is the lamp that shows that freedom lives." (Sir Patrick Devlin, *Trial by Jury* 1956).

"(T)he liberties of England cannot but subsist so long as this palladium remains sacred and inviolate" (Sir William Blackstone *Commentaries on the Laws of England Vol. IV*, 1769).

"[J]uries ... have a passionate and profound belief in and a commitment to the right of a defendant to be given a fair trial ... It is ... their birthright; it is shared by each one of them with the defendant. They guard it faithfully. The integrity of the jury is an essential feature of our trial process. Juries follow the directions ... to focus exclusively on the evidence and to ignore anything they may have heard or read out of court." (Judge LJ, *In the matter of B* (2006)).

"Out of all the citizens ... who in the course of any year find themselves in difficulty with the law only a small portion ... will be tried by a jury. The underlying logic of this situation we find puzzling in the extreme. If society believes that trial by jury is the fairest form of trial is it too costly and troublesome to be universally applied? ... But if jury trial is not inherently more fair given its extra cost and trouble what are the merits which justify its retention? Society appears to have an attachment to jury trial which is emotional or sentimental rather than logical." (The Roskill Committee on Fraud Trials 1986).

"The symbolic function of the jury far outweighs its practical significance ... this sentimental attachment to the symbol of the jury is dangerous. Adulation of the jury is based on no justification or spurious justification. It has fed public complacency with the English legal system and distracted attention from its evils ... The truth is that for most people who pass through the criminal justice system this palladium is simply not available and for those who can and do submit themselves to its verdict it will not necessarily safeguard their civil liberties." (Darbyshire 1991).

1. "THE LAMP THAT SHOWS THAT FREEDOM LIVES"

This ancient institution arouses strong emotions in the hearts of the English and Welsh, as it does with Americans. This is because, for centuries, jury trial was central to our legal systems. The use of ordinary people as fact finders in civil and criminal cases was and is perceived by some as the *only* democratic way of organising a legal system. The opinion surveys cited in the previous chapter show that most people have no idea that over 80 per cent of defendants to criminal

16–001

charges are dealt with by magistrates. Of the remainder who appear before the Crown Court, most plead guilty in front of a judge alone, therefore, only around one per cent of defendants receive a jury trial (see Ch.12). As for civil cases, the jury had almost died out by the mid twentieth century. Arguments for and against the jury are examined below.

2.   SELECTION OF JURORS

Widening jury participation from 2004

16–002   Jurors are drawn from the electoral roll. Random selection is not prescribed by the Juries Act but is a matter of practice. Prior to 2004, statutory excusals and avoidance of jury service destroyed randomness (Darbyshire 1991).

Selection

16–003   The Juries Act 1974, as amended, specifies that every adult, aged 18–75, who is on the electoral roll and who has lived in this country for at least five years is qualified to serve as a juror. The new juror summonsing service will allow anyone summoned to respond directly into the digitised system to share their availability or request to be excused, from 2019 or earlier. In our research for Auld LJ, for the Criminal Courts Review 2001, we (Darbyshire, Maughan and Stewart, 2001) examined jury research worldwide. We argued that selection from the electoral roll is a flawed system. Research as long ago as the 1960s, in the USA, demonstrated that electoral lists are not representative of communities. This has been confirmed in Australia and New Zealand. This is caused by such factors as population mobility and residential status, which are linked to class and income levels. Census data in England and Wales showed non-registration to be high among ethnic minorities, the 20–24 age group and renters. Some people do not register to vote in order to avoid council tax. By 1968, Federal US legislation required that in summoning jury pools, the voters' list should be supplemented with other source lists, such as drivers' licence and utility lists. We recommended copying this method. Auld adopted our recommendation in his *Review*. He considered that jury eligibility should be based on eligibility to vote not on inclusion on the roll. The Government rejected this. They said that instead, they would continue the work of the Electoral Commission to improve the quality of the electoral roll and ensure in particular that minority ethnic communities register themselves. My objections to this are threefold: it does not respond to our findings on population mobility or wilful refusal to register; no good reason was given for not adopting our recommendation; and thirdly, if the census is to be used as a test of the representativeness of the roll, then that too is defective, as there are gaps in the census. The same groups who did not register to vote also failed to complete the census, such as young men. Changes to the registration system for the electoral roll in 2014 mean that even more people are missing (BBC News).

Pre-2004: problems caused by statutory excusals, ineligibility and disqualification

"I am summon'd to appear upon a Jury, and was just going to try if I could get off." **16–004**
(Hawles' *The Englishman's Right: A Dialogue between a Barrister and a Jury-Man*
(1680))

Until 2003, the Juries Act disqualified some people from service and contained long lists of people who were ineligible or excusable as of right. For example, lawyers, judges, magistrates, members of the prison and probation services and the clergy were ineligible. The 1965 Morris Report considered that those with special knowledge or prestige attached to their occupations would be unduly influential over their fellow jurors. The Royal Commission on Criminal Justice 1993 (RCCJ) upheld this view but Auld (2001) did not agree.

Members of the armed forces, medical practitioners, chemists, vets, peers and MPs had a *right* to be excused, as did members of religious organisations, whose tenets or beliefs were incompatible with jury service, and those who had done jury service in the previous two years. In 1991, I complained that exempting long lists of people from jury service was the antithesis of randomness. The problems caused by the Act and the excusal rate were affirmed in 1999 by Home Office research by Airs and Shaw. 250,000 people were summoned for jury service every year. Of 50,000 summoned in 1999, only one third were available for service, about half of whom were allowed to defer to a later date. Of the remaining two thirds: 13 per cent were statutorily ineligible, or disqualified, or excusable as of right, 15 per cent failed to attend on the day, or their summonses were returned as "undelivered". 38 per cent were excused. As a result of their findings, a Jury Central Summoning Bureau (JCSB) was created. The excusal rate was high and inconsistent between Crown Court Centres so this was an attempt to regularise the position and tighten up on excusals.

The Jury Central Summoning Bureau reported to us (Darbyshire, Maughan and Stewart) in 2001 that, because of the rate of non-attendance and excusals, it was still necessary to summon four times as many jurors as were needed and six times as many as were needed in London (see, though, Thomas, 2007). We also found that if people simply did not respond to a jury summons, then they might not be pursued. It was left to each individual Crown Court to chase those who did not attend and in London there was no budget allocated for this. We recommended repeal of the categories of excusable as of right and ineligible in the Juries Act. Auld received a number of arguments to the same effect. He examined the regime in New York, where the law and procedure had been tightened up to prevent people avoiding jury service. The presumption in NY was that everyone should do jury service, with very limited grounds for excusal.

The solution—repealing ineligibility

Auld considered the reasons for making groups such as lawyers ineligible for jury **16–005**
service to be outdated: "People no longer defer to professionals … in the way they used to do" (2001, Ch.5). He also reviewed the traditional objection that if people who were connected with the criminal justice system did jury service, they would lack openness of mind but he thought they would be no more prejudiced

than shopkeepers or house owners who had been burglary victims. He acknowledged the objections to having judges serving on juries but concluded "I consider that it would be good for them and the system of jury trial if they could experience at first hand what jurors have to put up with." He was heartened by the fact that a number of US judges had had to do jury service and spoke warmly of it. Auld accordingly recommended that everyone should be eligible for jury service, save for the mentally ill and, as can be seen below, the law now reflects this, thanks to the Criminal Justice Act 2003.

The solution—abolishing the right to excusals

16–006 Scrutinising the list of excusable people, he noted that the Morris Committee reasoning was that such groups owed special duties to the state or were responsible for the relief of pain and suffering. Again, Auld felt that any problems could be dealt with by way of discretionary excusal. As for excusing those who had recently done jury service, he observed that if all these statutory exclusions were abolished, being summoned twice for jury service would occur less frequently.

The disqualified

16–007 Auld recommended that the category of the disqualified should not change and this was accepted by the Government. The Criminal Justice Act 2003 preserved the disqualification of those who have ever been sentenced to custody or its alternatives for five years or more, or who, in the last ten years, have been sentenced to custody or an alternative for three months. Those on bail are also disqualified. The 2003 Act Sch.33 continues the ban on mentally disordered persons. Those who cannot participate effectively as a juror because of physical incapacity may have their summons discharged by the judge.

Discretionary excusal

16–008 In our 2001 review of research, we found that people try to get out of jury service all over the world and the commonest excuses are childcare, family commitments, employment problems and loss of wages. Excusals were examined by Airs and Shaw. Auld noted the high excusal rate, 38 per cent, and recommended that where an excuse appears to be well-founded, Jury Central Summoning Bureau officers should aim to deal with it by way of deferral instead of excusal.

The statutory solution—The Criminal Justice Act 2003

16–009 The Government agreed with Auld's recommendations. Their 2002 White Paper, *Justice for All*, said "We believe that members of the community have the responsibility and a duty to carry out jury service if they possibly can". The Criminal Justice Act 2003 enacted their proposals. It amended the Juries Act s.1 to provide that virtually everyone should be qualified for jury service provided they are not mentally disordered or disqualified. Summoning officers are obliged to excuse serving members of the armed forces if their commanding officer certifies that their absence would be prejudicial to the efficiency of the armed service.

In *Justice for All*, the Government promised to improve jury service. Jurors had a right to be treated with respect and to expect minimal disruption to their personal lives. They agreed with our finding that too many jurors were kept hanging around. Jurors should be supported with more information and advice. They claimed that the Jury Central Summoning Bureau had shifted the balance from excusal to deferral and that this had increased the pool of potential jurors. The 2003 Act came into force on 2 April 2004 and the Government claimed that this would significantly increase the pool of potential jurors. They promised that only those who proved they could not defer service to another period within 12 months would be excused, and then only in exceptional circumstances. Their press release said that compelling reasons for *deferral* included death or illness of a close relative; health reasons; pre-booked holiday; being a serving member of the armed forces where absence would be detrimental; and religious festivals. Compelling reasons why eligible people could be *excused* included insufficient understanding of English, certain care responsibilities and being a member of a religious order or society whose beliefs are incompatible with jury service. This summarises the jury summoning guidance issued in 2009 and now on the gov.uk website, *Guidance for summoning officers when considering deferral and excusal applications*, discussed below, which contains this presumption: "The normal expectation is that everyone summoned for jury service will serve at the time for which they are summoned". Hardship may be grounds for deferral or excusal. Additionally, it says that if people find it difficult to get to court they can be offered another court. MPs can be allowed to sit outside their constituencies. Shift workers can ask for deferral. Those with physical disabilities should be treated sympathetically and so on. In its conclusions, the government clarified the position of those working for the Crown Prosecution Service (CPS). They should not sit on any case where the CPS is prosecutor, that is, most criminal cases. In response to concern that some of those summoned for jury service feared for their employment, the Employment Relations Act 2004 s.40 protects jurors from employment detriment or dismissal.

Public reaction to widening jury participation

When Auld published his 2001 proposals and during the passage of the 2003 Act through Parliament, as a bill, there were predictable objections. Newspapers came out in a rash of letters from doctors and nurses claiming that the National Health Service would collapse in their absence. My response to this is to repeat a calculation I made in 1997 (assisted by National Statistics) that we cited in our paper for Auld. Of all adults aged 18–70 in England and Wales, each person only had a one in six chance of being summoned for jury service during their eligible lifetime. Thanks to the changes made by the 2003 Act, a person's chances of ever doing jury service are now reduced. If doctors and nurses, like everyone else, now have, say, a one in 12 chance of doing a fortnight's jury service once in their

16–010

lifetimes, this is hardly going to cause the collapse of the NHS as we know it. Furthermore, those health care professionals who are not UK citizens will not be called for jury service.

Another battery of objections came from judges and lawyers, claiming that lawyer-jurors might have undue influence over others. One would surely hope, however, that lawyers and judges would have the integrity not to try to influence fellow jurors. By analogy, the old pre-2003 law did not exclude legal academics, or non-practising solicitors. I sat on two juries in 1990 and did not disclose that I taught law; nor did I try to sway my fellow jurors (Darbyshire 1990). Well aware of these objections, in 2003 the Government issued a consultation on "Jury Summoning Guidance", on deferral and excusals, in 2003. They reiterated Auld's reasoning:

> "Concerns have been raised about the possible effect on the fairness of the trial of allowing lawyers and others involved in the administration of justice to sit on juries. The fear is that they might exercise undue influence over their fellow jurors by virtue of their specialist knowledge of the justice system. However, the Government is satisfied that these concerns are unfounded. The American experience, where, in a number of states, judges, lawyers and others holding positions in the criminal justice system have sat as jurors for some time, is that their fellow jurors have not allowed them to dominate their deliberations. In England and Wales, a large number of people with extensive knowledge of the criminal justice system—legal academics, law students and civil servants working in criminal justice—currently do jury service. There is no evidence to suggest that the involvement of any of these groups in jury service has been a problem. More generally, the diluting effect of the process of random selection, and the group dynamic of the jury, serve to protect the integrity of the deliberative process."

16–011   Dyson LJ was the first judge to be called for jury service. One circuit judge had rejected him from a jury on the grounds that he knew him. This was silly because every trial judge knew the 37 Court of Appeal judges. Dyson wrote to the Lord Chief Justice to object that this was an unacceptable reason. In the meantime, he served on another jury. At the same time, a number of lawyers were attempting to avoid jury service, especially in the Old Bailey, by asking judges to be excused in trials where they knew the advocates. Some excusals were granted until the Recorder of London issued a local Practice Direction that this was unacceptable. Both Auld and the Government in its consultation paper had recognised that lawyers and judges might need to be excused if they knew trial participants. This problem has now been resolved by requiring judges or recorders to do jury service in an area in which they do not sit as a judge. Of course famous judges, such as Dyson were known to all judges and lawyers—but then so was Elizabeth Hurley when she did jury service in the Old Bailey. The Bar Council issued guidance, renewed in 2015, to barristers summoned for jury service. It warned them that it was neither necessary nor appropriate to conceal their profession, nor was it necessary to volunteer such information. They should remember they were sitting as one equal member of a tribunal of fact and not in their capacity as barristers. They should not offer advice or an opinion as to the law and they should not contradict the judge's direction on law. The Lord Chief Justice gave similar guidance to judges sitting as jurors.

Test cases on the 2003 Act reforms were heard by the law lords. Three appellants complained that they had had people in their juries who would have prejudiced a fair trial: police officers and a CPS lawyer: *R. v Abdroikov* (2007). The law lords upheld the claims of bias. Justice had not been seen to be done. Dissenting, Lord Rodger said that the judgment drove a coach and horses through the 2003 Act. Zander called this precedent "a troublesome decision". He was disappointed that the majority three were not persuaded by the powerful argument in the dissent that there are *twelve* jurors. Nevertheless, in *Hanif and Khan v UK* (2011), one juror was a police officer. He sent a note to the judge, saying that he knew a police officer who gave prosecution evidence. The judge established that they had worked together in the past though there was no connection with the juror in this case. The judge allowed the juror to continue, with a warning about impartiality. The ECtHR found that art.6 was violated. A judicial warning was insufficient to guard against the risk that the juror may, albeit subconsciously, favour the police evidence. A tribunal must be objectively as well as subjectively impartial. Note: the court surveyed many common law and other jurisdictions. The overwhelming majority made police officers ineligible to serve on juries. A number of law reform commissions had considered the issue since 2003. Scotland, Ireland, New South Wales and Western Australia had decided not to follow the English 2003 change to make police officers eligible. For detailed analysis, see Hungerford-Welch (2012), who called for Parliament to revisit this issue.

Randomness

The legal and philosophical sources of the notions of randomness and representativeness are difficult to discover. They do not appear in the Juries Act 1974, which, as we have just seen, significantly disrupted randomness until 2004, but there are statements elsewhere. The Morris Report (1965) said "a jury should represent a cross-section drawn at random from the community" and a 1973 Practice Note by the Lord Chief Justice stated "a jury consists of twelve individuals chosen at random from the appropriate panel". The obiter statement of Lord Denning in *Brownlow* (1980) reviewed the two "rival philosophies" as he called them, of our random jury and the highly selected US jury. He said:

16–012

> "Our philosophy is that the jury should be selected at random from a panel of persons who are nominated at random. We believe that twelve persons selected at random are likely to be a cross-section of the people and thus represent the views of the common man. Some may be moral. Others not. Some may be honest. Others not ... The parties must take them as they come."

Lord Denning's reference to the philosophy behind US jury composition acknowledges that while we believe in random selection, they believe that impartiality can only be guaranteed by a very elaborate selection system, by means of a "voir dire". This means the completion of questionnaires by potential jurors, who are then questioned in open court, plus a generous allocation of peremptory challenges exercisable by each party, to exclude those considered undesirable. In high profile US trials, such as the Rodney King beatings trials 1992–1993, the 1995 O.J. Simpson trial and the 2005 Michael Jackson trial, jury construction may take weeks or months and wealthy defendants like Simpson and Jackson spend thousands hiring expensive "jury consultants" to help them. Selection from the electoral roll in England and Wales is done randomly by computer, by the Jury Central Summoning Bureau, since 2000.

Race

16–013   In 2007, Thomas published the results of empirical research, discussed below, that suggested that BME groups were *not* underrepresented on juries in England and Wales. In the 1980s there had been complaints from black defendants that jurors were summoned from white areas. In one trial the judge ordered an adjournment and, in another, ordered a jury to be summoned from a different district. The CA has ruled, however, that a jury may not be racially constructed, in *R. v Smith (Lance Percival)* (2003), affirming *R. v Ford* (1989). The US Supreme Court has ruled likewise.

The Royal Commission on Criminal Justice (RCCJ) 1993 recommended that the prosecution or defence should be able to apply to the judge, pre-trial, for the selection of a jury containing up to three people from minority communities, in cases with a racial dimension where the defendant or alleged victim was non-white. We reiterated this in our 2001 paper for Auld and he adopted it. We concluded, on examining worldwide research on juries that, while the findings on gender and verdict and age and verdict are equivocal, there appeared to be a clear relationship between racial composition and verdicts. Research demonstrated that three jurors was the crucial number to have any impact on the verdict. We also pointed out that specially constructed juries are not unprecedented in English law. For over five centuries until 1870, foreigners had the right to be tried by a jury half composed of foreigners, *de medietate linguae*. The Law Society, Race Relations Committee of the Bar Council and the Commission for Racial Equality and others supported this recommendation.

Auld pointed out, as we had done, that minorities were underrepresented on juries because many did and do not register to vote, as disclosed by Airs and Shaw's 1999 research: 24 per cent of black citizens, 15 per cent Asian and 24 per cent other ethnic minority citizens did not register. He commented that a limited sample for his Review in three centres in 2000 "showed a noticeable lack of ethnic mix in jury trials at all three centres". Other solutions to the problem, contemplated by the RCCJ and by Auld would be to allow the judge to transfer a trial to an area with a better ethnic mix or amalgamate the jury panel with another jury panel from a mixed race area. He rejected these suggestions because it smacked of forum-shopping and could cause upset where a defendant and an alleged victim disagreed.

16–014   The first obvious objection to our recommendation, which we acknowledged, is that the type of racial construction we proposed destroys randomness. Auld considered this and weighed it against the problem that an estimated 400,000 crimes a year were racially motivated and this had recently been recognised by statute and, secondly, the philosophy of art.6 of the European Convention which requires objective impartiality. We recognised another objection to our suggestion for racial construction—a "thin end of the wedge" argument. If it were permitted in a racially charged case, why not allow parties to demand a jury of mixed sexuality in a "queer-bashing" case? Our research had indicated that white juries were or were perceived to be less fair to black than to white people. He thought the problems of racially constructing a jury were not insurmountable. The Summoning Bureau could ask people to disclose their ethnicity on receiving a summons. Initially attracted to Auld's recommendation, the Government eventually rejected it, in *Justice for All* (2002), para.7.29 because it would undermine the fundamental principle of randomness, and place a burden on courts to determine which cases should receive special treatment, and so on.

Important research by Thomas on *Diversity and Fairness in the Jury System* was published by the Ministry of Justice in 2007.

> "[T]he ... summoning process does not discriminate ... against BME groups: a representative section of the local BME community are summoned and serve as jurors in virtually all Crown Courts. [The research] also exposed a number of widespread myths ... There is no mass avoidance of jury service among the British public ... This was the reality of jury service in England and Wales even before the introduction of new juror eligibility rules in 2004, which have nonetheless increased participation in the jury system ... the case simulation research with real jurors showed that racially mixed juries in highly diverse communities did not discriminate against defendants based on the race of the defendant. This was despite the fact that race did influence the decisions of some individual jurors who sat on these juries in cases where race was not presented as an explicit element in the case. What remains to be answered is whether all-white juries, which decide cases in most Crown Courts, also do not discriminate against defendants based on race." (Summary)

Is the law working as intended?

As can be seen, Thomas challenged some of the assertions above, especially on the issue of avoidance of jury service. We return to Thomas below, to examine her 2010 findings on the effect of race on jury decision-making. In the meantime, we need to ask, is the law working as intended, to stop so may people being excused and is Thomas correct that there is no mass avoidance of jury service? The 2015–2016 Criminal Court Statistics show that of the 361,342 people summoned for jury service, 47,880 did not reply to their summons (and nothing happened to them). 96,907 (almost 27 per cent) were excused. 179,261 were supplied to courts. Some of these would then have then been excused by the judge. 60,269 (almost 17 per cent) were granted deferral to a later date. So, almost 50 per cent of those summoned were supplied to courts and an unknown number were then excused by judges. The government guidelines are clear that those who seek excusal should have their service deferred and excusal should only be granted in exceptional circumstances, yet far more were excused than deferred. The 13 per cent who failed to reply got away with it so I cannot say that our 2001 paper and Auld's recommendations achieved what we intended: forty per cent either did not reply or were excused. Therefore, on the evidence of current statistics, I still disagree with Thomas on whether there is "mass avoidance of jury service". See our interchange of letters (Darbyshire 2008).

16–015

Vetting

16–016   The group who are summoned for a particular date at a Crown Court and indeed appear there is called "the panel", from which juries are selected for trials over a certain period (usually two weeks) and the prosecution at this stage may exercise a problematic form of scrutiny known as "vetting" and then the prosecution and defence may exercise rights to challenge. It came to light in the 1970s that successive Attorneys General, using prerogative power, had been secretly vetting the backgrounds of potential jurors in politically sensitive trials. The AG was forced to reveal his guidelines on vetting. In 1980 the two divisions of the Court of Appeal gave conflicting rulings on the legality of vetting. In *R. v Sheffield Crown Court Ex p. Brownlow* (1980), the Civil Division ruled vetting by the police to be illegal but the Criminal Division, in *R. v Mason (Vincent)* (1981), held that *routine* police vetting was supportable as common sense. In response, the Attorney amended his guidelines, enhancing controls over vetting and distinguishing between: (a) vetting carried out by the police; and (b) "authorised checks", requiring his personal consent. New guidelines were issued in 2012. They stipulate that the prosecution will exercise its right to stand a juror by where the authorised check has revealed information justifying it, or

> "where a person is about to be sworn as a juror who is manifestly unsuitable and the defence agree … An example … is where … a juror selected for service to try a complex case is in fact illiterate".

The procedure for authorised checks is prescribed on the Attorney's web-pages.

> "2   The omission of a disqualified person from the panel is a matter for court officials—they will check criminal records …
>
> 3   There are, however, certain exceptional types of case of public importance … In such cases it is in the interests of both justice and the public that there should be further safeguards against the possibility of bias …
>
> 4   (a) cases in which national security is involved and part of the evidence is likely to be heard in camera, and (b) security and terrorist cases in which a juror's extreme beliefs could prevent a fair trial.
>
> 5   The particular aspects of these cases which may make it desirable to seek extra precautions are:
> a.   in security cases a danger that a juror, either voluntarily or under pressure, may make an improper use of evidence which, because of its sensitivity, has been given in camera,
> b.   in both security and terrorist cases the danger that a juror's personal beliefs are so biased as to go beyond normally reflecting the broad spectrum of views and interests in the community to reflect the extreme views of sectarian interest or pressure group to a degree which might interfere with his fair assessment of the facts of the case or lead him to exert improper pressure on his fellow jurors.
>
> 6   … it may be necessary to conduct a limited investigation of the panel … beyond … criminal records … a check may, additionally be made against the records of the Security Service …
>
> 7   No further investigation … should be made save with the personal authority of the Attorney General on the application of the Director of Public Prosecutions …

9   ... The Director will then decide ... what information ought to be brought to the attention of prosecuting counsel. The Director will also provide the Attorney General with the result of the authorised check ..."

The RCCJ 1993 recommended routine screening for criminal convictions.

Challenges to the Array

All parties have a common law right, preserved by s.12(6) of the Juries Act 1974, to challenge the whole panel, on the grounds that the summoning officer is biased or has acted improperly. For example this was attempted in *Danvers* (1982), by a black defendant, on the grounds that the all-white jury did not reflect the ethnic composition of the community.

    16–017

Challenges by the Prosecution

The prosecution may exclude any panel member from a particular jury by asking them to "stand by for the Crown" without reasons, until the whole panel, except for the last 12, is exhausted. Reasons, "cause", must be given for any further challenges but, with panels often consisting of 100 or more, the prosecution rarely needs to explain its challenges. The Roskill Committee (1986) recommended the abolition of this right but the Government disagreed. The Attorney General announced, in 1988, that the prosecution's right to stand a juror by without giving reasons would now be limited to two instances: to remove a "manifestly unsuitable" juror or to remove a juror after authorised vetting. This goes some way towards responding to complaints over the imbalance between prosecution and defence rights of challenge.

    16–018

Challenges by the Defence

Once the jury are assembled in court, the judge invites the juror to step down if she knows anyone involved in the case. The defence may then challenge any number of potential jurors for cause, (i.e. good reason acceptable to the judge) but what is an acceptable "cause" was qualified by a 1973 Practice Note issued by the Lord Chief Justice, who stated that it was contrary to established practice for jurors to be excused on grounds such as race, religion, political beliefs or occupation. It is also clear that the reasons must be those known to the defence and should not normally be ascertained by examining the potential juror in court. In other words, no practice exists such as the American "voir dire" system, above. There have been well-publicised exceptions. In the 1995–1996 Maxwell brothers' fraud trial, potential jurors were questioned on their views of the evidence because of prejudicial pre-trial publicity. In a trial of Dale Farm travellers for using vulnerable people as slaves, a questionnaire asked potential jurors whether their views would make it difficult or impossible to return verdicts based solely on the evidence: *R. v Connors* (2013).

    16–019

    Until 1989, the defence could make a certain number of peremptory challenges, that is, challenges without reasons. This right was progressively reduced then abolished by the Criminal Justice Act 1988. This resulted from the

Conservative Government's belief that the right to peremptory challenge was being abused and from the recommendation of the Roskill Committee that it be abolished. This leaves a gross imbalance between prosecution and defence rights of challenge. The abolition of peremptory challenge is in sharp contrast to the USA where, dependent on state law, each party usually has a generous number of "peremptories", to help them try to exclude unsympathetic jurors. Auld received very few suggestions that challenges be reintroduced in English law.

Excusal by the Judge

16–020   Under the Juries Act, the judge may discharge from service any juror about whom there is doubt as to "his capacity to act effectively as a juror" because of physical disability or insufficient understanding of English. Additionally, judges have a common law discretion to discharge jurors and they occasionally interpret this quite broadly, despite the fact that Criminal Practice Directions Division VI reiterates the principles of the 2003 legislation, set out above. This is in addition to the system of excusals and deferrals operated by the Jury Central Summoning Bureau. Each resident judge considers a weekly pile of letters seeking excusal and jurors make verbal requests to judges. In addition, jurors are summoned for a two week period so, in trials lasting more than two weeks, all potential jurors are given the chance to opt out. There are no statistics on excusals by judges. Sean O'Neill, crime and security editor of *The Times* said, in 2008:

> "I have reported on dozens of important criminal cases in the British courts, including every high-profile terrorist trial since 2003 ... Most big cases start with a parade of potential jurors queuing up to tell the judge why they should be excused because of holiday, work, illness or some other reason, the remnants—usually those not bright enough to come up with a half-decent excuse—are left to try some of the most complicated cases."

This standard practice before long trials (in instructions to judges in Criminal Practice Directions Division VI), plus the judge's discretion to entertain an appeal from the Summoning Bureau's decision (39B), must be taken account of when reading Thomas's findings and the statistics, above because those excused by the judge must be added to the 40 per cent who avoid jury service altogether.

3.   FUNCTION OF THE JURY

16–021   The purpose of having the jury is to enable the decision on fact to be taken by a small group from the community, rather than for it to be left entirely in the hands of the lawyers. After hearing the judge's "summing up" of the evidence and directions on the law, the jury retire and consider their verdict in private. In a civil case, they normally answer a series of questions set for them by the judge and advocates, which determines liability and they may set the level of damages awarded. In a criminal case, on the pronouncement of the verdict by the foreman of the jury, the accused is found either "guilty" or "not guilty". If "not guilty" the defendant is acquitted and is free to leave the court; if "guilty" he is convicted, and the judge sentences him. The jury plays no part in sentencing. Equally the jury has no part in decisions on law or legal procedure. A judge will often have to ask the jury to retire, so that she can hear arguments on and decide on a point of law. The judge routinely determines some points of law, procedure and admissibility of evidence before the jury are empanelled (Ch.12).

The decline of the civil jury

Civil juries declined in the twentieth century. Although a jury of eight may be called in the county court or 12 in the Queen's Bench Division, at the discretion of the judge, this is rare. In the following tort actions, s.69 of the Senior Courts Act 1981 grants a right to jury trial: malicious prosecution, false imprisonment and fraud, and it can be applied for in libel and slander, but it can be refused if prolonged examination of documents, or accounts, or other complex material is involved. In all other cases, the judge has a discretion to allow a jury trial. The trend away from civil jury trial was rapid. In 1933, 50 per cent of civil cases involved a jury. In *Ward v James (No.2)* (1966) a five-judge Court of Appeal (CA) decided that trial by judge alone should be the usual mode of civil trial.

16–022

The most important reason for the disuse of the civil jury was inconsistent and exorbitant damages awards. Examples include the £600,000 libel damages awarded to Sonia Sutcliffe, ex-wife of the "Yorkshire Ripper", against the publishers of *Private Eye*, which led Ian Hislop to comment: "If this is justice, I'm a banana". This was reduced to £60,000. The Courts and Legal Services Act 1990 s.8 provided for rules to empower the CA to substitute its own damages award. It has been easier to achieve consistency in damages awards for personal injuries because they are left to judges. Throughout the 1990s, juries made outlandishly high awards in defamation actions, much to the exasperation of the judiciary. Notice the disgust of Sir Thomas Bingham MR, in *John v MGN* (1995), an appeal in which the *Mirror* group succeeded in getting the CA to reduce to £75,000 the jury's award of £350,000 to Elton John, for alleging that he displayed symptoms of an eating disorder at a Hollywood party:

> "It is in our view offensive to public opinion ... that a defamation plaintiff should recover damages for injury to reputation greater, perhaps by a significant factor, than if that same plaintiff had been rendered a helpless cripple or an insensate vegetable."

Also in 1995, a jury award of £750,000 damages made to footballer Graeme Souness, against his ex-wife for calling him a "dirty rat" in the *People* newspaper, was settled, pending appeal, for £100,000. In 1996, four large damages awards against the Metropolitan Police in jury trials for actions such as false imprisonment provoked the Metropolitan Police Commissioner to call for judicial guidelines to be set down, similar to those in defamation cases. The Faulks Committee (1974) recommended that juries should no longer be available as of right in defamation actions for these reasons, which also provide some insight into why the civil jury declined.

- Judges were not as remote from real life as popularly supposed.
- Judges gave reasons, whereas juries did not.
- Juries found complex cases difficult.

- Juries were unpredictable.
- Juries trials were expensive (they are longer).

In the Defamation Act 2013, the presumption in favour of a jury trial in libel and slander cases is now reversed. They will be tried by judge alone, unless the judge orders to the contrary.

Coroners' juries

16–023   The coroner, whose task it is to inquire into sudden death can, and in some circumstances must, call a jury of seven to 11 people for the inquest. The coroner's jury, after hearing the evidence, returns a verdict on the cause of death. The issue of coroners' juries giving reasons is discussed in Ch.4.

4. MAJORITY VERDICTS

16–024   For centuries, the English legal system required that the verdict should be unanimous. In the 1960s there was increasing criticism of this requirement, particularly on the part of the police who pointed out that one member of the jury, if "nobbled" by the defendant or his supporters, could cause a retrial by simply refusing to agree with the other eleven. The Criminal Justice Act 1967 permitted a majority verdict of 10:2 to be accepted by the judge, or 10:1, or 9:1 if one or two jury members had been discharged. The jury must spend at least two hours seeking to achieve unanimity. If the verdict is "guilty" the fact that it is a majority verdict must be disclosed. Majority verdicts were permitted in civil cases from 1972. The law is now consolidated in the Juries Act 1974, as amended.

5. SECRECY

16–025   The secrecy of deliberations is protected. They deliberate alone in the jury room and disclosure of deliberations is a criminal offence. It used to be a contempt of court under the Contempt of Court Act 1981 s.8. This was thought to be a handicap to jury research. The 1993 Royal Commission recommended its amendment, as did the Law Commission, in their 1995 annual report but Auld disagreed, in his 2001 Review. He contemplated the view of Lord Hewart CJ, expressed in 1922, that the value of the jury's verdict lies only in its anonymity and the view of Glanville Williams, in *The Proof of Guilt*, 1955, that "the real reason for keeping the jury's deliberations secret is to preserve confidence in a system which more intimate knowledge might destroy" (p.205). Auld asked:

> "Should section 8 of the 1981 Act be amended to permit legitimate research (and, while we are about it, to enable the Court of Appeal, Criminal Division, to examine conduct in the jury room the subject of appeal)? Or is public confidence in juries' oracular verdicts so precious to our legal system that we should not put it at risk? Many fear that the very undertaking of intrusive research—that is, into how individual juries reach their decisions—could damage public confidence by sewing

doubts as to the integrity of verdicts ... On the other hand, such research might show that all is not well and that changes are needed." (p.166)

He considered our (2001) argument that there is a wealth of jury research, worldwide, from which lessons could be learned and most of it is of a non-intrusive nature. He cited the 1994 New York Jury Project and the 2001 New Zealand criminal trial jury study and concluded that ample lessons could be learned from non-intrusive research of this kind. He recommended no amendment to s.8. There should, instead, be careful consideration of all available existing research material throughout the common law world (summarised in our paper), with a view to identifying and responding appropriately to all available information about how juries arrived at their verdicts. If and to the extent to which such information was insufficient, jury research should be considered that did not violate the 1981 Act.

In 2005, the DCA published a consultation paper "Jury Research and Impropriety", again raising the question of whether s.8 should be amended. The paper stated that jury secrecy "has long been regarded as a cornerstone of the legal system" but in recent years, after the incorporation of the European Convention on Human Rights into English law

16–026

> "there has been increasing debate on whether the current law has got it right. Is there a risk that the necessary confidentiality of the jury process could lead to potential miscarriages of justice and, if so, is there a way of reducing this risk without fundamentally undermining the jury process?" (p.5)

The paper canvassed views on whether:

- any or all aspects of the way in which juries deliberate should be subject to research;
- there are circumstances in which a jury's deliberations should be subject to external investigation; and
- any aspect of the common law rule rendering inadmissible any evidence from jury deliberations should be clarified or amended.

The paper set out the Government's provisional views, proposing that any research into deliberations should only be allowed if permitted by the minister and undertaken in accordance with conditions agreed by him and the Lord Chief Justice, including confidentiality. As for impropriety, the paper set out the current law as stated in recent appeals, notably *R. v Mirza* (2004), below, and recommended that the law should be left as it is. Such allegations should be dealt with on a case-by-case basis. The paper explained the background to s.8: it had not been government intention in 1981 to prohibit bona fide research but, after lengthy deliberation on its dangers, Parliament made last-minute amendments to the Bill which precluded research. The potential benefits of research might include:

- Understanding the factors jurors consider important when determining guilt/innocence.
- Improving information, guidance and directions.

- Discovering what jurors think of the trial process.
- Examining whether all jurors are able to participate.
- Determining whether there is any evidence of gender/racial or other bias.
- Suggesting any other factors which would allow jurors to do their job better.

The risks included:

- Inhibiting the frankness of jury discussions.
- Undermining the finality of verdicts.
- Damaging public confidence in the jury system.
- Where the research is not bona fide or is slanted, exposing jurors to harassment.

They concluded that any change in the law must be designed to improve support for jurors. In 2008, some people raised concerns about jurors telling stories of their experiences to the newspapers. See, for instance, Bawdon. She reported on a rash of cases in which jurors had told the media that conviction verdicts in which they participated were wrong. As can be seen below, in 2013, the Law Commission recommended amending s.8 to permit academic jury research but the Government decided not to legislate on this. Thomas pointed out, in her 2013 article, that s.8 is commonly misinterpreted as precluding all useful research. She lists all the recent research achieved without breaching s.8.

6. ALLEGATIONS OF IMPROPRIETY OR BIAS

16–027 Occasionally, a defendant or a court hears allegations from a juror that there was something unsatisfactory about the deliberations or the way in which the jury arrived at their verdict and the trial court or the CA has to decide how far they can breach jury room secrecy to investigate. The 2005 consultation paper set out the common law rule, articulated in *R. v Mirza*, by Lord Hope, "the court will not investigate, or receive evidence about, anything said in the course of the jury's deliberations while they are considering their verdict in the retiring room." The consultation paper examined some problematic cases:

- *Ellis v Deheer* (1922): some of the jurors could not hear the verdict announced and disagreed with it. The CA declined to hear evidence of jury deliberations.
- *R. v Young* (1995): while staying overnight in a hotel, four jury members tried to contact the deceased via a ouija board. He allegedly told them the defendant had murdered him. The CA held that it could inquire into what took place in the hotel but not in the jury room.
- *R. v McCluskey* (1994): one of the jurors used a mobile phone to make a business call, during deliberations. The CA admitted evidence from him that he did have his phone.

Article 6 of the European Convention on Human Rights, as described in Chs 4 and 12, requires a fair trial. In *Remli v France* (1996) the ECtHR made it clear that the Convention imposes an obligation on the national court to check whether a tribunal was impartial. In *R. v Mirza*, the House of Lords (HL) held that the s.8 prohibition on the admission of jury deliberations did not breach art.6. The case law of the ECtHR had not undermined the principle of secrecy of jury deliberations. In *Gregory v UK* (1998), the ECtHR stressed that the tribunal, including the jury, must be impartial from a subjective as well as an objective point of view. In that case, one juror had passed a note to the judge during deliberations which read "Jury showing racial overtones. One member to be excused". The judge had warned the jury to decide according to the evidence and they returned a majority guilty verdict. The ECtHR acknowledged that jury room secrecy was fundamental and made no attempt to overturn the principle.

In *R. v Mirza*, the HL affirmed a line of cases on the common law prohibition against receiving evidence of deliberations. The rule only protected the secrecy of deliberations, not extraneous evidence of jury bias so was not disproportionate and therefore not in breach of art.6. The House recognised that there could be cases where evidence should be admitted that the jury had completely failed to discharge its duty, such as by using a ouija board. Lord Hope said it was the collective decision-making, free from outside interference, that gave jury trial its strength. The tribunal was presumed to be impartial until the contrary was proven. Attempts to soften the rule in the public interest should be resisted if jurors were to continue to perform their vital function of safeguarding individual liberty. The jury's introductory video should be amended to warn jurors to raise concerns before the verdict, when they could be investigated and dealt with by the trial judge. (Here, a juror had written *after* the trial, alleging prejudice by other jurors, and in the case joined to *Mirza*, called *Connor and Rollock* (2004), a juror alleged that her jury were prepared to find the accused guilty just for the sake of reaching a quick verdict.) The House said better information could be given to appeal courts so they could scrutinise allegations to the high degree required by art.6. The CA could call for a report from the trial judge. Issues of jury impropriety are dealt with at length in the Criminal Practice Directions VI.

After 2005, allegations of impropriety continued, sometimes with extremely **16–028** expensive results. *R. v Mirza* was applied in another HL decision, *R. v Smith (Patrick), R. v Mercieca* (2005). Here, a juror had written to the judge alleging coercion by some jurors of others and that deals were being done in order to reach a swift decision. The House upheld the trial judge's decision not to question the jurors about their deliberations. The judge had been correct to give the jury further directions and warn them not to be bullied but he was insufficiently comprehensive and emphatic. He should have given them a stern warning to follow his directions on law and to decide on their verdicts without pressure or bargaining.

In *R. v Karakaya* (2005), a juror downloaded information from the internet, for use in jury deliberations. The CA quashed the defendant's convictions on the ground that this offended against the principle of open justice. The public and the defendant should know the material considered by the decision making body. The prosecution and defence were entitled to a fair opportunity to address all the material considered by the jury. No evidence must be introduced after the jury retired. Jurors should not conduct their own private research. In *Attorney General v Scotcher* (2005), the HL upheld the contempt finding on a juror who had written to the defendant's mother expressing concern at the jury's deliberations. His desire to expose a miscarriage of justice was no defence.

In *R. v Cornwall* (2009) an outspoken *Sun* columnist, S, was the jury foreman with well-publicised views on knife-crime, drugs, immigration and sentencing but this was held not to be grounds for quashing the conviction. The difference between him and another juror was that he had expressed his views publicly. There was nothing to suggest that S was not faithful to his juror's oath. If a writer had expressed strong views about the *law*, he would be well-advised to draw this to the judge's attention. *R. v Gough* (1993) and *R. v Abdroikov* (2007) were considered: would a fair-minded and reasonable observer conclude that there was a real possibility or danger of bias?

By 2017, the frequency of allegations of jury nobbling, as in the *Twomey* case, and misconduct by jurors seemed to have increased and some judges fear that it is almost impossible to stop jurors researching the background to their cases on the internet. The first Facebook-related conviction for contempt of court took place in 2011. Joanna Fraill, a juror, and Jamie Sewart, an acquitted defendant, were convicted and jailed by the High Court after communicating on Facebook about the jury's deliberations during a multimillion pound drug trial in 2010, causing it to collapse: *Attorney General v Fraill* (2011). See Lord Judge CJ's speech on juries and the internet, 2010. In the memorable case of *Attorney General v Davey* (2013), a juror in a child-abuse trial posted this on Facebook: "Woooow I wasn't expecting to be in a jury Deciding a paedophile's fate, I've always wanted to fuck up a paedophile & now I'm within the law!" For an astonishing case of jurors hob-nobbing in the pub with a defendant, see *R. v Hewgill* (2011). The CA asked the Criminal Cases Review Commission to investigate what contact had taken place between the jurors and all the defendants. In *R. v Baybasin* (2013), however, the CA held that an inquiry should not be ordered where a complaint had been made post-verdict unless there was strong and compelling evidence. See a similar allegation of bias in *R. v Connors* (2013). Contrast this with *Pouladian-Kari* (2013), where the juror drew the judge's attention to his relevant professional knowledge and the subsequent conviction was quashed because the CA applied the standard bias test: whether a fair-minded and informed observer would have concluded there was a real possibility of unconscious bias.

16–029   The problem of jurors researching on the internet has been addressed in other countries, as can be seen from the Law Commission's consultation on contempt, below. Using post-verdict surveys with 239 jurors, the UCL Jury Project, led by Thomas (2013), investigated how jurors used the internet and what they understood improper conduct to be. 23 per cent were confused about the rule on internet use. 16 per cent believed they could not use the internet at all, five per cent believed there was no restriction and two per cent believed they could look for information about the case, provided it did not affect their judgment. 62 per cent were unaware of recent cases on juror misconduct like *Fraill*, despite the fact that some served at courts where these cases were posted on the jury lounge walls. Of the 78 per cent of jurors who had used the internet during the trial, 26 per cent had looked up information about the judge, lawyers, legal terms, or the parties, or visited the crime scene online, or discussed their jury service online. 82

per cent would have liked more guidance on conducting deliberations. Many felt they needed more guidance on what to do if they were confused on a legal issue or if something went wrong in deliberations. 100 per cent of those receiving written directions found them helpful. Stage two of Thomas's research is focusing on how to increase jurors' understanding of the rules on improper conduct. She recommended establishing clear court practices on access to internet-enabled devices and to take a research-based approach in attempting to change juror behaviour, assessing which methods of conveying information work best.

In 2013, in its 340th report, *Contempt of Court (1): Juror Misconduct and Internet Publications*, the Law Commission recommended a new criminal offence where a juror researches a case. They also recommended

> "a range of other measures designed to discourage and prevent jurors from undertaking research and from disclosing their deliberations ... greater education in schools ...; improving the information provided to jurors ...; changes to the wording of the juror oath to include an agreement to base the verdict only on the evidence heard in court; requiring jurors to sign a written declaration; informing jurors about asking questions during the trial; a statutory power for judges to remove internet-enabled devices from jurors where necessary and effective systems for jurors to report concerns. Finally ... we recommend the introduction of a specific, statutory, defence to a breach of section 8 of the Contempt of Court Act 1981, where, after the conclusion of the trial, a juror, in genuine belief that they are exposing a miscarriage of justice, discloses the content of jury deliberations to a court official, the police or the Criminal Cases Review Commission. We also recommend the introduction of an exception to the section 8 prohibition on jury research. This would allow for authorised academic research into jury deliberations, with a range of rigorous safeguards in place in order to protect the integrity of the jury's decision and the anonymity of jurors and parties to the trials." (1.23–1.24)

Accordingly, the Criminal Justice and Courts Act 2015 s.69 permits a judge to order jurors to surrender electronic devices. Section 71 creates a new imprisonable, extensive offence of "research by jurors", into information about the case, including information about the parties, lawyers, judge, evidence or the law. There is another new offence under s.72 of "sharing research with other jurors"; another offence under s.73 of engaging "in conduct from which it may be reasonably concluded that the person intends to try the issue otherwise than on the basis of the evidence presented in the proceedings on the issue". Disclosing jury deliberations becomes a specified offence under s.74. Prosecutions can only be instituted by the Attorney General. The Act spells out in detail that it is not an offence to disclose deliberation details for the purposes of investigating whether there has been a contempt of court. Section 8 of the Contempt of Court Act 1981, which made disclosing deliberations a contempt, is repealed. Judges now warn jurors of all of this but of course it will not stop them researching on the internet. The Act does *not* make an exception for academic research into jurors, contrary to the Law Commission's recommendation.

7. "JURY EQUITY" AND THE UNREASONED VERDICT

16–030   Jurors do not give reasons. An interesting historical survival is the rule that jurors cannot be punished if they bring in a perverse acquittal contrary to the direction of the judge. This was laid down in *Bushell's Case* in 1670 where two Quakers were charged with tumultuous assembly. The jury were ordered to convict, but instead returned a verdict of "not guilty". The judge sent the jury to prison until they paid a fine by way of punishment. On appeal, it was held that the fine and imprisonment could not be allowed to stand. In *R. v Wang* (2005), the HL affirmed that there were no circumstances in which a judge could direct a jury to convict, even in cases where the burden of raising a defence rested on the defendant and he had failed to discharge it. The jury were free to deliver an acquittal that the trial judge considered to be perverse. The *Ponting* trial of 1985 saw a jury bring in a verdict of "not guilty" in an Official Secrets Act case where a conviction had been expected. This freedom to ignore the law and resort to their consciences, is called "jury equity" in the UK and "nullification" in the USA. There are many more modern examples. For instance, there have been several acquittals of defendants who have used cannabis to relieve the pain of such illnesses as multiple sclerosis. An example of jury equity that met approval with the news media, as it seemed to reflect popular sentiment, occurred in 2009. Kenneth Batchelor was acquitted of murdering a would-be burglar. The circumstances were very similar to the Tony Martin case 10 years earlier. Burgess (2009) reported that:

> "[He] fired a shotgun at 'very close quarters' at 42-year-old Matthew Clements, who had climbed the scaffolding of his home to try to force open an upstairs window. Mr Batchelor had received a barrage of threatening phone calls from Mr Clements, a 20-stone nightclub bouncer, who was demanding maintenance money from the Batchelor family following a former relationship between his girlfriend and Mr Batchelor's brother Gary, which produced three children. The jury at Maidstone Crown Court took just one hour unanimously to acquit Mr Batchelor of the murder of Mr Clements who, the court heard, had an 'explosive temper' and had become 'fixated' with demanding money from the Batchelor family."

In our 2001 paper for Auld, we concluded that jurors could be asked to give reasons, or at least . . .

> "They could be given a series of questions, agreed between counsel and judge, as they are in civil trials. [See] Thaman's account of how the procedure works in Spain." (The New Zealand Law Commission recommended a series of sequential questions or a flow chart in complex trials, para.318.)

Auld pointed out that the ECtHR had ruled that the unreasoned verdict of a Danish jury was not a breach of the Convention. The problem with an unreasoned verdict in the English legal system is that it can make appeal difficult and it is an anomaly compared with other criminal tribunals. The magistrates and the district judge (magistrates' court) are both required by art.6 of the Convention to give reasoned decisions. Auld said:

"A reasoned judgment tells the parties why they have won or lost; it is more likely to be soundly based on the evidence than an unreasoned one; and, by its openness is more likely to engender public confidence in the decision-making system." (p.169)

He agreed with our 2001 suggestion of giving the jury a series of questions. Although this was not put into law or practice directions, the practice became much more common. By 2011, in *Sitting in Judgment*, I reported that all the circuit and High Court judges in my research sample had given written directions in some cases and some judges gave them in every case. In his 2015 Review Leveson said:

"In cases of complexity, Judges have more recently moved away from a purely oral exposition of the law and provided written directions in the form of "Route to Verdicts" identifying a logical progression of propositions which apply the law to the specific facts then being considered. Some also provide a copy of the directions of law so that the jury can have the precise terms of the directions to hand while deliberating. These developments are to be encouraged and should become the standard approach to be adopted in every case (p.75)."

As explained in the chapter on criminal procedure, this has at last found its way into the CrimPR.

Very importantly, in our 2001 paper for Auld, however, we added: "If jurors   **16–031**
are to be asked for reasons, then they must surely be told of their power to acquit in the face of condemnatory evidence, as an exercise of jury equity", but he reached the opposite conclusion on jury equity. He regarded the jury's ability to acquit or convict in the face of the law as "a blatant affront to the legal process and the main purpose of the criminal justice system—the control of crime". He surprised commentators by recommending that the law should be changed to declare that juries had no right to acquit in defiance of the law or disregard of the evidence (p.176). This recommendation outraged critics of the Auld Review and, unfortunately, destroyed much of its credibility. In 1991, I had attacked the rhetoric extolling the virtues of jury equity, which is sometimes irrational and can be unfair, using the same reasoning as Auld did 10 years later but it seems to me that suggesting that jury equity should be banned is pointless. The very reason why the British and Americans heap praise on the jury system is its ability to defy the law. It is argued that the jury acts as a check on officialdom, on the judge's power, and is a protector against unjust or oppressive prosecution, injecting jury "equity" by deciding guilt or innocence according to a feeling of justice rather than by applying known law to facts proven beyond reasonable doubt: for example Kalven and Zeisel said, in *The American Jury* (1966):

"It represents also an impressive way of building discretion, equity and flexibility into a legal system. Not least of the advantages is that the jury, relieved of the burdens of creating precedent, can bend the law without breaking it."

Unsurprisingly, in the furore on this point that followed publication of the *Review*, the Government did not follow this recommendation.

Taxquet v Belgium (2012) ECtHR is quite a worrying case for the English legal system. T applied to Strasbourg on the ground that there was a breach of art.6, because the jury had not given reasons for their decision. They were simply asked by the court's president to answer whether T was guilty of murder as perpetrator or through assistance or incitement and whether it was premeditated. The court unanimously held that, though there was no Convention requirement for jurors to give reasons, the accused and the public must be able to understand the jury's verdict. There must be sufficient safeguards in place, such as directions from the presiding judge and precise unequivocal questions, forming a framework on which the verdict is based. Ashworth's 2011 comment is very useful. He pointed out that 24 contracting states (signatories) of the European Convention on HR, have collaborative judge and jury systems, 10 have a traditional jury system and 14 have no jury trial. The UK, France and Ireland made submissions to the Grand Chamber, as interveners. The UK and Ireland argued that the judge's directions provided a sufficient safeguard.

For a thought-provoking, interesting argument on the jury's function and placing restrains on the jury, see Crosby's 2012 article. Noting the increased use of "route to verdict" directions, he said

> "my focus is on Devlin's two means of controlling juries—controlling what they see and controlling what they think—and I shall argue that at exactly the point at which growing internet use has made the first means increasingly difficult, strategies have been developed for more closely enforcing the second. My concern is that if jury nullification is desirable … then we should treat with caution any developments which would tend to undermine the jury's capacity to respond to a case differently from the professional lawyer on the Bench." (p.20)

8.   HISTORY

16–032   During its long history, the jury has completely changed its role. Generally, jurors should have no prior knowledge of the case, and will be able to reach their verdict entirely on the evidence presented at the trial. Originally, however, the jury's role was a combination of local police and prosecutor. Centuries before a paid police force was created, the responsibility for law and order lay with the community. This meant the local "jury" arrested suspected offenders, and then brought them before the visiting judge and swore, like prosecution witnesses, to the guilt of the accused. There was nothing unusual in this use of representatives in the early community. It can be seen also in the local inquiries which led to the creation of the Domesday Book, and the system of inquisitions post mortem, the inquiry held on a death as to the ownership of the lands and goods of the deceased. Throughout the Middle Ages juries were used in the settlement of civil disputes concerning the ownership and tenancy of land and the right to an advowson (the right to present to the living of a church).

It was only with the passage of centuries that the use of the jury as uninvolved judges of fact developed. Even then the original concept survived, leading to the distinction between the grand jury and the petty jury. The grand jury of 24 members met only at the start of assizes or quarter sessions in order to find a true bill of indictment against the accused. Since the accused had previously undergone the preliminary inquiry by magistrates, who had heard the prosecution case and had decided to commit the accused for trial, the decision of the grand jury became a complete formality. It was abolished by the Criminal Justice Act

1948. US jurisdictions retain the grand jury to indict the accused in certain cases. The petty (trial) jury of 12 emerged in the thirteenth century to replace trial by ordeal, condemned by the ecclesiastical authorities. It became increasingly distinct in its functions from the grand jury, although it long maintained its composition from *witnesses* of fact deciding matters from their local knowledge. In the fifteenth century the petty jury assumed its modern role in criminal trials as the adjudicator of fact.

In civil cases the jury appears to have had its origin in the Assizes of Clarendon in 1166, and the Assizes of Northampton in 1176, establishing the grand and petty assizes. Again the jury was at first called to decide a case from its local knowledge, but over time it became an impartial judge of the facts. The system allowed for trial to be in two parts. The local jury would hear and deal with the case, then send their findings to the judges at Westminster where the judgment would be given.

9. INROADS AND ATTEMPTED INROADS INTO THE CRIMINAL TRIAL JURY

Failed attempts to withdraw the right to elect jury trial

As explained in Ch.12, in cases of medium seriousness, called "triable either way", where the magistrates express no preference as to mode of trial, the defendant has the right to elect trial by magistrates in their court or judge and jury in the Crown Court. On the subject of the right to choose jury trial see Zander (2012):   **16–033**

> "The defendant's right to choose jury trial goes back not, as some maintain, to the Magna Carta, but only to the mid 19th century. The Administration of Criminal Justice Act 1855 gave magistrates jurisdiction to try simple larceny cases involving sums of under five shillings, but only if the defendant consented. The Summary Jurisdiction Act 1879 gave defendants the right to claim trial by jury for all offences carrying a maximum sentence of more than three months. Today that right applies to all either way offences."

Governments had been thinking of removing the right to elect jury trial long before the Royal Commission on Criminal Justice 1993 (RCCJ) recommended they do so. Drawing conclusions from Home Office and other research, they concluded that the system was not being used as intended. They found that, while defendants often opted for Crown Court trial in the belief that their chances of acquittal were greater, many nevertheless changed their plea to guilty at the Crown Court; defendants often opted for Crown Court trial in the mistaken belief that, if convicted, the Crown Court judge would impose a lighter sentence than magistrates. Magistrates sent a number of cases to the Crown Court where the defendant ultimately received a sentence within the magistrates' own sentencing powers. Governments (from 1965 or before, to 2017) perceive this as an enormous waste of money because proceedings in the magistrates' court are far cheaper than those in the Crown Court and this applies to sentencing proceedings, last minute guilty pleas and contested cases, trials. For instance, in 2010, Justice

Minister Ken Clarke said a last-minute guilty plea in the Crown Court cost just over £3,200, compared with under £300 in the magistrates' court.

The RCCJ recommended that the defendant should no longer have the right to insist on jury trial. Where prosecution and defence could not agree on mode of trial, the decision should be referred to the magistrates. The Commission was subject to academic criticism, especially by Professors McConville and Bridges, alleging that it had misinterpreted the Home Office research. Nevertheless, the (Conservative) Home Office published a consultation document, *Mode of Trial*, in 1995. They outlined three options designed to shift more cases from the Crown Court to the magistrates' courts:

1. The reclassification of more offences as triable only summarily, i.e. only in the magistrates' court.
2. The withdrawal of the defendant's option to insist on jury trial in the Crown Court.
3. A requirement that the defendant enter the plea before the trial/hearing venue is chosen.

The Government chose to enact the third and least draconian of these options. Given the sentimental attachment to jury trial in criminal cases, they realised it would be politically inexpedient to remove the defendant's right to opt for jury trial in all either-way cases. Instead, s.49 of the Criminal Procedure and Investigations Act 1996 (now amended) was passed. This requires magistrates, before determining mode of trial, to ascertain the accused's plea, in the hope of persuading the magistrates to keep more cases in the magistrates' court. This and the current procedure are explained in Ch.12. Before this plan could take effect, however, The Narey Report was published in 1997 and reiterated the recommendation that the defendant's right to elect jury trial be removed. In 1998, the newly elected Labour Home Secretary published *Determining Mode of Trial in Either Way Cases—A Consultation Paper*. It set out the familiar arguments on abolishing the defendant's right to elect jury trial, as follows.

For abolition

16–034
- The right was not ancient. It dated from 1855 and had nothing to do with Magna Carta.
- 22,000 defendants elected for Crown Court trial in 1997 but most changed their plea to guilty, after significant inconvenience and worry to victims and witnesses, and considerable extra cost.
- By definition, elected cases were those which magistrates had determined were suitable for themselves. The mode of trial decision should be based on objective assessment by the magistrates of the gravity of the case, not the defendant's perception of what was advantageous to him, such as a greater prospect of acquittal.
- It was questionable whether defendants opted for jury trial to defend their reputation, because nine tenths of those electing already had previous convictions.

- Most defendants chose jury trial because they wanted to delay proceedings, to apply pressure to the Crown to accept a guilty plea to a lesser offence, or to deter witnesses, or to put off the evil day.
- Few other jurisdictions allowed the defendant such an element of choice. In Scotland, the sheriff's court decided on the trial venue.

Arguments in favour of the status quo

- The right to elect jury trial helped to promote confidence in the criminal justice system.   **16–035**
- Whereas magistrates were broadly concerned with the seriousness of the offence, it was the defendant's reputation which the public saw as a justification for continuing to allow the right.
- When people who had never been accused of a crime defended the right, it was usually on the basis that they would want such a right if *they* were charged with something of which they were innocent.
- It was assumed that Crown Court trial was fairer. Defendants who chose it rightly believed they had a higher chance of acquittal.
- Some arguments went to the merits of trial by jury, for example, the jury's capacity to acquit contrary to legal proof of guilt.

One proposal in the paper was to take away the right of those defendants who had previous convictions and who had, therefore, already lost their reputations. Subsequently, Home Secretary Jack Straw introduced the Criminal Justice (Mode of Trial) Bill in 1999. This would have abolished the defendant's right to elect, placing the mode of trial decision in the magistrates' hands. The Bill attracted enormous opposition, notably from the Bar, the Law Society, the Society of Black Lawyers and from lawyers' groups such as the Legal Action Group (LAG). LAG argued the following (*Legal Action*, September 1998):

- The main reason defendants opted for jury trial was that they rightly saw their chances of obtaining justice in the Crown Court as significantly higher, as the acquittal rate was higher and many cases were dismissed by the judge. (For modern statistics, see the annual *Court Statistics*).
- Electing jury trial brought into play a range of other safeguards, such as greater disclosure of the prosecution case. (A point made by many other commentators.)
- Removing the right to elect would significantly disadvantage black defendants. Courtney Griffiths QC (*Counsel*, April 1999) added that research by the Runnymede Trust, in 1990, showed that, whereas under one third of white defendants, given the option, elected jury trial, 45 per cent of black defendants elected. This was an intelligent choice. Home Office research at Leicester magistrates' court showed white defendants had a substantially better chance of being granted bail. They were less likely to receive immediate custodial sentences than blacks.
- The suggestion that defendants elected jury trial to put off the evil day was not borne out by research.
- Delays would increase, caused by mini-trials about venue.

- When he was in opposition, Jack Straw had called the proposal "short-sighted".

Wolchover and Heaton-Armstong added:

- A defendant who delayed a guilty plea to obtain some advantage could not expect the same sentence discount as one who pleaded earlier and, since 1986, advocates had had a duty to warn defendants of this.
- Tactical elections for jury trial would continue to decline because of the introduction of the "plea before venue" procedure and because of s.48 of the Criminal Justice and Public Order Act 1994, which allowed the sentencing court to take account of the timing of the guilty plea.
- As defence counsel, their experience showed that the most frequent cause of a last minute plea was the defendant's loss of courage. Defendants did not choose jury trial to put off the evil day.
- The argument was about the loss of a traditional common law right.
- Loss of liberty was no less serious for an habitual thief than loss of good name for someone with no previous convictions.

Both the Bar and Law Society opposed the plan to abolish the right to elect. A number of other commentators emphasised that jury trial was inherently superior to summary trial, especially as listing a case for a Crown Court trial triggered a much more careful review of the case by the prosecution, which would often result in dropping the case or reducing the charges. This also implied that, if magistrates were to decide on mode of trial, they would be doing so on inadequate information.

16–036 Furthermore, at the Crown Court, a professional judge reviewed the strength and admissibility of the evidence, whereas magistrates were both fact-finders and arbiters of the law. Ley added that criminal defence solicitors in magistrates' courts were often ignorant of the law, as were magistrates' clerks. Some critics said that magistrates' courts were seen as police courts; magistrates were seen as part of the establishment and magistrates were not as socially and ethnically diverse as the jury. A *New Law Journal* editorial ((1999) 149 N.L.J. 549) argued that there were other ways of cutting down the cost and length of jury trials, such as reducing jurors to six, or cutting out the opening statement and permitting the judge to sum up only on law.

This first Bill was heavily defeated in the House of Lords, in 2000. A second Bill also failed. In 2001, in his Review, Auld reiterated the recommendation that the right to elect jury trial should be removed. After consulting on this, the Government received predictable responses from all the groups cited above, raising the same objections that they had already argued many times before. The Government therefore dropped plans to remove the right to elect. Instead, they passed the Criminal Justice Act 2003, enabling them to double magistrates' sentencing powers, as an alternative means of keeping more cases down in the magistrates' court, as discussed in Ch.12, but this has not yet been implemented. In 2011, history repeated itself. The Coalition government again raised the very same issue of how to save the waste of money and resources (as they see it) caused by trivial cases going to the Crown Court. In his 2010 consultation paper on legal aid, the Minister of Justice, Ken Clarke, said

> "Too many criminal cases that could adequately be dealt with in the magistrates' court are going to the Crown Court. Increasing numbers of those cases go on to plead guilty, often at a late stage in the proceedings. This is inefficient and ineffective for the criminal justice system as a whole and does not represent best value in legal aid expenditure."

The remainder of the quotation and discussion is in Ch.12, under the heading "Offences triable either way…".

Should we permit the defendant to elect trial by judge alone?

Auld thought that defendants in the Crown Court should be entitled to opt out of jury trial by choosing trial by judge alone. We discussed this in our 2001 paper for him. I have long argued (1991 and 1997) that it is inappropriate to speak of the "right" to jury trial in indictable cases which must go to the Crown Court, because the defendant has no choice. In these cases and cases where the defendant has opted for a Crown Court trial, if he pleads not guilty, then he will be tried by judge and jury. He cannot opt for trial by judge alone, or a "bench trial" as it is called in the USA. The English legal system is odd among common law systems, because the accused does have this choice in the USA, Canada, New Zealand and a number of Australian states. Doran and Jackson examined judge alone trials not only in Northern Ireland, in the Diplock Courts, but in other jurisdictions. Auld was persuaded to investigate this procedure in some depth. He found that in some Canadian provinces, up to 90 per cent of defendants opted for a bench trial. In the USA, judge alone trial tended to be chosen where prosecution and defence could not agree to a plea bargain but Auld found there were other defendants who preferred a judge alone trial, too:

16–037

- Those who believed themselves innocent in a factually or legally complex case who were anxious for the tribunal to understand their case.
- Defendants with technical defences who wanted fully reasoned decisions which would ease an appeal.
- Defendants charged with offences which attracted public opprobrium, such as sex or violent offences.
- Minorities who considered a judge to be more objective than a jury.
- Where there had been adverse publicity.
- Defendants in cases turning on alleged confessions or identification.
- Where local lower tier judges were well known to and trusted by the legal profession to conduct fair trials.

He recommended that defendants should, with the consent of the court, be able to opt for judge alone trial in cases tried on indictment. The Government accepted his recommendation. The Criminal Justice Bill 2003 aimed to introduce a procedure for trial by judge alone, where the accused requested it. This clause met opposition from the Conservatives and Liberal Democrats and did not survive into the Act. This was intensely frustrating to those of us who had campaigned for this change in the law. For my part, I cannot see a single logical reason why the accused should not be given the right to opt out of jury trial and be tried by judge alone. As I explained in the previous chapter, I drew attention to the illogicality of our present system, in 1997: in the magistrates' court, the defendant may be tried by three lay justices or a single district judge—he cannot choose between them; in a Crown Court trial he must be tried by judge *and* jury.

The judge's right to order trial by judge alone

Jury tampering

16–038   Section 44 of the Criminal Justice Act 2003 allows an application for a judge alone trial where there is a "real and present danger" of jury tampering, and other conditions are satisfied, as explained in Ch.12. The inclusion of s.44 resulted from lobbying by the police. As explained in Ch.12, after an unsuccessful appeal, the first defendants to be tried under this section, Twomey and others, were tried for a £1.7 million armed robbery at Heathrow, by Treacy J, sitting alone, in 2010. (The trial started at the Royal Courts of Justice but was moved to the Old Bailey after one defendant absconded.) At least two more trials were conducted by judge alone, in 2010, acting under the same section. This was condemned by the Criminal Bar Association as the thin end of the wedge in reducing trial by jury. See Fresco and Gibb, and Gibb, 2009 and 2010. As explained in Ch.12, the CA had ruled in *R. v T* (2010) against a jury trial which would have cost £1.5 million to £6 million for various levels of protection for the jury. Critical lawyers argued that the 800 year old right to jury trial was beyond price. Judges, all ex-lawyers themselves, are generally strongly in favour of jury trial and Lord Judge CJ was very sensitive to criticism of his Court of Appeal ruling in the *Twomey* case and the "thin end of the wedge" argument. He insisted "We believe in the jury system—every judge I know", when interviewed (2009). In *G.* (2011), jury tampering became apparent once the jury had retired. The judge decided that to continue with the trial herself would not be unfair. The CA upheld her decision and rejected G's argument that she should have stood down. "The normal approach remains that, assuming the necessary conditions are established, the case should continue and the attempt to disrupt the trial should fail" (Lord Judge). There are further examples of jury tampering such as *McManaman* (2016), where the CA held that where tampering was alleged, it was the duty of the police to place a senior officer in charge and act urgently.

Long and complex frauds

16–039   There has also been a long-standing concern by some that jury trial is inappropriate in long and complex frauds. Jurors' difficulty in understanding evidence is most acute in fraud trials and was considered by the Roskill Committee on Fraud Trials in 1986. Fraud trials are notoriously long (sometimes over 100 days), expensive and highly complicated. The Committee said:

> "The ... sophisticated world of high finance and international trading ... is probably a mystery to most or all of the jurors ... Even the language in which the allegedly

fraudulent transactions have been conducted will be unfamiliar. A knowledge of accountancy or bookkeeping may be essential to an understanding of the case. If any juror has such knowledge, it is by chance" (para.8.27).

The Committee recommended that the jury be abolished in complex criminal fraud cases and be replaced by a Fraud Trials Tribunal of a judge and two lay members. This debate was revived in 1992, following the Guinness trial and the Blue Arrow fraud trial, lasting over a year, and again in 1996, following the acquittals after the Maxwell trial. The suggestion was resurrected by Labour Home Secretary, Jack Straw, in 1998, in "Juries in Serious Fraud Trials", a Home Office consultation paper. In his *Review*, Auld considered fraud and other complex cases at length. He said the problem was compounded by the unrepresentative nature of juries, particularly in fraud and other complex cases. Even the Bar Council had acknowledged that it was difficult to find representative juries for long trials. The Serious Fraud Office had commented to him that these trials were often too much for jurors and ill health or claimed ill health was a cause of delay or severance. Auld 2001 listed the arguments for and against juries in cases of serious and complex fraud:

- jury trial was a hallowed democratic institution and the defendant's right in serious cases;
- random selection ensured fairness and independence;
- the question was usually one of dishonesty, essentially a matter for the jury, who because of their number and mix were better equipped than a smaller tribunal of professionals;
- there was no research evidence that they could not cope with long and complex cases or that their decisions were contrary to the evidence; and
- there was openness and impartiality in the parties having to explain the case to the jury in simple and digestible form and there was scope for improvement there.

On the other hand: **16–040**

- if juries were the defendant's peers, they ought to be experienced in the professional or commercial context of the alleged offence;
- the volume and complexity of evidence might make dishonesty difficult to determine;
- the length of such trials was an unreasonable intrusion into jurors' lives;
- juries in these trials were unrepresentative;
- long trials were a strain on the defendant, victim and witnesses;
- judges, with legal and forensic expertise, and/or specialist assessors would be better equipped to deal with such cases fairly and expeditiously;
- there would be the benefit of openness, since there would be a publicly reasoned and appealable decision; and
- the length of these trials was very costly to the public and unduly delayed the efficient disposal of other cases.

He contemplated the alternatives: special juries; judge alone; a panel of judges or a judge and lay members. He recommended that, as an alternative to jury trial in long and complex frauds, the nominated trial judge should be able to direct trial by himself, sitting with lay members or, where the defendant had opted for trial by judge alone, by himself. The Government responded to his recommendation in *Justice for All* (2002). They rejected the idea of using people experienced in complex financial issues because of the difficulty of recruitment so they proposed that such cases be tried by judge alone. They estimated this would not affect more than 15–20 trials a year. Accordingly, they introduced legislation. The Criminal Justice Act 2003 s.43, had it ever been implemented, would have allowed the prosecution to apply for a judge alone trial in a long and complex fraud case *but* the Government promised the Opposition that they would not activate this section without further research and consideration and it was never implemented and was repealed in 2012.

In March 2005, the Jubilee Line Extension corruption trial collapsed in the Old Bailey, after taking almost two years and wasting £60 million of public money. The trial had suffered massive delays and interruptions. One juror had already been removed, as he was suspected of benefit fraud. The trial finally collapsed when another juror said he could not afford to go on and a third said he was going on a six week holiday. The Attorney General ordered an immediate inquiry and Lord Woolf CJ, who was not in favour of judge alone trials, said jury trials should be organised so they took no longer than three months or, exceptionally, six months. The Bar, who also opposed removal of jury trial in such cases, supported his remarks. Naturally the case fuelled the revival of arguments in favour of ordering judge-alone trials in such cases. The Director of the Serious Fraud Office called for juries in serious fraud trials to be replaced. He thought a judge sitting alone or with assessors would provide the advantage of a reasoned decision. Some cases, he claimed, could not be tried in the suggested six months. The SFO's conviction rate fell from 70 per cent to 64 percent in 2004–2005. The AG put forward a draft statutory instrument to implement s.43. It was opposed by the Law Society, the Bar and JUSTICE. The Bar argued that trials collapsed through a lack of preparation not through the fault of jury trial. The Government established a review team on how to prosecute fraud. They introduced a single issue bill, the Fraud (Trials without a Jury) Bill. It was predictably defeated by the Lords. In order to avoid lengthy jury trials, the AG then decided to consult on whether to offer plea bargains (discussed in Ch.12) in serious fraud cases. She then published the *Attorney General's Guidelines on Plea Discussions in Cases of Serious or Complex Fraud*, in 2009. As can be seen from Ch.12, attorneys general and governments have clearly gone down the route of extreme plea bargains and deferred prosecution agreements, rather than wasting time and money on lengthy trials whose survival is fragile and whose outcome is highly unpredictable. Research by Julian showed that judges who presided over serious fraud trials strongly supported retaining the jury.

10. RESEARCH

Helping the jury to do their job

In our 2001 paper for Auld, we summarised all English language jury-research up   **16–041**
to 2001. There is a mass of American "jury research" since then. Much of it is not
worth reading as it consists of simple questionnaires that the public have
answered on the internet. The best UK research by far is Thomas's, in the UCL
jury project. In 2001, we (Darbyshire, Maughan and Stewart) made a number of
recommendations to help the jury perform their function of finding the facts and
applying them to the law as directed by the judge, based on our analysis of all the
relevant jury research. (Auld's responses are bracketed.)

1.   If English judges are to continue to sum up the evidence, they should be
       told not to recite their notes but to draw attention to the main points, to
       areas of conflict and to how the law applies to the issues of evidence. (Auld
       made similar recommendations in Ch.1, p.537.) In my later research on
       judges (2011), no judge that I observed simply repeated their notes. Indeed,
       I found that judges took great care to craft jury directions and sum up the
       evidence. See now reiteration of this recommendation by Leveson 2015,
       discussed above and in Ch.12.
2.   Juries in criminal trials should be given a series of questions to answer, as
       they are in civil trials (adopted by Auld). In my research on judges, I found
       in my research with judges (2011) that many judges did this, to try to help
       the jury structure their thoughts. As seen above, this was reiterated by
       Leveson 2015 and as explained in Ch.12, it is part of the CrimPR now.
3.   Juries have a great deal of difficulty in understanding and applying judicial
       directions. They should be rewritten by psycholinguists, taking account of
       the large body of research from the USA. (Auld went further than this,
       recommending that the judge should not direct the jury on law save by
       implication in the series of factual questions he puts to them.) In 2008, a
       judicial working party was considering how to simplify jury directions.
       They have moved away from specifying that the judge must use a particular
       form of words, in the 2017 *Crown Court Compendium*. In Thomas's
       in-depth empirical research (2010), she found that only 31 per cent of
       experimental jurors actually understood the directions fully in legal terms
       used by the judge and that written directions increased juror comprehension
       (and see her 2013 findings, above). Perry (2011), a former barrister and
       expert in plain English examined the 2010 Crown Court Benchbook, the
       predecessor to the *Compendium* (on jury directions) and suggested "One
       might start by editing out the hard words and elegant expressions from the
       Benchbook".
4.   Jurors should be given written directions on the law and pre-trial directions,
       where possible, as it is illogical and difficult for jurors to receive
       instructions on what evidence is important *after* they have heard it, as they
       now are. (Adopted by Auld at pp.522–523. He also recommended that
       judges should use visual aids where possible and be provided with
       PowerPoint and presentational software accordingly.) Judges do not

generally use PowerPoint but prosecutors commonly use it in complex cases. In my research on judges (2011), I found that each judge in the sample had used written jury instructions on at least one occasion and some used them quite often. At least one judge said he had increased his use of written instructions since he read the article by Madge (2006), wherein Judge Madge said he did it in all cases. See also, a speech by Moses LJ in November 2010. He reiterated Auld's suggestion that a list of questions should be given to the jury. He also said juries should be told of the defence before the trial starts, reiterated by Leveson 2015, discussed in Ch.12.

5.   Certain basic instructions, such as those on the burden and quantum of proof, could be pinned on the jury room wall. (Not discussed and not acted upon.)

6.   Juries have immense difficulty in understanding the quantum of proof "beyond reasonable doubt". When judges explain it to mean "sure", many jurors look for absolute proof of guilt, which is impossible. The word "sure" should be eliminated from the judges' explanation of BRD. (Not discussed.)

7.   Juries should be instructed to discuss the evidence before voting as this makes them deliberate more thoroughly. (Not discussed.)

8.   Real jurors in England and Wales experience a great inhibition against asking questions, often to the detriment of their deliberation. Encouraging jurors to ask questions, take notes occasionally and discuss the evidence at an interim stage may all help to keep them awake and alert and to make sense of the trial, to help them remember the evidence more accurately, to understand the case and make their deliberation more focussed. (Not discussed.)

16–042   We also made some recommendations to make life more comfortable for jurors, again resulting from our examination of jury research and personal accounts of jurors:

1.   Many people resent giving up time for jury service and the abiding memory of most jurors is boredom, waiting for a trial or for legal argument to take place in their absence. In long trials, the jury trial should proceed in the mornings, while jurors are more alert, and legal argument in the afternoons. In my later research on judges (2011, Ch.10), I found that some of them did this, as a matter of common sense.

2.   Heat, cold, boredom and their passive role may reduce jurors' arousal levels. Court managers should check courtroom temperatures and jurors should have breaks. This recommendation was ignored. Later, in my research on judges, I reported on many courtrooms that were far too cold, including one that was extremely cold, thanks to the judge. I reported the consequent and sometimes farcical effects this had on jurors.

3.   Small discomforts all irritate jurors. Court personnel should be more responsive and polite to them.

4.   Jury service can be emotionally and physically stressful.

5.   In long trials, we should copy the US system of sitting two or more "alternates" alongside the real jury, in case of illness or indisposition. Auld

adopted this last recommendation but the Government rejected it, to my frustration. As is obvious from the story told above, the Jubilee Line fraud trial would have been spared from collapse, at enormous cost, had this cheap and simple expedient been adopted.

Auld summarised our findings and made a number of suggestions for keeping the jury better informed and for providing them with better facilities, including working facilities, so they could carry on their business while waiting around. In 2002, the Government promised to continue their reforms of jury service to keep jurors better informed and ensure their time was not wasted. In 2004, the Home Office published findings on "Jurors' perceptions, understanding, confidence and satisfaction in the jury system: a study in six courts", by Matthews, Hancock and Briggs. The key findings were:

1.   Most respondents gained a more positive view of jury trial.
2.   Confidence in the jury system was closely associated with perceived fairness of the process and ability to consider evidence from different perspectives.
3.   A jury's representation of a broad spectrum of views was a key factor in jurors' confidence in the Crown Court trial.
4.   Jurors were very impressed with the professionalism and helpfulness of court personnel, especially the performance, commitment and competence of judges.
5.   The main impediment to understanding was legal terminology. Jurors felt evidence could sometimes be presented more clearly.
6.   Over half said they would be happy to do service again, reporting a greater understanding of Crown Court trial and a feeling of having performed an important civic duty.

As part of the inquiry into the collapse of the Jubilee Line fraud trial, above, Lloyd-Bostock and Thomas questioned jurors about their experience and how well they managed to cope with the evidence. The trial caused most of the jurors serious ongoing problems with employment, afterwards:

> "Return to work for seven of the 11 interviewed presented continuing problems nearly five months on. These include one who has been made redundant, one in an employment dispute, one required to undertake extensive re-training who has missed a definite and much desired promotion, and one signed off by his doctor as suffering from stress as a result of the work situation. A further three are back with their employers but report experiencing serious set backs in their positions because of their prolonged absence." (Lloyd-Bostock, 2005)

Jury decision-making

Most research into jury deliberation and decision making is conducted by constructing shadow juries or mock juries. They may be asked to sit in on a real trial, or, more usually, to watch an edited audio or videotape of a real trial. The drawbacks of this type of research are well known. The mock jurors often do not reflect composition of a real jury, as they are paid students. They are volunteers

16–043

not conscripts, like real jurors. They usually sit through a three hour video rather than a two day trial. Most importantly, they are not under the same pressure as real jurors, since their verdict will not affect a real victim and the liberty and reputation of a real defendant. Nevertheless, this is all that researchers can hope for, since they are banned from sitting in on jury deliberations in virtually all jury systems. Apart from this, a researcher's presence is bound to affect deliberations. In some US jurisdictions, researchers have been allowed to listen to audio-taped deliberations.

The 2005 DCA consultation paper, "Jury Research and Impropriety", discussed above, asked whether researchers should be allowed into the jury room. This question was rather pointless, I suggest, as virtually no respondent is likely to favour that and Parliament is highly unlikely to permit it. The paper also asked whether research should be permitted into jury deliberations. This could be conducted by asking jurors questions after they have served. Again, questioning jurors is not permitted in most jurisdictions, although many academics have for years advocated that it be permitted, as explained above. Nevertheless, Thomas has done an enormous amount of highly informative research by questioning real jurors but not about their deliberations. In our 2001 paper, as well as examining jury research, we (Darbyshire, Maugham and Stewart) also examined juror's personal accounts of jury service to test the cross-cultural applicability of foreign research, most of which is American. Among our findings, summarising this vast body of research were:

1. The most popular theory on how jurors individually consider the trial and verdict is the cognitive story model. The juror reorganises information into a narrative story by using the trial evidence, prior knowledge (which, as real jurors' accounts show, may be wrong) and what makes a complete story. Accounts of real English and Welsh jurors strongly support the story model and the research finding that the adversarial trial process presents evidence in a way which hampers the juror's construction of a story.

2. It is questionable how effective the average juror is at judging the truthfulness of a witness based on demeanour but real jurors' accounts show that many of them are influenced by whether they approve or disapprove of witnesses.

3. Although *Turnbull* allows a warning that even truthful and impressive witnesses can be in error, some American jurisdictions allow a much greater input from experts on the reliability of eyewitness evidence and other expert evaluation of different types of evidence.

4. The accounts of real jurors show they are frustrated by the fact that pieces of evidence have been excluded from the story and they speculate on what this evidence might be. They sometimes refer to jury trial as a game.

5. Jurors may be disproportionately influenced by evidence they are told to ignore and are influenced by previous convictions.

6. Joining defendants and multiple charges can confuse juries.

7. Juries are much better at remembering evidence than individual jurors but real juries sometimes argue in the jury room over the contents of the evidence.

8. Since juries consider the evidence more thoroughly when they are not "verdict driven", it maybe thought desirable to encourage them to discuss the evidence thoroughly before taking a vote on verdict. (The same point made by New Zealand Law Commission.)

2010 saw the publication of an extremely important piece of research by Thomas. It was large scale, using 68 simulated juries at Nottingham and Winchester, 668 post-verdict juror surveys and measuring average outcomes in 68,000 verdicts, nationwide, in 2006–2008. The main points (paraphrased) are as follows: **16–044**

- Verdicts of all-white juries did not discriminate against BME defendants.
- White juries in Winchester (a white area) had almost identical verdicts for white, black and Asian defendants but white juries at Nottingham (racially diverse, where almost all jurors are white) "had particular difficulty reaching a verdict involving a BME defendant or a BME victim". They were significantly more likely to convict a white D accused of assaulting a BME person than a white person.
- The only personal characteristic that appeared to affect juror decision-making was gender. Female jurors were more likely to be persuaded to change their vote.
- Examining 551,669 verdicts in 2006–2008, the study examined whether offence type and severity, court, or number of charges had any correlation to verdicts.
- The study *confirmed* that BME defendants were consistently more likely than whites to plead not guilty.
- BME defendants were three and a half times more likely to face a jury verdict relative to their representation in the population.
- There was a 63 per cent jury conviction rate for white and Asian defendants and a 67 per cent conviction rate for blacks.
- This strongly suggests that racially balanced juries are unnecessary for fairness BUT there are concerns about the *appearance* of fairness with all-white juries, especially at courts where mainly all-white juries try substantial numbers of BME defendants.
- At all Crown Courts, the proportion of BME defendants was greater than in the local population or BME jurors.
- HM Courts & Tribunals Service should, therefore, ensure that court users understand how representative juries are, locally.
- Only 12 per cent of all Crown Court charges were decided by jury deliberation; 59 per cent of all charges resulted in a guilty plea. Only 0.6 per cent of all verdicts were hung juries (juries which cannot reach a verdict).
- Juries convicted on 64 per cent of all charges, with the highest conviction rates in direct-evidence cases and the lowest where jurors had to be sure of the state of mind of D or V.
- Conviction rates rose with the number of charges: 40 per cent on one charge, 80 per cent where there were five charges.

- Contrary to popular belief and previous government reports, juries convicted in rape cases more often than not: 55 per cent (of 4,310 verdicts examined).
- Conviction rates in busy courts range from 69 per cent to 53 per cent. There were no courts with a higher acquittal than conviction rate.
- Most jurors at Blackfriars and Winchester *felt* they were able to understand directions but most at Nottingham felt they were difficult to understand.
- *BUT* only 31 per cent *actually understood* the directions fully in legal terms used by the judge.
- Written instructions increased juror comprehension. (As we said in 2001, in our paper for Auld …)
- Most jurors recalled media coverage of their trial only during the trial but in high-profile cases, 35 per cent remembered pre-trial coverage and 20 per cent of these said it was difficult putting this out of their minds.
- Some jurors looked for information on their trial on the internet.
- More should be done to instruct and continually remind jurors of the rules on impropriety.

For welcome examples of contemporary research, see Ellison and Munro. In 2010, Coen and Heffernan pointed out that we have not discussed juror comprehension of expert evidence much, in contrast with the USA. I would add that that indeed applies to all aspects of jury selection and functioning. In the meantime, a great deal could have been learned from our survey of the existing mass of research and from such projects as the New Zealand Law Commission's research which questioned real jurors. There is an enormous amount that can be done without questioning real jurors about their deliberations.

Public attitudes

16–045 Conversations with non-lawyers in England and Wales, like those in the USA, show they are firm supporters of the jury system, which is why all such attempts to remove the defendant's choice in either-way cases met with such strong opposition among lawyers and politicians. We finish this chapter on the same subject with which we commenced: attitudes towards the jury. In 2009, the Ministry of Justice published research by Roberts and Hough, who concluded:

> "It is striking that despite differences in the nature of the jury—as well as differences in the wording of specific survey questions—the positive reaction to the jury in England and Wales also emerges from surveys conducted in other common law countries … In addition, there is clear opposition in this country to proposals to restrict the right to trial by jury."

Bibliography
16–046 J. Airs and A. Shaw, "Jury Excusal and Deferral", Home Office RSD Research Study No.102, 1999, National Archives.
A. Ashworth, commentary on *Taxquet v Belgium* [2011] Crim. L.R. 236.
Auld LJ, *Review of the Criminal Courts of England and Wales* (2001) (The Criminal Courts Review), Ch.5.
BBC News website: "Electoral register 'down by 920,000'", 24 February 2015.

F. Bowden, "Silence was golden: why juries just can't keep quiet", *The Times*, 18 March 2008.

K. Burgess, "Homeowner Kenneth Batchelor cleared of murder after shooting dead intruder", *The Times,* 11 March 2009.

M. Coen and L. Heffernan, "Juror Comprehension of Expert Evidence: A Reform Agenda" [2010] Crim. L.R. 195.

Criminal Practice Directions CPD VII Trial 39.

K. Crosby, "Controlling Devlin's Jury: What the Jury Thinks, and What the Jury Sees Online" [2012] Crim. L.R. 15.

Judicial College, *Crown Court Compendium Part 1* (2017), containing guidance to judges on trial and jury management and directions (Judiciary website).

P. Darbyshire, "Notes of a Lawyer Juror" (1990) 140 N.L.J. 1264; "The Lamp That Shows That Freedom Lives—is it worth the candle?" [1991] Crim. L.R. 740; Letter to the editor [2008] Crim. L.R. 888; *Sitting in Judgment: The Working Lives of Judges* (Oxford: Hart Publishing, 2011), Ch.10, "Judges and Juries".

P. Darbyshire, A. Maughan and A. Stewart, "What Can the English Legal System Learn from Jury Research Published up to 2001?" available on the Kingston University website, research repository. It is summarised in P. Darbyshire, "What Can We Learn from Published Jury Research? Findings for the Criminal Courts Review 2001" [2001] Crim. L.R. 970.

Department for Constitutional Affairs, "Jury Research and Impropriety", Consultation Paper CP/04/05, on the DCA archived website, National Archives.

P. Devlin, *Trial by Jury* (London: Steven & Sons, 1956).

S. Doran and J. Jackson, "The Case for Jury Waiver" [1997] Crim. L.R. 155.

L. Ellison and V. Munro "Getting to (not) guilty: examining jurors' deliberative processes in, and beyond, the context of a mock rape trial" (2010) 30 (1) *Legal Studies* 74–97; "'Telling Tales': exploring narratives of life and law within the (mock) jury room" (2015) 35 (2) 201.

Home Office, *Determining Mode of Trial in Either Way Cases—A Consultation Paper*, 1998.

F. Gibb, "First trial without a jury for 400 years" *The Times*, 19 June 2009; A. Fresco and F. Gibb, "Lawyers fear more trials without jury…" and F. Gibb, "High cost of protection is eroding legal bastion". *The Times*, 1 April 2010.

HMCTS *Guidance for summoning officers when considering deferral and excusal applications* (2009) Gov.uk website.

P. Hungerford-Welch, "Police Officers as Jurors" [2012] Crim. L.R. 320.

J. Jackson and S. Doran, *Judge Without Jury: Diplock Trials in the Adversary System* (Oxford: Oxford University Press, 1995).

Lord Judge CJ was interviewed on *Law in Action*, BBC Radio 4, 27 October 2009; Lord Judge CJ, "Jury trials", speech, 19 November 2010, archived.

"Jury Summoning Guidance", December 2003, a consultation paper on the Department of Constitutional Affairs archived website.

R. F. Julian, "Judicial Perspectives on the Conduct of Serious Fraud Trials" [2007] Crim. L.R. 751–768.

Justice for All (2002), White Paper, CPS website.

Leveson LJ, *Review of Efficiency in Criminal Proceedings* (2015), Judiciary website.

N. Ley, on the superiority of Crown Court trial: (1999) 149 N.L.J. 1316.

S. Lloyd-Bostock, *Report on Interviews with Jurors in the Jubilee Line Case*, HM Crown Prosecution Service Inspectorate, 2005.

Lord Chancellor's Department, *Report of the Committee on Fraud Trials* (1986) LCO 36/95, "The Roskill Report", National Archives.

H.H. Judge Nic Madge, "Summing up—a Judge's Perspective" [2006] Crim. L.R. 817.

R. Matthews, L. Hancock and D. Briggs, "Jurors' perceptions...and satisfaction..." Home Office RDSD Findings 227 (2004).

Moses LJ, "Summing Down the Summing Up", Annual Law Reform Lecture, 23 November 2010.

M. Narey, *Review of Delay in the Criminal Justice System*, Home Office, 1997, National Archives

NZ Law Commission Report 69, *Juries in Criminal Trials*, 2001.

S. O'Neill, "Trial by jury no longer guarantees justice", *The Times*, 15 September 2008.

D. Perry, "direction", on jury directions, *Counsel*, March 2011.

Report of the Departmental Committee on Jury Service (The Morris Report) Cmnd.2627 (1965), National Archives.

J.V. Roberts and M. Hough, *Public opinion and the jury; an international literature review*, Ministry of Justice Research Series 1/09 (2009).

C. Thomas, *Diversity and Fairness in the Jury System,* Ministry of Justice Research Report 02/07 (2007) (see, however, P. Darbyshire, letter to the editor, 30 June 2008 [2008] Crim. L.R. 888); *Are Juries Fair?* Ministry of Justice Research Series 1/10; "Avoiding the Perfect Storm of Juror Contempt" [2013] Crim L.R. 483.

Wolchover and Heaton-Armstrong's arguments are at (1998) 148 N.L.J. 1614, and see 150 N.L.J. 158.

M. Zander, "A touch of bias?" (2007) 157 N.L.J. 1530; "The Right to Reform Trial by Jury" (2012) 176 J.P.N. 69.

Further reading and sources for updating this chapter

16–047 Free updates of this book are available on the Sweet & Maxwell website: *http://uklawstudent.thomsonreuters.com*.

Summary and revision: P. Darbyshire, *Nutshells English Legal System*, 10th edn (London: Sweet & Maxwell, 2016).

Guardian online.

Judiciary website.

The Legal Journals Index on *Westlaw*. Search case law and journals on *Westlaw* and *Lexis*. The Criminal Law Review, on Westlaw, is indispensable, as is Current Awareness.

The National Archives.

Ministry of Justice website.

Newspapers from databases; BBC News website.

Most jury research is published in social science journals and social science databases.

"Your Role as a Juror", Ministry of Justice YouTube videos.

PART 6

ACCESS TO JUSTICE

CHAPTER 17

Legal Aid

"The real difficulty in getting an adequate system of legal assistance is that some influential people do not consider that it is desirable. There is an idea that litigation is not a thing to be 'encouraged' ... It is noticeable that these same people do not suggest that wealthy persons or corporations should be discouraged from litigating ... This attitude may be seen in the Final Report of the Committee on Legal Aid for the Poor *... proposals to help poor people by a scheme similar to the National Health Insurance Acts were rejected on the ground that 'It is manifestly in the interests of the State that its citizens should be healthy, not that they should be litigious'. This attitude is a compound of ignorance and stupidity ... the ignorance being that of the upper classes."* (R.M. Jackson, *The Machinery of Justice in England* (1940), the first edition of the first ELS textbook, commenting on this crucial recommendation in 1928 that a National Legal Service should *not* be established).

"If Human Rights have come home, they are largely unemployed. There is all too often no wherewithal to protect or enforce them. The conditional fee provides at best a fig leaf to cover the nakedness of the legal system in protecting those in need of protection." (Lightman J, of the High Court, Chancery Division, 2003).

"It must surely be a short sighted economy for us to withdraw the availability of public funding from the under-privileged. It promotes the sense that the protection of the law is for the 'haves' and not the 'have-nots'." (Lightman J, 2007)

"He has spent the last six months in Guatemala providing a safe passage to local human rights lawyers. He does not carry a gun. His T-shirt symbolises the message: 'The world is watching, and there will be a hullabaloo if we come to any harm'." (Sir Henry Brooke, retired Lord Justice of Appeal, describing the unpaid work of a young solicitor, winner of a pro bono award, in a November 2007 speech to the Law Society.)

If the rule of law states that everyone should be equal before the law then, surely, this implies that everyone should have equal access to the law, the courts and legal services. Furthermore, the law presumes that we all know the law. Ignorance of the law is no defence to a civil or criminal action. I suggest, then, that one of the requirements of a civilised modern democracy must be the promotion of and access to information on our legal rights and duties. The first principle was broadly accepted in the English legal system from the middle of the twentieth century. It is supported by the European Convention on Human Rights 1950. Article 6, set out fully in Ch.12, requires fair trials and lays down the principles for the requirement of legal services. The section relevant to legal aid is as follows.

> "In the determination of his civil rights and obligations or of any criminal charge against him, everyone is entitled to a fair and public hearing ... Everyone charged with a criminal offence has the following minimum rights ... b. to have adequate

17–001

time and facilities for the preparation of his defence; c. to defend himself in person or through legal assistance of his own choosing or, if he has not sufficient means to pay for legal assistance, to be given it free when the interests of justice so require."

As can be seen, art.6 requires representation in criminal cases where "the interests of justice" require it. This phrase is identical to the test for granting criminal legal aid (LA) in England and Wales under the Poor Prisoners Defence Act 1903 and was doubtless copied from it by the UK lawyers who drafted the European Convention. The Convention also requires legal help or representation in civil cases, according to what the litigant needs to ensure "equality of arms" with the opposition. This must be determined on a case-by-case basis, as illustrated in Ch.4. The Lord Chancellor and his Ministry of Justice are responsible for legal services. He and his junior ministers are answerable in Parliament. The Legal Aid Agency, an executive agency of this Ministry, administers legal aid.

There was much use of the phrase "access to justice" in the 1990s. This means, broadly: being able to make full use of legal rights, through adequate legal services, i.e. advice, assistance and representation, regardless of means. It also means the ability to make full use of the court structure and rights of appeal. Legal services are dealt with here and access to justice in the civil courts and alternatives in Chs 10 and 11. The Royal Commission on Legal Services 1979 defined legal services as "services which should be available to any person or organisation requiring advice or assistance of a legal character, whether payment for the service is made from public or private funds".

17–002   Before the mid twentieth century, there was no systematic, statutory, widespread provision of legal aid (LA). In *civil* cases, poor people with less than £5 in capital could be represented in Royal Court (High Court) cases under the *in forma pauperis* procedure, placed on a statutory basis in 1494. Since poor people were rarely involved in proceedings in the Royal Courts, this was not much use. By 1875, free representation in *criminal* cases was limited to the dock brief system. A prisoner could obtain the services of a barrister for a one guinea plus a clerk's fee. The barrister could not refuse. Legal *advice* schemes were virtually unknown in the nineteenth century. Abel Smith and Stevens describe the very stilted development of LA and advice in the first half of the twentieth century. The Law Society, the solicitors' trade union, made sure that solicitors gained control over statutory schemes. The demand for accessible advice and civil representation became urgent in clearing a backlog of divorce cases, rendered more acute by the Second World War. Services were provided for the armed forces. In 1944–1945, the Rushcliffe Committee considered how best to provide legal services for those who could not afford them. The LA scheme established after this by the Legal Aid and Advice Act 1949 was to provide for services through the private practice lawyer who claimed a fee from the State. This model of delivery of publicly funded legal services is sometimes referred to as the *judicare* model and it was the LA model throughout the twentieth century. Their second recommendation, for a network of legal advice centres, staffed by fulltime state salaried lawyers, was never implemented. This would have been comparable with state-funded doctors' surgeries in the National Health Service. It was the refusal to adopt this recommendation that R.M. Jackson was criticising, above, in the quotation opening this chapter.

The Committee considered whether a state department or the local authorities should administer the system but, concerned that both of these had an interest in so many cases, they chose to leave administration in the hands of the Law Society. Leaving lawyers holding the purse strings was a curious policy, given that lawyers were the financial beneficiaries of the LA Fund and this is probably one of the reasons that by the 1980s at least half of all private practice solicitors earned some or most of their income from LA and provided many a lawyer with a comfortable income in the 1980s and 1990s. The 1949 Act was slow in being implemented because of lack of funds. Criminal LA arrived later, also delivered through private practice lawyers but dispensed via the courts. Legal advice was provided under a third scheme and dispensed to individual clients by their solicitors.

By the 1970s, when all three schemes were fully established, around 70 per cent of the population qualified for some kind of help. Sir Henry Brooke said, in his 2007 speech, that the LA scheme used to be the envy of the world and most lawyers, when he was in practice, undertook legally aided work. By 1988, the three schemes were put on a systematic basis in one statute, the Legal Aid Act 1988. At the same time, lawyers' fingers were at last taken off the purse strings. The Legal Aid Board was created to fund and manage the civil LA scheme and legal advice. Criminal LA, as before, was dispensed by the criminal courts, normally the court clerks in magistrates' courts. All types of aid were available only to those who passed a means test, requiring contributions from those who could afford it. The three types of aid had different means tests. Civil and criminal LA were subject to merits tests too.

Despite all of this provision, it proved to be inadequate. Sociologists and lawyers in the 1960s and 1970s exposed the continuing phenomenon of "unmet legal need", which occurs when someone has a legal problem which goes unsolved. The causes were identified and alternative legal services developed in the voluntary sector, outside the LA scheme, in an attempt to fulfil some of those needs. By the 1980s and 1990s, the LA budget was increasing out of control but, ironically, a diminishing percentage of the population was eligible for it and fewer cases were aided. It was clear that, whichever political party was elected in 1997, it would have to curb the LA budget and target it better to provide the right type of help to the right people. When New Labour were elected, they devised a new scheme under the Access to Justice Act 1999 but it was replaced in 2013 by the Coalition then Conservatives Governments' current mean-spirited scheme, under the Legal Aid, Sentencing and Punishment of Offenders (LASPO) Act 2012, which had a rough ride through Parliament. It is the stated aim of the current 2017 Conservative Government, like their Coalition and Labour predecessors, to drastically cut the number of criminal LA lawyers.

When reading evaluations of any legal aid or legal services scheme, I would invite the reader to bear in mind the following. The Law Society, representing solicitors, and Bar Council, representing barristers, are very powerful trade unions. Their publicity machinery promotes lawyers' financial interests. The press is flooded with comments from the profession when any change is proposed which affects them. They oppose most changes. They always argue that what they want is in the public interest. Their professional monopolies have maintained a stranglehold over legal services throughout the twentieth century and they

17–003

normally defend the interests of private practice lawyers. All of this is graphically illustrated in Ch.13. Much of the civil advice and help that people need, however, does not require complex legal knowledge. People in trouble need a lot of practical advice on matters such as debt and housing, that turns on the facts and can be delivered by non-lawyers, such as the volunteers who work for Citizens Advice. For example, most family law cases are disputes of fact and the family courts were generally portrayed as a "law free zone", in research on the working lives of judges, in *Sitting in Judgment* (2011). In criminal cases, however, it is crucial that most suspects are skilfully advised on their police interrogation and choice of plea, because they cannot be expected to understand the definition of a criminal offence in order to work out whether they are guilty of the offence charged or an alternative, or no offence. As we shall see, there is cause to be outraged by the current scheme, not on lawyers' behalf but on behalf the disadvantaged, the dispossessed and the incapacitated.

1. LEGAL AID FROM 2013, UNDER THE LASPO ACT 2012

17–004 In 2010, the Coalition government published a consultation called *Proposals for the Reform of Legal Aid in England and Wales*. This explains the policy behind the current Act, which replaces the Labour Government's scheme under the Access to Justice Act 1999. Lawyers are highly critical of the 2012 Act because its essential policy is that, instead of LA being available for everything unless specifically excluded, as under the 1999 Act and all previous statutes, we now have the reverse regime: LA is limited to those matters specified in the Act (Sch.1). The Act took the control of LA back within the Ministry of Justice, administered by an executive agency (s.38), called the Legal Aid Agency. The Legal Services Commission, the independent agency which formerly ran LA, was abolished (s.38). The Labour Government had already decided to do this, following Ian Magee's proposals in his review of the delivery of LA. The legal Services Commission had been criticised. In 2012, it had its accounts qualified for the fourth year running. The National Audit Office noted that it had paid mistaken, excessive fees of more than £20 million to LA lawyers, and £15 million went to recipients who were not eligible for help. I have emphasised key words in the 2012 Act's current scheme.

Section 1 makes the *Lord Chancellor*, Minister of Justice, responsible for the provision of LA. This is not new. Section 4 created a Director of Legal Casework to decide on LA in individual cases. He must comply with the LC's directions and guidance. The LC must not interfere. Section 8 defines *civil legal services* as including providing advice and assistance on law, legal proceedings and legal disputes. Services can include representation, *mediation* and assistance in other dispute resolution. This definition is not new but it is very important to the Government that help with mediation and ADR are provided for in a statute, because, like all governments since 1990, they emphasised the importance of using ADR instead of court proceedings, in order to reduce costs. Section 10 allows for LA provision in *exceptional* cases, where required under the Human Rights Act or EU law. As we will see, it is the narrow interpretation of this provision that is bitterly and regularly criticised, by 2017.

Section 11 requires the LC, in setting LA criteria, to take account of the *cost benefit* of legal service and resources *available*. The LC must take account of the applicant's *prospects of success* (not new), future demands for LA, whether alternatives are available, the importance to the individual, the *seriousness* of the issue, the applicant's conduct, and the public interest. The criteria re-emphasise *ADR*, including mediation. Section 15 allows the LC to make regulations about *criminal* LA. He must have regard to the *interests of justice*. Section 17 specifies that regulations will determine eligibility according to the applicant's financial *resources* and the interests of *justice*. These two tests, called *the means test* and *the merits test* have been applied to all types of criminal and civil LA since LA was invented. Section 19 provides for regulations permitting *courts* to grant LA: nothing new. Courts were always responsible for granting criminal LA. Section 23 allows for rules requiring people to pay a *contribution* towards their LA: not new. Section 25 allows for the *cost* of civil LA to be *recouped from property* recovered or *costs* secured in the case: not new. Section 26 provides that when *costs* are ordered in legally aided civil proceedings, they must be *reasonable*, taking account of the financial resources of all the parties, and their conduct.

Section 27 says that the LC is under no duty to provide the services by a means selected by the applicant. Services can be provided by *telephone* or other *electronic* means. This is not new. For instance, a police station detainee will often receive only telephone advice from a duty solicitor or other lawyer in the middle of the night. Section 27(4) provides that a recipient of *criminal* LA may select any representative who is authorised to provide criminal LA. This is not new. Free choice of lawyer is required by art.6 of the European Convention. This means that an applicant can never be restricted to representation by a public defender, as is the case in the USA. Section 29 requires the LC to produce a code of conduct for civil servants and LA providers. It must include duties to avoid discrimination and duties to the courts. Section 41 gives the LC, the Minister, 13 new powers to make regulations (delegated legislation). Ministers have always had sweeping delegated legislative powers to run LA schemes.

17–005

Schedule 1 lists the *types of civil legal services* that may be provided for, such as care, protection and supervision of children, special educational needs, child abuse, mental health and incapacity, community care, facilities for the disabled, appeals about benefits, family homes and domestic violence, family mediation, forced marriage, judicial review, habeas corpus (applications for release by the unlawfully detained), public authority abuse of power, breach of Convention rights, the Special Immigration Appeals Commission, immigration, loss of home, services for victims of gang-violence, human trafficking, harassment, inquests, pollution, equality, cross-border disputes, and terrorism prevention, among other services. The novelty here is the inclusion of such a long, detailed list in the Act. Ken Clarke LC explained that the aim was to stop LA branching out too far, as it did under Labour. Schedule 2 lists excluded services. Some are uncontroversial and have always been excluded: defamation, property conveyancing, will-making, trusts, company, partnership and business issues.

Very controversially, Sch.2 excludes a list of services formerly amenable to civil LA: claims for personal injury (first excluded by Labour in 1999, amid furore); claims in the torts of negligence, assault, battery, false imprisonment, breach of statutory duty, and trespass; property damage cases, state benefits, and criminal injuries. Negligence includes clinical negligence, which is intensely controversial. Critics were heartened by the fact that advocacy is provided for in a list of about 20 types of tribunal proceedings. A historic criticism of LA was that it did not provide tribunal representation.

2. THE POLICY BEHIND THE 2012 ACT

17–006   In 2010, the Coalition government replaced Labour. Ken Clarke became Minister of Justice and Lord Chancellor, with a remit to cut the justice budget drastically. His 2012 Act and policies created a new regime, replacing Labour's 1999 setup.

In *Legal Aid: Reforming Advocates' Graduated Fees* (2010), the Coalition Government consulted on aligning defence fees with (lower) prosecution fees, proposing to reduce fees over three years and to devise a new scheme for handling very high cost cases. This problem of the imbalance between prosecution and defence fees, making lawyering in Crown Court cases imbalanced, was identified about 20 years ago and lawyers had resisted repeated attempts to deal with it.

In 2010, Ken Clarke also published a consultation paper (CP12/10), *Proposals for the Reform of Legal Aid in England and Wales* Cm.7967. He said the legal aid system was one of the most expensive in the world and bore little resemblance to the scheme introduced in 1949. It covered a very wide range of issues, including some that should not require any legal expertise. There had been 30 consultations since 2006. Lawyers could not organise their practices against constant change. It was unsustainable. "I want to discourage people from resorting to lawyers whenever they face a problem, and instead encourage them, wherever it is sensible to do so, to consider alternative methods of dispute resolution which may be more effective and suitable." He said he was making reforms to the civil, criminal and family justice systems to make proceedings and the ELS less cumbersome and expensive. He was consulting on the Jackson recommendations on civil procedure, explained in Ch.10 of this book, and sentencing, asking David Norgrove to reform family procedure, and he would reform civil procedure to make greater use of mediation: "In the meantime, I have been working with the Home Secretary and the Attorney General on ways in which we can transform procedures in the criminal justice system" (Foreword). Here, I summarise the main policy points.

17–007   ● The Ministry of Justice needed to reduce its budget by 23 per cent, £2 billion. These proposals would cut legal aid costs by £350 million.

> "These proposals complement the wider programme of reform to move towards a simpler justice system: one which is more responsive to public needs, which allows people to resolve their issues out of court without recourse to public funds, using simpler, more informal, remedies where they are appropriate, and which encourages more efficient resolution of contested cases where necessary … It is an approach which demands that we make tough choices to ensure access to public funding in those cases that really require it, the protection of the most vulnerable in our society … ." (Foreword)

- Chapter 2: the key to efficient use of resources was reform of the criminal justice system: cutting bureaucracy, improving communication between agencies and case management. On sentencing: they would deliver a "rehab revolution", with sentence discounts to encourage the earliest possible guilty pleas. (His plan for *50 per cent* sentence discounts was shocking to the public and withdrawn by June 2011.) Restructured lawyers' fees would encourage this. In civil cases, the Jackson review of costs recommended more proportionality, and making success fees and "after the event" insurance in conditional fee cases irrecoverable.
- Chapter 4: no change in criminal legal aid eligibility.
- Chapter 5: set out proposals for eligibility changes in civil and family LA, including taking account of property equity. Contributions from clients' income should increase. Everyone with £8,000 disposable capital should contribute, including those on benefits. Everyone with £1,000 should pay a lump sum of £100, in addition to contributions from income, because this would encourage them to take a financial interest in the outcome of their case. There would be a £200,000 capital disregard, with £300,000 for pensioners, in most cases. The plan was to increase contributions from 20–30 per cent of disposable income.
- Remuneration for lawyers and other providers: competitive pricing should be introduced in crime (from police station to Crown Court), then family and civil. (This has proved so controversial, with lawyers' demonstrations and strikes in 2013–2014, that it was dropped in 2014, as explained below.) In the meantime, the structure of criminal fees would be altered, "to encourage … quicker and more efficient justice". This means he wanted to encourage earlier plea bargaining, as explained in Ch.12 of this book. Again, this was and is ferociously opposed.
- Chapter 7: set out proposals to reduce all civil and family fees "across the board" by 10 per cent. Barristers and solicitors were paid different civil fees, which was obviously unfair if they were doing the same work. The use of QCs in family cases should be controlled. They were used in care cases and paid up to £100,000.
- Chapter 8: experts' fees ought to be reduced by 10 per cent and move towards fixed or graduated fees with hourly rates for limited hours.
- Chapter 9: proposed alternative sources of funding, including using the interest from solicitors' client accounts, as in Australia, NZ, USA, South Africa, Zimbabwe and France; taking a proportion of legally aided claimants' damages towards a Supplementary Legal Aid Scheme; and encouraging legal protection insurance, as recommended by Jackson LJ. Unfortunately, private legal expenses insurance has been suggested by Lord Chancellors since the 1970s or earlier, and all research shows that the British have little appetite for it (Robins, 2010). While people are happy to insure pets for £12 a month, only one in seven of 2,000 consumers were prepared to pay £75 per year for legal expenses insurance.
- Chapter 10: proposed bringing LA within an executive agency of the MoJ, replacing the Legal Services Commission.
- Chapter 4: set out proposals to limit the scope of LA as follows.

- Target resourcing: the grant of LA should depend on the capacity of a person to represent themselves, the type of proceedings, adversarial or inquisitorial, the complexity of law and evidence. *Legal aid should be the "funder of last resort"*, the conditional fee agreement (no win no fee) being the first resort. The Ministry had taken account of other sources of advice. Other organisations, such as the voluntary sector, could provide advice on welfare and housing. The Government took account of other means of dispute resolution, such as ombudsmen and complaints procedures.

  "[We] propose a revised civil legal aid scheme which focuses resources on those cases where the litigant is at risk of very serious consequences. Examples include facing the removal of their children, physical harm, or homelessness, or where legal aid is justified to ensure a fair society through empowering citizens to hold the state to account or to meet our legal obligations, for example, in relation to reciprocal arrangements on international child abduction."

  Do bear this in mind when we examine the critiques of this current set up, below.
- The civil LA merits test would be retained.
- There is a massive annexe listing what was currently "in scope" in 2010–2011, what would be retained and what would be removed.
- "In scope" would include: children's care cases (where a local authority applies to take a child away from its parents); judicial review, except business cases, as before; matters covered by European or international agreements providing reciprocal access to legal assistance; cases where litigants are incapable of representing themselves, such as physically or emotionally vulnerable, elderly, frail, disabled people and asylum-seekers; immigration detention; international child abduction and family maintenance; claims against public authorities for abuse of power, breach of human rights and negligence; allegations of abuse and sexual violence; community care; debt where the client's home is at immediate risk; domestic violence; mediation in private family cases; housing; mental health; registration and enforcement of EU legislation judgments; children in private law children cases; help at inquests, harassment, care standards, gang violence injunctions; discrimination; environmental matters; EU cross-border litigation; appeals only on matters that fall "within scope".
- "Out of scope": the pre-existing exclusions such as will-writing and business disputes; money claims, such as consumer credit and contracts, except, for example, damages for child abuse or serious abuse of state power; cases resulting from the litigant's own decision, such as immigration; representation in inquests and tribunals, generally; ancillary relief (family property), without violence.

  "We propose to make changes to the courts' powers to enable the Court to redress the balance in cases where one party may be materially disadvantaged, by giving the judge the power to make interim lump sum orders against a party who has the means to fund the costs of representation for the other party. In doing so, the Court would also incentivise the contributing party to negotiate a settlement. The materially disadvantaged party could apply for an order at any stage of the proceedings, where they could demonstrate that they could not reasonably procure legal advice by any other means."

- "Out of scope" would be clinical negligence; criminal injuries; education, employment; housing, such as right-to-buy; welfare benefits; tort and other general claims.
- "Out of scope" would be private law children and family cases (estranged parents arguing about arrangements for children). "Legal aid is encouraging long, drawn-out and acrimonious cases which can have a significant impact on the long-term well-being of any children involved". (Comment: astonishingly wasteful cases like this, where self-centred parents battled for years, at the expense of the legal aid fund, were portrayed in the family judging chapter of Darbyshire, *Sitting in Judgment* (2011) *but* the consequences of this withdrawal have proven to be intensely problematic by 2017, as we shall see.)
- There should be a funding scheme for excluded cases, to meet our obligations under the European Convention on Human Rights. The proposed criteria would be: significant wider public interest, overwhelming importance to the client, or complexity.
- The paper emphasised telephone advice: "we will provide a simple, straightforward telephone service ... the single gateway to civil legal aid services", expanding the CLA helpline to include paid-for advice services.
- They acknowledged the potential increase in numbers of litigants in person but said many cases could be resolved out of court. Many would be in user-friendly courts or alternative fora. There was no evidence that whether a party was represented had an impact on the outcome of proceedings, according to research published by the Department of Constitutional Affairs, in 2005. (Comment: the author of this research, Professor Moorhead, claimed that the Ministry was misrepresenting his research. We saw in Ch.10 that these proposals disturbed judges, because they now have to cope with thousands more unrepresented litigants, in an adversarial process which presumes that the judge is a neutral umpire and the parties can do all the preparation and presentation themselves).
- Lawyers were paid more for guilty pleas in the Crown Court. The fees should be made more even, in triable-either-way (TEW) cases.
- Advocates and litigators were paid more for a cracked trial than an early guilty plea, sometimes double, regardless of whether extra work had been done. The paper proposed to harmonise guilty plea fees in indictable and serious TEW offences. They would increase guilty plea fees by 25 per cent, to encourage early guilty pleas. They would stop paying the extra 25–40 per cent fees in murder cases, aligning them with rape. (In 2010, Lord Judge CJ told the Justice Select Committee, in Parliament, that the LA system in crime and family work did not incentivise efficiency.)
- Litigators and advocates were paid according to the number of pages of prosecution evidence. This should be replaced with a better indicator of complexity.
- Three sets of fees applied in magistrates' courts: rural, urban and London. The London differential was not justified, given the supply of London solicitors.

- Some prosecution rates were significantly lower than defence rates.
- Fees in very high cost cases should relate to outputs not hours of input.
- In 2008–2009, LA payments to QCs and leading juniors cost £52 *million*. The average number of prosecution pages had increased by 65 per cent since 2004–2005. This reflected the use of mobile phone records as evidence.

3. OTHER PARTS OF THE SCHEME—WHAT HAS OR HAS NOT CHANGED

Administration

17–008 Under the (Labour) Access to Justice Act 1999, LA was administered by different non-governmental bodies. The civil "Community Legal Service" worked with local Partnerships, bringing together funders such as local authorities and charities with legal service providers, such as solicitors and volunteer advisers. Now the Legal Aid Agency which is within the Ministry administers LA.

The funding code

17–009 As before, the Code is prescribed by the Lord Chancellor. In his 2010 consultation, Ken Clarke LC said the old system was unsustainably expensive. They planned to reverse the funding presumption.

> "The existing legal aid scheme is very broad and allows public funds to be expended on any issue not explicitly excluded. In order to target legal aid resources in a more focused way on specific issues, we propose to specify the types of issue and levels of service which are available under the revised scheme in legislation ... Civil legal aid will not routinely be available for any other issue." (para.4.32)

Financial eligibility limits

17–010 These are updated by regulations, every April. Only clients with very low incomes and capital are entitled to fully funded legal services. Those whose income or capital fall above certain limits have to pay a contribution, assessed according to means. This is not new. Neither is the statutory charge: the LA fund may place a first "charge" on any real property, such as a house, recovered or preserved in legally aided proceedings. The logic is to ensure that people contribute towards the cost of their LA if they can; it encourages people to act reasonably and not to incur excessive costs and it puts them in a similar position to a privately paying client.

Contracting with providers

17–011 The introduction of general civil contracting by Labour in 1999 brought a massive shift in the funding model. Under the old scheme, any solicitor or barrister could provide LA but providers were now to be limited to those who had a contract. A provider had to demonstrate that they satisfied the quality criteria, evaluated by peer review. In the 2010 paper, the Coalition said in the short term they would be looking for efficiency savings and in the long term, civil and family work would be remunerated on the basis of competitive price tendering, a device that Labour and Conservative governments had threatened to introduce since the 1980s. It was always bitterly opposed by lawyers and in 2014, the Coalition Minister, Chris Grayling, had to withdraw these plans because lawyers went on strike.

Criminal defence

In 2000–2001, the Labour Government had announced proposals to develop a system of employed public defenders. Eight offices were introduced in 2001–2004.   **17–012**

From 2001, all solicitors' firms undertaking publicly funded criminal defence had to have a contract. Defendants are allowed to make a reasonable change of representatives at any time. The decision remains in the hands of the court because the judge or magistrates are free from any accusation of economic interest.

Means and merits test

The merits test for a criminal representation order is the "interests of justice test",   **17–013**
copied from the Poor Persons Defence Act 1906 and art.6 of the European Convention on Human Rights. The criteria are set out in the 2012 Act. They repeat the "Widgery criteria" developed in the 1960s and include likelihood of loss of liberty, livelihood, reputation, or that the case involves a substantial question of law, or the need to trace witnesses, or expert cross-examination, or that the accused may not be able to understand the proceedings, or present his own case, and so on. The Labour 1999 scheme originally scrapped the means test for representation in magistrates' courts. This had to be reinstated in 2006, because it turned out to be too expensive.

Conditional fee (no win no fee) agreements (CFAs) partly replaced LA

Speculative litigation was illegal under the common law offences of champerty   **17–014**
and maintenance, abolished in 1967, and was unenforceable in English law from the Statute of Westminster 1275, until the (Conservative) Courts and Legal Services Act 1990 permitted CFAs. In Scotland, it had long been legal. In the USA, a variety of contingency fees is permissible, the most common being that the lawyer takes a percentage of the sum recovered in litigation. By contrast, the English distaste for such deals was expressed by Blackstone in his *Commentaries on the Law of England* (1765): "This is an offence against public justice, as it keeps alive strife and contention, and perverts the remedial process of law into an engine of oppression" (quoted in Lord Mackay's consultation paper, below).

The Royal Commission on Legal Services 1979 agreed but the Conservative Courts and Legal Services Act 1990 permitted "no win no fee" (CFA) contracts, with the lawyer permitted to take a percentage uplift of 100 per cent above her normal fee if she won the case. CFAs were permitted in personal injury, insolvency and human rights cases. Labour, having condemned this, in 1995, as "little more than a gimmick designed to mask the chaotic state of the legal aid scheme", adopted CFAs as one of the main elements of their legal services policy, from 1999. Indeed, Lord Chancellor Irvine proposed abolishing *most* of civil LA and said litigants would instead be able to enter into private CFA contracts. This provoked an explosion of attacks from lawyers. Irvine was forced to make concessions. Research by the Policy Studies Institute on 197 CFA cases concluded they were not working well. Insurance companies warned of extra expense to them, as defendants, causing insurance premium inflation. Insurance lawyers complained that a windfall of extra fees would be paid to successful solicitors in uplifted fees for no good reason. Nevertheless, Labour's 1999 Act extended CFAs across the board. By 2010–2011, these warnings turned out to be prophetic. Worse, CFAs encouraged the "compensation culture" and uncontrollable civil costs which provoked the Jackson Review, all discussed in Ch.10. The Coalition Government went one step further in the 2012 Act and introduced *contingency* fees, following a recommendation of Jackson LJ's review of civil costs, as explained in Ch.10.

4. "ALTERNATIVE" LEGAL SERVICES

17–015 Alternatives grew out of the inadequacies of the original pre-1970 LA scheme but they have continued to flourish. "Unmet legal need" was identified by social research and social welfare lawyers in the 1960s. It occurs where someone has a legal problem but it goes unsolved through lack of access to legal services. As predicted, the 2012 Act generated more unmet need so there is by 2017 an overwhelming demand on these alternatives, as we shall see. Unmet need was (and is) caused by:

- the high cost of legal fees;
- fear of lawyers, fear of cost;
- lawyers' lack of training and unwillingness to serve poor clients' needs for advice in welfare law;
- the inaccessibility of lawyers' offices to poor or rural clients;
- the creation of new legal rights without the funding to enforce them;
- people's ignorance that the law could solve their problem;
- the fact that the LA schemes have always omitted certain services.

As a result, alternatives to private practice lawyers have been developed by radical lawyers, charities and others to try and fulfil these needs. Many can no longer be seen as alternatives because they have been absorbed into the mainstream, as charities have succeeded in securing contracts as service providers. Indeed, in the 2010 consultation, the Coalition government said they would take account of whether an alternative source of help existed, before granting LA. Some of these alternatives are now suffering a cut in funding as a result of the 2012 Act.

Law centres

From 1970 law centres, copied from US Neighbourhood Law Centres, were very   **17–016**
gradually established in poor areas, with a user-friendly, shop front image, where
employed lawyers, volunteers and paralegals provide advice and representation
on such matters as welfare law and immigration. They have always suffered from
vulnerable funding. Those financed by local authorities found they were biting
the hand that fed them, when they acted for groups suffering bad public housing.
Law centre funding has always been sporadic and sometimes they have to close
temporarily. By 2011 there were 55 law centres, plus affiliates and associated
members. By 2017, this is down to 45. For information, see the Law Centres
Network website and see evaluation below.

Citizens' Advice Bureaux

The Second World War exacerbated the need for advice and a thousand bureaux   **17–017**
were established by the end of the war. The Rushcliffe Committee 1944
recommended that they should be preserved. Expanding these was a policy of the
Thatcher government from 1979. In 2017, their website said they provided advice
at over 2,900 locations, with the aid of 23,000 volunteers, helping 2.7 million
clients face-to-face, and there were 36 million visits to their online advice pages,
in 2015–2016.

Advice centres

In the twentieth century, hundreds of independent advice centres grew up, some   **17–018**
providing general legal advice, some more specialised. In the first half of the
twentieth century, generalist advice centres were known as the Poor Man's
Lawyer, with lawyers providing free advice, usually in the evenings. Such centres
need to make a referral if substantive help is needed, beyond advice. During the
war, regional advice centres, staffed by solicitors and organised by the Law
Society, supplemented Citizens' Advice. Nowadays advice centres are sometimes
called law clinics and many are attached to university law schools. Organisations
and interest groups sometimes provide free specialist legal services, including
advice and representation, and make referrals. Examples are charities such as the
Child Poverty Action Group, Shelter (homelessness), Youth Access, The Money
Advice Trust, Dial UK (disability advice), Mind (mental health), the Refugee
Legal Centre, and so on.

Pro bono lawyers

There is evidence that the Romans used a pro bono system. During the 1990s,   **17–019**
both the Law Society and the Bar Council established pro bono groups to try to
persuade professionals to give some of their services free. The Free Representation Unit, a group of Bar students, was established in a pub in Chancery Lane in
1972. They practice advocacy by representing tribunal applicants. Another
example is the Citizens Advice Bureau in the Royal Courts of Justice, providing
help for litigants in person, where hundreds of lawyers work unpaid. Inspiring

examples of wide ranging pro bono work in this jurisdiction and by human rights lawyers abroad were given by Sir Henry Brooke, retired Lord Justice of Appeal, in the 2007 speech quoted at the opening of this chapter. In April 2011, a LawWorks (solicitors' pro bono) survey found that 65 per cent of law schools were engaged in pro bono activity. The National Pro Bono Centre was launched in 2010 and in 2016 they launched an online service to match lawyers with pro bono services needing experts. The Legal Services Act 2007 permits costs to be ordered to a winning lawyer, acting pro bono, and paid to the Access to Justice Foundation, which funds support networks for more pro bono work. Fraser (2013) suggested it could be made compulsory, as it is for applicants to the New York bar since 2015. This seems a great idea towards solving unmet legal need.

Other attempts from 1990 to enhance access to justice

17–020   The Conservative administrations of the 1990s devised various ways of enhancing access to justice, which were expanded under Labour from 1999. They attempted to draft laws in plain English and to make court procedures simpler and cheaper, providing advice leaflets in multiple languages. Mackay LC was given the crystal award by the Plain English Campaign for simplifying court leaflets. Judges are keen on this too. Lord Woolf CJ made it his personal mission to eliminate legal Latin. He was asked to simplify civil procedure. The "Woolf reforms" 1998 are described in Ch.10. Governments encouraged the use of alternative dispute resolution (ADR), as explained in Ch.11. Duty solicitor schemes, funded under the LA scheme, provide emergency help and representation in police stations and the magistrates' courts.

5.   REPETITIVE ATTEMPTS TO "REFORM" LA

17–021   I have been writing about LA since the 1980s. Depressingly, it raises the same perpetual problems as the National Health Service. Successive governments make sweeping changes via a new Act of Parliament, promising to eliminate the problems of spiralling cost, inefficiency, unmet need and unfair, patchy provision but we go round in circles, apparently incapable of finding an ideal or even a satisfactory system. Labour in 1999 then the Coalition in 2010 have made radical changes. The costs have been cut now, much more than government intended, but this has resulted in shocking examples of the denial of LA in deserving cases. In this next section, we see the problems of Labour's 1999 scheme, the immediate background to the current 2012 scheme.

Background to Labour's 1999 Act: uncontrolled cost and inefficiency

17–022   Throughout the late 1980s and 1990s, the Conservatives then New Labour from 1997 were determined to make radical reforms for these reasons:

- The cost was "spiralling out of control", according to Thatcher's Lord Chancellor, Lord Mackay, in 1986. LA was the only demand-led draw on the Treasury. Sometimes, in the 1990s, the cost rose by around 20 per cent per year, yet fewer people were aided. Separate representation for children, from 1989, and the development of duty solicitor schemes in police stations and the magistrates' courts, increased costs.

- Funders were uncoordinated. LA was designed to deliver legal services through the medium of private practice barristers and solicitors (the judicare model), therefore "alternative" legal services such as law centres received very little of the LA budget. They were dependent on a precarious mix of sources, such as charities, local authorities and other government departments.
- Criminal LA was administered unevenly by magistrates' courts, as demonstrated by research from the 1970s onwards. The Audit Commission criticised them eight years running in the 1990s for failure to apply the means test properly.
- "Fat cat lawyers" were charging the LA Board exorbitant fees.
- In 1999, Hazel Genn published a survey of how people solved their civil legal problems: *Paths to Justice*. People were disturbingly ignorant about their legal rights and obligations.

The 1999 Act and scheme were quite visionary and radical. Labour had had the simple idea of finding out how much money in total was spent on legal services provided via LA, plus the great variety of alternative legal services (charities and so on) and working out what people's needs were and how they could best be fulfilled, within this overall budget. Lawyers and "alternative" providers were to be funded from the same budget. They found people needed basic information and advice on rights and responsibilities, not necessarily to go to court. The idea was to assess need locally and match provision to need. But did the Access to Justice Act 1999 live up to its name? There was a mass of research and commentary by 2010.

Living with conditional fees

In *Nothing to Lose?* researchers Yarrow and Abrams (1999) reported that clients found CFAs confusing. In 2001, Moorhead and Scherr raised ethical questions over clients' lack of understanding of the risk they were taking. Research by Yarrow, *Just Rewards?* revealed that solicitors were using CFAs to overcharge.   **17–023**

In an important interpretive case, *Callery v Gray* (2001), Lord Woolf CJ, who designed the Civil Procedure Rules, and appellate colleagues, tried to make some sense of the mess over who should pay for success fees and insurance premiums attached to CFAs in claims about traffic accidents. They said that CFAs aimed to achieve access to justice for claimants who could not afford it so it was an inevitable consequence that *defendants* (insurance companies) should be subjected to additional costs. They felt that defendants should be able to limit success fees and insurance premiums to a reasonable amount. In cases like *Callery* which had a 98 per cent success rate, a "reasonable" success fee should be 20 per cent, a far cry from the crippling 100 per cent success fees that Jackson LJ found in his 2009 review of civil litigation costs had made civil litigation ridiculously expensive, as we saw in Ch.10.

Research in 2001 by accountants Stoy Hayward suggested that law firms "cherry picked" winnable cases. In 2004, Citizens' Advice published damning research, *No Win, No Fee, No Chance*, confirming this. People with meritorious but low value cases were left without a remedy. There was no regulation of the quality or cost of advice. Consumers, such as accident victims in hospital, were often subjected to high-pressure sales tactics. People thought CFA contracts were genuinely "no win no fee" and did not realise that they might have to pay the premium to insure against losing. Professor Moorhead found that only one third of lawyers were prepared to act on a "no win no fee" basis in employment cases because of the risks (Robins, 2009). A *Times* leading article "Sickness in Health", 21 December 2009, said that the Government's "noble goal", to make justice available to all, had become a "costly nightmare", as hospital payouts for clinical negligence had gone from nothing, two decades earlier, to £769 million per year, with much of the money going to lawyers. The NHS litigation authority complained to Jackson LJ during his 2009 civil costs review that the costs sought by claimants' lawyers were disproportionately high and were "indefensibly expensive".

On the other hand, others argued that CFAs boosted access to justice. Solicitor Adam Tudor wrote to *The Times* (8 February 2005) saying that since 1998, his firm alone had successfully represented over 100 libel claimants from all walks of life (LA was always unavailable for defamation). Wade (2009) argued that CFAs had helped credit crunch victims who would otherwise be unable to act against banks and so on, who had given them negligent financial advice. As discussed in Ch.10, Jackson LJ, in his review of civil costs, recommended that we abandon CFAs and legalise the more radical alternative of contingency fees, where the lawyer takes a share of damages. Consequently, these are permitted in the 2012 Act and called "damages based agreements".

Unmet need persists

17–024 The Law Society and Legal Action Group and Citizens Advice said that by 2003, so many solicitors' firms had given up doing legally aided work that there were "advice deserts", such as Kent, where there were no solicitors doing housing law.

In a 2003–2004 study for the Legal Services Research Centre of the Legal Services Commission, *Causes of Action: Civil Law & Social Justice*, Pleasance et al surveyed over 5,000 adults. The findings confirmed Genn (1999).

1. One third had experienced at least one civil law problem over 3.5 years.
2. One fifth took no action.
3. A million problems a year were left unsolved, as people did not understand basic rights.
4. Of those who took action, 37 per cent chose to handle their problems alone.
5. Socially excluded groups were especially vulnerable to civil justice problems, such as the homeless, lone parents and the unemployed.
6. Half of respondents reported multiple problems, such as personal injury leading to loss of home or income.
7. 15 per cent who sought advice did not obtain any, especially about homelessness and housing.

9.   People would often first discuss a problem with a doctor or social worker.
10. The more advisers a person was referred onto, the less likely they were to follow up all those referrals.

The official response was training Jobcentre staff to "signpost" the unemployed to advice and information; launching a telephone helpline, on benefits and education; putting information on the government website in 10 languages, establishing outreach clinics in town halls, community centres and GP's surgeries and so on.

In 2009, LAG published *The Justice Gap*. They argued that LA had fallen short of its original aims 60 years earlier (Robins).

Although problems occur in clusters, under the post-1999 scheme, advice became fragmented. Service providers' contracts limit them to advice on specific topics, so vulnerable people have to approach different advisers: Fox, Moorhead, Sefton and Wong.

Public defenders

Research was published in 2007 by Bridges, Cape, Moorhead and Scherr   **17–025**
evaluating the experimental public defenders' offices over a six year period. PDs operated at a high level of quality but their officers were more expensive to run than private lawyers' practices. By 2008, four of the eight were closed.

Law centres—still vulnerable

After 1999 the number of law centres increased to 65, including some mobile   **17–026**
services for rural areas, but they remain vulnerable to withdrawal of funding and they often close temporarily or permanently. As soon as the Coalition published its plans for the 2012 Act, law centres realised their legal aid income would dry up so some of them started charging a £100 flat fee for certain advice services, for the first time. This goes to the root of their existence. They were established to enhance access to justice by providing a free service.

Contracting, fixed fees, competitive tendering and trying to quality-control lawyers

The quality requirement under the new compulsory contracts exposed deficien-   **17–027**
cies and showed Labour's restrictions were justified. Research on advice by the Institute of Advanced Legal Studies in 2001 indicated room for improvement. Referral levels were poor and referrals were consistently late.

As Bridges and many others pointed out, the uncontrolled growth of LA since 1960 was linked to the massive increase in lawyers, who were not accountable for the *quality* of services they provided. His team's research, reported in *Standing Accused* (1994), exposed the appalling state of criminal defence. Barristers would appear in court having done no case preparation and not knowing the client from Adam. Some solicitors would send the office cleaner to sit behind counsel in court. Mostly, when someone asked to see a duty solicitor in a police station they would get anyone the duty solicitor chose to send. This book and the police uncovered widespread fraud by some solicitors who thought nothing of sending a secretary to sit behind counsel in court and charging the LA Board for a trainee solicitor. The Royal Commission on Criminal Justice 1993 found that most defence barristers did not meet their client until the morning of trial.

By 2003, once compulsory contracting was established, there were concerns that many firms were abandoning LA work. The Law Society found that 90 per cent of practitioners surveyed were dissatisfied, citing poor pay and excessive bureaucracy; 78 per cent threatened to drop or reduce LA work (*Gazette*, January 2003). The government said this was deliberate policy. They planned a significant cut in contracts, especially in London where they aimed to cut 488 providers to 150. Contracts would be awarded through competitive tendering.

17–028   The legal profession would not co-operate so a new consultation was issued, proposing that competitive tendering would initially be aimed at lower court work. In 2005, solicitor Andrew Keogh cynically opposed the rhetoric of his profession's leaders. Referring to the pre-1999 market, he argued:

> "Solicitors controlled the market; the state wrote the cheque … Only a fool could seriously believe the government will raise general remuneration rates given a total legal aid spend of £1.1bn on criminal defence services."

Also, when fixed fees for some work were introduced, lawyers complained bitterly. In 1993, Mackay LC introduced them in magistrates' courts. Solicitors sought a judicial review by the High Court and lawyers continue to use this method of attack whenever a Lord Chancellor has tried to curb their fees. Solicitors maintain that the amount they are paid does not allow them to provide an adequate service. Bridges' analysis showed that their argument lacked evidence and historical context. The growth in LA, especially in magistrates' courts, was linked to the rapid growth of the profession, in the 1970s and 1980s. Lack of quality had more to do with solicitors' inability to keep abreast with legal developments through having small case loads. Lawyers managed to resist for *30 years* all attempts to force them to compete in a tendering system and the last attempt in 2013 was scrapped.

The Legal Services Commission limited the suppliers of advice on asylum and immigration, in response to criticism by courts and others, that there were too many providers touting for business amongst asylum seekers and bringing hopeless cases.

The cost continued to rise

17–029   By 2004, LA was costing £2 billion per year, the largest LA budget in the developed world. The average case cost was still rising. Nevertheless, the Legal Action Group argued that this only represented 0.4 per cent of public spending, compared with £135 billion on benefits and £73 billion on the NHS. Family cases absorbed 80 per cent of the civil budget but most of the cost increase was caused by the rising cost of criminal defence. The causes were the abolition of the means test in magistrates' courts, the number of increasingly complex prosecutions brought by bodies such as the Serious Fraud Office and the creation of 360 new offences, in 1997–2004. Criminal defence overspent, reducing the money available for the civil and family cases. Critics argued it should be ring fenced. In

2005, the Legal Services Research Centre published *Demand Induced Supply? Identifying Cost Drivers in Criminal Defence Work*, by Professors Cape and Moorhead. They found the cost of LA on Crown Court cases had "risen dramatically" over 10 years. Government and prosecution policies had increased the number and seriousness of criminal cases and the amount of work that had to be done: increased police investigative power, greater use of technology in investigations (DNA testing, CCTV and so on). Procedural changes required defence lawyers to do more work. While crime had decreased, more of those arrested were prosecuted. There had been an increase in imprisonment rates. Means testing for criminal defence was reintroduced in 2006, claimed to save £35 million per year. In October 2009, Bowles and Perry for the Ministry of Justice compared spending in three common law countries and four European jurisdictions. They found that UK spending was unusually high, caused by a higher case load and higher average cost per case. The Legal Action Group pointed out, however, that although we have the most expensive LA system in Europe, other European countries have an inquisitorial system, where so much preparation is done by the court, not the client, so this cost is borne by the courts (and consequently, they have far more judges, to help people in court).

"Fat cats" and very high cost cases

Pre-1999, a significant portion of the budget was eaten up by very high cost cases. The media were scandalised about the high earnings of some barristers. In 1995, Lord Woolf MR advocated fixed fees and a stop to wasteful practices: unnecessary separate representation, use of two advocates and solicitors to sit behind counsel, and undue prolixity. The Lord Chancellor's Department (now Ministry of Justice) warned the Bar of the intention to fix fees. The Bar was hostile. In 1996, Lord Irvine, in opposition, said that one per cent of cases "swallowed up" 40 per cent of the criminal LA budget. In 1997, the LCD issued league tables of high paid barristers. A number earned over £400,000 for Crown Court work (and still do). Irvine attacked the price of lawyers. He famously told the House of Lords, "there are a significant number of QCs who earn a million pounds per annum ... Fat cat lawyers railing at the inequity of court fees do not attract the sympathy of the public." (*The Times*, 15 July 1997). In 1999, the Law Society joined in. The LC restricted the assignment of QCs in crime to cases where the defence involves substantial novel or complex issues of law or fact. In 2000, there was a 10 per cent cut in criminal defence fees, to reduce disparity between prosecution and defence, amid protests by the Bar. In 2001, the graduated fees scheme was introduced. By 2005, the problem of fat cats and high cost cases had worsened. Around one per cent of cases were absorbing 49 per cent of the criminal defence budget. In 2005, the Lord Chancellor announced reform of the management of large, complex cases. This is not to say that *all* legally aided lawyers are fat cats. Legally aided solicitors were among the worst paid public sector workers according to a *Guardian* survey in 2009, with an average salary below £25,000, less than prison officers and sewage plant workers: (2009) 159 N.L.J. 1641.

17–030

The 2004 "legal aid crisis" and "The Carter Reforms"

17–031   There was a battery of reviews in 2004. As well as repeating the well-known criticisms above, they made many points:

1.   The civil LA budget should be separated out.
2.   The government should develop a programme of public legal education.
3.   Government departments should recognise their role in creating demands on LA.
4.   ADR and consumer redress schemes should be promoted.
5.   Salaried services might tackle unmet need.
6.   Peripatetic (travelling) advisers should be used.
7.   There could be more use of private legal expenses insurance and CFAs.
8.   Over-specialisation could prevent a holistic approach by solicitors. There should be consortia to provide a one-stop shop for early advice and prevention.
9.   LA was restricted to those who had nothing. It excluded people of modest means and thus denied them access to justice.
11.   Community Legal Service Partnerships were not working as intended.
12.   Advice lines were not working as intended. Only 23 per cent of users were from target groups.

In response, the Legal Services Commission published a consultation, proposing to re-focus the LA scheme, in both family and civil cases, away from litigation and into early effective dispute resolution. In the CA, Lord Woolf, in *Anufrijeva v London Borough of Southwark* (2003) had criticised the disproportionate and "truly horrendous" cost of appeals under the Human Rights Act in maladministration cases. In 2005, the Department announced cuts in funding civil cases to promote early settlement, cutting eligibility for *representation* and increasing eligibility for *help* (advice and so on) to try and refocus on early troubleshooting. In 2006, the government asked Lord Carter of Coles to report on how to improve the purchasing of LA. His proposals were set out in *Legal Aid: a Market-Based Approach to Reform.* The government suggested best value tendering (yet again) for contracts; new responsibilities for Law Society and Bar Council to enhance quality of suppliers; fixed fees for solicitors in police stations, cutting costs related to waiting and travelling times; revised graduated fees for Crown Court advocates and a new graduated fee scheme for Crown Court litigators to reward earlier preparation and resolution of cases. Fees would be severely cut for the top-earning barristers (fat cats), to allow those at the lower end to be paid more; increased controls and audit capacity; standard fees for civil and family work and new graduated fees for solicitors in private law family and child care proceedings.

17–032   Willman, like other lawyers, was unsurprisingly critical. She said the most "galling aspect" of government plans was that "efficiency is equated with seeing large numbers of clients dealt with as cheaply as possible, regardless of the type of case or outcome". "Legal help" work was already unprofitable at £50–60 per hour in London and less outside. The Department published yet *another* paper in November 2006, including its scheme of fixed fees.

Keogh was prepared to defend the Carter proposals. The UK spent 10 times more on LA than its nearest rival. Meanwhile, lawyers demonstrated in Parliament Square in 2007 and sought judicial review of government plans on the Very High Cost Case Panel. The Carter plans were very heavily criticised by the House of Commons Constitutional Affairs Committee in a 2007 report but the government said it was going ahead. The Committee drew attention to a 32 per cent reduction in family providers. The government said provision was adequate. By 2008, all bodies representing criminal defence lawyers urged them not to sign the new contracts. Barristers boycotted a Very High Cost Cases (VHCC) panel so the LSC decided to create a panel of litigators and a list of accredited advocates for VHCCs. A convicted drug offender avoided a confiscation order of up to £4.5 million, because 30 barristers refused to act for the fixed fee of £175 per day. See Gibb (2008). In 2009, family graduated fees were cut. Lord Bach, LA minister, said average fees for private family disputes had risen from £800 to £1,450 in five years, "unsustainable". He said child protection work would receive an extra £4.4 million. The number of family LA practices dropped from 4,500 in 2000 to 2,800 (Gibb, 2009). The Law Society won a judicial review case in the High Court: *R. (on the application of the Law Society) v Legal Services Commission* (2010).

The Act came into force in 2013, then the Government proposed a further £220 million cut to the LA budget, in addition to the £350 million in 2013. They planned to cut lawyers' fees and introduce price competitive tendering (yet again) but dropped the latter. Barristers and solicitors staged a walkout from the criminal courts in 2014. So many independent barristers refused to take on serious criminal cases, "very high cost cases" (VHCCs) that courts suffered significant delays. In May 2014, Judge Leonard stayed (postponed) the proceedings in a complex land fraud because 70 sets of barristers' chambers had refused to defend the case. About £10 million had been spent in prosecuting the case and eight similar trials were queuing up behind. The CA immediately quashed his decision. The Ministry's unprecedented tactic in response was to employ a number of advocates, including QCs, to act as public defenders. In 2014, the Law Society published, on its website, all the ways in which money is wasted in the criminal process.

6. WHERE ARE WE NOW? CRITICISMS OF THE LASPO ACT 2012

Civil legally aided cases have dropped from about 130,000 a quarter in 2013, **17–033** before the Act came into force, to 40,000 per quarter by 2016. Spending on civil legal aid dropped by 20 per cent, from 2013 to 2015 and the number of social welfare cases fell from 470,000 to 53, by 2016. Ministry of Justice statistics showed that the number of LA providers continued to fall. In January 2017, the Minister of Justice published yet another consultation on an advocates graduated fee system, promising that fees would be based on the complexity of the case rather than the number of pages, yet this was identified as a problem by her predecessor as long ago as 2010, or earlier.

Parliamentary criticism

17–034   The most comprehensive assessment of legal aid now is the March 2015 report of
the all-party House of Commons Justice Committee, *Impact of changes to civil
legal aid under Part 1 of the Legal Aid, Sentencing and Punishment of Offenders
Act 2012*. I quote from the summary and add in details, updates, commentary and
the July 2015 Government response (Ministry of Justice), which is beside the
report on the Parliament website.

> "The Ministry's four objectives for the reforms were to:
> - discourage unnecessary and adversarial litigation at public expense;
> - target legal aid to those who need it most;
> - make significant savings in the cost of the scheme; and
> - deliver better overall value for money for the taxpayer.
>
> Our overall conclusion was that, while it had made significant savings in the cost of
> the scheme, the Ministry had harmed access to justice for some litigants and had not
> achieved the other three out of four of its stated objectives for the reforms."
> (Summary)

The government response dismissed this.

In 2014, the National Audit Office had warned that the evidence base for the
reforms was poor. The government had carried out no preparatory research.

> "Since the reforms came into effect there has been an underspend in the civil legal
> aid budget because the Ministry has not ensured that many people who are eligible
> for legal aid are able to access it. A lack of public information about the extent and
> availability of legal aid post-reforms, including about the Civil Legal Advice
> telephone gateway for debt advice, contributed to this and we recommend the
> Ministry take prompt steps to redress this." (Summary)

There was an annual underspend of £32 million. People mistakenly thought
LA was unavailable. The Ministry gave too little guidance. There was a shortfall
in exceptionally funded cases, including a shortfall in legally aided mediations
and an 85% shortfall in debt advice. The Government responded that they were
launching an enhanced digital service, which would fully inform people and their
advisers about legal aid eligibility and advice agencies.

17–035   The Committee heard evidence of one very vulnerable client with communication difficulties being unable to access the telephone gateway. The government
responded that they provided a free telephone interpreter in 170 languages,
Minicom and sign language webcam for deaf people, a callback facility for
people who could not afford the call and a freepost system. The Committee report
continued:

> "Parliament intended the exceptional cases funding scheme to act as a safety net,
> protecting access to justice for the most vulnerable. We are very concerned that it
> has not achieved that aim. We heard of a number of cases where, to our surprise,
> exceptional case funding was not granted" (Summary).

The Government had estimated that 3,700 applications would be granted
annually, yet only 151 had been granted in the previous 16 months. There were
"surprising" examples of refused applications:

"Details of cases refused exceptional cases funding include an illiterate woman with learning, hearing and speech difficulties facing an application which would determine her contact with her children; parents with learning difficulties who wished to contest their child's adoption but were £35 a month over the eligible financial limit; a women with 'modest learning difficulties' who the judge in the case told us was unable to deal with representations from the lawyer on the other side as a result of which she 'now faces possibly not seeing her child again'; and a destitute blind man with such profound learning difficulties he lacked litigation capacity." (p.14)

In their response, the Government insisted that the fund was designed to comply with human rights and EU requirements. The Justice Committee had received evidence that separated and trafficked children had difficulty in accessing advice. The Government responded that LA was available for asylum-seekers and trafficked people. Where LA was unavailable, unaccompanied children could get support from Law Centres and other charities. The Parliamentary Justice Committee moved on to family cases:

"Private family law was removed from the scope of legal aid, but those who can provide evidence of domestic violence are still eligible. We welcome the Ministry's efforts to ensure that victims of domestic violence are provided with the necessary evidence by healthcare professionals and its assurance that the types of evidence required are under continual review. However we are concerned by evidence we received that a large proportion of victims of domestic violence do not have any of the types of evidence required. We are also troubled by the potentially detrimental effects of the strict requirement that the evidence be from no more than 24 months prior to the date of application, which we consider should be a matter of discretion for the Legal Aid Agency in appropriate cases." (Summary).

They observed that common types of abuse, psychological and financial, were difficult to prove (Ch.4). The government did not accept that there was robust evidence that large numbers of victims were excluded but since 2015, they have relaxed the evidence criteria for domestic violence victims. The Justice Committee moved onto the topic of "advice deserts":

"We received evidence on the effects of the reforms on the legal aid market and providers of publicly-funded legal services. We were told by both the for-profit and not-for-profit sectors that the reforms have led to the cutting and significant downsizing of departments and centres dealing with such work, leading to concerns about the sustainability of legal aid practice in future. We are troubled by National Audit Office findings which indicate that there may already be 'advice deserts', geographical areas where these services are not available, and think that work to assess and rectify this must be carried out immediately." (Summary)

Nine law centres had closed—those which relied heavily on legal aid—but the capacity of the others had been significantly reduced, so centres now targeted specific groups of potential clients, rather than running an open door service. The charity Shelter had cut its housing advice by 40 per cent and debt advice by 60 per cent. Citizens Advice had lost 350 specialist advisers. Bodies like the Law Centres Network reported a surge in inquiries on topics now out-of-scope for LA, notably family, immigration and employment. Witnesses had said that if you effectively ration LA then the first, say, 100 clients get LA, which goes against the Act's aim of targeting the most needy (p.32). The NAO had found that in 14 local authorities, no new LA matters started in 2013-2014 and in a further 39 authorities, there were fewer than 49 new LA matters per 100,000 people (p.33).

17–036   The Government responded that it regularly reviewed supply, and there was sufficient capacity in all aspects of civil law in most geographical areas. Anyway, three commissioned research projects were due to report later in 2015. The Committee moved on to the topic of litigants in person.

> "There has been a substantial increase in litigants in person as a result of the Government's reforms, but the precise magnitude of the increase is unclear. More significant has been the shift in the nature of litigants in person, who are increasingly people with no choice other than to represent themselves and who may therefore have some difficulty in effectively presenting their cases. The result is that the courts are having to expend more resources to assist litigants in person and require more funding to cope, alongside increased direct assistance by the Ministry for litigants in person." (Summary)

The NAO had estimated that the additional cost generated by LiPs was £3.4 million in the family courts alone. A specific concern was that, while there was a ban in criminal cases on unrepresented alleged attackers cross-examining their alleged victims, there was no such ban in family courts:

> "In *P v D*, a father who was serving a 17 year jail sentence for repeatedly raping his wife and who, it was alleged, had also assaulted his elder daughters leading to one taking two overdoses at the age of 13, cross-examined all three women over an extended period during a hearing… ." (p.41)

The Government responded that whilst it sympathised in these cases, the Court of Appeal had pointed out that there were a number of case management options. For example, the judge or a magistrates' legal adviser could question the witness (the alleged victim) and this accorded with a Family Procedure Rules Practice Direction.

The Committee expressed surprise that cases involving adults who lacked capacity, where the Official Solicitor was involved, were not differentiated from other cases, because these were the most vulnerable people in society who were barred from conducting civil litigation themselves. The Government responded that just because people were vulnerable because of their incapacity, it did not mean that they were also financially vulnerable.

17–037   The Justice Committee were concerned at the increase in McKenzie friends representing people in court, as they were uninsured and the client had no remedy if they made a mistake. In some cases encouraging their use could be a counsel of despair. The government should consider regulating them. The Government said they had no current plans to regulate them but they were funding a Litigants in Person Support Strategy, in partnership with the Personal Support Unit, Advice Now, Law Works and other pro bono providers. The Committee moved on to the drastic decline in the uptake of mediation.

> "Also indicative of the lack of evidence on the effects the reforms would have has been the sharp reduction in the use of mediation, despite the Ministry's estimates that it would increase. We found that this was because the Ministry did not

appreciate what makes people seek mediation, with the end of compulsory mediation assessment, the removal of solicitors from the process, and the lack of clear advice from the Ministry all contributing. Unlike in other areas, however, the Ministry did act swiftly to remedy the problems." (Summary)

"...the MoJ estimated removing family law from scope would lead to an additional 9,000 Mediation Information and Assessment Meetings (MIAMs) each year. The opposite happened. Despite the continued funding of mediation the number of such meetings declined by an estimated 17,246 following the introduction of LASPO, a fall of 56 per cent. The NAO estimates that the MoJ underspend on mediation in 2013–14 was around £20 million." (p.53)

The NAO had concluded that the Ministry had a limited understanding of what influenced people to go to court. People did not now opt for mediation because prior to the 2012 Act, legally aided parties in private family law cases were obliged to attend a MIAM. Obviously, with the withdrawal of LA, this channel to mediation ceased. Nowadays, anyone in private family law proceedings is obliged to attend a MIAM but this only came into force in April 2014, which signified a lack of joined up thinking. Also, as people do not have solicitors, there is no-one to tell them about mediation. There was inadequate information explaining that mediation remained in scope for LA. The Ministry assumed the withdrawal of LA would provoke a culture change, persuading people to resolve their problems out of court. The fall in mediations and rise in LiPs shows they were wrong. The Government responded that, as the Committee acknowledged, it had worked swiftly with the mediation industry to provide policy solutions and new contracts provided for mediation providers at 171 further locations. Also, as of November 2014, the first session of all mediations was publicly funded, where one person was legally aided. Also they were launching a new communications campaign. The Committee concluded by criticising the cost benefit:

"The Ministry's significant savings are potentially undermined by its inability to show that it has achieved value for money for the taxpayer. The Ministry's efforts to target legal aid at those who most need it have suffered from the weakness that they have often been aimed at the point after a crisis has already developed, such as in housing repossession cases, rather than being preventive. There have therefore been a number of knock-on costs, with costs potentially merely being shifted from the legal aid budget to other public services, such as the courts or local authorities. This is another aspect of the reforms about which there is insufficient information; the Ministry must assess and quantify these knock-on costs if it is to be able to demonstrate it has met its objective of better value for the taxpayer.

It was clear to us that the urgency attached by the Government to the programme of savings militated against having a research-based and well-structured programme of change to the provision of civil legal aid. Many of the issues which we have identified and which have been identified to us could have been avoided by research and an evidence base to work from, as well as by the proper provision of public information about the reforms." (Summary)

The Government simply remarked that they had reservations as to whether wider costs could be properly monetised.

In the same month, the Parliamentary Human Rights Joint Committee reported on the UK's compliance with the UN Convention on the Rights of the Child. It concluded that the 2012 LA cutbacks were a "significant black mark" on the Government's human rights record.

Judges

17–038   Today's judges were all practising lawyers when legal aid was in its heyday, in the 1980s and 1990s. Many of them had made a good living out of the Legal Aid Fund. The growth in litigants in person has affected judges' capacity to manage cases properly and to keep cases moving swiftly through their courts. As the adversarial system is predicated on the idea that the parties bring to the court everything it needs, in terms of law, evidence and argument, this does not work where a party is unrepresented. In 2010, senior judges were swift to point this out when cuts were threatened. They warned of the burdens on the courts and their administration. Later, Lord Chief Justice Thomas made more than one speech from 2014 where he pointed out that unrepresented parties would be better off with an inquisitorial system but he also said in his annual report to Parliament that we had a justice system that was unaffordable to most people. Of course, judges, like many lawyers, have altruistic concerns about access to justice too. Before and after 2012, top judges have given speeches and been filmed for TV condemning the cutbacks. Three former appeal judges, Hooper, Moses and Sedley, led a group who wrote an open letter to the *Guardian* on 1 May 2015, "Legal Aid Cuts Threaten Our Very Democracy". It included academics, peers, doctors, representatives of lawyers groups, such as the Bar Council and radical lawyers' groups, such as the Legal Action Group. They recited the "eye-watering" statistics, as they called them, on the extent of the cuts, and used emotive language:

> "What the figures do not convey is the sheer human misery of being unable to get legal advice. GPs report a large increase in the number of patients who would have been assisted by advice on benefits, employment, debts and housing. Cuts to legal aid are literally making people sick…Politicians speak about access to justice as an optional extra that we simply cannot afford. But the introduction of legal aid, replacing the ad hoc "poor law" scheme of the 1920s and 1930s, came during a period of true austerity in the wake of the second world war…Without access to justice for all, inequalities take on a more dangerous edge which threatens the legitimacy of not just the justice system but our democracy."

Mr Justice Mostyn used a 2015 Magna Carta speech in Australia to attack the cuts. He said no-one had expected their "savagery". He quoted his decision in *MG & JG v JF* (2015) where he had analysed the "catalogue of cases" where judges had commented on the "gross injustices being meted out as a result of these reforms", including four judgments of the President of the Family Division. He quoted the retired appeal judge, Sir Anthony Hooper, as saying, at a 2015 meeting:

> "I'm completely depressed. I started out in the legal profession 30-odd years ago when we had as Rolls-Royce a system as you possibly could have. This has been destroyed gradually and then quickly over the past few years."

In March 2016, Charles J, Vice President of the Court of Protection, adjourned four test cases involving vulnerable people until the Legal Aid Agency, or central or local government agreed to pay for them to be represented. The ruling effectively halted the thousands of cases in the court's backlog (Bowcott 2016). In the 2016 Annual Report of the Court of Appeal Civil Division, Master Egan, Registrar of Criminal Appeals, said about ten per cent of leave applicants were unrepresented and the price was paid in difficult case management.

The Magistrates' Association estimates that a quarter of all litigants are unrepresented and some magistrates have resigned over cutbacks in LA or courts closures. A lot of people now represented themselves in bringing prosecutions and they needed considerable support.

Lord Justice Jackson revived the suggestion of a Contingency Legal Aid Fund, in a 2016 speech. This type of fund has been mooted since the 1970s and exists in other jurisdictions. It funds claimants' costs, win or lose. If the claimant wins, the fund recovers its costs, plus a share of the damages.

Pressure groups, lawyers and charities

LawWorks reported in 2016 that it had advised 35,000 people in its 223 clinics, an increase of 25 per cent. Another 11,000 people were referred on. The pressure group Transform Justice published *Justice Denied* in 2016. 90 per cent of respondents surveyed, mainly lawyers, reported an increase in unrepresented defendants in magistrates' courts and many expressed concern that they (naturally) did not understand what they were charged with. In a 2016 report, Amnesty International expressed concern that children were representing themselves in deportation cases. They had no idea how to complete forms or get help in immigration tribunal cases. In 2016, the Director of the Legal Action Group, Steve Hynes, and the representatives of two legal aid lawyers' groups wrote an open letter in *The Guardian* to Theresa May PM, urging a review of LA and reminding her of her appointment promise to serve everyone, not just the privileged few. Citizens Advice research found that 90 per cent of family LiPs reported a strain on health, jobs or finances. In 2016, the Law Society produced an interactive map of justice deserts. A 2016 survey by Ipsos MORI of 8912 people showed that 20 per cent of domestic violence sufferers thought they could not access legal aid. 86 per cent of respondents did not know that mediation was available for relationship breakdown. **17–039**

7. CONCLUSION

1. In the early twentieth century, we opted for the judicare model of provision of legal services in England and Wales, paying taxpayers' money in the form of fees to private practice lawyers rather and setting up a National Legal Service of salaried lawyers, like the NHS. This helped to encourage the enormous growth of lawyers, described in Ch.13, especially when we invented new resource intensive legal services, such as independent representation for children and duty solicitor schemes. **17–040**

2. Lawyers' capacity to protect their work and resist change should not be underestimated. The judicare model has suited them very well. The story in this chapter is testament to their tenacity. Competitive tendering was mooted in 1986. They have resisted countless attempts to introduce it. Remuneration rates for *some* legally aided work are now very low so there has been an exodus of law firms and many barristers from some legally aided work. In relation to criminal work, this accorded with the policy of successive governments to force out small firms.

3. We are said to have the world's most expensive LA system. All LCs since about 1986 have said this cannot go on.

4. When any Lord Chancellor tries to introduce a change in lawyers' remuneration, they bitterly oppose it and readily take the LC to the High Court in judicial review proceedings. I have lost count of these cases. If the LC tries to implement changes without adequate consultation, this provides grounds for review, hence the silly number of consultations. Judges are lawyers. The lawyers win most challenges in court. Lawyers think they also have the whip-hand because they can simply refuse to enter contracts for government funded work. Lord Chancellors panic, postpone their plans and issue yet another consultation. Lord Chancellors are generally lawyers too, incidentally.

5. If the number of LA practices is cut, this will not automatically deny citizens access to justice, *provided* there are suitable alternatives. Most people want advice and this can be supplied by phone, internet and bodies like Citizens Advice. All surveys find that most people with legal problems do nothing. A May 2014 survey for the Legal Services Board by Legal Futures found fewer than one in ten people with a legal problem sought advice from a lawyer. It concluded that this is sometimes entirely rational though a significant minority were characterised by powerlessness.

6. Government must provide adequate alternatives, or risk breaching art.6 of the European Convention on Human Rights.

7. Bureaucracy is a necessary corollary of quality control but lawyers ought to be accountable if they benefit from public funding, like anyone else. When they were unregulated, boasting that they were the world's best lawyers, they got away with scandalous behaviour and defrauding the old LA scheme, as exposed by the fascinating research reported in *Standing Accused*. They only have themselves to thank for further regulation.

8. For the latest evaluations, see the Law Society's review of LASPO and the SRA on unmet legal need, both 2017.

Bibliography

17–041 Note: all judges' speeches and lectures from 2014 are on the Judiciary website. Older ones are in the National Archives. There is a link on the Judiciary website to the URL, which is *http://webarchive.nationalarchives.gov.uk/ 20131202164909/http://judiciary.gov.uk/media/speeches/2013/index*.
The Access to Justice Act 1999.
F. Bawdon, on Yarrow and Abrams' research, "Nothing to lose?" (1999) 149 N.L.J. 1890.

CONCLUSION

Sir Henry Brooke, Second Annual Nottingham Pro Bono Lecture, 15 November 2007.

O. Bowcott, *The Guardian*, 10 March 2016 and many other *Guardian* articles.

R. Bowles and A. Perry, *An International Comparison of Publicly Funded Legal Services and Justice Systems*, MoJ research series 14/09 (2009).

Department of Constitutional Affairs, *Modernising Justice* (1998), White Paper, National Archives.

C. Fox, R. Moorhead, M. Sefton and K. Wong, "Community legal advice centres and networks: a process evaluation" (2011) 30(2) C.J.Q. 204–222.

M. Fraser, "Forced labour?" (2013) N.L.J., July, p.11.

H. Genn, *Paths to Justice—What People Do and Think About Going to Law* (1999).

Citizens' Advice, *Geography of Advice* (2004).

F. Gibb, "Drugs offender keeps £4.5m after 30 barristers refuse to take his case", *The Times*, 6 May 2008; "Vulnerable youngsters put at risk by plans to slash legal aid" *The Times*, 26 October 2009.

Jackson LJ, "The Case for a CLAF", speech, 2 February 2016.

A. Keogh, "Value for money or a leap into the unknown" (2005) 155 N.L.J. 157; "Carter—the crunch" (2006) 156 N.L.J. 1149.

The Law Society, *ACCESS DENIED? LASPO four years on: a Law Society review* (2017).

Lightman J, "The Civil Justice System and Legal Profession—The Challenges Ahead" (2003) C.J.Q. 235; the Edward Bramley Memorial Lecture, University of Sheffield, 4 April 2003; "Access to Justice", speech to the Law Society, 5 December 2007.

M. McConville, L. Bridges, J. Hodgson and A. Pavlovic, *Standing Accused* (1994).

R. Moorhead and A. Scherr on CFAs, "Midnight in the garden of the CFA people" (2001) 151 N.L.J. 274.

R. Moorhead and M. Robinson, "A Trouble Shared—legal problems clusters in solicitors and advice agencies" DCA research report 8/2006 (2006).

Mr Justice Mostyn, "Magna Carta and Access to Justice in Family Proceedings", speech, Sydney, 18–19 June 2015.

National Audit Office.

P. Pleasence et al., *Causes of Action: civil law and social justice*, 2004.

P. Pleasence, V. Kemp, and N.J. Balmer, "The Justice Lottery? Police Station Advice 25 Years on from PACE" [2011] Crim. L.R. 3.

J. Robins, "The Justice Gap" (2009) 159 N.L.J. 131; "The right call?" (2013) N.L.J., 12 July, p.10; "Pro bono: making a splash" (2013) N.L.J., 15 November, p.9; "Low Commission, high expectations" (2014) N.L.J. 7 February, p.11.

Solicitors Regulation Authority, *Improving access—tackling unmet legal needs* (2017).

Stoy Hayward's research on conditional fees: (2001) 151 N.L.J. 1078.

A. Wade, "Credit-crunch victims turn to no-win, no-fee for help", *The Times*, 7 May 2009.

S. Willman, "Access to justice or Tesco law?" (2006) 156 N.L.J. 1537.

Yarrow, *Just Rewards?* summarised at (2001) 151 N.L.J. 750.

Further reading and sources for updating this chapter

17–042 Free updates of this book are available on the Sweet & Maxwell website: *http://uklawstudent.thomsonreuters.com.*

Summary and revision: P. Darbyshire, *Nutshells English Legal System*, 10th edn (London: Sweet & Maxwell, 2016).

Westlaw Current Awareness was a primary research tool used for this chapter

Citizens' Advice: *http://www.citizensadvice.org.uk*

Counsel

Law Centres Network *http://www.lawcentres.org.uk*

The Law Society

The Law Society's *Gazette*

Legal Action Group website and *Legal Action*

Ministry of Justice news and statistics; answers to Freedom of Information questions.

National Audit Office

The New Law Journal, available on *Lexis*.

Parliament website, especially Justice Committee, Human Rights Committee and House of Commons Library briefing papers.

INDEX

LEGAL TAXONOMY
FROM SWEET & MAXWELL

This index has been prepared using Sweet and Maxwell's Legal Taxonomy. Main index entries conform to keywords provided by the Legal Taxonomy except where references to specific documents or non-standard terms (denoted by quotation marks) have been included. These keywords provide a means of identifying similar concepts in other Sweet and Maxwell publications and online services to which keywords from the Legal Taxonomy have been applied. Readers may find some minor differences between terms used in the text and those which appear in the index. Suggestions to *sweetandmaxwell.taxonomy@tr.com*.

All references are to paragraph number

INDEX

INDEX

Direct applicability
EU law, 3–026
Direct effect
decisions, 3–033
directives, 3–029
horizontal direct effect for directives, 3–032
horizontal or vertical direct effect, 3–030
international agreements, 3–034
introduction, 3–026
regulations, 3–028
state, 3–031
treaty articles, 3–027
UK law, 3–039
Director of Public Prosecutions
generally, 12–034
Disclosure
civil procedure, 10–023
Discrimination
bedroom tax, 4 053
introduction, 4–051
widowers, 4–052
District judges
civil procedure, 10–016
deputy district judges, 14–035
generally, 14–034
magistrates' courts, 14–037, 15–016
Diversity
judges
attempts to increase diversity,
14–070—14–078
emphasis on QCs, 14–065
exclusion of solicitors, 14–064
exclusion of women, 14–067
gays and lesbians, 14 068
introduction, 14–058
judicial working practices, 14–072
lack of social diversity, 14–060
legal profession, 14–073—14–078
more radical suggestion—a career judiciary,
14–079
problems of lack of diversity,
14 061—14 063
race, 14–066
requirements for appointment, 14–071
statistics, 14–059
what was government response to criticisms,
14–069
lawyers
educational background, 13–009—13–010
women and non-whites, 13–006—13–008
magistrates
age, 15–006
criticisms of lack of diversity, 15–004
disability, 15–009
enhancing diversity, 15–011—15–013
gender, 15–010
introduction, 15–005
race, 15–008
social class and politics, 15–007

Divisional Court
civil matters, 7–010
criminal matters, 6–006
"Domestic law"
types of law, 1–006
Domestic violence courts
see **Specialist domestic violence courts**
Double jeopardy
criminal procedure, 12–007
Drugs courts
generally, 7–006
Early neutral evaluation
alternative dispute resolution, 11 036
Ecclesiastical courts
generally, 6–021
Either way offences
generally, 12–072—12–073
Employment Appeal Tribunal
generally, 6–024
"English legal system"
adversarial procedure, 1–012
common law, 1–009, 1–011
comparison with other European systems
bad Europeans, 1 025
concept of law, 1–022
different branches, 1–019
different roots, 1–018
introduction, 1–017
judicial approach, 1–023
procedural differences, 1–024
public and private law, 1–021
sources of law, 1–023
written constitutions, 1–020
definition, 1–010
definition of "law", 1–002—1–003
hallmarks
adversarial procedure, 1–012
common law, 1–011
jury trial and morality, 1–013
lay magistrates, 1–014
introduction, 1–001
jury trial and morality, 1–013
keeping up to date, 1–027—1–028
lay magistrates, 1–014
mother of all common law systems,
1–015—1–016
personnel, 1–026
resources, 1–027—1–028
rule of law, 1–002—1–003
types of law
civil and criminal law, 1–007—1–008
common law and equity, 1–009
domestic and international law, 1–006
private and public law, 1–005
substantive and procedural law, 1–004
websites, 1–028
Equity
development, 8 010—8 014
generally, 1–009